An Introduction to
the Languages of the World

An Introduction
to the
Languages of the World

Anatole V. Lyovin

New York   Oxford
Oxford University Press
1997

Oxford University Press

Oxford   New York
Athens   Auckland   Bangkok
Calcutta   Cape Town   Dar es Salaam   Delhi
Florence   Hong Kong   Istanbul   Karachi
Kuala Lumpur   Madras   Madrid   Melbourne
Mexico City   Nairobi   Paris   Singapore
Taipei   Tokyo   Toronto

and associated companies in
Berlin   Ibadan

Library of Congress Cataloging-in-Publication Data

Lyovin, Anatole.
An introduction to the languages of the world / Anatole V. Lyovin.
p.   cm.
Includes bibliographical references and index.
ISBN 0-19-508115-3.   ISBN 0-19-508116-1 (pbk.)
1. Language and languages.   I. Title.
P371.L96   1996   410--dc20   95-6018

6 8 9 7 5

Printed in the United States of America
on acid-free paper

This book is dedicated to the memory of my mother, Valentina V. Lyovin (née Borotinski), without whose constant encouragement it could never have been completed.

Preface

This book is intended to be used in a course designed for students who have mastered the basic principles of linguistics but lack background information about the broad range of language phenomena (vowel harmony, ergative constructions, etc.) found in the world's languages, and who also need to learn a few facts about the existence of major language families, the distribution of major language groups, and so forth. It aims to offer students an opportunity to explore, at various levels, structures of very different, highly interesting languages without necessarily possessing a speaking or reading knowledge of these languages, as they would in normal language classes. At the same time, this book can serve as an introduction to language typology in general.

It should be emphasized that this text is not intended as an introduction to linguistics, since it presupposes some familiarity with such basic linguistics concepts as morpheme, phoneme, and basic articulatory phonetics terms. It is intended as a textbook for undergraduates who have already taken at least one advanced course in general linguistics and may also have taken an introductory course in phonetics. It is also intended for graduate students in linguistics who have already taken their required introductory courses in various branches of linguistics but otherwise have little background knowledge of the field. At the University of Hawaii at Mānoa, for example, a course for which this work would be assigned as a textbook requires as a minimum prerequisite an upper-division introductory course in general linguistics, which beginning graduate students who have no background in linguistics are required to take. Naturally, students who have had other linguistics courses (e.g., phonetics, phonology, and syntax) usually enjoy this course more and encounter fewer difficulties.

Even though this book is not intended as an introductory text in linguistics, certain concepts are reviewed in some detail in the introductory chapter because my experience as a teacher of beginning linguistics students has taught me to expect all sorts of misconceptions about what linguists mean when they say that certain languages are "genetically related." It is also not intended as a reference book, since it is limited in scope and coverage and certainly cannot compete with such books as Bernard Comrie's *The World's Major Languages* (New York: Oxford University Press, 1987), which contains in-depth articles on major languages and language families written by recognized experts in their respective fields. Lacking expertise in all the languages of the world, I have had to depend on the opinions of others without always being able to check the validity and accuracy of the latter. On the other hand, reference works are usually too technical and contain too many details for beginning students. In addition, they are not ideal as textbooks because, among other things, they do not contain such things as exercises and other addenda helpful to the instructor as well as students in introductory-level classes.

The need for such a textbook became apparent about twenty years ago when I began teaching a course on the languages of the world and found that there were simply no suitable textbooks for such courses, despite the existence of several books entitled "Languages of the World." (Most such books deal only with different writing systems found throughout the world.) It is only in recent years that up-to-date reference books on the languages of the world have appeared, that are suitable to be placed on the reserve shelf for courses on the subject.

This book surveys all the areas of the globe on a continent-by-continent basis. It does not concentrate on major languages, although most of the languages in the sketches may be considered so. Some languages were chosen because of their typological interest and not the socioeconomic prominence of their speakers. However, not all language types are represented. This would have required that the scope of this textbook be greatly expanded; as it is, it would be too difficult to cover the entire contents adequately in one semester. It would probably be best for the instructor to choose, on the basis of the interests of the students, which language sketches to assign and which to skip. It is hoped that students will read independently any materials not formally covered during the course.

Some exercises may prove too difficult for students with very little background in linguistics. Such exercises may be skipped entirely, or the instructor may provide clues and hints to the students in order to help them solve the problems more easily.

I would like to express my deep gratitude to the following individuals, who helped me in the preparation of this book: Riika Alanen, who helped me with the sample Finnish text; Greg Lee Carter, who suggested many key improvements for the sketch of Hawaiian; Emily Hawkins, who helped me in the selection of the sample Hawaiian text; Darius Kenyi Jonathan, who helped with the sketch of Arabic; Gillian Sankoff, who kindly provided the text for the Tok Pisin sketch and explained what it meant; Craig Volker, who kindly reviewed my sketch of Tok Pisin; Robert Blust, who clarified for me his classification of Austronesian languages; and Michael Forman, who offered many useful suggestions, especially on the chapter dealing with pidgin and creole languages. Thanks also go to Marion Sonomura. Finally, I must acknowledge the moral support provided by Byron W. Bender, my department chair at the University of Hawaii at Mānoa, in particular his unflagging faith that I would successfully complete this project. The anonymous readers for Oxford University Press critically reviewed an earlier draft of this book and provided many constructive comments. To all these kind people I say a heartfelt "Mahalo." If there are errors and omissions in this book, they are due to my lack of expertise in many areas.

Honolulu   A. V. L.
January 1996

Contents

CHAPTER 4 LANGUAGES OF ASIA   109

I. Turkic, II. Mongolian, III. Tungusic, IV. Korean-Japanese-
Okinawan, V. Ainu, VI. Paleosiberian, VII. Sino-Tibetan,
VIII. Hmong-Mien (Miao-Yao), IX. Tai-Kadai, X. Austronesian,
XI. Austroasiatic, XII. Dravidian, XIII. Burushaski, XIV. Afro-
Asiatic, XV. Indo-European, XVI. Uralic, XVII. Eskimo-Aleut

CHAPTER 5 LANGUAGES OF AFRICA   185

I. Afro-Asiatic (Afrasian) Family, II. Nilo-Saharan (Nilo-
Sahelian) Family, III. Niger-Congo Family, IV. Khoisan
Family, V. Austronesian, VI. Indo-European

CHAPTER 6 LANGUAGES OF OCEANIA   245

I. Austronesian, II. Papuan Languages, III. Australian

CHAPTER 7 NATIVE LANGUAGES OF THE AMERICAS   309

A. LANGUAGES OF NORTH AMERICA, 310

I. Eskimo-Aleut Family, IIA. Na-Dene Family, IIB. Haida Isolate,
III. Algonquian-Ritwan Family, IV. Muskogean Family, V. Natchez
Isolate, VI. Atakapa Isolate, VII. Chitimacha Isolate, VIII. Tunica
Isolate, IX. Tonkawa Isolate, X. Siouan Family, XI. Iroquoian
Family, XII. Caddoan Family, XIII. Yuchi Isolate, XIV. Yuman

Abbreviations

ablat. - ablative
acc. - accusative
act. - active
adess. - adessive
adj. - adjective, adjectival
adv. - adverb
allat. - allative
art. - article
asp. - aspect
caus. - causative
comit. - comitative
conj. - conjunction
dat. - dative
def. - definite
dem. - demonstrative
deriv. - derivational
det. - determiner
differ. - differing

elat. - elative
electr. - electrical
ess. - essive
excl. - exclusive
exper. - experience
fem. - feminine
1st pers. - first person
gen. - genitive
HCE - Hawaiian Creole English
honorif. - honorific
illat. - illative
imperat. - imperative
imperf. - imperfective
incl. - inclusive
indic. - indicative
iness. - inessive
inf. - infinitive
instr. - instrumental

interrog. - interrogative

irreg. - irregular

lit. - literally

loc. - locative

masc. - masculine

NC - noun class

neg. - negative

neut. - neuter

nom. - nominative

NP - noun phrase

obj. - object, objective

part. - partitive

particip. - participle

pass. - passive

perf. - perfective

pers. - person

PIE - Proto-Indo-European

pl. - plural

poss. - possessive

potent. - potential

preced. - preceding

prep. - preposition, prepositional

pres. - present

prog. - progressive

pron. - pronoun

ques. - question

relat. - relative

Russ. - Russian

SAE - Standard American English

2d pers. - second person

sing. - singular

sp. - speakers

sub. - subject

subord. - subordinate

suff. - suffix

Swed. - Swedish

term. - terminative

3d pers. - third person

tot. sp. - total number of speakers

transl. - translated

vb. - verb

vb. pref. - verb prefix

voc. - vocative

VP - verb phrase

An Introduction to
the Languages of the World

Chapter **1**   # Classification of Languages

Why bother classifying languages? There are several reasons why it is advantageous to do so. First, without a meaningful way of classifying languages we would not have an efficient framework within which to compare and contrast the numerous languages of the world. Second, a meaningful classificatory system allows us not only to arrange languages very neatly in their "pigeonholes" or "sample cases" like butterflies, but perhaps also to discover something new that we did not know before. Of course, not all classificatory frameworks are "meaningful" in this way; they may not always lead us to discover something new about the languages we are classifying or even display the truly important similarities and differences of these languages in a revealing and efficient way.

In the case of languages, it seems, it is necessary to have several different frameworks by means of which different important aspects of the world's languages are displayed for our inspection and perhaps we may be led to discover important correlations among various features.

GENETIC CLASSIFICATION

The oldest scientific way of classifying languages is into "language families." This method is called "genetic classification." Languages are considered to be "genetically related" if they can be shown (by using methods which will be discussed in some detail shortly) to be descended from the same parent language, or "proto-language." Thus, it can be shown that Russian and English are both descended from the same source language, dubbed Proto-Indo-European by linguists, and are therefore "genetically related" or "belong to the same language family."

How do linguists go about determining whether a given pair of languages belongs to the same language family? Basically, the process employed seeks to establish that there exist between such languages "systematic correspondences" that cannot be explained by any means save common origin of the languages in question.

A very common misconception concerning genetic relationship is that the related languages must somehow be "similar," especially in a superficial sort of way, that is, words in one language must show some phonetic resemblance to words with the same meaning in the other language. However, although very often this *may* be the case, especially if the languages in question are very closely related, it is *not* an absolute requirement for establishing genetic relationship. Furthermore, superficial resemblances can often be explained on the basis of such phenomena as borrowing, and therefore not only are they not necessarily present in the case of related languages, but they do not by themselves constitute valid proof that the two languages are genetically related. Linguistics departments often receive letters from well-meaning amateurs who, struck by some chance superficial similarities between languages spoken in widely separated corners of the globe, propose a new genetic alignment for the languages in question.

To establish that a pair of languages are genetically related one needs to demonstrate that *there are recurring sound correspondences between the words of the two languages which have roughly the same meaning and belong to the basic vocabulary.* The more such sound correspondences recur, the stronger the proof of genetic relationship.

Why *sound* correspondences? For the most part it seems that the connection between form (sound) and meaning of words is quite arbitrary. For example, there is no good reason why the English sequence of sounds *tree* should mean what it does, or for that matter that the same meaning is conveyed in Chinese by the sound sequence *shù*. It is true that there are some words in each language in which the connection between sound and meaning is not so arbitrary. For example, each language has some words like English *boom* and *buzz* (onomatopoeic expressions) which imitate the sounds they represent. Also, an exception to the general arbitrary nature of the connection between form and meaning are the so-called nursery words, such as *mama* and *papa,* which are found in most of the languages encountered so far.

These words are not entirely arbitrary because they have their origin in infants' babbling stage, which is governed by universal rules and tendencies built into each human baby's linguistic repertoire and are therefore independent of particular language. (Even so, there is still a large dose of arbitrariness in both onomatopoeia and nursery words. Take, for example, the onomatopoeia for rooster's crowing in English and Japanese: *cock-a-doodle-doo* and *kokekokko,* respectively. Or consider the following fact: in the Georgian language, spoken in the Caucasus region between Europe and Asia, *mama* means 'father' and *deda* means 'mother'.)

Another reason that sound correspondences are used to establish genetic relationship and not other formal characteristics of language, such as word order or structure of relative clauses, is that number of possible differences among languages in regard to these formal characteristics is surprisingly small: not all logically possible word orders actually occur among natural languages, and there seem to be only a few possible types of relative clause constructions. Thus, since the number of possibilities is so small, the likelihood of chance similarities and chance "correspondences" in these aspects of language structure is rather great. As we shall see when we discuss typological classification of languages, there are very compelling reasons for *not* taking typological parallels as proof of genetic relationship except in very special situations.

The sound correspondences have to 'recur'—some linguists prefer to say that the sound correspondences have to be "regular"—to ensure that they are not due to chance. It would be highly unlikely that by sheer chance there would arise a recurring correspondence between two sounds in two different languages in words meaning the same thing. For example, one can establish the following correspondence between English and Russian: English *s*:Russian *s*. This correspondence appears in such words as *son* and *sister* (Russian *syn* and *sestra,* respectively) as well as some other words. Of course, linguists do not look only for a couple of recurring correspondences to establish genetic relationship; they look for as many as they can find in order to strengthen their case in support of the genetic relationship claim. Also—and this cannot be emphasized enough—linguists do not look at individual correspondences in isolation: the comparativist who notes the existence of the *s*:*s* correspondence between English and Russian will also have to demonstrate that the rest of the sounds in the words which exhibit this correspondence also exhibit a recurring relationship. Thus, in our example it is possible to demonstrate that there is another recurring sound correspondence, *r*:*r*, in the word for *sister* (e.g., compare English *three* and Russian *tri*).

Why do we insist on "basic vocabulary," and what does this term mean? We have already eliminated two kinds of words from consideration—onomatopoeia and nursery words—because these words exhibit crosslinguistic similarities due to universal tendencies and a certain degree of nonarbitrariness in the connection between form and meaning. The reason we need to eliminate all but the basic, everyday type of vocabulary (usually said to consist of items such as names of body parts, kinship terms, natural phenomena not limited to a particular climate or place on earth, bodily functions, etc.) is that this type of vocabulary is not as readily borrowed from language to language as is other type of vocabulary.

Unfortunately for linguists, in certain circumstances everything may end up being borrowed, and therefore insisting on the basic vocabulary will not absolutely guarantee that one will eliminate all possible borrowings. There are two types of borrowing. In the usual situation only nonbasic vocabulary items tend to be borrowed: those items for which the borrowing language may not have handy terms, as in the case of new inventions, foreign philosophical concepts, imported fads, fashions, and so on. In the less usual case (but by no means very rare) there may be a prolonged contact, such that there is a high degree of bilingualism, or one language has such a marked prestige over the other language that the lower-prestige language borrows even basic vocabulary items. Not only is basic vocabulary borrowed in such situations but there is usually massive borrowing of vocabulary, which in turn may affect the rest of the grammar of the borrowing language. Such massive borrowings have occurred in the history of English (from French) and Japanese (from Chinese).

Massive borrowings usually leave some clues that they have occurred. For example, very often languages that have borrowed extensively from other languages, including basic vocabulary items, will have many doublets: two ways of referring to the same thing, one borrowed and one native. Thus, in Japanese there are two sets of numerals, one set borrowed from Chinese and the other the native Japanese set. Although the use of the two sets in Japanese is not random but usually depends on what is being counted, either set can be used when one is not counting anything in particular. The existence of such doublets immediately raises the suspicion that one member of such doublet has been borrowed, for languages usually avoid the luxury of having two different words for everything unless there is some external factor, such as prestige, that compels the borrowing language to tolerate such lexical redundancies.

If an intimate contact between various languages (whether genetically related or not) continues for a long time in a certain geographic area, that area may develop into a "linguistic area," that is, an area in which languages share a number of linguistic traits in common *not because these traits have been inherited from the same parent language but because these traits have diffused from one language into another.* On the Balkan peninsula, in southeastern Europe, we have an example of a linguistic area which involves related languages belonging to various branches of the Indo-European language family. One of the several features that is shared among the languages of this region is the presence of a postposed definite article, which is not an inherited feature from their ultimate parent language Proto-Indo-European but must have been a local innovation in one of the languages that somehow spread to other languages in the area.

An example of a linguistic area which involves languages that are not recognized as being genetically related is India. In India, there are languages belonging to three different language families: the Indo-Aryan group (belonging to the Indo-European language family), Dravidian (Dravidian language family), and Munda languages (Austroasiatic language family). In spite of being genetically unrelated, these language groups all share some linguistic features in common which must have diffused throughout the area from one language to another. One such feature here is the presence of series of retroflex consonants in all the languages of the subcontinent. Since neither Indo-European languages nor Austroasiatic languages outside of the area are noted as having this feature, and since it is clear that we have to reconstruct a retroflex series of consonants for Proto-Dravidian, it is reasonable to assume that retroflex consonants have diffused into Indo-Aryan and Munda languages from Dravidian. This is yet another reason why it is not very convincing to argue for genetic relationship solely on the basis of typological similarities.

Finally, we should ask ourselves whether it is possible to prove that some languages are *not* genetically related. Upon a moment's reflection one should realize that such a proof is strictly speaking not possible. After all, the fact that we have never seen a Martian does not necessarily *prove* that Martians do not exist. (In general, it is much harder to prove a negative hypothesis than a positive one: the discovery of even a single Martian would prove that Martians exist, but one would have to show that he has searched high and low in all the likely places for Martians and not found any before most people would finally accept the proposition that there are no Martians.) In the same way, just because one cannot at a given moment find the necessary evidence that a given pair of languages are genetically related does not necessarily mean that the languages in question do not have their ultimate origin in the same protolanguage. It may simply mean that the necessary evidence is quite difficult to find or even that such evidence is no longer available: After several millennia of separation the two languages in question as well as their basic vocabularies may have changed so much that the sound correspondences linguists can set up recur so few times that it is hard to convince anyone that any genetic relationship exists between these languages. It may well be that *all* the languages presently spoken in the world are genetically related; however, at present we do not have the means either to prove or disprove this hypothesis. It is estimated by some linguists that our present methods of establishing genetic relationship among languages work only for languages that have been separated from each other for less than five thousand years; at the same time it seems highly probable that human beings have been speaking for tens of millennia.

GENETIC SUBGROUPING

After establishing which languages are genetically related and which appear not to be, there are several other things that comparativists can do. First, they can attempt to reconstruct as much of the parent language of the related languages as possible. At present fairly reliable, though by no means perfect, methods of reconstructing the sound system, lexicon, and morphology are available. Much work is being done on establishing comparable methods for the reconstruction of the syntax of the parent language, but there is not yet any widely accepted comparative methodology for the reconstruction of syntax. This may be so because we seem to know more about the *synchronic* working of both phonology and morphology and therefore understand more how these components of grammar may change through time, whereas in syntax we haven't yet been able to hit upon the correct model for the description of the synchronic workings of syntax. (One of the requirements for a syntactic theory, then, would be that it must, among other things, offer a basis for explaining how syntactic change takes place.)

Second, comparativists may attempt to ascertain which among those languages that they have already determined to be genetically related are "more closely related" among themselves and which are more "distantly related." Again, what linguists mean by "closely related" is commonly misunderstood to mean 'superficially more similar to each other', and therefore it must be stressed that this expression, "more closely related," has a special, technical meaning in this context.

Later we shall look at some concrete examples from real languages; for the sake of clarity, let us look at a simple hypothetical case first. Suppose that you have just examined three different languages X, Y, and Z and determined that all three of them are genetically related. As you begin to reconstruct the sound system of their protolanguage you come to the conclusion that several sound changes that you have posited must have taken place in the history of both X and Y. Both X and Y appear to have changed a word-final -*m* to -*n* and a word-final -*k* to a glottal stop. In addition, both X and Y have devoiced all obstruents (stops, fricatives, and affricates).

How can we explain why X and Y share these three changes? There are several possible answers. First, it could be a coincidence that both X and Y underwent the same changes. However, the more such shared changes there are, the less likely it is that this phenomenon results entirely from coincidence. Coincidence as an explanation is likely only if all the changes that X and Y have in common are very common sound changes that are well-motivated on phonetic grounds. Even so, it would be highly improbable that two separate languages would undergo a whole series of *identical* sound changes through sheer coincidence. If the sound changes shared are not so usual or the number of such shared changes argues against chance, another possible explanation offers itself: the shared changes must have taken place not when X and Y were already separate languages but before they became separate languages. That is, there was an *intermediate protolanguage,* Proto-XY, during the existence of which these changes took place, and then X and Y split into separate entities each of which had its own separate development from that point on.

The relationship among X, Y, and Z can be represented by means of a "family tree diagram" (see Figure 1.1). This diagram allows us to explain the shared changes between X and Y by proposing that the split between X and Y was a later phenomenon that the split of the ancestor of X and Y, Proto-XY, and Z. Thus languages X and Y are considered to be 'more closely related' to each other than either is to Z. (It should also be noted that although for the sake of illustration we have used sound changes, the shared changes or innovations may consist of other types of changes, say, lexical or morphological, or even a combination of all types of changes.) Note that even though

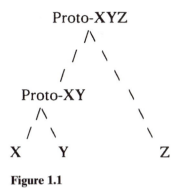

Figure 1.1

X and Y have been declared to be more closely related to each other than either is to Z, X and Z may share a number of similarities that are not shared by X and Y, the 'closely related' languages. Thus, superficially at least, X and Z may look as if *they* were the more closely related pair, and usually beginners jump to the conclusion that these indeed are the most closely related languages. What tends to be forgotten is that the basis for determining which languages are more closely related is *not* superficial resemblances, which may be due largely or even entirely to *shared retentions* of the features of the ancestor language of the entire family, but *shared innovations or changes*. Accordingly, unless one has reconstructed the protolanguage (at least in outline form) of the entire family one cannot do genetic subgrouping because the latter task requires a determination of which features of the protolanguage have changed in each language and which have been retained in each language.

The method of genetic subgrouping just described and the family tree diagram that is usually used to display the results of such subgrouping both suffer from serious deficiencies because they assume certain things that are not always actually true. First, it is quite possible that the reason why X and Y have some innovations in common is that various changes diffused from X to Y and vice versa *after* X and Y had become differentiated languages. In such a case it would, of course, be erroneous to ascribe the shared innovations to a period when X and Y were still a part of the same language. The tree diagram, too, implies that once split, languages cannot influence each other, which is quite incorrect. The existence of the Balkan linguistic area and similar phenomena elsewhere disproves this. In addition, the family tree diagram seems to imply that splits between languages are neat, clean breaks which happen at a particular moment in time. Such "breaks" may occasionally occur when an entire section of population moves suddenly to a far off location, or when for some other reason communication is cut off between various groups of people speaking the same language, but usually we encounter situations in which dialectal differences gradually build up over the course of time; different dialects continue to be spoken in the vicinity of each other and continue to influence each other linguistically. Finally, there is no specific point at which we can say that two dialects of the same language have become separate languages in their own right. One may argue that one such point is reached when the two variants are no longer mutually intelligible. However, mutual intelligibility itself is a continuum without sharp, neat breaks.

Another method of subgrouping, called "lexicostatistics," is used quite often in those cases where the protolanguage of the family has not been reconstructed yet or the data on individual languages—especially on the historical changes that have taken place in them—are severely limited. (Very often in such cases the only thing a linguist has to work with are word lists of the languages involved.) Basically, this method involves calculating the percentages of "shared cognates," that is, words traceable to the same historical source, in the basic vocabularies of the languages being subgrouped. In the example that we discussed, the same family tree would be obtained if languages X and Y were to be found to share, say, 80 percent of basic vocabulary in common whereas the percentage of shared basic vocabulary that either X or Y shares with Z is significantly lower than 80 percent (say around 50 percent).

Most linguists do not consider lexicostatistics to be a very reliable tool for subgrouping for several reasons. Lexicostatistics simply counts the number of shared cognates without ascertaining whether this sharing of cognates is a result of lexical innovations, lexical retentions, or borrowing from each other or from outside sources. If we consider that in the first place genetic subgrouping was set up to explain the phenomenon of shared innovations in related languages, it becomes obvious why a method that ignores the distinction between innovations and retentions is regarded as being a very crude tool for subgrouping. Second, normally one looks at all kinds of innovations, sound changes, lexical changes, morphological changes, and the like, all of which strengthen the case for a particular subgrouping, whereas lexicostatistics looks only at the lexicon. Finally, lexicostatistics sometimes poses a very peculiar problem for anyone who wants to draw a family tree on the basis of lexicostatistical data—what to do when, say, X and Y have 75 percent of basic vocabulary in common and Y and Z share 75 percent, but X and Z share only 50 percent in common. (On the basis of the above, X and Y should belong to the same branch, and Y and Z should belong to the same branch, but X and Z should not, which is a paradoxical situation.) Difficulties such as these have made most linguists wary of lexicostatistics.

I now review the method of establishing genetic relationship and doing genetic subgrouping by examining some data from real languages. To keep things simple, only a small portion of the relevant data will be presented (see Table 1.1).

There are no consonant clusters or word-final consonants in Samoan and Hawaiian. Maranao is a language spoken in the Philippines.

ESTABLISHING GENETIC RELATIONSHIP

First of all, even though this may seem obvious from Table 1.1, we must *formally* show that these languages are all genetically related by demonstrating that there are at least some recurring sound correspondences among all of

Table 1.1

GLOSS	MALAY	SAMOAN	MARANAO	HAWAIIAN
1. 'two'	dua	lua	dua	lua
2. 'five'	lima	lima	lima	lima
3. 'sky'	laŋit	laŋi	laŋit	lani
4. 'to cry'	taŋis	taŋi	ula'ul	kani
5. 'louse'	kutu	'utu	kutu	'uku
6. 'lobster'	udaŋ	ula	udaŋ	ula
7. 'I'	aku	a'u	aku	a'u
8. 'rafters'	kasaw	'aso	kasaw	'aho
9. 'mistake'	salah	sala	sala'	hala
10. 'eye'	mata	mata	mata	maka
11. 'pandanus'	pandan	fala	raguruy	hala
12. 'hibiscus'	baru	fau	wagu	hau
13. 'house'	balay	fale	walay	hale
14. 'coconut'	ñiur	niu	niug	niu
15. 'hardwood'	teras	toa	tegas	koa
16. 'die'	mati	mate	matay	make
17. 'way, path'	jalan	ala	lalan	ala
18. 'drink'	minum	inu	inum	inu

ŋ = velar nasal consonant
ñ = palatal nasal
' = glottal stop

them. For example, one can establish the recurring correspondences for the data given (see Table 1.2).

Note that many other sets of recurring sound correspondences can be found in the data, but they do not necessarily involve basic vocabulary items. (For example, $b:f:w:h$ correspondence which occurs in the items for 'hibiscus' and 'house'.) On the other hand, many of the nonbasic vocabulary items listed exhibit the same correspondences as the basic vocabulary items. (For example, the item for 'hardwood' exhibits the same initial consonant correspondence as correspondence 3 in Table 1.2.) This latter fact suggests that at least some of the nonbasic vocabulary items are not borrowed forms

Table 1.2

MALAY	SAMOAN	MARANAO	HAWAIIAN	ITEM
1. l	l	l	l	2, 3, 9, etc.
2. m	m	m	m	2, 10, 16
3. t	t	t	k	10, 16
4. u	u	u	u	1, 7, 18
5. a	a	a	a	1, 2, 9, etc.
6. i	i	i	i	2, 3, 18

but inherited from the common parent or protolanguage of these four languages.

It should also be pointed out that although it looks as if all four languages in question are genetically related, not all of their vocabulary items, whether basic or nonbasic, are necessarily cognate (i.e., traceable to the same source). Since even the basic vocabulary may be replaced through semantic change, we do not necessarily expect that all the basic vocabulary items be cognate in the related languages. (For example, compare the Maranao word for 'to cry' in Table 1.1).

GENETIC SUBGROUPING

Now that it has been formally established that all the languages in our sample seem to be genetically related, I will attempt to establish which of the languages are more closely related to each other, specifically, which of the languages share a period of common development after the split from the parent language of all four of the languages we have cited. In other words, we have to look for innovations which are shared by two or more related languages.

Once we have established that certain languages are genetically related, we no longer need to exclude the nonbasic vocabulary items from our consideration. Of course, we still have to be on the lookout for possible loanwords, but once we have established what the "regular" sound correspondences are in the basic vocabulary of these languages we can consider those nonbasic items that exhibit the same sound correspondences to be also cognate. If these languages are related, it stands to reason that at least some of their nonbasic vocabulary items are also cognate. (One of the ways we identify possible borrowings is by observing which items exhibit unexpected sound correspondences.)

The correspondences cited in Table 1.2 to establish genetic relationship are not useful for genetic subgrouping, with the possible exception of correspondence 3. All the other sound correspondences listed are *identities*, that is, each language has exactly the same reflex of the protophoneme, and therefore, if we are looking for shared innovations, or changes that took place only in *some* of the related languages, these correspondences are not very helpful.

Correspondence 3 turns out to be of little help also because it is not possible to determine without more evidence whether the Hawaiian language alone has innovated (by changing *t* to *k*) or whether Malay, Maranao, and Samoan have innovated by changing *k* to *t*. If we could show the latter case to be correct, we could then claim that the three languages just mentioned are more closely related to each other than any of them is to Hawaiian. (Given more evidence, which we won't cite here, it becomes clear that it is Hawaiian alone that has innovated in this case.)

By adding sound correspondences that are derived both from basic and nonbasic vocabulary items we can observe that the languages in question seem to fall into two groups (see Table 1.3).

Table 1.3

MALAY	SAMOAN	MARANAO	HAWAIIAN	ITEM
7. d	l	d	l	1, 6
8. s	Ø	s	Ø	15, 14
9. h	Ø	'	Ø	9
10. t	Ø	t	Ø	3
11. m	Ø	m	Ø	18
12. ŋ	Ø	ŋ	Ø	6
13. g	Ø	r	Ø	14

Let us first compare correspondence 1 in Table 1.2 with the correspondence 7 in Table 1.3. Correspondence 1 has *l* in all four languages, and it is therefore not unreasonable to assume that this correspondence most likely reflects **l* of the protolanguage. In correspondence 7 on the other hand some languages have *l* (Samoan and Hawaiian) and some have *d* (Malay and Maranao). In this instance there are at least two possible explanations that we may consider: (1) Malay and Maranao have changed the original **l* to *d* under some conditions but preserved it as *l* under some other conditions. (2) The original protophoneme **d* is preserved as such in Malay and Maranao but is shifted everywhere to *l* in Samoan and Hawaiian.

Since both *l* and *d* appear in pretty much the same environments in Malay and Maranao—initially in items 1 and 2 or between vowels as in items 6 and 9 in Table 1.1—it is not possible to formulate a rule which would correctly predict when the hypothetical **l* became *d* and when it stayed *l* in Malay and Maranao. Furthermore, since the comparative method does not allow us to posit an unconditioned phonemic split (positing that some **l*'s shifted to *d* irregularly) we must reject the first hypothesis and look at another alternative.

The second alternative, on the other hand, does not go counter to the usual assumption of the comparative method that sound changes are regular: there are no *d*'s in either Hawaiian or Samoan which have not shifted to *l*. Therefore, we accept the second hypothesis, which means that it is Hawaiian and Samoan that share an innovation in common: **d → l*.

In addition, correspondences 8 through 13 offer additional evidence for a closer genetic relationship between Samoan and Hawaiian. Although most of these correspondences do not recur in our data, the words in which they occur are clearly cognate since they exhibit many of the regular correspondences established on the basis of basic vocabulary. What these cases all share is that Malay and Maranao exhibit various consonants whereas Samoan and Hawaiian have zero reflexes. Also, these correspondences all occur at the end of words. Here, too, there are two logical alternatives. (1) Malay and Maranao have added various consonants at the end of words; (2) Samoan and Hawaiian have deleted all word-final consonants.

Again, it is not possible to justify accepting the first hypothesis since it is obvious that this would go counter to the usual assumptions of the comparative method: Malay and Maranao did *not* add a consonant at the end of every word (compare 'five' and 'lobster'), and there is no way to account for different consonants being added after identical vowels (compare 'sky' and 'to cry' in Malay).

On the other hand, if we posit that Samoan and Hawaiian have dropped all word-final consonants, there are no counterexamples in our data to account for. Moreover, deletion of word-final consonants is a more common phenomenon than epenthesis, or insertion, of word-final consonants (although the latter does occasionally occur). The clincher is provided by some evidence from Samoan and Hawaiian that the word-final consonants in Malay and Maranao represent a shared retention from the protolanguage. For example, the passive form of the verb 'to drink' in Hawaiian is *inumia,* which retains the original ending of the verb stem (*m*) because of the following passive suffix *-ia*. (Similarly, Samoan also shows internal evidence suggesting that word-final consonants were deleted.)

To sum up, I have established that Samoan and Hawaiian share at least two innovations (sound changes) in common: (1) shift of **d* to *l* in all environments, and (2) deletion of all word-final consonants. Therefore I conclude that Samoan and Hawaiian are more closely related to each other than either is to Malay or Maranao. But what about Malay and Maranao? Don't they look "more closely related" because their forms are so similar? Although it would be rather tedious to demonstrate, it is indeed not possible to establish on the basis of the data given that Maranao and Malay have any innovations in common. All that they share are the retentions. That is, they look very much alike because they are both comparatively conservative languages, not because they have changed in a similar manner. Thus in spite of their superficial similarity, they by definition do not qualify as 'more closely related'.

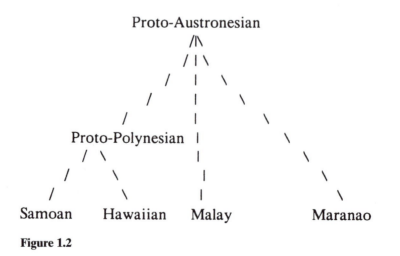

Figure 1.2

Accordingly, the interrelations among these languages can be schematized by means of a tree diagram (see Figure 1.2). Other types of diagrams representing genetic subgrouping are possible, but while they are in many respects more accurate than the tree diagram, the tree diagram remains the most popular way of representing genetic subgrouping. In this book the tree diagram is the primary visual means of accounting for genetic subgrouping, but the reader is cautioned about the limitations of this kind of representation.

TYPOLOGICAL CLASSIFICATION OF LANGUAGES

Languages may also be classified according to the type of their structure. Such a classification is potentially much more revealing, since genetically related languages are not necessarily also similar in structure, whereas by claiming that two languages belong to the same *type* of language one does claim that they share at least some similarities. Thus, for example, saying that Russian and English are genetically related merely makes the claim that these two languages have a common origin but does not necessarily imply that the two languages have preserved many common features. Thus a person who knows English would not on the basis of such a claim expect that Russian would necessarily be similar to English in respect to word order. On the other hand, if one is told that both English and Russian are Subject + Verb + Object languages, then one would know that at least in regard to basic word order (and even in respect to the order of other types of syntactic constituents) the two languages are very similar.

Actually, genetic and typological classification supplement each other very well: the former tells us something about the origins of a particular language, whereas the latter tells us something about the structure of that language. Typological classification is not yet as fully developed a science as is genetic classification. The reason for that is that until relatively recently linguists had not identified the really important, fundamental features on which we should base the typological classification of languages. After all, languages may differ from each other in many ways, and since all languages differ from each other in at least *some* respects, a classification of languages that took into account *all* the features would be too cumbersome and lead to a taxonomy in which each individual language would be a separate type. In the past, there were many proposals for a meaningful typological taxonomy of languages focusing primarily on morphology; in recent years there have also been very interesting proposals for syntactic taxonomy, and even one for a holistic approach that combines salient features of phonology, morphology, and syntax.

PHONOLOGICAL TYPOLOGY

One may classify languages into tone languages, pitch-accent languages, and dynamic accent languages. Each of these categories can perhaps be further subdivided. For example, one can subdivide tone languages into those that have (underlyingly) only level tones and those that in addition to level tones, have contour tones (i.e., tones which change pitch direction). One can also subdivide dynamic accent (stress) languages according to whether the placement of stress is predictable or unpredictable in them.

It is possible to classify languages also according to other features of their phonological systems. For example, one can classify languages according to the number of vowel phonemes in their phonological system, and then further subclassify the languages according to the particular vowels found in each system. For such type of language classification one may turn to the pioneering work of Trubetzkoy (1969), who, however, was not primarily interested in typological classification for its own sake. Also, Hockett (1955) presents a discussion of phonological typology based on the American structuralist model of phonology.

Morphological Typology

Morphological structure has been the traditional basis for language classification, and those readers who are interested in a fairly detailed overview of the history of language classification based on morphology may wish to consult Horne (1966). Here I provide only a summary of important aspects of morphological typology.

In spite of many terminological differences (and some terminological confusion) various scholars working in this field in the nineteenth and early twentieth centuries more or less agreed that there are three or four major types of language. Each of the four traditional morphological types listed below is followed by the name of a language usually cited as supposedly epitomizing that type. The usual terms referring to each type of language appear in parentheses. (Since different typologists define these terms somewhat differently, the terms in question are cited here only for reference.)

> Type I: Classical Chinese *(analytic/isolating)*
>
> Type II: Turkish *(agglutinative)*
>
> Type III: Latin *(fusional/synthetic/inflected)*
>
> Type IV: Eskimo *(polysynthetic/incorporating)*

Although one may discuss the main differences among the four language types under various rubrics, I focus here only on the most salient ones, emphasizing some aspects that were not necessarily emphasized by the scholars who set up the original typological schema.

The main division should be made between Type I and Type II languages, on the one hand, and the Type III and Type IV, on the other. The feature that is the main differentiator here is the transparency of word structure: In Type I and Type II languages the morphological makeup of words is crystal clear and the function of various morphemes is relatively easy to ascertain, whereas in Type III and Type IV languages word structure tends to be obscured by various factors. (Note that it *tends* to be obscured but is not necessarily obscured in all cases.)

Although Turkish and other Type II languages tend to have long, morphologically complex words consisting of series of affixes attached to the root or stem morpheme, and Classical Chinese (Type I) has relatively short words and extremely few affixes, in both language types the morphological structure of words is completely transparent because the boundaries between adjacent morphemes are seldom obscured (i.e., morphological cuts are seldom in doubt), nonautomatic morpheme alternants (i.e., morphologically conditioned allomorphs) are few or even nonexistent, there are no morphemes whose status as independent morphemes is questionable (such as various morphemes which merely connect other morphemes to each other, thematic vowels, conjugation markers, etc.), and affixes usually have a well defined grammatical function.

In languages belonging to Type III and Type IV, the morphological structure of words may be obscured by the presence of "empty morphemes" (such as *cran-* in *cranberry*), suppletion, and other types of nonautomatic morpheme alternants. Also, such languages tend to have a fair number of portmanteau morphs and even what I call "portmanteau morphemes." An example of a portmanteau morph is French *au* which is the realization of a sequence of two morphemes: the preposition meaning 'to' and the masculine definite article, both of which have independent realizations in other environments. An example of a portmanteau morpheme is the suffix *-i* in the Latin word *fili-i* 'of the son', which signals at the same time masculine gender, singular number, and genitive case, none of which is ever signaled in Latin by an independent morpheme.

The difference between a Type I language and a Type II language is the same as the difference between a Type III and a Type IV language: Type I and Type III languages have relatively less affixation than Type II and Type IV; what in languages of Types I and III is expressed by independent words very often may, or even must, be expressed by bound affixes in languages belonging to Types II and Type IV. In general, Type III languages have more affixation than Type I languages but not as much as Type II or Type IV. Although languages belonging to Type I have very few affixes, it does not mean that their words are not morphologically complex—usually languages of this type allow quite free compounding of stem or root morphemes within a word.

Languages belonging to Type I and Type III place a relatively greater burden on syntax than do languages belonging to Type II and Type IV, which place a relatively greater burden on morphology. Type I languages especially tend to have a fairly rigid word order to signal various grammatical relations between words. That is not to say that languages belonging to other types may not have a fairly rigid word order as well; we are talking here of natural tendencies, not necessarily rigid laws. In this case "natural tendency" has a reasonable explanation: it is only natural that languages with little affixation should employ word order to mark at least some grammatical relations, and the fewer morphological devices there are in a language for marking such relations, the more likely it is that syntactic devices such as word order will be used instead.

In order to illustrate the "spirit" of the structure exemplifying each type of language, a few fairly typical sentences from Classical Chinese, Turkish, Latin, and Yup'ik Eskimo are cited, together with a morpheme-by-morpheme translation and an idiomatic English translation, followed by a brief commentary on the salient aspects of the grammatical structure of the example sentences.

In all the examples to follow, the romanized version of the sentence or phrase uses spaces to mark word breaks and dashes to mark morpheme breaks. The morpheme-by-morpheme translation of the examples marks word breaks by slashes and morpheme boundaries by pluses. (This format is followed throughout the book.)

Type I: Classical Chinese

A. 下　馬　人　車　中

xià　mǎ　rù　chē　zhōng

descend/ horse/ enter/ chariot/ middle

'[He] got off the horse [and] got into the chariot.'

B. 松　下　問　童　子

sōng　xià　wèn　tóng　zǐ

pine/ under/ ask/ lad/ diminutive marker

'Under the pine trees [I] asked the boy.'

C. 楚　莊　王　賜　群　臣　酒

Chǔ　Zhuāng　Wáng　cì　qún　chén　jiǔ

name of a region/ proper name of a person/ king/ bestow/ flock/ official/ wine

'King Zhuang of Chu bestowed wine on his ministers.'

D. 豬　人　立　而　啼

zhū　rén　lì　ér　tí

pig/ man/ stand/ and/ cry

'The pig stood up [like a] man and cried.'

The morpheme *xia* can act as a verb (as in sentence A where it was translated as 'descend') or as a postposition (as in sentence B where it is translated as 'under'). Likewise *ren,* which usually functions as a noun ('man'), appears in an adverbial function in sentence D without any formal marking. This illustrates one of the secondary traits of Type I languages: One and the same morpheme may sometimes act as a different part of speech depending on the context *without any morphological marking to signal the different function.*

Sentence C illustrates the fact that word order alone marks three different grammatical relationships among the noun phrases: the subject (King Zhuang), the indirect object (his ministers), and the direct object (wine).

There are no true affixes in the preceding examples; all the words cited are stem morphemes. The only morpheme that seems to act as an affix is *zi*, the diminutive. However, this morpheme appears also as an independent stem meaning 'son' or 'offspring'.

No morphemes cited in the previous examples have any allomorphs (insofar as this can be determined from the logographic writing system); however, Early Classical Chinese does have some fused portmanteau morphemes.

Type II: Turkish

A. Köy-ün-den çık-ma-mış köy-lü bu mesele-ler-i anla-r-mı

village + third person possessive + from/ come + negative + past participle/ village + characterizing suffix/ demonstrative/ problem + plural + object marker/ understand + aorist + interrogative

'Does the villager who has not left his village understand these problems?'

B. Ev-ler-im-iz-den gel-mi-yor-d-um

house + plural + first person possessive + possessor pluralizer + from/ come + negative + progressive + past + first person

'I was not coming from our houses.'

It is fairly evident from the preceding examples that both nouns and verbs in Turkish may consist of relatively long strings of morphemes: a stem followed by a series of suffixes. What is not readily apparent from the examples is that allomorphy is overwhelmingly regular. (However, there are *some* irregularities present even in the two example sentences: The progressive aspect marker *yor,* for example, violates the rules of Turkish vowel harmony.) In addition there is a marked absence of portmanteau morphemes; concepts such as number, case, tense, aspect, and person are all marked by separate, independent morphemes.

Type III: Latin

A. Fili-us patr-em am-at

offspring + nominative singular masculine/ father + accusative singular masculine/ love + third person singular present indicative

'The son loves the father.'

B. Pater fili-um vid-et

> father + nominative singular masculine is here repre-
> sented by a zero allomorph/ offspring + masculine ac-
> cusative singular/ see + third person singular present
> indicative

'The father sees the son.'

The examples provided show only a moderate amount of affixation, which is normal for languages of this type. There are several examples of portmanteau morphemes (e.g., -us which at once shows case, gender, and number). Moreover, it is not always clear where the morphological cuts should be made. For example, the suffix representing third person indicative present has two allomorphs in the examples given: -at and -et. It may be argued that -t should be isolated as the marker of the third person singular; the vowels a and e would then be allomorphs of a present indicative morpheme. Alternatively, one could also recognize the vowels as independent morphemes signaling the verb conjugation. In either analysis there is a large element of arbitrariness involved, and the presence of such forms as am-ō ('I love'), in which the indicative present or conjugation marker morpheme is missing, complicates the morphological analysis since -ō is clearly a person marker regardless of what else it may be said to mark.

Finally, it is typical of Type III (as well as Type IV) languages that most root or stem morphemes are bound. That is, they cannot appear alone as independent words in the language. This is true of most of the roots given in the two preceding Latin examples, and perhaps one could make a very convincing argument that all Latin roots are bound. (For example, *fili* 'offspring' can appear as independent word in the vocative singular masculine, but only because the vocative singular masculine suffix is represented by a zero allomorph with this root.) Of course, affixes in all types of languages tend to be bound morphemes.

Type IV: Yup'ik Eskimo

A. Angyar-pa-li-yugnga-yugnar-quq-llu

> boat + big + make + be able + probably + third person singular indicative intransitive + also

'Also, he can probably make big boats.'

B. Angut-em ner-aa neqa

> man + relative singular case/ eat + third person singular transitive indicative/ fish

'The man eats the fish.'

Example A not only illustrates a long string of affixes but also the fact that languages of this type often "incorporate" direct and indirect object nominals along with some of their modifiers by attaching them to a verb root. This is generally done only in case the object nominals are indefinite, as in example A. In those cases where the object is definite, the latter is expressed by an independent word (cf. example B).

It should be emphasized here that the presence of pronominal subject and object affixes attached to the verbs does not qualify a language as being incorporating.

Besides having portmanteau morphemes (e.g., third person singular indicative transitive), Yup'ik Eskimo has extremely complicated morphophonemics (e.g., suffixes which cause deletion of the preceding consonant and those that do not) which render many a morpheme boundary opaque.

In languages of this type, word order is not as important as the order of morphemes in a word. The same is true to a lesser extent in the case of Type II languages.

Perhaps it is not an exaggeration to say that languages of this type have a potentially infinite number of words. I could determine no theoretical limit on the number of affixes that can be appended to a single Yup'ik Eskimo word. In languages belonging to the other three types, a similar potential "infinity of words" effect may be achieved by means of compounding, which involves combining two or more stems or roots into single words. It should be noted, however, that languages differ significantly in the extent to which such processes are allowed to go. For example, English allows only a moderate amount of compounding, whereas German is famous for its very long compounds, which are often cited to amuse speakers of moderately compounding languages. The following example, cited from Uspenskij (1957:307), was seen in a German stamp catalogue. (Here plus signs mark the potential word breaks within the compound. The morpheme breaks are left unmarked.)

> Kaiser + Wilhelm + Jerusalems + reise + gedächtnis + brief + karten + post + marke

> 'Kaiser Wilhelm's Jerusalem trip commemorative postcard stamp'

At this point the reader may legitimately wonder, To which of the above four types of languages does English belong? The answer to this question is not, unfortunately, a straightforward one. Although English shares many features with Type I languages such as Classical Chinese, it also shares some features with languages such as Latin. For example, the English words *fish* and *man* can both be used as either verbs or nouns without any special marking to indicate when they are used as verbs and when as nouns. In English, too, it is the word order alone that marks the case relations among the three noun phrases in the following sentence: "Peter gave John the book."

On the other hand, English has a lot of irregular morphology, including suppletion and portmanteau allomorphs (e.g., foot + PLURAL = feet), which makes it look more like a Type III language. In addition, there are even a few examples of words containing long sequences of affixes, the allomorphs of which are perfectly regular, suggesting the type of structures common in Type II languages (e.g., the word *anti-dis-ESTABLISH-ment-ari-an-ism*). Thus, one may conclude that, typologically speaking, English is neither fish nor fowl: it is a typological anomaly. It turns out that most of the world's languages do not fit neatly within the categories of traditional morphological typology.

To remedy this problem, at least in part, Edward Sapir (1921) proposed a rather complicated refinement of the traditional morphological typology, but his schema provided up to 2,870 "pigeonholes" into which languages could be placed and was therefore too cumbersome. In addition, it did not completely do away with the problem of what to do with languages such as English which have features typical of different major typological classes of languages. Today it seems clear that any classificatory schema that attempts to pigeonhole an entire *language* within a typological schema cannot avoid at least some degree of arbitrariness.

Eventually, Joseph Greenberg (1960) hit upon the idea that one need not necessarily pigeonhole entire languages as belonging to one clearly delineated type or another. Instead, he proposed that one could calculate the *degree* to which a certain typologically important feature is present in a given language. Thus, for example, one could calculate the average ratio of prefixes per word by counting how many prefixes and how many words are found in a given representative passage in a given language. This is clearly a superior way of typologizing languages for the following reasons:

1. It avoids the arbitrariness of having to decide just how many prefixes (or whatever other feature) a language must have before it is labeled as "a prefixing language."

2. It reflects better the true nature of the language in that, for example, those languages that have a number of prefixes which are rarely used will have a very low index of prefixation, just like languages that have a very small inventory of prefixes to begin with. In the old schema, which was an "all or nothing" kind of classification, a language having only one or two prefixes would be classified as a prefixing language just like a language that had hundreds of different prefixes, and only languages that had no prefixes of any kind would be classified as nonprefixing.

3. It provides the possibility of comparing different *styles* in the same language in regard to certain typologically relevant features, thus recognizing that a language is not a perfectly homogeneous entity but has typologically quite distinct variants.

In his article, Greenberg proposes the following typological indexes:

1. *Degree of synthesis* involves the ratio of morphemes to words. Note that this index seems to combine the degree of affixation and the degree of compounding into one index.

2. *Index of agglutination* involves the ratio of agglutinative constructions (i.e., combinations of morphemes whose allomorphs are completely automatic in that environment) per morph junctures (i.e., the total number of morpheme junctures within a given word). Type II languages would naturally have a very high index of agglutination.

3. *Compositional index* is the ratio of roots per word. In other words, this index measures the degree of compounding in a given language.

4. *Derivational index* is the ratio of derivational morphemes per word. (We do not need to concern ourselves here with Greenberg's distinction between derivational and inflectional affixes.)

5. *Gross inflectional index* is the ratio of inflectional morphemes per word.

6. *Prefixial index* is the ratio of prefixes per word.

7. *Suffixial index* is the ratio of suffixes per word.

8. *Isolational index* is the ratio of instances of significant order per total nexus. Stated more simply, this index measures the degree of significant word order in a language. One might argue that this particular index is more syntactic than morphological in nature or that it at least straddles the line between the two.

9. *Pure inflectional index* is the ratio of instances of nonconcordial (see next index) inflectional morphemes per nexus.

10. *Concordial index* is the ratio of instances of concordial inflectional morphemes (in other words, morphemes which signal some kind of grammatical agreement) per nexus.

Curiously, despite some initial interest, nothing was done to improve and develop further Greenberg's indexes. That may be because the attention of linguists interested in language typology, including that of Greenberg himself, turned to syntactic typology, which blossomed because of a general shift of interest to syntactic phenomena stimulated by Noam Chomsky's generative syntax.

SYNTACTIC TYPOLOGY

The development of syntactic typology owes much both to Noam Chomsky, whose ideas greatly stimulated interest in matters syntactic in general, and to Joseph Greenberg, whose interest in language typology and language universals led him to take up the theory of *implicational universals* and to illustrate it by citing chiefly syntactic phenomena. (The theory of implicational universals was originally formulated by the Prague School linguist Roman Jakobson in 1958.) In an article entitled "Some Universals of Grammar with Particular Reference to the Order of Meaningful Elements," published in 1963, Greenberg demonstrated that the presence of a certain syntactic feature often implies the presence of one or more other features. For example, he noted that languages with dominant VSO (Verb + Subject + Object) word order are almost always prepositional (i.e., they have prepositions rather than postpositions) and that there is a very strong tendency for SOV languages to be postpositional.

The foregoing observations cited from Greenberg's article illustrate the principle of implicational universal very well: given that a language has VSO as the basic word order we can automatically assume that such a language has prepositions instead of postpositions, and given the fact that a language has SOV as the basic word order we can reasonably expect (though not assume with total certainty) that this language will have postpositions instead of prepositions. Moreover, in SOV languages attributive adjectives and relative clauses precede the nouns they modify, whereas in SVO languages they usually follow.

Of course, the implicational chaining need not stop with just one implication. It is quite possible, for example, to find a whole chain of implications where the presence of feature X implies the presence of feature Y, which in turn implies the presence of feature Z, and so on. It should also be noted that such implicational relationships are not limited solely to the domain of syntax but can be found in other components of grammar as well.

The discovery of implicational universals is a very important development for linguistic typology for two reasons. First, it allows for a more economical typological schema: if we choose the basic classificatory categories on the basis of those features that by universal simplication entail the presence of a large number of other important features, we need only state that a given language has this feature to imply, by universal convention, a whole series of other features as well. For example, by classifying a language as having SOV as its basic word order we imply that it is also a postpositional language.

Second, the existence of implicational universals alerts us to many phenomena that require explanation; that is, linguistic theory must explain why there are such interrelationships between various grammatical features. In turn, our search for such explanations usually leads us to discover even more hidden facts and relationships in language. Thus, what starts as a "merely" typological, classificatory endeavor eventually leads to ever expanding understanding of the workings of language.

It is not possible here to go into all the recent developments in syntactic typology. Here I shall only note that the basic word-order typology is the fundamental feature of syntactic typology. For a well written account of current developments in syntactic typology and typology in general, the reader is especially urged to consult the works of Bernard Comrie and William Croft listed in the bibliography at the end of this chapter.

LEXICOSEMANTIC TYPOLOGY

Among the various possible classifications of language on the basis of linguistic structure one may also mention classification on the basis of the features of the lexicon, though no one has yet proposed a fully developed classificatory schema based on the features of the lexicon. One often sees in the more popular works on linguistics claims that there are hundreds of monomorphemic words for camel in Arabic, similarly large number of monomorphemic words for different types of snow in Eskimo, large numbers of different words for coconut in Pacific Island languages, and so on. Such claims usually turn out to be grossly exaggerated since Eskimo and English are not so different in the number of their monomorphemic words for 'snow', as Pullum (1991) points out, but to the extent that languages may actually differ somewhat in this respect, it may be worthwhile to consider the possibility of establishing some kind of classification on the basis of lexical differences among various languages.

At the moment it is not clear whether a comprehensive and meaningful classificatory schema could be constructed on the basis of such observations, but perhaps in the future a typology of languages based on the peculiar features of the lexicon will prove useful. Various works in ethnosemantics and cognitive anthropology certainly provide a good basis for such a schema. At present there are already many cross-language comparative studies of such phenomena—antonym systems (Wirth, 1982), kinship terminology and numeral systems (Greenberg, 1978), and basic color terms (Berlin and Kay, 1969)—that can form a basis for some kind of lexicosemantic typology.

HOLISTIC TYPOLOGY

The existence of implicational universals and the fairly lengthy implicational chains that are involved in some of them have stimulated many scholars to look for implicational universals that would tie together important features on all major levels of linguistic structure, from phonology to morphology and syntax. Of course, such a global, holistic approach, if feasible, would be the ultimate typological classification in terms of its economy and elegance. Unfortunately, since things usually turn out to be much more complicated and messy in "real life" than the elegant theories claim them to be, a careful scholar needs to exercise an even greater degree of skepticism when evaluating any new theory that appears to be too elegant and economical. Basically, it seems that various typological schemas that have been constructed on the basis of implicational universals suffer from the same malady, namely that many "universals" turn out to be merely universal tendencies rather than universals in the true sense of this term.

A good example of a holistic typological schema is found in Patricia Donegan and David Stampe's 1983 article. Simply stated, the authors' argument is that phrase and word accent are correlated with the basic word order, and determine also whether a language will be mostly prefixing or suffixing, whether it will have case-relation marking by means of affixation or not, whether it will tend to be tonal or not, and so on. The authors present quite interesting arguments in favor of their hypothesis that links all these seemingly disparate elements of language structure together into one coherent theory of language type. Much needs to be done, however, to validate the main claims of this theory as well as to make the necessary refinements.

SOCIOLINGUISTIC CLASSIFICATION

One may also classify languages according to their sociolinguistic roles, that is, what roles they play in the societies that use them. For example, some languages are now only used in written form or only in church services (liturgical languages such as Coptic or Latin, both of which were originally used for other purposes as well), some are used as second languages for prestige or for other special purposes. Languages have different degrees of prestige, official status, and different social uses to which they are put. What complicates matters in such a classification is the fact that one and the same language may have very different functions in different societies that use it. For example, Classical Arabic is mostly a liturgical language in non-Arab Muslim countries, whereas in Arab countries it (actually a modified version of it called Modern Literary Arabic) is used as a formal written language, in education, in formal discourse, and as an intermediary language to be used with Arabs from other countries whose colloquial language may be quite different from the local colloquial Arabic.

A preliminary attempt to formulate a sociolinguistic framework of language classification may be found in W. Stewart (1962). A brief summary of it is also given in Horne (1966:3–4). Kloss (1968) classifies entire nations in terms of the status of the languages spoken in them in a somewhat elaborate schema designed for "language planning" purposes.

Finally, we should mention the possibility of sociolinguistic/ethnolinguistic classification based on the ethnography of speaking or ethnography of communication studies. Simply stated, such studies concentrate on the complex interrelationship between language use in particular speech communities with various social, economic, ethnographic, and cultural factors in these speech communities. For example, the phenomenon of turn-taking in conversation may be studied crosslinguistically to determine what may be the universal and what are the speech-community particular phenomena involved. Another example is the series of studies concerning the dimension of volubility/taciturnity in different speech communities: Is volubility or taciturnity prized more in the community, and under what circumstances?

Ethnography of speaking is a field that was initiated by Dell Hymes in the 1960s because he felt that linguistics, anthropological linguistics, and sociolinguistics were all ignoring certain important language phenomena that were crucial for our understanding of how language is actually used in different speech communities. Since then there have been numerous studies in the field, many of which have focused on crosslinguistic cross-cultural aspects of the ethnography of speaking, thus laying the foundation for a sociolinguistic/ethnolinguistic language typology. (Only a small sample of the relevant literature will be cited in the bibliography at the end of this chapter. The works by Duranti and Philipsen and Carbaugh, however, may be consulted for references to other important work in this area.)

EXERCISES

1. Establishing Genetic Relationship

The data below contains lexical items from Finnish and Hungarian. Your task is to decide whether or not one can establish that these two languages are genetically related *based solely on the given data*. If you decide that it is not possible to do so, discuss the difficulties and your reasoning. If you decide that it is possible to establish the genetic relationship in this case, cite the relevant evidence for your claim.

GLOSS	FINNISH	HUNGARIAN
1. child	lapsi	gyermek
2. church	kirkko	templom
3. six	kuusi	hat
4. fire	tuli	tűz
5. head	pä	fő
6. three	kolme	három
7. cracker	keksi	keksz
8. water	vesi	víz
9. fish	kala	hal
10. sun	aurinko	nap
11. winter	talvi	tél
12. sugar	sokeri	czukor
13. tree	puu	fa
14. tongue	kieli	nyelv
15. eye	silmä	szem
16. blood	veri	vér
17. death	kuolema	halál
18. zero	nolla	nulla
19. son	poika	fiú
20. under	ala	allá
21. hear	kuulla	hall
22. heel	suoni	ín
23. nose	nenä	orr
24. soap	saippua	szappan
25. soft	pehmeä	puha
26. ice	jää	jég
27. nest	pesä	fészek
28. bird	lintu	lud ('goose')
29. breast	süli	öl ('lap')
30. half	puoli	fél
31. egg	muna	mony
32. hand	käsi	kéz
33. heart	sydän	szív
34. two	kaksi	két
35. hundred	sata	szás
36. mouth	suu	száj
37. what	mitä	mi

Note: Forms are cited in the standard orthography for Finnish and Hungarian. In Finnish, [y] stands for the high front rounded vowel, and [ä] stands for a low front unrounded vowel. In Hungarian stress mark indicates vowel length; combination *sz* represents [s], whereas an *s* not followed by *z* is [š]; *cs* is [č], and *c* is [ts]. The letter *y* indicates that the preceding consonant is palatalized. In both languages, the letter *j* stands for the palatal semivowel.

II. Typology Exercise 1

Choose two different passages of English of about two hundred words each and perform a simple morphological analysis on them. One of the passages chosen should consist of a running conversation, whereas the other should be an example of a narrative in formal, literary style. Calculate the degree of synthesis and the compositional index for the two passages. If either of the indices is significantly different for the two passages, how do you account for the difference?

III. Typology Exercise 2

Examine the following data from four different languages and determine which morphological type is exemplified by each. Give a brief justification for your decision in each case.

Language A (based on Lillooet Salish)

> tuxp-elic'e-ʔen-č-eš
>
> buy + clothing + transitive verb marker + first person singular object + third person singular transitive subject
>
> 'He bought me some clothes.'

Language B (Quechua)

> 'ika-y-ku-man-lya p"awa-sa-n-ku-ču
>
> flower + first person + plural + to + also/ fly + progressive + present + plural + question
>
> 'Are they flying to my flowers also?'

Language C (Samoan)

> ua alu le teine i le fale-ma'i [both *fale* and *ma'i* can be independent words]
>
> perfective/ go/ the/ girl/ to/ the/ house + sick
>
> 'The girl has gone to the hospital.'

Language D (Nepali)

> y-as khol-ā māthi sãgh-u thi-yo
>
> that + oblique case/ river + oblique case/ across (postposition)/ bridge + non-oblique case, masculine ending/ past tense allomorph of *hunu* 'to be' + third person singular preterite indicative
>
> 'Across that river there was a bridge.'

SELECTED BIBLIOGRAPHY

Genetic Classification

Arlotto, Anthony. 1972. *Introduction to historical linguistics.* Boston: Houghton Mifflin. (A very readable elementary-level introduction to genetic classification, comparative method, and allied topics.)

Haas, Mary R. 1969. *The prehistory of languages.* Janua Linguarum, series minor no. 57. The Hague: Mouton. (A more technical work which emphasizes the comparative method as it is applied to unwritten languages, especially American Indian languages.)

Hock, Hans Heinrich. 1991. *Principles of historical linguistics.* 2d ed. Berlin: Mouton de Gruyter. (A very thorough and well-written advanced-level introduction to historical linguistics and comparative method.)

Lehmann, Winfred P. 1992. *Historical linguistics.* 3d ed. London: Routledge. (Elementary-level introduction to genetic classification, comparative method, and allied topics. One chapter is devoted to language typology.)

Typological Classification

Anderson, E. 1978. Lexical universals of body-part terminology. In J. H. Greenberg, ed., *Universals of human language.* vol. 3, 335–68. Stanford: Stanford University Press.

Berlin, Brent, and Paul Kay. 1969. *Basic color terms: Their universality and evolution.* Berkeley and Los Angeles: University of California Press.

Comrie, Bernard. 1989. *Language universals and linguistic typology: Syntax and morphology.* 2d ed. Chicago: University of Chicago Press. (An excellent overview of the more recent developments in language typology; very readable even though it is not an elementary introduction to the topic.)

Croft, William. 1990. *Typology and universals.* Cambridge: Cambridge University Press. (This work's emphasis and general orientation make it an excellent companion volume to Comrie's text.)

Donegan, Patricia Jane, and David Stampe. 1983. Rhythm and the holistic organization of language structure. In John F. Richardson et al., eds., *Papers from the parasession on the interplay of phonology, morphology and syntax,* 337–53. Chicago: Chicago Linguistic Society. (Somewhat difficult reading for those with little background in linguistics.)

Greenberg, Joseph. 1960. A quantitative approach to the morphological typology of language. *International Journal of American Linguistics* 26:178–94.

———. 1966. Some universals of grammar with particular reference to the order of meaningful elements. In Joseph Greenberg, ed., *Universals of language,* 73–113. 2d ed. Cambridge: M.I.T. Press.

———. 1975. Research on language universals. *Annual Review of Anthropology* 4:75–94. (Explains the interconnection between language universals research and language typology.)

———. 1978. Generalizations about numeral systems. In J. H. Greenberg, ed., *Universals of human language,* vol. 3, 249–95. Stanford: Stanford University Press.

Hockett, Charles. 1955. *Manual of phonology.* Indiana University Publications in Anthropology and Linguistics, Memoir 2. Bloomington: Indiana University Press; rpt. Chicago: University of Chicago Press, 1979.

Horne, Kibbey M. 1966. *Language typology: 19th and 20th century views.* Washington, D.C.: Georgetown University Press. (A very condensed account of various language typology schemas, mostly based on morphology.)

Lehmann, Winfred P., ed. 1978. *Syntactic typology: Studies in the phenomenology of language.* Austin: University of Texas Press. (A collection of articles dealing primarily with word order typology and various implicational universals connected with the latter.)

Lyovin, Anatole. 1981. Bibliography of linguistic typology. *Working Papers in Linguistics* (Dept. of Linguistics, University of Hawaii at Manoa), 13(2):75–94. (Although not very accessible, this bibliography would be very useful for those who want to do further reading on the topic.)

Pullum, Geoffrey K. 1991. *The great Eskimo vocabulary hoax, and other irreverent essays in the study of language.* Chicago: University of Chicago Press.

Sapir, Edward. 1921. *Language.* New York: Harcourt, Brace and World. (Includes a lengthy section on language typology.)

Sociolinguistic Classification

Duranti, Alessandro. 1988. Ethnography of speaking: Towards a linguistics of the praxis. In Frederick J. Newmeyer, ed. *Linguistics: the Cambridge survey.* Vol. 4: *Language: The socio-cultural context,* 210–28. Cambridge: Cambridge University Press. (Contains a very good bibliography on ethnography of speaking as well as a good, short overview of the field.)

Gumperz, John J., and Dell Hymes, eds. 1972. *Directions in sociolinguistics: The ethnography of communication.* New York: Holt, Rinehart & Winston.

Hymes, Dell. 1974. *Foundations in sociolinguistics: An ethnographic approach.* Philadelphia: University of Pennsylvania Press. (The first two chapters are of special relevance. Chapter 2 illustrates how language communities differ from each other in their attitudes toward volubility and taciturnity.)

Kloss, Heinz. 1968. Notes concerning a language-nation typology. In Fishman, J. A., C. A. Ferguson, and J. Das Gupta, eds., *Language problems of developing nations,* 69–85 John Wiley.

Philipsen, G., and D. Carbaugh. 1986. A bibliography of fieldwork in the ethnography of speaking. *Language in Society* 15:387–97.

Saville-Troike, Muriel. 1989. *The ethnography of communication: An introduction.* 2d ed. Oxford: Basil Blackwell. (This is a standard introductory text in the field.)

Scollon, Ronald, and Suzanne B. K. Scollon. 1979. *Linguistic convergence: An ethnography of speaking at Fort Chipewyan, Alberta.* New York: Academic Press.

Stewart, William A. 1962. An outline of linguistic typology for describing multilingualism. In *Study of the role of second languages in Asia, Africa, and Latin America,* 15–25. Washington, D.C.: Center for Applied Linguistics of the Modern Language Association of America.

Chapter **2**   Classification of
Writing Systems

Writing is only a secondary aspect of language, that is, it is only a means of symbolizing spoken languages, often a very imperfect means at that. However, since we are more frequently confronted with unfamiliar and exotic looking foreign scripts than actual foreign languages as they are spoken, and since we shall encounter several exotic scripts in the language sketches, it will not do to omit discussing the various scripts of the world. Here the emphasis will be on the typology of the writing systems that are currently in use rather than on the historical development of writing and the ancient scripts.

Just like languages themselves, writing systems can be classified either genetically, according to their historical origin, or typologically, according to various criteria. In the case of writing systems, however, it is more revealing to discuss their typological classification before discussing their genetic classification.

TYPOLOGICAL CLASSIFICATION

Writing systems may differ from each other in many different ways, and therefore it is necessary to make a judicious choice of the aspects on which to base the typological criteria for classification. For example, one may choose to classify writing systems according to the inventory of shapes that they employ for their symbols. Although this turns out not to be a very enlightening classification, it does actually have some practical use—it may help us design a "writing-system identification aid" of some kind (perhaps computerized) that would be useful to people who have to identify quickly the language in which certain written materials are written. For general purposes, however, a typology based on what the basic graphic units represent is more revealing and meaningful.

According to the criterion just mentioned, one can identify four basic types of writing: (1) pictographic, (2) logographic (or morphemographic), (3) syllabic, and (4) alphabetic.

Pictographic writing is, strictly speaking, not a *system* of writing at all since it uses no recognizable graphic units but simply pictures of items or situations. To be sure, pictographic writing may be highly stylized, but it is open-ended since any new symbols may be added to suit the situation. Finally, it represents meaning without any intervening levels of language structure, unlike the other types of writing in which symbols represent some kind of linguistic unit. Thus it is "language-neutral" though not necessarily "culture-neutral" since its pictures or symbols may be stylized or decipherable only by persons familiar with the culture of the writer.

For example, Figure 2.1 may be easily interpreted as representing a man spearing a pig, regardless of what language or languages are known to the reader, but it does not represent any particular sentence or sentences in any particular language. An English-speaking reader may, for example, "read" this pictograph as 'A man is spearing a pig' or as 'A pig is being hunted by a man'.

This language neutrality is both an advantage and a disadvantage of pictographic writing. On the one hand it is convenient that a pictograph may be understood regardless of what language a reader knows. For this reason, we still use pictographs to designate such things as 'danger' (skull and cross-bones), 'crossroads' (a cross), and so forth. In Europe, where many different languages are spoken in a relatively small area, fairly stylized pictographic signs are widely used in railway stations and airports to help foreign visitors locate such essential things as money exchanges, toilets, and restaurants. A few examples are provided in Figure 2.2.

On the other hand, pictographic writing has many severe deficiencies. For example, it cannot be used to write down a poem that one has just composed since a picture or a set of pictures does not represent a particular phrase or

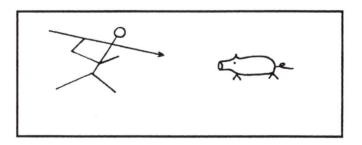

Figure 2.1

elevator   waiting room   ladies' beauty shop

Figure 2.2

sentence in any particular language. Abstract notions cannot be directly "written down," but only hinted at indirectly by ingenious means. (For example, a man breaking his chains could represent the notion "freedom.") Being open-ended, this writing type cannot be adapted to take advantage of modern inventions such as the typewriter and the word processor (at least not simply). At best it can be used either for conveying very rudimentary messages to readers who come from different countries and do not share common languages or as a very primitive mnemonic device in the absence of true writing.

It is therefore not surprising that no modern language uses pictographic writing as defined here as its principal means of writing. One can easily imagine how frustrating it would be to try to write down a great poem using pictographs that don't represent any particular sentence in any language: The beauty of poetry, after all, is largely the result of a masterful combination of content and particular words arranged in a particular order and exhibiting a particular rhythm, and it cannot be adequately conveyed or symbolized by pictographs that only represent content, and that very imprecisely.

Logographic writing is a true writing system in that it represents linguistic units of a particular language. In this type of writing, each basic graphic unit represents a morpheme. Actually, the term *logographic* is not entirely appropriate since *logo-* means 'word' in Greek, and this writing does not have a separate symbol for each different word. However, it is true that in isolating languages many words consist of a single morpheme, and Chinese, which uses logographic writing, is an isolating language. The terminological confusion seems to have arisen because, as in many languages, those languages that use a logographic system of writing have a number of words that consist of a single morpheme and are therefore written by representing each morpheme with a single logograph. As far as I know, there is no writing system, past or present, having a different symbol for each word. Such a system would have been extremely unwieldy and difficult to learn since every language has a vast number of different words, and those languages in which new word formation (through compounding, as in German) is very easy and highly productive have an infinite number of words—at least potentially. Accordingly, a better term for this type of writing would have been *morphemographic*, but this latter term does sound somewhat awkward and is not in current usage. (For alternative terminology, see the discussion of Peter Daniels' schema at the end of this section.)

The reader may be puzzled why the terms *ideogram* and *ideograph* are not used in this book in reference to Chinese characters or logographic writing in general. Whatever the intent of the original coiners of the term 'ideograph' was, it is evident that subsequently at least some have misconstrued the meaning of this term to mean that an ideograph represents ideas directly, rather than any linguistic unit in any particular language. In other words, since the term causes misunderstanding it is not appropriate for use in reference to Chinese characters. As it is, there are many misconceptions being propagated about the Chinese writing system even by those who ought to know better. Those who are interested in the Chinese writing system and wish to go beyond myth and misconceptions about it should read John De Francis' book (1984) listed in the bibliography at the end of this chapter.

Chinese is the only modern language that still uses what is to a large extent, if not entirely, a logographic system of writing. In addition, Japanese and Korean (as written in South Korea) use borrowed Chinese logographs along with other, natively developed, forms of writing. In the past, Chinese characters or logographs were also used by the Vietnamese and Koreans in North Korea, as well as by some other nationalities. (For the historical development of the Chinese logographic script see the following section on the genetic classification of the writing systems.)

In the following Chinese sentence, each individual character represents a different Chinese morpheme:

我	不	是	中	國	人
Wǒ	bù	shì	zhōng	guó	rén
I	not	be	middle	country	person

'I am not Chinese.'

Note also that in the above Chinese sentence each morpheme consists of a single syllable. Thus, one can easily reach a mistaken conclusion that Chinese writing is basically syllabic. However, on closer inspection of the Chinese writing system one can see that totally homophonous syllables are written differently if they refer to different morphemes:

事   是

                      vs.

shì: 'thing, affair'   shì: 'be (copula)'

In a true *syllabic* writing system each basic symbol represents a syllable. In terms of the number of separate symbols that have to be learned, a syllabary is much more economical than a logographic writing system since all languages have more different morphemes than they have different syllables. For example, large dictionaries of Chinese contain up to fifty thousand different entries for individual characters, and even when one sifts away the obsolete characters occurring only once or twice in some ancient texts and variant shapes of the same character, the total number of remaining characters is still in the tens of thousands, whereas the number of different syllables in any given Chinese dialect is at most a few hundred. (It should be noted that the average literate Chinese knows only about five thousand logographs at most.)

The most familiar syllabic writing system in common use today is that of Japanese. Actually, Japanese uses two different syllabaries although basically only one would be adequate to write anything in Japanese. The origin of these two syllabaries, *hiragana* and *katakana,* will be discussed in the next section of this chapter; here it may be noted that *hiragana* is primarily used to write native Japanese words, whereas *katakana* is usually used to write foreign loanwords (unless the loanwords in question are from Chinese, in which case Chinese logographs are usually used), some onomatopoeic expressions, and some exclamations.

In terms of efficiency and economy, a syllabary is much better than a logographic system of writing. However, for languages with a very large number of different syllables the number of separate syllabic characters is still prohibitively high. Languages like Japanese and Hawaiian have a very simple syllable structure and therefore have few different syllables—for example, all Hawaiian syllables have CV or V canonical shape—and therefore a syllabic system of writing is not too unsuitable for them. On the other hand, English syllable structure is much more complex, and therefore the number of different syllables is high. Consider, for example, the fact that each of the following English words consists of one syllable each, a *different* syllable, and therefore in syllabic writing would have to be written with a totally different symbol: sprays, spray, prays, pray, rays, ray, trips, strips, screams.

Here are a few examples of Japanese words written in the *hiragana* syllabary:

た	こ			こ	こ	ろ		
ta	ko	=	'octopus'	ko	ko	ro	=	'heart'

こ	と		
ko	to	=	'thing' or 'Japanese musical instrument'

Note that in the hiragana syllable signs one cannot isolate those graphic elements which represent vowels from those representing consonants. Thus the symbols which are read *ta* and *to* do not have an element that can be identified with the consonant *t,* nor can one find a common element that represents the vowel *o* if one compares the symbols used for writing syllables *ko* and *to.* Note also that *koto* 'thing, affair' and *koto* 'Japanese musical instrument', when written logographically, using Chinese characters, look quite different (since they are different morphemes) than when they are written with the *hiragana* syllabary:

koto 'thing' = 事   koto 'musical instrument = 琴

An *alphabetic* writing system is potentially the most economical and efficient one since in it each basic symbol represents an individual segment or a phoneme, and each language has many fewer individual segments or phonemes than it does different syllables (and, as previously mentioned, each language has fewer syllables than it has morphemes). The reason that this efficiency and economy is only potential is that alphabetic systems in actual use may for various reasons become very complicated over time. For example, English orthography is replete with arbitrary spellings, and although it is basically alphabetic, there are letters that actually stand for more than one segment (e.g., *x* in *ox*) and sequences of letters that represent single sounds (e.g., *th* in *think*). In addition, there are the so-called silent letters which now have no sound value, although they may have had sound value at the time the spelling of the words in question was set (e.g., *gh* in *dough*).

A note of caution must be given here regarding the Korean *hangŭl* alphabet, in which the basic alphabetic symbols are arranged into clusters of letters representing syllables. Although each cluster does indeed represent a syllable, each graphic cluster can be easily analyzed into its component units which represent individual segments of Korean. For example, *mikuk saram* ('American person') is written by alphabetic symbols clustering into four compound symbols, one for each syllable—*mi-kuk-sa-ram*—but one can easily isolate the individual symbols for *m*, *k*, and the vowel *a*:

미	국	사	람	=	mi	k	sa	ra
						u		m
mi	kuk	sa	ram			k		

Finally, it is necessary to point out that writing systems in actual use in the world today are rarely completely homogeneous typologically. Thus, Japanese writing uses both syllable signs and logographs and should therefore be characterized as a 'mixed syllabic/logographic type', and even English can be shown to use a few symbols which are clearly logographic and is thus not purely alphabetic. (For example, numerals such as 1 'one' and 2 'two' and miscellaneous symbols such as & 'and' and $ 'dollar'.)

In deciphering unknown scripts, scholars pay special attention to the number of different symbols that appear in the undeciphered inscriptions. If the number of different symbols is much larger than 200, the script is suspected of being a logographic system (or at least partially so); if there are fewer than 200 but more than about 40, the script is suspected of being a syllabary; if there are fewer than 40 different symbols, the script is suspected of being an alphabet. Once the type of script has been determined, one can begin to look for other clues that may eventually lead at least to a partial decipherment.

The typological schema given above is actually deficient in some respects since there are some systems intermediate between those cited. A fuller typo-

Table 2.1

TYPE	DEFINITION	EXAMPLE
Logography	assigns a morpheme (usually a word) to each symbol	Archaic Sumerian?
Logosyllabography	logograms used for their syllabic as well as their semantic values	Sumerian, Chinese
Syllabography	assigns a syllable possible in the language to each symbol	Vai (Liberia)
Abjad	assigns a consonant to each symbol	Phoenician
Augmented abjad	includes some syllabograms as well	Ugaritic
Alphabet	assigns a segment (consonant or vowel) to each symbol	Greek, vocalized Hebrew
Augmented alphabet	includes some syllabograms as well	Coptic
Neosyllabary	assigns a consonant plus a particular vowel to each basic symbol and modifies the basic symbol in a (fairly) systematic fashion to denote other vowels or the absence of vowels	Ethiopic

Source: Daniels (1990:730)

logical schema is presented by Peter T. Daniels (1990:730) and is cited in Table 2.1.

As can readily be seen, Daniels rightly excludes pictographic writing from his schema because pictographic writing is really not a *system* of writing. He also correctly classifies Chinese as being a "logosyllabographic" type of system in which symbols stand for syllables as well as individual morphemes. He does not seem certain whether there is or ever has been a purely logographic system in which symbols represent only morphemes, not syllables, but believes that Sumerian writing in its early stages may have belonged to this type. There is no need to say much about his syllabography and alphabet types because these are equivalents to what we have called syllabic and alphabetic types in our discussion. There are several other categories in this classificatory schema that need some comment and a word of explanation.

Abjad is the term coined on the basis of the pronunciation of the first three letters of the early Semitic alphabets. The big difference between abjad and an alphabet is that in the latter there are symbols for all the segments, both vowels and consonants, whereas in abjad there are letters only for consonantal segments. In other words, an abjad is a consonantal alphabet. The Arabic script discussed in the "Sketch of Modern Literary Arabic" is an alphabet derived from an abjad.

Augmented abjad has, in addition to symbols for consonants, also some symbols representing syllables.

Augmented alphabet is an alphabet that has, besides the symbols for vowels and consonants, also some symbols representing syllables. To the example of Coptic, given by Daniels in his chart, we may add Cyrillic script which has letters for such syllables as *yu, ya, yo* (cf. "Sketch of Russian").

Neosyllabary is a system partway between an alphabet and a syllabary in that basic letters represent a consonant plus an inherent vowel of some kind (usually *a* or *ə*) and a number of diacritics representing vowels differing from the inherent one. In addition, there are various means of indicating when the inherent vowel is absent. Most of the neosyllabaries, although not all, as Daniels' example of Ethiopic indicates, are scripts either used in India or based on Indian scripts. A good example of a neosyllabary is Tibetan writing, described in the "Sketch of Classical Tibetan."

GENETIC CLASSIFICATION OF WRITING SYSTEMS

According to Gelb (1963:60), the following seven "Oriental" scripts may have arisen independently of each other in the area stretching from the Mediterranean to China (although there are scholars that see connections between some of them):

1. Sumerian in Mesopotamia, 3100 B.C.
2. Proto-Elamite in Elam, 3000 B.C.
3. Proto-Indic in the Indus Valley, around 2200 B.C.
4. Chinese in China, 1300 B.C.
5. Egyptian in Egypt, 3000 B.C.
6. Cretan in Crete and Greece, 2000 B.C.
7. Hittite in Anatolia and Syria, 1500 B.C.

Besides those ennumerated there are, of course, other scripts that arose in other parts of the world (e.g., Mayan script in Mesoamerica). Most of the latter as well as the scripts descended from them are presently extinct; of the foregoing scripts only Chinese is still used (in a somewhat changed form), along with Japanese syllabaries which are descended from it. Also, if some of the scholars studying ancient Near Eastern scripts are correct, although Egyptian script itself is extinct its numerous descendants are now used all over the world.

At its very beginning, Egyptian writing was clearly mnemonic/pictographic in that symbols did not stand for particular words or morphemes of the Egyptian language, nor did their arrangement follow the order of words or morphemes of the Egyptian language. The most frequently cited example of earliest Egyptian writing, the Narmer palette, which has been dated around 3000 B.C., is clearly pictorial in character, representing a king's victory over his enemies. On the other hand, this is not merely a picture of a victory parade: there is an attempt to record the name of the king by the *rebus principle* (see Figure 2.3), the number of the slain enemies, who the latter were, and so forth.

Figure 2.3 *The Narmer palette. From J. E. Quibell in* Zeitschrift für ägyptische *Sprache, xxxvi (1898) pls. xii f, as reproduced in Gelb (1963:73).*

At a later stage of development, although the symbols themselves appear to be pictures of the objects they represent, the Egyptian writing is clearly logographic because the symbols are arranged in a particular order, mirroring the order of morphemes in the Egyptian language, and there is increased use of the rebus principle: some of the symbols are used merely for their sound value. To illustrate, let us make an analogous example using English. It is difficult to invent a suitable symbol that will unambiguously represent the English morpheme 'son'. We could draw a small male figure, but that could also be interpreted to represent 'boy'; we could instead borrow a symbol for 'sun', say, a circle with rays coming from it, since our word for the sun is completely homophonous with our word for male offspring. Of course, if we did as suggested above, one and the same symbol would now stand for two different morphemes, 'sun' and 'son'. In most contexts, there would probably be no problem in guessing which morpheme is meant. Since in some contexts, however, such ambiguity would be troublesome and undesirable, one may add a little disambiguating mark, a picture of a human being to the side, to indicate that in a particular instance the morpheme referred to is not the sun in the sky, but the morpheme which refers to a human being and only *sounds like* the morpheme for the bright body in the heavens (see Figure 2.4).

Both the Chinese and Egyptian writing systems (as well as others) eventually came to employ the device of the rebus in the course of their development. In Chinese, the majority of the characters used today employs the rebus principle, so much so that one may even argue that Chinese writing is more of an elaborate syllabary than a purely logographic system as defined here. For example, the word for *horse* is pronounced mǎ in Mandarin. The character for *horse* in turn often, but not always, appears as a phonetic clue in compound characters built on the rebus principle:

馬   罵   媽

mǎ = 'horse'   mà = 'to scold'   mā = 'mother'

Essentially, both Chinese and Egyptian logographic systems consisted of a number of basic characters/logographs that represented easily depicted objects and a larger number of compound symbols which consisted of combinations of the basic symbols. In these combinations some of the basic symbols

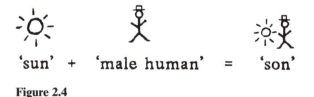

'sun' + 'male human' = 'son'

Figure 2.4

had the role of a semantic clue (indicating the broad semantic category to which a given morpheme belongs, e.g., "some kind of tree," "some kind of speech," "some kind of liquid") and some had the function of a phonetic clue ("pronounced like . . .")

Since a logographic system of writing places a very heavy burden on learners' memory because it has a large number of different symbols, it is only natural that sooner or later someone would realize that one can use the phonetic clues *alone* simply to spell all the morphemes as sequences of *sounds*, dispensing with semantic clues and symbols that represent morphemes directly. Those of us who are used to alphabetic writing usually assume that speakers of all languages are aware of individual segments or phonemes of their language. However, it turns out that illiterate speakers of all languages are much more conscious of syllables as units of their language than individual segments. In addition, all the phonetic clues used in Chinese represented single syllables *since Chinese morphemes themselves were essentially one syllable in length.* Thus it is not surprising to see several syllabaries evolving from Chinese. (See the following discussion of the development of the Japanese *kana* syllabaries from Chinese logographs.)

Although in Egyptian, as well as in other languages for which writing was developed rather early, there are many morphemes that consist of more than just one syllable, a syllabic type of system tended to evolve just the same since a system which has symbols only for single syllables is, of course, much more economical than the one which also has symbols for polysyllabic morphemes.

For various reasons not discussed here, a true syllabic writing system did not develop in China itself, although according to De Francis (1984) Chinese writing is in fact a clumsy and elaborate syllabary. In Japan, however, two syllabaries were developed from Chinese logographs at roughly the same time. After borrowing the Chinese characters in the seventh century A.D., the Japanese for the most part wrote everything in the Chinese language. In other words, the written language itself was borrowed from China along with the characters themselves. Even in government documents, however, Japanese proper names had to be written in some way, and since the Japanese proper names did not consist of Chinese morphemes there were no Chinese logographs to write them. Thus, Japanese had to use some Chinese characters only for their sound value, ignoring their semantic value, in order to transcribe Japanese names just as in Modern Chinese foreign proper names such as 'Malay' are arbitrarily transcribed by two characters: mǎ 'horse' and lái 'come'. Unfortunately, since there was no way to indicate which characters were being used only for their sound and which for their Chinese meaning, reading documents written in such a way was very difficult.

An additional impetus for developing a syllabary in Japan was provided by the existence of Japanese poetry, which somehow had to be recorded in Japanese and could not be recorded in Chinese as the government documents had been.

Eventually two methods were developed to signal those characters which were being used only for their sound (i.e., syllabic) value. One method was to write such characters cursively, leaving the characters used for their meaning written in a more printed style. Thus was created the syllabary that is called *hiragana* in Japanese. Here are a few *hiragana* syllable signs along with their Chinese-character originals in "printed style":

かく加 (ka)   むく無 (mu)   たく太 (ta)

The other method was developed primarily by Buddhist monks who wanted a means of indicating the pronunciation of rare Chinese characters that cropped up here and there in the Buddhist holy writings. This method consisted of using parts of Chinese characters to stand for the sound value of the whole Chinese character. The result of this method is called *katakana* syllabary in Japanese. The following are a few *katakana* syllable signs, along with the Chinese characters whose abbreviated or truncated versions they are:

カく加 (ka)   イく伊 (i)   タく多 (ta)

In Ancient Egypt the evolution of writing ran a similar course: Certain logographic elements began to be used primarily for their sound value and thus the system ceased to be a purely logographic one. However, according to Gelb's (1963) rather controversial theory in the Egyptian case a somewhat peculiar situation developed: The original logographs being used for their sound value represented *syllables* as in the case of Japanese *kana,* but unlike the latter in which all the vowels are differentiated, the Egyptian "syllabary" did not differentiate the vowels. Thus, for example, in Japanese *kana* syllables such as *ka, ki, ko, ke, ku* all have completely different symbols to represent them, whereas in Egyptian a symbol came to represent a particular consonant sound followed by a vowel—*any vowel.* In essence, then, Egyptian writing differentiated only the consonants, and vowels were only "understood" as following the consonants. For this reason, most scholars dispute the claim that Egyptian writing evolved into a syllabary and claim instead that Egyptian writing evolved into an alphabet which had symbols only for the consonants. For conflicting views on this issue, see Gelb (1963:166–9), Coulmas (1989:137–57), and Daniels (1990).

Although this also is still disputed by a many scholars, it does appear likely that Egyptian phonological writing provided the basis for the so-called Semitic alphabets or, using Daniels' term, abjads, among which was the crucial Phoenician script that was eventually borrowed by the Greeks. In borrowing the Phoenician script, the Greeks may have misunderstood their Phoenician teachers and added separate symbols for vowels: since Phoenician letters had names beginning with the consonant sounds which the letters represented, it was only natural that the Greeks did not recognize the Phoenician consonant sounds which the Greek language lacked as sounds at all and took the second sound in the name of the letter to be the value of the symbol. Thus, for example, the first letter of the Phoenician alphabet was called *'aleph* and represented a glottal stop, a sound that did not exist as a phoneme in Greek. It was very natural, then, for a Greek learner to assume that *'aleph* represented the sound of the vowel *a*. Similarly, Phoenician letters which represented various pharyngeal and laryngeal sounds not found in the inventory of Greek phonemes ended up being interpreted by the Greeks as representing other vowel sounds. However, it may also be true that we are underestimating the Greeks here: they may have quite consciously hit upon the idea of using the "useless" Phoenician letters for the vowel sounds.

Whether the addition of the vowel symbols by the Greeks was truly due to a mistake or a stroke of genius is not all that important. What is important is that with the changes added by the Greeks we get the first true alphabet in which both vowel segments and consonant segments are marked by symbols of equal status.

Eventually, the Greek alphabet spread to the Romans, who in turn spread it all over Europe. In addition, the Greek alphabet was the main basis of the Cyrillic alphabet used primarily by the Slavic peoples who were Christianized by the missionaries from Byzantium and not Rome. Cyrillic is also used in various parts of the former Soviet Union to write some Turkic and other non-Slavic minority languages. At the moment, however, many of these languages seem to be on the point of switching to their earlier native scripts or Roman script as various nationalist movements in many regions reassert independence from Russia. A Cyrillic-based alphabet was also used for writing Mongolian in the Mongolian People's Republic, but with the collapse of communism and reassertion of Mongolia's independence from Russian influence, there too the government has decided to switch back to the old script, based on Uighur script, which continued to be used in Inner Mongolia (an autonomous region of China).

Some Semitic script (but it is not known exactly which) must have provided the basis for Brahmi script in India, which is the basis not only of all the current alphabets of India but of those used in Southeast Asia (Burmese, Cambodian, Thai, Laotian, etc.) as well as Tibetan.

Tibetan in turn was the basis of the so-called *'Phags-pa* script which was devised in the middle of thirteenth century A.D. by an influential Tibetan monk during the Mongol occupation of China and adjacent regions for writing various languages of the Mongol empire, including Chinese. In turn, *'Phags-pa* script must have been known to the Koreans who devised the Korean *hangŭl* alphabet around A.D. 1446 since some of the letters of Korean and *'Phags-pa* alphabets are too similar to each other to be mere coincidence.

A number of minor scripts still in use are inventions of individuals who were familiar with the writing scripts of other peoples and cannot be said to have descended directly from either the Chinese or the Egyptian writing or any other ancient writing. Sequoia's Cherokee syllabary (1820–24) and the

Armenian alphabet designed by Mesrop Mashtots (A.D. 362–440) are two examples.

EXERCISES

I. Typology Exercise I

a. Devise a purely logographic script to write the following English passage. (If you know how to write Chinese characters, you may attempt to use Chinese characters to write English morphemes.)

> The powerful chief of the Blackfeet attacked the invaders at the mountain pass and defeated them. He took two hundred prisoners, including Chief Eagle Feather.

b. Attempt to convey the gist of the preceding message pictographically. Instead of actually drawing the picture you may just *describe* what kind of picture or series of pictures you might draw. How might you convey the proper names? If you run into any unexpected difficulties in accomplishing the assigned task, be sure to explain in detail what they are.

II. Typology Exercise 2

Examine the three different scripts given below and determine what *type* of writing is represented by each. Briefly explain the reasoning which led you to your conclusion in each case. (Note that both the scripts and the languages are made up in order that those who may be already familiar with a variety of scripts would not have an unfair advantage over others. The first line is script, and the second line is a phonemic transcription.)

Script A

       гфц шгм чвгф ц

       kamani wikara umikama ni

       'Did Kamani bring his sword?'

Script B

       @ Z ◎ Z ‖‡ ßℍ

       kad taka ugura taka maridu marakat

       'When did the man take the donkey?'

Script C

       ḳwòq̧cw Øz̧o̧w̄q c̀z̧q̇

       mangetukan warganut kereto

       'Virtue is always triumphant.'

Figure 2.5

III. Typological Exercise 3

Figure 2.5 contains some pictograms designed to convey simple ideas to travelers in airports. See if you can decipher the "message" of each pictogram. Give a brief statement about your reasoning in each case. Do you think that all of the pictograms would be understood by all people? (For example, would an ordinary villager from a Third World country who has only a fourth grade education understand them?) Why?

SELECTED BIBLIOGRAPHY

Coulmas, Florian. 1989. *The writing systems of the world.* Oxford: Blackwell Publishers. (This is one of the best modern accounts about the subject.)

Daniels, Peter T. 1990. Fundamentals of grammatology. *Journal of the American Oriental Society* 110(4):727–31. (This short article is very important because it presents a well thought out typological schema for writing systems as well as some important views on the historical development of writing.)

Daniels, Peter T., and William Bright, eds. 1995. *The world's writing systems.* New York: Oxford University Press. (This is the most up-to-date reference on the subject.)

De Francis, John. 1984. *The Chinese language: Fact and fantasy.* Honolulu: University of Hawaii Press. (The main purpose of this book is to debunk some of the myths that have arisen in connection with Chinese writing.)

———. 1989. *Writing: Its diversity and essential oneness.* Honolulu: University of Hawaii Press. (This work seriously challenges many traditional concepts concerning the nature of writing, especially pictographic and logographic writing.)

Gelb, I. J. 1963. *A study of writing.* 2d, rev. ed. Chicago: University of Chicago Press. (One of the classic works on writing systems and their origin. Gelb is particularly strong on Middle Eastern scripts and their development, but not so strong on Chinese writing. In addition, some of his views are highly controversial.)

Gilyarevskiy, R. S., and V. S. Grivnin. 1970. *Language identification guide.* Moscow: Nauka Publishing House. (This is one of several books that attempt to help one identify a language through its writing system, including special diacritics, etc.)

Katzner, Kenneth. 1975. *The languages of the world.* New York: Funk & Wagnalls. (The title of this book is somewhat misleading since it is more a guide to various scripts of the world than to languages. It nevertheless gives more information on each language than Gilyarevskiy and Grivnin.)

Nakanishi, Akira. 1982. *Writing systems of the world: Alphabets, syllabaries, pictograms.* Rutland, Vt.: Charles E. Tuttle. (Contains a number of good illustrations of various scripts.)

Sampson, Geoffrey. 1985. *Writing systems: A linguistic introduction.* London: Hutchinson.

Trager, George L. 1972. *Language and languages.* San Francisco: Chandler. (Part III of this book gives a surprisingly thorough description of the major writing systems of the world, though one may argue with the author's characterization of the Chinese writing system.)

Chapter 3   Languages of Europe

Before I launch into an enumeration of the various language families found in Europe, a few prefatory words are in order about the scope of the coverage, the sources on which the following presentations are based, and even the author's handling of some genetic classifications which have caused a great deal of controversy in recent years.

First, the coverage is not intended to be encyclopedic and exhaustive because there exist many excellent reference sources which may be consulted by students wishing to know more details about classification of particular languages, geographical distribution of languages, and the number of speakers of individual languages. My aim has been to strike a balance between overwhelming the readers with too much detailed information about various languages and the controversies involving their genetic classification and giving too superficial an account. To make the account simpler and shorter the coverage emphasizes the living languages rather than the extinct ones, although on occasion references are made to extinct languages as well. After each chapter there is a bibliography which will provide a good basis for readers who want to know more about some specific topic.

Thus, for more details about the genetic classification of individual languages, readers may consult Grimes (1992), Ruhlen (1987), and Bright et al. (1992). Although Ruhlen's book is very controversial because it promotes the views of Joseph Greenberg, which are opposed by many linguists as lacking scientific validity, it contains detailed accounts about the development and evolution of genetic subgrouping schemas for all the language families of the world. (Of course, one must not fall into the error of thinking that the very latest schemas of genetic classification or genetic subgrouping must be the most correct, but must examine the data and the principles on which they are based.) For the most part, I have tried to follow Bright et al. in matters of genetic classification and genetic subgrouping of the various languages. In cases deviating from that source, other references are cited.

For the numbers and distribution of speakers of various languages, I followed in the main Grimes (1992) although I am aware of the much more detailed coverage in the Kloss and McConnell (1974–84) volumes.

As for the controversial topics that have stirred the linguistic community in the recent and not so recent past, I felt that it would be highly remiss to avoid any mention of Joseph Greenberg's Amerind and Indo-Pacific hypotheses, Paul Benedict's Austro-Tai and Austro-Tai-Japanese hypotheses, and the Nostratic hypothesis being championed by Shevroshkin et al. In the case of the Altaic hypothesis, which already has a venerable history and cannot be considered a recent development, it seemed a disservice to the readers to dismiss the whole matter with a mere mention in a footnote. Thus, all of these ideas are mentioned and briefly described in this text, and bibliographical references are given for scholarly articles which argue both for and against these hypotheses. On the other hand, since this is, after all, an introductory textbook, it would be out place to include lengthy accounts of such controversies.

The language groups and language families of Europe discussed next appear according to the number of their speakers in Europe. Language families whose members are found primarily in Europe are discussed in detail in this chapter. However, since some language families spill over onto other continents, as is the case for both Uralic and Indo-European language families, whose members are found in Asia as well, some mention of these language families is given in other chapters as appropriate. (The same policy holds for the language families and groupings found primarily on continents other than Europe.)

I. INDO-EUROPEAN

The vast majority of the languages currently spoken in Europe belong to this family, which is one of the most extensively studied language families in the world. Here I discuss in some detail various branches of the Indo-European language family, including those that encompass languages spoken in Asia as well as some that have become extinct.

1. CELTIC

It is estimated that there are fewer than 2 million speakers of languages belonging to this branch. At one time, before the invasion of Germanic and Slavic tribes from the east and the expansion of the Roman Empire from the south and east, this branch had a very wide distribution throughout Europe (France, southern Germany, Austria, the Danube River basin, the British Isles, as well as colonies in Greece, Spain, Italy, and even Asia Minor). At present, however, there are essentially small pockets of speakers left in the British Isles and France. The chief representatives are *Irish*, which is an official language of Eire, the Irish Republic, where it is spoken on a daily basis only among the rural population in the west of the country (120,000 sp., with about 670,000 more people elsewhere who speak it as a second language), *Scottish Gaelic* in Scotland (94,000 tot. sp., of which 5,000 are in Canada), *Welsh* in Wales (580,000 sp., most of whom are bilingual in English and Welsh), and *Breton* (685,250 sp., half of whom are bilingual in Breton and French) in Brittany (France) and some in Canada.

The earliest inscriptions date from around A.D. 100 and are in *Gaulish*, the language of ancient Gaul.

2. GERMANIC

There are more than 400 million speakers of languages belonging to this branch. In terms of the number of speakers, this is the largest branch of the Indo-European language family. There are three major subbranches of Germanic, but one of these, *Eastern*, has become extinct.

a. West Germanic

This branch contains *English*, its nearest relative *Frisian* (spoken on some islands off the coast of Holland and Germany and elsewhere in Holland by 700,000 sp.), as well as *Low* and *High German*. It is estimated that there are 403 million first-language speakers of English and as many as 800 million if second-language speakers are included. *Dutch*, including *Flemish* (20 million sp. of the two combined in Holland, Belgium, and the former Dutch colonies), *Afrikaans* (5.8 million sp. in South Africa) are all now considered to be independent languages, whereas *Plattdeutsch* (a cover term for northern German dialects) is considered to be a dialect of German. However, historically all of these are classified as belonging to the *Low German* subbranch of West Germanic.

High German includes all the German dialects spoken to the south of *Plattdeutsch,* and includes standard German (119 million sp. in Germany and worldwide, 6 million of whom are in the United States) and *Yiddish* (about 2,080,000 sp. worldwide, of whom about 1.6 million are in the United States, 215,000 in Israel, and 220,000 in the former Soviet Union), the language spoken by the Ashkenazic Jews from Central and Eastern Europe. (Yiddish is written in Hebrew letters and includes loanwords from Hebrew and other languages besides the Germanic vocabulary.)

Although English and Frisian are close relatives and share a lot of common vocabulary, they are not mutually intelligible languages. Generally speaking, English is not a typical Germanic language because after the Norman Conquest of England (eleventh century A.D.) English vocabulary came under a strong influence of Norman French. In addition, English has also borrowed a large number of Latin and even Greek words, and thus its vocabulary is no longer as Germanic as that of, say, standard German.

b. North Germanic

This subbranch includes (1) *West Norse* languages: *Icelandic* (250,000 tot. sp.) and *Faroese* (about 41,000 sp.), which is spoken on the Faroe Islands (administrated by Denmark) located between Iceland and Scotland, and (2) *East Norse* languages: *Swedish* (10 million tot. sp., with 7,825,000 in Sweden, 340,600 in Finland, and 626,102 in the United States); *Danish* (5,280,000 tot. sp., of whom 5 million are in Denmark, 7,830 in Greenland, and 194,462 in the United States); *Norwegian* (5 million tot. sp., 612,862 of whom are in the United States) is considered primarily a West Norse language which has been greatly influenced by Danish, an East Norse language.

c. East Germanic

This subbranch consists of *Gothic,* which became extinct around the sixteenth century A.D. Gothic was spoken in various enclaves stretching from the Black Sea to Spain.

The earliest inscriptions in a Germanic language date from the third century A.D. and are written in *Old Norse.* However, the earliest extensive text is a translation of the Bible into Gothic by Bishop Wulfila in A.D. 350.

3. ITALIC

There are almost 600 million speakers of languages belonging to this branch. This branch had several subbranches, but only one of them survives. The surviving branch consists of the descendants of *Latin* (originally the language of Rome only, other areas of Italy speaking languages that were later supplanted by Latin), which is the protolanguage of the so-called *Romance* languages.

The earliest inscriptions are in Latin and date from sixth century B.C.

Besides the major Romance languages—*French* (109 million first-language speakers, of whom 51 million are in France); *Occitan* (10,204,500 sp. in the south of France, most of whom are bilingual in French); *Spanish* (266 million tot. sp., of whom 28 million are in Spain, the rest in Central and South America); *Portuguese* (154 million first-language speakers of whom 125 million are in Brazil and 10 million in Portugal); *Italian* (40 million tot. sp. for standard Italian) and its major dialects *Neapolitan-Calabrese* (7,047,000 sp. in southern Italy), *Piemontese* (3 million sp. in northwestern Italy), *Sicilian* (4,680,715 sp. on Sicily), *Venetian* (2,109,502 sp. in northern Italy); and *Rumanian* (23 million tot. sp.), *Catalan* (spoken in northeastern Spain by 8.5 million sp. and by 260,000 sp. in France)—there are also many others—*Romansch* or *Rheto-Romance* (spoken in Switzerland by about 65,000 sp.), *Sardinian* (spoken on the island of Sardinia by about 1.5 million sp.), *Friulian* (spoken in the northeastern part of Italy, bordering on Austria and the Republic of Slovenia, by

600,000 sp., most of whom also speak standard Italian), and *Ladino* or *Judeo-Spanish* (spoken by 160,000 Sephardic Jews, with 100,000 sp. in Israel and the rest scattered in other countries bordering on the Mediterranean). *Ladino* should not be confused with *Ladin* or *Dolomite* (sometimes also called *Ladino*), which is spoken by up to 35,000 sp. in the Italian Tyrol.

Rumanian is totally surrounded by speakers of non-Romance languages and is a language of the descendants of Romans who colonized the Roman province of Dacia before the invasion of various Slav and Magyar (Hungarian) tribes that cut off Rumanian from other Romance languages. Rumanian has borrowed extensively from its Slavic neighbors.

4. GREEK

There are about 12 million speakers of *Greek* (primarily in Greece and Cyprus, with about 1.5 million in the United States and 344,000 in the former Soviet Union). This branch consists of only one language, Greek, and its dialects. The earliest inscriptions, in an ancient dialect called *Mycenaean Greek,* date from about 1400 B.C. *Modern Greek* has been influenced by Turkish and Italian and differs significantly in both grammar and vocabulary from *Classical Greek (Attic).* However, the formal style, called *katharevousa,* which until about a decade ago was still in use especially as a literary language (as opposed to *dhimotiki* or informal, colloquial style), is quite close to Classical Greek.

5. ALBANIAN

This branch, too, consists of a single language, *Albanian,* and its dialects. There are about 4 million speakers of Albanian, primarily in Albania, the Kosovo region of Yugoslavia (1.7 million sp.), and smaller communities in Greece and Italy. The language has borrowed extensively from Slavic, Greek, Latin, Italian, and Turkish.

There are two main dialects: *Tosk* in the south, which forms the basis of the standard language, and *Geg* in the north. The two dialects are said to be mutually unintelligible.

The earliest inscriptions date from the sixteenth century A.D.

6. BALTO-SLAVIC

There are about 400 million speakers of languages belonging to this branch (primarily belonging to the *Slavic* subbranch). This branch is sometimes split into two separate branches of Indo-European, but many linguists consider it a single branch that, in turn, has two separate subbranches.

a. Baltic

This includes *Lithuanian* (3,557,000 tot. sp.) and *Latvian* (1,554,000 tot. sp.), both spoken in the Baltic countries of Lithuania and Latvia, respectively, and *Old Prussian* (a language which used to be spoken in East Prussia but became extinct in the early eighteenth century). There are fairly large groups of

Lithuanian speakers (292,820) and Latvian speakers (50,000) in the United States.

The oldest records (a vocabulary list) are in Old Prussian and date from A.D. 1300. Lithuanian is considered to be the most conservative of all the living Indo-European languages and is therefore extensively studied by Indo-Europeanists.

b. Slavic

This subbranch is split into three main groups.

i. Western

This consists of *Polish* (40,522,000 sp., with 2,437,938 sp. in the United States), *Czech* (11,730,000 tot. sp.), *Slovak* (5,360,000 tot. sp.), and *Sorbian*. *Sorbian,* also called *Lusatian,* is a Slavic pocket located within the German-speaking area (70,000 sp. in eastern Germany) and is not to be confused with *Serbian,* which is one of the languages of Yugoslavia and Bosnia-Herzegovina.

ii. Southern

This consists of *Serbo-Croatian* (19 million tot. sp., spoken in the Republic of Croatia, Bosnia-Herzegovina and elsewhere in Yugoslavia), *Macedonian* (2 million sp. in Republic of Macedonia) and *Slovene* or *Slovenian* (2,218,000 sp. in the Republic of Slovenia), and *Bulgarian* (9 million sp. in Bulgaria). Bulgarian and Macedonian are very similar in that in both the elaborate case ending system which is still present in all other Slavic languages has been largely eliminated in favor of prepositions.

iii. Eastern

This group consists of *Russian* (270 million sp., including those who speak it as a second language), *Ukrainian* (45 million sp. primarily in Ukraine), and *Byelorussian* (10 million sp.). The last language is also known as *White Russian* and is spoken in the Belarus Republic just east of Poland.

All Slavic languages are mutually intelligible to a very high degree. The oldest inscriptions date from ninth century A.D. and are in *Old Church Slav(on)ic,* probably a variant Southern Slavic dialect spoken near the Greek town of Thessaloniki at the time the Greek missionaries began converting the local Slavic tribes to Christianity.

7. ARMENIAN

This is another branch that consists of a single language, *Armenian,* which is spoken by about 5,527,000 speakers, primarily in the Republic of Armenia, Iran, Lebanon, Egypt, Syria, and Turkey. Smaller enclaves of Armenians are found elsewhere, for example, the United States (175,000 sp., mainly in California). The vocabulary of Armenian contains many Iranian loanwords, and early scholars thus considered Armenian to be an Iranian language.

The oldest inscriptions date from the fifth century A.D. These inscriptions are written in the Greek alphabet. Later, an Armenian monk devised a special alphabet for Armenian language which is in use to the present day.

The following branches of Indo-European are or were found outside of Europe (in Asia).

8. INDO-IRANIAN

Roughly 400 million speakers speak languages belonging to this branch (mainly its *Indic* subbranch). This branch consists of two subbranches.

a. Iranian

This includes *Farsi,* or various dialects of *Persian* (30 million sp. in Iran, Afghanistan, and Pakistan), *Tajik* (2,898,000 sp. in Tajikistan), *Pashto* (8,300,000 sp., mostly in Afghanistan and Pakistan, some in Iran), *Baluchi* (1,390,000 sp. in Pakistan, Iran, and Afghanistan), and other languages including *Kurdish* (13 million sp.) which is spoken in various areas of Turkey, Iran, and Iraq, and *Ossete* (700,000 sp. mostly in the Caucasus region of the former Soviet Union). The oldest inscriptions are in *Old Persian* and date to 550 B.C.

b. Indic or Indo-Aryan

This includes most of the languages spoken in Northern India such as *Hindi* (182 million first-language speakers, 300 million sp. if second language speakers are included), *Punjabi* (20 million sp.), *Gujarati* (30 million sp.), *Marathi* (50 million sp.), and so forth, *Bengali* (152 million tot. sp. in Eastern India and Bangladesh), *Nepali* (16 million sp. in Nepal and India), *Sinhala* (11,836,000 sp. in Sri Lanka), and *Urdu* (41,260,000 sp. in Pakistan and India).

Included in this group are also *Romani* (usually referred to as "Gypsy") languages and dialects which are found from Spain and Ireland in the west all the way to India in the east. The latest hypothesis concerning the origin of the Gypsies (many of whom prefer to be called Roma, since they consider the name "Gypsy" a pejorative term) is that they are descendants of the Rajputs of northwestern India who fled India after being defeated by Islamic invaders in the Middle Ages, eventually reaching various parts of Europe by different routes. Their dialects have borrowed heavily from the languages of the regions which they passed through, but some still retain their basic Indic character and vocabulary, unlike, for example, *Anglo Romani,* which is basically English but uses many *Romani* lexical items (spoken in the United Kingdom by 135,000 sp.).

It is estimated that there are from 6 million to 10 million *Romani* speakers in the world, with speakers of *Vlach* and *Balkan Romani* being the most numerous (1.5 million sp. and 1 million sp., respectively).

Dardic languages present some problems for classification. According to Baldi (1983:65), the best that can be said about them at this time is that they are probably Indic but have been strongly influenced by Iranian languages. The chief representative of this group is *Kashmiri* (3 million sp. in India and Pakistan).

The earliest records in an Indic language are the orally transmitted religious hymns in *Vedic Sanskrit* which were probably composed as early as 1400 B.C. but were not actually written down until more than a thousand years later when writing came to India from the Middle East.

Sanskrit (the language of Hindu holy scriptures) was at one time considered by Indo-Europeanists to be the most conservative Indo-European language, but subsequent discoveries, especially that of Hittite, have led most scholars to believe that Sanskrit had innovated extensively and had evolved toward a more inflected/synthetic type of language than Proto-Indo-European had been.

9. ANATOLIAN

This branch has been extinct for a long time. Originally consisting of several languages spoken in Asia Minor (in what is now Turkey), it was discovered only in this century. The discovery of this branch caused Indo-Europeanists to revise their theories concerning what the Proto-Indo-European language was like typologically.

The major representative is *Hittite.* Inscriptions in this language date back to 1400 B.C. and are the earliest known inscriptions in any Indo-European language. Other extinct languages belonging to this group are *Luwian* and *Lycian.*

10. TOCHARIAN

This, too, is an extinct branch. It was represented by two closely related languages named *Tocharian A* and *Tocharian B,* which were spoken in several oases in Chinese Central Asia (Xinjiang Autonomous Region). Texts date from seventh century A.D. and are mostly Buddhist religious writings. Most likely these languages were the source for a number of very early loanwords in Chinese that include words for 'honey', 'grape', and so on. (Though the words in question are believed to be of Indo-European origin there are those who dispute this.)

Before the discovery of Tocharian by scholars in this century, the Indo-European language family was thought to consist of two major branches, the Western or *kentum* branch and the Eastern or *satem* branch, which correlated well with the geographical distribution of the daughter languages (see Table 3.1). The basis for this division was the difference in the development of the velar consonants in the two branches ($*\hat{k}$ = fronted velars; $*k$ = plain velars; $*kw$ = rounded velars) (see Figure 3.1). However, Tocharian, the easternmost Indo-European branch known, turned out to more like a western Indo-European language with regard to several developments. In Tocharian, PIE $*\hat{k}$ and

Table 3.1

EASTERN	WESTERN
Balto-Slavic	Celtic
Armenian	Germanic
Albanian	Italic
Indo-Iranian	Greek
	Anatolian

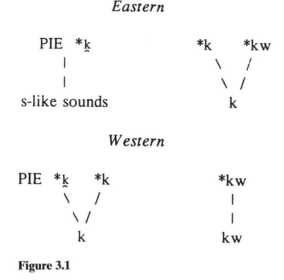

Figure 3.1

k were merged into k, as in the West; at the same time Tocharian was like an Eastern Indo-European language in that it merged labiovelars (*kw*, etc.) with plain velars as well (see Figure 3.2).

Thus, the Tocharian language belongs neither to a *kentum* nor to a *satem* branch, and the neat two-way division of the Indo-European language family into two primary branches turns out to be not entirely tenable. For this reason also the family tree diagram of Indo-European does not reflect this two way classification, since the innovations involved are believed to have spread from one branch to another like waves after the various branches had split from the parent language.

The terms *kentum* and *satem* refer to different developments of the Indo-European word for 'hundred' which had a PIE *ḱ-* (a velar stop produced further front than regular velar consonants) as its initial consonant in the Western and Eastern Indo-European languages, respectively: PIE *ḱmtóm* 'hundred' (see Table 3.2).

In terms of morphology, Indo-European languages can be divided into two major groups, the conservative and the innovating. The conservative languages typically have a number of case inflections, a relatively free word order, show gender/number/case agreement in the adjectives and other nominal

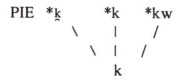

Figure 3.2

Table 3.2

WESTERN	EASTERN
Latin *centum* (pron. *k*entum)	Russian *sto*
Greek he-*katon*	Lithuanian *šimtas*
Welsh *cant* (pron. *k*ant)	Sanskrit *śata*
(Tocharian *kant*)	Avestan *satəm*

modifiers, and are in general highly inflected, synthetic languages. The inno-vating ones typically have fewer case endings or none at all, mark case rela-tions by word order and prepositions, tend to lose gender distinctions in nouns and personal endings in verbs, and are in general more analytical than synthetic. Good examples of modern conservative languages are Serbo-Croa-tian, Russian, Lithuanian, and most Slavic languages in general, except Bul-garian and Macedonian. Typical examples of the innovating ones are English and French. Of course, *all* languages are to some extent innovating, and therefore the distinction made here is only a rough one.

Most modern Indo-European languages have SVO word order (with the notable exceptions being most Indo-Iranian languages, which tend to be SOV, and Celtic languages, which are VSO) and are nominative/accusative rather than ergative. (Again, Indo-Iranian languages are the exception.)

II. URALIC

This family also extends from Europe to Asia. Major European languages that belong to this family are *Finnish, Estonian,* and *Hungarian.* The rest are minor languages spoken in the northern regions of European and Asian parts of the Russian Federation.

Uralic languages are commonly grouped into two primary branches: *Samoyedic* and *Finno-Ugric.*

1. SAMOYEDIC BRANCH

This group is further subdivided into *Southern Samoyed* (*Selkup,* 3,000 sp.) and *Northern Samoyed* (*Enets,* 250 sp.; *Nenets* or *Yurak Samoyed,* 30,000 sp.; *Nganasan,* 900 sp.) All of these languages are spoken in Siberia; *Nganasan* is the northermost language spoken in Siberia.

2. FINNO-UGRIC BRANCH

This branch is further subdivided into two major subbranches.

a. Ugric branch

This branch is further subdivided into two major language groups.

i. Hungarian or Magyar, consisting of Hungarian.
There are 14,423,000 total speakers, of which 10,553,000 are in Hungary, the rest being scattered in the neighboring countries of Rumania, Yugoslavia, Slovakia, etc. The ancestors of modern Hungarians arrived into present-day Hungary around A.D. 896 after a series of migrations from a region just west of the Urals as a part of a military coalition of Magyar and various Turkic tribes. The earliest inscriptions in Hungarian date back to about A.D. 1200.

ii. Ob-Ugric
This language group consists of *Vogul* or *Mansi* (about 3,800 sp. in the Russian Federation) and *Ostyak* or *Khanty* (about 14,280 sp. in the Russian Federation).

b. Fennic Branch

This is in turn subdivided into three subbranches.

i. Permic
Votyak or *Udmurt* (714,000 sp.); *Ziryan* or *Komi* (327,000 sp.); *Komi-Permyak* (151,000 sp.).

ii. Baltic-Finnic
Finnish (5,538,000 sp. in Finland, 300,000 in Sweden, 214,168 in the United States, especially in Minnesota and Michigan). The earliest written documents date back to the 1530s.
Estonian (1,100,00 sp., mainly in Estonia).
Karelian (138,000 sp. in the Karelian Autonomous region in the Russian Federation and 40,000 sp. in Finland). An oath formula inscribed on birch bark in the thirteenth century A.D. is the oldest known Balto-Finnic inscription.
A separate subbranch of *Baltic-Finnic* is *Lappish* or *Saame* (12,000 sp. of different dialects in Finland, Sweden, Norway, and the Russian Federation). However, there are some scholars who feel that this group of languages may form a branch of Fennic, not Baltic-Finnic. In other words, these languages are considered by some to be more distantly related to the Baltic-Finnic languages.

iii. Volgaic
This consists of two language groupings, *Mordvinian,* which embraces two somewhat divergent languages: *Moksha* (428,333 sp.) and *Erzya* (856,667 sp.); and *Cheremis* or *Mari* (700,000 sp.).
It is also believed by some linguists that *Yukaghir* (800 sp. in Eastern Siberia and Kamchatka), which is usually grouped together with the so-called *Paleo-Siberian* languages, is genetically related to Uralic languages, but proof of this connection seems to be lacking at this time. In addition, Uralic and Altaic (discussed in the next chapter) languages used to be linked together by some scholars into one superfamily, Ural-Altaic, on the basis of both lexical and typological features that these languages share. However, very few linguists believe in the Ural-Altaic hypothesis these days.

Some linguists feel that there is enough evidence to link this family with Indo-European. Again, it is clear that Uralic speakers were from very ancient times in contact with Indo-European speakers—it may even turn out, as some scholars have speculated, that Proto-Indo-European and Proto-Uralic were neighboring languages—and that there has been steady borrowing from Baltic languages, Iranian languages, Slavic and Germanic languages. In fact, Finnish loanwords from Germanic are often cited as having preserved some very archaic Germanic features. Thus, although genetic relationship cannot be ruled out between Indo-European and Uralic, it is at present difficult, if not impossible, to ascertain which similarities are due to genetic relationship and which to diffusion of linguistic traits across language family boundaries.

Finally, there are speculations about possible links between Uralic and Dravidian and Uralic and Eskimo-Aleut. For information on the latter hypothesis, see Bergsland (1959).

Typologically Uralic languages range from agglutinative (e.g., Finnish) to synthetic/inflected (e.g., Estonian). According to Janhunen (1992:208), Proto-Uralic was agglutinative, had SOV order, two grammatical cases (accusative and genitive), and three local cases (dative, locative, and ablative). (Compare modern Finnish, which has fifteen cases, and Hungarian, which has twenty-three, but some of the latter are found with only few stems. Most of the Hungarian cases are innovations.)

There is usually fairly complex verb morphology in Uralic languages. The most striking feature is that Uralic languages have special negative verbs that are used as auxiliary verbs to negate other verbs. (Cf. Finnish *en ota* 'I do not take' to *emme ota* 'we do not take'. Note that *e-* is the stem of the negative verb, and the personal suffixes *-n* and *-mme* are attached to it.)

There are some typologically quite interesting phenomena in Uralic languages. First, in Estonian, there is a three-way quantitative contrast in both vowels and consonants. Thus Estonian has short, long, and extra long vowels and consonants. Second, a number of Uralic languages, but not all, exhibit what is called *consonant gradation*. Basically, this gradation takes place before the vowel of a closed syllable: long stops become short, and short stops become voiced. For example, in Finnish *akka* 'old woman' becomes *akat* when *-t*, the plural suffix is added and causes the final syllable to be closed, and *pata* 'cooking pot' becomes *padat*.[1]

Most Uralic languages also exhibit *vowel harmony*. Since this is a fairly important phenomenon that is referred to later, I here give a general outline of what it involves. First, there are two basic types of vowel harmony: partial harmony, in which only some feature or features of vowel segments "harmonize" or agree throughout the word or morpheme, and total harmony, which involves copying all the vowel features. Thus in Finnish there is total harmony after *h*: *maa* 'land' becomes *maa-han* in illative singular, *pää* 'head' becomes *pää-hän, puu* 'tree' becomes *puu-hun, pii* 'flint' becomes *pii-hin,* and so forth.

Second, vowel harmony differs from language to language with respect to its domain. That is, the vowels may harmonize only within a morpheme, or only within a noncompound word, and so on. (In Finnish, for example, vowel harmony extends throughout noncompound words, but not compounds.)

Finally, in partial vowel harmony there are number of features that may harmonize:

1. *Labial* (lip rounding) harmony. According to Collinder (1965:65), labial harmony occurs in Hungarian, Eastern Cheremis, and Selkup, all languages which have been under Turkic influence. (Turkic languages themselves exhibit labial harmony.)

2. *Palatal* harmony. This can also be called front/back harmony. Palatal harmony occurs in most Uralic languages except in *Lappish, Votyak, Ziryene, Northern Vogul,* and most *Estonian* dialects including *Standard Estonian.*[2]

3. *Vertical* or high/low harmony is not found in Uralic languages and seems to be somewhat rare in general. Modern Lhasa Tibetan is said to exhibit this type of vowel harmony.

III. LANGUAGES OF THE CAUCASUS

This is not universally recognized as a single language family but a preliminary geographic grouping of languages. All thirty-eight or so languages belonging to this group are spoken in the region of Caucasus mountains which straddle the borders of Turkey, Iran, and the Caucasus republics (primarily Georgia) and autonomous regions of the former Soviet Union. Genetic classification of these languages still presents many problems, but the current consensus is that they should be temporarily grouped into at least three, if not four, language families. (Some authorities prefer two, and there are some who consider all of these language groups to be genetically related.) B. G. Hewitt (1992:220–27) lists four language groups, each of which clearly contains genetically related languages.

1. NORTHWEST CAUCASIAN OR ABKHAZ-ADYGE GROUP

The languages of this group are spoken mainly in the northwestern part of the Caucasus region, but some of them are also spoken in scattered pockets elsewhere. They are *Abkhaz* (91,000 sp. in the Abkhaz Autonomous Republic in Georgia and 4,000 in Turkey) and *Abaza* (29,000 sp. in the Karachay-Cherkess Autonomous Oblast of the former Soviet Union and 5,000 to 30,000 in Turkey), *Ubykh,* which is now most likely extinct, was spoken only by an 80 year old man in Turkey according to the last report; *Adyghe* or *West Circassian* (109,000 sp. in the Adyghe Autonomous Oblast of the former Soviet Union, 71,000 in Turkey, 44,000 in Jordan, and 25,000 in Syria) and *Kabardian* or *East Circassian* (368,000 sp., most in the Kabardo-Balkar Autonomous Republic and the Karachay-Cherkess Autonomous Oblast of the former Soviet Union, some in Turkey).

Typologically, these languages are *ergative,* lack the distinction between active and passive, and have SOV word order. They have complex verb morphology but relatively simple noun morphology. The verbs show agreement with subject, object, and indirect object in respect to class of the noun. They are generally agglutinative in structure, with prefixes outnumbering suffixes.

One of the interesting features of these languages is that they possess very rich consonant phoneme inventories but only very few vowel phonemes. Thus, for example, Ubykh has been analyzed as having as many as 82 consonant phonemes (including such series as plain, rounded, palatalized, and glottalized), but only two vowel phonemes.

Since ergativity is mentioned again in connection with Basque language and elsewhere, a brief explanation of the term is given here. For more details and specific examples, however, see "Sketch of Classical Tibetan" in the chapter on the languages of Asia as well as references to ergativity in the index.

In *nominative/accusative* languages such as English, the subject of a transitive verb and a subject of an intransitive verb have the same case marking (or no overt marking). In contrast, a direct object of a transitive verb is marked as having a different case from the subject:

> He slept. (*He* in this sentence is a subject of an intransitive verb.)
>
> He saw him. (*He* is a subject of a transitive verb, whereas *him* is a direct object.)

Thus, in nominative/accusative languages all subjects are marked for the same case, and the contrast is between subjects as a group and objects.

In ergative languages, however, the subject of an intransitive verb and the direct object of a transitive verb have the same case marking (called *absolutive*), whereas the subject of a transitive verb is marked by a different case (called *ergative*). Another feature of such languages is that they often do not have a distinction between active and passive constructions.

2. NORTH CENTRAL CAUCASIAN OR NAKH GROUP

This consists of the following languages, all spoken in the northern Caucasus region of the former Soviet Union: *Chechen* (900,000 sp.), *Ingush* (200,000 sp.), *Batsbi* (2,500 to 3,000 sp.).

3. NORTHEAST CAUCASIAN GROUP

This group is subdivided into three subgroups.

a. Avar-Andi-Dido

This subgroup includes the following languages of the Daghestan Autonomous Republic of the former Soviet Union: *Avar* or *Daghestani* (483,000 sp.), *Andi* (8,000–9,000 sp.), *Dido* or *Tsez* (7,000 sp.).

b. Lak-Dargwa

This subgroup consists of two languages spoken in Daghestan: *Lak* (100,000 sp.) and *Dargwa* or *Dargin* (287,000 sp.).

c. Lezgian

This subgroup consists of *Lezgi* (383,000 sp.), and *Tabassaran* (75,000 sp.), plus a number of minor languages spoken in primarily in Daghestan.

There is now some evidence that the last two groups should be considered a single language group called *Northeast Caucasian* or *Nakh-Daghestanian* with *Nakh* and *Daghestanian* as its immediate constituents.

Typologically the languages belonging to the last two groups are ergative, although they do show some nominative/accusative traits. The basic word order is SOV. As opposed to the Abkhaz-Adyge languages, their verb morphology is very simple, whereas their noun morphology is very complex. (Tabassaran is reported to have as many as forty-eight cases.) Nouns are divided into masculine, feminine, animate (nonhuman), and inanimate.

4. SOUTH CAUCASIAN OR KARTVELIAN GROUP

The most prominent language of this group is *Georgian* (the native language of Joseph Stalin), which has the largest number of speakers of any Caucasian language: 3,571,000 in the Republic of Georgia, 1,000 to 10,000 in Iran, 40,000 in Turkey, with smaller numbers elsewhere. The other languages belonging to this group are *Svan* (35,000 sp. in northwestern part of Republic of Georgia), and *Laz,* spoken primarily in Turkey by up to 90,000 sp. (for 30,000 of whom this is the first language).

Instead of being ergative languages as many languages of the Caucasus are, both *Georgian* and *Svan* exhibit active/nonactive typology in which subjects of intransitive verbs divide into "active" and "non-active." Active subjects pattern like subjects of transitives and are agentive in nature (e.g., 'I run'), whereas nonactive subjects pattern like objects of transitive verbs and are nonagentive in nature (e.g., 'I die').[3]

In this group of languages both SVO and SOV word orders are found, sometimes in the same language.

According to Hewitt (1992), the three northern language groups may all be genetically related, but the southern group does not seem to be related to any of the other groups.

The majority of Caucasus languages share a number of traits, including a limited set of similar lexical items and phonological, morphological, and grammatical features. For example, most of them are ergative to some degree, have glottalized ejective and pharyngeal consonants, show subject and object agreement prefixes on the verb, and are generally agglutinative in structure. If these shared features are not due to genetic ties between these language groups, then we can say that they are most likely due to diffusion, and that Caucasus is a *linguistic area*. Klimov (1965:77) rightly points out, however, that the Caucasus region is, geographically speaking, a very unlikely candidate to be a linguistic area: the mountainous terrain greatly hinders communication and contact between various settlements. Therefore Klimov suspects that what we are dealing with here is really divergence from a common ancestor language which cannot yet be firmly established because the comparative studies of the Caucasus languages are still in their infancy. On the other hand, one must point out that all Caucasus languages show large numbers of loanwords from Iranian languages, Turkic languages, and Arabic (through the spread of Islam). Presumably, therefore, the mountainous terrain does not entirely prevent language contact.

IV. BASQUE

This is a language family that has only one member since *Basque* or *Euskara* is a *language isolate*. (However, there are some who feel that dialect differences within Basque are so great that we should talk about several Basque languages instead.) It is spoken by a relatively small number of people in the region of the Pyrenees, the mountain range separating France from Spain. There are 615,000 speakers in Spain and 90,000 speakers, mostly older people, in France. There are also about 8,000 immigrant speakers of Basque in the United States. Most speakers of Basque are probably bilingual, speaking Basque and either French or Spanish.

Certain linguists and philologists have attempted to show that *Basque* is related to some languages of the Caucasus, but their evidence is not very convincing. The same is true in the case of various attempts to link *Basque* with some native languages of the Americas and Burushaski, a language isolate spoken in Pakistan. (There seems to be a definite trend among amateur linguists to attempt genetic linkages between various "linguistic orphans," i.e., language isolates.)

Attempts to link *Basque* with some of the languages of the Caucasus and Burushaski (in the Himalayas) are motivated to a large extent by the fact that *Basque,* most of the Caucasian languages, and Burushaski indeed share a few typological traits—for example, ergativity—which are not found in other language groups in Europe.

The following two examples from Saltarelli (1988;vi–vii) illustrate the ergative case marking in Basque:

emakume-*ak* gizon-*a* ikus-ten d-u

/woman + sing. ergative suffix /man + sing. absolutive suffix /see + habitual/ 3d pers. absolutive object agreement + transitive auxiliary/(Present tense and third person singular subject agreement are not overtly marked in the last word.)

'The woman sees the man.'

gizon-*a* kale-an d-a-go

/man + sing. absolutive/ street + sing. locative suffix/ 3d pers. absolutive + pres. tense + be

'The man is in the street.'

According to Saltarelli (1988), Basque is a morphologically ergative, highly inflected language which has sixteen nominal cases and qualifies as an agglutinative language. (However, he also says that syntactically Basque acts like a nominative/accusative language in that notions such as "subject" and "object" are more relevant to the description of the language than "absolutive" and "ergative," i.e., "subject of an intransitive verb" versus "subject of a transitive verb.") Although it has a relatively free word order on account of its rich system of inflections, its neutral word order appears to be Subject Object Verb. The adjectives and genitives precede the nouns they modify. Its sound pattern is influenced by the various languages with which it has had contact: Latin, Spanish, and the Gascon dialect of Occitan French.

V. TURKIC

The only major European representative of this family is *Turkish,* which is spoken in the European part of Turkey and by minority populations in Cyprus, Greece, Bulgaria, and parts of former Yugoslavia, especially Bosnia-Herzegovina and Macedonia. This language grouping is discussed in detail in the chapter on Asian languages since most of its members are found in Asia.

SKETCH OF RUSSIAN

A. GENETIC CLASSIFICATION AND GENERAL BACKGROUND

Russian belongs to the Eastern subbranch (along with Ukrainian and Byelorussian) of the Slavic branch of the Indo-European language family and is spoken by about 270 million people, including 153,655,000 who consider it their native language, primarily in the Russian Federation. Because it was the language of the largest ethnic group in the former Soviet Union, it is still taught and used in the non-Russian regions of the Commonwealth of Independent States even though local languages have now become the main official languages in most of the former Soviet republics. (In all of the newly independent Baltic countries, but especially in Latvia, there are fairly large Russian-speaking minority populations.) In addition, Russian was fairly widely taught as a foreign language in the former Soviet bloc countries as well as in some developing nations which used to receive technical assistance from the Soviet Union. However, it was never as widely taught or spoken as one would expect given the political and military status of the former Soviet Union in the world. Since Slavic languages are to a large extent mutually intelligible, many Slavs just do not bother learning Russian because they feel that they can communicate adequately with Russians by speaking their own native language. For example, a Czech or a Bulgarian may use Czech or Bulgarian, respectively, when speaking to a Russian and be reasonably sure that much of what they say will be understood by the latter. (In addition, not learning Russian or learning it badly was one of the ways that people in the

Eastern bloc countries used to show opposition to the dominance of their countries by the Soviet Union.)

It is predominantly a synthetic type language with SVO/AN (Subject + Verb + Object; Adjective + Noun; Noun + Genitive) word order with a fairly complicated morphology and phonology.

Russian has borrowed extensively from other languages. In the past it was influenced by various Turkic languages, Finno-Ugric (Uralic) languages, Greek, Latin, and Germanic languages. In more recent times a large number of terms, especially technical terms, were borrowed from German, Dutch, French, and even more recently, English.

B. ALPHABET AND ORTHOGRAPHY

The alphabet used to write Russian as well as other Slavic languages whose speakers belong to the Greek Orthodox Church (i.e., Serbian, Macedonian, Bulgarian, Ukrainian, and Byelorussian) is based on an alphabet whose creation is traditionally ascribed to Saints Cyril and Methodius, ninth-century Greek Orthodox missionaries to the Slavs. Most of the letters of the Cyrillic alphabet, as it is called, are derived from the Greek alphabet; letters for some of the sounds that did not have Greek equivalents were borrowed from Hebrew and Syriac alphabets.

Some other languages that use or have used Cyrillic are Mongolian (only in the Mongolian Republic—in Inner Mongolia, a part of China, the old Mongolian script has always been used), though recently even in the Mongolian Republic the old Mongol script is being revived; Uzbek, Kazakh, and many other minority languages of the former Soviet Union.

At the time of this writing there are reports that Tajikistan is planning to revert to the Arabic script for Tajik, and that Azerbaijan is switching to Latin script for Azeri. At present, however, in both countries the Cyrillic-based script is still in use along with Arabic-based script and Latin-based script respectively.

Rather than being listed according to the traditional alphabetic order, the Russian Cyrillic letters have here been divided into three different categories in order to facilitate somewhat the learning of their values (see Table 3.3). In group I are the letters which have roughly the same shape and sound value in both Russian and English; in group II those Russian letters that look like English letters but have a very different sound value in Russian are listed; in group III are those Russian letters which are not found in the English (Roman) alphabet. The symbols in square brackets are the IPA phonetic symbols for the sound values of each Russian letter. The rightmost column gives the standard romanization of each Cyrillic letter.

The letters ь and ъ originally represented a very short (reduced) high front vowel and a very short (reduced) high back vowel, respectively. The letter ь indicates that the preceding consonant is palatalized, whereas ъ indicates that the preceding consonant is not palatalized even though it is in a palatalizing environment (i.e., before a front vowel or before a letter that represents a

Table 3.3 RUSSIAN CYRILLIC ALPHABET

GROUP I			GROUP II			GROUP III		
А	[a]	a	Е	[je]	e	Б	[b]	b
К	[k]	k	Н	[n]	n	Г	[g]	g
М	[m]	m	Р	[r]	r	Д	[d]	d
О	[o]	o	С	[s]	s	Ж	[ʒ]	ž
Т	[t]	t	У	[u]	u	З	[z]	z
			Х	[x]	x	И	[i]	i
			В	[v]	v	Й	[j]	j
						Л	[l]	l
						П	[p]	p
						Ф	[f]	f
						Ц	[ts]	c
						Ч	[tɕ]	č
						Ш	[ʃ]	š
						Щ	[ɕ:]	šč
						Ь	silent	'
						Ъ	silent	"
						Ы	[ɯɨ]	y
						Э	[e]	è
						Ю	[ju]	ju
						Я	[ja]	ja
						Ё	[jo]	jo

sound beginning in a palatal glide). (The letter ъ is found only rarely in modern Russian spelling.)

Here are some examples of Russian words in Cyrillic (with marked stress) and their romanization and gloss:

спу́тник = sputnik (sputnik, traveling companion, artificial satellite)

Роси́я = Rossija 'Russia'

Аме́рика = Amerika 'America'

това́рищ = tovarišč 'comrade, friend'

Москва́ = Moskva 'Moscow'

Кита́й = Kitaj 'China'

Although Russian orthography is not as complicated and arbitrary as that of English, it is also based more on etymology than on what is actually pronounced or on what could be justified on the basis of a synchronic phonological analysis of the sound system. For example, what is written хорошо (xorošo) 'good, well'[4] is actually pronounced [xarašó] because unstressed *o*'s are pronounced as *a*'s in the standard dialect of Russian (for more details, see the discussion of vowel reduction in the following section). The second vowel of this morpheme is sometimes stressed and is then actually pronounced as *o* (as in xoróšyj—masc. sing. adj. form), and therefore one might argue that it is underlyingly an *o*. However, the first *o* of this word is never stressed and therefore never pronounced as *o*; therefore spelling it as *o* can be justified only on historical, etymological grounds and on the basis of pronunciation in some nonstandard dialects of Russian (some of which lack the rule which changes unstressed *o*'s and *a*'s).

C. PHONETICS AND PHONOLOGY

The sound system of Russian is dominated by the opposition between plain (in some instances velarized) and palatalized consonants, and therefore most consonant phonemes come in pairs (see Table 3.4).

The patterns of stress are very complicated; in practical terms it is necessary to learn stress with most individual lexical items. There are some rather critical minimal pairs for stress such as *pisát'* = 'to write' versus *písat'* = vulgar for 'to urinate'.

Velar consonants are palatalized (more accurately, fronted) before /i, e, j/, but there is no phonological contrast between plain and palatalized velars as in the case of labials and dentals. /r/ and its palatalized counterpart are trills though they are not as long as those found in Spanish or in the Scottish dialects of English. /l/ is heavily velarized in all positions so that phonetically there is really no plain l-sound in Russian.[5]

In many variants of standard Russian /t'/ and /d'/ are affricated. /š'/ and /č'/ are both laminal (i.e., produced by the tongue blade), whereas /š/ and /ž/ are apical (i.e., produced by the tongue tip). In some varieties of Russian /š'/ is pronounced as a combination of a palatalized laminoalveolar fricative and a homorganic affricate. In many dialects, however, it is simply a tense, palatalized laminoalveolar fricative of rather long duration with just a hint of an affricate component at times. /ž'/ is a rather rare phoneme, but it appears in a few fairly common vocabulary items. In word-final position all voiced obstruents are devoiced.

Table 3.4 CONSONANT PHONEMES OF RUSSIAN

Labials		Dentals		Alveopalatals		Velars
PLAIN	PAL.	PLAIN	PAL.	PLAIN	PAL.	PLAIN
p	p'	t	t'			k
b	b'	d	d'			g
		ts = c			č' = č	
f	f'	s	s'	š	š' = šč	x
v	v'	z	z'	ž	ž'	
m	m'	n	n'			
		r	r'			
		l	l'			

Table 3.5   VOCALIC PHONEMES OF RUSSIAN

i		u
e		o
	a	
	semivowel:	
	j	

After nonpalatalized consonant phonemes (except velars), /i/ has the allophone [ɯɨ], a diphthong whose first, nonsyllabic element is a high back unrounded vowel and whose syllabic nucleus is a high central vowel. (Velar consonant phonemes have fronted allophones before front vowel phonemes and /j/.)

In unstressed syllables some of the vowel contrasts are neutralized: unstressed *o* becomes *a*, unstressed *e* becomes *i*, and even unstressed *a* becomes *i* after palatalized consonants. (There are some exceptions to these rules but they are not given here.) For example: гора [gará] 'mountain', but горы [góruɨ] 'mountains'; семья [s'im'já] 'family', but семьи [s'ém'ji] 'families'. Thus, in unstressed syllables the five vowel system is reduced to a three vowel system: /i/, /u/, and /a/.

D. MORPHOLOGY

Nouns

The nouns have three genders: masculine, feminine, and neuter. Feminine nouns usually end in -*a* in nominative singular, and neuter nouns usually end in -*o* or -*e* in nominative singular. There are several different declensions. For example,

> vodá = 'water' (fem. noun, cognate with English 'water')
>
> ogón' = 'fire' (masc. noun; cf. *ign*-ite)
>
> dérevo = 'tree' (neuter noun, cognate with English 'tree')

Calvin and Hobbes

Figure 3.3

Table 3.6 Sample Noun Paradigms

	'WATER'	'FIRE'	'TREE'
Singular			
Nom.	vodá	ogón'	dérevo
Gen.	vodý	ognjá	déreva
Acc.	vódu	ogón'	dérevo
Dat.	vodé	ognjú	dérevu
Instr.	vodój	ognëm[6]	dérevom
Prep.	vodé	ogné	déreve
Plural			
Nom.	vódy	ogní	derév'ja
Gen.	vód	ognéj	derév'jev
Acc.	vódy	ogní	derév'ja
Dat.	vodám	ognjám	derév'jam
Instr.	vodámi	ognjámi	derév'jami
Prep.	vodáx	ognjáx	derév'jax

There are two numbers—singular and plural. Though there are some traces of an older dual number, the latter is not a living category in modern Russian.

All nominals (as well as adjectives that modify them) are inflected for six cases: *Nominative* which marks the subject of the verb; *genitive,* which marks the possessor, occurs after some prepositions, and is also used to mark a direct object after negated verbs; *accusative,* which marks a direct object after non-negated verbs and also occurs after certain prepositions; *dative,* which marks an indirect object and also occurs after certain prepositions; *instrumental,* which marks the instrument or means whereby an action is performed and has many idiomatic uses; and *prepositional,* which occurs only after a limited set of prepositions (see Table 3.6).

There are also a very restricted set of nouns which retain the *vocative* case as well from the older language. Older forms of Russian had this case (which is used to call or address someone) but lost it except for some words which are fairly intimately connected with church life; the more conservative language used in the Russian Orthodox liturgical services has, in other words, exerted a conservative influence on these particular words. Thus, *Bog* 'God' (nominative case) has the vocative form *Bože* 'oh God!'

There are no definite and indefinite articles in Russian.

Adjectives

Adjectives must agree in gender, case, and number with the nouns they modify. For example:

> bol'šój kon' 'big horse' (masc. nom. sing.)
>
> bol'šája kóška 'big cat' (fem. nom. sing.)

bol'šóe dérevo 'big tree' (neut. nom. sing.)

bol'ším kóškam 'to big cats' (fem. dat. pl.)

As can be seen from these examples, Russian adjectives usually precede the nouns they modify; however, for special effects, especially in poetry, the order may be reversed or the adjectives may be placed far from the nouns they modify as long as the agreement unambiguously indicates which adjective goes with which noun.

Diminutive forms

Both nouns and adjectives in Russian can have a variety of diminutive suffixes which can sometimes even be piled up one after another:

> górod 'town, city'; gorod-ók 'small town'; gorod-óč-ek 'a tiny town'; gorod-óč-eč-ek 'a teency-weency town'

Besides indicating the small size of something, diminutive also expresses endearment (and more rarely these days, deprecation) and therefore plays a large role in baby talk and in the sweet talk between lovers:

> Pëtr 'Peter', but Péten'ka 'dear Petie' or Pét'ka 'Pete (the servant, or someone of similarly low social status, or someone with whom the speaker is angry, annoyed, etc.)

Even adjectives can be inflected with diminutive endings:

> belýj 'white', but bélen'kij 'tiny white' (note that this means something like 'tiny and white', not 'a little bit white')

Patronymics

A source of endless confusion for the readers of Russian novels in English translation are the patronymics which Russians use instead of middle names. The patronymics indicate whose son or daughter a person is. It is considered respectful enough to address someone only by his or her first name followed by the patronymic (omitting the last name and any title of respect).

Patronymics as well as Russian last names are really derived adjectives and as such must agree in gender, case, and number with the nouns they modify, that is, with the first or Christian name of a person. This is what creates confusion among the uninitiated non-Russian readers since, depending on the sex of the person, both the patronymic and the last name will look different in the case of a brother and sister:

> Iván Ivánov-ič Ivanóv = 'Ivan, son of Ivan, Ivanov'
> Eléna Ivánov-na Ivanóv-a = 'Helen, daughter of Ivan, Ivanov'

Verbs

Russian verbs are inflected for person, number, tense, aspect, and in some instances for gender. (Participles, which are in fact adjectives derived from verbs, must agree in gender, case, and number with the nouns they modify, just like any other adjectives.) The tenses are present, past, and future. There are two aspects, perfective and imperfective, with perfective marking actions which are viewed as either being completed or which will be completed in the future, and the imperfective marking actions which are not viewed as having a definite end or which are ongoing without a definite end in sight. The imperfective and perfective forms cannot be automatically derived from each other, and the student of Russian must, accordingly, learn both the perfective and imperfective forms of each individual verb (see Table 3.7). The following illustration presents the active conjugation of the Russian verb 'to give' in both aspects. Note that in the present tense there is only imperfective aspect. (What looks morphologically like present perfective has future perfective meaning.)

Infinitives

> Perf.: dat'; imperf.: davát'

Imperative Forms

> Imperf. sing.: daváj, pl. davájte; perf. sing.: daj, pl. dájte

Participles

> Imperf. act.: dajúščij ('giving one'); imperf. pass.: daváemyj ('one being given')

> Perf. act.: dávšij ('having given'); perf. pass.: dánnyj ('one having been given')

Gerunds

> Perf.: dávši; imperf.: davávši

Note that gerunds do not show gender, number, and case agreement with the nominals whose logical modifiers they are:

> *Peredávši* pakét, mál'čik ušël.

> 'Having handed over (gerund) the parcel, the boy went away'.

> *Peredávši* pakét, dévočki ušlí.

> 'Having handed over (gerund) the parcel, the girls went away'.

Compare this with the following:

> Mál'čik *peredávšij* pakét ušël.

> 'The boy, the one having handed over (participle showing masc. sing. nom. agreement) the parcel, went away.'

Table 3.7 INDICATIVE VERB FORMS

	PRES. IMPERF.	PAST IMPERF.	PAST PERF.	FUT. IMPERF.	FUT. PERF.
1st pers. sing.	dajú	davál/a/o	dal/á/ó	búdu davát'	dam
2d pers. sing.	daëš'	davál/a/o	dal/á/ó	búdeš' davát'	daš'
3d pers. sing.	daët	davál/a/o	dal/á/ó	búdet davát'	dast
1st pers. pl.	daëm	daváli	dáli	búdem davát'	dadím
2d pers. pl.	daëte	daváli	dáli	búdete davát'	dadíte
3d pers. pl.	dajút	daváli	dáli	búdut davát'	dadút

There is also a full passive paradigm, but except for the passive participles, passive forms are usually confined to the written language and sound too bookish when used in conversation.

The alternate forms of the verbs in the past tense (e.g., *daval*, *davála*, *daválo*) show agreement in gender and number with their subject. Thus *ja daval* 'I was giving' or 'I used to give' implies that the speaker ('I') is masculine; if a woman were speaking, she would say *ja davála* instead. Note that the past tense forms do not show person agreement, only the gender/number agreement, in contrast to verb forms in other two tenses. This rather strange situation arises from the fact that past tense forms were originally past participles which had to agree in gender, number, and case with the subject nouns or pronouns.

The Russian equivalent of the verb *to be* is not used in the present tense as a copula verb. Where English says 'I am a student' or 'I am sick' Russian says literally 'I student' *(ja studént)* and 'I sick' *(ja bólen)*.

Beside the large number of verb inflections there is also a very rich system of verb derivation: by adding various affixes one can derive a large number of verbs from a single root creating new stems which differ subtly in meaning. For example, from the basic root *stuk* 'knock' one can form the following verbs (all cited in their infinitive form):

> stučat' (imperf.) 'to knock, keep on knocking'
>
> stuknut' (perf.) 'to knock (once)'
>
> postukivat' (imperf.) 'to keep on knocking intermittently'
>
> postučat' (perf.) 'to knock intermittently once'
>
> dostučat'sja (perf.) 'to knock until there is a result'
>
> nastučat'sja (perf.) 'to have one's fill of knocking'
>
> rasstučat' (perf.) 'to knock something apart'
>
> rasstučat'sja (perf.) 'to knock away with abandon'

E. SYNTAX

The unmarked or basic word order in Russian is Subject + Verb + Object, as in English. Adjectives normally precede the nouns they modify. In general, however, the Russian word order is less fixed than that of English because the gender/number/case suffixes in nouns, case suffixes in pronouns, and case/gender/number agreement suffixes in participles and adjectives indicate fairly unambiguously what modifies what, what is the subject of a sentence, the object, and so forth. In fact, the normal word order is often violated for stylistic reasons and when various elements of the sentence are topicalized. For example, both of the following Russian sentences basically mean 'My cat bit your dog' in spite of the radical difference in word order that would affect the meaning of the sentence in English:

Mojá kóška ukusíla tvojú sobáku.

My cat bit your dog

(Normal word order in answer to the question, 'What happened?')

Tvojú sobáku ukusíla mojá kóška.

Your dog bit my cat

(In answer to the question, 'What happened to my dog?')

Note that the Russian sentence meaning 'Your dog bit my cat' would have the same word order as the immediately preceding sentence, but the nouns would have very different endings:

Tvoj-*á* sobák-*a* ukusíla moj-*ú* kóšk-*u*.

Interrogative Sentences

Interrogative sentences in Russian often have the same word order as declarative sentences, especially if they are content questions and there is a question word in the sentence:

Ty byl tam.

You were there

Kogdá ty byl tam?

When you were there

'When were you there?' (Note the subject and verb position switch in the English equivalent.)

If there is no question word in the sentence (as in yes-or-no questions) particle *li* is placed right after the word which is being questioned and the questioned word is placed at the beginning of the sentence:

Byl *li* ty tam?

Were ques. you there

'Were you [actually] there?'

Vy li byli tam?

You (pl.) ques. were there

'Was it you [and not somebody else] who were there?'

But the most common way of forming yes-no questions is just to use a question intonation.

Relative Clauses

Relative clauses which modify nouns follow their head nouns. Other subordinate clauses usually precede the elements they modify. Like English, Russian employs relative pronouns as markers of relative clauses:

> Koška, kotóraja ukusila sobáku, ubežala.
>
> Cat which bit dog ran away
>
> 'The cat which bit the dog ran away.'

> Kogdá ty pri šël, on uže byl p'jan.
>
> When you came he already was drunk
>
> 'When you came he was already drunk.'

Negation

Like Spanish and some other languages (including many nonstandard dialects of English), Russian employs double negation. The multiple negatives do not cancel each other out, but redundantly signal and reinforce the negative aspect of the statement:

> On nikogdá ne xóčet pojtí nikúda so mnoj.
>
> he never not wants to go nowhere with me
>
> 'He never wants to go anywhere with me.'

Another important feature of negation in Russian is the different case marking of direct object NPs after negated verbs (genitive) and after non-negated verbs (accusative):

> Ja vižu košku
>
> I see cat (acc.)
>
> 'I see [a] cat.'

versus

> Ja ne vižu koški
>
> I neg. see cat (gen.)
>
> 'I don't see [a] cat.'

The genitive case is also used instead of the expected nominative case to mark the logical subject in existential sentences which have been negated:

> Vodá est'
>
> water (nom.) exists
>
> 'There is water.'

versus

> Vodý net
>
> water (gen.) not [exist]
>
> 'There is no water.'

F. SAMPLE TEXT
Russian Text[7]

(1) У Абакýмова был тóже голосóк с громовы́ми раскáтами, и он умéл им припугнýть. Но сейчáс он чýвствовал, что кричáть бы́ло бы беспóмощно и несоли́дно. Он пóнял, что арестáнт э́тот трýдный.

(2) И тóлько предупреди́л:

(3) — Слýшайте, заключённый. Éсли я с вáми мя́гко, так вы не забывáйтесь . . .

(4) — А éсли бы вы со мной грýбо — я б с вáми и разговáривать не стал, граждани́н мини́стр. Кричи́те на свои́х полкóвников да генерáлов, у них сли́шком мнóго в жи́зни есть, им сли́шком жáлко этого всегó.

(5) — Скóлко нýжно — и вас застáвим.

(6) — Ошибáетесь, граждани́н мини́стр! — И си́льные глазá Бобы́нина сверкнýли нéнавистью. — У меня ничегó нет, вы понимáете — нет ничегó! Женý мою и ребёнка вы уже не достáнете — их взялá бóмба. Роди́тели мои́ — ужé ýмерли. Имýщества у меня́ всегó на землé — носовóй платóк, а комбинезóн и вот бельё под ним без пýговиц (он обнажи́л грудь и показáл) — казённое. Свобóду вы у меня давнó óтняли, а вернýть её не в вáших си́лах, и́бо её нет у вас самогó. Лет мне óтроду сóрок два, срóку вы мне отсы́пали двáдцать пять, на кáторге я уже был, в номерáх ходи́л, и в нарýчниках, и с собáками, и в бригáде уси́ленного режи́ма — чем ещё мóжете вы мне угрози́ть? чегó ещё лиши́ть? Инженéрной рабóты? Вы от э́того потеря́ете бóльше. Я закурю́.

(7) Абакýмов раскры́л корóбку «Трóйки» осóбого вы́пуска и пододви́нул Бобы́нину:

(8) — Вот возьми́те э́тих.

(9) — Спаси́бо. Не меня́ю мáрки. Кáшель. — И достáл «беломóрину» из самодéльного портсигáра. — Вообщé, пойми́те и передáйте там, кому нáдо вы́ше, что вы сильны́ лишь постóльку, поскóльку отбирáете от людéй не

всё. Но челове́к, у кото́рого вы отобра́ли всё — уже́ не подвла́стен вам, он сно́ва свобо́ден.

Literal Morpheme-by-Morpheme Translation

Superscripted numbers in the following translation refer to notes at the end of this section. In order to keep things uncluttered, some morpheme breaks have been ignored. (Hyphens indicate morpheme breaks; slashes indicate word breaks.) Grammatical features of words which are not overtly marked, are marked by zero allomorphs, or are marked by morphemes which have not been identified in the text are provided in parentheses. An equal sign indicates a more idiomatic rather than a literal translation. All translations of appropriate content morphemes appear in **boldface** type for easier identification. Original punctuation has been retained in both the romanized Russian and the translation in order to facilitate the matching up of various "levels of representation" of the text. (Note that Russian allows what in English would be considered run-on sentences.)

(1) *U Abakúmov-a by-l tóže golos-ók s grom-ový-mi raskát-ami,*
At, near, by (loc. prep.)/ **Abakumov** (proper noun) + masc. gen. sing./ **exist, be** + past tense (masc. sing.)/[1] **also**/ **voice** + diminutive suffix (masc. nom. sing.)/[13] **with**/ **thunder** + **ous** + masc. instr. pl./ **roll** + masc. instr. pl./,

i on umé-l im pripugnú-t'. No sejčás on čúvstvova-l, čto krič-át'
and/ **he**/ **know how** (imperf.) + past tense (masc. sing.)/ 3d pers. masc. pron., instr. case = **with it**/ **frighten** (perf.) + inf./. **But**/ **now**/ **he**/ **feel** (imperf.) + past tense (masc. sing.)/ that (relat. pron.)/ **yell** + inf./

bý-l-o by bes-pómošč-no i ne-solíd-no. On pónja-l, čto arestánt ètot trúdn-yj.
be + past + neut. sing./ **would**/ without + help (= **helpless**) + neut. nom. sing./[2] **and** / **non** + **solid** + neut. nom. sing./[2] **He**/ **understand** (perf.) + past (masc. sing.)/ **that** (relat.) **prisoner** (masc. nom. sing.) / **this** (masc. nom. sing.)/ **difficult** + masc. nom. sing./[3]

(2) *I tól'ko predupredí-l:*
And/ **only**/ **warn** (perf.) + past (masc. sing.):

(3) *Slúša-j-te zaključënnyj. Ésli ja s vámi mjágk-o, tak vy*
Listen (imperf.) + imperat. + 2d pers. pl./ **prisoner** (masc. nom. sing.). If/ I/ **with**/ **you** (instr. pl.)/ **soft** + adverb suffix/,[4] **so**/ you (nom. pl.)

ne zabyvá-j-te-s' . . .
/ **not**/ **forget** (imperf.) + imper. + 2d pers. pl.- reflexive/[5] . . .

(4) *A ésli by vy so mnoj grúb-o — ja b s vámi i razgováriva-t' ne sta-l,*
But/ **if**/ **would**/ **you** (nom. pl.)/ **with**/ **me** (instr.)/ **rough** + adv./[4] — I / **would**/ **with**/ **you** (instr. pl.)/ and (= **even**)/ **speak** (imperf.) + inf./ **not** / **begin,** become (perf.) + past (masc. nom. sing.),

graždanín minístr. Krič-í-te na svoix polkóvnik-ov da generál-ov,
citizen (masc. nom. sing.)/ **minister** (masc. nom. sing.)/ **Yell** + imper. + 2d. pers. pl./ **at**/ **own** (masc. acc. pl.)/ **colonel** + masc. acc. pl./ **and**/ **general** + masc. acc. pl./,

u nix slíškom mnógo v žízn-i est', im slíškom žálko èto-go vse-gó.
at/ they (gen. pl.)/ **too/ much/ in/life** + fem. dat. sing./ **(there) is**/, **(to) them**
(dat. pl.)/[1] **too/ much/ sorry** (neut. nom. sing.)/ **this** + neut. gen. sing./ **all** +
neut. gen. sing./.[6]

(5) *Skól'ko nú žno — i vas zastávi-m.*
How much (= **as much as**)/ **necessary** (neut. nom. sing.)/ — **and** (= **also**)/**you**
(acc. pl.)/ **force** (perf.) + 1st pers. pl. (future).

(6) *Ošibá-ete-s', gra ždanín minístr! — I síl'ny-e glaz-á Bobýnin-a*
Mistake (verb, perf.) + 2d pers. pl. + reflexive/,[7] **citizen** (masc. nom. sing.)/
minister (masc. nom. sing.)/ — **And/ strong** + masc. nom. pl./ **eye** + masc.
nom. pl./ **(of) Bobynin** + masc. gen. sing./

sverknú-l-i nénavist'-ju. — U ménja nič-egó net, vy poníma-ete — net
flash (perf.) + past + masc. pl./ **hatred** + fem. instr. sing./. **At** / **me** (gen.)/
nothing + neut. gen. sing./ **not exist,** not be/,[1] **you/ understand** + 2d pers. pl./
— **not exist,** not be (pres.)/

nič-egó! Žen-ú moj-ú i rebënk-a vy užé ne dostán-ete — ix vzja-l-á
nothing + neut. gen. sing./! **Wife** + fem. acc. sing./ **my** + fem. acc. sing./ **and/**
child + masc. acc. sing./ **you** (nom. pl.)/ **already/ not/ get** (perf.) + 2d pers. pl.
(future)/ — **them** (acc. pl.)/ **take** (perf.) + past- fem. sing./

bómba. Rodítel-i mo-í — u žé úmer-l-i. Imú ščestv-a u menjá vse-gó
bomb (fem. nom. sing.)/ **Parent-** masc. nom. pl./ **my** + masc. nom. pl./ — **al-**
ready/ die (perf.) + past + masc. pl./ **Possession** + neuter gen. sing./ **at/ me**
(gen.)/ **all** + neut. gen. sing./

na zeml-é — nos-ovó-j platók, a kombinezón i vot bel'ë pod nim
on /earth + fem. dat. sing./ — **nose** + adj. suff. + masc. nom. sing./**kerchief** +
masc. nom. sing./ **whereas/ overalls** (masc. nom. sing.)/ **and/ here/ underwear**
(neut. nom. sing.)/ **under/** him[8] (= **it**, masc. instr. sing.)/

bez púgovic (on obnaží-l grud' i pokazá-l) — kazënn-oe. Svobód-u vy u
without/buttons (fem. gen. pl.)/ (/**he** (nom.)/ **bare** (perf.) + past (masc. sing.)/
and/ show (perf.) + past (masc. sing.)/ — state-owned[9] + neut. nom. sing./
Freedom + fem. acc. sing./ **you** (nom.)/ at (= **from**)/

menjá davnó ótnja-l-i, a vernú-t' eë ne v vá š-ix síl-ax, íbo eë net u
me (gen.)/ **long ago** (adv.)/ **take away** (perf.) + past + masc. pl./, **but**, and/ **re-**
turn (perf.) + infinitive/ her (= **it**, fem. acc.)/ **not/ in/ your** + fem. prep. pl./
power + fem. prep. pl./, **for** (conjunction)/ her[10] (= **it**), fem. gen. sing.)/ **not**
exist, not be/ **at/**

vas sam-ogó. Let mne ót-rodu sórok dva, srók-u vy mne otsýpa-l-i
you (gen.)/ self (= **yourself**) + masc. gen. sing./.[1] **Years** (masc. gen. pl.)/ me
(= **to me**, dat.)/ **from** + **birth** (adv.)/ **forty** (nom.)/ **two** (nom.)/, **(prison) term**
+ masc. gen. sing./ **you** (nom.)/ me (= **to me**, dat.)/ **pour** (perf.)[11] + past +
masc. pl./

dvádcat' pjat', na kátorg-e ja u žé by-l, v nomer-áx xodí-l, i v
twenty (acc.)/ **five** (acc.)/, on, **in/ convict labor** + fem. prep. sing./ **I** (nom.)/ **al-**
ready/ be + past (masc. sing.)/, **in/ number** + masc. prep. pl./ **go**, walk (imperf.) + past (masc. sing.)/, and, **also/ in/**

na-rúč-nik-ax, i s sobáka-mi, i v brigád-e usílenn-ogo režím-a — čem
on + hand + deriv. noun suff. (= **handcuff**) + masc. prep. pl./, **and**, also/ **with**/
dog + fem. instr. pl./, **in**/ **brigade** + fem. prep. sing./ **(of)** **strengthened** +
masc. gen. sing./ **regimen** + masc. gen. sing./ — what (= **with what**, instr.
sing.)/

e ščë móž-ete vy mne ugrozí-t'? čegó liší-t'? Inženér-noj rabót-y?
still, more/ **can** (imperf.) + 2d. pers. pl. (pres.)/ **you** (nom. pl.)/ **me** (dat.)/
threaten (perf.) + inf./? what (= **of what**, gen sing.)/ **deprive** (perf.) + inf./?
Engineering + fem. gen. sing./ **work** + fem. gen. sing./?

Vy ot èto-go poterjá-ete ból'še. Ja zakur-jú.
You (nom. pl.)/ **from**/ **this** + neut. gen. sing./ **lose** (perf.) + 2d. pers. pl. (future)/ **more**/. **I** (nom.)/ **smoke** (perf.) + 1st pers. sing. (future)/.

(7) *Abakúmov raskrý-l koróbk-u 'Trójk-i' osób-ogo výpusk-a i*
Abakumov (masc. nom. sing.)/**open up** (perf.) + past (masc. sing.)/ **box** +
fem. acc. sing./ **(of)** **'Troika'** + fem. gen. sing./ **special** + masc. gen. sing./ **edition** + masc. gen. sing./ **and**/

pododvínu-l Bobýnin-u:
move closer (transitive verb, perf.) + past (masc. sing.)/ **(to)** **Bobynin** +
masc. dat. sing./:

(8) *Vot voz'm-í-te èt-ix.*
Here/ **take** (perf.) + imperat. + 2d pers. pl./ **this** + fem. gen. pl./.[12]

(9) *Spasíbo. Ne menjá-ju márk-i. Kášel'. — I dostá-l*
Thanks/. **Not**/ **change** (imperf.) + 1st pers. sing. (pres.)/ **brand** + fem. gen./.[10]
Cough (masc. nom. sing.)/. **And**/ **get**, obtain (perf.) + past (masc. sing.)/

'belo-mór-in-u' iz samo-dél'-n-ogo portsigár-a. — Voobščé, pojm-í-te
'white + **sea'** + augmentative + fem. acc. sing.'/[13] **from**/ **self** + **make** + adj.
suffix + masc. gen. sing./ **cigarette holder** + masc. gen. sing./. — **In general**
(adv.)/, **understand** + imperat. + 2d pers. pl./

i peredá-j-te tam, komú nádo výše, čto vy sil'n-ý liš' postól'ku,
and/ **report**, transmit (perf.) + imperative + 2d pers. pl./ **there**/ whom (= **to
whom**, dative sing. relat. pron.)/ **necessary**/ **higher**/, **that** (relat.)/ **you** (nom.
pl.)/ **powerful**, strong + masc. pl./ **only**/ insomuch/,

poskól'ku ne ot-birá-ete ot ljud-éj ne vsë. No čelovék, u kotór-ogo vy
how much (= **inasmuch as**)/ **not**/ from (= **away**) + **take** (imperf.) + 2d pers.
pl. (present)/ **from**/ **people** + masc. gen. pl./ **not**/ **all** (neuter acc. sing.)/. **But**/
man (masc. nom. sing.)/, at (= **from**)/ **whom** + masc. gen. sing./ **you** (nom. pl.)/

ot-obrá-l-i vsë — užé ne pod-vlást-en vam, on snóva svobóden.
from (= **away**) + **take** (perf.) + past + masc. pl./ **all** (neuter acc. sing.)/ — **already**/ **not**/ under + power (= **subordinate**) + adj. (masc. nom. sing.)/ you
(= **to you**, dat. pl.)/, **he** (nom.)/ **again**/ **free** (masc. nom. sing.)/.

NOTES

1. The most common way to express possession in Russian is by means of the following construction: Preposition *u* ('near, at, by') + possessor (noun or pronoun) in
the genitive case + form of the verb 'to be, exist' (this is sometimes omitted) + thing
possessed in the nominative case. For example,

U Iván-a (gen.) est' sáxar (nom.). = 'Ivan has sugar.'

The negative counterpart of such a construction is the same except that instead of the verb 'to be, exist', *net* ('not to be, not to exist') is used. In addition, the thing possessed is marked by genitive case:

U Iván-a net sáxar-a. = 'Ivan does not have any sugar.'

2. Neuter nominative singular forms of adjectives can often be translated as impersonal constructions in English:

Xólodn-o. = '[It is] cold.'

Note also that neuter nominative singular forms of adjectives also act as adverbs. What function such a form has in a given sentence must be determined from the context.

3. The copula verb is not used in the present tense in Russian.

4. Some verb such as *obraščat'sja* 'to treat' whose object is marked by preposition *s* ('with') is understood here.

5. That is, 'do not forget yourself'.

6. The Russian construction which means 'someone is sorry about something' or 'someone regrets something' is quite different in structure from its English equivalent:

> Subject (who feels sorry) in the dative case + be (the past form is in the neuter singular) + žálko ('sorry, regrettable', neuter nominative singular) + person or thing one is sorry for or about in the genitive case:

> Iván-u (dative) bý-l-o (was, neut. nom. sing.) žálk-o (regretable, sorry, neut. nom. sing.) konj-á (horse, gen. sing.). = 'Ivan was sorry about/for the horse.' Lit. 'To Ivan it was sorry, regretable of the horse.'

It must be pointed out that the Russian construction is ambiguous in meaning: the above example may mean either that Ivan was sorry for the horse (because the horse was suffering from pain, for example), or that he felt sorry to lose, sell, give away, etc. the horse in question.

7. Lit. 'you mistake yourself'. This expression is similar to French 'Vous vous trompez'.

8. 'Him' because the Russian noun for 'overalls', the antecedent, is a masculine singular noun.

9. This adjective is derived from the Russian noun *kazná* which means 'treasury' and can also mean 'state treasury'. Things that have been bought using funds from the state treasury belong to the state.

10. 'Her' because the antecedent 'freedom' is a feminine noun in Russian. The form is genitive because it refers to the direct object of a negated verb.

11. 'Pour' in the sense of 'pour out a measure of grain'. Here this verb is being used as a slang equivalent of 'to give (a prison term)'.

12. This is a partitive use of the genitive case signaling that the object in question is not completely or fully affected by the verb: 'Take (some) of these'.

13. Augmentative suffix here is used to suggest coarseness, crudeness, and commonplaceness rather than large size of the object.

The diminutive suffixes (as used, for example, in reference to Abakumov's voice) are sometimes also used to refer to crude, big things, etc., when sarcasm is intended.

Idiomatic Translation by Author

(1) Abakumov[8] also had quite a loud voice, like rolling thunder, and knew how to frighten people with it. But now he felt that shouting would betray helplessness and weakness. He understood that this prisoner was a difficult one.

(2) And so he merely gave a warning:

(3) "Listen, prisoner. Just because I treat you nicely you mustn't forget yourself . . ."

(4) "If you treated me roughly I wouldn't even bother talking with you, citizen minister.[9] You can shout at your colonels and generals; they have so much in their lives, they would be too sorry to lose it all."

(5) "As much as may be necessary—we can force you, too."

(6) "That's where you are wrong, citizen minister." And Bobynin's piercing eyes flashed with hatred. "I have nothing, you understand, nothing! My wife and my child you can't reach any longer—a bomb got them. My parents have already died. All my earthly possessions consist of a handkerchief, and the overalls as well as the underwear without buttons[10] which I wear beneath it (here he opened the overalls at the chest and showed his underwear) belong to the state. Freedom you took from me long ago, and are powerless to restore to me, for you have no freedom yourself. I am forty-two years of age, and you have saddled me with a twenty-five-year prison term. I have already been a convict laborer, carried a prison number, been in handcuffs, been guarded by dogs, and been in a strict discipline labor brigade. What else can you still threaten me with? What else can you deprive me of? Engineering work? You are going to lose more from this . . . I am going to smoke."

(7) Abakumov opened a pack of "Troika," special edition,[11] and pushed it over to Bobynin:

(8) "Here, take some of these."

(9) "Thanks, I don't switch brands. Cough, you see." And he took out a coarse "Belomor" [12] from a homemade cigarette holder. "In sum, understand what I am saying and report it to whomever it may concern higher up that you are powerful only insofar as you do not take everything away from people. You see, a man from whom you have taken everything is no longer in your power; he is free again."

SKETCH OF FINNISH

A. GENETIC CLASSIFICATION AND GENERAL BACKGROUND

Finnish is a member of the Finno-Ugric branch of the Uralic language family and is to a large extent mutually intelligible with Karelian. It is spoken by more than 6 million people (5,538,000 in Finland, 300,000 in Sweden, and 214,168 in the United States).

Typologically, Finnish is considered to be predominantly agglutinative language (with some synthetic traits as well) with a very rich morphology and SVO word order. (Most of the Uralic languages have SOV word order, but Finnish, Hungarian and some other languages which have been greatly influenced by the neighboring Indo-European languages have SVO.)

Finnish vocabulary has been influenced very much by Indo-European languages: some Iranian language (cf. *sata* 'hundred'), early Germanic (cf. *kuningas* 'king'), Baltic languages (cf. *silta* 'bridge' < Lithuanian *tìltas*), Russian (cf. *risti* 'cross' < Russ. *krest*), and Swedish (cf. *joulu* 'Christmas, Yule'). In modern times it has also borrowed some words from French and English (cf. *romaani* 'novel', *hotelli* 'hotel'). The Iranian and Germanic loanwords seem to be the earliest. Early Germanic loanwords in Finnish are very important for the reconstruction of the Proto-Germanic language and are usually cited in connection with this endeavor.

The earliest written records in Finnish date back to the 1530s and consist primarily of Christian religious materials. The *ethnonym* 'Finn' may be of Germanic/Scandinavian origin and could be connected with the verb 'to find', that is, Finns were considered 'finders or hunters'.

B. PHONETICS, PHONOLOGY, AND ORTHOGRAPHY

The items in parentheses indicate sounds that are found only in relatively recent loanwords, except for the apostrophe which is the way orthography sometimes indicates the glottal stop. The glottal stop occurs only syllable-finally. The glottal stop reflects an earlier -*k*. It is not marked at all in the orthography and is rarely pronounced in Standard Finnish as such: it is pronounced as a glottal stop only if the following word begins in a vowel; otherwise it assimilates to the initial consonant of the following word.

All of the native consonants except the glottals, /j/, and /v/ have long counterparts (written double in the orthography: *tt, pp, ll,* etc.). The long /ŋ/ is

Table 3.8   FINNISH CONSONANT PHONEMES

LABIALS	DENTALS	PALATALS	VELARS	GLOTTALS
p	t		k	ʔ(')
(b)	d		(g)	
(f)	s	(š)		h
v	(z)			
	(ts/c)	(tš)		
m	n		ŋ	
	l			
	r			
		j		

Table 3.9   FINNISH VOWEL PHONEMES

FRONT UNROUND	FRONT ROUND	BACK UNROUND	BACK ROUND
i ii	y yy		u uu
e ee	ö öö		o oo
ä ää		a aa	

written *ng*, whereas the short [ŋ] is written as *n* (and occurs only before *k*). Finnish voiceless stops are not aspirated (even before stressed vowels).

Voiced stops are not found initially in native words. Medially, *d* occurs in native words and contrast with *t*. (See the section on Consonant Gradation.)

Double vowels indicate long vowels in the orthography and contrast with their short counterparts. Orthographic *ä* and *ö* are [æ] and [ø], respectively. In the neighborhood of back vowels, *i* and *e* have somewhat backer allophones.

There are also the diphthongs listed in Table 3.10.

Finnish orthography is quite regular; there are no silent letters: every letter is pronounced. However, as was indicated, the glottal stop is rarely written, and long /ŋ/ is written *ng*.

Stress

Stress is normally on the first syllable of a word; secondary stresses are usually on the third or fourth syllable in words of more than three syllables, and then on every other syllable except the last.

Vowel Harmony

Vowel harmony in Finnish extends only within a single noncompound word. There are three groups of vowels:

Group 1. Back vowels *a, o, u* (along with their long counter-

Table 3.10   FINNISH DIPHTHONGS

ei	äy	eu
äi		
ui		
ai		au
oi		ou
öi	öy	
yi		
ie		
	yö	uo
		iu

parts and diphthongs that contain back vowels as one of their elements)

Group 2. Front rounded vowels and low front unrounded vowel *ö*, *y*, and *ä*, (along with their long counterparts and diphthongs containing one of these vowels as elements)

Group 3. Front non-low unrounded vowels *i* and *e* (and their long counterparts and diphthongs containing these vowels)

In native Finnish words vowels belonging to the first two groups do not mix with each other; the third group vowels, *i* and *e*, may mix with either of the first two groups and are therefore called neutral vowels. Thus there are noncompound Finnish words which contain the following vowel patterns:

1. Words that have only back vowels: *kaura* 'oats', *talo* 'house', etc.
2. Words that have only the front rounded vowels along with the low front unrounded vowel: *tyttö* 'girl', *tytär* 'daughter', *pyörä* 'wheel', etc.
3. Words in which the neutral vowels mix with back vowels (Group 1): *Suomi* 'Finland', *keskus* 'middle', etc.
4. Words in which the neutral vowels mix with front rounded and low front unrounded vowels (Group 2): *järvi* 'lake', *pesä* 'nest', etc.
5. Words in which only the neutral vowels *i* or *e* are found: *hirsi* 'log', *tiede* 'science', etc.

It is important to note that if the first syllable contains one of the neutral vowels, the vowel of the second syllable determines what vowels may follow: if it is also a neutral vowel, then following vowels must be front vowels, that is, either the neutral vowels or Group 2 vowels.

In foreign loanwords the preceding rules are often violated, and, as was indicated earlier, these rules do not apply across word boundaries or between stem morphemes even in native Finnish compound words:

kuvernööri 'governor' < French gouverneur (*u* + *ö*)

työhuone 'workroom' < työ 'work' 1 huone 'room' (*y*,*ö* + *u*,*o*)

Vowel harmony is a very important feature of the Finnish language since it determines the allomorphs of a very large number of suffixes that may be attached to a stem.

Consonant Gradation or Softening

Voiced stops are not found initially in native Finnish words and are somewhat rare in the medial position as well. This is because Finnish voiced stops are derived from their voiceless counterparts when the basic or underlying voiceless consonants are found in a noninitial closed syllable, that is, a syllable that ends in a consonant and is preceded by a vowel or a voiced consonant (and sometimes *h*). This phenomenon becomes readily apparent when one compares the nominative singular and genitive singular forms of some nouns:

> tieto 'knowledge': tiedo-n gen. sing.
>
> äiti 'mother': äidi-n gen. sing.

(Note that *tiede* 'science' seems to have an unexpected *d* in an open syllable. Actually, this word ends in a glottal stop, which is not always pronounced or marked orthographically in modern Finnish, and thus the second *t* of the stem is really in a closed syllable: ti-e-de'.)

However, consonant gradation does not only involve voicing but a number of other changes as well. The short voiceless stops probably all became simply voiced stops in closed syllables originally, but eventually the voiced bilabial stops derived by this process became voiced labiodental fricatives ([v]), and the voiced velar stops (which also were most likely fricativized to [γ]) were eventually dropped altogether except after a nasal:

> leipä 'bread': leivä-n gen. sing.
>
> ripa 'handle, grip': riva-n gen. sing.
>
> jalka 'foot': jala-n gen. sing.
>
> sika 'pig': sia-n gen. sing.

but

> matka 'journey, trip': matka-n gen. sing. (*k* is not dropped here because it is preceded by a voiceless stop *t*.)
>
> kaupunki (*nk* = [ŋk]) 'town, city': kaupungi-n (*ng* = [ŋŋ]) gen. sing.

Second, the long voiceless stops do not voice but simply become short in the same environment, thus creating surface contrast between /t/ and /d/ in closed syllables:

> soppa 'soup': sopa-n gen. sing.
>
> juttu 'tale': jutu-n gen. sing.
>
> kakku 'cake': kaku-n gen. sing.

Finally, some consonant clusters in this position are affected by progressive assimilation:

> rinta 'chest': rinna-n gen. sing.
>
> valta 'power': valla-n gen. sing.
>
> kerta 'time, occasion': kerra-n gen. sing.

There are other complications, which for the sake of brevity are not mentioned here. However, it should be noted that recent loanwords and people's names often do not exhibit consonant softening:

> auto 'car, auto': auto-n gen. sing., not *audo-n

These phenomena are sometimes called consonant "softening" or "weakening" for the following reasons. As is to some extent true of the Finnish example, this type of change involves a chain of developments that eventually lead to loss or deletion of the consonants involved. For example, voiceless obstruents become voiced, then fricativized, then some kind of semivowels, and the latter are eventually dropped. In Finnish it was the original *k* that eventually dropped; the original *p* was voiced and then became fricativized, and the original *t* became ð and was then changed to *d* in Standard Finnish under the influence of Swedish. The long voiceless stops become short, and this usually means that they in turn become more vulnerable to the same processes that caused the voicing and fricativization of the original short voiceless stops. To sum up, there seems to be a natural tendency (not only in Finnish but in general) that leads to a chain of developments that finally culminates in deletion of segments:

> long voiceless stops → short voiceless stops → (short) voiced stops → voiced fricatives → semivowel-like segments → zero

Except for the shortening of long stops, all the developments cited here are most likely to happen between vowels; what is somewhat unusual in the Finnish case is that this happens only in closed syllables and not more generally between vowels.

c. Morphology

In general, Finnish words tend to be much longer than English words. This is not just because Finnish is an agglutinative language and tends to have long strings of affixes; it also results from the tendency of Finnish stem morphemes to be polysyllabic, unlike English stem morphemes, which are usually monosyllabic. In addition, Finnish seems to employ more compounding than English.

Nouns

Noncompound nouns in Finnish have the following structure:

> Stem + (deriv. suffix or suffixes) + (plural) + case + (possessive suffix)

For example:

> ravinto-lo-i-ssa-ni
>
> 'nourishment' + loc. deriv. suffix + plural + iness. case + 'my'
>
> 'In my restaurants.'

The items in parentheses are nonobligatory elements of a Finnish noun. The plural marker is *-t* in the nominative and accusative (when it is followed by zero, since nominative and accusative cases in the plural have no overt marking in Finnish) and *-i-* before other case suffixes. In addition, it has an automatic allomorph *-j-* when it is found between two vowels.

The possessive endings sometimes cause the case and number marking to be neutralized.

Nominative and genitive singular and nominative plural:

> talo-ni 'my house, my house's, my houses'
>
> talo-si 'your house, your house's, your houses'
>
> talo-nsa 'his house, his house's, his houses'
>
> talo-mme 'our house, our house's, our houses'
>
> talo-nne 'your house, your house's, your houses'
>
> talo-nsa 'their house, their house's, their houses'

but

> talo-ssa-ni 'in my house'
>
> talo-i-ssa-ni 'in my houses'

and so on.

Cases

There is a very large number of cases, but not all are equally productive.

1. *Nominative.* This case does not have a special marker, but the allomorph of the plural with this case is *-t*, instead of the *-i* which appears with most other cases. This case is used to mark the subject of a sentence.

Many Finnish nouns appear to have special oblique stems to which the non-nominative case endings and the *-t* nominative plural are added. (In other words, the oblique stem is used in all the situations where the stem is followed by an overt, i.e., nonzero, suffix of some sort.) For example, *nainen* 'woman' has an oblique stem *naise-*, and thus *naise-t* is the nominative plural form for this noun; *rukous* 'prayer' has an oblique stem *rukoukse-*; and so on. The reason for this situation is that a number of phonological rules apply to the stem if no suffix is added:

> rukoukse → rukouksi (final *e* goes to *i*)
>
> rukouksi → rukouks (final *i* is deleted in words of three syllables or more)
>
> rukouks → rukous (final consonant cluster simplification)

2. *Genitive.* This case is marked by suffix *-n*. It signals possession and is used in some impersonal constructions. It used to be the case that marked an indirect object, and that usage is preserved in some expressions like *Jumala-n kiitos* 'Thanks be to God'.

3. *Accusative.* In the singular this case is marked by *-n*, just like the genitive, but in the plural the form is the same as in the nominative. (There is also an alternative form in the singular which is identical with the nominative.

This case marks the direct object of a verb if that verb is viewed as affecting the whole object; nouns expressing distance covered, time passed, and the like, are also put in this case.

4. *Partitive.* The marker for this case is *-(t)ä/-(t)a.* (The elements enclosed in parentheses are dropped in certain environments; the vowel alternations are due to the operation of vowel harmony rules.) This case has many uses, the chief of which is to signal that an object is affected only partially by the verb or that the effect is not real. Thus, it is used to mark the direct object after negated verbs, the direct object of verbs that indicate an ongoing action, or verbs that express thoughts, wishes, hopes, and so forth. It is also used after numbers, to indicate the notion "some," and as measures in such expressions as 'one pound of potatoes' where 'of potatoes' is simply the noun 'potato' in partitive case.

Even the subject may be in the partitive case: in negative sentences and interrogative sentences in which *ole-* 'to exist', *näky-* 'to be visible', and *kuule-* 'to be audible' are the main verbs:

> Tä-ssä kylä-ssä ei ole suutari-a.
>
> this + iness./ village + iness./ neg. vb./ be/ cobbler + part.
>
> 'There is no cobbler in this village.'

5. *Essive: -na/-nä.* This case signals the site of an action, the time at which an action takes place, and the state or temporary character of something or someone:

> joulu-na 'at Christmas'
>
> Poika-na minä e-n tunte-nut hän-tä
>
> boy + ess./ I (nom.)/ neg. vb. + 1st pers. sing./ know + past participle active/ he + part.
>
> 'As a boy I did not know him.'

6. *Adessive: -lla/-llä.* This case also indicates location in time or space, the price at which a thing is bought, and sometimes instrument or manner in which an action is performed. This case is also used to indicate the possessor in such constructions like *Minu-lla on kirja,* 'I have a book' (lit., 'At me is book'), which is very similar to the expression of possession in Russian (cf. "Sketch of Russian").

7. *Inessive: -ssa/-ssä.* This case expresses the notion of within some place or time, occupation in which a person is engaged, and location with abstract concepts, for example 'He lives in poverty.'

> Suome-ssa 'In Finland'
> päivä-ssä 'within a day'

8. *Allative: -lle.* This case expresses the direction towards which an action or movement takes place as well as to indicate the beneficiary of an action. In other words, it is used to indicate an indirect object.

> Pane-n kirja-n pöyda-lle.
>
> put + 1st pers. sing./ book + acc./ table + allat.
>
> 'I will put the book on the table.'

> Me hanki-mme tei-lle uude-t sukse-t.
>
> we/ get + 1st pers. sing./ you + allat./ new + pl./ ski + pl.
>
> 'We will get you new skis.'

9. *Ablative: -lta/-ltä.* This case has many different functions.

a. It expresses the notion 'from' in relation to a surface or vicinity of something:

> Lintu lens-i kato-lta.
>
> bird / fly + imperf./ roof + ablat.
>
> 'A bird flew off the roof.'

b. It is also used with the meaning of 'on' with verbs of seeking and finding:

> Löys-i-n soimukse-n lattia-lta.
>
> Find + imperf./ ring + acc./ floor + ablat.
>
> 'I found the ring on the floor.'

c. It is also used to express the cause of some hindrance:

> E-n voi-nut nukku-a koira-n haukunna-lta.
>
> neg. vb. + 1 sg./ be able + past participle act./ sleep + inf. I/ dog + gen./ barking + ablat.
>
> 'I could not sleep for the barking of the dog.'

d. Finally, it marks what may be translated as the subject of verbs expressing loss, lack, or deficiency in general:

> Häne-ltä kuol-i äiti.
>
> he + ablat./ die + imperf. (3d pers. sing./ mother
>
> 'His mother died.' (Lit. 'from him died mother')

10. *Elative: sta/stä.* This case mainly indicates movement from inside of something, 'out of', etc. It also indicates 'for' with verbs of buying selling or exchanging.

> Tule-n kylä-stä
>
> come + 1st pers. sing./ village + elat.
>
> 'I come from a village.'

In addition, it has a large variety of functions such as indicating cause or origin, what a thing is made out of, separation from a thing, the subject of verbs of impression. An example of the latter usage would be *Minu-sta tuntuu, että* . . . 'It seems to me that . . .' It also indicates the direct object of the verb 'to like':

> Pidä-tte-kö häne-stä?
>
> like + 2d pers. pl. + interrog./ she + elat.
>
> 'Do you like her?'

11. *Illative: -Vn/-hVn/-sVn/-hVn* (V = copy of the final vowel of the preceding morpheme. There are a number of somewhat irregular allomorphs of this case suffix.) This case expresses movement into something, goal, or activity:

> Mene-n talo-on.
>
> go + 1st pers. sing./ house + illat.
>
> 'I am going into the house.'

It also signals the time at which something is done or the use to which a thing is put.

12. *Comitative: -ne.* This case indicates close relation with something, 'in the company of', 'provided with', 'belonging to'. It is attached only to the plural stems, and in addition the nouns must have a possessive suffix added to them:

> Se ol-i rakennus mon-i-ne huone-i-ne-en.
>
> it/ be + imperf./ building/ many + pl. + comit./ room + pl.
> + comit. + 3d sing. poss. (special allomorph)
>
> 'It was a house with many rooms.'

13. *Translative: -ksi/-kse.* This case indicates what something turns 'into', that is, change of state:

Lumi muttu-i vede-ksi.

snow/ turn + imperf./ water + transl.

'The snow turned to water.'

14. *Instructive or Instrumental: -n*. This case is used almost always in the plural even though only a singular object is involved. It basically marks the manner or the means whereby an action is accomplished. Adjectives in the instructive case serve as adverbs.

Hän ol-i om-i-n avu-i-n pääs-syt päämääräa-nsä

he/ be + imperf./ own + pl. + instr./ ability + pl + instr./ reach + past participle act./ goal + 3d pers. sing. poss.

'He reached his goal by his own abilities.'

yksi 'one' but yksi-n 'alone'.

15. *Prolative: -tse*. This case expresses the concepts 'by way of' or 'along'. For example, *meri-tse* 'by sea'. It is not a very productive case and is used only with a limited number of nouns. (Instead various prepositions governing different cases are used.)

16. *Abessive: -ttä/-tta*. This case expresses absence of the object to which this case ending is added. In other words, it signals the concept 'without': *raha-tta* 'without money'. In modern Finnish this case is usually replaced by *ilman* followed by the noun in the partitive case: *ilman rahoja* 'without money.'

Nine of the Finnish cases form three coordinated sets that were originally linked morphologically and semantically:

> *General:* + talo-ksi *(Transl.)* change of state toward something
>
> Ø talo-na *(Essiv.)* state of being
>
> − talo-a < *-ða < *-ta *(Part.)* being part of something
>
> *Internal:* + talo-on < *hen < *sen' *(Illat.)* movement into something
>
> Ø talo-ssa < *-s-na *(Iness.)* being inside something
>
> − talo-sta < *s-ta *(Elat.)* movement out of something
>
> *External:* + talo-lle < *-len' *(Allat.)* movement toward something
>
> Ø talo-lla < *-l-na *(Adess.)* being near something

> — talo-lta < *-l-ta *(Ablat.)* movement away from
> something

From these examples we can see that -s- at one time signaled internal location, -l- external location, and that these suffixes combined with other case
suffixes to form complex cases involving movement toward (+), movement
away from (−), and the absence of movement (Ø).

Pronouns

The personal pronouns are as follows (oblique stems are in parentheses):

1st pers. sing. minä (minu-)	1st pers. pl. me (mei-)
2d pers. sing. sinä (sinu-)	2d pers. pl. te (tei-)
3d pers. sing. hän (häne-)	3d pers. pl. he (hei-)

Since the Finnish verbs are marked for person, the first and second person
pronoun subjects are usually omitted; however, the third person subject pronouns are not.

It should be noted that in Finnish the third person singular pronoun does
not show any gender distinctions. Thus, *hän* may mean either 'he' or 'she'.
(For 'it', a demonstrative pronoun *se* is used.)

As in many languages, the second person plural pronoun and other forms
marked for second person plural (verb forms, nouns with possessive suffixes,
etc.) are used in reference to a single person to express respect for that person.

Like English, Finnish also has demonstrative, relative, and interrogative
pronouns, but these will not be listed here.

Verbs

The Finnish verb paradigm includes several forms.

1. Present Indicative
This form of the verb is also used for future indicative; there is no separate
future tense in Finnish.

1st pers. sing. laula-n	1st pers. pl. laula-mme
2d pers. sing. laula-t	2d pers. pl. laula-tte
3d pers. sing. laula-V (laulaa)	3d pers. pl. laula-vät/vat

V = doubling of the final vowel of the stem unless the stem already ends
in a long vowel, in which case the stem remains unchanged. The third person
plural ending changes according to the rules of vowel harmony:

> laula-vat 'they sing' vs. syö-vät 'they eat'

2. Imperfect or Preterite Indicative
This form of the verb is derived according to the following formula:

> Stem + i + personal endings

The personal endings are the same as in the present indicative except that third person singular has Ø ending (i.e., no vowel lengthening).

> laulo-i-n < laula-i-n 'I sang, I was singing'

3. Perfect Indicative Active
This form of the verb employs *ole-* 'be' as an auxiliary verb which takes the personal endings, followed by the past participle active of the main verb. The latter form is composed of a verb stem followed by the suffix *-nyt/-nut.*

> ole-n laula-nut 'I have sung'

4. Pluperfect Indicative Active
This is formed by the imperfect indicative form of the auxiliary verb *ole-* 'be' followed by the past participle active of the main verb:

> ol-i-n laula-nut "I had sung'

5. Imperative Mood

> syö-' 'eat! (2d pers. sing.)
>
> syö-köö-n 'let him eat!' (3d pers. sing.)
>
> syö-kää-mme 'let us eat!' (1st pers. pl.)
>
> syö-kää-(tte) 'eat!' (2d pers. pl.)
>
> syö-köö-t 'let them eat' (3d pers. pl.)

As can be seen from the preceding examples, the second person singular imperative form is a stem followed by the glottal stop (which comes from an original *-k*), whereas in the other forms of the imperative there is an imperative suffix, *-kää/-kaa* in the first and second person plural and *-köö/-koo* in the third person, which is then followed by personal endings. Note that *-tte* of the second person plural is usually omitted.

6. Conditional Mood
This form is made by suffixing *-isi* to the verb stem and then adding personal endings:

> puhu-isi-n 'I would speak'

7. Potential or Concessive Mood
This mood is not used much in the colloquial. It implies doubt or uncertainty or an assumption. The present tense form is made as follows: Verb stem + ne + personal ending

> Kylä-n naise-t naura-ne-vat
>
> village + gen./ woman + pl. (nom.)/laugh + potent. + 3d
>   pers. pl.
>
> 'Perhaps the women of the village will laugh'.

The perfect form is made as follows: Present potential form of *ole-* (which is irregular: *lie-*) + pers. suffix + active past participle. For example:

> lie-ne-n sano-nut 'I may have said'.

8. Participles

a. Present participle active: Verb stem + *-vä/-va* + case

> Hän on Jumala-a *pelkaä-vä* mies
>
> He/is/God + part./ fear + pres. particip./ man
>
> 'He is a God-fearing man'.

b. Present participle passive: Verb stem + passive marker *(-tä/-ta/-ttä/-tta)* + *-vä/-va* + case

> *syö-tä-vä-t* siene-t
>
> eat + passive + pres. particip. + pl./ mushroom + pl.
>
> 'edible mushrooms'

c. Past participle active: Verb stem + *-nyt/-nut* + case

d. Past participle passive: Verb stem + passive marker (see above) with the final vowel elided + *-y/-u*

> *Puhuu-tt-u* puhe on kuin *ammu-tt-u* nuoli.
>
> speak + pass. + past particip. pass./ word/is/like/shoot + pass. + past particip. pass./ arrow
>
> 'A spoken word is like an arrow shot'.

9. Infinitive

Finnish grammars list four different infinitive forms, only the first of which really corresponds to the infinitive form of English in its functions; the rest are really *deverbal nouns* (i.e., nouns that are derived from verbs) which have developed very specialized functions.

a. Infinitive I: This is the form of the verb that is usually given as the citation form for verbs in the Finnish dictionaries. It does not take case endings as other Finnish infinitives. It is formed from the verb stem by adding suffix *-tä/-ta*, which ends in a glottal stop ' (usually omitted in both spelling and pronunciation) that actually closes the syllable and causes the *t* to become *d*:

> syö-dä(') 'to eat'

This form of the infinitive suffix is attached to stems ending in a diphthong or a long vowel; after stems ending in a short vowel, the *d* of the suffix is dropped:

> luke-a 'to read, study'

This form is used very much like the infinitive in English expressions such as the following:

> The book is good *to read.*
>
> I want *to read.*

b. Infinitive II: This is chiefly a literary form that occurs only in inessive and instructive cases. It is formed by attaching suffix *-te'* to the verb stem. The suffix in question behaves exactly like the infinitive I suffix in respect to the voicing and loss of the *t*.

> Inf. I: sano-a 'to speak'
>
> Inf. II: sano-e-ssa (with inessive case suffix)

With inessive case ending this infinitive is used to express an action that goes on simultaneously with the action expressed by the main verb; thus it can be used in the function of an English subordinate clause introduced by 'while':

> Tädi-n kaata-e-ssa kahvi-a kuppe-i-hin tijott-i Eeva ikkuna-sta ulos.
>
> aunt + gen it./ pour + inf. II + iness./ coffee + part./ cup + plur. + illat./ stare + imperf./ Eeva (nom.)/ window + elat./ outside
>
> 'While [her] aunt was pouring coffee into the cups, Eve stared out of the window'.

c. Infinitive III: This form is made by attaching the suffix *-mä/-ma* to the verb stem. Basically, this form acts usually as a noun or adjective and as such may take all the case endings:

> elä- 'live' + -mä = 'life'
>
> sano- 'say' + ma = 'message, report'

d. Infinitive IV: This form is formed by adding suffix *-minen* (oblique stem *mise-*) to the verb stem. It functions mainly like English gerunds:

> Syö-minen on sairaa-lle aivan mahdotonta.
>
> eat + inf. IV/ is/ invalid + allat./ quite/ impossible/
>
> 'Eating is quite impossible for an invalid.'

Negation

To express negation Finnish uses a special verb of negation which acts as a sort of auxiliary. It shares this feature with many Uralic and Altaic languages. This verb, which one may translate as 'not to be, not to exist' is inflected as any other Finnish verb:

e-n 'am not'   e-mme 'we are not'

e-t 'you are not'   e-tte 'you (plur.) are not'

ei-Ø 'he, she, it is not'   ei-vät 'they are not'

Thus, to express 'I don't know' in Finnish one says *e-n tiedä'*, where *e-n* is the negative verb in the present tense with a personal suffix and *tiedä'* is a special negative form of the verb *to know*. The tense is then usually marked by addition of the appropriate suffixes to the stem of the verb of negation, not to the infinitive, but there are some complications as well:

1. Neg. of present indicative: e-n tiedä 'I don't know'
2. Neg. of imperfect indicative: e-n tien-nyt 'I didn't know'
3. Neg. of perfect indicative: e-n ole tien-nyt 'I haven't known'
4. Neg. of pluperfect indicative: e-n ollut (< ol-nut) tien-nyt 'I hadn't known'
5. Negative imperative: äl-kää-mme pelät-kö 'Let us not fear'

Note: *äl-* is the irregular imperative stem of the negative verb; *-kää-* is the regular imperative suffix (cf. imperative mood in earlier section); *-kö/-ko* is the suffix that must be attached to the stem of the main verb in this construction.

6. Negative conditional: e-n puhu-isi 'I would not speak'

For the sake of brevity, examples of negation in the passive constructions will be omitted here.

To express such words as 'nobody' and 'nowhere', the suffix *-kään/-kaan* is added to corresponding interrogative pronouns. (In such cases, the *-ka/-kä* extension of the interrogative stems is dropped.)

Ku-ka on tuo-lla? 'Who is there?': Ei *ku-kaan* 'Nobody'.

Instead of *ja* 'and' + verb of negation, *-kä* is suffixed to the verb of negation in the following clause:

E-mme anna e-mme-*kä* ota mit-ään.

neg. vb. + 3d pers. pl./ give/ neg. vb. + 3d pers. pl. + and/
take/ what + any/

'We shall not give and not take anything.'

The suffix *-ään* in this example is an allomorph of the suffix *-kään/-kaan* which was mentioned earlier.

Passive Construction

Finnish passive construction is different from English passive construction in several respects. First, Finnish passives have only the third person singular form. Second, Finnish passive constructions are really impersonal constructions in which the subject is an impersonal (usually only implicitly understood) 'it'. Thus, it is not possible to construct in Finnish a literal equivalent of the English sentence, 'Mary was kissed by John'.

1. Present indicative passive: This form is made according to the following formula: Verb stem + passive stem marker *(-tä/-ta/-ttä/-tta)* + -Vn (in which V is a copy of the preceding vowel)

> Tää-llä *ele-tä-än* hauskasti

> here + adess./ live + passive stem marker + passive ending/ pleasantly

> 'One lives pleasantly here'. More lit. '[It] is lived pleasantly here'.

2. Imperfective indicative passive: This form is made according to the following formula: Verb stem + passive stem marker + i + Vn

> Kirje-i-tä saa-t-i-in säänöllisesti.

> letter + pl. + part./ receive + pass. + imperf. + Vn/ regu-larly

> 'Letters were received regularly. One received letters regu-larly'.

3. Perfect and pluperfect passive: These are made very much like their active counterparts with the auxiliary verb *ole-* in appropriate tenses, followed by the passive past participle:

> on lue-tt-u 'It has been read. One has read.'

> ol-i lue-tt-u 'It had been read. One had read.'

4. Potential passive: For the sake of brevity, only an example of the present tense form will be given here:

> puhu-tta-ne-en

> speak + passive stem marker + potential + passive ending

> 'There may be words spoken. One may speak'.

D. SYNTAX

Agreement or Concord

In Finnish, adjectives and demonstratives must agree in number and case (but not gender, since Finnish does not have any) with the nouns they modify.

The verbs must agree in person and number with their subject except that in the spoken language third person plural subjects usually govern verbs that are marked as being third person singular: tytö-t *laula-a* instead of tytö-t *laula-vat* for 'The girls are singing'.

Interrogative Sentences

Finnish interrogative construction is very similar to the Russian interrogative construction:

a. Content questions with question words do not have any special marking:

>Kuka tulee 'Who is coming?'

b. In yes/no questions *-kö/-ko* is added to the word that is being questioned and that word is moved to the beginning of the sentence, just as in the case of the words after which the interrogative particle *li* is attached in Russian:

>Tulee-*ko* hän? 'Is he coming?' ('Is he coming or not?')

>Hän-*kö* tulee? 'Is it *he* that is coming (and not someone else)?'

Negative questions add *-ko/-kö* to the verb of negation:

>Ei-vät-*kö* tiedä? 'Didn't they know?'

Relative and Other Dependent Clauses

As in English, relative clauses are introduced by relative pronouns (which cannot be omitted as is sometimes done in English). The relative pronoun agrees with its antecedent in number but takes the case ending that is appropriate to its grammatical role in the subordinate clause:

>Kirjee-t, jo-i-sta kerro-i-n, o-vat pöydä-llä

>letter + pl. (nom.)/, relat. pron. stem + pl. + elat. case/ talk + imperf. + 1st pers. sing./, be + 3d pers. pl./ table + adess. case/

>'The letters about which I was talking are on the table'.

When the relative clause precedes the main clause or when the antecedent is not expressed, interrogative pronouns are used instead of a relative pronoun to introduce the relative clause:

>Se minkä sano-i-n on totta.

>that (nom.) what (acc.)/ say + imperf. + 1st pers. sing./ is/ true

>'What I said is the truth'.

Embedded interrogative sentences are marked with the interrogative particle, just like interrogative main clauses:

>E-n tiedä, on-*ko* hän suomalainen.

>neg. vb. + 1st pers. sing./ know (inf.)/, is + interrog. particle/ he / Finnish/

>'I do not know whether he is a Finn'.

Tiedä-tte-*kö*, on-*ko* hän ranskalainen?

know + 2d pers. pl. + interrog./, is + interrog./ he/ French/

'Do you know whether he is French?'

E. SAMPLE TEXT

Finnish Text[13]

(1) MEIDÄN SUOMALAISTEN SAUNA

(2) Missä ikänä Suomessa kulkee ja näkee asunnon, voi tarkkaava silmä havaita jonkin matkan päässä asuntorakennuksesta metsikön reunassa tai veden partaalla pienen hirsisen rakennuksen saunan.

(3) Sauna on suomalaisen kylpylaitos, ja jokaisella perheellä, köyhimmälläkin, on oma saunansa, jossa kylvetään vähintäin kerran viikossa. (4) Vain kaupungeissa ja tiheissä asutuskeskuksissa sekä laitosten yhteydessä on yhteisiä saunoja.

(5) On vaikeata antaa niin täsmällistä määritelmää siitä, mikä suomalainen sauna on, että sen perimmäinen olemus sen avulla selviäisi, eikä se ainakaan suomalaisen omalta kannalta liene niin tarpellistakaan, sillä suomalaiset ovat ainakin tuhannen vuoden ajan käneet saunassa ryhtymättä sitä määrittelemään tai selittämään, ja silti se—ainakin sen vieläkin yleinen muoto savusauna—on yhä kautta vuosisatojen perusominaisuuksiltaan pysynyt samanlaisena. (6) Ilman ulkoapäin tulleita kehoituksia ja opetuksia, ilman paljon maksavaa valistustyötä, ilman apurahoja ja mallipiirustuksia on jokainen kodin perustaja rakentanut itselleen saunan usein ennen kuin itse asumuksen.

(7) Saunan ympärille kiertyy suomalaisen elämä syntymästä kuolemaan asti: (8) Siitä hän ammentaa terveyttä hyvinä päivinä, ja siitä hän hakee parannusta sairauksien sattuessa. (9) Sauna merkitsee jokaiselle suomalaiselle nautintoa ja virkistystä. (10) Melko varmasti näillä seikoilla on oma tärkeä osuutensa siihen, että sauna on elänyt ja jatkuvasti elää voimakkaana Suomen kansan elämässä. (11) Sauna ei ole vain välttämätön terveydenlähde, vaan myös suuri ja korkeamman luokan nautintoväline. (12) Suomessa onkin tapana—kuten muinaisissa ritarilinnoissa—valmistaa sauna hyville ja tervetulleille vieraille. (13) Sauna tarjotaan yhtä hyvästä sydämestä vieraitten nautintoa silmälläpitäen kuin mitkä muut herkut tahansa ja vastaanotetaan kiitollisuudella. (14) Sauna on ja tulee varmaan olemaan Suomessa vieraileviin ulkomaalaisiin nähden parhaita mainosvälineitä.

Literal Morpheme-by-Morpheme Translation

Superscripted numbers in the following translation refer to the notes at the end of this section. In order to keep things less cluttered, some morpheme breaks—especially those involving derivational affixes)—have been ignored. (Hyphens indicate morpheme breaks; slashes indicate word breaks.) Grammatical features of words which are not overtly marked, are marked by zero allomorphs, or are marked by morphemes that have not been identified in the text are provided in parentheses. An equal sign indicates a more idiomatic rather than a literal translation. All translations of appropriate content morphemes appear in **boldface** for easier identification. Original punctuation has been retained in both the Finnish text and the literal translation in order to facilitate the matching up of the various "levels of representation" of the text.

(1) *Mei-dän suoma-lais-ten sauna*
we + gen. (= **'our'**)/ **Finn** + **-ish** (deriv. suff.) + gen. (pl.)[1]/ **sauna**/

(2) *Mi-ssä ikä-nä Suome-ssa kulke-e ja näke-e asunno-n, voi tarkkaa-va silmä*
where + iness./ **no matter** + ess./ **Finland** + iness./ **walk** + 3d pers. sing.[2]/ **and**/ see + 3d pers. sing.[2]/ **dwelling, residence** + acc./, **can** (3d pers. sing.)/ **observe** + pres. particip. act. (nom.)/ **eye** (nom.)/

havai-ta jonkin matka-n pää-ssä asunto-rakennukse-sta metsi-kö-n reuna-ssa
perceive + inf. I/ **some**/ **trip, journey** + gen./ **distance,** extremity + iness./ dwelling, residence + building, structure + elat. (= **'from the house'**)/ forest + diminutive deriv. suff. + gen. (= **'grove's'**)/ **edge, border** + iness./

tai vede-n partaa-lla piene-n hirs-ise-n rakennukse-n, sauna-n.
or/ **water** + gen./ **edge, shore** + adess./ **small** + acc./ **log** + **made of** (deriv. suff.) + acc./ **building, structure** + acc./, **sauna** + acc./

(3) *Sauna on suoma-laise-n kylpy-laitos, ja jokaise-lla perhee-llä, köyh-immä-llä-kin,*
sauna/ **is**/ **Finn** + **-ish** (deriv. suff.) + gen./ **bath** + **facility, institution** (nom.)/, **and**/ **every** + adess./ **family** + adess./ + **poor** + superlative (= **-est**) + adess. + **even** (clitic)/

on oma sauna-nsa, jo-ssa kylve-tä-än vähintäin kerran viiko-ssa.
be, exist (3d pers. sing.)(= **'has'**)[3]/ **own, particular**/**sauna** + 3d pers. sing. poss./, relat. pron. + iness. (= **'in which'**)/**bathe** + pass. stem + 3d pers. sing./ **at least**/ **once**/ week + iness./.

(4) *Vain kaupunge-i-ssa ja tihe-i-ssä asutus-keskuks-i-ssa se-kä laitos-ten yhteyde-ssä on yhteis-i-ä sauno-j-a.*
only/ **city, town** + pl. + iness./ **and**/ **dense, thick** + pl. + iness./ settlement, colony + middle, center + pl. + iness. (**in population centers**)/ it + and (clitic) (= **'as well as'**)/ **institution** + gen. (pl.)[1]/ connection, association + iness. (= **'in connection with'**)/ **exist,** be (3d pers. sing.)/ **general, common** + pl. + part./ **sauna** + pl. + part/.

(5) *On vaikea-ta anta-a ni-in täsmällis-tä määritelmä-ä siitä, mikä suoma-lainen sauna on,*
be (3d pers. sing.)(= **'it is'**)/ **difficult, troublesome** + part./ **give** + inf. I/ this + instr. (= **'so, thus'**)/ **exact** + part./ **definition** + part./ **about the fact that**/, **what**/ **Finn** + **-ish** (deriv. suff.) (nom.)/ **sauna** (nom.)/ **be** (3d pers. sing.)/,

että se-n per-immä-inen ole-mus se-n avu-lla selviä-isi,
that (conj.)/ **it** + gen./ end + superlative + adj. suff. (nom.) (= **'utmost, es-sential'**)/ be + deriv. suff. (= **'being, essence'**) (nom.)/ help + adess. (= **'with the help of'**)/ **clear up** + conditional (3d pers. sing.)/,

ei-kä se ainakaan suoma-laise-n oma-lta kanna-lta lie-ne ni-in tarpellis-ta-kaan,
neg. vb. (3d pers. sing.) + and (clitic)(= **'nor'**)/ **it**/ **at any rate**/ **Finn** + **-ish** (de-riv. suff.) + gen./ **own, particular** + ablat./ **point of view** + ablat./ be (irreg. stem form) + potential (3d pers. sing.) (= **'may be'**)/ **so, thus, this way**/ **neces-sary** + part. + **even** (clitic)/,

si-llä suoma-laise-t o-vat aina-kin tuhanne-n vuode-n aja-n käy-neet sauna-ssa ryhty-mä-ttä
it + adess. (= **'for'**) (conj.)/ **Finn** + -ish (deriv. suff.) + pl. (nom.)/ be + 3d pers. pl. (= **'have'**)[4]/ **at least**/ **thousand** + gen./ **year** + gen./ time + gen. (= **'during the time of'**)/ **go, visit** + past particip. act. (nom. pl.)/ **sauna** + iness./ undertake, take steps to, start + inf. III + abess. (= **'without finding it necessary to'**)/[5]

si-tä määrittele-mä-än tai selittä-mä-än, ja silti se—aina-kin se-n vielä-kin yle-inen muoto savu-sauna—
it + part./ **define** + inf. III + illat.[6]/ **or**/ **explain** + inf. III + illat.[6]/, **and**/ **still, yet, however**/ **it** (nom.)/ —**at least**/ it + gen. (= **'its'**)/ **even yet**/ **general, com-mon**/ **shape, form** (nom.)/ **smoke, fume** + **sauna** (nom.)/ —

on yhä kautta vuos-i-sato-j-en perus-ominaisuuks-i-lta-an pysy-nyt sama-n-laise-na.
be (3d pers. sing.) (= **'has'**)[4]/ **still, continually**/ **through**/ year + pl. + hundred + pl. + gen. (= **'centuries'**)/ basis, foundation + character, characteristic, pe-culiarity + pl. + ablat. + 3d pers. sing. poss. (= **'as far as its basic characteris-tics are concerned'**)/ **remain** + past particip. act. (nom.)/ **same** + gen. + **kind** (deriv. suff.) + ess.[7]/.

(6) *Ilman ulkoapäin tul-le-i-ta kehoituks-i-a ja opetuks-i-a, ilman paljon maksa-va-a valistus-työ-tä,*
without/ **from outside** (adv.)/ **come** + past particip. act. + pl. + part./ **advice, suggestion** + pl. + part./ **and**/ **instruction** + pl. + part./, **without**/ **much**/ cost + pres. particip. act. + part. (= **'expensive'**)/ enlightenment, education, cul-ture + work + part. (= **'work of enlightenment'**),

ilman apu-raho-j-a ja malli-piirustuks-i-a on jokainen kodi-n perusta-ja rakenta-nut
without/ **aid, assistance** + money + pl. + part. (= **'grants, stipends'**)/ **and**/ image, model + drawing, design, plan + pl. + part. (= **'blueprints'**)/ be (3d pers. sing.) (= **'has'**)[4]/ every (nom.)/ **home** + gen./ basis, establish + agentive deriv. suff. (nom.)(= **'home founder'**)/ **build, construct** + past particip. act. (nom.)/

itse-lle-en sauna-n usein ennen kuin itse asumukse-n.
self + allat. + 3d pers. possess. (= **'for himself'**)/ **sauna** + acc./ **often, most frequently**/ **before**/ than/ self (= **'itself'**)/dwelling, **residence** + acc./

(7) *Sauna-n ympäri-lle kierty-y suoma-laise-n elämä synty-mä-stä kuole-ma-an asti:*

sauna + gen./ **around** + allat. / **revolve** + 3d pers. sing./ **Finn** + **-ish** (deriv. suff.) + gen./ **life** (nom.)/ be born + inf. III + elat. (= **'from birth'**)/ die + inf. III + illat. (= **'until death'**)/ until, up to/:

(8) *Sii-tä hän ammenta-a terveyt-tä hyv-i-nä päiv-i-nä, ja sii-tä hän hake-e parannus-ta sairauks-i-en sattu-e-ssa.*

it + elat. (= **'from it'**)/ he ~ **she** (nom.)/ **acquire, ladle** + 3d pers. sing./ **health** + part./ **good** + pl. + ess./ **day** + pl. + ess./, **and**/ it + elat. (= **'from it'**)/ **he** ~ **she**/ **seek, request** + 3d pers. sing./ **cure, improvement** + part./ **illness** + pl. + gen./ happen, occur + inf. II + iness. (= **'when they occur'**).[8]

(9) *Sauna merkitse-e jokaise-lle suoma-laise-lle nautinto-a ja virkistys-tä.*

sauna (nom.)/ **mean** + 3d pers. sing./ **every** + allat./ **Finn** + -ish (deriv. suff.) + allat./ **enjoyment, pleasure** + part./ **and**/ **relaxation, recreation, refreshment** + part./.

(10) *Melko varma-sti nä-i-llä seiko-i-lla on oma tärke-ä osuute-nsa sii-hen,* **quite**/ **certain** + **ly**/ **this** + pl. + adess./ **factor,** circumstance + pl. + adess./ be (3d pers. sing.) (= **'have'**)[3]/ **own** (nom.)/ **meaningful, important, significant** (nom.)/ **part, role, share** + 3d pers. possess./ it + illat. (= **'for the fact'**)/,

että sauna on elä-nyt ja jatkuva-sti elä-ä voimakkaa-na Suome-n kansa-n elä-mä-ssä.

that (conj.)/ **sauna**/ be (3d pers. sing.)(= **'has'**)[4]/ **live** + past partic. act. (nom.)/ **and**/ **continuous** + **ly**/ **live** + 3d pers. sing./ **strong, powerful** + ess./ **Finland** + gen./ **people** + gen./ **life** + iness./.

(11) *Sauna ei ole vain vältä-mä-tön terveyde-n-lähde, vaan myös suuri ja korkea-mma-n luoka-n nautinto-väline.*

sauna (nom.)/ neg. vb. (3d pers. sing.)/ **be**/ **only**/ avoid + inf. III + neg. suff. (= **'necessary, essential, indispensable'**)/ **health** + gen. + **source, spring** (nom.)[7]/, **but**/ **as well**/ big, **great** (nom.)/ **and**/ high + comparative + gen. (= **'more exalted, superior'**)/ **class, type** + gen./ **pleasure, recreation** + instrument, **means** (nom.)/.

(12) *Suome-ssa on-kin tapana—kuten muinais-i-ssa ritari-linno-i-ssa—*

Finland + iness./ be (3d pers. sing.) (= **'exists, there is'**) + **also** (clitic)/ **custom** + ess.)/   —**as,** how/**ancient** + pl. + iness./   **knight** + **castle** + pl. + iness./—

valmista-a sauna hyv-i-lle ja terve-tulle-i-lle viera-i-lle.

prepare, make ready + inf. I/ **sauna** (acc.)[9]/ **good** + pl. + allat./ **and**/ **welcome** + pl. + allat./ **guest** + pl. + allat./.

(13) *Sauna tar jo-ta-an yh-tä hyvä-stä sydäme-stä viera-i-tten nautinto-a silmä-llä-pitä-e-n*

sauna/ present, offer + pass. stem + pass. ending (= **'one offers'**)/ one + part. (= **'just as, equally'**) / **good** + elat. / **heart** + elat./ **guest** + pl. + gen./ **pleasure, recreation** + part./ eye + adess. + keep, hold + inf II + instr. (= **'keeping in view, mindful of'**)/

kuin mitkä muu-t herku-t tahansa ja vastaanote-ta-an kiito-llisuude-lla.

as, than/ **any** (acc.)/ **other** + pl. (acc.)/ **treat, delicacy** + pl. (acc.)/ **whatsoever**/ **and**/ receive, accept + pass. stem + pass. ending (= **'one accepts'**) / thanks + expression + adess. (= **'with thanks'**)/.

(14) *Sauna on ja tule-e varmaan ole-ma-an Suome-ssa vieraile-v-i-in ulko-maa-lais-i-in*

sauna/ be (3d person sing.) (= **'is'**)/ **and**/ **come** + 3d pers. sing.[10]/ **surely, certainly**/ **be** + inf. III + illat./ **Finland** + iness./ **visit, spend time as guest** + pres. partic. act. + pl. + illat./ outside + land, country + dweller + pl. + illat. (= **'for foreigners'**)/

näh-de-n parha-i-ta mainos-väline-i-tä.

see + inf. II + instr. (= **'as regards, concerning'**)[11]/ **best** + pl. + part./ advertising, publicity + means, instrument, medium + pl. + part. (= **'means of advertising'**)/.

NOTES

1. In the plural, the allomorph of the genitive suffix contains a linking element *-te-* whose presence sometimes causes the plural suffix to be deleted (depending on what precedes) and which itself may drop the *-t* under various conditions.

2. Third person singular indicative form of the verb, without an overtly expressed subject, is often used in an impersonal sense: *one walks, one sees,* and so forth.

3. The Finnish possessive construction has the following structure: possessor (marked by adessive case) + third person form of verb *ole-* 'to be, exist' + what is possessed (marked by nominative case). This construction is very similar to the Russian possessive construction (cf. "Sketch of Russian").

4. The verb *ole-* 'to be, exist' is also used as an auxiliary verb in forming the past perfect form of the verb.

5. The abessive case form of the infinitive III signifies action not performed, absence of the action expressed by the verb stem, and so on: 'without V-ing, not performing V'.

6. The illative case form of the infinitive III signifies an aim or destination, an action which is to be done or should be done, or for which one is prepared or suited.

7. Although, as in English, Finnish compounds very often involve only the stem morphemes (e.g., *sana-kirja,* lit. 'word' + 'book' = 'dictionary') with only the last stem in the compound being inflected for case, Finnish also has compounds in which the first stem is followed by case marking as well (e.g., *terveyde-n-lähde,* health + gen. + spring (nom.), lit. 'health's spring' = 'source of health').

8. Infinitive II + inessive case usually indicates an action taking place at the same time as that expressed by the main verb. Thus, such forms can be translated into English as subordinate temporal clauses: 'when V, while V-ing'.

9. In the singular, the accusative case may appear marked with the suffix *-n* or have the same form as the nominative singular form. Because of the limitations of space the difference in the usage of the two forms is not explained here.

10. Since Finnish does not have a special future tense, the future is sometimes marked by *tulee* 'to come', used as an auxiliary verb.

11. This word, when used as a kind of a postposition, governs the illative case.

Idiomatic Translation by Author

(1) OUR FINNISH SAUNA

(2) No matter where in Finland one walks and sees a house, an observant eye may notice, at some distance from the house, at the edge of a small forest or some body of water, a small structure made of logs, the sauna.

(3) Sauna is the bathing facility of the Finns, and every family, even the poorest, has its own sauna where one bathes at least once a week. (4) Only in cities and densely populated areas and in connection with institutions are there public saunas.

(5) It is difficult to give such a precise definition of what a Finnish sauna is that would help make clear what its essential nature is, and from a purely Finnish point of view at least such a definition may perhaps be completely unnecessary, for Finns have been using the sauna for at least a thousand years without finding it necessary to define or explain it, and yet its general form, that of smoke sauna,[14] has remained the same throughout the centuries as far as its basic characteristics are concerned. (6) Without advice or instruction from outside, without expensive work of enlightenment, without grants-in-aid or blueprints, every founder of a home has constructed for himself a sauna, very often before the residence itself.

(7) A Finn's life revolves around the sauna from the time he is born to the time he dies: (8) From it he draws good health during good days and from it he seeks cures for his illnesses when they befall him. (9) To every Finn sauna means enjoyment and reinvigoration. (10) It is fairly clear that each of these factors has its own important role in that the sauna has been and continues to be a very powerful force in the life of the Finnish people. (11) Sauna is not only an essential source of health but is also a great and superior type of pleasure source. (12) In Finland it is the custom, just as in ancient castles of the knights, to prepare a sauna for good and welcome guests. (13) Sauna is offered with the aim of providing pleasure to one's guests just as cordially as any other treat whatsoever, and one accepts it with an expression of gratitude. (14) Sauna is and will certainly continue to be one of the best means of advertising for foreigners visiting in Finland.

EXERCISES

1. Loanwords in Finnish

Examine carefully the following loanwords from various European languages in Finnish and formulate as many general observations as you can about the way Finnish adapts foreign words to the Finnish phonological system. (Take note, for example, what regular sound substitutions occur and what phonotactic or syllable structure constraints Finnish imposes on foreign words. For the purposes of this exercise you may assume that, unless otherwise indicated, foreign originals are pronounced roughly as in English. For example, you may assume that in the language from which Finnish borrowed the word *pankki* 'bank' this word, as in English, also began with *b* and ended in *k*. Ignore random or unsystematic changes.) Give a brief explanation for each type of adjustment that you discover in the data.

sohva 'sofa'	Tukholma 'Stockholm'
lamppu 'lamp'	kahvi 'coffee'
koulu 'school'	kapteeni 'captain'
silkki 'silk'	lasi 'glass'

piippu 'pipe'	musiikki 'music'
tohtori 'doctor'	kaasu 'gas'
tirehtööri 'director'	ruusu 'rose'
kulta 'gold'	tanssi 'dance'
pastori 'pastor'	Englanti 'England'
tikku 'stick'	konjakki 'cognac'
kupari 'copper'	pankki 'bank'

Ranska 'France' < Franska (<Swed.)

rouve 'married woman, Mrs.' (cf. German Frau)

evankeliumi 'gospel' < evangelium

risti 'cross' < Russ. krest

tavara 'goods' < Russ. tavar (<továr)

2. Comparative/Typological Exercise

Examine the following data from Finnish *(Uralic)*, Turkish *(Turkic)*, and Sanskrit *(Indo-European)* and then list the similarities that are found in the personal and possessive endings as well as the interrogative pronouns in these languages.

Could these similarities be due to (1) coincidence, (2) borrowing from language to language, (3) genetic relationship of these languages, (4) some universal tendencies of languages, or (5) combination of some of these causes and of some other causes that you may think of? Discuss briefly the pros and cons of the alternative explanations mentioned.

Finnish (Uralic)

Interrogative pron.: kuka 'who' (The *-ka* part is a kind of extension which is added to monosyllabic forms of various Finnish pronouns.)

	POSSESSIVE SUFFIXES ON NOUNS	PERSONAL SUFFIXES ON VERBS
1st pers. sing.	-ni (< -mi)	-n (<-m)
2d pers. sing.	-si (< -ti ~ -ði)	-t
3d pers. sing.	-nsa' (<-sen ~ -zen)	-Ø
1st pers. pl.	-mme' (<'mek)	-mme'
2nd pers. pl.	-nne' (<-'tek)	-tte'
3d pers. pl.	-nsa' (<-sek ~ -zek)	-vat (<-va + t)*

*This ending is a combination of an old present tense marker and a plural marker. In other words, there is really a zero personal marker in the third person plural form, at least from a diachronic point of view.

Turkish (Turkic)

Interrogative pron.: kim 'who'

	POSSESSIVE SUFFIXES ON NOUNS	PERSONAL SUFFIXES ON VERBS
1st pers. sing.	-mi/-m	-m
2d pers. sing.	-in/-n	-sin
3d pers. sing.	-i/Ø	-dir/Ø
1st pers. pl.	-im-iz/-m-iz	-iz
2nd pers. pl.	-in-iz/n-iz	-sin-iz
3d pers. pl.	-ler-i	-dir-ler/-Ø

Note that Turkish forms are subject to the rules of Turkish vowel harmony. (See the next exercise.) The presence and absence of the initial vowel in some of the suffixes is determined by the final segment of the preceding morpheme: vowel-initial endings are found after consonants, whereas consonant-initial endings are found after vowels. Note also that the order of affixation is the same for Finnish and Turkish affixes in nouns: Noun stem + plural + case suffix + possessive pronoun suffix.

Sanskrit (Indo-European)

Interrogative pron.: kas 'who' (masc. nom. sg.), kim (neut. nom. sing.), kā (fem. nom. sing.)

PERSONAL ENDINGS ON THE VERB 'TO BE' IN THE PRESENT TENSE			
1st pers. sing.	as-mi	1st pers. pl.	s-mas
2d pers. sing.	as-i	2d pers. pl.	s-tha
3d pers. sing.	as-ti	3d pers. pl.	s-anti

RECONSTRUCTED PROTO-INDO-EUROPEAN PERSONAL ENDINGS ATTACHED TO THE VERB STEM *bher-* 'TO CARRY, BEAR'			
1st pers. sing.	*bher-ō	1st pers. pl.	*bher-omes
2d pers. sing.	*bher-esi	2d pers. pl.	*bher-ete
3d pers. sing.	*bher-eti	3d pers. pl.	*bher-onti

Note that as a rule, Indo-European languages do not have personal possessive suffixes on nouns.

3. Turkish Vowel Harmony Rules (Vowel Harmony Typology)

Like Finnish, Turkish also has vowel harmony. However, although there are some similarities between the two languages, there are also some differences. (For example, Turkish does not have a "neutral vowel category" as far as vowel harmony is concerned.) Examine the Turkish data given in the following table and (1) formulate the rules of Turkish vowel harmony, and (2) compare and contrast these rules with the vowel harmony rules of Finnish which were given in the "Sketch of Finnish." Note that the Turkish vowel system contains the following vowels: *i, e* (front unrounded vowels); *ü, ö* (IPA [y], [ø] = front rounded vowels); *ı* ([ɨ]), *a* (= nonfront unrounded vowels); *u, o* (back or 'nonfront' rounded vowels).

GLOSS	NOUN	N + MY	N + PL.	N + PL. + MY
1. 'stone'	taş	taşım	taşlar	taşlarım
2. 'face'	yüz	yüzüm	yüzler	yüzlerim
3. 'donkey'	eşek	eşekim	eşekler	eşeklerim
4. 'banana'	muz	muzum	muzlar	muzlarım
5. 'fish'	balık	balıkım	balıklar	balıklarım
6. 'tooth'	diş	dişim	dişler	dişlerim
7. 'ear'	kulak	kulakım	kulaklar	kulaklarım
8. 'flower'	çiçek	çiçekim	çiçekler	çiçeklerim
9. 'eye'	göz	gözüm	gözler	gözlerim
10. 'son'	oğul	oğulum	oğullar	oğullarım
11. 'arm'	kol	kolum	kollar	kollarım

NOTES

1. There are also situations where a consonant is dropped or assimilates to the following consonant. For more details, see Collinder (1965:67–73) and the "Sketch of Finnish" at the end of this chapter.

2. See "Sketch of Finnish" in this chapter for more details about vowel harmony as it operates in Finnish.

3. For details about active/nonactive typology, cf. B. G. Hewitt (1987).

4. Stress is normally omitted in Russian orthography except in textbooks for language learners.

5. Cf. Avanesov (1984:119–20). This goes counter to the hypothesis that a language cannot have phonetically "marked" (i.e., less common or articulatorily complex) segments unless it also has their "unmarked" counterparts.

6. Note that *ë* always receives the stress and that therefore words which have this letter need not be marked for stress in transcription.

7. The following passage is taken from Aleksandr I. Solženicyn [Solzhenitsyn]. 1968. *V pervom krugu* [In the First Circle]. London: Flegon Press, 1968. The text follows the punctuation of the Russian original. The paragraphs are numbered for easier reference to the literal translation which follows.

8. Abakumov was a high official in the Soviet state security apparatus during Stalin's time.

9. Bobylin, being a prisoner, cannot address Abakumov as "comrade minister," which would have been the normal way for an ordinary Soviet citizen to address such an official: Prisoners and other "enemies of the state" could not be considered "comrades" of Soviet officials.

10. According to Soviet prison regulations of that time, prisoners were for some reason forbidden to wear clothing with buttons.

11. Special, high quality editions of cigarette brands and some other products were made for higher Soviet officials and were available only to them. ("Troika" is the Russian word for a three-horse sleigh or wagon.)

12. This was one of the cheapest brands of cigarettes and was named in honor of the construction of the Belomor Canal (White Sea Canal) which was built largely with prison labor.

13. This passage, written by H. J. Viherjuuri, is taken from Robert Austerlitz. 1966. *Finnish reader and glossary.* Indiana University Publications, Uralic and Altaic Series, vol. 15, Bloomington: Indiana University Press, 42–3.

14. That is, a sauna without a chimney, made of earth, also used for smoking fish, ham. (From note in Robert Austerlitz' *Finnish reader and glossary.*)

SELECTED BIBLIOGRAPHY

General

Bright, William, et al., eds. 1992. *International encyclopedia of linguistics.* New York: Oxford University Press. 4 vols. (Contains authoritative and up-to-date entries on all language families and many individual languages.)

Campbell, George L. 1991. *Compendium of the world's languages.* New York: Routledge. 2 vols. (Contains language samples from many languages of the world along with brief information about each.)

Comrie, Bernard, ed. 1987. *The world's major languages.* New York: Oxford University Press. (Good sketches of major languages and overviews of some major language families are given by experts.)

Fraenkel, Gerd. 1967. *Languages of the world.* Boston: Ginn. (An extremely brief, nontechnical survey.)

Grimes, Barbara. 1992. *Ethnologue: Languages of the world.* Dallas, Texas: Summer Institute of Linguistics, Inc. 12th ed. (Periodically updated, this work also contains a separate index volume.)

Grimes, Joseph Evan, and Barbara Grimes. 1993. *Ethnologue: Language family identity.* Dallas, Texas: Summer Institute of Linguistics, Inc.

Kamei, Takashi, and Rokurō Kōno, eds. 1988–1992. *Gengogaku daijiten. Sekai gengo hen.* 4 vols. Tokyo: Sanseidō Press. (A very up-to-date Japanese linguistic encyclopedia, with entries on various languages and language families.)

Katzner, Kenneth. 1986. *The languages of the world.* Rev. ed. London: Routledge & Kegan Paul. (Contains samples of world's languages in native script and very brief information on each cited language.)

Kloss, Heinz, and Grant McConnell, gen. eds. 1974–1984. *Linguistic composition of the nations of the world.* Québec: Les Presses de l'Université Laval. (A number of volumes of this monumental work, each under different editors, have already appeared. Because the information in them is somewhat harder to use than that given in Grimes (1992) and since the latter already incorporates most of the information contained in this work, this work is not cited in this textbook.)

Meillet, Antoine, and Marcel Cohen, eds. 1952. *Les langue du monde, par un groupe de linguistes sous la diréction de A. meillet et Marcel Cohen.* 2d ed. Paris: E. Champion. (The classic survey of the languages of the world; now quite outdated, but still of some interest.)

Moseley, C., and R. E. Asher, gen. eds. 1994. *Atlas of the world's languages.* London: Routledge. (This is the most comprehensive linguistic atlas of the world's languages to date.)

Ruhlen, Merritt. 1987. *A guide to world's languages. Vol. 1: Classification.* Stanford: Stanford University Press. (Ruhlen is a veteran of the Stanford University Language Universals Project. He is also known as an apologist for the very sweeping genetic classification hypotheses of his mentor Joseph Greenberg. Vol. 2 gives language data, and vol. 3 will deal with language universals.)

Indo-European Languages

Baldi, Philip. 1983. *An introduction to the Indo-European languages.* Carbondale and Edwardsville: Southern Illinois University Press. (A very readable introductory overview of the various branches and languages of this family, both living and extinct. Good bibliography.)

———. 1987. Indo-European languages. In Bernard Comrie, ed., *The world's major languages,* 33–67. New York: Oxford University Press.

Cardona, George. 1987a. Indo-Aryan languages. In Bernard Comrie, ed. *The world's major languages,* 440–7. New York: Oxford University Press.

———. 1987b. Sanskrit. In Bernard Comrie, ed., *The world's major languages,* 448–69. New York: Oxford University Press.

Coleman, R. G. G. 1987. Latin and the Italic languages. In Bernard Comrie, ed., *The world's major languages,* 180–202. New York: Oxford University Press.

Comrie, Bernard. 1987. Slavonic languages. In Bernard Comrie, ed., *The world's major languages,* 322–8. New York: Oxford University Press.

Green, John N. 1987. Romance languages. In Bernard Comrie, ed., *The world's major languages,* 203–9. New York: Oxford University Press.

Hawkins, John A. 1987. Germanic languages. In Bernard Comrie, ed., *The world's major languages,* 68–76. New York: Oxford University Press.

Joseph, Brian D. 1987. Green. In Bernard Comrie, ed., *The world's major languages,* 410–39. New York: Oxford University Press.

Lockwood, W. B. 1972. *A panorama of Indo-European languages.* London: Hutchinson University Library. (A readable overview, very similar to Baldi 1983. Includes the Lord's Prayer in many of the languages, including several creoles and pidgins based on Indo-European languages.)

Mallory, J. P. 1989. *In search of the Indo-Europeans: Language, archeology and myth.* London: Thames and Hudson.

Payne, J. R. 1987. Iranian languages. In Bernard Comrie, ed., *The world's major languages,* 514–22. New York: Oxford University Press.

Schmalstieg, W. R. 1980. *Indo-European linguistics: A new synthesis.* University Park: Pennsylvania University Press.

Szemerényi, O. 1980. *Einführung in die vergleichende Sprachwissenschaft.* 2d ed. Darmstadt: Wissenschaftliche Buchgesellschaft. (Currently the most authoritative handbook.)

Watkins, Calvert. 1992. Indo-European languages. In William Bright et al., eds. *Inter-*

national encyclopedia of linguistics. Vol. 2: 206–12. New York: Oxford University Press.

Windfuhr, Gernot L. 1987. Persian. In Bernard Comrie, ed., *The world's major languages,* 524–46. New York: Oxford University Press.

Uralic Languages

Abondolo, Daniel. 1987. Hungarian. In Bernard Comrie, ed., *The world's major languages,* 577–92. New York: Oxford University Press.

Austerlitz, Robert. Uralic languages. In Bernard Comrie, ed., *The world's major languages,* 567–76. New York: Oxford University Press.

Bergsland, Knut. 1959. The Eskimo-Uralic hypothesis. *Journal de la Société Finno-ougrienne,* 61:1–29.

Collinder, Björn. 1965. *An introduction to the Uralic languages.* Berkeley and Los Angeles: University of California Press. (A fairly thorough and not too technical introduction to the comparative studies of the Uralic languages, but somewhat dated.)

Collinder, Björn, comp. 1969 [1957]. *Survey of Uralic languages. Grammatical sketches and commented texts with English translations.* Stockholm: Almquist & Wiksells.

Comrie, Bernard, et al., eds. 1981. *The languages of the Soviet Union.* Cambridge: Cambridge University Press. (Chapter 3 is devoted to brief sketches of those Uralic languages spoken in the former Soviet Union.)

Janhunen, Juha. 1992. Uralic languages. In William Bright et al., eds., *International encyclopedia of linguistics.* Vol. 4:205–10. New York: Oxford University Press.

Koizumi, Tamotsu. 1981. Uraru shogo. In Hajime Kitamura, ed., *Sekai no gengo,* 81–111. Kōza Gengo, vol. 6. Tokyo: Taishūkan shoten.

Languages of the Caucasus

Dzidziguri, Shota. 1969. *The Georgian language.* Tbilisi: Tbilisi University Press. (This work gives a good overview of the history of the study of the Georgian language and its origins and a fairly detailed bibliography, but it unfortunately offers little insight into the structure of the Georgian language itself.)

Hewitt, B. G. 1981. Caucasian languages. In Bernard Comrie et al., eds., *Languages of the Soviet Union,* 196–237. New York: Cambridge University Press.

———. 1987. Georgian: Ergative or active? *Lingua* 71:319–40.

———. 1992. Caucasian languages. In William Bright et al., eds., *International encyclopedia of linguistics,* 1:220–7. New York: Oxford University Press.

Klimov, Georgij Andreevič. 1965. *Kavkazskie jazyki.* Moscow: Nauka Publishing House. (This overview is very good although it is already somewhat dated.)

Klimov, Georgij Andreevič, and M. E. Alekseev. 1980. *Tipologija kavkazskix jazykov.* Moscow: Nauka Publishing House. (A thorough exploration of the important typological features of the Caucasus languages.)

Kuipers, Aert H. 1976. *Typologically salient features of some North-West Caucasian languages.* Lisse: The Peter de Ridder Press. (The author attempts to show that some languages of the Caucasus have no vowel phonemes whatsoever.)

Basque

de Rijk, Rudolf P. G. 1992. Basque. In William Bright et al., eds., *International encyclopedia of linguistics,* 1:162–9. New York: Oxford University Press.

Saltarelli, Mario. 1988. *Basque.* London: Croom Helm. Croom Helm Descriptive Grammar Series.

Tovar, Antonio. 1957. *The Basque language.* Transl. from Spanish by H. P. Houghton. Philadelphia: University of Pennsylvania Press.

Russian

Avanesov, R. I. 1984. *Russkoe literaturnoe proizno šenie.* Moscow: Prosveščenie.

Comrie, Bernard. 1979. Russian. In Timothy Shopen, ed., *Languages and their status,* 91–151. Cambridge, Mass.: Winthrop. (A very readable, non-technical description of the language.)

Comrie, Bernard. 1987. Russian. In Bernard Comrie, ed., *The world's major languages,* 329–47. New York: Oxford University Press.

Sussex, Roland. 1992. Russian. In William Bright et al., eds., *International encyclopedia of linguistics,* 3:350–8. New York: Oxford University Press.

Vinokur, G. O. 1971. *The Russian language: A brief history.* London: Cambridge University Press. (Translation from the Russian 1957 edition.)

Finnish

Branch, Michael. 1987. Finnish. In Bernard Comrie, ed., *The world's major languages,* 593–617. New York: Oxford University Press.

Hakulinen, L. 1961. *The structure and development of the Finnish language.* Indiana University Publ., Uralic and Altaic Series, vol. 3. Bloomington: Indiana University Press.

Karlsson, Fred. 1992. Finnish. In William Bright et al., eds., *International encyclopedia of linguistics,* 2:14–7. New York: Oxford University Press.

Lehtinen, Meri. 1962. *Basic course in Finnish.* Indiana University Publ., Uralic and Altaic Series, vol. 27. Bloomington: Indiana University Press.

Whitney, Arthur. H. 1956. *Finnish.* Teach Yourself Books. Sevenoaks, Kent: Hodder and Stoughton. (Most of the examples cited in the Finnish sketch have been taken from this work.)

Chapter **4**   # Languages of Asia

It is somewhat difficult to come up with a sensible, nonarbitrary way of determining the order in which the languages of Asia are to be discussed. Neither the purely directional approach (listing languages in the order that they are found from, say, east to west) nor the approach of listing languages and language families according to the number of their speakers seems quite appropriate here for various reasons. What shall be followed here is basically a variation on the first approach: languages and language families of Asia will be listed mainly in terms of their geographical location; in addition, various possible genetic or areal linkages between the language families will also be taken into consideration, which will entail several different "passes" in different directions. Thus, we shall begin by going from west to east, listing language families that have been grouped by some into the so-called Altaic language family. Then we shall turn southwards through East Asia to Southeast Asia and from there westward to South Asia and so on. Finally, language families that are only peripherally present in Asia will be briefly mentioned.

I. TURKIC

The *Turkic* language family contains a fairly large number of different languages spoken from the Balkans (SE Europe) to the Central Asian regions of both China and the former Soviet Union. The earliest written records are from the beginning of the eighth century and are in *Orkhon*

Turkic. According the Comrie's (1992) overview, Turkic may be subdivided into the following five groups.

1. BOLGAR OR BULGAR

This branch consists of *Chuvash* (1,440,000 sp. in the Chuvash Autonomous Republic east of Moscow on the Volga River). This language is very different from all other Turkic languages, and according to some scholars it may form a separate branch which branched off Proto-Turkic before all the other Turkic subgroups.

2. EASTERN TURKIC

This includes *Uighur* (6,749,500 sp. of whom 6,500,000 are in China, most of the rest in the former Soviet Union) and *Uzbek* (15,013,000 tot. sp., mostly in Uzbekistan, the rest in China).

3. NORTHERN TURKIC

This includes *Altai* (51,600 sp. in the Gorno-Altai Autonomous Region of the Russian Federation), *Tuvan* (191,000 tot. sp., of whom 166,000 are in the Tuvin Autonomous Region of the Russian Federation and 24,700 are in the Mongolian Republic), and *Yakut* (316,000 sp. in the Yakut Autonomous Republic in the Russian Federation along the Lena River).

4. SOUTHERN TURKIC

The more prominent members of this subgroup are *Turkish* or *Osmanli* (50 million tot. sp., of which more than 46 million are in Turkey), *Azeri* (14 million sp. or more, with 7,757,000 in Iran, the rest mostly in the Azerbaijan Republic, and some in Iraq, Turkey, and Syria), *Crimean Tatar* (375,000 sp., mostly in Uzbekistan, some in Rumania and elsewhere), *Salar,* (55,000 sp. in Western China provinces of Qinghai, Gansu, and Xinjiang), *Gagauz* (166,000 sp., mostly in Moldova, with some in Ukraine and Kazakhstan), and *Turkmenian* (3,131,000 tot. sp., of whom 2,028,000 are in Turkmenistan and 380,000 in Afghanistan).

5. WESTERN TURKIC

This subgroup includes *Karachai-Balkar* (191,000 sp. in the Karachay-Cherkess Autonomous Region of the Russian Federation), *Kumyk* (189,000 sp. in southern Dagestan Autonomous Republic), *Bashkir* (1,000,000 sp. in the Bashkir Autonomous Republic in the Russian Federation), *Volga Tatar* (5,493,000 sp. mostly in the Tatarstan Republic), *Karakalpak* (about 293,000 sp. in Karakalpak Autonomous Republic in Uzbekistan along the Amu Darya and the southern part of the Aral Sea), *Kazakh* (7,600,000 sp., most of whom are in Kazakhstan, some in China), and *Kirghiz* (2,020,000 sp., of whom 1,906,000 are in Kyrgyzstan and 111,000 in Western China).

Turkic languages are for the most part still very similar to each other, and there is a high degree of mutual intelligibility among many of them.

II. MONGOLIAN

According to Binnick (1992), the *Mongolian* family is divided into two sub-branches, *Eastern Mongolian* and *Western Mongolian*.

1. EASTERN MONGOLIAN
This is subdivided into three subbranches.

a. Dagur Subbranch
Dagur or *Daghur* (about 60,000 sp. stretching from Inner Mongolia to Xinjiang in Western China). Some varieties of *Dagur* have been influenced by the neighboring Tungusic languages. This influence led some scholars to believe that Dagur was a Tungusic language.

b. Monguor Subbranch
The chief representative of this group is *Tu,* which has about 90,000 speakers in the Qinghai province of China. This branch has been somewhat influenced by various Tibetan dialects spoken in the region.

c. Oirat-Khalkha Subbranch
This, in turn, is subdivided into two more branches.
i. *Khalkha-Buriat Subbranch*
This is represented by *Khalkha Mongolian* (1,885,000 sp. mostly in the Mongolian Republic) and *Buriat* (353,000 sp. in the Buriat-Mongol Autonomous Republic around Lake Baikal in the Russian Federation).
ii. *Oirat-Kalmyk-Darkhat Subbranch*
This is represented by *Oirat-Kalmyk* (274,000 sp. mainly in the Kalmyk Autonomous Republic between the Don and Volga rivers in the Russian Federation).

2. WESTERN MONGOLIAN
This branch is represented by an almost extinct language called *Mogholi* or *Mogul,* which is spoken by about 200 speakers, mostly elderly, in two villages near Herat, Afghanistan. Mogholi is not mutually intelligible with any of the other Mongol languages.

The oldest substantial written record in Mongolian is the *Secret history of the Mongols* which was compiled around A.D. 1240.

III. TUNGUSIC

The main representatives of this family are *Manchu* (with 70–1,000 sp. it is now almost extinct as a spoken language, though up to 4,299,159 people in China consider themselves ethnic Manchus), *Xibe* or *Xibo* (27,000 sp. in Xinjiang, Western China), and a number of tribal languages spoken by a relatively few speakers in Eastern Siberia and Northeastern China: *Goldi* or

Nanai (7,190 mother-tongue speakers of whom most are in the Russian Federation around the confluence of Amur and Ussuri rivers, the rest in China), *Evenki* (24,000 tot. sp., of whom 12,000 are in the Russian Federation on Sakhalin Island, 10,000 in China, and 2,000 in Mongolia), and *Even* or *Lamut* (about 7,170 sp. scattered in the Yakut Autonomous Republic and Kamchatka peninsula in the Russian Federation).

IV. KOREAN-JAPANESE-OKINAWAN

This language family has two branches.

1. KOREAN

The only representative is *Korean* (65,015,000 tot. sp., of whom 42 million are in South Korea, 20 million in North Korea, 1,763,870 in China, 604,000 in Japan, 389,000 in the former Soviet Union, and 249,000 in the United States).

2. JAPANESE-OKINAWAN

This branch consists of *Japanese* (117 million sp., of whom 116 million are in Japan, 527,000 in the United States, and 380,000 in Brazil), and various *Okinawan* languages (each with a relatively few speakers, but as a group totaling 900,000).

Although various Okinawan languages/dialects are not mutually intelligible with Japanese and even with each other, there is no doubt that the Okinawan and Japanese are genetically related. On the other hand, even though such scholars as Sam Martin (1991a, 1991b) have presented fairly convincing evidence that Korean and Japanese-Okinawan languages are genetically related, there still remains some skepticism in the scholarly community regarding this genetic linkage. All the languages in question are typical SOV languages and share a large number of grammatical traits; however, it is not easy to find cognates between Korean and Japanese, which suggests that if Japanese and Korean are indeed related, the relationship is a very distant one.

V. AINU

Although the total number of ethnic Ainus is somewhere around 15,000 (mostly in Japan, 1,500 in the Pacific region of the Russian Federation), the Ainu language itself is spoken as a second language by very few elderly people located on the island of Hokkaido, the northernmost island of Japan, and on southern Sakhalin (Russian Far East). Originally, the Ainus also occupied the northern half of the main Japanese island of Honshu (as many place names there attest), but they were gradually pushed northward by Japanese settlers. They are now for the most part fully integrated into the Japanese culture.

Racially the Ainus are quite unlike the Japanese—they are Caucasoid and tend to have much more body hair than Japanese. Their languages also appear to be unrelated, although there has obviously been some borrowing between them. The basic word order is SOV, as in Japanese.

In the 1960s there was an attempt to demonstrate the genetic relationship between Ainu and Indo-European, but this hypothesis did not gain much acceptance. More recently Patrie (1982) attempted to link it to Altaic, but the evidence was based on what turned out to be unreliable data on the Ainu language and was therefore flawed. Most scholars still prefer to consider Ainu as language isolate.

Turkic, Mongolian, and *Tungusic* languages are considered by a fairly large group of scholars to constitute the *Altaic* language family. In addition, some scholars consider *Korean-Japanese-Okinawan* and *Ainu* to be part of this family. In the past, the "core" *Altaic* family was linked by some scholars, mainly on the basis of shared typological features, to the *Uralic* family (the "Ural-Altaic hypothesis"), but in recent years most scholars have abandoned the latter hypothesis.

The Altaic hypothesis is by no means accepted by everyone in the field, and there is much controversy surrounding it. There seems to be a consensus that the various languages within individual "branches" of Altaic are indeed genetically related, but there is still considerable doubt that the various branches themselves are genetically linked to each other.

For example, there is no question that all so-called Turkic languages are all mutually related, or that the various Mongolian languages are mutally related. However, there is considerable doubt among linguists that Mongolian and Turkic languages are genetically related. Scholars like Sir Gerald Clauson (1956) point out that *Turkic* and *Mongolian* languages have been in continuous contact with each other over a long span of time and that their contact very likely goes back a long time into prehistory. In addition, it is indisputable that these two groups of languages have borrowed much lexical material and even some morphological material from each other. Finally, he points out that when the earliest written records of the two groups are compared, there are *fewer* similarities between them when one should expect there to be more similarities as one gets closer to the protolanguage from which all these languages have sprung. In other words, he believes that there has been language *convergence* caused by a prolonged intimate contact between the two groups and that the two groups are not genetically related. (This would explain why there are so few cognates involving basic vocabulary that are shared among all the Altaic groups.)

On the other hand, scholars like Nicholas Poppe and Roy Andrew Miller have actually set up recurring sound correspondences among Altaic languages and have even reconstructed Proto-Altaic sound system, lexical and morphological material, and so on, more or less in the same manner as scholars have done for more accepted language families. They argue that it is unreasonable to dismiss their work simply because there is proof that at least some borrowing has indeed taken place among all three core Altaic languages and that it is unfair to impose more stringent criteria on their proof of genetic relationship among Altaic languages than are imposed elsewhere.

The addition of Korean, Japanese, Okinawan, and Ainu languages to the "Altaic" family is even more controversial because even some supporters of the Altaic hypothesis do not accept the evidence adduced in support of the inclusion of these languages into Altaic.

In connection with Japanese relationship to Altaic it should be mentioned that some time ago a Japanese scholar by the name of Susumu Ono (1970) suggested that Japanese language is a blend of an Altaic *superstratum* language and an Austronesian *substratum* language. (In brief, he believes that a strong group of Altaic-speaking invaders conquered Japan and imposed its language on the Austronesian-speaking natives who were already there. However, the Austronesian speakers introduced some of the linguistic traits of their own language—for example, the CV syllable structure prevalent in the Oceanic branch of Austronesian—into the Altaic language of their conquerors. Although this is still an unproven hypothesis, there is some archeological evidence showing that there were indeed migrations of peoples from the Asian mainland into Japan as well as from the south.)

Even more controversial and less accepted than the Altaic hypothesis is the so-called Nostratic hypothesis which lumps together Indo-European, Afroasiatic, Kartvelian (Caucasus), Uralic, Altaic, and Dravidian into one super language family. Originally articulated by two Russian linguists in the sixties this hypothesis is now championed by several scholars in the United States as well. For an overview of this hypothesis consult Kaiser and Shevroshkin (1988).

VI. PALEOSIBERIAN

This is not an established language family as such, but a geographical grouping of languages (like "Languages of the Caucasus" in the preceding chapter) spoken in northeastern Siberia. Attempts to link these languages with the language families of North America have so far not been successful.

Among several languages of this group that have now been recognized as being genetically related is the *Chukotko-Kamchatkan* family (formerly called *Chukchi-Kamchadal*), which consists of the following languages: *Chukchi* (14,000 sp. on Chukotka peninsula), *Kamchadal* (400 sp. on Kamchatka peninsula), *Koryak* (7,900 sp. on Kamchatka), *Kerek* (400 sp. at Cape Navarin), and *Alutor* (2,000 sp. on Kamachatka peninsula). The rest of the languages in this geographical grouping are best considered as language isolates for the time being.

Ket (sometimes also called *Yenisey Ostyak*) is spoken by fewer than 1,100 people along the Yenisey River. Attempts to link this language with Sino-Tibetan have not been very convincing.

Yukaghir (800 sp. at the mouth of the Kolyma River) is now thought by some to be distantly related to the Uralic family, but formal proof is yet to come.

Gilyak or *Nivkh* (1,500 sp. on the island of Sakhalin).

Sometimes the Eskimo-Aleut language family and Ainu are also included in this geographical grouping of languages.

Besides the geographic location of the foregoing languages, another reason for grouping them (even though they are not all genetically related) is that some linguists consider them to be somewhat typologically similar to each other, perhaps due to diffusion from language to language.

According to Comrie (1981:238), however, the so-called Paleosiberian languages are not particularly similar to one another typologically, although it seems that all of them tend to be agllutinative to a certain degree and mostly exhibit the SOV word order. At the same time it is true that there are some important typological differences among them: Ket, for example, unlike the rest of the Paleosiberian languages, has several phonemic tones, discontinuous root morphemes and infixes, and few nonfinite verb forms; Nivkh or Gilyak has a well developed system of noun classifiers, something which is lacking in the other languages; and Chukchi and Koryak are ergative languages and have vowel harmony, unlike the rest.

VII. Sino-Tibetan

Although preliminary classifications (based on deficient data) have been attempted for this family (e.g., by Sten Konow and Robert Shafer) much more work needs to be done before a reasonably accurate classification of all the Sino-Tibetan languages can be given. At the moment, only two major branches have been fairly firmly established as such.

1. Sinitic

This branch contains Chinese and its "dialects," some of which are in fact mutally unintelligible languages (estim. 1 billion tot. sp.). (For a more detailed statement on Sinitic language groups, cf. "Sketch of Mandarin Chinese" in this chapter.)

Sinitic languages are tonal, to a large extent monosyllabic, and analytic/isolating in type. Most of them have SVO word order with modifiers preceding the words modified. The earliest written records go back to about 2000 B.C. or even earlier.

2. Tibeto-Burman

According to Matisoff (1991:481), the Tibeto-Burman branch has the following subbranches.

a. Kamarupan

This subbranch is in turn divided into three groups.

i. Kuki-Chin-Naga

Most of the languages belonging to this group are spoken in the region where the borders of Assam (India), Burma, and Bangladesh meet. Some of the chief languages belonging to this group are *Lushai* (330,000 sp. in India, 12,500 in Burma, and 1,041 in Bangladesh), *Thado* (125,000 sp. in India, 26,200 in Burma), *Ao Naga* (about 80,000 sp. in Assam), *Sema* (65,000 sp. in central and southern Nagaland, Assam), *Angami Naga* (43,569 sp., mainly in western Nagaland), *Konyak Naga* (95,000 sp. in northeast Nagaland, Assam), *Tangkhul Naga* (72,000 sp. in Manipur, Ukhul, Nagaland), and *Lepcha* or *Rong* (65,000 sp. of which most are found in Sikkim and Bhutan, some in Nepal).

ii. Abor-Miri-Dafla

This group includes *Adi* (110,000 sp.) and *Miri* (334,000 sp.), both found mostly in Assam, some in Tibet, and *Dafla* or *Nisi* (33,000 sp. in Assam).

iii. Bodo-Garo

This group includes *Bodo* (600,938 tot. sp., with 600,000 in India and the rest in Nepal) and *Dimasa* (70,000 sp. in Assam, Nagaland) in the plains of Assam, and *Garo,* spoken by 504,000 speakers of which 411,000 are in the hills of Assam and 92,800 are in Bangladesh.

b. Himalayish

The main representative of this group of languages is *Tibetan* (tot. sp. 4,035,000, of which 3,870,068 are in China, 60,000 in Nepal, 100,000 in India, 3,000 in Bhutan, and smaller groups in Switzerland and the United States) and its dialects. (For a statement regarding the dialects of Tibetan, see "Sketch of Classical Tibetan" in this chapter.)

In addition there is a large number of languages spoken primarily by relatively small groups of people in Nepal; the chief non-Tibetan language belonging to this group is *Newari* (500,000 sp. in Nepal), which has several divergent dialects and has been greatly influenced by the neighboring Indo-Aryan languages.

c. Qiangic

This includes *Qiang* (102,768 sp. in Western Sichuan, China), which has a number of dialects some of which may be separate languages.

d. Kachinic

This includes *Kachin* or *Jinghpaw* (tot. sp. 631,108, of which 530,900 are in Northern Burma, 93,008 in Yunnan, China, and 7,200 in India).

e. Lolo-Burmese

This in turn has the following subbranches.

i. Burmish

This includes *Burmese* and its various dialects (a total of 22 million sp., of which 21,553,000 are first-language speakers in Burma [now officially called Myanmar], with about 3 million sp. who speak it as a second language in that country, and about 100,000 sp. in Bangladesh), *Atsi* or *Tsaiwa* (63,000 sp., of whom 13,000 are in Burma and 50,000 in China), *Lashi* (55,500 sp. in Burma), and *Maru* (98,700 sp. in North Burma and parts of China bordering on Burma).

ii. Loloish

This includes *Lisu* (635,000 sp., of whom 126,000 are in Burma, 480,960 in China, and 13,000 in Thailand), *Yi* or *Nyi* (tot. sp. 5,453,448, of which most are in Southwestern China), *Akha* (tot. sp. 280,200, of which 150,000 are in China, 100,200 in Burma, 25,000 in Thailand, and 5,000 in Laos), *Lahu* (tot. sp. 580,000, of which 67,400 are in Burma, 304,174 in China, about 2,500 in Laos, and 23,000 in Thailand), and *Naxi* or *Moso* (245,154 sp., mostly in Yunnan, China). It is also thought that the *Tangut* language of the medieval Hsihsia (Xixia) kingdom belonged to this group.

f. Baic

This subgroup is represented by one language, *Bai* or *Minjia,* which is spoken by 1,131,124 people in Yunnan, China. Because this language has been thoroughly influenced by Chinese—for some dialects Matisoff (1991:484) claims up to 70 percent Chinese loanwords—it is now difficult to ascertain the exact place of this language within the family.

g. Karenic

This includes *Pho* or *Pwo* (1,209,800 sp. in Burma and 60,000 sp. in Thailand) and its closely related *Taungthu* (560,000 sp. in Burma and 600 in Thailand); *Sgaw* (1,284,700 sp. primarily in the Irrawaddy Delta in Burma), and *Kayah* or *Red Karen* (210,000 sp. in Burma and 77,900 in Thailand). Karenic languages, unlike their other Sino-Tibetan neighbors, have SVO word order instead of the more usual SOV word order. Karenic languages have been influenced to some extent by Burmese, but they remain unlike Burmese in several respects.

Sino-Tibetan languages tend to be analytic/isolating in type, monosyllabic, and tonal. However, not all of the Sino-Tibetan languages exhibit these characteristics. For example, Classical Tibetan as well as many modern dialects of Tibetan spoken on the periphery of Tibet are not tonal languages, and tonal contrasts in Burmese and Kachin may be a relatively recent secondary development.

Among the languages of the Himalayan region there is a group that has been given the name "pronominalized Himalayan languages." In contrast with other Sino-Tibetan languages, which do not show much affixation in general, languages belonging to this group have subject and even object affixes in verbs. Some authorities believe that this feature is the result of diffusion from Munda languages (Austroasiatic), whereas others feel that this feature is a very conservative one and should perhaps be reconstructed for Pronto-Sino-Tibetan.

In the past it was very widely accepted as fact that Tai (Daic) languages, Vietnamese, and Hmong-Mien languages are also members of the Sino-Tibetan language family, and some scholars still maintain this view. In recent years, however, a number of linguists working on languages in the area have come to consider Vietnamese to be an Austroasiatic language that has been heavily influenced by Chinese; Paul Benedict has proposed that Tai languages are related to Austronesian languages; and the genetic affiliation of the Hmong-Mien languages with Sino-Tibetan languages has been seriously questioned. The chief difficulty is that all of the said language groups have obviously been influenced by Chinese and perhaps other Sino-Tibetan languages and exhibit lexical and typological similarities to the former. Therefore, it is often very difficult to determine which structural features and even lexical items are truly native and which have been borrowed from Chinese, especially because much of the borrowing must go back to prehistoric times.

There have also been speculations that Ket (cf. Peleosiberian languages) and the Na-Dene (Eyak-Athapascan) languages of North America are genetically related to Sino-Tibetan. The latter hypothesis was first put forth by Edward Sapir and was later championed by Robert Shafer, who published a number of very unsystematic lexical comparisons of the two families. Neither of these hypotheses has gained much acceptance among linguists in general.

VIII. HMONG-MIEN (MIAO-YAO)

Hmong-Mien languages are often listed, especially by Chinese linguists, as forming a branch of the Sino-Tibetan language family, but since there is considerable uncertainty about their genetic affiliation they are discussed here as a separate language group. Clearly these languages have been greatly influenced over a long period of time by Chinese and perhaps also by their neighboring Tai-Kadai languages in many respects. Until it is determined just what has been borrowed and what is original Hmong-Mien, the genetic affiliation of this language group will remain uncertain.

There are two major branches.

1. HMONG OR MIAO

This branch includes the following groups: *Xiangxi Hmong,* spoken by 440,000 speakers in Western Hunan province of China; *White Hmong* or *Hmong Daw,* spoken by 30,000 speakers in Thailand and 70,000 sp. in the United States; *Blue Hmong* or *Hmong Njua,* spoken by 100,000 speakers in Laos, 33,000 in Thailand, and about 4,000 in the United States; *Qiandong Hmong,* with 900,000 speakers in southeast Guizhou, northeast Yunnan, Hunan, and Guangxi (also some in Thailand and Vietnam); and *Chuanqiandian Hmong* or *Flowered Hmong,* with 1,150,000 speakers in southwest Guizhou and Guangxi, Sichuan, Yunnan, northern parts of Vietnam, Thailand, and Laos. According to the 1982 census, altogether there are 5,030,897 Hmong speakers of all groups in China alone.

2. MIEN OR YAO

This branch is represented by various dialects spoken by about 300,000 speakers in Vietnam, 30,000 speakers in Thailand, 60,000 speakers in Laos, and 740,000 speakers in China (out of a total of 1,402,676 people who consider themselves ethnic Mien). The Mien speakers in China are spread around in Guangxi, Guangdong, Yunnan, Hunan, and Guizhou provinces. The total number of speakers of Mien dialects/languages is estimated to be 1 million.

According to Cao (1987), the common characteristics exhibited by both Hmong and Mien branch languages are as follows:

1. Stops, affricates, as well as fricatives, laterals, and nasals exhibit aspirated vs. unaspirated contrast.
2. Syllable finals tend to be very simple in structure; only nasals -*n* and -ŋ may appear as syllable-final elements in Hmong languages, whereas Mien languages in addition have a few oral stop finals.
3. All of these languages have a relatively large number of lexical tones, as many as twelve in some cases. (Some Hmong languages are reported to have up to five *level* tones besides having *contour* tones such as rising and falling.) Tone *sandhi*[1] is common, and tones show a definite relationship to syllable-initial consonants. Thus, for example, aspirated consonant initials only appear in certain tones.
4. All of them have *noun classifier*[2] systems, which are relatively complex.
5. Modifying adjectives, as in Tai languages, always follow the noun they modify.
6. However, noun classifier phrases, nouns, and pronouns in possessive relation to the head noun all precede the latter.
7. Case relations are signaled by word order (SVO) and grammatical particles.

The features which are common to all languages of the Hmong branch only:

1. Hmong languages have uvular stops which are lacking in Mien languages.
2. Hmong languages have syllable-initial consonant clusters such as stop + liquid, nasal + oral stop.
3. They have an especially large number of monosyllabic words.
4. Besides singular and plural, there is also dual number, especially in the pronouns.
5. The noun classifier may modify a noun without a number and is placed before the head noun.
6. Demonstratives, nouns, verbs, or adjectives used as modifiers are placed after the head noun.

The following are the traits common only to the Mien branch languages:

1. They lack uvular consonant initials which are found in the Hmong languages.
2. They have syllable-final stop endings like *-p* and *-t*, whereas Hmong languages have only *-n* and *-ŋ* as syllable-final consonants.
3. They have two sets of numbers, one native and one borrowed.
4. They have special ordinal numbers.
5. Demonstratives and measure words when used as noun modifiers precede the head noun.

IX. TAI-KADAI

This language family consists of three groups.

1. TAI

The most important members of the *Tai* branch are *Thai* or *Siamese* (20 million sp. in Thailand), *Northern Tai* (6 million sp. in Thailand and about 3,000 in Laos, some in China), *Southern Tai* (4,550,000 sp. in Thailand), *Black Tai* or *Tai Dam* (500,000 sp., mostly in Vietnam), *Laotian* (3 million), and *Shan* (2,530,000 tot. sp., of whom 2.5 million are in Burma and the rest in Thailand).

Note that "Tai" is usually used as the name of the branch, whereas "Thai" is used to refer to the main language of Thailand.

2. KAM-SUI

The *Kam-Sui* branch is represented by *Dong* or *Kam* (about 1,430,000 sp. in southeast Guizhou, western Hunan, and northern Guangxi provinces of China), *Sui* (286,487 sp. in Guìzhōu and Guǎngxī, China), and some other minor languages, all spoken within China.

3. KADAI

Some of the *Kadai* languages are *Li* (817,562 sp. mainly on the island of Hǎinán off the southern coast of China), *Gelao* (about 6,000 sp. out of about 60,500 ethnic population, most of whom are in southern China, some in Vietnam), *Ongbe* (500,000 sp. on Hainan island, China), *Laqua* (5,000 sp. in Vietnam), and others. In-depth studies of some of the Kadai languages have only recently become available. It is expected that some realignments in the genetic subgrouping of the entire Tai-Kadai language family will be forthcoming as a result.

Tai-Kadai languages have been very strongly influenced by Chinese and some other languages, but especially by Chinese. It is very likely that Chinese itself has borrowed from Tai languages. Chinese historical records show that Tai-Kadai speaking peoples used to be located much further north than they are found now, covering large portions of China south of the Yangtze River.

The basic word order of these languages is generally SVO, and adjectives usually follow the nouns they modify. All of the *Tai-Kadai* languages are also tonal and tend to be monosyllabic and isolating.

Tai-Kadai has been linked by Paul Benedict to Austronesian. His "Austro-Thai hypothesis" will be discussed later.

X. AUSTRONESIAN

Since most of the languages belonging to this large family are found in Oceania, the family as a whole will be discussed in detail in the chapter on the languages of Oceania. The most important Austronesian languages spoken on the Asian mainland (Southeast Asia) are Malay and the Chamic languages.

In his famous article published in *American Anthropologist,* Paul Benedict (1942) proposed that Tai languages, Kadai languages (about which very little was known at the time), and "Indonesian" (i.e., Austronesian languages) are genetically related. Until that time it was generally accepted that Tai languages were related to the Sino-Tibetan languages, especially to the Chinese. Benedict has since amassed an impressive array of evidence in support of his theory. Much of this evidence has been criticized by Austronesianists as being spurious, but even so he nevertheless convinced some Austronesianists that these language families are indeed genetically related. Benedict calls this "superfamily" *Austro-Thai* and has published much on the subject.

Benedict now considers the Hmong-Mien languages also to belong to Austro-Tai and recently proposed that Japanese be included as well. Both of these additions have met little acceptance. More recently, even some of those who originally were quite sympathetic to the Austro-Thai hypothesis have come to doubt the link between the Tai-Kadai family and Austronesian. As Graham Thurgood (1993) points out, the Tai-Kadai words that have Austronesian cognates exhibit irregular correspondences, which to him means that such items are very likely loanwords from Austronesian in Tai-Kadai rather than being inherited from the putative ancestor language Proto-Austro-Tai.

It is interesting to note in this connection that in his original article in which he first proposed the linkage between Austronesian and Tai-Kadai languages, Benedict cited the Kadai forms of some numbers which clearly showed resemblance to the Austronesian forms for the same numbers. Benedict concluded at the time that the Thai numbers (as well as numbers in other Tai languages) were borrowed from Chinese and that the Kadai languages had retained the original numbers (inherited from Proto-Austro-Tai). However, it is also possible that whereas Tai languages have borrowed from Chinese, Kadai languages have borrowed from Austronesian languages. In other words, words for numbers may be borrowed from the neighboring languages, and it would be strange to argue, without citing some cogent reason, that in one case such borrowing must have occurred but in the other it was not likely to have occurred.

XI. AUSTROASIATIC

This family is thought to have two major branches, Western and Eastern, which are typologically very divergent from each other.

1. MUNDA OR WESTERN

This branch consists of two groups.

a. Nahali or Nihali

There are 5,000 speakers in Madhya Pradesh and Maharashtra, Northeastern India. The genetic affiliation of this language is controversial.

b. Munda

This subbranch is also found in Northeastern India. It consists of a fairly large number of languages the chief of which are *Santali* (3,840,000 tot. sp., of whom 3,693,558 are in India, 100,000 in Bangladesh, and 40,000 in Nepal), *Mundari* (850,000 sp. in Assam and Bihar, India), *Ho* (749,793 sp., mainly in Bihar and Orissa, India), *Sora* (270,000 sp., mainly in Orissa, India), *Korku* (320,000 sp., mainly in Madhya Pradesh, India), *Juang* (13,000 sp. in Orissa, India), and *Korwa* (14,246 sp., mainly in Bihar and Madhya Pradesh, India). Munda speakers live in the mountains and plateaus of Madhya Pradesh, Bihar, and Orissa and are surrounded by Indo-European and Dravidian speakers, whose languages have greater social prestige.

Munda languages appear to have been greatly influenced by their Indo-European and Dravidian neighbors. Typologically they are agglutinative, and very long sequences of affixes may be found, especially in verbs. There is even noun-incorporation (e.g., in Sora) which is usually a feature of polysynthetic/incorporating languages. Nouns are divided into two major categories: animate and inanimate. Case relations are signaled by word order, postpositions, and pronominal affixes. The basic word order is SOV. In general, these languages are typologically quite different from their relatives which belong to the *Eastern* branch of the family.

2. MON-KHMER OR EASTERN

This branch consists of a number of subbranches.

a. Nicobarese

This subbranch consists of six different languages with a total of 22,100 speakers on Nicobar Islands, which are under Indian administration.

b. Northern Mon-Khmer

This subbranch has a number of subbranches itself.

i. Khasi or Khasian

This subbranch consists of *Khasi* (535,000 sp., mainly in Assam, India, and Bangladesh).

ii. Palaungic
This subbranch consists of a large number of minor languages spoken in scattered pockets located in Thailand, Laos, Burma, and Yunnan (China). *Parauk* (648,991 tot. sp., 348,000 of whom are in Burma and 298,591 in China) is one of the more prominent languages belonging to this group.

iii. Khmuic
This subbranch consists of several languages spoken in northern Laos and northern Thailand, the chief of which is *Khmu* (340,000 tot. sp.)

c. Eastern Mon-Khmer
This is further subdivided into three subbranches.

i. Khmeric
This consists of a single language: *Khmer* (7 million sp. or more, mainly in Cambodia, with 700,000 in Vietnam, 10,000 in Malaysia, and 4,000 or more in Thailand).

ii. Bahnaric
This includes about thirty-five minor languages spoken in central and southern Vietnam, southern Laos, and eastern Cambodia. *Bahnar* (85,000 sp. in Vietnam) is one of them.

iii. Katuic
This branch includes a number of minor languages scattered in Vietnam, Laos, Thailand, and Cambodia.

d. Viet-Muong or Vietic
This includes *Vietnamese* (55,438,000 tot. sp., of whom 54,450,000 are in Vietnam, 600,000 in the United States, 300,000 in Cambodia, and 11,995 in China) and a number of minor languages spoken in northern Vietnam and northern Laos.

e. Monic
This includes *Mon* (about 935,000 tot. sp., of whom 835,100 are in Burma and 70,000 to 100,000 are in Thailand) and *Nyahkur* (300 to 1,000 sp. in central Thailand).

f. Aslian
This subbranch consists of several minor languages spoken in southern Thailand and adjacent areas of Malaysia: *Kensiu* (3,000 sp. in Malaysia and 300 in Thailand), *Temiar* or *Northern Sakai* (11,593 sp. in Malaysia), and others, with altogether about 40,000 speakers.

The languages of the *Mon-Khmer* group are mostly prefixing and tend to be monosyllabic. There is usually a large number of vowel contrasts. Some of the languages, notably Vietnamese, have developed tones, and some may be considered to be in a transition stage from nontonal to tonal languages. The most commonly found word order is SVO. Vietnamese has borrowed massively from Chinese, especially during the Tang dynasty, when Vietnam (Annam) came under strong cultural and political influence of China, and was even written with Chinese characters (like Korean and Japanese) until Western Christian missionaries introduced the Roman alphabet.

On the basis of some lexical and typological similarities some linguists speculate that Austroasiatic languages are very distant relatives of Sino-Tibetan and others connect Austroasiatic and Austronesian, but there is very little convincing evidence so far to support either of these hypotheses.

XII. DRAVIDIAN

Most of the languages belonging to this family are spoken in South India and parts of Sri Lanka (Ceylon). An exception of this is *Brahui* (200,000 sp.), which forms a Dravidian pocket in Baluchistan (West Pakistan). The existence of this Dravidian pocket deep in the Indo-Iranian language area strongly suggests that Dravidian languages originally extended much further north before being pushed to the south by the invading Indo-Iranian tribes (Indo-Europeans) in prehistoric times.

Not too long ago a group of Scandinavian scholars put forth the claim that the ancient inhabitants of Harappa and Mohenjo Daro (Indus Valley civilizations) were Dravidian speaking, but evidence for this is somewhat tenuous even though the hypothesis itself is not an unreasonable one given what was said previously about the earlier distribution of Dravidian speakers. The evidence presented by the Scandinavians consists of a putative decipherment of seal inscriptions found at the two sites mentioned above. Since the inscriptions in question are extremely short, any decipherment based on them is in principle highly difficult if not impossible. Accordingly, the validity of the claim that the script has been successfully deciphered is somewhat questionable. For a recent summary concerning the Indus script decipherment, see Parpola (1994).

Brahui, a language belonging to the *Northwest* branch of Dravidian, has been influenced to a great extent by Baluchi (an Iranian language). Other Dravidian languages, especially those that have a long literary tradition, have been to a large extent influenced by Indic languages, especially Sanskrit (through the spread of Hinduism), and have in their turn influenced their Indic (Indo-European) and Munda (Austroasiatic) neighbors. Thus, for example, it is believed that the presence of retroflex consonants in Indic and Munda languages is due to diffusion from Dravidian.

In general, Dravidian languages are mostly agglutinative in type although they do not exhibit very elaborate chains of affixes as are found in such agglutinative languages as Turkish. Some of them have also developed a number of synthetic/inflectional traits. The word order is relatively fixed (usually SOV). One of the more unusual typological features of Dravidian is the presence (in Tamil and the reconstructed Proto-Dravidian) of a three-way phonological contrast: dental consonants vs. alveolar consonants vs. retroflex consonants. On the basis of this contrast and the racial features of Dravidian speakers, some scholars have hypothesized that Dravidian languages are genetically linked to the Australian aborigine languages (many of which also exhibit this uncommon contrast). No further proof has been adduced in support of this claim.

There is also a hypothesis that Dravidian is related to Uralic languages. This latter claim is based on some lexical similarities which may be due to borrowing in prehistoric times.

Dravidian languages are divided into four major branches.

1. SOUTHERN DRAVIDIAN (SOMETIMES CALLED DRAVIDA)

This branch is represented by *Tamil* (about 50 million tot. sp., most of whom are located in Tamil Nadu, India; 3,346,000 sp. are in Sri Lanka and 1,000,000 are in Vietnam; smaller groups are scattered in Southeast Asian countries, South Africa, Fiji, and Mauritius), *Malayalam* (26 million in Kerala, India), *Kannada* (26,890,000 mostly in Karnataka and adjacent states of India), as well as minor languages such as *Kodagu* (93,000 sp. in Karnataka, India), *Tulu* (1,157,000 sp. in Karnataka, India), *Toda* (800 sp.), and *Kota* (900 sp.). The last two languages are spoken by tribal people in the Nilgiri Hills of Tamil Nadu (southern India).

2. SOUTH-CENTRAL DRAVIDIAN OR ANDHRA BRANCH

This consists of *Telugu* (54 million sp., mostly in Andhra Pradesh and parts of the neighboring provinces of India), *Kui* (508,000 sp. in Orissa, Andhra Pradesh, Madhya Pradesh, and Tamil Nadu, India), and *Gondi* (about 2 million sp. in Madhya Pradesh, Maharashtra, and Orissa, India).

3. CENTRAL DRAVIDIAN

This branch consists of a number of languages spoken in Madhya Pradesh, Karnataka, Bihar, and Orissa: *Parji* (20,000 sp.), *Kolami* (88,000 sp.), and *Naiki* (1,000 sp.).

4. NORTHERN DRAVIDIAN

This branch consists of *Brahui* (200,000 sp.) spoken in Pakistan, Brahui, isolated geographically from the rest of the Dravidian languages, is strongly influenced by Baluchi, a neighboring Iranian language. Other languages are *Kurukh* (1,264,000 sp. in the Indian states of Bihar, Madhya Paradesh, Orissa), and *Malto* (95,000 sp. in Bihar and West Bengal, India).

XIII. BURUSHASKI

Burushaski is a language isolate spoken in Kashmir (in the Hunza-Nagir area, which is controlled by Pakistan) by about 40,000 speakers. It is surrounded by speakers of Dardic (Indo-European), Iranian (Indo-European), and Tibetan (Sino-Tibetan) languages, but the area is very remote and isolated, and linguistic contact is primarily with Dardic languages, especially Shina. Attempts to link it with languages of the Caucasus, Basque, and some other languages primarily on the basis of typological similarities remain very unconvincing. It is believed that many speakers of Dardic languages in the area once spoke languages related to Burushaski.

It is an ergative language with an SOV word order. Its phonological inventory is very much like that of its Indic and Dardic neighbors (except that there are no aspirated voiced stops) with the addition of uvular stops and fricatives, which are lacking in Indic languages. It is also reported to have at least three distinct tones.

All Burushaski nouns are divided into four semantically determined classes:

1. Noun class referring to male humans.
2. Noun class of female humans.
3. Noun class of animate nonhumans and certain objects such as fruits, parts of trees and objects made of wood, and some natural phenomena, especially heavenly objects such as the moon.
4. Noun class of nonanimate objects.

These classes play a role in verb morphology where there are suffixes showing class agreement with the third person subjects and prefixes showing the same for the direct and indirect objects. This feature is very reminiscent of similar phenomena in the Nakh-Dagestanian languages of the Caucasus and is usually cited in support of the hypothesis that Burushaski is genetically related to these languages.

Another interesting feature of Burushaski is that some nouns *must* appear with possessive prefixes. These are nouns that may be considered to be "inalienable possessions" of people and animals. This would include parts of the body, such things as the noun 'name', nouns denoting certain emotions, and so forth, although there are some strange items included as well such as 'stick' and 'pillow'.

XIV. Afro-Asiatic

Since most of the branches of this family are found in Africa this family is discussed in the chapter on the languages of Africa. (It is believed that the protohome of this family was in Africa.)

Modern languages belonging to this family and spoken in Asia are the Eastern Arabic dialects (of the Arabian peninsula, Iraq, Syria, Jordan, and Lebanon), Israeli Hebrew in Israel, Assyrian (Eastern Syriac) in Syria, Iraq, and so on, and other Aramaic languages spoken primarily in Syria and Lebanon.

XV. Indo-European

Most of the modern branches of this family are centered in Europe, and therefore this family as a whole is discussed in the chapter on the languages of Europe. The Asian languages belonging to this family are found in Iran,

Afghanistan, India, Pakistan, Bangladesh, and Sri Lanka; for the most part they belong to the Indo-Iranian branch of the family.

XVI. URALIC

The languages belonging to this family are discussed in the chapter on the languages of Europe since the most prominent languages belonging to this family, Finnish and Hungarian, are spoken in Europe.

Asian representatives of this family are languages belonging to the Samoyedic branch of the family in northern Siberia and, if it is indeed related to Uralic, the Yukaghir language spoken in eastern Siberia and Kamchatka peninsula. The latter language is usually classified as a "Paleosiberian language."

XVII. ESKIMO-ALEUT

The languages of this family are primarily centered in Alaska, and therefore this family will be discussed in the chapter on the languages of the Americas. As far as can be determined, this is the only language family that is found in both Asia and North America, even though it is believed that all native languages of the Americas are ultimately descended from those languages that were brought by migrants from Asia who came in many waves across the Behring Strait. In the case of Eskimo-Aleut, the presence of this family on the Asian continent is due to remigration back to Asia from Alaska, and not to a group of speakers remaining behind in Asia after the migration of the rest to North America.

Some classifications include Eskimo-Aleut in the Paleosiberian language grouping which is discussed later in this chapter. This is done primarily on geographical grounds.

SKETCH OF MANDARIN CHINESE

A. GENETIC RELATIONSHIP AND GENERAL BACKGROUND

Chinese is a member of the *Sinitic* branch of the Sino-Tibetan language family. It is spoken by over 1 billion people in a large number of dialects in the People's Republic of China (PRC), Republic of China (Taiwan), Hong Kong, Singapore, Malaysia, and Indonesia. There are also substantial emigrant communities in Vietnam, Thailand, Burma, and other parts of the world, including North America.

The major divisions are as follows.

1. MANDARIN (NORTH, INTERIOR CHINA)

A total of 730,900,000 people, or about 70 percent of Chinese population, speak one of the Mandarin dialects. There are four subgroups.

a. Northern

This includes Héběi, Hénán, Shāndōng, Northern Ānhuī, northeastern provinces (old Manchuria) as well as parts of Inner Mongolia.

b. Northwestern

This includes Shānxī, Shǎnxī, Gānsù, Qīnghǎi, Níngxià and parts of Inner Mongolia.

c. Southwestern

This includes Sìchuān, Yúnnán, Guìzhōu, northwest Guǎngxī, Húběi, and northwest Húnán.

d. Eastern or Jiāng-Huái

This includes dialects spoken in central Ānhuī, and Jiāngsū north of the Yangtze River, and in the region of Nánjīng (Nanking).

2. WÚ (CENTRAL COAST, INCLUDING SHANGHAI)

This dialect group has 77,175,000 speakers, or 7.5 percent of the population. It is further divided into two subgroups.

a. Northern

This includes dialects spoken in the region of Jiāngsū south of the Yangtze.

b. Southern

This includes dialects spoken in Zhèjiāng.

Basically, in this case the two groups differ mainly in the degree to which they have preserved the distinctive Wú vocabulary: the Southern Wú dialects have preserved more of it, whereas the Northern have been greatly influenced by the neighboring Mandarin dialects in this respect.

3. XIĀNG (HÚNÁN PROVINCE)

This group has 36,015,000 speakers, or 3.5 percent of the total population. It is often divided into Old and New Xiāng, mainly on the basis of which dialects have preserved more distinctive Xiāng features (*Old Xiāng*) as opposed to those which have been strongly influenced by Mandarin (*New Xiāng*), just as is done in the case of Wú dialects.

4. YUÈ OR CANTONESE (GUǍNGDŌNG AND GUǍNGXĪ PROVINCES, SOUTHERN COAST AND INTERIOR)

This group has 53,900,000 total speakers, of whom 46,305,000 are in the PRC (4.5 percent of the population), 5,292,000 in Hong Kong, 748,010 in Malaysia, 500,000 in Vietnam, 498,000 in Macau, 314,000 in Singapore, 180,000 in Indonesia, 29,400 in Thailand, 12,800 in New Zealand, 6,000 in the Philippines, and the rest in smaller communities elsewhere. Most of the Chinese in the

United States are Cantonese dialect speakers. The dialect of Canton (Guăngzhōu) is considered to be the standard.

5. HAKKA OR KÈJIĀ (SCATTERED IN SOUTH CHINA)

This dialect group has 25,725,000 speakers in China, or 2.5 percent of the population; the total number of speakers is 27,365,000.

6. GÀN (JIĀNGXĪ PROVINCE AND SOUTHEAST CORNER OF HÚBĚI)

This dialect group has 20,580,000 speakers, or 2 percent of the population.

7. MĬN (FÚJIÀN, PARTS OF GUĂNGDŌNG, TAIWAN, HĂINÁN, SOUTHERN COAST)

This dialect group has the following subdivisions.

a. Western

This includes some dialects in western Fújiàn such as Jiànyáng and Shàowŭ.

b. Eastern

This subgroup in turn has two subbranches.

i. Northern (Fùzhōu)

Total number of speakers is 10,537,000, of whom 10,290,000 are in the PRC (1.2 percent of the population).

ii. Southern (Hokkien) (Amoy, Taiwan)

Total number of speakers is 45,305,000, of whom 25,725,000 are in the PRC (2.5 percent of the population), 1,948,581 in Malaysia, 14,177,800 in Taiwan, 1,170,000 in Singapore, 1,081,920 in Thailand, 700,000 in Indonesia, 493,500 in the Philippines, and 10,000 in Brunei.

Some scholars consider Mĭn dialects spoken on Hăinán island as a third subbranch of Eastern Mĭn.

The standard official language is *Pŭtōnghuà*, the Mandarin of Peking shorn of its purely local Peking expressions. It is the medium of instruction in both the PRC and the Republic of China on Taiwan, though in some regions of the PRC (notably the Cantonese dialect areas) schools use the local dialect in addition to the standard language. The overseas Chinese communities (in most of which Mĭn and Cantonese speakers form the majority) are also increasingly using standard Mandarin Chinese in their schools.

Although the written language is understood throughout China by educated, literate speakers regardless of their dialect, oral communication between speakers whose dialects belong to different dialect groups is often very difficult or even impossible. This is because the dialectal differences are sometimes greater than those found, for example, between English and Dutch, and because the logographic system of writing used in China is not as directly tied to pronunciation as an alphabetic system. Thus, a Chinese character that has the same meaning in all the dialects may have a very different sound value from dialect to dialect.

The greatest degree of difference exists between Mandarin and Mĭn dialect groups. It is only tradition that still makes people refer to these two groups as being "dialects" of the same language rather than two different languages. The greatest linguistic diversity is found on the coast of China, whereas in the interior, where Mandarin dialects stretch from Burma all the way to the border between China and Russia, there is still much mutual intelligibility among dialects.

The government of the PRC is in the process of carrying out a language engineering project on a vast scale. The basic objective of this project is to unify various regions of China by facilitating communication among speakers of different dialect groups. To accomplish this task the government is promoting language standardization, that is, learning of Mandarin by all students, no matter where they are living in China, and by promoting various script reforms in order to increase literacy. The ultimate goal of the orthographic reforms is total conversion to writing in *pīnyīn,* that is, a roman alphabet for Chinese. (However, this policy may change in time, since there is some opposition to total conversion.) Before total conversion to an alphabetic writing system can take place, however, the masses of the people have to be taught to speak and understand the standard language, since romanization of individual dialects would impede communication from dialect to dialect. Schoolchildren and adults are now being taught the standard language, but many adults cannot yet speak Mandarin well. (In Taiwan, the government has been successful in teaching everyone Mandarin, even older, illiterate people, but the government on Taiwan did not have to contend with the vast population of the Chinese mainland.)

As an interim measure, a large number of Chinese characters, especially the more commonly used ones, have been officially and even unofficially simplified for the sake of convenience. (The simplified characters used in the PRC have not yet been sanctioned by the government on Taiwan.)

Chinese has greatly influenced the languages of its immediate neighbors through the overwhelming cultural prestige of the Chinese civilization and culture in East and Southeast Asia. Japanese, Korean, Vietnamese, and Thai have borrowed extensively from China at different times. All of the mentioned languages, except Thai, have also borrowed the Chinese system of writing. Vietnamese, however, has abandoned it completely in favor of romanization introduced by Catholic missionaries, and Korean is in the process of abandoning Chinese characters, though to a certain extent they are still used. (North Korea has completely abandoned Chinese characters in favor of the native Korean alphabet, *hangŭl,* whereas in South Korea characters are still used, especially for writing people's names.)

Recent archeological discoveries in Northern Thailand suggest that civilization may have spread northward from non-Chinese lands into the Chinese territory, which in turn suggests that Chinese, too, may have borrowed from its southern neighbors, most likely the Tai-speaking peoples (Tai-Kadai) which populated southern China before the time of Chinese expansion into the region. In recent times, Chinese has borrowed some words from English and other European languages, but Chinese has resisted large-scale borrowings such as took place in Japanese.

The earliest written texts in Chinese go back to around seventeenth century B.C. (or perhaps even earlier) and consist mostly of logographic inscriptions on oracle bones (bones and turtle shells used in fortune telling).

B. PHONETICS, PHONOLOGY, AND ORTHOGRAPHY

The majority of Chinese morphemes consist of a single syllable, and that is why Chinese is often cited as an example of a *monosyllabic language*. The latter term is very often misunderstood to mean that such a language has only monosyllabic *words*, which certainly is not true of any Chinese dialect or, for that matter, any known language in the world. Although Mandarin is to a very large extent monosyllabic, it has a preponderance of disyllabic *words* and a number of disyllabic morphemes (e.g., *bòhe* 'mint'), some of which are actually loanwords from other languages. Also, the so-called diminutive suffix -*ér* is for the most part realized as a nonsyllabic element (i.e., this suffix is phonetically *less* than one syllable in length). Be that as it may, the phonological system of any Chinese dialect is best described in terms of syllable structure which is essentially morpheme structure as well rather than in terms of individual segments. The following formula summarizes the structure of the Mandarin Chinese syllable:

(C) (G) V (N or G) + Tone

C = consonant

G = glide (nonsyllabic vowel)

V = full vowel

N = nasal consonant

Tone is an obligatory component of every syllable although tonal distinctions are neutralized in unstressed syllables under special conditions which are difficult to formulate. Note that only tone and a full vowel must be present in every syllable. Other elements may or may not be present. Also, not all combinations of consonants, glides, and vowels are permitted. For example, velar consonants, dental affricates and fricatives, and retroflex affricates and fricatives are not found before high front vowels or palatal glides.

Table 4.1 INVENTORY OF MANDARIN SYLLABLE-INITIAL CONSONANTS

Labials	p (b)	pʰ (p)	m (m)	f (f)	
Dental stops, nasal, liquid	t (d)	tʰ (t)	n (n)		l (l)
Dental affricates and fricatives	ts (z)	tsʰ (c)		s (s)	
Retroflex affricates and fricatives	tʂ (zh)	tʂʰ (ch)		ʂ (sh)	ʐ (r)
Laminoalveolar affricates and fricatives	tɕ (j)	tɕʰ (q)		ɕ (x)	
Velars	k (g)	kʰ (k)		x (h)	

Forms in parentheses are the equivalents in the official *pīnyīn* romanization currently being used in the PRC.

Laminoalveolar affricates and fricatives are articulated by the tongue blade making a constriction against the alveolar ridge, with the rest of the tongue in a raised position. This series may be viewed as a palatalized counterpart of the retroflex series of consonants which are articulated with the tongue tip only (just behind the alveolar ridge).

Inventory of Tones

Peking Mandarin has only four contrastive tones. In general, Mandarin dialects have fewer tones than non-Mandarin dialects spoken in South China.

1.	˥	55	(in rom. ˉ over the vowel)
2.	˧˥	35	(in rom. ´ over the vowel)
3.	˨˩˧	213	(in rom. ˇ over the vowel)
4.	˥˩	41	(in rom. ` over the vowel)

These tone symbols were devised in 1930 by the famous Chinese linguist Y. R. Chao. The relative pitch is represented in terms of an imaginary five-point scale, five being the highest point and one being the lowest. The tones can then be represented either graphically, as in the first column, or numerically, as in the second column. Thus, the first Mandarin tone is a level, relatively high tone. The second is a high rising tone; it starts somewhat below the register of the first tone and rises in pitch to the level of the first tone. The third is a relatively low falling-rising tone, and the fourth is a high falling tone. The first and the third tones are also relatively longer in duration than the other two.

The so-called neutral tone which appears in some weakly stressed syllables (usually on the second syllable of a compound word or disyllabic morpheme) is realized in different ways depending on the tone of the preceding syllable. In general it is realized as a short, level (or nearly so) tone which is mid to low in register. (In romanization it is left unmarked.)

A tone three syllable preceding another tone three syllable changes its tone to tone two (45), but this change (called *tone sandhi*) is constrained by syntactic considerations such as whether the two syllables in question are immediate constituents. Tone three before a syllable with tone other than three loses its rising portion (i.e., it becomes 21).

Note that high vowels [i], [y] (a high front rounded vowel), and [u] when not preceded by a consonant are pronounced with an initial homorganic glide and are written in pīnyīn as *yi, yu,* and *wu* respectively. In general, if there is no syllable-initial consonant, the glides [i̯], [y̯], and [u̯] are written as *y, y,* and *w* respectively. The high front rounded vowel [y] is written as *ü* after *n* and *l;* otherwise, it is written as *u* (because it may occur only after laminoalveolar consonants and the palatal glide after which [u] is not found. (In other words, [y] and [u] are in contrastive distribution only after [n] and [l].) For example:

> *wu* = [u̯u], but *yu* = [y̯y]
> *cu* = [tsʰu], but *qu* = [tɕʰy]
> *nu* = [nu], but *nü* = [ny]

Table 4.2 **INVENTORY OF PERMITTED COMBINATIONS OF VOWELS, GLIDES, AND FINAL NASALS—i.e., RHYMES**

i (i)	u (u)	y (u, ü)	a (a)	ɤ (e)	o (o)
in (in)	u̯ən (un)	yn (un)	an (an)	ən (en)	
i̯en (ian)	u̯an (uan)	y̯en (uan)			
i̯aŋ (iang)	u̯aŋ (uang)				
iŋ (ing)	uŋ (ong)	yŋ (iong)	aŋ (ang)	əŋ (eng)	
i̯e (ie)	u̯o (uo)	y̯e (ue, üe)			
i̯ou̯ (iu)					ou̯
i̯au̯ (iao)			au̯ (ao)		
i̯a (ia)	u̯a (ua)				
	u̯ai̯ (uai)		ai̯ (ai)		
	u̯ei̯ (ui)			ei̯ (ei)	
				ɚ (er)	

Pīnyīn romanization equivalents are given in parentheses.

Sound Distribution

Velars, retroflex consonants, and dental affricates and fricatives do not occur before [i], [i̯], [y], and [y̯]. After retroflex consonants /i/ is realized as [ʅ] (a retroflex high central vowel), whereas after dental fricatives and affricates it is realized as [ɿ] (an apical high central vowel).

Note that only [-n] and [-ŋ] appear as syllable-final consonants. (Historically, final [-m] merged with [-n], and non-nasal final consonants were dropped. The latter are still reflected as a glottal stop in some Mandarin dialects.)

Note also that two homorganic glides cannot appear in the same syllable: *i̯ai̯ and *u̯au̯ are not possible combinations in Modern Standard Mandarin.

Rhotacized Finals

In addition to the syllable-finals given in the preceding list there are also finals that are a blend of one of the above finals with the suffix -*ér*. This suffix is usually but not exclusively added to nouns, and its morphological function is not always clear. In any case, it always loses its own independent syllabic status and merges with the preceding syllable, causing any final nasal to drop, but the trace of the nasal consonant [ŋ] remains as nasalization on the vowel. (For example, *míng* + *ér* gives [mĩɚ̃] = 'tomorrow'.)

The resultant endings have as final element a retroflex or r-colored vowel (very similar to the vowel in American pronunciation of 'err').

C. MORPHOLOGY AND SYNTAX

Chinese words are best classified into different parts of speech on the basis of their function in sentences rather than on the basis of any formal or morphological properties, since one and the same morpheme may often function as a different part of speech in different contexts without any derivational affixes being added. (This aspect is not nearly as strong in modern Mandarin as it was in Classical Chinese.) For example, *xià* may function either as a verb or as a kind of locative postposition:

> (a) Wǒ *xià* shān.
>
>> I *down* mountain
>>
>> 'I descend the mountain.'
>
> (b) Shān *xià* yǒu rén.
>
>> mountain *down* exist person(s)
>>
>> 'There are people below the mountain.'

Pronouns

There are no gender distinctions of any kind in Chinese pronouns, but because of the influence of European languages, in modern times the third person pronoun is written with different logographs depending on whether it means 'he', 'she', or 'it'. (In other words, the gender distinction is made only graphically.) The third person pronoun is very rarely used to refer to inanimate things.

There is also a polite form of the second person pronoun, *nín,* which can be used both in the singular and plural.

Though this distinction is not very commonly observed in the standard language, Peking Mandarin itself has two different forms for the first person depending on whether or not the person addressed is being included:

> wǒmen = 'exclusive we' (excludes person being spoken to)
>
> zámen = 'inclusive we' (includes person being spoken to)

Examples:

> (a) *Wǒmen* qù kàn diànyǐng.
>
>> we go look movie (lit., 'electric shadow')
>>
>> 'We are going to the movies (but not you).'
>
> (b) *Zámen* qù kàn diànyǐng.
>
>> we go look movies
>>
>> 'We (including you) are going to the movies.'

Table 4.3 MANDARIN CHINESE PERSONAL PRONOUNS

PERSON	SINGULAR	PLURAL
1st pers.	wǒ	wǒmen
2d pers.	nǐ	nǐmen
3d pers.	tā	tāmen

Nominals and Nominal Constructions

Although Mandarin pronouns regularly show distinction between singular and plural number, nouns do not show such a distinction. Thus, *rén* can mean either 'person' or 'persons' depending on the context. When necessary to indicate plurality unambiguously, modifiers such as 'many' are used. In addition, the plural suffix *-men* which occurs in the pronouns may be added to nouns denoting persons.

Noun Classifiers

There is no gender system as in Russian, French, and many other European languages, but instead nouns can be grouped into classes depending on what *noun classifier* (somewhat similar to such English terms as 'three head of cattle') is used with them when they are counted or when they are modified by a demonstrative. Note that there are several classifiers which are determined by the general shape of the object being counted. The following examples illustrate only a few (out of several dozen) of these noun classifiers:

yī *zhī* qiānbǐ

one/ classifier for long, cylindrical objects/ pencil (lit., 'lead writing instrument')

'one pencil'

sān *wèi* kèrén

three/ polite classifier for human beings/ guest

'three (honored) guests'

nèi *ge* rén

that/ ordinary classifier for persons/ person

'that person'

Note that *ge* can be used as a general classifier; that is, it can be used with any noun, especially those for which there is no special classifier.

Noun Compounding

Noun compounding is a very productive process in Chinese. Much of the technical (as well as nontechnical) vocabulary consists of various compounds using native morphemes instead of being borrowed from another language. (In English, for example, most of the technical vocabulary consists of combinations of Greek and Latin morphemes whose meaning is generally not known to English speakers who have not studied these two languages.) Therefore, Chinese technical terms are often very "transparent" morphologically, and one can guess at their meaning much more successfully than would be the case with English technical words whose meaning one does not know to begin with:

> fēijī = lit. 'fly engine' = 'airplane'
>
> biànyāqì = lit. 'change (electr.) pressure implement' = 'transformer'
>
> fādiànjī = lit. 'emit electricity engine' = 'electric generator'

Verbs and Adjectives

Chinese verbs are not inflected for person and number. Adjectives, which in Chinese are a subclass of verbs, do not show any agreement with the nouns they modify. Both verbs and adjectives can be followed by the grammatical particle *le*, which is a marker of the perfective aspect and also functions as an indicator of a new state or situation. (In other words, one must recognize two different morphemes that happen to sound the same but have different functions.)

> Tiān hēi le.
>
> sky/ black/ new situation.
>
> 'The sky darkened.' (I.e. 'the sky has become dark.')

> Wǒ chī fàn le.
>
> I/ eat/ cooked rice/ perfect.
>
> 'I ate rice' or 'I finished eating.'

> Wǒ bú qù le.
>
> I/ not/ go/ new situation
>
> 'I am no longer going.' (I was going to go, but changed my mind = new situation.)

Tense is marked not by inflection but by time words or by some other lexical indicators of time. A perfective marker usually implies that an action took place in the past, and future action is often implied by such verbs as *yào* 'want' or *xiǎng* 'think':

> *Míngtiǎn* wǒ qù kàn diànyǐng.
>
> *tomorrow*/ I/ go/ look/ movie
>
> 'I shall go to see a movie tomorrow.'

> Wǒ yào qù kàn diànyǐng.
>
> I/ want/ go/ look/ movie
>
> 'I want to go to see a movie.'

The verb 'to be' has several functions in English all of which are expressed by different verbs in Chinese. (Note that this state of affairs is not all that unusual in the world's languages even though it is quite different from English.)

'I *am* a student.' (BE used as a copula verb.)

Wǒ *shì* xuéshēng.

I be student

'I *am* at home.' (BE used as a locative verb.)

Wǒ *zài* jiā

I/ be (at)/ home

'There *is* a person at the door.' (BE used as an existential verb.)

Yǒu rén zài ménkǒur.

exist/ person/ be at/ door

The existential verb *yǒu* is used in possessive constructions such as the following:

Wǒ *yǒu* liǎng běn shū.

I/ *exist*/ two/ classifier for books/ book

'I have two books.'

The preceding example shows that at least in some cases what one might regard to be the subject of the Chinese sentence is in reality the *topic* of the sentence. Thus, the sentence may be translated more literally as 'As for me, there exists a book'. In other words, 'the book' may be regarded as the subject of the verb 'to exist' since it is the book which 'does' the existing, whereas 'I' is merely the topic about which the rest of the sentence supplies some information.

Resultative Verb Compounds

Some verbs can be combined directly with other verbs, such that the first verb indicates the main action while the second verb indicates the result of that action:

Tā *xià sǐ* le wǒ.

he/ *frighten*/ *die*/ perfect./ I

'He/she frightened me to death.'

Wǒ kàn jian tā.

I/ look/ perceive/ he

'I see him.'

Negation

There are two negatives which precede the words they negate: *méi* is used to negate the existential verb *yǒu* and verbs in the perfective aspect, whereas *bù* is used with other verbs and adjectives:[3]

Wǒ *bú* qù.

I *not* go

'I am not going.'

Wǒ *méi* (yǒu) qù.

I/ not/ (exist)/ go

'I haven't gone.'

The perfective particle *le* is obligatorily deleted when the verb is negated by *méi*. Optionally, *yǒu* 'exist' may be inserted between the negative *méi* and the main verb in the perfective. In addition, it should be noted that *bù* is also used to negate verbs which are followed by *le* that marks new situation rather than perfective aspect.

Word Order and Case Relations

The basic word order is SVO as in English; modifiers, including relative clauses, generally precede the words they modify. Since direct objects are not distinguished from subjects or topics by case markers, word order is important and relatively fixed:

Wǒ mà Zhāng Sān.

I/ scold/ Zhang San (proper noun)

'I scold Zhang San.'

Zhāng Sān mà wǒ.

Zhang San/ scold/ I

'Zhang San scolds me.'

Case relations, such as locative and instrument, are usually signaled by means of preposed verbs instead of case suffixes (as in Russian) or by prepositions (as in English):

> Wǒ *zuò* fēijǐ *dào* Běijīng qù.
>
> I/ *sit*/ plane/ *arrive*/ Peking/ go
>
> 'I am going to Peking by plane.'

> Wǒ *yòng* yàoshi kāi mén.
>
> I/ *use*/ key/ open/ door
>
> 'I open the door *with* a key.'

> Wǒ *bǎ* nèi-běn shū sòng *gěi* tā le.
>
> I/ *take*/ that + classifier for books/ send/ *give*/ him/ perf.
>
> 'I sent that book *to* him.'

Note that in the preceding sentence *bǎ* acts as an indicator of the direct object. This construction is used primarily when the direct object is a definite NP. Elsewhere, the direct object is usually unmarked for case.

Passive Construction

The passive construction is also signaled by a special verb and has *adversative* value, that is, it implies that the patient of the action expressed in the main verb was in some way unpleasantly affected by it; the agent of the passive construction is usually marked by the verb *bèi*, 'to suffer':

> Wǒ *bèi* tāmén kànjian le.
>
> I *suffer* they see perfect.
>
> 'I was seen by them (and that was somehow unpleasant for me).'

Note that even intransitive verbs can be passivized in Chinese:

> Wǒ *bèi* tā pǎo le.
>
> I *suffer* he run perfect.
>
> 'He ran away on me.'

The adversative passive, like the noun classifiers discussed earlier, seems to be an areal feature found in a continuum that stretches from Southeast Asia through China and on to Japan and Korea.

Interrogative Sentences

Interrogative sentences that contain question words (i.e., "content questions") do not add anything or change their word order. To change statements into questions ("yes-or-no questions") one may either add an interrogative particle such as *ma* at the end of the sentence or use the Verb + negative + Verb construction:

> Shéi qù?
>
> who/ go
>
> 'Who is going?' (Content question)

> Nǐ qù ma?
>
> you/ go/ interrog. particle (plus interrog. intonation on the particle *ma*)
>
> 'Are you going?' (Yes-or-no question)

> Nǐ qù bú qù?
>
> you go not go
>
> 'Are you going?' (Yes-or-no question)

Relative and Other Subordinate Clauses

Relative clauses precede the head nominals and are connected to them by the subordinating particle *de* (which functions also as a possessive marker):

> Zuótiān lái *de* rén shì wǒ *de* péngyǒu.
>
> yesterday/ come/ *de* (= relative clause marker)/ person/ be/ I/ *de* (= possessive marker)/ friend
>
> 'The person who came yesterday is my friend.'

Conditional clauses are usually introduced by *yàoshi* 'if', but this subordinate conjunction can be optionally omitted:

> (Yàoshi) nǐ bú yào qù, wǒ yě bú yào qù.
>
> (if)/ you/ not/ want/ go/, I/ also/ not/ want/ go
>
> 'If you do not want to go, I don't want to go.'

Some temporal subordinate clauses are in fact relative clauses with *shíhóu* 'time' as the head noun:

Tā lái de shíhóu, nǐ hái méi dào Shànghǎi.

He/ come/ subordinating particle/ time/ you/ still/ not/ arrive/ Shanghai

'When he came you still had not arrived to Shanghai.'

Other temporal clauses consist of a subordinate clause unmarked by *de* but followed by a time adverbial which is used as a kind of postposition:

Tā lái le yǐhòu, wǒmen qù kàn diànyǐng.

He/ come/ perf./ afterward/, we/ go/ look/ movies

'After he comes we shall go to see a movie.'

D. SAMPLE TEXTS

The first sample selection is a Táng dynasty poem written by Zhāng Jì, who lived in the eighth century A.D. It is included here not only to illustrate the terse beauty of Chinese poetry, but also for a typological reason: Chinese classical poetry is the best example of isolating/analytical language structure, since almost all case relations and other grammatical relations between words are signaled primarily by word order, not by affixation or even grammatical particles. (Grammatical particles are avoided in Chinese classical poetry wherever possible.)

Of course, one must keep in mind that the language of poetry may differ significantly from the spoken colloquial or even literary prose. In Chinese, because terseness is highly esteemed, the presence of grammatical particles in a poem would be considered 'unnecessary clutter'.)

The second selection is a short prose story[4] written in modern literary Mandarin. It is actually a modern retelling of a story from one of the Chinese classics. (Superscripted numbers in the following sections refer to the notes which follow each text.)

Poem

Chinese text

楓	橋	夜	泊			
月	落	烏	啼	霜	滿	天
江	風	漁	火	對	愁	眠
姑	蘇	城	外	寒	山	寺
夜	半	鐘	聲	到	客	船

Literal Morpheme-by-Morpheme Translation

FĒNG	QIÁO	YÈ	BÓ			
MAPLE	BRIDGE	NIGHT	ANCHOR (VB)			

Yuè	*luò*	*wū*	*tí*	*shuāng*	*mǎn*	*tiān*[1]
moon	fall	raven	cry	frost	fill	sky
jiāng	*fēng*	*yú*	*huǒ*	*duì*	*chóu*	*mián*[1]
river	maple	fish (vb)	fire	face	sad(ness)	sleep
Gū	*sū*[2]	*chéng*	*wài*	*Hán*	*Shān*	*sì*
Soochow		city	outside	Cold	Mountain	temple[3]
yè	*bàn*	*zhōng*	*shēng*	*dào*	*kè*	*chuān*[1]
night	half	bell	sound	reach	guest	boat

NOTES

1. Each line of the poem is seven syllables long. The rhyme scheme is *aaba,* but in modern pronunciation *chuān* (= [ʈʂʰuan]) 'boat' does not rhyme very well with *tiān* (= [tʰien]) 'sky' and *mián* (= [mi̯en]) 'sleep'. There are also somewhat complicated rules governing the sequences of tones in each line.

2. Gūsū is an ancient name for present-day Sūzhōu, a town not too far from Shànghǎi, famous for its beautiful women and gardens.

3. The Cold Mountain Temple and the Maple Bridge right next to it are still in existence and have become quite an attraction, especially for Japanese tourists who come to visit this famous temple, hear its bell, and buy hanging scrolls on which this poem, well known in Japan, is beautifully inscribed by local calligraphers. On New Year's Eve, thousands of Japanese tourists jam the street near the temple to hear the midnight bell as it tolls in the New Year. (Japanese study Chinese classical poetry just as in the old days students in the West used to study Latin poetry.)

Idiomatic Translation[5]

ANCHORING AT NIGHT AT THE MAPLE BRIDGE

> The moon goes down, a raven cries, frost fills the sky.
> River maples, fishing fires, facing sadness [I] lie.
> Outside Soochow city
> The sound of Cold Mountain Temple's midnight bell
> Reaches the visiting boats.

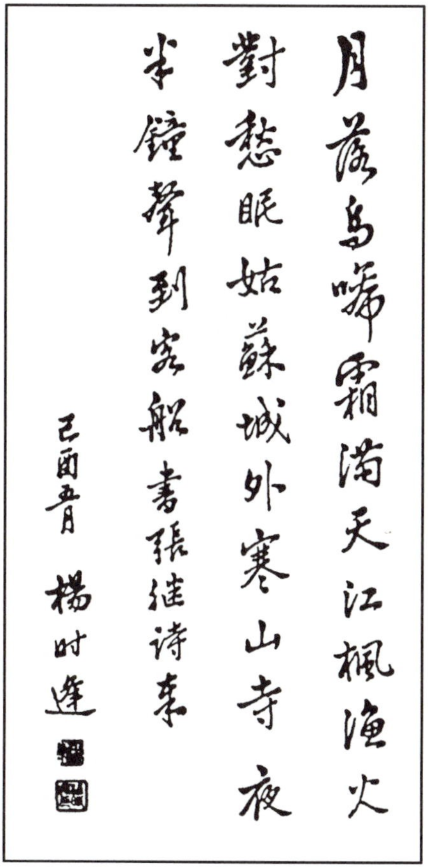

Figure 4.1   *"Anchoring at Night at the Maple Bridge," written in semicursive style.*

Modern Written Style

Chinese Character Text

(1) 有一個楚國人過江的時候，他的劍從船上掉到水裡去。
(2) 他馬上在船邊上刻了一個印子，說：我　的劍是從這兒
掉下去的。　(3) 船停了，他就按照他刻了印的地方下水
去找。　(4) 船已經動了，可是劍沒動。　(5) 找劍這
樣找法不是糊塗嗎？

Figure 4.2 *In 1981 the People's Republic of China issued a set of five stamps depicting the story of the foolish man from Chu who lost his sword. The first stamp in the set includes the text of this story in the original Classical Chinese.*

Romanized Text and Literal Morpheme-by-Morpheme Translation

(1) *Yǒu yí ge Chǔ guó rén guò jiāng de shíhóu*

exist/ one/ classifier for persons/ Chu[1]/ country/ person/ cross, pass/ river[2]/ subordinating particle/ time[3]

tā de jiàn cóng chuān shàng diào dào shuǐ lǐ qù.

he/ subord. partic./ sword/ from/ boat/ top = 'on'/ fall/ reach, arrive/ water/ inside/ go[4].

(2) *Tā mǎshàng zài chuān biān shàng kē le yí ge yìnzi shuō:*

he/ immediately[5]/ (be) at/ boat/ side/ top = 'on'/ carve/ perf./ one/ general classifier/ mark/ say

'Wǒ de jiàn shì cóng zhèr diào xià qù de'.

I/ subord. partic./ sword/ be/ from/ here/ fall/ down/ go[4]/ subord. partic.[6]

(3) *Chuān tíng le, tā jiòu ànzhào tā kē le yìnzi de dìfāng xià shuǐ qù zhǎo.*

boat/ stop/ perf./ he/ then[7]/ according to/ he/ carve/ perf./ mark/ subord. partic./ place/ down, descend/ water/ go/ seek, look for

(4) *Chuān yǐjīng dòng le, kěshi jiàn méi dòng.*

boat/ already/ move/ perf./ but/ sword/ not[8]/ move

(5) *Zhǎo jiàn xiàng zhè yàng zhǎo fǎ bú shì hútú ma?*

seek/ sword/ like, be similar/ this/ kind/ seek/ way, method/ negative/ be/ silly, nonsense/ interrog. particle

---

NOTES

1. Chu is the name of an Ancient Chinese kingdom located in Central China.

2. In Classical Chinese literature *jiāng* refers specifically to the Yangtze River. In modern Chinese it may refer to any river. This word is believed by some to be a very old loanword from some Austroasiatic language.

3. Cf. temporal subordinate clauses in the sketch.

4. 'Go' here has the function of signaling movement away from the speaker, in much the same way as the German verb prefix *hin-*.

5. Lit., 'horse top' = 'on a horse'.

6. This 'then' is a sequential action marker.

7. The head noun here is "understood" to be the same as the topic "sword". Therefore, literally the sentence is 'My sword is (one) which fell down from here'. This type of construction is often used to express past actions.

8. Remember that *méi* negates verbs which have perfective aspect and that the perfective marker *le* itself is obligatorily deleted if the verb is negated.

Idiomatic Translation

While a certain man from the country of Chu was crossing a river, his sword fell into the water from the boat. He immediately carved a mark at the side of the boat, saying, "My sword fell down from here."

After the boat stopped [at the other side of the river], he went down into the water to seek his sword according to the position of the mark which he had carved. However, the boat had already moved [from the place where he had lost his sword], whereas the sword had not. Isn't this way of looking for the sword a rather silly one?

SKETCH OF CLASSICAL TIBETAN

A. GENETIC RELATIONSHIP AND GENERAL BACKGROUND

Tibetan is a member of the *Himalayish* subbranch of the Tibeto-Burman branch of Sino-Tibetan. It is spoken by an estimated total of 4,035,000 speakers in a variety of dialects, the chief of which is the dialect of Lhasa, the capital. The bulk of the speakers is concentrated in the Tibet Autonomous Region of China; the rest are scattered in the various Chinese provinces adjoining Tibet, especially Sìchuān and Qīnghǎi (for a total of 3,870,065 speakers in China), as well as in Nepal (60,000), Sikkim, Bhutan (about 8,500), and various parts of India (100,000).

The earliest written records in Tibetan date from the seventh century A.D. It was about that time that Buddhism was imported into Tibet from India along with the writing system. For many centuries thereafter the culture and language of Tibet were under a strong influence of Indic culture. Although relatively few words from Sanskrit and other Indic languages were borrowed into Tibetan directly there are many *loan translations* (*calques*) from these languages, especially Sanskrit.

An example of a typical loan translation is the following epithet of Buddha that was translated almost morpheme-by-morpheme into Tibetan:

> Sanskrit: *Tathāgata* = thus + go + past participle + masculine nom. sing. = 'one who has gone thus'
>
> Tibetan: *de.* + *bzhin.* + *gshegs.* + *pa.* = that + like + went + nominalizer

(The period in romanized Tibetan represents the syllable boundary symbol, which is an obligatory element of Tibetan orthography.)

In turn, Tibetan has strongly influenced Mongolian ever since Mongols embraced Tibetan Buddhism as their religion.

Currently the Tibetan language in areas under Chinese control is undergoing rapid changes. Lhasa dialect has been designated as the standard language of the Tibetan national minority and is taught in the schools of all regions of Tibet. Thousands of new terms are being introduced into the language in connection with the importation of new political and scientific concepts from China proper. Some of these loanwords are direct loans from standard Chinese (Mandarin), but the majority of them are also loan translations from that language. (The tradition of making loan translations rather than direct loans from other languages was rather firmly set at the time when the first Buddhist texts were translated into Tibetan from Sanskrit.)

There is an extensive literature which consists mostly of Buddhist texts and commentaries. Because some of the Buddhist texts were preserved only in their Tibetan translation and because Tibetan Buddhism (Lamaism, Tantric Buddhism) has developed in a unique fashion, Tibetan language is extensively studied by buddhologists. Purely secular literature has been almost nonexistent until recently except for some historical chronicles, folk tales, and poetry.

Although there are many dialects of Tibetan, some of which are probably not mutually intelligible, the written language is fairly uniform throughout Tibet. This is because the written language does not reflect any modern dialect but is essentially a somewhat modified version of the classical language of the seventh century A.D. The modification involves infusion of more modern vocabulary and a somewhat confused attempt to reflect the verb morphology of modern Lhasa Tibetan. This amalgam of ancient and modern features is called Modern Written Tibetan. In this sketch only the more conservative Classical Tibetan rather than Modern Written Tibetan or the colloquial dialect of Lhasa will be described.

In spite of the very large divergences between the written language and modern vernaculars which impede universal literacy in Tibet, there are no plans for major reforms of the written language in the near future. Chinese linguists consider that no reforms are possible until the dialect of Lhasa is more widely spoken and understood, since the written language of the future will have to be based on this dialect. To switch to Lhasa colloquial as the written language now would mean that large numbers of Tibetans would be unable to understand this new written language, and to allow the number of different written languages based on different colloquial standards would hinder communication among different regions. (The dialects of Central Tibet, including that of Lhasa, have undergone many more radical sound changes, especially involving consonants, than the dialects in the peripheral regions.)

According to Rerix (1961: 19–25) modern Tibetan dialects may be grouped into following branches.

a. Central Tibetan Group

This includes the *Ü* (*Dbus.*) and the *Tsang* (*Gtsang.*) subgroups. The former includes the dialect of Lhasa, the capital, and the latter includes the dialect of Shigatse. The dialect of Lhasa and dialects closely related to it have undergone many phonological mergers and in general are some of the most innovating dialects of Tibetan. The dialect of Shigatse is somewhat more conservative and is closer to the written language.

For example, the written Tibetan form *dbus.* is pronounced [y:] (a long rounded high front vowel) in Modern Lhasa Tibetan. The initial consonant cluster *db-* has been deleted, the vowel has been fronted because of the *-s* final and then has been lengthened to compensate for the dropping of the *-s* itself. In addition, the final *-s* also caused a falling tone to develop in this syllable, and the voicing of the consonants in the original initial consonant cluster determined the register of the tone: low. Thus the resultant tone in this word is a low falling tone (↘).

b. South Tibetan Dialects

This includes the *Lho.* and *Gro.mo.* valley dialects located in southern Tibet as well as the dialects of Sikkim and Bhutan. In Bhutan, *Dzongkha* or *Lhoka* speakers number from 5,100 to 8,500. The characteristic feature of these dialects is the telescoping of disyllabic lexical items into monosyllables:

> *sde.pa.* 'regional official' is pronounced [dep] in these dialects.

According to official data, there are up to nine different dialects in Bhutan, some of which may be called different languages. The linguistic boundary is located along the Dpal.le.la. Pass: to the west and northwest of it the Bhutanese population speaks Tibetan dialects which are close to those spoken in Gro.mo valley, whereas to the east, the population speaks Assamese (Indo-Aryan) and in Mon.yul. a dialect which seems to belong to an independent, little-known southeastern group of Tibetan dialects. In northern Bhutan, along the Tibetan border, the nomadic population speaks a special dialect called *'Brog.skad.* or 'nomad dialect'. (This term seems to be used elsewhere to refer to other dialects of Tibetan and even to non-Tibetan languages that have been adopted by the Tibetan population. For example, one dialect of Shina (a Dardic language spoken in Baltistan, Pakistan, is called *Brokskat* or *Brokpa*).

c. Southwestern Dialects

This includes *Shar.pa.* (*Sherpa*), spoken in northeastern Nepal (14,126 sp.) and in Sikkim and India (10,170), *Kagate* (800 to 1,000 sp., also in Nepal), *Garhwali* (not to be confused with the Indo-Aryan language of the same name), and *N'amkat.* Tibetan dialects spoken in Nepal have been strongly influenced by the surrounding languages.

d. Western Dialects

This group consists of two subgroups. The first is that of Mnga'.ris. or *Stod.skad.* (Upper Tibet speech), which covers a vast but sparsely populated territory. There is little dialect differentiation here, and the second group consists of transitional dialects from central ones to those of the extreme west of Tibet. This latter group includes the *Spiti* dialect.

The second group consists of dialects spoken at the extreme western end of the plateau: *Balti* (*Sbalti*), which has a total of 300,000 speakers, mainly in Pakistan, with 40,136 in India (Kashmir); *Ladakhi* with 56,737 speakers in Indian-controlled Kashmir; *Zankar* (*Zangskari*) with 5,000 speakers in Kashmir and possibly in Tibet; *Purig* with 135,000 to 148,000 speakers in Northern Kashmir, and *Garzha*. Most of the speakers of these dialects are Muslims and some even use the Arabic alphabet to write their language. The Balti dialect is considered to have preserved some very archaic features.

e. Northern Dialects

These dialects are spoken by a number of nomadic groups that inhabit the northern grasslands such as the following: *Nub.hor., Rgya.sde., Nang.chen., Byang.pa.,* and *'Dam.sog.*

The northern dialects, as in general all nomadic dialects, are characterized by the conservative aspects of their sound systems as well as of their lexicons.

f. Northeastern Dialects

This group includes the *Amdo,* the *Banak,* and *Golok* (about 90,000 sp. in the Chinese province of Qīnghǎi) dialects, each of which has its own variant forms. These dialects are especially important for Tibetan comparative linguistics as they have preserved quite archaic phonological and lexical features.

g. Eastern Dialects

This includes all the *Kham* (*Khams.*) dialects (11,400 tot. sp.), the chief of which are those of Chamdo (Chab.mdo.), Derge (Sde.dge.), Hor, and so on.

h. Extreme Eastern Dialects

These are dialects spoken in the Chinese province of Sìchuān and are called *Qiǎng* by the Chinese. The most interesting dialect of this group is that of *Gyarung,* which may turn out not to be really a dialect of Tibetan but an independent Tibeto-Burman language. (Note that most Sino-Tibetanists would now agree with Rerix about this point and would not classify *Qiǎng* as being a dialect of Tibetan.)

i. Southeastern Dialects

To this group belong the dialects of Mon.yul., Kong.po., and others, in Bhutan and along the Tibetan-Assamese border. These are the least studied dialects of Tibetan but are known to have very conservative lexicon.

In Tibet one can easily observe the following correlation: those dialects which have preserved many consonant clusters and consonantal contrasts found in Classical Tibetan (the peripheral dialects) tend to remain nontonal languages, whereas dialects like those in the central regions, which have lost almost all consonant clusters and have merged many consonantal contrasts, have developed lexical tones.

B. ORTHOGRAPHY, PHONETICS, AND PHONOLOGY

Tibetan script is an adaptation of an Indic script used in northern India in the seventh century A.D. and still bears a fairly close resemblance to such Indic scripts as the *Devanagari* which is used for Hindi and other languages of north India and Nepal. In turn, Tibetan script was the basis for the so-called *'Phags-pa* script or alphabet introduced to China during the Mongol domination (A.D. 1280–1368). It was designed by a Tibetan lama to serve as a "universal" alphabet for all the different languages of the Mongol empire spoken at the time (including Chinese), but after the expulsion of the Mongols from China this alphabet also fell into disuse. Before its total demise, however, it may have influenced the creation of the native Korean alphabet, but this is disputed by some scholars.

The Tibetan writing system is essentially alphabetic, but, like Indic scripts and other scripts based on them, it possesses some features of a syllabary. (In Chapter 2 this type of writing was classified as a neosyllabary, a type which is intermediate between a true syllabary and an alphabet.) The basic graphemes represent consonants followed by the inherent vowel *a*. The rest of the vowels are indicated by a system of diacritic symbols which 'cancel' the inherent vowel *a*. Thus, when vowel diacritics are added, the system may be viewed as being alphabetic; when there are no overt symbols for vowels, however, the graphemes represent syllables and not just the consonants, and in this respect the system is syllabic.

In Table 4.4 the Tibetan letters are given along with their Wylie romanization (cf. Wylie, 1959) and the phonetic transcription of the consonant component of the symbol. They are arranged in the traditional Tibetan alphabetic sequence used in Tibetan dictionaries. Note that this order, reflecting Indic linguistic tradition, shows superior understanding of articulatory phonetics in that velars are neatly followed by alveopalatals (laminoalveolars), which in turn are followed by dentals and then bilabials. In other words, the consonants are arranged according to their place of articulation from the back part of the oral cavity to the front. Within each series they are arranged according to the manner of their articulation: voiceless unaspirated, voiceless aspirated, voiced unaspirated, and voiced nasal stops.

There are several variants of the Tibetan alphabet, the two most widely used being *dbu.can.* and *dbu.med.* The former is the more formal printed style, which includes the top horizontal element of those characters that have such an element, whereas the latter script is more cursive in style and abbreviated, with the horizontal stroke element on the top missing. Here only the *dbu.can.* variant will be illustrated.

As already pointed out, vowel *a* is inherent in every letter and is therefore unmarked in Tibetan script. When vowel symbols are added to the base char-

Table 4.4 TIBETAN ALPHABET

Tib. alph	ཀ	ཁ	ག	ང
Wylie rom.	*ka.*	*kha.*	*ga.*	*nga.*
IPA	[ka]	[kʰa]	[ga]	[ŋa]
Tib. alph.	ཅ	ཆ	ཇ	ཉ
Wylie rom.	*ca.*	*cha.*	*ja.*	*nya.*
IPA	[tça]	[tçʰa]	[dʐa]	[ɳa]
Tib. alph.	ཏ	ཐ	ད	ན
Wylie rom.	*ta.*	*tha.*	*da.*	*na.*
IPA	[ta]	[tʰa]	[da]	[na]
Tib. alph.	པ	ཕ	བ	མ
Wylie rom.	*pa.*	*pha.*	*ba.*	*ma.*
IPA	[pa]	[pʰa]	[ba]	[ma]
Tib. alph.	ཙ	ཚ	ཛ	
Wylie rom.	*tsa.*	*tsha.*	*dza.*	
IPA	[tsa]	[tsʰa]	[dza]	
Tib. alph	ཝ	ཞ	ཟ	འ
Wylie rom.	*wa.*	*zha.*	*za.*	*'a.*
IPA	[wa]	[ʐa]	[za]	[ɦa]*
Tib. alph	ཡ	ར	ལ	ཤ
Wylie rom.	*ya.*	*ra.*	*la.*	*sha.*
IPA	[ja]	[ra]	[la]	[ça]*
Tib. alph	ས	ཧ	ཨ	
Wylie rom.	*sa.*	*ha.*	*a.*†	
IPA	[sa]	[ha]	[ʔa]	

*The exact sound value of this Tibetan letter is not known. Modern dialects have various sound values for this letter, and therefore comparative evidence is somewhat contradictory. It may actually have had various functions, sometimes representing a particular sound, sometimes being merely an orthographic device, and sometimes a manner of articulation marker. In modern Lhasa Tibetan this letter is in some lexical items pronounced as a nasal consonant homorganic with the following consonant. Most of the time, however, it is not pronounced at all.

†Wylie romanization does not mark the presence of the glottal stop.

acter, this inherent *a* is suppressed. The following are the various combinations of *m* + a vowel:

   ma. = མ (vowel not marked)

   mi. = མི   *mu.* = མུ

   me. = མེ   *mo.* = མོ

The raised dot marks the syllable boundary and is very important for determining when the inherent vowel *a* is present or absent as well as where one syllable ends and the other begins. For example, in the following combinations the presence of the syllable boundary symbol indicates whether we are dealing with a single syllable, in which case only one inherent *a* surfaces, or with two syllables, in which case both *a*'s have to appear:

ལས་ = *las.*　　but　ལ་ས་ = *la.sa.*

One way that the position of *a* in the syllable may be indicated is by means of ligatures, or subscript and superscript letters. No vowel can come between one of the latter and the letter to which they are attached:

གལ་ = *gal.*　　but　གླ = *gla.* (ག + subscript ལ)

In some cases, the symbol for ' is used as an orthographic device to signal the position of the vowel with respect to the consonants within the same syllable. For example, *bag.* and *bga.* are both possible syllables in Tibetan. Since there is no *b* superscript or *g* subscript, there is no way to indicate unambiguously whether the vowel *a* should come between *b* and *g* or after *g* in *bg.* Therefore, ' is written if *a* must come after *g*, and if it is not written, then it is assumed that the vowel comes between *b* and *g*:

བག་ = *bag.*　　but　བགའ་ = *bga.*

The proper romanization for *bga.* in Wylie's system is actually *bga'.* since Wylie transcribes the symbol འ by an apostrophe wherever it appears regardless of whether or not it happens to be merely an orthographic device. The same symbol is used to transcribe diphthongs:

ང་ = *nga.*　　but　ངའི་ = *nga'i.*

Superscripts and subscripts:

རྒ་ = *rga.*　(superscript ར over ག)

གྲ་ = *gra.*　(subscript ར under ག)

གྱ་ = *gya.*　(subscript ཡ under ག)

གྭ་ = *gwa.*　(subscript ཝ under ག)

Other letters do not change their basic form as either subscripts or superscripts. For example, the syllable *sgo.* is written like this: སྒོ་

It should be noted that the Tibetan alphabet has symbols for transcribing long vowels, retroflex consonants, voiced aspirates stops, and other elements of Sanskrit. For the sake of brevity, these are not listed in this sketch.

Finally, there is one more complication, and that involves two different ways of writing the sequence of *g* + *y*:

གྱ　　and　གཡ

In order to disambiguate between the two, Wylie romanization has *gy* for the former and *g'y* for the latter. (The difference in spelling most likely indicates that there was a morpheme boundary or even a reduced vowel between the consonant and the glide in the latter case. In Modern Lhasa Tibetan, the former combination is pronounced as a palatal stop, whereas the latter combina-

Table 4.5 TIBETAN CONSONANTS

BILABIALS	DENTALS	DENTALS	PALATO-ALVEOLARS	VELARS	GLOTTALS
p	t	ts	tɕ	k	ʔ
pʰ	tʰ	tsʰ	tɕʰ	kʰ	
b	d	dz	dʐ	g	
m	n		ɳ	ŋ	
		s	ɕ		h
		z	ʐ		ɦ
	ɬ				
	l				
			j	w	

tion is pronounced without any trace of the initial stop, i.e., with initial *y* glide only.)

In addition to the dot marking the syllable boundary, Tibetan orthography uses a number of punctuation marks, the chief of which is a vertical line whose function roughly corresponds to our comma or semicolon.

Phonetics and Phonology

Besides the consonant and vowel segments listed in the tables, Tibetan had another consonant segment, a voiceless lateral fricative [ɬ], which was written as a digraph, a combination of *l* + *h*. (There was no equivalent sound in the Indic languages and therefore no single letter for representing this Tibetan sound.)

The Classical Tibetan vowel system consisted basically of the following five vowels (listed in their Tibetan alphabetical order): *a, i, u, e,* and *o*.

There is no provision in the orthography for marking tones. It is believed that Classical Tibetan was not a tone language. Tones in some modern dialects are believed to have arisen as compensation for the loss of various consonantal contrasts.

The contrast between the voiceless aspirated and voiceless unaspirated series of consonants plays a very minor role since the two series of consonants are for the most part in complementary distribution: both series are found only in the syllable-initial position; the aspirated series can be preceded only by ' ([ɦ]), *m*- or zero, whereas the unaspirated series is usually preceded by some consonant other than ' or *m*-.

There are no underlying diphthongs; all the diphthongs are derivable from underlying sequences of monophthongs.

The syllable structure of Classical Tibetan is somewhat complex because it allows a rather large number of consonants to begin a syllable. For example, *brgy*- and *bsgr*- are possible syllable-initial clusters. The structure of the rest of the syllable is less complex: A syllable may end in a vowel, or a vowel followed by nasal, a voiced stop, a liquid, or *s*. Final voiced stops may be followed by *-s* to yield the following final consonant clusters: *-bs* and *-gs*. (There is a surface constraint against sequences of homorganic consonants in the syllable-final position. Thus, *-ds* is not a permissible syllable-final consonant cluster. A less general constraint operates in the syllable-initial position where *s* and the liquids may combine with homorganic consonants, but sequences of homorganic stops, or homorganic nasals are not allowed.)

There is some reason to believe that the original syllable structure was much simpler, probably something like the following:

(C) + (a glide or a liquid) + V + (C)

The more complex syllable structure is very likely the result of sound changes that first reduced and then deleted the vowels of the various prefixes and suffixes thus resulting in long sequences of syllable-initial consonants. This deletion was perhaps motivated by the placement of stress on the stem syllable.

c. MORPHOLOGY AND SYNTAX

By the time of the earliest inscriptions in Classical Tibetan much of the earlier affixal morphology had become fossilized and opaque. For example, it is possible to isolate a prefix *g-* in such Tibetan numbers as *gcig.* 'one', *gnyis.* 'two', and *gsum.* 'three', but unless one resorts to comparative evidence it is not possible to assign any specific meaning or function to this prefix. What will be described in this section is only the more productive and functional morphology of Classical Tibetan.

Structure of the Noun Phrase

A noun phrase whose head is not a pronoun but a nominal of some kind has the following structure: Head nominal + (Adjective) + (Demonstrative) + (Plural) + (Indefinite particle) + Case particle

> *mi./chen.po./ de./ rnams./ la.*
>
> man/ large/ that/ pl./ dat. case
>
> 'to those large men'

In this formula only the head nominal and case marking are obligatory constituents; everything else is optional. The demonstrative and the indefinite particle are mutually exclusive. An adjective or a demonstrative may precede the noun it modifies if it is followed by a genitive case marker:

Adjective or demonstrative + genitive case + Nominal

It should be noted that for the most part Tibetan adjectives function grammatically like nominals and can themselves serve as heads of noun phrases.

Number

Singular is unmarked; plural is usually also unmarked for inanimate nouns (except in some texts which have been translated from Indic languages). For pronouns and nouns the most common plural marker is *rnams.* Other plural suffixes are *dag., cag.,* and a few other rarer ones. It is curious to note that *dag.* very often is used to mark plural in vocative constructions, and, in texts translated from Sanskrit, represents Sanskrit dual number which is not a morphological category in Tibetan itself.

The singular/plural distinction is strictly observed only in the pronouns. With nominals, especially if the sense is clear from the context (as when a number modifies a noun) plural is only optionally marked.

Indefinite Particle

Contrary to some old grammars of Tibetan written by Western missionaries, there is no definite article in this language, although a sense of definiteness is often signaled by the demonstrative *de.* 'that'. Indefiniteness is signaled by particle *cig.,* which is derived from *gcig.* 'one'. Unlike *gcig.,* which is invariable, the indefinite particle changes its initial consonant depending on the final segment of the preceding morpheme:

> *zhig.* / sonorants (nasals, liquids, vowels)＿＿＿
>
> *shig.* / s＿＿＿
>
> *cig.* / *b, d, g* ＿＿＿ (In the syllable-final position these consonants were probably voiceless unless followed directly by some voiced consonant or a vowel.)

After a plural marker or a number the indefinite particle can be translated as 'about' or 'some':

> *dge.slong.* / *lnga.* / *brgya.* / *zhig.*
>
> monk/ five/ hundred/ indef.
>
> 'About 500 monks'

Cases

Case relations are marked by postposed particles which govern the entire noun phrase to which they are attached. (There is no case/number agreement in Tibetan; gender agreement is very marginal and appears mostly in texts translated from Sanskrit.)

1. Absolutive

This case has no overt marker in Tibetan. A nominal or a pronoun in this case acts as *a direct object of a transitive verb* or as *a subject of an intransitive verb.* The subject of a transitive verb must be in the instrumental/ergative case. This type of case relationship marking is called ergative as opposed to accusative case marking in which both the subject of a transitive verb and the subject of the intransitive verb have the same case marking (nominative), whereas the direct object has a different case marking (accusative). (Cf. "Sketch of Russian" for an example of accusative type case marking.)

2. Genitive

> *gi.* / velars (*g* and *ng*)____
>
> *gyi.* / liquids and nonvelar nasals____
>
> *-i* / vowels____
>
> *kyi.* / *d, b, s*____

This case marks possession and subordination in general. Relative clauses (which always precede the head and can be regarded as nominalized sentences), adjectives and demonstratives[6] which precede the head nouns (cf. the preceding statement of the order of various constituents in the Tibetan noun phrase) are placed in the genitive to signal their subordination to the head nominal:

> *dngul. btang.* + *ba* + *'i. mi.*
>
> money (lit. 'silver')/ gave + nominal particle + gen./ man
>
> 'the man who gave the money'

3. Instrumental/Ergative

The marker for this case is a combination of the genitive marker and *-s*. The only difference is that it is simply *-s* after vowels, not *-is*, which one might otherwise expect.

As already stated, this case marks the subject of a transitive verb. It also marks the instrument whereby an action is performed. From the word order and the context it is usually clear which of the nominals marked with the instrumental case is the subject (i.e., agent) and which is the instrument:

> *Rgyal.po-s. mi. de. ral. gri-s. bsad.*
>
> king + instr./ man/ that/ sword + instr./ killed
>
> 'The king killed that man with the sword.'

Added to nominalized clauses, this case usually marks 'cause':

> *shin.tu. bka'.ba. yin.-pa-s*
>
> very/ difficult/ be + nominal particle + instr.
>
> 'because (it) is very difficult'

4. Locative

The marker for this case is *na.*, which does not vary in shape. It marks a stationary position in time or space. After verbs, it has the function of conditional clause marker ('if').

> *de. na.*
>
> that/ loc.
>
> 'then' or 'there'

> *de - 'i. tshe. na.*
>
> that + gen./ time/ loc.
>
> 'at that time'

5. Dative

The marker for this case is *la.* (invariable). It marks the indirect object of a verb or general direction toward which an action is taking place. It is also used to mark simple location. With some verbs it marks the logical direct object:

> *a.ma-la. ltos.*
>
> mother + dat./ look (imperat.)
>
> 'Look at mother!'

One of its other uses is to mark the possessor in possessive constructions like the following:

> *Nga. la. ral.gri. yod.*
>
> I/ dat./ sword/ exist
>
> 'To me there is a sword.' = 'I have a sword.'

6. Ablative

The markers for this case are *nas.* and *las.* (both invariable). After nouns these markers may be used more or less interchangeably to signal the source from which an action proceeds ('from'). Originally, these two morphemes probably had distinct functions and may have arisen from combinations of *na.* and *la.* with the instrumental case. Even in Classical Tibetan they are not interchangeable in all situations.

> *Rta. nas.* or *las. lhung.*
>
> horse/ ablat./ fell
>
> '(He/she) fell from a horse.'

Las. is used in comparative constructions like 'than' in English to mark the standard to which something is being compared:

> *Gser. las. rdo.rje. dkon.pa. yin.*
>
> gold/ ablat./ diamond/ precious/ copula vb.
>
> 'Diamonds are more precious than gold.' (Note that there is no inflection on the adjective to signal a comparative construction.)

After present and past forms of the verb *las.* and *nas.* (but more commonly *nas.*) are used to mark subordination (usually temporal but sometimes causal) of that verb and its clause to another verb in the sentence:

> *Ba.glang. sgo. gzhan. du. song. nas. stor. ro.*
>
> bull/ door/ other/ term./ went/ ablat./ became lost/ sentence final particle
>
> 'The bull, after having gone through another door, became lost.'

As already pointed out *nas.* and *las.* incorporate the instrumental marker, and this explains some of their more idiomatic uses:

> *Lag.pa. nas. mi. de. 'dzin.pa.*
>
> hand/ ablat./ man/ that/ grasp
>
> '(He/she) grasped that man by the hand.' (Lit. 'took that man by means of on the hand'. Note that the hand in question does not belong to the subject of the sentence.)

Those who are familiar with Japanese should note that uses of *las./nas.* parallel the uses of Japanese *yori* and *kara* respectively.

7. Terminative Case

The marker for this case has the following allomorphs:

> -*r.* (also *ru.*)/ vowels_____
>
> *su./ s*_____
>
> *tu./ g, b*_____
>
> *du./* nasals, liquids, *d*_____

This case has a large variety of functions some of which duplicate those of other cases: (a) to mark motion toward or into something (like dative), (b) to indicate location in space and duration in time (like locative), (c) to make manner adverbials out of adjectives, (d) to mark what something becomes or turns into, and (e) to indicate purpose. (And a number of other uses which cannot be neatly summarized here.)

> *Grong.khyer. du. 'jug.pa.*
>
> city/ term./ enter
>
> 'enter the city'

> *Khyim. du. yod.*
>
> house/ term./ exist
>
> '(He/she) is at home.'

> *myur. du.*
>
> quick/ term.
>
> 'quickly, soon'

> *Chang. dug. tu. gyur.*
>
> beer/ poison/ term./ became
>
> 'Beer became poison.'

> *thos.pa. + r. snyan.pa.*
>
> hear + term./ pleasant
>
> 'pleasant to hear'

> *nyin.pa. + r.*
>
> day + term.
>
> 'during the day'

Structure of the Verb Phrase

There are four basic forms in the Classical Tibetan verb paradigm:

Present:		Verb theme		*sgrim.* 'to hold fast'
Past:	*b* +	Verb theme	+ *s*	*bsgrims.*
Future:	*b* +	Verb theme		*bsgrim.*
Imperative:		Verb theme	+ *s*	*sgrims.*

Tibetan verbs are not inflected for person or number. The *b*- prefix which appears in the past and future forms is generally not affixed to plain roots (i.e., roots that do not have any prefixes; verb themes are composed of prefixes whose morphological function is frequently quite obscure, plus a verb root) and is therefore absent in most verbs beginning in a single consonant. Moreover, this prefix as well as suffix -*s* (past and imperative forms) are deleted by phonological rules which prevent certain sequences of consonants from appearing on the surface. For example, *b*- is deleted if the verb theme begins in a cluster of consonants which contains a bilabial consonant. (Generally, sequences of homorganic stops, affricates, and nasals are not allowed either syllable-initially or syllable-finally.) This deletion of affixes often leads to homophonous forms within the same paradigm; the ambiguous forms are often replaced by periphrastic constructions based on the present tense form in combination with various auxiliary verbs.

A fairly large number of verbs exhibit *vowel ablaut* (unpredictable morphophonemic alternation of vowels) in addition:

Present:	*byed.* 'do'
Past:	*byas.*
Future:	*bya.*
Imperative:	*byos.*

The verb 'to do' is irregular in that it has -*d* in the present. Verbs whose present tense form contains either *i* or *u* as a root vowel very rarely exhibit vowel ablaut. In Table 4.6 are some of the more common vowel ablaut patterns in verb stems.

For the sake of brevity, numerous exceptions and some very common affixual and ablaut patterns have been omitted from this description, but the foregoing summary holds true for a very large number of Tibetan verbs.

Other major verb inflections include the prefix *s*- which turns various stems into transitive verbs (often causative):

bug.pa. 'hole' : *sbug.pa.* 'to pierce'

'gyur.pa. 'to become' vs. *sgyur.pa.* 'to transform, to cause to become'

Table 4.6

PRESENT	PAST	FUTURE	IMPERATIVE
a	a	a	o
e	a	a	o
o	a	a	o

Subordination Markers

There are several suffixed particles that signal that the verb to which they are attached is a verb in a subordinate clause of some kind:

1. Subordinating Absolute Particle

> *ste.* / vowels, non-apical nasals and stops____
>
> *de.* / d____
>
> *te.* / other dental consonants____

This particle may be suffixed to the present, future, and past forms of the verb, but it is usually found after the past tense forms. Its function is to link two or more clauses in the same sentence whether or not these clauses have the same subject:

> *De-s.   rdo. zhig. blangs. te.   'phangs.pa.*
>
> that + instr./ stone/ indef./ took/ subord./ threw
>
> 'He (lit. 'that one'), having taken a stone, threw (it).'

> *Rgyal.po-s. khrims. bca'. / ste.   bzang. la. / bya.dga'. bster.*
>
> king + instr./law/ enacted/ subord./ good/ dat./ reward/ bestowed
>
> 'The king having made the law, the good people were rewarded.'

2. Continuative Subordinating Particle

cing. (The initial consonant of this morpheme exhibits the same morphophonemic changes as that of the indefinite particle.)

Although this particle can be suffixed to various forms of the verb except the imperative it is usually suffixed to the present tense form. It often denotes an action or state taking place or existing at the same time as the action or state expressed by the main verb of the sentence. In short it links two or more verb phrases if the action expressed by their verbs is roughly contemporaneous:

> *De-'i. drung. na. tha.ga.pa. zhig. thags.'thag. cing. 'dug. pa. de 'i. steng. du. lhung.*
>
> that + gen./   front/   loc./   weaver/   indef./   weave/ continuative/ sit/ nominal particle/ that + gen./ top/ term./ fell
>
> '(He) fell on top of a weaver, that (one) who was sitting and weaving in front of it (the wall).'

Main Verb Inflections

a. Interrogative Particle

> *'am.* / vowels____
>
> *Cam.* / C____ (i.e., copy of the preceding consonant + *am.*)

This particle marks interrogation in those sentences (yes-or-no questions) that do not contain a question word like 'who' or 'what'. (The latter type of interrogative sentences have the normal word order and have no special marking.)

> *Khyod. kyis. glang. brnyas. sam.*
>
> you/ instr./ bull/ borrowed/ interrog. particle
>
> 'Did you borrow the bull?'

b. Sentence Final Particle

> *'o.* / vowels____
>
> *Co.* / C____ (i.e., copy of the preceding consonant + *o*)

This particle marks a somewhat emphatic end of a sentence, and since the main verb phrase comes at the end of the Tibetan sentence, can be considered to be the main verb phrase marker or even the main verb marker. Sometimes it has the force of a copula verb when the latter has been optionally deleted and there are no other sentence-final verbs; some scholars believe that it was originally a copula verb itself:

> *Nga-s. glang. brnyas.-so.*
>
> I + instr./ bull/ borrowed + final particle
>
> 'I borrowed the bull.'

> *De-'i. gdong.pa. mjes. kyang.-ngo.*
>
> that + gen./ face/ beautiful/ even + final part.
>
> 'His face is even beautiful.'

Existential, Locative, and Copula Verbs

Existential, locative, and copula verbs are not inflected for tense and do not have imperative forms. (The same is true of many intransitive verbs in general.)

yod. 'exist, be located'

yin. 'be (copula)'

'dug. 'be, sit' (combines functions of copula and existential verbs)

Negation

Negative particles immediately precede the words they negate such as verbs, adjectives, and adverbs.

ma. is used to negate *yod.* and *yin.* (but see below), past tense forms of other verbs, and negative imperatives (prohibitions). The latter are formed with the present tense form of the verb, not with the imperative:

ma. lta.	vs.	*ltos.*
neg. / look		look! (imperat. form)
'Don't look!'		'Look!'

Mi. negates most adjectivals, the existential verb *'dug.*, and present and future forms of other verbs.

The negative particle *ma.* coalesces with *yod.* and *yin.* to form contracted forms *med.* and *min.* respectively.

Med. is also used as a privative suffix in contrast with *can.*, a posessive suffix:

dbu.med.	vs.	*dbu.can*
head/ privative suff.		head/ possess. suff.
'headless'		'headful' (i.e., 'having a head')

(The preceding terms happen to be names of two variants of the Tibetan script.)

Word Order

The basic word order is Subject + Object + Verb. As already noted, adjectives usually follow the nouns they modify and adverbs usually precede the verbs they modify.

Relative Clauses

Relative clauses usually precede their heads and are really nominalized verb phrases that are then linked to the head noun by the genitive case marker. If they follow the head noun, they are not marked in any special way as being relative clauses, but simply end in a nominal particle.

Table 4.7

PLAIN FORM	HONORIFIC FORM
lus. 'body'	*sku.* 'body'
mgo. 'head'	*dbu.* 'head'
lag. 'hand'	*phyag.* 'hand'
mig. 'eye'	*spyan.* 'eye'
rna. 'ear'	*snyan.* 'ear'
rta. 'horse'	*chibs.* 'horse'
'dug. 'exist'	*bzhugs.* 'exist'
nyal.ba. 'to sleep'	*gnal. gzim.pa.* 'to sleep'

bgo.ba/. med.-pa -'i./ mi./ rnams.

clothes/ not have-nominalizer (nominal particle) + gen./
pers./ pl.

Or (less common):

mi. bgo.ba. med.pa. rnams

person/ clothes/ not have + nominalizer/ plural

'people who do not have clothes'

Honorifics

Although the classical language did not have as elaborate a system of honorifics as Modern Lhasa Tibetan now has, it did have quite an impressive
number of doublets, especially nouns (and a few verbs), one honorific, applied to possessions and actions of persons higher in status than the speaker,
and one a plain form, used in informal conversation among friends or to refer
to one's own actions or possessions when speaking to strangers or superiors.
More often than not such doublets consist of totally dissimilar lexical items
(see Table 4.7).

D. SAMPLE TEXT

The sample text below is taken from the third chapter of the biography of the
famous Tibetan Buddhist saint Milarepa (*Mi.la.ras.pa.,* A.D. 1040–1123). The
biography was written by Gtsan.smyon. He.ru.ka. (A.D. 1452–1507) and describes in fairly plain language the spiritual journey of Milarepa from being a
practitioner of black magic and a murderer to being an enlightened saint. Although the setting is exotic Tibet more than 900 years ago, even those readers
who are not at all familiar with Tibet and Tibetan culture will easily understand what Milarepa had to go through on his way to enlightenment, his en-

counters with such universal human foibles as greed, hatred, indifference, and ignorance in himself and others. In sum, the biography was written with such sincerity and compassion that the reader can easily forget the exotic setting and empathize with Milarepa simply as a fellow human being who had to contend with many of the same things that we have to go through no matter where or in what century we live.

The setting of the excerpt is as follows. On his deathbed, Milarepa's father made Milarepa's paternal aunt and uncle promise to look after his widow and children. However, after his death, the aunt and uncle broke their promise and robbed the bereaved family of almost all their possessions. Filled with grief, hatred, and yearning for revenge, the betrayed widow hopes that Milarepa will eventually learn black magic and take a terrible revenge on his aunt and uncle. And so Milarepa is sent off to study but, being a young man, soon forgets what it is that he must do. It is this point in the story that the excerpt describes.

If you want to learn what happened next, there is a fairly good English translation of Milarepa's biography, reference to which is given in connection with the idiomatic translation of the passage which follows the morpheme-by-morpheme translation.

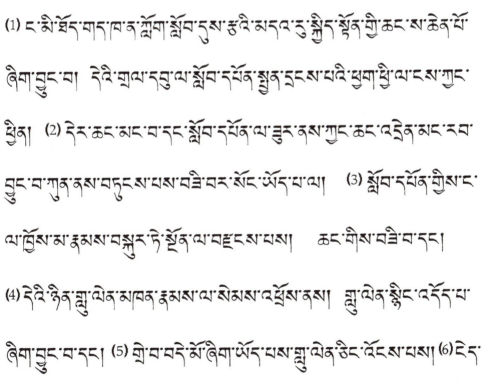

Figure 4.3 *Tibetan Text*

རང་གི་ཁང་པའི་མདུན་ན་ཡར་ལམ་ཡོད་པས་སྐྱིའི་ཐད་དུ་སྐྱིབས་རུང་བླ་བྲང་རས་

པས། ཨ་མ་ནང་ན་ཡོས་རྫོང་ཀྱིན་ཡོད་པས་ཐོས་ནས། (7) ཙེ་ཟེར་སྐད་འདིའི་

འའི་བུའི་སྐད་འདྲ། ཉིད་མ་སྐད་ཀྱི་སྒྲུག་པ་ནི་ས་ཐོག་ན་མེད་པས་ཁོའི་བླ་ལེན་མི་

ཐད་སྐྲམ་ནས་ཡིད་མ་ཆེས་པར་བསླུས་པས། (8) ང་ཡིན་པར་ཤེས་ནས་ཏ་ལས་ཏེ།

སྐྲ་པ་གཡས་སུ་བོར། ཡོས་དགུགས་གཡོན་དུ་བོར། (9) ཡོས་རྫོང་འཕྲོ་འཚོག་

དུ་བཅུག་ལག་པ་གཡས་སུ་ཡོག་པ་ཞིག་ཕྱིར། གཡོན་དུ་ཐལ་བ་སྒུར་གང་ཕྱིར།

(10) སྐྲས་རིང་བ་ལ་བབས། བྱུང་བ་ལ་མཆོངས་ནས་ཕྱིར་ཐོན་བུང་སྟེ། (11)ཐལ་བ་

དེ་གདོང་ལ་བདག བ་ ཡོག་པ་དེ་མགོ་ལ་ལན་འབབ་བརྒྱབས་ནས། (12) ཡབ་

མི་ལ་ཤེས་རབ་རྒྱལ་མཚན་ཁྱིད་ལ་བུ་འདི་འདུ་སྐྱེས་སོ། (13) ཁྱིད་རབས་ཆད་

གདན་བ། ཉིད་མ་སྐད་ཀྱི་ལས་སྐོས་ལས་གཟིགས་དང་ཟེར་ཨ་མ་ལུག་ཅིག་

བརྒྱལ་ནས་འགྱིལ་འདུག་པའི་ཚེ། (14) སྲིང་མོ་ཡང་ཐོན་བུང་སྟེ། ཨ་ཇོའི་

བསམ་བློ་ལ་ཨ་མ་ལ་ཕྱོས་དང་ཟེར་དུ་ཞིང་འདུག་པ་ལ། བདེན་སྐྲམ་ནས།

(15) ང་རང་ཡང་མཆི་མ་མང་པོ་འོར། (16) དེད་མིང་སྲིང་གཉིས་ཀྱིས་དུ་བའི་དང་

ནས་ཨ་མའི་ལག་པ་མཉེད་ཅིང་བོས་པས་དར་ཅིག་ནས་བརྒྱལ་བ་སངས་ཏེ་

ལངས་བུང་ནས། (17) དུ་བའི་གདོང་གིས་ང་ལ་ཅི་རེ་བལྟས་ནས། (18)བུ་རང་རེ་

Figure 4.3 *(continued)*

མ་སྨྱང་པས་སྐྱག་པ་ས་ཐོག་ན་མེད་པ་ལ་ཁྱིད་སྐྱུ་ཨིན་པ་དན་པ་རང་འདུག་གས!

(19) ང་མ་རྐན་མོ་ནི་བསམ་མནོ་གཏོང་གིན་ཨི་སྐྱག་པ་དང་དུ་ཐོབ་མིན་པ་མི་འདུབ

ཟེར། (20) སྐྱེ་སྐྱགས་འདོན་ཞིང་རེད་མ་སྨྱད་གསུམ་ཀ་ཌུས་སོ།།

Figure 4.3 *(continued)*

Literal Morpheme-by-Morpheme Translation

The superscripted numbers in this section refer to notes at the end of the section. Many notes are needed because in Tibetan the same morpheme may have quite a number of different grammatical functions that have to be determined from the context. (This is especially true of various particles.)

(1) *Nga. Mi.thod.gad.kha.-na. klog. slob. dus. Rtsa'-i. mda'.-ru., skyid.-ston.-gyi. chang.-sa. chen.po. zhig. byung.-ba.,*
I/ **Mithodgadkha** (place name) + loc./ **reading**/ **learn** (pres.)/ **time**[1]/ **Rtsa** (place name) + gen./ **lower part of a valley** + terminative[2]/ happiness + feast, banquet (= **'wedding feast**) + gen./ beer + place = **'beer drinking bout'**/ **big**/ indefinite/ **took place** (past of *'byung.*) + nominal particle,[3]

de'-i. gral.-dbu.-la. slob.-dpon. spyan.-drangs.-pa'-i. phyag. phyi.-la. nga-s. kyang. phyin.,
that + gen. (= **'its'**)/ row, class + head (honorific) (= seat at the head of the table, i.e., **'presider at a feast'**) + dat.[4]/ teach + master (= **'teacher'**)/ eye (honorif.) + invited (past of *'dren*) (= honorific compound for **'invite'**) + nominal particle + gen.[5]/ hand (honorif.) + after, behind (= **'attendant, servant'**) + dat./ **I** + instr.[6]/ **also**/ went,

(2) *de-r. chang. mang.-ba. dang. slob.-dpon.-la. zur.-nas. kyang. chang. 'dren. mang. rab. byung.-ba. kun.-nas. btungs.-pa-s. bzi.-ba-r. song. yod.-pa.-la.,*
that + term. (= **'there'**)/ **beer**/ **be much** + nominal particle/ **and**/ teach + master (= **'teacher'**) + dat./ **side** + ablat./ **also**, even/ **beer**/ **invite**, pour out/ **much**, very/ **plentiful**/ happened, **came about** (past of *'byung.*) + nominal particle/ **all**/ ablat./ **drank** (past of *'thung.* + nominal particle + instr.[7]/ **drunk** + terminative[8]/ **became**, went (past of *'gro.*)/ exist + nominal particle + dat.,[9]

(3) *slob.-dpon.-gyis. nga.-la. khyos.-ma.-rnams. bskur.-te. sngon.-la. brdzangs.-pa-s., chang.-gis. bzi.-ba. dang.,*
teach + master (= **'teacher'**) + instr./ **I** + dat. (= **'to me'**)/ **present**, gift + nominal particle + plural/ **handed over,** entrust (past of *skur.* + subord. particle)/ before, **ahead** + dat./ **sent off** (past of *rdzong.*) + nominal particle + instr.[7]/, **beer** + instr. / **intoxicated**, drunk + nominal particle/ **and**,[10]

(4) *de'i. nyin. glu.-len.-mkhan.-rnams.-la. sems. 'phros.-nas., glu.-len. snying.-'dod.-pa. zhig. byung.-ba. dang.,*

that + gen.[11]/ **day**/ song + sing + agentive suffix + pl. (= **'singers'**) + dat./ spirit, **mind**/ proceed, issue, go on, **continue**[12] + ablat.[13]/, **song** + **sing**/ mind, heart + desire (= **'desire,** wish) + nominal particle/ indef./ **became,** came about (past of *'byung.*) + nominal particle/ **and,**

(5) *gre.-ba. bde.mo. zhig. yod.-pa-s. glu. len.-cing. 'ongs.-pa-s.,*
throat (= **'voice'**) + nominal particle/ **good,** happy/ indef./ exist, **have** + nominal particle + instr.[7]/ **song**/ **sing** + continuative particle/ **came** (past of *'ong.*) + nominal particle + instr.[7]

(6) *nged. rang.-gi. khang.-pa'-i. mdun.-na. yar.-lam. yod.-pa-s. sgo'-i. thad.-du. slebs. rung. glu. blangs.-pa-s.,*
I, we/ self + gen. (= **'our own'**)/ **house** + nominal particle + gen./ **front** + loc./ upper + road (= **'shortcut'**)/ **exist** + nominal particle + instr.,[7]/ **door** + gen./ forward direction + term. (= **'up to'**)/ **arrived,** reached (past of *sleb.*)/ even, **be capable,** able/ **song**/ **sang** (past of *len.*) + nominal particle + instr.,[7]

a.ma. nang.-na. yos. rngod.-kyin.-yod.-pa-s. thos.-nas.,
mother/ **inside** + loc./ **roasted barley**/ **parch** + progressive aspect particle + exist[14] + nominal particle + instr.[7]/ **heard**[15] + ablat.,[13]

(7) *ci. zer. skad. 'di. ni. nga'-i. bu'-i. skad 'dra., nged. ma.-smad.-kyi. sdug.-pa. ni. sa. thog.-na. med.-pa-s.*
what?/ **say**[16]/ **voice**/ **this**/ topic marker[17]/ I + gen. (= **'my'**)/ **son** + gen./ **voice**/ **be like,** similar/, **we**/ **mother** + **children**/ **misery** + nominal particle/ topic marker[17]/ **earth**/ top + loc. (= **'on'**)/ **not exist**[18]/ + nominal particle + instr.[7]

kho. ni. glu. len. mi. thad. snyam. nas. yid.-ma.- ches.-pa-r. bltas.-pa-s.,
he/ topic marker[17]/ **song**/ **sing**/ negative/ **right,** straight[19]/ **think**/ ablat.[13]/ mind + neg. + believe + (= **'not believe'**) nominal particle + terminative[20]/ **looked** (past of *lta.*) + nominal particle + instr.,

(8) *nga. yin.-pa-r. shes.-nas. ha.las.-te., skam.-pa. g'yas.-su. bor., yos.-dkrugs. g'yon.-du. bor.,*
I/ be + nominal particle + termin.[21]/ **perceive,** apprehend, know + ablat.[13]/ **be astonished,** frightened + subord. particle/, **tongs** + nominal particle/ **right side** + term.[22]/ **threw** (past of *'bor.*)/, **barley** + **stirring stick**/ **left side** + term.[22]/ **threw** (past of *'bor.*),

(9) *yos. rngod. 'phro. 'tshig.-tu. bcug. lag.-pa. g'yas.-su. yog.-pa. zhig., khyer., g'yon.-du. thal.-ba. spar.-gang. khyer.,*
barley/ **parch**[23]/ proceed, **continue** / **burn,** destroy by fire + term.[24]/ **let,** caused (past of *'jug.*)/ **hand** + nominal particle/ **right** + term.[2]/ **poker,** stick for stirring fire + nominal particle/ indef./ **took,** brought (past of *'khyer.*)/, **left** + term.[2]/ **ashes,** dust + nominal particle/ handful + full, measure (= **'handful'**)/ **took,** brought (past of *'khyer.*),

(10) *skas. ring.-ba.-la. babs., thung.-ba.-la. mchongs.-nas. phyi-r. thon. byung.-ste.,*
step/ **steep,** long + nominal particle + dat./ **descended,** went down (past of

'bab.)/ **low,** short + nominal particle + dat./ **leaped over**[15] + ablat./ **outside** + term.[22]/ **appear,** emerge/ became (past of *'byung.*)[25] + subord. particle

(11) *thal.-ba. de. gdong.-la. btab., yog.-pa. de. mgo.-la. lan. 'ga'. brgyabs.-nas.,*
ashes + nominal particle/ **that/ face** + dat./ **threw** (past of *gtong.*)/, **poker** + nominal particle/ **that/ head** + dat.[26]/ **time/ few/ hit** (past of *rgyab.*) + ablat.[13],

(12) *yab. Mi.la. Shes.rab. Rgyal.-mtshan. khyed.-la. bu. 'di.-'dra. skyes.-so.;*
father (honorif.)/ **Mila/ Wisdom/ Victory** + **Sign** (with preceding two words = proper name)/ **you** + dat./ **son/** this + like (= **'such'**)/ **was born** (past of *skye.*) + final particle;

(13) *khyed. rabs.-chad. gda'-.ba., nged. ma. smad.-kyi. las. skos.-la. gzigs. dang. zer. a.ma. yug. cig. brgyal. nas. 'gyel. 'dug.-pa'-i. tshe.,*
you/ lineage, generation + rent, torn (= **'a person whose lineage is broken off'**)/ **be** (elegant) + nominal particle[3]/, **we/ mother** + **children** + gen./ destiny, **fate** + dat./ **look,** see (honorif.)/ imperat.[27]/ **say**[16]/ **mother/ moment,** short space of time/ indef./ **faint/** ablat.[13]/ be carried away, **overcome/ be,** exist + nominal particle + gen./ **time,**[28]

(14) *sring.mo. yang. thon. byung.-ste., a.jo'-i. bsam.-blo.-la. a.ma.-la. ltos. dang. zer. ngu.-zhing. 'dug.-pa.-la., bden.-snyam.-nas.,*
sister (of a male)/ **also/ came out,** appeared (past, of *'thon.*)/ became, came about (past of *'byung.*)[25] + subord. particle/ **elder brother** + gen./ thought + mind (= **'thinking'**) + dat.[9]/ **mother** + dat.[26]/ **look** (imperat. of *lta.*)/ imperat.[27]/ **say**[16]/ **weep** + continuative particle/ **be,** stay[29] + nominal particle + dat.[9]/ true, truth + think, sense (= **'come to one's senses'**) + ablat.,[13]/

(15) *nga-.rang. yang. mchi.-ma. mang.po. shor.,*
I + self (= **'I myself'**)/ **also/ tear** + nominal particle/ **many/ came out** (past of *'chor.*),

(16) *nged. ming.-sring. gnyis.-kyis. ngu.-ba'-i. ngang.-nas. a.ma'-i. lag.-pa. mnyed.-cing. bos.-pa-s. dar.cig.-nas. brgyal.-ba. sangs.-te. langs. byung.-nas.,*
we/ brother + **sister/** two (= **'the two of us'**) + instr./ **weep** + nominal particle + gen./ state, nature, mood (= **'in a state of tears'**) + ablat.[13]/ **mother** + gen./ **hand** + nominal particle/ **rub** (between the hands) + continuative particle/ **called by name** (past of *'bod.* + nominal particle + instr.[7]/ **a little while** + ablat.[13]/ faint + nominal particle/ disspelled (past of *sang.*) (= **'awakened from faint**) + subord. particle/ **stood up,** arose (past of *lang.*)/ became (past of *'byung.*)[25] + ablat.[13],

(17) *ngu.-ba'-i. gdong.-gis. nga.-la. ce.re. bltas.-nas.,*
weep + nominal particle + gen./ **face,** countenance + instr./ I + dat. (= 'me')[26]/ staring, fixed gaze/ looked (past of *lta.*) (= **'looked at me fixedly'**) + ablat,[13]

(18) *bu. rang.re. ma.smad.-pa-s. sdug.-pa. sa-.thog-.na. med.-pa.-la. khyod. glu. len-.pa. dran.-pa. rang. 'dug.-gam.,*

son, child[30]/ **we**/ **mother** + **children** + nominal particle + instr./ **misery,** affliction + nominal particle/ **earth** + **top** + loc./ **not exist**[18] + nominal particle + dat.[9]/ **you**/ **song**/ **sing** + nominal particle/ **think of,** recall + nominal particle/ **even** (emphatic)/ **be,** exist + question particle,

(19) *nga. ma. rgan.mo. ni. bsam.mno. gtong-.gin. yi.mug.-pa. dang. ngu. bro.-ba. min.pa. mi.'dug. zer.,*

I/ **mother**/ **old**/ topic marker[17]/ thinking/ let, let in (= with prec. **'think,** consider') + immediate pres. marker/ **be despondent,** despair + nominal particle/ **and**/ **weep**/ desire, **wish**/ **not be** + nominal particle/ negative/ **be,** exist[31]/ **say,**[16]

(20) *smre.sngags. 'don.-zhing. nged. ma.smad. gsum.-ka-s. ngus.-so.*

lamentation/ **utter** + continuative particle/ **we**/ **mother** + **children**/ three + substantivizer (= **'the three'**) + instr.[6]/ **wept** (past of *ngu.*) + sentence final particle

---

NOTES

1. One would ordinarily expect *slob.pa'i.dus* here, that is, a relative clause whose head is the word *dus.* 'time': 'at the time I was studying . . .' Perhaps this is more of a compound rather than a relative clause, and that is why the expected markers are missing.

2. Terminative case is used here to mark location.

3. Verb forms are very often followed by a nominal particle; some linguists consider all such verb forms to be nominalizations, but in many cases it makes little difference whether one considers them to be simply verbs or derived nominals.

4. Dative case here is used to indicate purpose.

5. The sentence in the Tibetan original text seems to split the constituents of the relative clause by placing the head noun in the middle of it. The more usual Tibetan construction would be something like the following one: *de'-i. gral.-dbu.-la. spyan.-drangs.- pa'-i. slob.-dpon.-la. 'phyags.-phyi.-la. ngas. kyang. phyin.* = 'I also went as an attendant to [my] teacher who had been invited [there to serve] as the guest of honor at the feast.'

6. It is not clear why a subject of what seems to be an intransitive verb ('go, weep') is marked with the instrumental/ergative case instead of the expected absolutive case in these instances.

7. The sequence Verb + nominative particle + instrumental is another nonfinite verb form; sometimes it has the force of a subordinate clause of cause ('since, because . . .'), but most of the time it can be translated into English by a participial construction: 'My teacher having drunk all . . .'

8. Terminative case here marks what one becomes.

9. Dative marker *la.* is sometimes used as a conjunction 'and' (especially to connect two imperatives).

10. Conjunction *dang.* 'and' in Tibetan goes with the preceding clause; that is, the potential pause comes after it, not before it as in English.

11. The demonstrative modifying a noun may precede it, but then it must be linked to the latter by means of the genitive marker.

12. This probably means something like 'my mind kept dwelling on the singers'.

13. Ablative case particle after verbs also marks a nonfinite clause, very often an adverbial subordinate clause of time ('after VP . . .').

14. The Verb + *kyin.* + *yod.* construction seems to indicate a continuing action which is taking place at this very moment in the present or at some very particular moment in the past, simultaneous with some other event: 'Mother was just then in the process of parching barley . . .'

15. Some verbs have oblique forms identical with that of the present tense form. Thus, *thos.* 'hear' can mean either 'hear' or 'heard' depending on the context. When necessary various auxiliary verbs and periphrastic constructions are used along with the present tense form to mark other tenses and the imperative mood.

16. Verb *zer.* is used to signal a quotation. Sometimes it comes at the end of the quote and sometimes it is embedded within a quotation, often as a second element. It is sometimes very difficult to figure out exactly where a quotation begins and ends since there are no punctuation marks to signal its boundaries.

17. Topic marker *ni.* adds a certain degree of emphasis to an NP or a clause after which it appears; it sometimes seems to have a contrastive function as well.

18. This appears to be a kind of truncated comparative construction: 'since there is no suffering on earth (greater than that of) us, mother and children . . .' Milarepa's mother keeps using this expression as a kind of formula; thus it is no wonder that the comparison marking has been ellided for brevity.

19. Most likely the sense here is: 'it is not proper for him to be singing'.

20. Terminative case here forms a kind of manner adverbial phrase: 'not believing-ly' (= 'in disbelief').

21. Terminative case marker is also used to mark an NP or subordinate relative clause which is the direct object of a verb of knowing, perceiving, etc.: 'Perceiving that it was me . . .'

22. Here terminative case indicates the direction of a motion.

23. Parched barley, as well as other parched grains, is the staple food of Tibetans.

24. Terminative case is used here to connect two verbs, 'cause' and 'burn'.

25. The past tense form of *'byung.* is used as a kind of past tense or perfective auxiliary verb, especially in those cases when the main verb has no special past tense form different from the present tense form.

26. With some verbs *la.* (dat. particle) is used to mark a direct object. This is somewhat parallel to such English verb phrases as 'look at something' in which the object of the verb 'look' is marked by the preposition 'at'. Note also that one would have expected the immediately preceding NP ('that poker') to be marked as being instrumental, but the original text does not mark it so.

27. After a verb, *dang.* (which usually means 'and') is sometimes used to signal imperative mood, especially in the case of verbs which do not have an imperative form different from the present tense form.

28. Here we have an example of a relative clause, whose head noun is 'time', that acts as an adverbial subordinate clause of time: 'when . . . , at the time of . . .'

29. The verb *'dug.* often appears with *zhing.* and other markers of continuing action as a sort of progressive aspect auxiliary.

30. *Bu.* 'child, son' is here used as a vocative: 'Oh son!'

31. The force of the two negated verbs in a row ('it is not + it exists not') seems to be 'if not X, there is nothing else but . .': 'I can only despair and cry . . .'

Idiomatic Translation[7]

While studying at Mithogekha, one day I accompanied my tutor to the lower valley of Tsa, where he was invited to preside at a wedding feast. Drinking much beer, not only what I poured for him but also what all the others poured for him, my tutor became drunk. He sent me ahead with the presents he had received. I also was drunk. Hearing the singers, I too had a desire to sing, and having a good voice, I sang as I went along. The road passed in front of my house, and I was still singing when I arrived at the door. In the house my mother was roasting barley and heard me. "What is this?" she said to herself. "That sounds like the voice of my son. But how could he be singing while we are so miserable?" And not believing what she heard, she looked outside. As soon as she recognized me she cried out in surprise. Her right hand dropped the tongs; her left hand dropped the whisk; and, leaving barley to burn, she took a stick in one hand and a handful of ashes in the other. She ran down the big steps, leaped over the little ones, and was outside. She threw the ashes in my face, struck me several times on the head, and shouted, "Father Mila Banner of Wisdom, is this the son that you have begotten? He is not worthy of you. Look at our fate, mother and son!" And with this she fainted.

At this moment my sister came running up and said, "Elder brother, what are you doing? What has happened to mother?" And her weeping brought me to my senses. Then I too shed many tears. We rubbed our mother's hands and called her name. After a moment she came to herself and got up. Then, fixing her tear-filled eyes on me, she said, "Since we are the most unfortunate people on earth, is it proper to sing? When I think of it, I, your old mother, am consumed by despair and can only cry." Then, lamenting loudly, all three of us began to weep.

EXERCISES

1. Comparison of Modern Lhasa Tibetan and Written Tibetan[8]

Compare the spelling (Written Tibetan) of the following words and their pronunciation in Modern Lhasa Tibetan. Assuming that the spelling more or less reflects an older stage of the Tibetan language, what general sound changes have occurred between that stage and the stage of Modern Lhasa Tibetan? How can the tones of the latter be predicted from the spelling?

In order to answer the latter question you will have to take into consideration a number of factors, such as the quality of syllable-initial consonants, vowel length, and even the silent letters, that is, letters which are no longer pronounced. You should remember that in the romanization of Written Tibetan a consonant + h sequence does not represent a sequence of phonemes but single unit phonemes; thus, kh = [kʰ]; lh = [ɬ], and so on. Note also that the data has been somewhat simplified for the purposes of this exercise. For explanation of Chao's tone letters, cf. "Sketch of Mandarin Chinese" in this chapter.

2. Comparison of Tibetan and Chinese

Classical Tibetan and Mandarin Chinese are considered to be members of the same language family, Sino-Tibetan. However, that does not necesarily mean that they are very similar in most respects. After reading the sketches of these two languages in this chapter, compile a list of major differences and similarities between the two. (For example, Classical Tibetan was not a tone lan-

Table 4.8

WRITTEN TIBETAN	LHASA TIBETAN	GLOSS
1. *kha.*	kʰa ˩	'mouth'
2. *sa.*	sa ˩	'earth'
3. *rigs.*	ʐi ˩	'race, lineage'
4. *sems.*	sem ˩	'heart, mind'
5. *sha.*	ɕa ˩	'flesh'
6. *shar.*	ɕaː ˥	'east'
7. *chang.*	tɕʰaŋ ˥	'beer'
8. *khong.*	kʰoŋ ˥	'he, she'
9. *gsum.*	sum ˥	'three'
10. *stong.*	toŋ ˥	'thousand'
11. *nub.*	nu ʔ ˥	'west'
12. *bod.*	pø ʔ ˥	'Tibet'
13. *phag.*	pʰa ʔ ˩	'pig'
14. *mdun.*	tỹ ˥	'front'
15. *ring.*	ʐiŋ ˥	'long'
16. *za.*	sa ˥	'eat'
17. *mdung.*	tuŋ ˥	'spear'
18. *sgam.*	kam ˥	'box, chest'
19. *lags.*	la ˦	'yes'
20. *zas.pa.*	sɛ ˦ pa ˩	'food'
21. *lcags.*	tɕa ˩	'iron'
22. *sbrul.*	tʂy ˥	'snake'
23. *dkar.po.*	kaː ˦ po ˩	'white'
24. *mdzes.*	tse ˦	'beautiful'
25. *lha.*	ɬa ˩	'god'
26. *la.*	la ˥	'mountain pass'

guage, whereas Mandarin Chinese is. In both, however, plural number is only optionally marked on nouns, whereas it is obligatory in the pronouns.) Do the differences outnumber the similarities or vice-versa? You should be careful not to include language universal features in your list of similarities. (For example, both languages have both vowel and consonant phonemes.)

3. Altaic Typological Traits

Examine carefully the structure of the following sentences in Turkish, Korean and Japanese (all thought by some scholars to be members of the Altaic language family) and list all the structural similarities shared by all these languages as far as that can be determined from the data given. Then compare Classical Tibetan (Sino-Tibetan) example sentence to see how many of these shared features are also shared by a supposedly unrelated, non-Altaic language. What different possible explanations can you think of for the shared features among all these languages?

Turkish

Köy-ün-den çık-ma-mış köy-lü bu mesele-ler-i anla-r-mı?

village + his + from/ leave + not + past participle suff./ village + characterizing suffix/ this/ problem + pl. + def. obj./ understand + aorist + interrog.

'Does a villager who has not left his village understand these problems?'

Korean

Mikuk-esə o-si-n kyosu-nim-tŭl-i Səul-e-to ka-si-pni-k'a?

America + from/ come + honorif. + past tense dependent clause vb. marker/ professor + polite title + pl. + sub./ Seoul + to + also/ go + honorif. + formal statement + interrog.

'Are the professors who came from America going to Seoul also?'

Japanese

Kinoo kono hoteru ni toma-tta sensei wa moo Tookyoo e kaeri-mashi-ta-ka?

yesterday/ this/ hotel/ at/ stay + past/ teacher/ topic marker/ already/ Tokyo/ to/ return + polite suffix + past + interrog.

'Has the teacher who stayed at this hotel yesterday returned to Tokyo already?'

Classical Tibetan

Kyod.-kyis. khyim.-bdag. las. brnyas.-pa-'i. ba.glang. de. khyim.-gyi. nang-du. btang.-ngam?

you + ergative/ house + owner/ from/ borrowed/ (past of *brnya.* + nominalizing suffix + genitive/ bull/ that/ house + gen./ inside, interior + terminative/ let in (past of *gtong.* + interrog.

'Did you let into the house that bull which you borrowed from the master of the house?'

4. *Case Relation Marking in Various Languages*

Compare and contrast the marking of case relations (i.e., the various means whereby these languages signal different case relations) in Mandarin Chinese, Classical Tibetan, Russian, and English. You may refer either to the sketches in this and the previous chapters or refer to more detailed descriptions of these languages in the various reference grammars referred to in the bibliographies.

5. Hmong (Miao) Languages and Chinese

Examine the data in Table 4.9 from three different Hmong dialects (languages?) and Mandarin Chinese and then answer the following questions:

a. On the basis of this data can it be shown that the three Hmong languages are genetically related?

b. On the basis of this data can it be shown that Mandarin Chinese and Hmong languages are related?

c. Is there any evidence in the data to suggest that Hmong languages have been influenced by some Chinese dialect? (Note that Hmong languages are not spoken in the immediate vicinity of Peking Mandarin speakers. In Yunnan province they are in contact with Southwestern Mandarin speakers; elsewhere they are in contact with speakers of Chinese belonging to Sinitic language groups other than Mandarin.)[9]

Table 4.9

MIAO A	MIAO B	MIAO C	MANDARIN	GLOSS
1. u^{35}	$ə^{33}$	$tl̥e^{31}$	$ṣuei^{213}$	'water'
2. pu^{35}	pi^{33}	pe^{43}	san^{55}	'three'
3. $pʐei^{35}$	lu^{33}	$plou^{43}$	$sʅ^{41}$	'four'
4. $ʐi^{33}$	za^{31}	zi^{24}	pa^{55}	'eight'
5. pa^{53}	pa^{44}	pua^{44}	pai^{213}	'hundred'
6. mpe^{53}	$pɛ^{44}$	mpo^{44}	$çye^{45}$	'snow'
7. $noŋ^{42}$	$noŋ^{13}$	$naŋ^{13}$	y^{213}	'rain'
8. $pə^{53}$	pi^{44}	pu^{44}	$ṣuei^{41}$	'sleep'
9. $ta^{35} mpa^{53}$	pa^{44}	$mpua^{44}$	tsu^{55}	'pig'
10. $ɲin^{33} haŋ^{33}$	$ʐen^{31} haŋ^{31}$	$ʐen^{31} haŋ^{31}$	$jin^{55} xaŋ^{45}$	'bank'
11. $tɕi^{35} pa^{33}$	$ti^{35} pa^{31}$	$ti^{24} pa^{31}$	$ti^{41} pa^{55}$	'eighth'
12. nhe^{35}	$nhɛ^{33}$	$n̥o^{43}$	$zʅ^{41}$	'sun'
13. $noŋ^{31}$	$naŋ^{55}$	nau^{31}	$tsʰʅ^{55}$	'eat'
14. hu^{33}	fu^{31}	fu^{31}	xu^{45}	'lake'
15. pei^{31}	$paŋ^{55}$	$paŋ^{31}$	xua^{55}	'flower'
16. $me^{33} ṣei^{53}$	$mɛ^{31} sei^{55}$	$me^{24} ṣuei^{55}$	$mo^{41} ṣuei^{213}$	'ink'
17. $moŋ^{33}$	$moŋ^{11}$	mo^{21}	$tɕʰy^{41}$	'go'
18. to^{35}	to^{33}	to^{43}	$ṣən^{55}$	'deep'
19. le^{44}	$lɛ^{35}$	lo^{44}	$tuan^{213}$	'short'
20. $ntɯ^{44}$	ta^{35}	nte^{55}	$tsʰaŋ^{45}$	'long'
21. $ʐoŋ^{33} zi^{35}$	$ɣu^{44} ɛ^{44}$	$ʐoŋ^{31} zi^{24}$	$zuŋ^{45} ji^{41}$	'easy'
22. zi^{35}	zi^{35}	zi^{24}	ji^{41}	'10,000'
23. a^{44}	i^{33}	i^{43}	ji^{55}	'one'
24. $tɕi^{35} zi^{33}$	$ti^{35} zi^{31}$	$ti^{24} zi^{43}$	$ti^{41} ji^{55}$	'first'
25. $tɕi^{35} wu^{53}$	$ti^{35} vu^{55}$	$ti^{24} wu^{43}$	$ti^{41} wu^{213}$	'fifth'

Note that in item 16 ('ink'), the Mandarin Chinese word is morphologically complex: The first syllable means 'India ink (stick)' and the second means 'water' (i.e., 'liquid'). Chinese use ink sticks which they partially dissolve by rubbing them on an ink stone on which they pour a bit of water whenever they need ink for writing with the traditional Chinese writing brush.

6. Honorifics, Ellipsis, and Pronouns in Japanese[10]

In Japanese, personal pronouns are used very sparingly mainly because Japanese possesses a highly developed system of honorifics and humilifics which makes it possible for the interlocutors to understand who is being referred to without resorting to the use of personal pronouns. In addition, Japanese allows much more ellipsis than English and does not require pronominal "dummy" subjects such as are required in English in sentences like 'It is raining'. These features of Japanese are well illustrated by the following example of a typical short conversation in Japanese. After examining the word-by-word translation (with some key morphemes also explained) of the conversation and the notes that follow, try to translate the Japanese passage into idiomatic English, inserting pronouns into your English translation wherever appropriate.

(1) Mrs. Nakada: *Ara, moo sanji desu ne. Kore kara kaimono ni ikanakute wa narimasen.*

exclamation of surprise/ already/ three o'clock/ be/ tag question/. this/ from (= 'just now')/ shopping/ to/ not going/ topic marker/ won't do (= 'must go')

(2) Mrs. Tanaka: *Kaimono ni irassharu n desu ka?*

shopping/ dat. marker (here it marks purpose)/ go (honorif.)/ connecting morpheme (need not be translated into English)/ be/ interrog.

(3) Mrs. Nakada: *Hai, ashita wa shujin no haha no tanjoobi desu node . . . .*

yes/ tomorrow/ topic marker/ husband (plain)/ poss. marker/ mother (plain)/ poss. marker/ birthday/ be/ because, since

(4) Mrs. Tanaka: *Ja, nanika purezento o o-kai ni narimasu no?*

well then/ some/ present/ obj. marker/ honorif. prefix + buy/ dat. marker/ become (= *o-kai ni naru* = honor. 'to buy')/ interrog. used by women

(5) Mrs. Nakada: *Hai, depaato e mairimasu. Nanika ii aidia ga at-tara oshiete kudasai.*

yes/ department store/ to/ go (humilific)/. some/ good/ idea/ sub. marker/ exist, have + if/ teach, tell (gerund)/ give — imperative (from superior to an inferior)

(6) Mrs. Tanaka: *Donna mono ga o-suki desu ka?*

what kind/ thing/ sub. marker/ honorif. prefix + like/ be/ interrog.

(7) Mrs. Nakada: *Kiru mono yori mo taberu mono ga suki nan desu.*

wear/ thing/ than/ even/ eat/ thing/ sub. marker/ like/ connecting morpheme (need not be translated into English)/ be

(8) Mrs. Tanaka: *Jaa, keeki o sashiage-tara ikaga deshoo ka?*

well then/ cake/ obj. marker/ give, present (to a superior) + if/ how/ would be/ interrog.

(9) Mrs. Nakada: *Demo shujin ga keeki o katte kimasu.*

but, however/ husband/ sub. marker/ cake/ obj. marker/ buy/ come

(10) Mrs. Tanaka: *O-kaa-sama wa chokoreeto ga o-suki desu ka?*

honorif. prefix + mother + polite title/ topic marker/ chocolate/ subject marker/ honorif. prefix + like/ be/ interrog.

(11) Mrs. Nakada: *Hai, daisuki desu kedo, chokoreeto wa musume ga kaimasu. Honto ni nani o age-tara ii n deshoo ne. O-taku no go-shujin no o-kaasama wa donna mono ga o-suki desu ka?*

yes/ very much like/ be/ although/ chocolate/ topic marker/ daughter (plain)/ sub. marker/ buy/. real/ dat. marker (= 'really')/ what/ give (by inferior to a superior) + if/ good/ connecting morpheme/ would be/ tag question (= 'you see')/. honorif. prefix + house, family/ poss. marker/ honorif. prefix + husband/ poss. marker/ honorif. prefix + mother/ topic marker/ what kind/ thing/ sub. marker/ honorif. prefix + like, be fond of/ be/ interrog.

(12) Mrs. Tanaka: *Uchi wa nandemo suki desu kara, kooyuu mondai wa nai desu ne. Go-shujin to ojoosan wa maitoshi onaji mono o purezento nasaru n desu ka?*

home, family (plain)/ topic marker/ anything, everything/ like/ be/ because, since/ such/ problem/ topic marker/ not exist/ be/ tag question (= 'you see')/. honorif. prefix + husband/ and/ daughter, young lady (honorif.)/ topic marker/ every year/ same thing/ obj. marker/ present/ do (honorif.)/ connecting morpheme/ be/ interrog.

(13) Mrs. Nakada: *Hai, soo desu. Dewa, tonikaku itte mi-mashoo.*

yes/ so, thus/ be/. well then/ anyway/ go/ will see, let see (= 'go and see')

Note that Japanese is an SOV language. Case relations are indicated by means of postposed particles. You ought to be able to figure out the meaning of this conversation very easily, except for a couple of constructions which may seem strange to an English speaker.

a. 'Must' in Japanese is usually expressed by a construction which could be translated literally into English as 'as for not doing X, that won't do'. See (1).

b. Copula verb *desu* is sometimes used as a kind of polite auxilary with another verb. For example see (2), *irassharu* + connecting morpheme *n* + *desu* is a somewhat less formal equivalent of *irasshai-masu*. It does not have to be translated into English in such cases.

c. In (7) you will encounter the Japanese comparative construction: **X** *yori* (*mo*) **Y** + subject marker + *suki* = 'likes **Y** more than **X**'. Note also that the object of liking is marked as a subject, because in Japanese *suki* really means something like 'is likable, is desirable' (i.e., it is not a transitive verb) and cannot take a direct object.

d. In (9) *katte kimasu* can be translated as 'buy and bring'.

e. Most of foreign loanwords in Japanese are nouns; however, most of these can be easily made into verbs by the addition of *suru* 'to do'. Thus, for example, *purezento* 'present' can be made into a verb 'to make a gift or a present': *purezento suru*. In (12) *purezento nasaru* is an honorific equivalent since *nasaru* is the honorific equivalent of the plain verb *suru*. The humilific equivalent of *suru* is *itasu*. Note that humilifics are usually used in reference to one's self, honorifics only in reference to others (whether they are people being addressed or third persons), whereas plain forms can be used for either depending on the level of politeness and the context. For example, *iku* plain for 'to go' can be used in reference to one's self when one is not being especially polite, or in reference to other persons. However, the honorific equivalent *irassharu* cannot be used in reference to one's self, and the humilific *mairu* is used only in reference to one's self or one's family members when talking very politely to somebody of higher status.

NOTES

1. This term is fully explained in the "Sketch of Mandarin Chinese."

2. This term is also explained in the "Sketch of Mandarin Chinese."

3. Note that *bù* changes to *bú* before syllables in the fourth tone. This seems to be a dissimilatory type of *tone sandhi* which affects only a few common morphemes.

4. This selection is taken from Y. C. Liu (1960:15).

5. The English translation of this poem is cited from Chao (1957:274), who in turn cites it from C. W. Luh's *On Chinese Poetry,* published in Peiping in 1935.

6. For an example of a demonstrative preceding its head noun, cf. example 4.b on the following page.

7. This translation is cited from Lobsang Phuntsok Lhalungpa, transl. 1984. *The life of Milarepa.* Boulder, Col.: Shambhala Publ., 22–3.

8. The Lhasa Tibetan data is based on that found in Zhōngyāng Mínzúyuàn Shǎoshǔ Mínzú Yǔyán Yánjìusuǒ, ed., *Zhōngguó shǎoshǔ mínzú yǔyán.* Chengdu: Sìchuān Mínzú Chūbǎnshè, 1987.

9. The data is taken from Fùshì Wáng, ed. 1985. *Miáoyǔ jiǎnzhì.* Beijing: Mínzú chūbǎnshè. Superscripts in Table 4.9 indicate tones. For explanation, see page 132.

10. For this exercise I consulted with my wife, Emiko Lyovin, a native speaker of Japanese, whose invaluable help I hereby acknowledge.

SELECTED BIBLIOGRAPHY

General

Egerod, Søren. 1991. Far Eastern languages. In Sydney M. Lamb and E. Douglas Mitchell, eds. *Sprung from some common source,* 205–31. Stanford: Stanford University Press. (Interesting account not only of the genetic connections among the languages in the region but also of the various typological features of these languages.)

Ramsey, S. Robert. 1987. *The languages of China.* Princeton: Princeton University Press.

Shibatani, Masayoshi. 1990. *The languages of Japan.* New York: Cambridge University Press. (Contains good information on Japanese and Ainu languages.)

Zograf, G. A. 1960. *Jazyki Indii, Pakistana, Cejlona i Nepala.* Moscow: Izdatel'stvo "Nauka".

Turkic

Comrie, Bernard. 1992. Turkic languages. In William Bright et al., eds., *International encyclopedia of linguistics.* Vol. 4:187–90. New York: Oxford University Press.

Kornfilt, Jaklin, 1987. Turkish and the Turkic languages. In Bernard Comrie, ed., *The world's major languages,* 619–44. New York: Oxford University Press.

———. 1992. Turkish. In William Bright et al., eds., *International encyclopedia of linguistics.* Vol. 4:190–6. New York: Oxford University Press.

Menges, Karl H. 1968. *The Turkic languages and peoples: An introduction to Turkic studies.* Wiesbaden: Otto Harrassowitz.

Mongolian

Binnick, Robert I. 1992. Mongolian languages. In William Bright et al., eds. *International encyclopedia of linguistics.* Vol. 2:434–7. New York: Oxford University Press.

Poppe, Nicholas. 1970. *Mongolian language handbook.* Washington: Center for Applied Linguistics.

Street, John C. 1963. *Khalkha structure*. Uralic and Altaic Series. Vol. 24. Bloomington: Indiana University.

Tungusic

Comrie, Bernard. 1981. Altaic languages. In Bernard Comrie et al., *The languages of the Soviet Union,* 39–91. Cambridge: Cambridge University Press.

———. 1992. Altaic languages. In William Bright et al., eds., *International encyclopedia of linguistics.* Vol. 1:48–51. New York: Oxford University Press.

Dörfer, Gerhard. 1985. *Mongolo-Tungusica*. Wiesbaden: Otto Harrassowitz.

Korean-Japanese-Okinawan

Kim, Nam-Kil. 1987. Korean. In Bernard Comrie, ed., *The world's major languages,* 881–98. New York: Oxford University Press.

———. 1992. Korean. In William Bright et al., eds., *International encyclopedia of linguistics.* Vol. 2:282–6. New York: Oxford University Press.

Martin, Samuel E. 1991a. Morphological clues to the relationships of Japanese and Korean. In Philip Baldi, ed., *Patterns of change, change of patterns: Linguistic change and reconstruction methodology,* 483–510. New York: Mouton de Gruyter.

———. 1991b. Recent research on the relationships of Japanese and Korean. In Sydney M. Lamb and E. Douglas Mitchell, eds., *Sprung from some common source,* 269–92. Stanford: Stanford University Press.

Shibatani, Masayoshi. 1987. Japanese. In Bernard Comrie, ed., *The world's major languages,* 855–80. New York: Oxford University Press.

———. 1992. Japanese. In William Bright et al., eds., *International encyclopedia of linguistics,* Vol. 2:248–52. New York: Oxford University Press.

Syromjatnikov, N. A. 1972. *Drevnejaponskij jazyk*. Moscow: Izdatel'stvo "Nauka". (Suggests genetic relationship between Japanese and Austronesian.)

Ainu

Tamura, Suzuko. 1981. Ainugo. In Hajime Kitamura, ed., *Sekai no gengo,* 415–45. Tokyo: Taishūkan shoten.

'Altaic'

Clauson, Sir Gerard. 1956. The case against the Altaic theory. *Central Asiatic Journal* 2(3):181–7. (This is one of the early attacks against the Altaic hypothesis.)

Miller, Roy Andrew. 1971. *Japanese and other Altaic languages*. Chicago: University of Chicago Press. (The author presents evidence for including Japanese in Altaic.)

———. 1991. Genetic connections among the Altaic languages. In Sydney M. Lamb and E. Douglas Mitchell, eds., *Sprung from some common source,* 293–327. Stanford: Stanford University Press. (Miller tries to rebut various critics of the Altaic hypothesis, starting with Sir Gerald Clauson.)

Ono, Susumu. 1970. *The origin of the Japanese language*. Tokyo: Kokusai Bunka Shinkokai. Translation of *Nihongo no kigen*, originally published in 1957. (Ohno sets out his hypothesis that Japanese is an Altaic language with an Austronesian substratum).

Ooe, Takao. 1981. Arutai shogo. In Hajime Kitamura, ed., *Sekai no gengo,* 115–48. Tokyo: Taishūkan shoten. (Kōza gengo, vol. 6)

Patrie, James. 1982. *The genetic relationship of the Ainu language*. (Oceanic Linguistics Special Publication, no. 17.) Honolulu: University of Hawaii Press. (Concludes that Ainu is an Altaic language.)

Poppe, Nicholas. 1960. *Vergleichende Grammatik der altaischen Sprachen. Teil 1, Vergleichende Lautlehre.* Wiesbaden: Otto Harrassowitz.

———. 1965. *Introduction to Altaic linguistics.* Wiesbaden: Otto Harrassowitz.

Shirokogoroff, S. M. 1970. *Ethnological and linguistical* [sic] *aspects of the Ural-Altaic hypothesis.* The Netherlands: Oosterhout. (A reprint of *Tsing Hua Journal,* Anthropological Publications, vol. 6, originally published in Peiping, China, in 1931.)

Sunik, O. P., ed. 1971. *Problema obščnosti altajskix jazykov.* Leningrad: Nauka.

Unger, J. Marshall. 1991. Japanese and what other Altaic languages. In Philip Baldi, ed., *Patterns of change, change of patterns: Linguistic change and reconstruction methodology,* 547–64. New York: Mouton de Gruyter. (This is one of the more recent critical attacks on the Altaic hypothesis, especially on the inclusion of Japanese in Altaic.)

'Nostratic'

Kaiser, M., and V. Shevroshkin. 1988. Nostratic. *Annual Review of Anthropology* 17:309–29. (An overview of the Nostratic hypothesis written by its proponents.)

Paleosiberian

Comrie, Bernard. 1981. Paleosiberian and other languages. In Bernard Comrie, ed., *The languages of the Soviet Union,* 238–78. Cambridge: Cambridge University Press.

———. 1992. Siberian languages. In William Bright et al., eds., *International encyclopedia of linguistics,* Vol. 3:429–32. New York: Oxford University Press.

Miyaoka, Osahito. 1981. Kyū ajia shogo. In Hajime Kitamura, ed., *Sekai no gengo,* 393–411. Kōza gengo, vol. 6, Tokyo: Taishūkan shoten.

Sino-Tibetan

Benedict, Paul. 1972. *Sino-Tibetan: A conspectus.* Contrib. ed. James A. Matisoff. Cambridge: Cambridge University Press. (This classic work is now somewhat outdated but should be consulted by all who are interested in this language family.)

DeLancey, Scott. 1987. Sino-Tibetan languages. In Bernard Comrie, ed., *The world's major languages,* 797–810. New York: Oxford University Press.

———. 1992. Sino-Tibetan languages. In William Bright et al., eds., *International encyclopedia of linguistics.* Vol. 3:445–9. New York: Oxford University Press.

Hale, A. 1982. *Research on Tibeto-Burman languages.* The Hague: Mouton.

Hashimoto, Mantarō. 1981. Shina-chibetto shogo. In Hajime Kitamura, ed., *Sekai no gengo,* 149–70. Kōza gengo, Tokyo: Taishūkan shoten.

Matisoff, James A. 1991. Sino-Tibetan linguistics: Present state and future prospects. *Annual Review of Anthropology* 20:469–504. (This is an excellent overview of the Sino-Tibetan family of languages as well as languages which are only sometimes included as possible members of the family. Includes very good typological information about all of the language groups concerned.)

Shafer, Robert. 1966–73. *Introduction to Sino-Tibetan.* Wiesbaden: Otto Harrassowitz. (This work contains a wealth of material but is already quite dated.)

Hmong-Mien

Cǎo, Cuì-yún. 1987. Miáoyǎoyǔ tèdiǎn gaìyào. In Zhōngyāng Mínzúyuàn Shǎoshǔ Mínzú Yǔyán Yánjiùsuǒ, ed., *Zhōngguó shǎoshǔ mínzú yǔyán,* 403–5. Chengdu: Sìchuān Mínzú Chūbǎnshè. (The special characteristics of Hmong-Mien languages are cited from this work.)

Tai-Kadai

Diller, Anthony. 1992. Thai. In William Bright et al., eds., *International encyclopedia of linguistics*. Vol. 4:149–56. New York: Oxford University Press.

———. Tai languages. In William Bright et al., eds. *International encyclopedia of linguistics*. Vol. 4:128–31. New York: Oxford University Press.

Hudak, Thomas John. 1987. Thai. In Bernard Comrie, ed., *The world's major languages*, 757–75. New York: Oxford University Press.

Strecker, David. 1987. Tai languages. In Bernard Comrie, ed., *The world's major languages*, 747–56. New York: Oxford University Press.

'Austro-Tai'

Benedict, Paul. 1942. Thai, Kadai and Indonesian: A new alignment in Southeastern Asia. *American Anthropologist* 44:576–601. (In this famous article Benedict first presented his evidence that Tai languages are most likely genetically related to Austronesian languages rather than to Sino-Tibetan.)

———. 1975. *Austro-Thai language and culture, with a glossary of roots*. New Haven: Human Relations Area Files Press. (Considerably more evidence here than in Benedict 1942 is presented, much of it rather controversial.)

———. 1986. *Japanese/Austro-Tai*. Ann Arbor: Karoma Press. (Benedict proposes that Japanese is also a part of Austro-Tai.)

Thurgood, Graham. 1993. Tai-Kadai and Austronesian: The nature of the historical relationship. Paper presented at the *Conference of Asia-Mainland/Austronesian Connections*, Honolulu, May 10–13, 1993.

Austroasiatic

Diffloth, Gérard and Norman Zide. 1992. Austro-Asiatic languages. In William Bright et al., eds., *International encyclopedia of linguistics*, Vol. 1:137–42. New York: Oxford University Press.

Nguyễn, Dình-Hoà. 1987. Vietnamese. In Bernard Comrie, ed., *The world's major languages*, 777–96. New York: Oxford University Press. (Vietnamese is not a typical Austroasiatic language since it has been very much influenced by Chinese.)

Sakamoto, Yasuyuki. 1981. Ōsutro-ajia shogo. In Hajime Kitamura, ed., *Sekai no gengo*, 173–96. Kōza gengo, vol. 6. Tokyo: Taishūkan shoten.

Schmidt, W. 1906. Die Mon-Khmer Völker, ein Bindeglied zwischen Völkern Zentral-Asiens und Austronesiens. *Archiv für Antrhopologie* 5:59–109. (This is the article which launched the so-called Austric hypothesis which genetically links the Austroasiatic family with the Austronesian family.)

Dravidian

Andronov, M. S. 1970. *Dravidian languages*. Moscow: Izdatel'stvo "Nauka".

Krishnamurti, Bh. 1992a. Dravidian languages. In William Bright et al., eds., *International encyclopedia of linguistics*, Vol. 1:373–8. New York: Oxford University Press.

———. 1992b. Telugu. In William Bright et al., eds., *International encyclopedia of linguistics*. Vol. 4:137–41. New York: Oxford University Press.

Steever, Sanford B. 1987. Tamil and the Dravidian languages. In Bernard Comrie, ed., *The world's major languages*, 725–46. New York: Oxford University Press.

———. 1992. Tamil. In William Bright et al., eds., *International encyclopedia of linguistics*. Vol. 4:131–6. New York: Oxford University Press.

Burushaski

Berger, Hermann. 1974. *Das Yasin-Burushaski (Werchikwar): Grammatik, Texte, Wörterbuch*. Wiesbaden: Otto Harrassowitz. (One of the very few modern accounts of the language.)

Klimov, G. A., and D. I. Èdel'man. 1970. *Jazyk burušaski.* Moscow: Izdatel'stvo "Nauka."

Chinese

Chao, Yuen Ren. 1930. A system of tone letters. *Le Maître Phonétique,* troisième série, vol. 30:24–7.

———. 1968. *A grammar of spoken Chinese.* Berkeley: University of California Press. (Although not very up to date in its theoretical framework, this is a very good and usable reference grammar.)

Forrest, R. A. D. 1965. *The Chinese language.* 2d, rev. ed. London: Faber & Faber. (Emphasis on historical and comparative aspects of Chinese.)

Kratochvil, Paul. 1968. *The Chinese language today: Features of an emerging standard.* London: Hutchinson University Library.

Li, Charles N. 1992. Chinese. In William Bright et al., eds., *International encyclopedia of linguistics.* Vol. 1:257–63. New York: Oxford University Press.

Li, Charles N., and Sandra A. Thompson. 1979. Chinese: Dialect variations and language reforms. In Timothy Shopen, ed, *Languages and their status,* 295–335. Cambridge, Mass.: Winthrop.

———. 1981. *Mandarin Chinese: a functional reference grammar.* Berkeley and Los Angeles: University of California Press. (A more modern approach than that used in Chao's reference grammar; more emphasis on syntax.)

———. 1987. Chinese. In Bernard Comrie, ed., *The world's major languages,* 811–33. New York: Oxford University Press.

Norman, Jerry. 1988. *Chinese.* Cambridge Language Surveys. Cambridge: Cambridge University Press. (This is most up-to-date general work available in English and gives a very thorough overview of all aspects of the Chinese language.)

Tibetan

Chang, Kun. 1992. Tibetan. In William Bright et al., eds., *International encyclopedia of linguistics.* Vol. 4:156–60. New York: Oxford University Press. (This is basically an overview of Modern Lhasa Tibetan.)

Chang, Kun, and Betty Shefts. 1964. *Manual of spoken Tibetan (Lhasa dialect).* Seattle: University of Washington Press. (For those interested in comparing Classical Tibetan and the modern dialect of Lhasa, this is a fairly good source, especially since there are accompanying tapes which can be ordered with the book. This is, however, a language textbook, not a reference grammar.)

Das, Sarat Chandra (Rai Bahadur). 1960. *Tibetan-English dictionary.* Alipore, West Bengal: West Bengal Government Press. (Originally published in 1912.) (Although there are now more recently compiled dictionaries, this is still a very good dictionary and is commonly found in American libraries.)

Hodge, Stephen. 1990. *An introduction to Classical Tibetan.* Warminster, Wiltshire, U.K.: Airs & Phillips. (Contains reading passages with glossaries and grammatical notes.)

Hu, Tan. 1988. A comparative study of tonal and toneless Tibetan dialects. [In Chinese.] In Paul K. Eguchi, ed., *Languages and history in East Asia: Festschrift for Tatsuo Nishida on the occasion of his 60th birthday,* 75–92. Kyoto: Shokado.

Jaeschke, H. A. 1958. *A Tibetan-English dictionary (with an English-Tibetan vocabulary).* London: Kegal Paul. (Reprint of the 1881 original edition.) (This is another fairly common dictionary of Classical Tibetan.)

Lalou, Marcelle. 1950. *Manuel élémentaire de tibétain classique.* Paris: Librarie d'Amérique et d'Orient, Adrien Maisonneuve. (This is a fairly good, but short, reference grammar of Classical Tibetan with many examples from various Tibetan literary works.)

Miller, Roy, 1956. *The Tibetan system of writing.* Washington, D.C.: American Council of Learned Societies, Program in Oriental Languages, Publ. ser. B, Aids No. 6. (This interesting work relates the pronunciation of modern Lhasa Tibetan and the traditional Tibetan writing system. It shows how Lhasa tones are reflected in the spelling, i.e., from what segments the tones arose.)

————. 1970. A grammatical sketch of Classical Tibetan. *Journal of the American Oriental Society* 90:74–96. (A somewhat different view of the language than what has been presented in this book.)

Parfionovich, Y. M. 1982. The written Tibetan language. Moscow: Nauka Publishing House. Transl. from the original Russian by S. S. Glitman. (This is a fairly straightforward sketch of Modern Literary Tibetan, with references to Classical Tibetan as well.)

Rerix, Ju. N. 1961. *Tibetskij jazyk.* Moscow: Izdatel'stvo "Nauka". (A good sketch of Classical Tibetan.)

Wilson, Joe Bransford. 1992. *Translating Buddhism from Tibetan.* Ithaca, N.Y.: Snow Lion Publications. (In spite of its somewhat misleading title, this is really a very good, comprehensive modern introductory grammar of Classical Tibetan.)

Chapter 5 Languages of Africa

In Africa, as elsewhere, there has obviously been some diffusion of linguistic features from one family to another (e.g., tones into Afro-Asiatic languages, and clicks from Khoisan languages into a number of Bantu languages). Thus, even though speakers of Hausa are racially quite distinct from most other Afro-Asiatic speakers in that they are Negroid whereas the majority of Afro-Asiatic speakers are not, and even though Hausa has tones which most Afro-Asiatic languages do not, Africanists no longer dispute the classification of Hausa as a member of the Afro-Asiatic language family.

According to Welmers (1973:78), with a very few exceptions the languages of Africa south of the Sahara are tone languages regardless of their genetic affiliation. Thus, all known languages that belong to the Chadic branch of the Afro-Asiatic family are tonal, and according to Hetzron (1987a:650) Omotic and some Cushitic branch languages are also tonal. All the studied languages belonging to the Khoisan and the Nilo-Saharan language families are tonal. Finally, a very large majority of languages belonging to the Niger-Congo language family are also tonal. Exceptions are Wolof, Serere, and Fula of the Atlantic branch, as well as Swahili, which is a Bantu language.

Since it is highly improbable that tone developed independently in all four language families mentioned, one must consider it very likely that at least this feature has diffused across genetic boundaries throughout most of the continent, perhaps because tone is a feature which is more easily diffused than others. (Note that there has been apparently similar diffusion of tone in East and Southeast Asia.)

The language families of Africa may perhaps be best discussed in terms of their geographical location from north to south.

I. AFRO-ASIATIC (AFRASIAN) FAMILY

According to Zaborski (1992:36), this family is divided into the following branches.

1. EGYPTIAN BRANCH

The only more or less modern language belonging to this branch is *Coptic,* which probably became extinct in the sixteenth century and now survives only as a liturgical language used by the adherents of the Coptic Christian Church in Egypt. (The extinct *Ancient Egyptian* also belonged to this branch. Modern Egyptian is a dialect of Arabic.)

Although now extinct, Egyptian is a very important branch of the Afro-Asiatic language family since its written records cover a period from about 3000 B.C. to about A.D. 1500, a time span of 4,500 years, and are among the oldest written records in any language. The Ancient Egyptian language was the language of a great ancient empire and civilization and therefore continues to fascinate, especially its hieroglyphic system of writing, which was briefly referred to in Chapter 2.

Basically, Egyptian hieroglyphic writing was a mixed system that included alphabetic elements as well as logographic elements. However, the alphabetic elements did not constitute a true alphabet since some signs represented single consonants, some two, and some three, and there was no provision for indicating vowels at all. Therefore, Ancient Egyptian texts are usually romanized without any vowels but only with consonant and semivowel letters. Earlier stages of Ancient Egyptian had VSO word order.

2. SEMITIC

The languages belonging to this branch cover most of North Africa, all of the Arabian peninsula, Iraq, Israel, Lebanon, Syria, and much of Ethiopia, as well as the island of Malta and parts of Iran and Turkey. According to Hetzron (1992:413), this branch is further subdivided into the following subbranches.

a. East Semitic or Akkadian

The languages belonging to this subbranch were all very important languages of the ancient Middle East but are now extinct: *Akkadian,* including its two variants, *Assyrian* and *Babylonian,* spoken from about 3,000 B.C.E to the beginning of the Common Era in the area of what is now modern Iraq.

b. West Semitic

This branch is further subdivided into two subbranches.

i. Central Semitic

This in turn is subdivided into two groups.

a. Aramaic

This is another important branch of Semitic because its various older representatives were widely used in the ancient Middle East. *Syriac,* a Late Aramaic language, retains its importance as the liturgical language of many Asian Christian churches (such as the Syrian Orthodox church).

According to Hoberman (1992:98), there are four major groups of Aramaic languages spoken today: (1) the *Ma'lūla* group in Syria (19,215 sp.); (2) *Tūrōyo* or *Suryoyo,* in southeastern Turkey and in Syria (about 50,000 tot. sp.); (3) *Northeastern Aramaic* (167,000 or more speakers), in a region straddling northern Iraq and adjacent parts of Iran and Turkey; and (4) *Modern Mandaic* (number of speakers unavailable), in Khuzistan, Iran.

b. South-Central Semitic

This subgroup in turn is subdivided into two groups:

1. *Arabic.* The main representative of this group is *Arabic* (over 160 million sp.), which has a number of dialects, many of which are not mutually intelligible. Speakers of different dialect groups use Modern Literary Arabic, which is a modified form of Classical Arabic, the language of the Muslim sacred book, the Koran, as a formal spoken and written language. (Cf. "Sketch of Modern Literary Arabic" in this chapter for further information about dialects of Arabic.)

Maltese (spoken by about 330,000 sp. on the island of Malta in the Mediterranean) is so different from other Arabic dialects, including the Maghribi (North African) dialects to which it is most closely related, that most linguists consider it to be a separate language. It has been much influenced by European languages, especially Italian, and since the majority of Maltese are Christians, Classical Arabic is not used by Maltese as a formal language and therefore does not exert a conservative influence on Maltese language as it does on other Arabic dialects.

2. *Canaanite.* The chief modern representative is *Hebrew* (est. 4 million tot. sp., of whom 2,709,000 are in Israel and 101,686 are in the United States). This was almost (but not quite) a dead language by the time of Christ, although it remained in wide use as the liturgical language of Judaism. It was "resurrected" in this century to serve as the official language of the state of Israel. (At the time of Christ, the chief language of Palestine was Aramaic, another Semitic language. Later on, Jews in the diaspora spoke various languages: Arabic in Arabic countries, Ladino, a dialect of Spanish, in the countries of the Mediterranean Europe, and Yiddish, a German dialect, in East and Central Europe.)

In addition, several ancient languages, the most important of which was *Phoenician* (spoken on the coast of Lebanon, in Carthage, and various Phoenician colonies in the Mediterranean) belonged to this group.

ii. South Semitic

This subbranch includes the Semitic languages of Ethiopia: *Amharic* (10 million first-language speakers, plus 9 million second-language speakers in Ethiopia), *Tigrinya* (4 million sp. in Eritrea), *Tigré* (600,000 sp. mostly in Eritrea, some in Sudan), *Central West Gurage* (542,000 sp. in Ethiopia) and *East Gurage* (200,000 sp. in Ethiopia).

In addition, the so-called South Arabian languages (not the same as Arabic!) also belong to this subbranch. *Mahri,* a language spoken by 50,000 speakers in Oman, 3,537 in Kuwait, and unspecified number of speakers in Saudi Arabia and Yemen, is one of the representatives of this group.

3. CUSHITIC BRANCH

The languages belonging to this branch are spoken in and around Ethiopia. The chief representatives are *Somali* (5,620,000 sp., of whom 4,018,500 are in Somalia, 888,000 in Ethiopia, and the rest in Kenya, United Arab Emirates, and Djibouti), *Hadiyya* (2 million sp. in Ethiopia), *Oromo* or *Galla* (4,840,000 tot. sp., of which 4,734,000 are in Ethiopia and the rest in Kenya), *Western Oromo* (5,750,000 sp., mostly in Ethiopia and some in Egypt), and *Afar* or *Danakil* (more than 600,000 sp., of whom 400,000 are in Ethiopia and 200,000 in Djibouti).

In addition, there are some scholars who think that languages once classified as being West Cushitic should be considered as a separate branch of Afro-Asiatic family called *Omotic.* This is still a very controversial issue since the so-called *Omotic* languages are very different from each other and exhibit few common traits.

Omotic is supposed to include 40 languages spoken in southern Ethiopia by more than 2 million speakers. The language with the largest number of speakers is *Wolaytta,* reportedly spoken by 2 million people.

4. BERBER

This branch is represented by a number of languages scattered over North Africa from Senegal to Egypt. Most of them have borrowed extensively from their neighboring Arab dialects and are spoken by nomadic tribesmen. According to Ruhlen (1987:93, 320), there are three major subbranches of this branch.

a. Eastern Berber

Representatives of this subgroup are the minor languages *Awjilah* (spoken in Cyrenaica, Lybia) and *Sawknah* (spoken in Tripolitania, Lybia). (No information is available on the number of speakers of either of these languages.)

b. Northern Berber

The chief representatives of this branch are *Tamazight* (spoken by 3 million sp., of whom 1.8 million are in Morocco, the rest in Algeria), *Tachelhit* (spoken by 3 million sp. in Morocco), *Tarifit* or *Riff* (1 million sp. in Morocco);

Kabyle (2,537,000 tot. sp., of whom 537,000 are in France and the rest in Algeria).

c. Tamasheq

This subgroup is represented by *Tahoua Tamajeq (Tuareg)* (360,000 sp. or more, of whom 300,000 or more are in Niger, 50,000 to 60,000 in Mali), *Air Tamajeq* or *Tuareg* (25,000 sp. in Niger), *Timbuktu Tamasheq* (about 250,000 sp. in central and northwestern Mali, and 10,000 in Burkina Fasso), and *Hoggar Tamahaq* (25,000 sp. mostly in Algeria, some in Niger and Lybia).

5. CHADIC BRANCH

Chadic languages are spoken in West and Central Africa just below the Sahara (mainly in parts of Nigeria, Niger, Cameroon, and Chad). According to Newman (1992:253), the Chadic branch is further subdivided into four major branches.

a. West Branch

This branch is represented by the most important Chadic language, *Hausa* (25 million tot. sp., including first- and second-language speakers, of whom most are in Nigeria and Niger, some in Cameroon, Togo, and Burkina Faso). Hausa also serves as a trade language among othe ethnic groups in the region.

b. Biu-Mandara Branch

This subgroup includes a large number of languages (more than 60). Its major representatives are *Bura* (250,000 sp. in Nigeria), *Higi* (180,000 sp. in Nigeria), *Kilba* (100,000 sp. in Nigeria), *Mafa* (136,000 sp. in northern Cameroon and 2,000 in Nigeria), and *Central Margi* (200,000 sp. in Nigeria).

c. East Branch

This subbranch contains about 30 languages, most of which are spoken by fewer than 40,000 speakers. The chief among them are *Nancere* (50,000 sp. in southwestern Chad), *Gabri* (40,000 sp. in southwestern Chad), and *Mubi* (36,000 sp. in south central Chad).

d. Masa Branch

This subgroup is represented by *Marba* (100,000 sp. in southwestern Chad), *Masa* (183,000 tot. sp., of whom 103,000 are in northern Cameroon and 80,000 in southwestern Chad), and *Musey* (120,000 tot. sp., of whom 100,000 are in southwestern Chad and 20,000 in northern Cameroon).

There are two features which are fairly widely distributed among the Afro-Asiatic languages. For example, most of these languages (with the exception of the languages belonging to the Egyptian branch) have a three-way contrast in obstruents: voiced, voiceless, and emphatic. The so-called emphatic consonants are realized as pharyngealized or velarized consonants in many

Semitic and Berber languages, as glottalized ejectives in the Semitic languages of Ethiopia, South Arabian (not the same as Arabic), Cushitic, and Omotic languages, and as imploded consonants in the Chadic languages. Which realization of the emphatic series will be found appears to be an areal phenomenon. Many of these languages also have pharyngeal fricatives which are generally rare in other language families (although Khoisan languages are reported to have pharyngealized vowels).

With the exception of Chadic, Cushitic, and Omotic branches, Afro-Asiatic languages exhibit another somewhat unusual feature: most of their verb roots (from which nouns can be derived as well) can be characterized as consisting of three consonant segments (with semivowels counting as consonants) which are not associated with any vowel or vowels, and the vowels which appear in the various forms of the verb can be analyzed as belonging to inflectional or derivational morphemes, that is, as infixes, as discontinuous morpheme infixes, or as prefixes and suffixes. (Cf. "Sketch of Modern Literary Arabic" in this chapter for a fuller explanation of this phenomenon. This feature is especially prominent in Classical Arabic.)

According to Hetzron (1987a:652), the dominant word order in Semitic, Egyptian, and Berber branches is VSO, although Amharic (Ethiopian Semitic) is SOV; languages of the Chadic branch are mostly SVO (but VSO order is also found), and Cushitic branch languages are almost all SOV.

II. Nilo-Saharan (Nilo-Sahelian) Family

This language family has not yet been studied very extensively, and there are some scholars who seriously doubt that all the languages included in it are genetically related. There is also disagreement about the genetic subgrouping of this family. Roughly speaking, these languages are sandwiched between the Afro-Asiatic languages (to the north) and the Niger-Congro languages (to the south).

Racially the speakers of this family of languages are similar to the speakers of the languages belonging to the Niger-Congo family.

Nilo-Saharan languages are tonal, have mostly SVO word order (a few have SOV, and some have VSO, which is more common in Afro-Asiatic) with adjectives following the nouns they modify, have complicated morphology, and have internal flection. (Changes within a given morpheme itself, such as those observed in English words 'foot' and 'feet', are referred to as 'internal flection'.) Some languages have grammatical gender, but none have the complex noun class systems that are found in many Niger-Congo languages.

According to Dimmendaal (1992:100), who basically follows Greenberg's (1963) classification, this family is subdivided into six subbranches.

1. Chari-Nile

This branch has three major subbranches and one minor one.

a. Berta

This branch is represented by a single language, *Berta,* spoken by about 50,000 people, of whom 28,000 are in Ethiopia, the rest in Sudan.

b. Central Sudanic

Some languages belonging to this branch are *Moru* (70,000 sp. in Sudan), and *Madi* (232,920 sp., of whom 214,920 are in Uganda, the rest in Sudan).

c. East Sudanic

This branch includes a number of fairly important languages which are spoken by a substantial number of speakers.

The chief representatives are *Luo* (spoken by 3,243,000 sp., of whom 3,036,000 are in Tanzania, the rest in Kenya), *Maasai* (657,000 sp. almost equally divided between Kenya and Tanzania), *Nuer* (800,000 tot. sp., of whom 740,000 are in Sudan, the rest in Ethiopia), and the various *Dinka* languages, spoken by about 2 million people in Sudan.

Ancient Nubian, a language known from various written materials (mostly Christian texts) dating as far back as A.D. 795, belongs in this group, as do its various descendants such as *Kenuzi-Dongola* (about 1 million sp., of whom 170,000 are in Sudan, the rest in Egypt), and *Nobiin* or *Fadidja* (338,000 sp. in Egypt).

d. Kunama

This branch is represented by a single language, *Kunama* (perhaps as many as 70,000 sp. in Ethiopia).

2. FUR

Fur (or *Fora*) is spoken by 500,000 speakers in western Sudan and by 1,086 in Chad.

3. KOMUZ

This subbranch is represented by a few languages spoken on the Ethiopia-Sudan border such as *Gumuz* (90,000 sp., of whom 50,000 are in Ethiopia and the rest in Sudan).

4. MABAN

This subbranch is represented by fewer than ten minor languages spoken in Chad.

Maba (or *Mabangi*) has 56,000 speakers in Chad and perhaps 9,000 in Sudan. The majority are reported to be bilingual in Arabic; *Masalit* has a total of 200,000 speakers, of whom 115,000 are in Sudan and 73,000 in Chad.

5. SAHARAN

The chief representative is *Kanuri* (*Kanuri-Yerwa*), which is spoken by about 3.5 million speakers, of which 3 million or more are in northeastern Nigeria, 100,000 or more in Chad, and 56,500 in Cameroon.

6. SONGHAI

Songhai is spoken by a total of 528,000 speakers, of which 400,000 are in Mali, 93,000 in Niger, and 34,131 in Burkina Fasso. It was formerly the language of an empire centered around Timbuktu. This language is said to be very distantly related to the rest of the Nilo-Saharan, and there are some scholars who dispute its genetic relationship with the latter.

III. NIGER-CONGO FAMILY

The total number of speakers of languages that belong to this family of languages is about 200 million. According to K. Williamson's (1989:21) overview of this family, the latter is divided into three main branches.

1. KORDOFANIAN

This branch is represented by a small group of minor languages spoken in Sudan the total number of whose speakers does not exceed 200,000.

Some of the languages belonging to this branch are *Tegali* (80,000 sp. in Sudan), *Koalib* (24,000 sp. in Sudan), and *Katla* (22,000 sp. in Sudan).

2. MANDE

These languages are spoken in Sierra Leone, Niger, and Liberia (somewhat to the east of the West Atlantic subbranch). Major representatives are *Kpelle* (408,176 sp. in Liberia), *Maninka* (1,651,200 or more speakers, of whom 1,525,000 are in Guinea, 96,000 in Guinea Bissau), *Bambara* (1,500,000 sp. spread around Mali, Côte d'Ivoire, or Ivory Coast, Senegal, Gambia, and Burkina Faso), and *Mende* (1,016,000 sp., of whom are 16,462 in Liberia, the rest in Sierra Leone).

3. ATLANTIC-CONGO

This branch in turn has a very large number of subbranches and covers most of Africa south of the Sahara, Sudan, and Ethiopia with the exception of the parts of South Africa, Namibia, Angola, and Tanzania that are occupied by the speakers of languages belonging to the Khoisan family, and, of course, those in which Afrikaans and English are spoken.

The following are three major subbranches of this branch.

a. Atlantic

These languages are spoken in Guinea, Cameroon, Senegal, Sierra Leone, and neighboring countries. The chief representatives are *Fulacunda* (1,436,000 sp., of whom 1,172,000 are in Senegal, 169,000 in Guinea Bissau, and 94,120 in Gambia), *Fuuta Jalon* (2,576,000 sp. or more, of whom 2,440,000 are in Guinea, 136,000 in Sierra Leone), plus various other so-called *Fulani* languages (the total number of speakers of all the Fulani languages is estimated to be somewhere between 8 million and 10 million), and *Wolof* (3 million sp., which includes about 1 million second-language speakers in Senegal and a few in Mauritania).

b. Volta-Congo

This subgroup has five subbranches.

i. Kru

Representative languages are *Northeastern Krumen* (17,000 sp. in Côte d'Ivoire, or Ivory Coast) and *Southern Krumen* (27,000 sp. in Côte d'Ivoire).

ii. Kwa

Representatives of this subbranch are *Akan,* also known as *Twi, Fanti,* and *Ashanti* (4,300,000 sp. in Ghana), *Éwé* (1,980,000 sp., of whom 1,350,000 are in Ghana, the rest in Togo), *Fon-Gbe* (1,030,000 sp., of whom 27,189 are in Togo, the rest in Benin), and *Baule* (1,500,000 sp. in Côte d'Ivoire).

It should be noted that in the earlier classifications of this family, the Kwa branch has a much broader scope and covered many more languages than in this formulation. This is somewhat confusing, since there still is a branch called Kwa in the new formulation, only its extension has been radically narrowed.

iii. Benue-Congo

This group of languages has eleven subbranches which will not be listed here. It is represented by languages spoken on the coast of the Gulf of Guinea, from Côte d'Ivoire and into Nigeria. The main non-Bantu representatives are *Yoruba* (16 million sp. in Nigeria, also some in Togo and Benin), *Igbo* (12 million sp. in Nigeria), *Edo* or *Bini* (1 million sp. in Nigeria), *Nupe* (1 million sp. in Nigeria, *Efik* (spoken by 36,000 native-language speakers, of whom 26,300 are in Nigeria, the rest in Cameroon; if second-language speakers are included, the total number of speakers is 3,500,000) and *Katab* (32,370 sp. in Nigeria).

A very important subbranch of this subbranch in *Bantu.* This subbranch contains a very large number of languages and occupies a larger territory than all the other subbranches of Niger-Congo put together. It is believed that Bantu languages originated in central Nigeria and gradually spread as far as South Africa. Most of the languages spoken by large numbers of people belong to the Bantu subgroup.

Swahili (1,300,000 first-language speakers; 30 million if second-language speakers are included; some sources claim up to 50 million sp. for Swahili). Swahili is used as an official language in many countries of East Africa and as a lingua franca in adjacent regions. (Cf. "Sketch of Swahili" in this chapter for more details about this language.)

Shona (7 million sp. of whom 2,811,090 are in Zimbabwe, the rest mostly in Zambia, some in Mozambique).

Rwanda or *Kinyarwanda* (6,205,300 or more speakers, of whom 5 million are in Rwanda, 867,300 in Uganda, 250,000 in Zaire, and 88,000 in Tanzania).

Kirundi (5 million sp., mainly in Burundi, some in Tanzania). This language is mutually intelligible with Rwanda and is essentially a variant of the same language.

Zulu (5,964,000 sp., of whom 5,683,000 are in South Africa, 37,480 in Malawi, 14,880 in Swaziland, and 228,000 in Lesotho).

Xhosa (5,902,200 sp. in South Africa).

Gikuyu or *Kikuyu* (4,356,000 sp. in Kenya).

Tswana (3,304,650 sp., of whom 2,424,000 are in South Africa, 840,000 in Botswana, 29,350 in Zimbabwe, and 11,300 in Namibia).

Kongo or *Kikongo* (3,217,000 sp., of whom a million each are in Zaire and Angola, the rest in Congo).

Southern Sotho (2,959,000 sp., of whom 1,742,000 are in South Africa, the rest in Lesotho).

Northern Sotho (2,348,000 sp. in South Africa).

Ganda (2,362,000 sp. or more, of whom 2,352,000 are in Uganda, the rest in Tanzania).

Swazi or *Swati* (spoken by 1,436,300 sp., of whom 854,000 are in South Africa, and 582,300 are in Swaziland).

iv. Dogon

The representative language is *Dogon* (500,000 sp., of whom 312,000 are in Mali, the rest in Burkina Faso).

v. North Volta-Congo

This consists of two smaller groups.

   a. Gur

Languages of this subbranch are located east of the Mande group in northern Ghana and Upper Volta. Chief representative is *Mooré* or *Mossi* (4 million sp., 15,063 of whom are in Togo, the rest in Burkina Faso).

   b. Adamawa-Ubangi

The languages of this subbranch are spoken in central Nigeria, Cameroon, the Central African Republic, northern Zaire, and western Sudan.

Representative languages are *Gbaya* (861,000 or more speakers, of whom 729,000 are in the Central African Republic, the rest in Cameroon), *Ngbaka* (753,000 sp., of whom 750,000 are in Zaire, the rest in the Central African Republic), and *Masana* (150,000 sp. in Cameroon).

c. Ijoid

This group consists of such languages as *Ijo* (about 400,000 sp. of different varieties) and *Defaka,* which are spoken in the Niger River Delta region in Nigeria.

Niger-Congo languages are usually tonal (with the exception of those mentioned at the beginning of this chapter). The basic word order is most often SVO (except in Ijo and Mande, which are SOV).

Many languages in West Africa share what seems to be an areal feature that is not very common elsewhere in the world: doubly articulated stops, which involve a simultaneous velar and bilabial closure. Some languages have doubly articulated nasals as well as oral stops. Here are two examples from Yoruba which contain doubly articulated oral stops:[1]

[ak͡pá] 'arm'   [àg͡bà] 'old'

A very interesting feature of some Atlantic languages is *consonant ablaut,* also known as *permutation.* For example, in Fulani,[2] the morpheme for 'dog' has the following allomorphs depending on the suffix which follows the stem:

rawaa-ndu 'dog'   *dawaa*-di 'dogs'   *ndawa*-kon 'small dogs'

This example shows that the initial consonant of the morpheme meaning 'dog' alternates between *r, d,* and *nd.* In Fulani there are other such ablauting series of consonants: *b-w-mb, k-h-k,* and so on. Since suffixes that end in a nasal consonant (e.g., *-kon*) all require the prenasalized consonant as the initial of the stem, it is believed that this permutation or consonant ablaut may have arisen as a kind of assimilatory process which took place at the time when the morphemes which are now suffixes were independent words that usually occurred *before* the stem morpheme.

According to Welmers (1973:78), in Niger-Congo languages simple nouns are combinations of an affix + noun stem, although in some languages (e.g., Igbo, Efik, and Yoruba) this structure is very poorly represented. Most sub-branches of Niger-Congo (excluding Mande and those which were earlier considered to form a separate branch called Kwa: Yoruba, Igbo, Akan, Bini, etc.) use a system of noun classes similar to noun gender in Indo-European languages. However, the number of separate noun classes is much larger than three genders found in Indo-European, and they are not connected with sex (cf. Latin or Russian masculine, feminine, and neuter). These noun class systems are especially prominent in the Bantu languages. In Swahili, for example, there are at least six separate noun classes. As in Indo-European languages, adjectives, demonstratives, and other types of noun modifiers have to agree in gender and number with the noun they modify. (Cf. "Sketch of Swahili in this chapter for details.)

The Bantu languages of South Africa have been influenced by languages belonging to the Khoisan family and have click sounds in their phonological inventories (e.g., Xhosa, Zulu).

It may be appropriate at this point to say a few words about some of the tone phenomena found in African tone languages that are not found in Asian tone languages. Although these phenomena are not necessarily limited to tonal languages belonging to the Niger-Congo language family, all the features to be discussed are also found in the Niger-Congo family.

According to Welmers (1973), rather than dividing tone languages into *register* (i.e., languages that have mainly level tones at various pitch heights, so that features such as "high," "low," and "mid" are the distinguishing features) and *contour* (i.e., languages that have tones that change their pitch, so that "rising," "falling," "rising-falling," etc., are the distinguishing features) tone languages, as Kenneth L. Pike did in his early work on tone languages, it would be more meaningful to divide tone languages into *discrete level* tone languages and *terraced level* tone languages.

1. *Discrete level* tone languages, according to Welmers (1973:81), are those in which "each level tone is restricted to a relatively narrow range of absolute pitch (absolute for a given speaker under given environmental conditions) within a phrase, and these tonemic ranges are discrete—never overlapping, and separated by pitch ranges which are not used—throughout the phrase, though they may tilt downward at the very end of the phrase in a brief final contour." In other words, in such languages the high tone is always higher than any mid or low tone in the same phrase and is realized pretty much the same no matter where in the phrase it is located.

2. In *terraced level* tone languages, on the other hand, the tonemic ranges of tones may overlap, and "what is significant is not the absolute pitch (for a given speaker under given conditions) of a syllable in a phrase, as in discrete level language, but the pitches of nonlow syllables relative to preceding non-

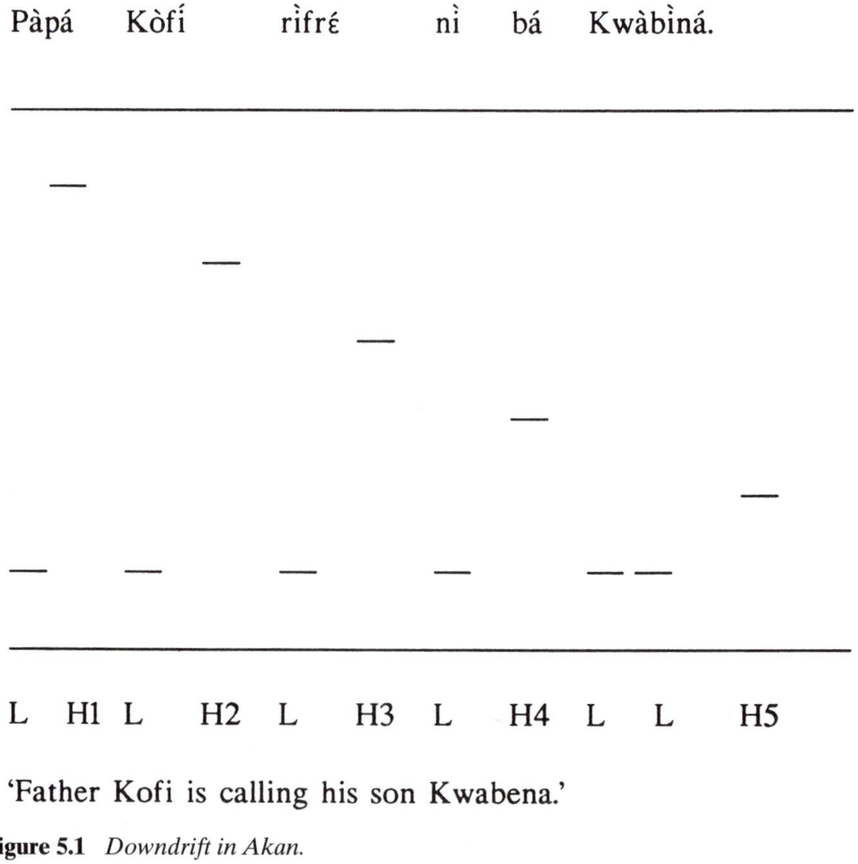

Pàpá   Kòfí   rìfrέ   nì   bá   Kwàbìná.

L   H1 L   H2 L   H3 L   H4 L   L   H5

'Father Kofi is calling his son Kwabena.'

Figure 5.1 *Downdrift in Akan.*

low syllables." An example from Akan of the phenomenon called *downdrift*, taken from Kropp Dakubu (1988:70), may clarify what is meant here.

In the example shown in Figure 5.1, each successive high tone is lowered after each low tone (which itself remains at the same level throughout). (In the commonly accepted Africanist usage high tone is indicated by ´ over a vowel and low tone by ` over a vowel.) In other words, in Akan the realization of the high tone depends on the pitch level of the preceding high tone, which is in turn conditioned by the preceding high tone (better termed "non-low"), and so on. Thus the number of actual levels of pitch is at least theoretically unlimited. The sequence of nonlow pitches in a phrase can be likened to a series of descending terraces or steps. That is why tone languages of this type are called terraced level.

As already pointed out, the pitch value of the low tone remains constant throughout the phrase in Akan. According to Ladefoged (1982:231), however, in Hausa, which exhibits a similar phenomenon, both low and high tones are higher at the beginning of the sentence than they are at the end. Thus a high tone at the end of the sentence may have the same absolute pitch as a low tone at the beginning of the same sentence. This, of course, means that the absolute values of different phonemes may overlap in the same sentence in Hausa.

3. *Downstep.* In the Akan downdrift example, the ever lower pitched realizations of the nonlow (high) tone are due to the presence of intervening low tone syllables preceding each lower realization. Thus one may view downdrift as a kind of tone assimilation. In many African tone languages, however, such lowering may also occur in situations where there does not seem to be any apparent cause for pitch lowering. That is, a high tone may be lowered after a high tone, but this is not dissimilation either since in such languages unlowered high tones may also follow a high tone. For example, in Efik there are the following words.[3]

/óbòŋ/[‾   ] 'sugar cane'

/óbóŋ/[‾ ‾] 'mosquito'

/óboˈ/[‾ ¯] 'chief'

From just these examples, one might well conclude that Efik has three level tones: high, mid, and low. However, more data, especially that involving words and phrases of more than two syllables, shows that the so-called mid tone is actually the same thing as the lowered nonlow in the Akan downdrift example, because whole series of successively lower realization of this mid tone can be found. Welmers suggests that languages like Efik should be considered as having two tonemes, high and low, and a special "process phoneme" or "downstep phoneme" which causes downdrift-like pitch lowering but is itself not a toneme (= "tone phoneme").

4. *Floating tone.* Some African languages also have what is termed *floating tones*, that is, tones that seem to be associated with particular morphemes but are *not* associated with any syllable of these particular morphemes. (Note that some sources call these *dangling tones*.) Instead these tones are realized

on syllables to which the morphemes in question are attached. Gregersen (1977:35) provides the following examples from Sukuma (a Bantu language spoken in Tanzania) in which some words have an associated floating tone that must be realized on the second syllable of the subsequent word if it is to be realized at all:

> akasɔla (−H) 'he chose'
>
> akabɔna (+H) 'he saw'
>
> akasɔla balemi 'he chose farmers'
>
> akabɔna balémi 'he saw farmers'

In some African languages particular tones are associated with particular grammatical constructions and some morphemes have only tonal realizations (i.e., they are not associated with any segmental phonemes but are a sort of "tonal replacive" which changes the tone of other, segmental morphemes), phenomena that are very foreign to Asian tone languages.

IV. KHOISAN FAMILY

The languages belonging to this family are found primarily in southwestern Africa (Kalahari desert region), but there are a few small pockets of Khoisan speakers in Tanzania. Originally these languages occupied a much larger territory, but they were then pushed into the less hospitable desert areas by the more aggressive Bantu tribes from the north and the white settlers from the south. Now only about 160,000 people speak languages belonging to this family.

Most of the Khoisan speakers are racially distinct from their Bantu neighbors. They have a yellowish skin and tend to be very short in stature.

According to Greenberg (1963), Khoisan is divided into three branches, two of which are represented by single languages. (Note that various unusual symbols represent the click sounds found in these languages.)

1. SOUTHERN AFRICA

This branch is further subdivided into three subbranches.

a. Northern

This group includes *Kung-Ekoka* (also called *!Kung, !Xu*) spoken by 5,000 speakers, mostly in Namibia, but also some in Angola, *Kung-Gogabis* (also called *//Au, Kaukau, Koko*), spoken by 3,000 speakers in Namibia, and *Kung-Tsumkwe* (also known as Ju'oasi) spoken by 3,000 speakers in Namibia and partly in Angola.

b. Central

This group is represented by *Nama* (also known as *Khoi* or *Hottentot*), which has 133,000 speakers in South Africa and Namibia; *San* (*Saan*), which has 16,000 speakers in Namibia; *Xun* (*Hukwe*), which has 9,000 speakers in Angola and 2,000 in Namibia; and *Kwadi* (or *Cuepe*), which has 15,000 speakers in Angola.

c. Southern

A representative of this subbranch is /*Hua-owani* (1,000 to 1,500 sp. in southern Kalahari, Botswana).

2. SANDAWE

This branch is represented by a single language, *Sandawe*, which is spoken by 70,000 people in Tanzania.

3. HADZA

This branch is also represented by a single language, *Hatsa* (or *Hadza*), which is spoken by about 200 speakers southeast of Lake Victoria in Tanzania. (It should be noted that some Africanists question the validity of linking Hadza and Sandawe with the rest of Khoisan languages as well as linking Sandawe and Hadza with each other. If these scholars are right, the latter two languages should be considered language isolates.)

Khoisan languages exhibit a number of unique linguistic features. It is believed that only Khoisan languages (as well as a few Bantu languages influenced by them) have clicks which are used for speech sounds, but, according to Gregersen (1977:32) there have been unconfirmed reports that a Cushitic language spoken in Kenya and some unspecified South American Indian languages also have clicks. There are bilabial (found only in Southern Khoisan), dental, palatoalveolar, palatal, and lateral clicks. In addition, the clicks can be voiced or voiceless, aspirated or unaspirated, and oral or nasalized. Click sounds, however, are somewhat restricted phonotactically: they may occur only at the beginning of stems.

Table 5.1 shows the commonly used symbols for transcribing click sounds. It is to be noted that the orthographic traditions for the Khoisan languages and Bantu languages are very different.

The voiceless clicks are indicated by means of the basic symbol, the voiced by a prefixed *g-* followed by the basic click symbol, and nasalized clicks by a prefixed -ŋ. In general, the consonant inventories of Khoisan languages are very large, rivaling those of the Caucasus languages, and even vowel inventories are sometimes complex because in addition to the distinction of nasal versus oral vowels, there may be also pharyngealized vowel phonemes.

Table 5.1 SYMBOLS USED TO TRANSCRIBE CLICKS

KIND	IPA	KHOISAN ORTHOGRAPHY	BANTU ORTHOGRAPHY
Bilabial		☉	
Dental	ʇ	|	c
Palatoalveolar	ʗ	!	q
Palatal		=|=	
Lateral	ʖ	‖	x

The most common basic word order is said to be SVO (but OSV is also reported for some languages). Some languages have grammatical gender based on sex. Verb morphology is somewhat complex, and sometimes totally different lexical items are used to express the same action depending on whether it is being performed by a single person or by more than one person.

V. AUSTRONESIAN

This family will be discussed in more detail in the chapter on the languages of Oceania because most languages that belong to this family are found outside of Africa.

The sole representative of this family in Africa is *Malagasy* and its dialects (about 10 million sp.) on the island of Madagascar. Its nearest relatives are some languages spoken on Borneo (Western Austronesian branch).

The basic word order in Malagasy is VOS. Malagasy has borrowed vocabulary items from various Bantu languages, especially Swahili, from Arabic and such European languages as French and English, but its Austronesian genetic affinities are not in doubt.

VI. INDO-EUROPEAN

English and French are still very influential in many former British and French colonies in Africa, especially in those African countries in which a large number of very different native languages are spoken and there are not yet clear national languages emerging. There are a number of noteworthy African writers and poets who write primarily in English or French.

The case of *Afrikaans* is very special since it is not merely an imported colonial language but something that grew and developed in South Africa from the language of the Dutch settlers that started arriving there in the latter half of the seventeenth century. Since it is considered to be a language separate from Dutch, it deserves to be classified as an Indo-European language of Africa.

Afrikaans is spoken by about 6 million people in South Africa and surrounding African countries. Compared to Standard Dutch it looks rather simplified; there are many loanwords from Malay, Portuguese, other European languages, and various African languages, and therefore some have argued that Afrikaans is really a creole based on Dutch. The validity of this hypothesis, however, is still being disputed.

Since until relatively recently Africa had been under the political control and strong cultural influence of the various European powers, there have arisen in Africa many contact languages, pidgins, and creoles, the more prominent of which will be discussed in Chapter 8.

Sketch of Modern Literary Arabic

A. Genetic Relationship and General Information

Arabic belongs to the *Semitic* branch of the Afro-Asiatic family of languages, more specifically, to the Central subbranch of the West Semitic subbranch. The oldest Arabic inscriptions go back to the fourth century A.D., but inscriptions in this language are not numerous until the Islamic times beginning a couple of centuries later.

Modern Arabic has a large number of dialects, many of which are not mutually intelligible. Perhaps the greatest differences are found between Maltese, which is often considered a separate language, and the rest. On formal occasions, and in formal writing, Modern Literary Arabic, based on the Classical Arabic language of the Koran (Qurʔān), the sacred book of Islam, is used instead of the local vernacular dialects. Most of the speakers of Maltese are Christians unfamiliar with the Koran, and since Maltese do not usually learn Classical Arabic in school, that would help explain why Maltese has diverged so much from the rest of the Arabic dialects, which are constantly under the conservative influences of Classical Arabic. (Christian Arabs living in places such as Lebanon and Syria also sometimes study the Koran in order to learn good Classical Arabic.)

Aside from Maltese (which is closest to the Arabic dialects of North Africa), regional dialects form two main groups: (1) *Eastern Arabic,* which includes dialects spoken in Mesopotamia, Syria, Lebanon, Israel, the Arabian peninsula, Egypt, Sudan, and Zanzibar (Tanzania), and (2) *Western Arabic,* which includes dialects spoken in North Africa: Libya, Morocco, Algeria, Tunisia, and Mauritania. In addition, in each region there is also a significant dichotomy between the dialects of the city dwellers and those of the nomadic Bedouins. The dialect with the largest number of speakers is *Egyptian Arabic* (43,026,000 sp.).

Classical Arabic (used for religious purposes) and Modern Literary Arabic coexist in various Arab countries with the local varieties of Arabic. The Modern Literary Arabic (Modern Standard Arabic) is used for communiction with speakers of other Arabic dialects (interdialectal communication), for formal speeches, formal documents, serious literature, and so forth, whereas the local dialect is used primarily for ordinary oral communication and for such nonserious literature as comic books and joke books. This situation in which there are two very different variants of the same language used in the same community for well defined separate purposes is called *diglossia.*

Since according to the Islamic tradition the Koran is not to be translated (being a direct record of the word of God), all Muslim faithful are expected to learn Arabic in order to be able to read and understand their holy scripture. All prayers are also said in Arabic. This means that in non-Arab Muslim countries as well, Classical Arabic is widely read if not actually spoken and thereby exerts a great influence on the local languages, for instance, on Persian in Iran and on Turkish in Turkey. In turn, the Arabic language is itself influenced by the surrounding languages, especially Persian and Turkish, and in recent times has also borrowed words from European languages, especially French, English, and Italian. In this respect various regional dialects of colloquial Arabic differ from each other since each has borrowed words from a different European language. Thus, for example, Syrian, Lebanese, Tunisian, Moroccan, and Algerian varieties have borrowed more from French, Libyan more from Italian, and Egyptian and Sudanese more from English.

The English language has a large number of Arabic loanwords, some of which have entered English via Spanish. (Spain was once almost entirely occupied by Arabs.) Some of the loanwords can be easily spotted because they contain the Arabic definite article *al-*:

> *alcohol*
>
> *algebra*
>
> *alchemy* (this is actually a Greek word that was borrowed via Arabic)

Others do not contain the definite article:

> *syrup*
>
> *sherbet* (note the similarity in the root consonants of these two words!)
>
> *nadir*
>
> *zenith*

It should be noted that many astronomical terms, including names of some stars (e.g., *Aldebaran*), are of Arabic origin.

Roughly speaking, there are about 160,388,600 speakers of different variants of Arabic, plus an indeterminate number of those who are nonnative speakers but who have learned Classical Arabic for religious purposes. About half of the native speakers are in Africa, and the other half is in the Middle East. There are about 330,000 speakers of Maltese.

B. PHONETICS AND PHONOLOGY

i. Consonant Sounds

There is much variation in the pronunciation of Modern Literary Arabic, as one might expect. After all, Modern Literary Arabic is not a native language of any speaker and therefore tends to be influenced by the sound systems of local dialects. The phonological system cited in Table 5.2 follows Kaye (1987:668–9).

The dotted consonants are the emphatic (pharyngealized) counterparts of the plain dental consonants (not retroflex consonants which are also very often marked by a subscript dot). /ẓ/ varies in value from [ẓ] to [ð] depending on the region. /ḷ/ is a very marginal phoneme, since it occurs only in a few contexts, primarily in the name of God: /ʔaḷḷa:h/.

The pharyngealized consonants exert a lowering and backing effect on the neighboring vowels. Pharyngeal and uvular phonemes exhibit similar effects.

Table 5.2 CONSONANT PHONEMES OF MODERN LITERARY ARABIC

	STOPS	AFFRI-CATES	FRICA-TIVES	NASALS	LIQUIDS	SEMI-VOWELS
Bilabials	b			m		w
Labiodentals			f			
Interdentals			θ ð			
Dentals	t d		s z	n	l r	
Emphatic Dent.	ṭ ḍ		ṣ ẓ		ḷ	
Alveopalatals		dʒ	ʃ			
Palatals						j
Velars	k		χ			
Uvulars	q		R			
Pharyngeals			ħ ʕ			
Glottals	ʔ		h			

/ʕ/ is phonetically a creaky-voice, pharyngealized resonant (there does not seem to be much air friction if there is any at all) that mimics the following vowel, or if such does not exist, the preceding one. /ħ/, on the other hand, is a true voiceless pharyngeal fricative. /R/ is a voiced *uvular* fricative, and /χ/ is its voiceless counterpart. Note that the last two fricatives are often described as being velar, not uvular, perhaps because in some speakers' pronunciation they are in fact velar.

It is interesting to note the gaps in the system. For example, there is no /p/ corresponding to /b/, and no /g/ corresponding to /k/. This is the result of various historical developments. For example, /dʒ/ comes from an older /*g/. (Note that the Egyptian colloquial Arabic has [g] in those cases where Modern Literary Arabic has /dʒ/.)

ii. Vowels

Modern Literary Arabic has the classical three-vowel phonemic system which is doubled to six by the fact that vowel length is also phonemic (see Table 5.3).

The chief aspect of the system is that there is a great dichotomy between vowel allophones found in the environment of emphatic and uvular and pharyngeal consonants on the one hand and those in the environment of plain consonants on the other. (The former have a lowering and backing effect on the vowels.) For example, the phoneme /a/ is realized as [æ] after plain consonants or even as [ɛ] if it is found before /j/, whereas it is realized as [ɑ] in the environment of pharyngeal, pharyngealized, or uvular consonants.

**Table 5.3 VOWEL PHONEMES OF
MODERN LITERARY ARABIC**

/i:/		/u/	/u:/
	/a/	/a:/	

C. ARABIC ORTHOGRAPHY

The Arabic alphabet consists primarily of letters for the consonants, the vowels being marked by diacritics or diacritics in conjunction with certain consonant letters used as auxiliary vowel markers. The letters may have up to four different *allographs:* independent, word-initial, medial, and final.

Arabic is written from right to left. There is no cursive versus print dichotomy in Arabic writing since all writing is essentially cursive. However, there are several different styles of script.

Some of the letters cannot be connected to letters that follow; for such letters only the independent and "final" forms are given in Table 5.4.

Table 5.4   THE ARABIC ALPHABET (ABJAD)

NAME	IPA	INDEPENDENT	FINAL	MEDIAL	INITIAL
alif	[ʔ]	ا	ا		
ba:	[b]	ب	ـب	ـبـ	بـ
ta:	[t]	ت	ـت	ـتـ	تـ
tha:	[θ]	ث	ـث	ـثـ	ثـ
ji:m	[ʤ]	ج	ـج	ـجـ	جـ
ḥa:	[ħ]	ح	ـح	ـحـ	حـ
kha:	[x]	خ	ـخ	ـخـ	خـ
da:l	[d]	د	ـد		
dha:l	[ð]	ذ	ـذ		
ra:	[r]	ر	ـر		
za:	[z]	ز	ـز		
si:n	[s]	س	ـس	ـسـ	سـ
shi:n	[ʃ]	ش	ـش	ـشـ	شـ
ṣa:d	[ṣ]	ص	ـص	ـصـ	صـ
ḍa:d	[ḍ]	ض	ـض	ـضـ	ضـ
ṭa:	[ṭ]	ط	ـط	ـطـ	طـ
ẓa:	[ẓ]	ظ	ـظ	ـظـ	ظـ
'ain	[ʕ]	ع	ـع	ـعـ	عـ
ghain	[ʀ]	غ	ـغ	ـغـ	غـ
fa:	[f]	ف	ـف	ـفـ	فـ
qa:f	[q]	ق	ـق	ـقـ	قـ
ka:f	[k]	ك	ـك	ـكـ	كـ
la:m	[l]	ل	ـل	ـلـ	لـ
mi:m	[m]	م	ـم	ـمـ	مـ
nu:n	[n]	ن	ـن	ـنـ	نـ
ha:	[h]	ه	ـه	ـهـ	هـ
wa:w	[w]	و	ـو		
ya:	[j]	ي	ـي	ـيـ	يـ

In addition there are some special ligature forms. For example, a *la:m* followed by an *alif* is written not as ل but as لا.

Note that in the table of Arabic consonant symbols, the final form of each letter is shown after *mi:m*, the medial form between *mi:m* and *alif*, and the initial form before an *alif*.

Vowel Marking

The short vowels are marked by diacritics written above or below the consonant symbol:

ها: = هَ .

هu: = هُ .

هi: = هِ .

The long vowels are marked by a combination of the diacritic symbol for *a, u,* and *i* and followed by *alif, wa:w,* and *ya:* respectively.

(Note that sometimes *ya:* also appears as the symbol for vowel length in *a:* as well.)

ها: = هَا.

هu: = هُو .

هi: = هِي .

Note that, except in the Koran, the diacritics for short vowels are very seldom used.

The glottal stop is marked by a special diacritic called *hamza,* which is seldom used alone but needs a consonant symbol (*alif, wa:w* or *ja:*) as a "seat." (Originally, *alif* by itself represented the glottal stop, but this function has been taken over by the *hamza.*)

ʔanta ('you') = أَنْتَ.

If a consonant is not followed by a vowel, a small circle called *suku:n* is written above the consonant letter:

xamru ('wine') = خَمْرُ.

Gemination, or doubling of the consonants, is indicated by a diacritic called *shadda,* which is also written above the consonant affected:

xamma:ru ('wine merchant') = خَمَّارُ.

The indefinite suffix *-n* (the addition of which is traditionally called *nunation* in Arabic grammar) is written by doubling the diacritic symbol for the preceding vowel:

xamr-u-n = ('a wine', nominative case) = خَمْرٌ.

xamr-a-n = ('a wine', accusative case) = خَمْرً.

xamr-i-n = ('a wine', genitive case) = خَمْرٍ .

There is a slight complication in that indefinite masculine nouns add an *alif* as a seat for the nunation in the accusative case unless the word ends in a glottal stop preceded by *a:*. Thus, xamr-a-n should actually be written as خَمْرًا .

Historical Note

The modern Arabic script is derived from the cursive form of the Aramaic script (Nabatean) which had several inadequacies for writing Arabic.

1. It had developed ligature forms that neutralized the graphic distinctions among various letters. Thus, *b, t, n,* and *j* were not adequately differentiated or not differentiated at all in some positions.

2. Aramaic did not have symbols for some Arabic sounds. For example, there was no symbol for representing the Arabic voiceless interdental fricative [θ].

These problems were eventually solved by the addition of diacritic symbols. Vowel diacritics were added in imitation of Hebrew writing practices which had developed among the Jews (writing in Hebrew).

Arabic script was used and is still being used to write many languages other than Arabic: Urdu (Indo-European) in Pakistan, Pashto and Dari (Indo-European) in Afghanistan, Uighur (Turkic) in China, Tibetan dialects (Sino-Tibetan) spoken by Tibetan Muslims in Kashmir, Persian (Indo-European) in Iran, and so forth. Most Turkic languages used to be written in Arabic script, but in modern times have switched to romanization (as in Turkey itself) or to Cyrillic-based alphabets (as in the former Soviet Union). There are various diacritics which are added to Arabic letters in order to write sounds that are found in various non-Arab languages but are not found in Arabic.

D. MORPHOLOGY

i. Nominal Morphology

Nouns can be either feminine or masculine in gender, inflected for definiteness or indefiniteness, and are marked by one of the three cases: nominative, accusative, and genitive.

Masculine nouns are unmarked for gender, whereas most, though not all, feminine nouns are marked by a feminine suffix *-ah/-at*. The formula for an indefinite noun is as follows: Noun stem + (fem. suffix) + case suffix + indef. suffix.

The schema for a definite noun is just slightly different: def. article + noun stem + (fem. suffix) + case suffix.

Table 5.5 shows all the possible inflections of the masculine noun meaning "wine" except for number.

The nominative case is used to mark the subject; accusative to mark the direct object and to derive adverbs and prepositions from nouns, whereas the

Table 5.5 CASE MARKING

	NOMINATIVE	ACCUSATIVE	GENITIVE
Indefinite	xamr-u-n	xamr-a-n	xamr-i-n
Definite	al-xamr-u	al-xamr-a	al-xamr-i

genitive is used to mark the possessor and is the case governed by almost all Arabic prepositions.

Arabic, like most Semitic languages, has a special possessive construction in which the possessed noun appears in the so-called *construct state*. The possessed noun must come first and cannot have either the definite article or the nunation (indefinite suffix). That is then followed by a noun in the genitive which may or may not have the definite article attached:

> bajt-u radʒul-i-n
>
> house + nom./ man + gen. + indef.
>
> 'the house of a man'
>
> bajt-u r-radʒul-i
>
> house + nom./ def. article + man + gen.
>
> 'the house of the man'

All possessed nouns are grammatically definite even though they are not overtly marked for definiteness.

Nouns can be singular, dual, or plural in number. Dual is formed by means of affixation of the singular form; plural, on the other hand, is formed either by suffixation (called "sound plural") or by internal flexion (called "broken plural").

Examples of sound duals and plurals:

> masc. dual: bajt-aːn 'two houses'
> fem. dual: malik-at-aːn 'two queens'
> masc. pl.: muslim-uːn 'Muslims'
> fem. pl.: malik-aːt 'queens'

Broken plurals:

> radʒul 'man' vs. ridʒaːl 'men'
> kitaːb 'book' vs. kutub 'books'

There are many patterns of broken plurals, and one has to memorize which noun takes what pattern. The masculine sound plural is used primarily with participles of the derived forms of the verb and with adjectival forms with the suffix *-i:j*. The broken plurals are morphologically related to the collective noun forms.

As far as the gender of a noun is concerned, for the most part one can predict it on the basis of semantic criteria. For example, nouns referring to female entities, body parts that come in pairs, and names of most countries are feminine, whereas nouns that do not belong to one of these categories are masculine. Most feminine nouns actually have the feminine suffix *-ah/-at* (the first form is the allomorph that appears before a pause) by which one can recognize them.

Adjectives behave very much like substantives and do not really form a class separate from that of nouns. The most common adjectival suffix is *-i:j*, but the adjectives derived by means of this suffix can also act as nouns:

> miṣr 'Egypt'
>
> miṣr-i:j 'Egyptian'(adjective)
>
> al miṣr-i:j 'the Egyptian' (subst.)

There is also a derived comparative/superlative form of the adjective which is a combination of affixes and internal flexion: *ʔa-CCaC* for masculine (The C's stand for the triconsonantal root, explained later) and *CuCC-a:* for feminines:

> ʔaħsan-u radʒul-i-n
>
> finest + nom./ men + gen. + indef.
>
> 'finest of men'
>
> al malik-at-u l-dʒuml-a:
>
> def. art./ queen + fem. suffix + nom./ def. art. + most beautiful + feminine suff.
>
> 'the most beautiful queen'

In the last example the *a* of the definite article is elided because the preceding word ends in a vowel. This kind of vowel deletion is a regular feature of Arab phonology.

ii. Pronouns

Personal suffixes marking subjects of verbs will be given in the paradigms cited in the section on verb morphology. The independent pronoun forms can be seen in Table 5.6.

Note that Arabic has dual number as well as singular and plural. In addition, it is somewhat unusual in that it has gender distinction not only in the third person but in the second person as well. (There is no gender distinction in the dual, however.)

Table 5.6 PERSONAL PRONOUNS

1st sing. masc.	ʔana:				1st pl.	naħnu
2d sing. masc.	ʔanta	2 dual	ʔantuma:		2d pl. masc.	ʔantum(u:)
2d sing. fem.	ʔanti		ʔantuma:		2d pl. fem.	ʔantunna
3d sing. masc.	huwa	3 dual	huma:		3d pl. masc.	hum(u:)
3d sing. fem.	hiya		huma:		3d pl. fem.	hunna

The suffix forms of the pronouns are shown in Table 5.7. Suffix forms of the pronouns are used to mark possession when attached to nominals and as "objects" of prepositions (which are largely nominals in origin); attached to verbs they mark pronominal direct objects. Note that the first person singular has several variants: the first one is used only as a direct object form; the second one is used as a possessive suffix, and the third one is an older form which survives in some environments.

> kalb-i: 'my dog'   ḍaraba-ni: 'he hit me'   ʕaṣa:-ja 'my stick'

Table 5.7 SUFFIX FORMS OF THE PERSONAL PRONOUNS

1st sing.	-ni:, -i:, -ja			1st pl.	-na:
2d sing. masc.	-ka	2 dual	-kuma:	2d pl. masc.	-kum(u:)
2d sing. fem.	-ki		-kuma:	2d pl. fem.	-kunna
3d sing. masc.	-hu	3 dual	-huma:	3d pl. masc.	-hum(u:)
3d sing. fem.	-ha:		-huma:	3d pl. fem.	-hunna

iii. Verb Morphology

Arabic has a very rich verb morphology involving a large number of inflectional patterns as well as a number of fairly productive derivational ones. Arabic, like other Semitic languages, has consonantal roots which for the most part consist of no more and no less than three consonants, and to which vowel infixes and various prefixes and suffixes are added. Given a *triconsonantal root* and the productive patterns of the language, a speaker of Arabic can generate an impressively large paradigm of derived and inflected forms that would take several pages just to list. There are also some biconsonantal forms and quadriconsonantal roots (also called *biliteral* and *quadriliteral* roots), but they will not be discussed in this sketch.

In addition to the inflections of the verb which will be illustrated later there are about a dozen derivational patterns. (Note that one of the differences between inflection and derivation is that it is not always possible to predict the meaning of a derived form.) Most of them are illustrated below. In order to keep the proper perspective on the richness of Arabic verb morphology, bear in mind that each of the following patterns can in turn take all the inflections that will be discussed after this. For example, consider derived verbs from the triconsonantal root SLM 'peace':

SaLiMa = 'be safe, well' (Pattern I)

SaLLaMa = 'greet (denominative), make safe, protect, surrender (transitive)' (Pattern II, causative, intensive)

SaLaMa = 'make peace with, treat peaceably' (Pattern III)

ʔa-SLaMa = 'submit, turn Muslim' (i.e., 'submit to God') (Pattern IV)

ta-SaLLaMa = 'receive the surrender, turn Muslim' (Pattern V, reflexive of Pattern II)

ta-Sa:LaMa = 'make peace together' (Pattern VI, reciprocal)

i-S-ta-LaMa = 'kiss (the Black Stone)' (Pattern VIII)

ista-SLaMa = 'submit, keep to the middle of the road' (Pattern X)

Passive Paradigm

The passive paradigm of the verb is very similar to the active one except that the stem is KuTiB in the perfective (instead of KaTaB) and KTaB in the imperfective (instead of KTuB); in addition, the vowel of the prefix in the imperative is *u* instead of *a*.

KaTaB-a 'wrote' (Perf. active); KuTiB-a 'was written' (Perf. pass.)

ja-KTuB-u 'is writing' (Imperf. active); ju-KTaB-u 'is being written' (Imperf. pass.)

The passive participle is *ma*-KTu:B.

In Arabic passive constructions, the agent NP cannot be expressed. (This is not a rare phenomenon among the languages of the world.) If agent NP must be expressed, the statement must be reworded in active voice.

qutila Zaydun 'Zayd was killed'

'Zayd was killed by Mohammed' cannot be expressed using passive voice.

Tenses, Aspects, and Moods

Perfect has only one mood, whereas the imperfect has, besides the indicative, four other moods: *subjunctive,* used in subordinate clauses after verbs of wishing; *jussive,* used for the second person negative imperatives (prohibitions) and for the imperatives of the first and third persons ('let us . . .', 'let him . . .'); *energetic,* used in solemn statements, especially after oaths, in commands and wishes; and *imperative.* The energetic mood is rarely used. In

Table 5.8 ACTIVE VERB PARADIGMS

a. Perfective

1st sing.	KaTaB -tu
2d sing. masc.	KaTaB -ta
2d sing. fem.	KaTaB -ti
3d sing. masc.	KaTaB -a
3d sing. fem.	KaTaB -at
2d dual	KaTaB -tuma
3d dual masc.	KaTaB -a:
3d dual fem.	KaTaB -ata:
1st pl.	KaTaB -na
2d pl. masc	KaTaB -tum
2d pl. fem.	KaTaB -tunna
3d pl. masc.	KaTaB -u:
3d pl. fem.	KaTaB -na

b. Imperfective

	INDICATIVE	SUBJUNCTIVE	JUSSIVE	ENERGETIC
1st sing.	ʔa- KTuB -u	ʔa-KTuB -a	ʔa- KTuB	ʔa- KTuB -anna
2d sing. masc.	ta- KTuB -u	ta- KTuB -a	ta- KTuB	ta- KTuB -anna
2d sing. fem.	ta- KTuB -i:na	ta- KTuB -i:	ta- KTuB	ta- KTuB -anna
3d sing. masc.	ja- KTuB -u	ja- KTuB -a	ja- KTuB	ja- KTuB -anna
3d sing. fem.	ta- KTuB -u	ta- KTuB -a	ta- KTuB	ta- KTuB -anna
2d dual	ta- KTuB -a:ni	ta- KTuB -a:	ta- KTuB -a:	ta- KTuB -a:nni
3d dual masc.	ja- KTuB -a:ni	ja- KTuB -a:	ja- KTuB -a:	ja- KTuB -a:nni
3d dual fem.	ta- KTuB -a:ni	ta- KTuB -a:	ta- KTuB -a:	ta- KTuB -a:nni
1st pl.	na- KTuB -u	na- KTuB -a:	na- KTuB	na- KTuB -anna
2d pl. masc.	ta- KTuB -u:na	ta- KTuB -u:	ta- KTuB -u:	ta- KTuB -unna
2d pl. fem.	ta- KTuB -na	ta- KTuB -na	ta- KTuB -na	ta- KTuB -a:nni
3d pl. masc.	ja- KTuB -u:na	ja- KTuB -u:	ja- KTuB -u:	ja- KTuB -unna
3d pl. fem.	ja- KTuB -na	ja- KTuB -na	ja- KTuB -na	ja- KTuB -a:nni

c. Imperative Mood

2d sing. masc.	u- KTuB
2d sing. fem.	u- KTuB -i:
2d dual	u- KTuB -a:
2d pl. masc.	u- KTuB -u:
2d pl. fem.	u- KTuB -na

Note that all imperative forms have the imperfective form of the stem. Active participle: Ka:TiB general, perfect is used for the past; the imperfect is used for the present and past (for actions that are viewed as ongoing, not having a definite end), and, with a prefix *sa-*, the future.

In conditional sentences either the perfect or the jussive may be used in both clauses.

E. SYNTAX

i. Word Order

Modern Literary Arabic has a variety of orders which are used depending on the type of constituents found in the sentence, but generally it is classified as a VSO language. Modern Arabic dialects, on the other hand, are reported to be mostly SVO.

If there is no verb in the sentence, the order is *Subject + Complement* (or *Predicate*):

> Zaydun mari:dun
>
> 'Zayd (is) ill.'

If the predicate is a verb, the order is usually *Verb + Subject + Object + (Adverbial complements)*:

> za:ra Zaydun ʕAmran
>
> 'Zayd visited Amr.'

However, if the subject happens to be a pronoun it usually precedes the verb:

> huwa za:ra ʕAmran
>
> 'He visited Amr.'

Adjectivals follow the nouns they modify, but the demonstratives precede their heads:

> al-luRatu l ʕarabi:jatu
>
> the + language/ the/ Arab
>
> 'the Arabic language' (Lit. 'the language the Arab')

ii. Case Relation Marking

As already noted in the section on nominal inflections, Arabic nouns as well as nouns acting as adjectives are marked for three surface cases: Nominative, Accusative, and Genitive, the first two of which normally mark such case relations as *Agent* and *Patient* respectively. Case relations other than these two are marked by means of prepositions (most of which govern the Genitive case).

Since modern colloquial Arabic dialects have lost the case endings of Classical Arabic due to the loss of final short vowels, case relations in them are signaled by word order and various prepositions.

iii. Agreement and Predication

Nominals acting as adjectives must agree with the nouns they modify in gender (if the noun is singular), in case, and in definiteness.

> busta:n-u-n kabi:r-u-n
>
> garden + nom. + indef./ big + nom. + indef.
>
> 'a big garden'

> al-busta:n-u l kabi:r-u
>
> the + garden + nom./ the/ big + nom.
>
> 'the big garden'

All broken plurals (cf. the section on noun morphology) are grammatically collective nouns in the feminine singular and therefore they may be modified by adjectives in their feminine singular form (with the feminine suffix) instead of the broken plural form of the adjective itself:

> ridʒa:l-u-n kabi:r-at-u-n
>
> men (broken plural) + nom. + indef./ big + fem. + nom. + indef.
>
> 'big (important) men'

The following alternative has the adjective in its broken plural form without any gender marking:

> ridʒa:l-u-n kiba:r-u-n
>
> men (broken plural) + nom. + indef./ big + (broken plural) + nom. + indef.
>
> 'big (important) men'

Possessed nouns are grammatically definite (even though they are not preceded by the definite article), and therefore adjectives modifying them must also be definite:

kalb-u-hu l-kabi:r-u

dog + nom. + his/ the + big + nom.

'his big dog'

iv. Relative Clauses

If the antecedent noun phrase is definite, the relative clause is introduced by the relative pronoun *al-laði:* (more accurately, relative pronoun *laði:* which is preceded by a definite article) which agrees in gender and number with the antecedent. (It also agrees in case, but that is apparent only in the dual.)

ar-radʒul-u l-laði: qatala ʔab-i:

the + man + nom./ the + who/ killed/ father + my

'The man who killed my father.'

Note that in this example the -*l* of the definite article assimilates completely to the initial consonant of the following word. This assimilation occurs before all coronal consonants (i.e., consonants articulated by the tongue tip or tongue blade).

If the head NP which a relative clause modifies is in an oblique case (i.e., non-nominative), the relative pronoun must be supplemented by a personal pronoun object in the relative clause:

ar-radʒul-u l-laði: qatala-hu ʔab-i:

the + man + nom./ the + who/ killed + him/ father-my

'The man whom my father killed.'

When the head which the relative clause modifies is indefinite, the relative clause is added without the relative pronoun:

raʔaj-tu radʒul-a-n dʒa:ʔa

saw + I/ man + acc. + indef./ came (3d pers. sing. perf.)

'I saw a man who came.'

F. SAMPLE TEXT

The following text is a short story from *One Thousand and One Nights,* which is a source of wonderful tales both short and long, familiar to people the world over, especially in their expurgated versions for children.[4] Divisions in the Arabic text are marked with Arabic numbers in heavy parentheses. (Do not forget that Arabic is written from right to left!) In the literal morpheme-by-morpheme translation section, the superscripted numbers refer to the notes that follow that section.

Arabic Text

» ١ « كَانَ خَمَّارٌ يُسَافِرُ بِخَمْرٍ لَهُ وَمَعَهُ قِرْدٌ وَ كَانَ يَمْزُجُ
الْخَمْرَ بِالْمَاءِ نِصْفَيْنِ » ٢ « وَ يَبِيعُهُ بِسِعْرِ الْخَمْرِ » ٣ « وَ
الْقِرْدُ يُشِيرُ إِلَيْهِ أَنْ لَا تَفْعَلْ فَيَضْرِبُهُ فَلَمَّا فَرَغَ مِنْ بَيْعِ الْخَمْرِ
» ٤ « وَ أَرَادَ الرُّجُوعَ إِلَى بَلَدِهِ رَكِبَ الْبَحْرَ » ٥ « وَ قِرْدُهُ مَعَهُ وَ
خُرْجٌ فِيهِ ثِيَابُهُ » ٦ « وَ الْكِيسُ الَّذِي جَمَعَهُ مِنْ ثَمَنِ الْخَمْرِ
» ٧ « فَلَمَّا سَارَ فِي الْبَحْرِ اسْتَخْرَجَ الْقِرْدُ الْكِيسَ مِنْ مَوْضِعِهِ
» ٨ « وَ رَقِيَ الدَّقَلَ وَ هُوَ مَعَهُ حَتَّى صَارَ فِي أَعْلَاهُ وَرَمَى إِلَى
الْمَرْكَبِ بِدِرْهَمٍ » ٩ « وَ إِلَى الْبَحْرِ بِدِرْهَمٍ فَلَمْ يَزَلْ ذَلِكَ دَأَبَهُ
حَتَّى قَسَمَ الدَّرَاهِمَ نِصْفَيْنِ

Literal Morpheme-by-Morpheme Translation

(1) *ka:na χamma:r-u-n ju-sa:fir-u bi-χamr-i-n la-hu, wa maʕa-hu qird-u-n, wa ka:na ja-mzudʒ-u l- χamr-a bi-l-ma:ʔ-i niṣf-ajni,*
3d sing. masc. perf. of 'become, **be**'[1]/ **wine merchant**[2] + nom. + indef./ 3d sing. masc. + **travel** + (imperf.)/ by, **with** + **wine** + gen. + indef./ **to** + **him**[3]/, **and**/ **with** + **him**/ **monkey** + nom. + indef./, **and**/ 3d sing. masc. perf. of 'become, **be**'[1]/ 3d sing. masc. + **mix** + (imperf.)/ **the** + **wine** + acc./ by, **with** + **the** + **water**/ **half** + dual (ACC)[4]/,

(2) *wa ja-bi:ʕ-u-hu bi siʕr-i l-χamr-i*
and/ 3d sing. masc. + **sell** + (imperf.) + **it**/ **at, with**/ **price** + gen.[5]/ **the** + **wine** + gen./

(3) *wa l-qird-u ju-ʃi:r-u ʔilaj-hi, ʔan la: ta-fʕal, fa ja-ḍrib-u-hu, fa lamma: faraʀa min bajʕ-i l-χamr-i*
and/ **the** + **monkey** + nom./ 3d sing. masc. + **sign** + (imperf.)/ **to-him**/, **that** (conj.)/ negat./ 2d sing. masc. + **do** (jussive)[6]/, **and**[7]/ 3d sing. masc. + **beat** + (imperf.) + **him**/ **and**/ **when, after**/ 3d sing. masc. perf. of '**finish**'/ from (= '**with**')/ **sell** + nominalizing suff.[8]/ **the** + **wine** + gen./

(4) *wa ʔarada r-rudʒu:ʕ-a ʔila: balad-i-hi, rakiba l-baḥr-a,*
and/ 3d sing. masc. perf. of '**want**'/ **the**[9] + **return**[10] + acc./ **to**/ town, **home-town** + gen. + **his**/ 3d sing. masc. perf. of '**ride**'/ **the** + **sea** + acc./,

(5) *wa qird-u-hu maʕa-hu, wa χurdʒ-u-n fi:hi θija:bu-hu,*
and/ **monkey** + indef. + **his**/ **with** + **him**/ **and**/ **saddle bag**[11] + nom. + indef./ **in** + **it**/ **clothes** + nom. + **his**/,

(6) *wa l-ki:s-u l-laði dʒamaʕa-hu min θaman-i l-χamr-i,*
and/ **the** + **purse** + nom./ **the** + **which** (masc. sing.)/ 3d sing. masc. perf. of
'collect' + **it**[12]/ **from**/ **price**[13] + gen./ **the** + **wine** + gen./

(7) *fa lamma: sa:ra fi-l-baħr-i, sta-χradʒa l-qird-u l-ki:s-a min ma-wḍiʕ-i-hi*
and/ **then,** so/ 3d sing. masc. perf. of **'be far'**/ **in** + **the** + **sea** + gen./
causative + 3d sing. masc. perf. of **'pull out'**/ **the** + **monkey** + nom./ **the** +
purse + acc./ **from**/ loc. + put, **place**[13] + gen. + **his**/

(8) *wa raqija d-daqal-a wa huwa maʕa-hu ħatta: ṣa:ra fi: ʔaʕla-hu wa rama:*
ʔila l-markab-i bi dirham-i-n
and/ 3d sing. masc. perf. of **'climb'**/ **the**[9] + **mast** + acc./ **and**/ he, it (= the
purse)/ **with** + **him**/ **until**/ 3d sing. masc. perf. of **'reach'**/ in, **to**/ **top** + **its,** his/
and/ 3d sing. masc. perf. of **'throw'**/ **into**/ **the** + **ship**[14] + gen./ by, **with**[15]/
dirham + gen. + indef./

(9) *wa ʔila l-baħr-i bi dirham-i-n wa falam jazal ða:lika daʕba-hu ħatta:*
qasama d-dara:him-a niṣf-ajni.
and/ **into**/ **the** + **sea** + gen./ by, **with**[15]/ **dirham** + gen. + indef./ **and**/ **then**[16]/
3d sing. masc. jussive of **'remain,** stay' /**that** (masc. sing.)/ **practice** + **his**/
until/ 3d sing. masc. perf. of **'divide'**/ **the**[9] + **dirhams** (broken plural of
dirham) + acc./ **half** + dual (oblique form).[4]

NOTES

1. Perfective of *KWN* is here used as an auxilary verb to mark past tense with the imperfect (which usually implies a continuing action in the present): 'It came to pass that as a certain wine merchant was travelling . . .'

2. The KaTTa:B pattern marks habitual involvement with whatever is expressed by the root. Thus, 'one habitually involved with wine' = 'wine merchant'.

3. *La* + personal pronoun construction is often used to indicate possession: 'wine to him' = 'his wine'.

4. Dual endings have only the distinction between nominative and oblique. That is, there is no distinction between genitive and accusative in the dual, but here the oblique case represents what would otherwise be an accusative case marking.

5. This is the so-called construct state construction; that is, the first noun is marked neither for definiteness or indefiniteness and is followed by a definite noun in the genitive case. The result is a definite noun compound: 'the price of wine' or 'the price of the wine'.

6. *La:* + jussive = negative imperative or prohibition.

7. The use of *fa* 'and' instead of *wa* implies that the following is somehow the consequence of what has been said in the preceding clause, whereas *wa* is neutral in this regard. Thus *fa* may be translated 'and so . . .'

8. This is an infinitive of the verb 'to sell' (i.e., a deverbal noun).

9. In connected speech, the initial vowel *a* of the definite article is deleted after a word ending in a vowel. In addition, the *l* of the article assimilates completely to the following consonant if the latter is coronal, that is, a sound produced by the tongue tip or the tongue blade.

10. This is the infinitive form of 'to return'.

11. The root *XRJ* means 'to pull out.' Perhaps the connection with pulling is that a saddle bag was originally made from skins of animals 'pulled' off the carcasses.

12. Cf. the section on the relative clause construction in this sketch.

13. This is a deverbal locative noun = 'place where the action expressed in the root occurs'. Such nouns can readily replace relative clauses referring to locations.

14. This is a deverbal locative noun form of *RKB* 'to ride'; thus it is more literally translated as 'something one rides in, a conveyance'.

15. The Arabic verb 'to throw' is an intransitive verb and therefore cannot have a direct object in the accusative case. What would be the logical object of English 'throw' must be expressed as an instrument.

16. *falam* is short for *falamma:. falam* may govern jussive.

Idiomatic Translation

A wine merchant used to travel in wine he had, and a monkey was with him. He mixed wine with water half and half and sold it at the price of wine. The monkey signed to him: don't do that, so he beat it. When he had finished selling the wine and wanted to go back to his town, he rode on the sea having with him the monkey and the saddle bags in which were his clothes and the purse which he had collected from the price of wine. When he was well at sea, the monkey pulled the purse from its place and climbed the mast, it (the money) being with him, till he reached the top. He threw one dirham into the ship and one into the sea, and that continued to be his practice till he had divided the dirhams into two halves.

SKETCH OF SWAHILI

A. GENETIC AFFILIATION AND GENERAL BACKGROUND

Swahili belongs to the *Bantu* subbranch of the *Benue-Congo* branch of the *Niger-Congo* language family. According to some reports, for example, Myachina (1981:1), Swahili is spoken by 50 million people if the second-language speakers are included. Other sources do not estimate the total number of speakers to be as high. According to Grimes (1992), there are only 1,300,000 first-language speakers of Swahili of whom the largest group (313,200) is in Tanzania, where Swahili is the official language, and the total number of speakers in all Africa, including second-language speakers, is only about 30 million. Figures given by Hinnebusch (1992) agree with those given by Grimes.

Originally a language spoken by a relatively small number of people living on the east coast of Central Africa, Swahili became a trade language and a *lingua franca* (an intermediary language used by groups of speakers who do not speak each other's language), probably because some kind of intermediary language was needed between the Arab traders and the local indigenous population. (The name of the language, Swahili, is derived from the Arabic word for 'coast'.) From the coast it gradually spread inland and seaward, and now besides Tanzania it is also spoken in Kenya, Uganda, Comoro Islands, parts of Mozambique, Zaire, Somalia, and Madagascar. It is reported that in some places a pidginized form of Swahili is spoken.

Four major dialect variants are found on the coast.

1. *KiUnguja* (Southern Swahili) was originally spoken on the island of Zanzibar and is now also spoken on the African mainland in Tanganyika. (Both regions now constitute the state of Tanzania.)

2. *KiMvita* (Northern Swahili) is spoken on Mombasa island and other parts of Kenya.

3. *KiAmu* (Northern Swahili) is spoken on the island of Lamu (northern coast of Kenya) and the coastal areas opposite the said island.

4. *KiMwani* is spoken in northern Mozambique.

Originally, Swahili was written in Arabic script, but starting in the middle of the nineteenth century the Arabic script was replaced by the Roman alphabet. The *KiUnguja* dialect is the basis of Standard Swahili, which is described in this sketch.

B. PHONETICS, PHONOLOGY AND ORTHOGRAPHY

Note that all segments in Table 5.9 are cited in IPA. Their Standard Swahili orthographic equivalents are cited in the parentheses.

In addition, Swahili has two syllabic nasals, m̩- and n̩-, which appear in the word-initial position before nonsyllabic segments (except *w* and *j*). For the most part this distinction is predictable, but there are a few cases in which these nasals contrast with their nonsyllabic counterparts. The difference between syllabic nasals and nonsyllabic nasals is not marked by the orthography.

Asterisked segments are found only in Arabic loanwords, and many Swahili speakers substitute other sounds for them. For example, *kh* (voiceless velar fricative) is often pronounced *h*, and *gh* (voiced velar fricative) is pronounced as *g*.

Voiced stop phonemes are realized as imploded voiced stops everywhere except after tautosyllabic nasals; there they have plain (nonimploded) allophones. Likewise, the palatal phoneme /ʄ/ is realized as an imploded palatal stop except after a tautosyllabic nasal (a nasal consonant belonging to the

Table 5.9   PHONEMES OF SWAHILI

CONSONANTS AND SEMIVOWELS						VOWELS		
p (p)	t (t)		tʃ (ch)	k (k)		i (i)		u (u)
pʰ (p)	tʰ (t)		tʃʰ (ch)	kʰ (k)		e (e)		o (o)
ɓ (b)	ɗ (d)		ʄ (j)	ɠ (g)			a (a)	
f (f)	*θ (th)	s (s)	ʃ (sh)	*x (kh)	h (h)			
v (v)	*ð (dh)	z (z)		*ɣ (gh)				
m (m)	n (n)		ɲ (ny)	ŋ (ng)				
	r (r)							
	l (l)							
			j (y)	w (w)				

same syllable as the phoneme in question) where it is realized as a plain (nonimploded) postalveolar affricate [dʒ].

In some Swahili dialects *r* is replaced by *l*. After an underlying syllabic *n*-prefix (cf. noun class prefix *N*- in the next section) voiceless stops and affricates become aspirated, even though the nasal which triggers this aspiration is deleted and does not appear on the surface. The orthography doesn't mark the phonetic contrast between the voiceless unaspirated consonants and the voiceless aspirated ones.

Swahili also exhibits vowel assimilation that is rather interesting typologically because it involves a class of mid vowels as opposed to a class of high and low vowels. For example, certain verb suffixes appear either with vowel *i* after stems containing *i, u, a*, or with vowel *e* after stems containing *e* or *o*:

> *pig-ia, pig-iwa; fund-isha, fund-ishwa* vs. *end-ea, end-esha; on-ea, on-eka*

Stress is regularly placed on the penultimate syllable. Exceptions to this are some Arabic loanwords, but even these exceptions are often made to conform to the general rule.

Some people who speak a tone language as their native language and speak Swahili as a second language pronounce Swahili with tones.

c. MORPHOLOGY

Typologically Swahili appears to be very agglutinative although it also has some synthetic traits such as irregular or morphologically conditioned allomorphs of some morphemes. Like most Bantu languages it is predominantly a prefixing language, but it does have a number of suffixes as well.

Nouns and Their Modifiers

The major inflection on nouns and their modifiers consists of noun class/number prefixes (gender/number prefixes); adjectives and demonstratives as well as verbs governed by nouns have to show class/number agreement with the noun. For example:

> *Wa*-tu *wa*-zuri *wa*-wili *wa*-le *wa*-meanguka.
>
> NC2p + person/ NC2p + good/ NC2p + two/ NC2p + that/ NC2p + fell down
>
> 'Those two good persons fell down.'

(NC2p = *WATU* class plural prefix. NC stands for 'noun class', 2 stands for the customary class designation, and *p* stands for plural, since the words in this class are all plural. See below for more discussion.)

Note that since the subject of the sentence in the preceding example is a noun belonging to the *WATU* class, the verb must have the *wa*- prefix indicating agreement with the class/number of the subject noun. Similar agreement must be shown in the case of direct object noun as well if the latter is definite or if there is a special emphasis on the object:

> Ni-li-soma *ki*-tabu.
>
> I + past + read/ NC7s + book
>
> 'I read (past) a book.'

versus

> Ni-li-*ki*-soma *ki*-tabu.
>
> I + past + NC7s + read/ NC7s + book
>
> 'I read (past) *the* book.'

Adjectives, demonstratives, and numerals (nominal modifiers in general) follow the noun they modify, and there is a preferred order of such elements as illustrated in the first Swahili example given in this section above. (For a more detailed statement on word order see the section on syntax.)

Scholars working on Bantu languages prefer to consider singular and plural noun class prefixes as belonging to different noun classes, rather than being simply singular and plural variants of the same noun class. This is because in some cases, the plural classes are not merely plural but have other functions as well, as will become apparent from the following discussion.

By and large, the Swahili noun classes are determined by the semantic features of the nouns themselves; they are not largely arbitrary as noun gender is in the Indo-European languages. However, nouns which have been borrowed from other languages sometimes do not fit the semantic category of the noun class, and some of the Proto-Bantu nouns classes have merged in Swahili. Both of these factors contribute in some degree to the apparent arbitrariness of the classes in some cases.

The following are the noun classes of Swahili.

1. NC1s: *m-tu* ('person') Class
The prefix for this class is *m-* or *mw-* or *mu-* (before stems in vowels). Nouns belonging to this class refer mostly to human beings except for the following: *m-dudu* 'insect' and *m-nyama* 'animal'. Some names of family relationship belong to another class; nevertheless, their modifiers exhibit NCl class agreement.

2. NC2p: *wa-tu* ('people') Class
The prefix for this class is *wa-* or *w-* before a vowel. Nouns belonging to this class are plurals of the nouns belonging to NCls class.

3. NC3s: *m-ti* ('tree') Class
The prefix for this class is *m-* before consonants and *mw-* or *mu-* before vowels. Thus the marking for this class is identical with the NC1s prefix. However, there are overt differences between the allomorphs of various agreement prefixes for this class and the agreement prefixes for the NC1s.

This class includes nouns referring to trees and plants. (However, the fruits of the plants belonging to this class belong to another class!) In addition it contains nouns that refer to various products made of wood, names of some natural phenomena such as 'river', 'mountain', and 'moon', and names of some parts of the body such as 'heart' and 'leg'.

4. NC4s: *mi-ti* ('*trees*') Class

The prefix for this class is *mi-*. Nouns belonging to this class are plurals of the nouns belonging to NC3s.

5. NC5s: *ji-* Class

The prefix for this class may have various shapes: *Ø-*, *j-* or *ji-*. The most productive allomorph of this prefix is the zero allomorph.

This class is actually a combination of two originally separate classes in Bantu: the class that contained *augmentatives* (described later) derived from other noun classes, and a noun class that contained nouns referring to round objects. Thus this class contains nouns referring to various fruits such as *chungwa* 'orange', other round objects such as *yai* 'egg', and even *ziwa* 'lake'. In addition there are also some nouns that belong to this class but do not quite fit the semantic categories mentioned above.

The augmentatives are derived from nouns belonging to other noun classes by prefixing *ji-* which replaces the prefix of the original noun class. For example, *m-tu* 'man, person' (NC1) becomes *ji-tu* 'giant'.

6. NC6:*ma-* Class

The prefix for this class is *ma-*. Besides being the plural of NC5 nouns, it has some other functions as well. It includes nouns referring to liquids, for instance, *ma-ji* 'water', in which case this prefix does not signal plurality but collectivity. It can also be used to make plurals of classes other than NC5 (as a kind of innovation in the language), and in the augmentatives it indicates plurality but does not replace the augmentative prefix *ji-* itself. Thus, the plural of *ji-tu* 'giant' is not, as one might expect, *ma-tu,* but *ma-ji-tu* where *ma-* signals class and plurality, and *-ji-* signals the augmentative.

7. NC7s: *ki-tu* ('*thing*') Class

The prefix for this class is *ki-* before consonants and *ch-* before vowels. With few exceptions, all nouns belonging to this class refer to inanimate objects. It is curious to note that the Arabic loanword *kitabu* 'book', has been analyzed by the Swahili borrowers as consisting of *ki-* (class/gender prefix) followed by the stem *tabu* and placed within this class, even though in Arabic the *ki-* portion is actually part of the stem and not a prefix at all.

Among the inanimate things included in this class one may especially single out the names of languages such as *Ki-Swahili* 'Swahili language', *Ki-Ingereza* 'English language', and so on.

This class also includes *diminutives,* which are derived from other classes by means of the NC7s prefix:

> *ki-toto* 'baby' derived from *m-toto* 'child' (NC1s)

Finally, this class includes nouns refering to some physical defects.

> *ki-lema* 'a cripple'

8. NC8p: *vi-tu* ('things') Class

The prefix for this class is *vi-* before consonants and *vy-* before vowels (except *-i*). Besides being the plural counterpart for NC7 this prefix is also used to form adverbs from nouns:

> *vi-zuri* 'well' < *-zuri* 'good, beautiful'

9. NC9s: N- Class

Usually the prefix for this and the following class is given as consisting of a morphophoneme *N* which has the following realizations: Before voiceless segments, *N* is realized as zero, but it causes voiceless stops and affricates to become aspirated; before *b* and *v* it is realized as *m-*; before all other consonants it is realized as *n-*, and before vowels as *ny-*.

This class contains family names, most animal and insect names, some fruit names, most foreign loanwords, and a whole series of other miscellaneous groups of nouns such as names of musical instruments, names of parts of the body, names of buildings and their parts, and names of some countries and parts of the world (but many names of countries belong to the NC11s class instead).

10. NC10p: N- Class

The noun prefix for this class is identical with the one for NC9s (i.e., morphophoneme *N*). However, the agreement prefixes for the two classes are not everywhere homophonous, and therefore the two classes are formally distinct.

This class is the plural counterpart for NC9s, but in addition it is used to mark the plural of NC11s nouns and those NC5s nouns which have a zero allomorph of the noun class prefix.

11. NC11s: *u-* Class

The prefix for this class is *u-* or *w* before a vowel. This class is a combination of two originally separate Bantu classes, and is therefore sometimes referred to as the noun class 11/14.

A large group of nouns belonging to this class are abstract nouns derived from other nouns or from adjectives:

> *zuri* 'beautiful'> *u-zuri* 'beauty' (in abstract sense only)
>
> *moja* 'one'> *u-moja* 'oneness, unity'

Other nouns belonging to this class denote substances which can be regarded as collections of many small things (like English *mass nouns*):

> *u-dongo* 'soil'
>
> *u-gali* 'porridge'
>
> *u-nga* 'flour'

At the same time some nouns belonging to this class are names of objects which refer to single units from a group or collection of such objects:

> *u-shanga* 'bead' (cf. *shanga* 'beads')

It also contains nouns referring to long or elongated objects and some natural phenomena:

>*u-zi* 'thread'
>
>*u-pepo* 'wind'

Names of many countries also belong to this class:

>*U-Ganda* 'Uganda' (lit. 'Ganda nation')
>
>*U-Ingereza* 'England'

Compare *Ki-Ingereza* (NC7s) 'English language' and *Wa-Ingereza* (NC2p) 'English people, Englishmen'.

The peculiar thing about the names of countries belonging to this class is that they govern NC9s concordial agreement, not NC11s concordial agreement.

12. NC15: *ku-* Class

The prefix for this class is *ku-* before consonants and *kw-* before vowels. Note that it is traditionally designated as being noun class 15, not 12. This is because some of the original Bantu classes were lost in Swahili whereas some have merged (for example, class 11 and class 14).

This class contains the infinitives of Swahili verbs, that is, nouns derived from verbs:

>*ku-soma* 'to read, reading'
>
>*ku-piga* 'to beat, beating'

There are no plural counterparts to this and the following classes.

13. NC16: *pa-* Locative Class

The prefix for this class is *pa-*. Only one word belongs to this class: *mahali* 'place(s)'. Adjectives or verbs agreeing with this word take the prefix *pa-* even though this word itself does not take the *pa-* prefix. (This word happens to be a loanword from Arabic which has replaced the original Swahili word. That is why it does not show the expected class prefixes.)

>mahali *pa*-moja
>
>place / NC16 + one
>
>'one place'

Otherwise, this and the following noun classes (usually termed "locative classes") do not have nouns which are permanent members of these classes. The noun class prefixes of all these classes are used to show agreement with nouns which have the general locative suffix *-ni* (and all noun classes except NC1, NC2, and NC15 can take this suffix). NC16 *pa-* expresses a position on the surface of something or a close location of something, whereas other locative noun classes express other locative relationships which will be described below.

14. NC17: *ku-* Locative Class

The prefix of this locative noun class is *ku-* and it signals that the noun (which has the locative suffix *-ni*) is the goal of the movement, distance, and location whose exact whereabouts are unknown to the speaker.

15. NC18: *mu-* Locative Class

The prefix of this locative noun is *mu-* and it signals location within something ('something' being expressed by a noun with the *-ni* suffix).

Here are a couple of examples from Myachina (1981:32) illustrating how the locative classes work:

> Kuna wa-tu *shamba-ni p-angu.*
>
> there are/NC2p + person/ field (NC5s noun) + loc. suffix/ NC15 + my
>
> 'There are people *in* my field.'

> Ni-na-enda *shamba-ni kw-angu.*
>
> I + pres. progressive + go/ field (NC5s noun) + loc. suffix/ NC17 + my
>
> 'I am going *to* my field.'

As can be guessed from these examples, some of these so-called noun classes actually involve *derivation* rather than what we usually think of when we talk about grammatical gender in nouns. Unlike gender in Indo-European languages, which seems to be an "inherent" property of particular noun stems, in Swahili gender is "movable." That is, in Swahili one and the same stem can appear with various class prefixes:

> *m*-toto 'child'
>
> *ki*-toto 'little child, baby'
>
> *u*-toto 'childhood'

This phenomenon is not entirely without parallels in Indo-European languages. For example, German diminutives formed with the suffixes *-chen* and *-lein* are all neuter in gender regardless of what gender the nondiminutive form of the noun belonged to. (Cf. *das Mädchen* 'girl'—neuter gender.)

Personal Pronouns

Since pronominal subject prefixes are obligatorily attached to most verb forms (excluding impersonal constructions and certain modal prefixes which do not co-occur with subject prefixes), independent pronoun forms are used mostly for emphasis; otherwise, they are usually omitted.

'It' and 'they' not referring to persons have emphatic pronouns which are actually reduplicated NC prefixes:

> *kiki* 'it' (NC7s in reference to a book, for example)
>
> *vivi* 'they' (NC8p in reference to books, for example)

**Table 5.10   SWAHILI PERSONAL
PRONOUNS AND
PERSON MARKING**

I. INDEPENDENT FORMS

---

mimi 'I'	*sisi* 'we'
wewe 'you' (sing.)	*ninyi* 'you' (pl.)
yeye 'he, she'	*wao* 'they'

II. SUBJECT PREFIXES (ON VERBS)

---

ni- 'I'	*tu-* 'we'
u- 'you (sg.)'	*m-* 'you (pl.)'
a- 'he, she'	*wa-* 'they'

III. OBJECT PREFIXES (ON VERBS)

---

ni- 'me'	*tu-* 'us'
ku- 'you (sg.)'	*wa-* 'you (pl.)'
m- 'him, her'	*wa-* 'them'

Possessive Constructions

To express possession Swahili uses the following construction: possessed noun + concord prefix agreeing with the NC of the possessed noun + possessive marker + possessor noun

> *ki-tabu ch-a m-toto*
>
> NC7s + book / NC7 + possessive marker / NC1s + child
>
> 'The child's book.'

Possessive pronouns—'my', 'your', and so on—are combinations of a NC prefix showing class agreement with the possessed noun followed by the possessive morpheme and a person marker:

> *wa-toto w-a-ngu*
>
> NC2p + child / NC2p + poss. morpheme + 1st pers. sing.
>
> 'my children'

However, in the case of some very common nouns that refer to family relationships the possessive pronoun complex is attached as a suffix to the possessed noun itself:

> *babangu* 'my father' instead of *baba y-a-ngu*

Verb Morphology

The verb morphology of Swahili is very complex: long strings of prefixes may precede a verb root, and a moderate number of suffixes (some of which are derivational) may follow it. Only a very cursory outline will be given here. To simplify the presentation, all references to allomorphs will be omitted, even in those cases where allomorphy is phonologically conditioned.

The least inflected form of the Swahali verb (as in most languages) is the imperative singular form:

> *soma* 'read!' (compare *someni* 'read!'—plural imperative)

In the following schema of the Swahili verb structure, habitual aspect prefix *hu-* may replace the subject prefix + the tense/aspect prefix; verbs prefixed with *hu-* do not show class/number agreement with the subject noun (but may have a pronominal subject prefix after *hu-*) and are "tenseless"— the tense of such verbs is to be inferred from the context.

Negative prefixes cause special complications and will be discussed separately.

The morphological structure of the Swahili verb is considered next.

i. Prefixal complex

> *sub. + tense/aspect + (sub. agr. + relative formant) + obj. + stem*

a. Subject Prefix

This can be either a pronominal prefix or a NC prefix showing agreement with the NC of the subject noun.

b. Tense/Aspect Prefixes

a- simple present; *na-* present progressive; *li-* simple past; *me-* present perfective; *ta-* future; *ja-* 'not yet' (with negative); *ki-* 'when, if . . .'; *ka-* consecutive 'and'; *nga-* present conditional; *ngali-* past conditional (combination of *nga-* conditional + *li-* past).

c. Subject Agreement + Relative Formant

These two go together and are not as obligatory elements in the verb as the other prefixes listed. Below are a few examples of relative constructions containing these prefixes in the verb:

> *m-toto a-li-y-e-soma ki-tabu*
>
> NC1s + child/ NC1s + past + NC1s + relative formant + stem/ NC7s + book
>
> 'the child who read a book'

> *ki-tabu a-li-ch-o-ki-soma m-toto*
>
> NC7s + book/ NC1s + past + NC7s + relative formant + NC7s (obj. agreement) + stem/ NC1s + child
>
> 'the book which the child read'

There are various complications with such relative constructions since the order of various morphemes is different in different tenses, and there is a special negative construction in which tense marking is neutralized.

There are special relatives of place as well:

Ha-tu-jui a-li-k-o-kwend-a.

neg. + we + know/ NC1s (3d sing. pron. agr.) + past + NC17 (indef. loc.) + relative formant + go + indicative

'We do not know where he went.'

d. *Object Slot*

This, too, may be either a personal pronoun prefix or a NC prefix agreeing with the noun class of the object noun.

ii. *Suffixal complex:*

stem + (causative) + (benefactive/locative) + (passive) + mood

a. *Causative*

This is marked by an underlying suffix *-y* which surfaces as palatalization of the preceding consonant. Thus, *-k* becomes *-sh*, *-g* and *-d* (and sometimes *-b*) become *-z*, and so on.

b. *Benefactive/Locative*

This is usually marked by the *i-/e-* suffix (cf. discussion of vowel assimilation in Swahili in the phonology section):

A-li-ni-andik-i-a barua.

he + past + me + write + benef. + indic./ letter

'He wrote to me a letter.'

As can be seen from this example, this prefix indicates that the object of this verb is a person or entity for whose benefit the action expressed by the verb is taking place.

Passive

This is marked by suffix *-w*.

Mood

Indicative mood is marked by *-a*, and subjunctive by *-e*. In some analyses of Swahili the suffix *-a* is considered to be simply an obligatory verb stem ending, perhaps because it also appears in the imperative mood (at least in the singular imperative). In such analyses the subjunctive is accordingly analyzed as being a replacive morpheme which replaces this otherwise obligatory stem final vowel *-a*.

Besides the above affixation there are many derivational patterns, some involving other suffixes and others involving such things as reduplication:

> *FUMB-a* 'to close'; *fumb-u-a* 'to unclose' (*conversive*); *fumb-ik-a* 'is closed' (*stative*); *fumb-a-fumb-a* 'keep on closing'; *fumb-an-a* 'close together' (*reciprocal*)

'To Be' and 'To have'

The verb 'to be' in Swahili is somewhat irregular in that its root is a monosyllable *wa* which, however, does not appear in all the forms of this verb; instead, another root *li* is used, and even that is totally dropped in particular environments:

> *u-li-ku-wa*
>
> you (sing.) + past + NC15 (*ku-* is usually added to verb roots which consist of a single syllable) + be (*wa* allomorph)
>
> 'you were'

> *u-li-y-e*
>
> you (sing.) + be (*li* allomorph) + NC1s + relative formant
>
> 'you who are'

> *ni*
>
> I (+ Ø allomorph of 'to be')
>
> 'I am'

There is also an emphatic copula construction:

> *ndi-mi*
>
> emphatic copula + 1st pers. sing. suff. (< truncated form of the independent pronoun *mimi*)
>
> 'It is I.'

Note also such forms as *nipo* 'I am here' which consist of a person prefix followed by a zero allomorph of the copula which in turn is followed by NC16 (loc. noun class) + relative formant.

The form *ni* (and its negative counterpart *si*) can be used without regard to noun classes when 'be' is used simply as a linking copula verb.

'To have' is expressed by a combination of 'be' followed by the associative or comitative marker *na*:

U-li-ku-wa na fedha?

you (sing.) + past + NC15 (required prefix for monosyllabic
   verb roots) + be/ comit. marker/ money

'Did you have money?' (Lit., 'Were you with money?')

Ki-banda ki-na vy-umba vi-tatu.

NC7s + hut/ NC7s + comit. marker/ NC8p + room/ NC8p
   + three

'The hut has three rooms.'

Note that in the preceding example, the verb 'to be' has a zero allomorph,
and therefore the subject agreement prefix is attached to *na* directly.

To express existence locative noun class prefixes are added to the verb 'to
be' followed by *na*:

Ku-na wa-tu njia-ni?

NC18 + (∅ allomorph of 'to be') + comit. marker/ NC2p +
   person/ road + loc. suffix

'Are there people on the road?'

Negation

Negation is signaled by prefixes *ha-* and *si-* with the latter allomorph appearing in place of the expected sequence *ha* (neg.) + *ni* (1st pers. sing.) and in
such constructions as the relative construction, subjunctive, and conditional:

h-a-ta-kuwa

neg. (*a*-vowel deleted before another *a*) + future + be

'He won't be.'

si-wi

neg. + be

'I am not.'

Note that in the preceding example the final vowel of the verb stem *wa* is
changed from *a* to *i*. This happens only in the negative forms of simple present and progressive present.

ch-akula ki-si-ch-o (< ki-o)-toshe

NC7s + food/ NC7s + neg. + NC7s + relative formant +
   sufficient

'food which (is, will be, was) insufficient'

The tense here is ambiguous because tenses are neutralized in negative relative constructions.

> *h-a-ku-soma*
>
> neg. + 3d pers. sing. + past tense + read
>
> 'He did not/has not read.'

Note that *li-* simple past and *me-* perfect are both replaced by *ku-* in negative forms of the verb.

D. SYNTAX

Word Order

The basic word order in Swahili is SVO, and modifiers generally follow what they modify. Assertive and interrogative sentences have the same word order. Interrogative sentences differ from assertive ones only in intonation or contain question words.

The order of various nominal modifiers is a mirror image of the usual order of such elements in English:

> *noun + adjective + number + demonstrative*   or   *posessive pronoun*

Thus 'my two big baskets' would be literally 'baskets big two my' in Swahili. (*Vikapu vikubwa viwili vyangu.*)

Case Relations

The difference between subject and direct object is usually signaled by word order but since subject and object prefixes on the verb can also encode subject versus object, they take precedence over the word order. This means that since the subject and object prefixes not only indicate what is the subject and what is the object of the verb to which they are attached but also agree in gender/number with the noun phrases to which they refer, the latter may appear in any order without any confusion arising about their case status. The only case affix is the locative *-ni*, which can be attached to nouns belonging to most noun classes. (Cf. pp 223–24, where the so-called locative noun classes are discussed.) Various locative and instrumental relations are signaled by various prepositions.

For example, the agent NP in a passive sentence is marked by preposition *na* ('associative' or 'comitative'):

> *M-toto a-li-pig-wa na baba y-ake.*
>
> NC1s + child/ NC1s + past + beat + pass./ comit. prep./
>   father (NC9s)/ NC9s + his
>
> 'The child was beaten by its father.'

As we have already seen (on page 227), indirect object is indicated by a special benefactive suffix added to the verb, and at the same time there is an object prefix showing agreement with the indirect object noun. (Indirect object noun precedes the direct object noun in the verb phrase.)

For emphasis object may be placed at the beginning of the sentence, but only if the concord morphemes on the verb clearly indicate which NP is the subject and which the object, and this is the case only if the head of the subject NP and the head of the object NP belong to different noun classes:

> *Ki-tabu wa-na-ki-soma wa-toto.*
>
> NC7s + book/ NC2p + pres. progressive + NC7s + read/
> NC2p + child
>
> 'The children are reading the book.'

Even though a NC7s noun occupies the usual subject NP position in the foregoing sentence, the order of prefixes in the verb clearly shows that the subject of this sentence must be a NC2p noun since a NC2p prefix appears in the subject agreement slot and a NC7s prefix appears in the object agreement slot.

Interrogative sentences have the same word order as assertive sentences. They differ from the latter only in intonation or in the presence of interrogative words which may come either at the beginning or at the end of a sentence.

Concord

As already discussed in the morphology section, nominal modifiers—adjectives, demonstratives, numbers, and so forth—must show noun class agreement with the noun they modify. In addition, in most cases verb forms, too, are inflected to show agreement with the noun class of their subjects, and sometimes in addition with the noun class of the object noun.

If a sentence has several subject NPs belonging to different noun classes, the subject concord prefix on the verb agrees with the noun class of the subject NP closest to the verb.

However, the rules of concord are not altogether straightforward. For example, nouns which refer to animate beings but do not belong to either NC1s or NC2p nevertheless require the concord markers of NC1s or NC2p:

> *M-na vi-boko wa-kubwa mto-ni.*
>
> NC18 + comit. (= 'there are in')/ NC8p + hippopotamus/
> NC2p + big/ river + loc. suffix
>
> 'There are large hippos in the river.'

In addition there are some other concord complications which for the sake of brevity will not be listed here.

Relative and Other Subordinate Clauses

Because Swahili has such a rich derivational and inflectional morphology, its syntax is relatively uncomplicated. For example, as was already discussed under verb morphology, there is a special affix that makes a relative form of the verb; thus, there is no need for such things as relative pronouns to signal relative clauses:

> *wa-li-soma* 'they read (past)' : *wa-li-o-soma* 'those who read (past)'

However, there is yet another way to make a relative clause by using *amba,* which was originally a verb meaning 'to say' but is now a frozen form that acts very much like an English relative pronoun:

> Huyu ni m-toto *amba-y-e* kesho ha-ta-kuja shule.
>
> this/ is/ NC1s + child/ *amba* + relative formant + NC1s/ tomorrow / neg. + future + come/ school
>
> 'This is the child who will not be coming to school tomorrow.'

Note that *amba* still takes the relative formant suffix with the noun class concord affix showing agreement with the noun class of the head noun. The *amba* construction is a relatively recent innovation in Swahili.

Other types of subordinate clauses are introduced by various conjunctions. Subordinate clauses that express purpose or intention may or may not be introduced by a subordinate conjunction such as *ili* or *kusudi.* In either case, the verb must be in the subjunctive mood:

> *Wa-li-ondoka kusudi wa-end-e bara Hindi.*
>
> NC2p + past + leave/ (with the) intention (to)/ NC2p + go + subjunctive/ mainland, continent/ India
>
> 'They left with the intention to go to India.'

E. SAMPLE TEXT

The following short texts are taken from Perrot (1951:139), who in turn cites them from the Swahili language newspaper *Maendeleo* ("Progress"). They constitute two short letters from different readers, one arguing against Swahili and the other arguing for the use of Swahili. Such arguments concerning the status of Swahili seem to have been rather common just before independence came to various countries of East Africa.

The superscripted numbers in the literal morpheme-by-morpheme translation refer to the notes which follow that section.

Swahili Text

(1) KɪSWAHILI KIONDOSHWE

(2) Maneno mengi yatumikayo katika lugha ya KiSwahili yametoka katika lugha za WaArabu, WaZungu na WaHindi. (3) KiSwahili kilipatikana hasa katika sehemu za pwani, nacho ni lugha ya kibiashara. (4) Hakuna watu ambao kabila lao au taifa lao ni la KiSwahili. (5) Ingefaa tuiondoshe lugha hiyo sasa kabila lugha zetu wenyewe hazijaharibiwa.

(6) Ubaya wa KiSwahili ni nini? (7) Kitaondoshwa kwa sababu ni mchanganyiko wa maneno ya KiArabu, KiZungu KiHindi, na KiBantu? (8) Hii si sababu hata kidogo. (9) Hata KiIngereza ni mchanganyiko wa Ki-Latini na lugha nyingine za ULaya. (10) KiSwahili hutuletea faida nyingi. (11) Husaidia WaAfrika wasiojua KiIngereza kusikizana na WaZungu. (12) Husaidia WaAfrika wa makabila mbalimbali kusikizana. (13) Husaidia WaAfrika wanaokijua kusoma magazeti na matangazo ya serikali. (14) Vitabu vilivyopigwa chapa katika KiSwahili ni vingi sana na vyenye maana kabisa katika maendeleo yetu. (15) KiSwahili kitaendelea na kitazidi kusitawishwa mpaka kiwe chema zaidi ya jinsi kilivyo sasa.

Literal Morpheme-by-Morpheme Translation

(1) KI-SWAHILI KI-ONDOSH-W-E

NC7s + **Swahili** (language)/ NC7s + causat. of *ondoka* **'go away'** [1] + pass. + subjunctive/

(2) *Ma-neno m-engi* [2] *ya-tumi-ka-y-o katika lugha y-a Ki-Swahili ya-metoka katika lugha z-a Wa-Arabu, Wa-Zungu na Wa-Hindi.*
NC6 + **word**/ NC6 + **many,** much/ NC6 + **use,** employ + stative + NC6 + relative/ **in**/ (NC9s) **language**/ NC9s + **of**/ NC7s + **Swahili**/ NC6 + pres. perfect + **go out,** come out/ in, **out of,** off/ (NC10p) **language**/ NC10p + **of**/ NC2p + **Arab**/ NC2p + **European**/ **and**/ NC2p + **Indian.**

(3) *Ki-Swahili ki-li-pati-ka-na hasa katika sehemu z-a pwani, na-ch-o ni lugha y-a ki-biashara.*
NC7s + **Swahili**/ NC7s + past + obtain, get + stative + reciprocal or associative (= **'was obtainable'**)/ **especially**/ **in,** out of/ (NC10p) **portion,** fraction/ NC10p + **of**/ **coast**/ **and** + NC7s + relative formant/ [3] **be**/ (NC9s) **language**/ NC9s + **of**/ NC7s + **commerce.**

(4) *Ha-kuna wa-tu amba-o kabila la-o au taifa la-o ni l-a Ki-Swahili.*
neg. + be, **exist** (impersonal) [4]/ NC2p + person, (= **'people'**)/ relative pron. + relative formant (NC2p)/ **tribe**/ NC5s + **their**/ **or**/ **nation**/ NC5s + **their**/ **be**/ NC5s + **of**/ NC7s + **Swahili** [5]/.

(5) *I-nge-faa tu-i-ondosh-e lugha hi-yo sasa kabila lugha z-etu w-enyewe ha-zi-ja-haribi-wa.*
NC9s + conditional + **be proper,** useful/ **we** + NC9s (obj.)/ causat. of *ondoka* **'to go away'** [1] + subjunctive/ (NC9s) **language**/ **this** (already

mentioned) + NC9s/ **now**/ **tribe** (NC10p) language/ NC10p + our/ NC2p + self (with preceding word = **'our own'**)[2]/ neg. + NC10p + **yet** + **destroy, spoil** + pass./.

(6) *U-baya w-a Ki-Swahili ni nini?*
NC11s + **bad**/ NC11s + **of**/ NC7s + **Swahili**/ **be**/ **what**/?

(7) *Ki-ta-ondosh-wa kwa sababu ni m-changany-ik-o w-a ma-neno y-a Ki-Arabu, Ki-Zunga, Ki-Hindi, na Ki-Bantu?*
NC7s + future + causative form of *ondoka* **'go away'**[1] + pass./ by, with, for/ reason (with previous word = **'because'**) / **be**/ NC3s + mix + stative + nominalizer (= **'mixture'**)/ NC3s + **of**/ NC6 + **word**/ NC6 + **of**/ NC7s + **Arab**/, NC7s + **Europe**/, NC7s + **Hindi**/ **and**/ NC7s + **Bantu**/?

(8) *Hii si sababu hata ki-dogo.*
this (NC9s)/ **not be**/ **reason**/ **even**/ NC7s + **small**[6]/.

(9) *Hata Ki-Ingereza ni m-changany-ik-o w-a Ki-Latini na lugha ny-ingine z-a U-Laya.*
even/ NC7s + **English**/ **be**/ NC3 + mix + stative + nominalizer (= **'mixture'**)/ NC3 + **of**/ NC7s + **Latin**/ **and**/ (NC10p) **language**/ NC10p + **other**/ NC10p + **of**/ NC11s + **Europe**/.

(10) *Ki-Swahili hu-tu-let-e-a faida ny-ingi.*
NC7s + **Swahili**/habitual[7] + **us** + **bring** + benefactive + indicative/ (NC10p) **advantage**/ NC10p + **many**/.

(11) *Hu-saidia Wa-Afrika wa-si-o-jua Ki-Ingereza ku-sikiza-na na Wa-Zungu.*
habitual[7] + **help**/ NC2 + **Africa**/ NC2p + neg. + relative + known (= **'those who do not know'**)/ NC7s + **English**/ NC15 + **listen**[8] + reciprocal/ and, **with**/ NC2p + **European**/.

(12) *Hu-saidia Wa-Afrika w-a ma-kabila mbali-mbali ku-sikiza-na.*
habitual[7] + **help**/ NC2p + **Africa**/ NC2p + **of**/ NC6p + **tribe**/ far (= **'different'**)/ NC15 + listen + reciprocal (= **'to understand each other'**)/.

(13) *Hu-saidia Wa-Afrika wa-na-o-ki-ju-a ku-soma ma-gazeti na ma-tangaz-o y-a serikali.*
habitual[7] + **help**/ NC2p-**Africa**/ NC2p + present + relative formant + NC7s + **know** + indic./ NC15 + **read**/ NC6p + **newspaper**/ **and**/ NC6p + proclaim + nominalizer (= **'proclamations'**)/ NC6p + **of**/ **government.**

(14) *Vi-tabu vi-li-vy-o-pig-w-a chapa katika Ki-Swahili ni v-ingi sana na vy-enye maana kabisa katika ma-endele-o y-etu.*
NC8p + **book**/ NC8p + past + NC8p + relative formant + hit + pass. + indic./ mark (*piga chapa* = **'to print'**)/ **in**/ NC7s + **Swahili**/ **be**/ NC8p + **many**/ **very**/ **and**/ NC8p + **having,** becoming/ **meaning,** reason/ entirely, **absolutely**/ **in**/ NC6 + continue, **progress** + nominalizer/ NC6s-**our**/.

(15) *Ki-Swahili ki-ta-endele-a na ki-ta-zidi ku-sitawi-sh-wa mpaka kiwe chema zaidi ya jinsi kilivyo sasa.*
NC7s + **Swahili**/ NC7s + future + **continue,** progress + indic./ **and**/ NC7s + future + **increase**/ NC15 + **prosper** + causative + pass. + indic./ **until,** up to, as far as/ NC7s + subjunctive form of **'to be'**[9]/ NC7s + **good**/ **more**/ **than**/ **how**/ NC7s + **be** + NC8 + relative[10]/ **now**/.

NOTES

1. The original shape of the causative suffix was *-i* (*-y* before another vowel). It caused the stem final consonant to palatalize and spirantize (i.e., become a fricative) but in most cases no longer appears itself. Thus *-k* becomes *-sh*, *-d* becomes *-z*, etc.

2. When two vowels come together in Swahili, depending on the vowels and the environment, some of the vowel sequences monopthongize, whereas in some cases one of the vowels is deleted: *ma* + *engi* = *mengi* (monopthongization); *wa* + *enyewe* = *wenyewe* (deletion of the first vowel).

3. This appears to be a sequence consisting of *na-* (conjunction *and*), noun class concord morpheme, followed by the relative morpheme *-o-*. Literally translated, this sequence means something like 'and which . . .'

4. The negative prefix *ha-* does not co-occur with subject prefixes; thus such constructions are impersonal. Literally, the Swahili construction which means 'to have something' consists of the verb complex meaning 'to be with' + what is possessed.

5. The Swahili construction *'be'* + *possessive marker with concord + complement Y* has the meaning 'X is characterized or characterizable as *Y*'.

6. The NC7s concord prefix on *ki-dogo* does not mean that this adjective modifies some NC7s noun. In this case the NC7s prefix signals adverbial usage: 'at all, even a bit'. (It is, however, more usual to derive adverbs from adjectives by prefixing NC8p prefix to the latter.)

7. Habitual aspect marker *hu-* does not co-occur with the subject agreement prefixes nor with tense prefixes. It may, however, be followed by a pronoun subject prefix.

8. *Sikizana* is a combination of *siki* 'hear' + *-za-* (causative) + *-na* (reciprocal). Thus it means literally 'make each other hear', but here it really means 'understand each other'.

9. In the relative clause introduced by *mpaka* 'until' the verb has to be in the subjunctive mood: 'Until it [Swahili] is . . .' (Note also that the Swahili verb 'to be' has a number of somewhat irregular forms.)

10. Subordinate clauses of manner or degree are introduced by *jinsi* ('manner', 'way'), and the verb complex in such clauses must contain, among other things, the relative formant *-vyo-* with NCp8 concord. (NC8p prefix is often used to derive manner adverbials from adjective stems.)

Idiomatic Translation

LET SWAHILI BE DONE AWAY WITH[5]

Many words which are employed in Swahili language have originated from the languages of the Arabs, the Europeans, and Indians. It really belongs to certain portions of the coast and is a trade language. There are no people whose tribe or nation can be characterized as being "Swahili." It would be good if we get rid of this language now while our own tribal languages have not yet been destroyed.

What is the evil of Swahili? Shall it be done away with because it is a mixture of Arabic words, words from European languages, Hindi words and Bantu words? That is not at all a [good] reason. Even English is a mixture of Latin and other languages of Europe. The Swahili language brings us many advantages. It helps Africans who do not know English to understand and be understood by Europeans. It helps Africans of different tribes to understand each other. It helps those Africans who know it to read newspapers and government proclamations. Books which have been published in Swahili are very many, and this fact has a great significance for our progress. Swahili language will expand and continue to flourish until it is even better than it is now.

EXERCISES

1. Swahili Text

Translate the following Swahili passage into idiomatic English using the glossary and notes that follow as well as the "Sketch of Swahili" as reference:

MALEZI MABAYA[6]

Mara kwa mara tunawaona watoto wengi ambao hawana heshima na adabu nzuri kwa *wakubwa* wao, au pengine kwa wageni wanaofika katika mji fulani. Nimeona katika miji, hasa Nairobi, Mombasa na Dar es Salaam, mama wengine wenye watoto ambao hawawapeleki shuleni kusoma. Basi, mama hawa wakimwona mgeni, humwambia mtoto, "Mwombe peni *ukanunue* mkate." Mtoto huondoka *na kumwamkia* yule mtu shikamuu kubwa, halafu akamwomba peni *la* mkate. Peni lile mtoto hunyang'anywa *na* mama akanunua sigareti ama kitu kingine *apendacho* yeye.

GLOSSARY

A		-baya	bad, evil
a-	NC1s (subj.)		
adabu	good manners	**C**	
a-ka-mw-omb-a		-ch-	NC7s (< -ki)
a-ka-nunu-a			
ama	or, either	**E**	
amba-	who (relat.)	-e	subjunctive
amba-o		-engi	many, much
-amb-i-a	tell, say to	-engine	some, other
-amk-i-a	greet	-enye	having
a-penda-ch-o		**F**	
au	or	fulani	certain
		-fik-a	arrive
B		**G**	
basi	well, so	-geni	stranger

H

ha-	negat. pref.
halafu	afterward
hasa	especially
ha-wa	these (NC2p)
ha-wa-na	they don't have
ha-wa-wa-peleki	
heshima	honour
hu-	habitual aspect
hu-nyang'any-wa	
hu-mw-amb-i-a	
hu-ondok-a	

I

-i-	benefactive
-ingine	some, other

J

-ji	town, village

K

k-	NC7s
-ka-	consecut. (and)
-kate	bread
katika	in
ki-	NC7s
-ki-	when (vb. pref.)
k-ingine	
ki-tu	NC7s + thing
ku-	NC15
kubwa	big, large
ku-mw-amk-i-a	
ku-som-a	
kwa	to, toward

L

l-	NC5s
l-a	NC + of
-le	that
-lezi	upbringing
li-	NC5s
li-le	

M

m-	NC3s
ma-	NC6
ma-baya	
ma-lezi	
mama	mother
mara	time
-me-	pres. perfect.
mi-	NC4p
mi-ji	
m-ji	
m-kate	
m-toto	
m-tu	
-mw-	him, her (obj.)
mw-omb-e	

N

n-	NC10p (or NC9s)
na	and, with
-na-	pres. progress.
ni-	I
-ni	locat. suff.
-nunu-a	buy
-nyang'any-a	rob
n-zuri	

O

-o-	relative formant
-omb-a	ask, beg
-on-a	see
-ondok-a	go away

P

-peleki	send
-pend-a	like
pengine	sometimes
peni	penny

S

shikamuu	greeting
shule	school
shule-ni	
sigareti	cigarette
-som-a	read

T

-toto	child
tu-	we
-tu	person
tu-na-wa-on-a	

U

u-	you (sing.)
u-ka-nunu-e	

W

w-	NC2p
wa-	NC2p
-wa-	NC2p
-wa	passive
wa-geni	
wa-ki-mw-on-a	
wa-kubwa	
wa-na-o-fik-a	
wa-o	NC2p + their
wa-toto	
w-engi	
w-engine	
w-enye	

Y

yeye	she, he
yu-	NC1s
yu-le	

Z

-zuri	good, beautiful

NOTES

a. *Mara kwa mara:* 'From time to time.'
b. *wa-kubwa:* Lit. 'the big ones' = 'elders, grown ups'
c. *u-ka-nunu-e:* '(And) so that you may buy . . .'
d. *na ku-mw-amk-i-a:* When two actions are closely associated the verbs expressing these actions may be joined by *na* (associative or comitative marker) and the second verb is then prefixed by *ku-* (infinitive marker, i.e., NC15).

e. *l-a:* Lit. 'of'; however, here it would be more appropriate to translate this as 'for'.

f. *na:* In passive construction the agent of the action expressed by the verb is marked by *na* (associative/comitative marker).

g. *a-penda-ch-o:* 'Which (NC7s concord) she likes.'

---

2. Analysis of !Xũ (Khoisan)[7]

A. *!Xũ* is a Khoisan language spoken in Northwest Kalahari. Examine the *!Xũ* sentences below and their English glosses and then answer the questions that follow.

Data

a. Mi meni i!a.	'I answer you.'
b. I!a n!aro mi.	'You teach me.'
c. N!eng ho mi.	'The eland sees me.'
d. !Hwã ho n!eng.	'The man sees the eland.'
e. Da'ama ho n!eng.	'The child sees the eland.'
f. N!'hei ho n!eng.	'the lion/lions see(s) the eland.'
g. De'ebi ho n!eng.	'The children see the eland.'
h. N‖ae ho n!eng.	'The men see the eland.'
i. N'eu ho mi.	'The elder sees me.'
j. N'eusi ho mi.	'The elders see me.'

Questions

i. What signals case relations in this language?

ii. What is the basic word order?

iii. How is number marked on nouns?

B. Analyze the !Xũ data below and on the basis of your analysis attempt to explain the *differences in the pronouns.*

a. Da'ama ho !hwã	'The child sees the man.'
Ha ho ha.	'It (child) sees him (man).'
b. De'ebi ho n!eusi.	'The children see the elders.'
Si ho si.	'They (children) see them (elders).'
c. !Hwã wi dz'heu.	'The man helps the woman.'
Ha wi ha.	'He (man) helps her (woman).'
d. Eiya ‖xoma de'ebi.	'Mother pities the children.'
Ha ‖xoma si.	'She (mother) pities them (children).'
e. ǀWara o !ae-kx'ao.	'The baboon sees the hunter.'
Ha o ha.	'It (baboon) sees him (hunter).'
f. ǀWara o eiyasi.	'The baboons see the mothers.'
Hi o si.	'They (baboons) see them (mothers).'
g. ‖'Hao kwa ǀwara.	'The badger fears the baboons.'
Ha kwa hi.	'It (badger) fears them (baboons).'
h. ‖'Hao kwa ǀwara.	'The badgers fear the baboons.'
Hi kwa hi.	'They (badgers) fear them (baboons).'

i. N!'hei-leri kwa da'a. 'The wasp fears fire.'
   Ha kwa hi. 'It (wasp) fears it (fire).'
j. N!'hei-leri kwa da'asi. 'The wasps fear fires.'
   Hi kwa hi. 'They (wasps) fear them (fires).'
k. Dz'heu o ≠xanu. 'The woman sees the book.'
   Ha o hi. 'She (woman) sees it (book).'
l. Dz'heu o ≠xanusi. 'The woman sees the books.'
   Ha o hi. 'She (woman) sees them (books).'
m. Dz'heu ll'ama xore. 'The woman buys the belt.'
   Ha ll'ama hi. 'She (woman) buys it (belt).'
n. Dz'heusi ll'ama xoresi. 'The women buy the belts.'
   Si ll'ama hi. 'They (women) buy them (belts).'

3. Loanwords in Swahili

Swahili has borrowed very heavily from both Arabic and English. In doing so it has adapted the original words to fit into the phonological patterns of Swahili. Examine the data below and determine what general adaptations have taken place. Pay special attention to the final vowels in the Swahili forms. (The data for this exercise comes from E. C. Polomé. 1967. *Swahili language handbook*. Washington, D.C.: Center for Applied Linguistics.)

Loanwords from Arabic

adaba	(< Ar. ʔadab)	'good manners'
kisi	(< Ar. qis)	'estimate'
ratibu	(< Ar. rattib)	'arrange'
wakati	(< Ar. waqt)	'time'
madini	(< Ar. maʕdin)	'metal'
maki	(< Ar. maʕq)	'thickness'
milki	(< Ar. milk)	'possession, dominion'
kaburi	(< Ar. qabr)	'grave, tomb'
dhaifu	(< Ar. daʕiif)	'weak'
fariji	(< Ar. farridʒ)	'comfort'
shahamu	(< Ar. ʃaḥm)	'fat, lard'
duni	(< Ar. duun)	'inferior, low'
sakifu	(< Ar. saqqif)	'make a stone floor'
kuzi	(< Ar. kuuz)	'earthenware pitcher'

Loanwords from English

burashi		'brush'
bulangeti		'blanket'
reli	(< rail)	'railway'
eropleni		'aeroplane'

skrubu		'screw'
paipu	(< pipe)	'motor horn'
stimu	(< steam)	'power (of electricity)'
kilabu		'club'
madigadi		'mudguard'
stesheni		'station'

NOTES

1. These examples are cited from Peter Ladefoged. 1982. *A course in phonetics*. New York: Harcourt Brace Jovanovich, 150.

2. Examples are taken from Gregersen (1977:86).

3. These examples are cited from Nishie (1981:289).

4. The story, as well as its English translation, are cited from Arthur Stanley Tritton (1943:23–4), the text from which most of the Arabic examples cited in this sketch are taken. The morpheme-by-morpheme translation is my own.

5. This translation is a slightly revised version of the one that is given in Perrott (1951:167–8).

6. This is a portion of a text from Perrott (1951:150) who in turn cites it from the Swahili-language newspaper *Maendeleo*. Idiomatic translation of this text is given in Perrott (1951:169) in case you want to check your translation.

7. The data for this exercise is taken from J. W. Snyman. 1970. An introduction to the *!Xũ language*. Cape Town: A. A. Balkema. The orthography of the original text has been preserved except for one or two symbols for clicks.

SELECTED BIBLIOGRAPHY

General

Greenberg, J. H. 1963. *The languages of Africa*. Bloomington: Indiana University Press. (Greenberg's classification of African languages did not receive universal acceptance when it first came out, and it has now been substantially revised by other scholars.)

Gregersen, E. A. 1977. *Language in Africa: An introductory survey*. New York: Gordon and Breach. (This is a fairly easy-to-read introduction for the nonspecialist and covers a broad range of topics.)

Heine, Bernd. 1976. *A typology of African languages: Based on the order of meaningful elements*. Kölner Beiträge zur Afrikanistik, vol. 4. Berlin: Dietrich Reimer Verlag.

———. 1992. African languages. In William Bright et al., eds., *International encyclopedia of linguistics*, 31–6. New York: Oxford University Press.

Heine, Bernd, Thilo C. Schadeberg, and Ekkehard Wolff, eds. 1981. *Die Sprachen Afrikas, mit zahlreichen Karten und Tabellen*. Hamburg: Helmut Buske Verlag.

Nishie, Masayuki. 1981. Afurika no shogengo. In Hajime Kitamura, ed., *Sekai no gengo*, 261–308. Kōza gengo, vol. 6. Tokyo: Taishūkan shoten.

Welmers, William E. 1973. *African language structures*. Berkeley and Los Angeles: University of California Press. (Presents an overview of the phonology, morphology, and syntax of all the language groups found in Africa. It is a more advanced introductory overview than Gregersen's book, but at the same time very readable and even entertaining.)

Afro-Asiatic

Bender, M. Lionel. 1992. Amharic. In William Bright et al., eds., *International encyclopedia of linguistics*, 51–6. New York: Oxford University Press.

Bergsträßer, G. 1983. *Introduction to the Semitic languages*. Winona Lake, Ind.: Eisenbrauns. (Translation by P. T. Daniels of the German original, *Einführung in die semitischen Sprachen*, Munich: Max Hueber, 1928; 2d. ed. 1963.)

Berman, Ruth A. 1992. Hebrew: Modern Hebrew. In William Bright et al., eds., *International encyclopedia of linguistics*, 118–23. New York: Oxford University Press.

Diakonoff, Igor M. 1965. *Semito-Hamitic languages: An essay in classification*. Moscow: Nauka Publ.

Hetzron, Robert. 1987a. Afroasiatic languages. In Bernard Comrie, ed., *The world's major languages*, 645–53. New York: Oxford University Press.

———. 1987b. Hebrew. In Bernard Comrie, ed., *The world's major languages*, 687–704. New York: Oxford University Press.

———. 1987c. Semitic languages. In Bernard Comrie, ed., *The world's major languages*, 654–63. New York: Oxford University Press.

———. 1992. Semitic languages. In William Bright et al., eds., *International encyclopedia of linguistics*, 412–7. New York: Oxford University Press.

Hoberman, Robert, D. 1992. Aramaic. In William Bright et al., eds., *International encyclopedia of linguistics*, 98–102. New York: Oxford University Press.

Moscati, Sabatino, et al. 1964. *An introduction to the comparative grammar of the Semetic languages: Phonology and morphology*. Porta linguarum orientalium, n.s. 6. Wiesbaden: Otto Harrassowitz.

Newman, Paul. 1992a. Chadic languages. In William Bright et al., eds., *International encyclopedia of linguistics*, 253–4. New York: Oxford University Press.

———. 1992b. Hausa. In William Bright et al., eds., *International encyclopedia of linguistics*, 103–9. New York: Oxford University Press.

Sasse, Hans-Jürgen. 1992. Cushitic languages. In William Bright et al., eds., *International encyclopedia of linguistics*, 326–30. New York: Oxford University Press.

Smirnova, M. A. 1960. *Jazyk hausa*. Moscow: Nauka Publ.

Steiner, Richard C. Hebrew: Ancient Hebrew. In William Bright et al., eds., *International encyclopedia of linguistics*, 110–8. New York: Oxford University Press.

Zaborski, Andrzej. 1992. Afro-Asiatic languages. In William Bright et al., eds., *International encyclopedia of linguistics*, 36–7. New York: Oxford University Press.

Nilo-Saharan

Bender, Marvin Lionel, ed. 1989. *Nilo-Saharan language studies*. Vol. 2. Hamburg: Buske.

Dimmendaal, Gerrit J. 1992. Nilo-Saharan languages. In William Bright et al., eds., *International encyclopedia of linguistics*, 100–4. New York: Oxford University Press.

Tucker, A. N. 1940. *The Eastern Sudanic languages*. Publ. for the International Institute of African Languages and Cultures. London: Oxford University Press. (This contains fairly detailed sketches of various languages belonging to the Eastern Sudanic group.)

Zavadovskij, Ju N. and E. B. Smagina. 1986. *Nubijskij jazyk*. Moscow: Nauka Publ. (This work sketches both Ancient Nubian and its modern descendents.)

Niger-Congo

Bendor-Samuel, John. 1992. Niger-Congo languages. In William Bright et al., eds., *International encyclopedia of linguistics*, 93–100. New York: Oxford University Press.

Bendor-Samuel, John, and Rhonda L. Hartell, eds. 1989. *The Niger-Congo languages.* Lanham, Md.: University Press of America. (This book contains articles by different scholars who discuss in some detail various branches and subbranches of the family as well as the typological features exhibited by the languages in question.)

Bird, Charles, and Timothy Shopen. 1979. Maninka. In Timothy Shopen, ed., *Languages and their speakers,* 59–111. Cambridge, Mass.: Winthrop.

Koval', A. I. and G. B. Zubko. 1986. *Jazyk fula.* Moscow: Nauka Publ.

Kropp Dakubu, M. E., ed. 1988. *The languages of Ghana.* International African Institute, African languages/Languages Africaines, occas. publ. no. 2. London: Kegan Paul Internat.

Nikiforova, L. A. 1981. *Jazyk volof.* Moscow: Nauka Publ.

Oxotina, N. V. 1961. *Jazyk zulu.* Moscow: Nauka Publ.

Pulleyblank, Douglas. 1987a. Niger-Kordofanian languages. In Bernard Comrie, ed., *The world's major languages,* 959–70. New York: Oxford University Press.

———. 1987b. Yoruba. In Bernard Comrie, ed., *The world's major languages,* 971–90. New York: Oxford University Press.

Tokarskaja, V. P. 1964. *Jazyk malinke (mandingo).* Moscow: Nauka Publ.

Williamson, Kay. 1989. Niger-Congo overview. In John Bendor-Samuel and Rhonda L. Hartell, eds., *The Niger-Congo languages,* 3–45. Lanham, Md.: University Press of America.

Khoisan

Snyman, J. W. 1970. An introduction to the *!Xũ language.* Cape Town: A. A. Balkeme. (Published for the Department of African Languages, School of African Studies, University of Capetown.)

Arabic

Awde, Nicholas, and Putros Samano. 1987. *The Arabic alphabet, how to read and write it.* London: Al Saqui Books.

Bateson, Mary Catherine. 1967. *Arabic language handbook.* Center for Applied Linguistics, Washington, D.C. (A very readable account.)

Fischer, Wolfdietrich. 1992. Arabic. In William Bright et al., eds., *International encyclopedia of linguistics,* 91–8. New York: Oxford University Press.

Fleisch, H. 1956. *L'Arabe classique: esquisse d'une structure linguistique.* Beirut: Imprimerie catholique.

Kaye, Alan S. 1987. Arabic. In Bernard Comrie, ed., *The world's major languages,* 664–85. New York: Oxford University Press.

Tritton, Arthur Stanley. 1943. *Teach yourself Arabic.* Philadelphia: D. McKay for the English University Press. (Most of my examples and the sample text in the sketch of Classical Arabic are taken from this work.)

Wright, W. 1896. *A grammar of the Arabic language.* 3d ed. (Reprinted, 1951). Cambridge: Cambridge University Press. (Very thorough, but at the same time very old-fashioned reference-type grammar.)

Yushmanov, N. V. 1961. *The structure of the Arabic language.* Translated from Russian by Moshe Perlmann. Center for Applied Linguistics, Washington, D.C.

Swahili

Haddon, Ernest B. 1955. *Swahili lessons.* Cambridge: W. Heffer and Sons.

Hinnebusch, Thomas J. 1979. Swahili. In Timothy Shopen, ed., *Languages and their status,* 204–93. Cambridge, Mass.: Winthrop.

————. 1992. Swahili. In William Bright et al., eds., *International encyclopedia of linguistics,* 99–106. New York: Oxford University Press.

Loogman, Alfons. 1967. *Swahili reading with notes, exercises and key.* Duquesne Studies: African Series, no. 2. Pittsburgh, Penn.: Duquesne University Press.

Myachina, E. N. 1981. *The Swahili language: A descriptive grammar.* Translated from original Russian by G. L. Cambell. Languages of Asia and Africa series, vol. 1. London: Routledge and Kegan Paul.

Perrott, D. V. 1951. *Teach yourself Swahili.* London: English Universities Press. (Most of my examples in the sketch of Swahili as well as the sample texts are taken from this book.)

————. 1965. *Concise Swahili and English dictionary.* New York: David McKay.

Polomé, E. C. 1967. *Swahili language handbook.* Washington, D. C.: Center for Applied Linguistics.

Stevick, E. W., J. G. Mlela, and F. N. Njenga. 1963. *Swahili basic course.* Washington, D. C.: Department of State, Foreign Language Institute.

Wald, Benji. 1987. Swahili and the Bantu languages. In Bernard Comrie, ed., *The world's major languages,* 991–1014. New York: Oxford University Press.

Whitley, W. H. 1969. *Swahili: The rise of a national language.* London: Methuen.

Chapter 6   Languages of Oceania

Geographically speaking, Oceania includes Australia and the majority of the island territories lying in the central and southern Pacific and Indian oceans. Linguistically, this vast area stretches from Taiwan in the north, New Zealand in the south, Madagascar (off the coast of Africa) in the West, and Easter Island, or Rapa Nui (Chile), in the east.

There are three different language groups recognized in the region: Austronesian, Australian, and Papuan languages. Only the first two of these are widely recognized to be language *families;* the last is a geographical grouping which is a catch-all category for all those languages in the region that do not belong to either the Austronesian or the Australian language families, since convincing proof has yet to be presented that they are all genetically related. It should be mentioned here, however, that Greenberg (1971) proposed that all Papuan languages, the extinct Tasmanian, and Andamanese languages constitute a super language family which he called *"Indo-Pacific."* Although it is now clear that at least some major Papuan language groups are genetically related, there has been no proof acceptable to most linguists that Greenberg's Indo-Pacific hypothesis as a whole is valid.

In this chapter we shall survey the language groups in order of the numerical strength of their speakers.

I. AUSTRONESIAN

The total number of speakers of languages belonging to this family is about 240 million. It probably is the language family with the most individual languages in existence, though some of the languages have very few speakers.

There is still much work to be done in terms of subgrouping, and therefore there is some controversy concerning various groupings which will be listed below. For example, not all scholars are agreed on the number of primary branches of this family, but there seems to be a consensus that there are at least three primary branches (referred to collectively as "Formosan branches") on Formosa (Taiwan) and one primary branch outside of Formosa.[1]

1. TSOUIC

This branch consists of *Tsou,* which is spoken by about 500 speakers in west central mountains of Taiwan.

2. ATAYALIC

This branch consists of *Tayal* or *Atayal* (41,000 sp. in the northern mountains of Taiwan) and *Seediq* of which *Taroko* (25,000 sp. in the northern mountains of Taiwan) is the major dialect.

3. PAIWANIC

This branch consists of *Paiwan* (53,000 sp. in the southern and southwestern mountains of Taiwan), *Amis* (130,000 sp. on Taiwan's east coast), and about a dozen minor languages. Some scholars, including Blust, question the validity of this grouping.

The problem with the genetic subgrouping in the Formosan branches is that the languages belonging to them have existed side by side for thousands of years in a relatively small geographical space and have therefore influenced each other over the years to such an extent that it is difficult to separate the shared innovations due to shared intermediate protolanguages from the shared innovations due to diffusion across genetic boundaries.

4. MALAYO-POLYNESIAN

This term was for some time used to refer to the entire Austronesian family, but here it is used to designate a branch of the family. This branch is in turn divided into the following subbranches.

a. Western Malayo–Polynesian

This branch includes a large number of languages, including some of the major languages of the family. Rather than listing further subgroups as such, the languages belonging to this branch are listed roughly in geographical order.

In Micronesia, the following three languages belong to this group: *Chamorro* (73,000 tot. sp., of whom 60,000 are on Guam and 13,500 on the

Northern Mariana Islands, Micronesia), *Palauan* or *Palau* (15,000 sp. in Belau, Guam, and Western Carolines, Micronesia), and *Yapese* (5,000 sp. on Yap, Caroline Islands, Micronesia).

The position of *Yapese* in this group is questioned by many since no one has yet demonstrated that it must belong to this group. A number of scholars (including Blust) have recently proposed that this language belongs to the Oceanic subgroup.

The languages of the Philippines also belong to this group and include, among others, the following languages.

Tagalog, which is also known as *Pilipino,* the national language of the Republic of the Philippines (10,500,000 first-language speakers, but is understood by more than 15 million people), *Cebuano* (12 million), *Ilocano* (5.3 million sp.), *Hiligaynon* (4.5 million), and *Samar-Leyte,* or *Waray-Waray* (2,180,000 sp.).

Languages of Indonesia (excluding Irian Jaya, the western part of New Guinea, where various Papuan languages are spoken), Malaysia, and Madagascar.

Indonesian (Bahasa Indonesia), which has 6.7 million native speakers and about 110 million speakers if second-language speakers are included, its variant *Malay (Bahasa Malaysia),* which has a total of 17,526,000 first-language speakers (of whom 10 million are in Indonesia, the rest mainly in Malaysia), *Javanese* (70 million native sp.), *Madurese* (9 million), *Sundanese* (25 million), *Balinese* (3 million or more) in Indonesia, *Bugis (Buginese* or *Bugi),* which is spoken by about 2.9 million sp., most of whom are on Celebes, and *Malagasy* (10 million on Madagascar), plus a large number of others.

If only native speakers of a language are counted, *Javanese* has the greatest number of speakers of all the Austronesian languages.

On the Asian mainland, besides Malay, which has already been mentioned, there are scattered pockets of Austronesian languages that also belong to this branch. Chief among them are the *Chamic* subgroup languages, which are spoken by less than 500,000 people in isolated pockets in Vietnam and Cambodia. Representative languages are *Eastern Cham* (80,000 sp. mostly in Vietnam) and *Western Cham* (155,000 sp. mostly in Vietnam, and some in Cambodia).

This branch of Austronesian languages also includes those which have the earliest written records in the family: *Old Cham's* earliest inscription is dated A.D. 829, *Old Malay's* earliest inscriptions dated around A.D. 683, and Old Javanese, whose earliest records date back to the ninth century A.D. (All of these languages were written in scripts borrowed from India.)

b. Central-Eastern

This subbranch in turn consists of two major branches.

i. Central Malayo-Polynesian

This includes some hundred odd languages spoken in the Moluccas (Maluku) and Lesser Sunda Islands.

ii. Eastern Malayo-Polynesian

In turn this is subdivided into two subbranches.

a. South Halmahera–West New Guinea

This includes about forty-five minor languages spoken for the most part in coastal Irian Jaya (Indonesia), and coastal New Guinea.

b. Oceanic

This subbranch contains over 450 languages, or about half of the total for the Austronesian family as a whole. The branches and subbranches of *Oceanic* are too numerous to list here in full. Generally speaking, a number of very small subbranches are found in coastal New Guinea and adjacent islands as well as in Vanuatu (New Hebrides) and Loyalty Islands (administratively part of New Caledonia).

The most important subbranch, *Remote Oceanic,* covers most of Micronesia and all of Polynesia. It in turn has a number of branches and subbranches. The more important groups of languages belonging to this subbranch are *Micronesian* and *Central New Hebrides.*

Except for *Palauan, Yapese, and Chamorro,* all of which belong to the *Western Malayo–Polynesian* branch, as well as *Nukuoro* and *Kapingamarangi,* which are *Polynesian* (described later), the *Micronesian* subgroup includes all the languages of Micronesia. Among the chief languages of this group are *Ikiribati (Gilbertese)* with 64,000 or more speakers, mainly in Kiribati; *Trukese* (45,000 sp., including second-language speakers), and *Marshallese* (29,500 sp.).

Remote Oceanic also includes *Fijian* (285,000 first-language speakers, 500,000 if second-language speakers are included), *Rotuman* (8,580 sp. in Fiji and Rotuma Island), and the Polynesian subgroup: *Samoan* (297,400 sp., of whom 140,000 are in Samoa, 32,400 in American Samoa, 15,000 in Hawaii, 90,000 on the U.S. west coast, and 19,711 in New Zealand); *Maori* (100,000 sp. in New Zealand, all of whom are bilingual in English); *Tongan* (108,000 sp., mostly in Tonga); *Tahitian* (124,262 tot. sp.); *Hawaiian* (only about 100 first-language speakers, 2,000 sp. if second-language speakers are included); and a score of lesser known languages with a small number of speakers: for example, *Rapanui (Pascuense),* spoken by 2,500 speakers on Easter Island, which is governed by Chile.

It should be noted that a number of scholars question the validity of the Remote Oceanic subgroup.

It is very difficult to make general statements about Austronesian languages as they are spread over such a large area and are typologically quite diverse. As a rule, Western Malayo–Polynesian languages appear to be more conservative than languages belonging to other branches of Malayo-Polynesian both in phonology and in morphology. Most Oceanic languages have lost word-final consonants and have simplified consonant clusters. (Many of the languages, like Hawaiian, have no consonant clusters at all.)

Basic word order for Austronesian is predominantly VOS on Taiwan, the Philippines, and adjacent parts of Borneo and Sulawesi. It is SVO in much of western Indonesia, eastern Indonesia, and Melanesia. A number of the Austronesian languages of New Guinea are SOV, as a result of contact with Papuan languages. Polynesian languages are VSO, as is Malagasy.

As was already stated in the chapter on the languages of Asia, Paul Benedict considers Austronesian languages to belong to his "Austro-Tai" language family, along with Tai-Kadai languages, Hmong-Mien languages, and Japanese. Other scholars have attempted to link Austronesian with Altaic, Indo-European, Austroasiatic (the so-called Austric hypothesis), and even Sino-Tibetan (specifically Sinitic), but so far none of these hypotheses has been thoroughly explored and confirmed by solid evidence.

In recent years a great deal of interest has been devoted to the question of where the original homeland of the Proto-Austronesian language family must have been located. There are two different but complementary approaches that may be taken in order to determine where the original homeland of any protolanguage (i.e., "protohome," or *Urheimat* in German) was located.

1. One can employ the principle that the area of greatest linguistic diversity within a given language family must be the area which was settled earliest by the speakers of languages belonging to the language family in question, and that areas of little linguistic diversity must be the areas of more recent settlement. This principle is derived from the observation of linguistic situation in the areas for which we have ample historical documentation concerning the settlement and expansion of speakers of various languages. For example, it is clear that the most pronounced differentiation among the various dialects of American English is found on the Atlantic seaboard, which was settled earliest by European colonists, and that the farther West one goes, the less dialect differentiation can be found. In China, too, the spread of Mandarin into southwestern China and northeastern China has been relatively recent, and that accounts for the fact that there is still much similarity between Mandarin dialects spoken in Sichuan and Yunnan (southwestern China) and the dialects spoken in northeastern China (former Manchuria). On the other hand, on the coast of China, areas settled by Chinese-speaking peoples much earlier, there are sometimes very deep linguistic divisions even among adjacent speech communities.

2. The other basis for determining where the original homeland must have been involves reconstructing the vocabulary of the protolanguage and then examining this vocabulary for clues as to the material culture of the speakers of the protolanguage, including terms for flora and fauna. Thus, it is argued that if the protolanguage had the word for coconut, its speakers must have lived in a tropical area where coconuts are found. In addition, archeologists may attempt to match up various prehistoric archeological sites with a particular reconstructed protolanguage, based on the presence at the archeological sites of artifacts, animals, evidence of cultivation of various crops, and so forth, all of which match the presence in the reconstructed protolanguage of lexical items for such items.

Unfortunately, this strategy is not without its pitfalls since words for various artifacts, unfamiliar plants and animals, may be diffused from language to language, and, if borrowed rather early—before major sound shifts have taken place in the borrowing languages—may no longer be recognizable as loanwords and thus be reconstructed as part of the original vocabulary.

Blust (1988) and Bellwood (1991) attempt to apply both of the foregoing approaches in determining the protohome of Austronesian. (Bellwood tentatively accepts Paul Benedict's Austro-Tai hypothesis and therefore talks about the possible protohomeland of Austro-Tai as well.) They both come to the conclusion that the most likely protohomeland for Austronesian was coastal south China where, according to archeological evidence, there were Neolithic settlements whose inhabitants developed rice and sugar cane cultivation, domesticated water buffalo and other cattle, and had such implements as plows, axes, and canoes. In addition, if Benedict's hypothesis is correct, the earliest split, that between Tai-Kadai and Austronesian languages most likely occurred there since Tai-Kadai languages are still spoken in the general area of south China and the Formosan branch of Austronesian, a branch involved in the primary split within the Austronesian language family, is still spoken on an island off the coast of south China.

As the Austronesian language speakers expanded gradually in various directions, this expansion resulted in further splits from the family tree, and as the speakers developed new artifacts or encountered new plants and animals in their new habitats, lexical items for these new things were added to their languages. Thus, for example, lexical items for things such as taro, breadfruit, yam, banana, sago, and coconut cannot be reconstructed for Proto-Austronesian, but they can be reconstructed for Proto-Malayo-Polynesian (the parent language of one of the major branches of Austronesian), which was likely spoken in an area further south of the Proto-Austronesian homeland, in the lands bordering on the Sulawesi sea.

II. PAPUAN LANGUAGES

As already stated at the beginning of this chapter, although Joseph Greenberg considers all Papuan languages to be part of his "Indo-Pacific" family, it might be more judicious to treat Papuan languages as a geographic grouping for the time being until better evidence can be adduced for the genetic relationship among all the languages in question.

Note that *Tasmanian,* the extinct group of languages of the island of Tasmania off the southeastern coast of Australia, is claimed by Greenberg to belong, along with the Papuan languages, to his Indo-Pacific family, even though very little data survives today on this language. Recently, however, more materials on this language group have come to light, and on the basis of these materials some scholars now believe that Tasmanian may have been related to the languages of Australia. Also included in Greenberg's Indo-Pacific is *Andamanese,* a group of languages spoken on Andaman islands (governed by

India) by small groups of people. (There is very little published material on these languages.)

Disregarding Tasmanian and Andamanese, twelve separate groupings of Papuan languages are posited by Wurm (1982); most of these are found in various parts of New Guinea, Central Solomons, Bouganville, and Timor, that is, they are the non-Austronesian languages of Melanesia and adjacent areas. (In addition, there are a number of languages whose status is uncertain.)

1. TRANS-NEW GUINEA

This group has a large number of branches and subbranches and covers the whole of the mainland New Guinea except northwestern Irian Jaya (which is part of Indonesia) and northwestern Papua New Guinea, but in addition includes the languages belonging to the Timor-Alor-Pantar group spoken in the Lesser Sundas region of Indonesia. It is considered to be the most controversial grouping in Wurm's classification of Papuan languages.

Excluding branches that consist of single languages, this family is divided into the following major branches.

a. Main Section

This subbranch in turn consists of two major subbranches.

i. Central and West Trans-New Guinea

This subbranch has 12 subbranches which will not be listed here. Some of the major languages belonging to this group are *Enga* (164,750 sp. in Enga Province, Papua New Guinea), *Kuman,* which is also known as *Chimbu* (71,731 sp. in Chimbu Province, Papua New Guinea), *Awyu* (18,000 sp. on the south coast of Irian Jaya, Indonesia), *Kaeti* (spoken by 10,000 sp. in Irian Jaya, Indonesia, and adjacent areas of Papua New Guinea), *Kombai* (10,000 sp. in Irian Jaya, Indonesia), *Ngalum* (spoken by 18,000 sp. on the border between Irian Jaya, Indonesia, and Papua New Guinea), *Yonggom* (spoken by about 17,000 sp. in Western Province, Papua New Guinea and in Irian Jaya, Indonesia).

ii. East Trans-New Guinea

The main languages in this group are *Ewage-Notu* (spoken by 12,000 sp. in Oro Province, Papua New Guinea), *Kunimaipa* (10,000 sp. in Central Province and Morobe Province, Papua New Guinea), *Mailu* (6,000 sp. in Central Province, Papua New Guinea) and *Tauade* (spoken by about 8,620 sp. in Central Province, Papua New Guinea).

b. Eleman

The chief representative here is *Toaripi,* spoken by 23,000 speakers in Gulf Province, Papua New Guinea.

c. Inland Gulf

This group consists of only four languages of which *Tao-Suamato* (500 sp. in Western Province, Papua New Guinea) is the largest in terms of the number of speakers.

d. Kaure

This consists of about five minor languages of which *Kaure* (500 sp. in Irian Jaya) has the largest number of speakers.

e. Kolopom

This consists of three languages, the largest being *Kimaghama* (3,000 sp. on Frederik Hendrik Island off southeast coast of Irian Jaya, Indonesia).

f. Madang-Adelbert Range

The main languages of this group are *Amele* (spoken by 5,300 sp. in Madang Province, Papua New Guinea) and *Sumau* (spoken by about 2,510 sp. in Madang Province, Papua New Guinea).

g. Mek

This group consists of nine languages, of which the chief representatives are *Hmanggona* (spoken by 8,000 to 10,000 sp. in Irian Jaya, Indonesia) and *Ketengban* (spoken by 7,000 to 10,000 sp. in Irian Jaya, Indonesia, near the Papua New Guinea border).

h. Nimboran

This consists of five languages of which the chief is *Nimboran* (3,500 sp. in Irian Jaya, Indonesia, near the border with Papua New Guinea).

i. North Trans-New Guinea

This group includes a large number subbranches. Most of the languages have very few speakers. Some of the major languages belonging to this group are *Amanab* (6,800 sp. in West Sepik Province, Papua New Guinea, and in Irian Jaya, Indonesia), *Kilmeri* (2,200 sp. in West Sepik Province, Papua New Guinea), and *Waris* (3,160 sp. in West Sepik Province, Papua New Guinea, and in Irian Jaya, Indonesia).

j. Pauwasi

This consists of four languages of which *Emumu* (1,100 sp. Irian Jaya, Indonesia) has the largest number of speakers.

k. Senagi

This group consists of two languages, of which *Angor* (about 2,570 sp. in West Sepik Province, Papua New Guinea) has more speakers.

l. South Bird's Head-Timor-Alor-Pantar

This group consists of ten languages, of which the chief ones are *Kasuweri* (2,500 sp. in Irian Jaya, Indonesia) and *Kemberano* (spoken by 1,500 sp. in Irian Jaya, Indonesia).

m. Teberan-Pawaian

This subgroup consists of three languages: *Dadibi* (10,000 sp. in Southern Highlands Province, Papua New Guinea), *Folopa* (spoken by 3,000 sp. in Gulf Province and Southern Highlands Province, Papua New Guinea), and *Pawaia* (spoken by about 2,920 sp. in Chimbu Province and Gulf Province, Papua New Guinea).

n. Trans-Fly-Bulaka River

This group contains a large number of subbranches and about 30 languages. The chief representatives are *Bamu* (4,400 sp. in Western Province, Papua New Guinea), *Northeast Kiwai* (4,400 sp. in Western Province, Papua New Guinea), and *Southern Kiwai* (spoken by 9,700 sp. in Western Province, Papua New Guinea).

o. Turama-Kikorian

This consists of only three languages, the largest of which is *Kairi* (spoken by 1,000 people in Gulf Province, Papua New Guinea).

2. WEST PAPUAN

This proposed family is subdivided into two major subbranches.

a. Bird's Head

The chief representatives of this group are *Mai Brat* (20,000 sp. or more in Irian Jaya, Indonesia), *Moi* (4,000 sp. on Salawati Island, Irian Jaya, Indonesia), *Mpur* (5,000 sp. in Irian Jaya, Indonesia), and *Tehit* (spoken by 8,500 sp. in Irian Jaya, Indonesia).

b. North Halmahera

The chief representatives are *Galela* (spoken by 20,000 to 25,000 sp. on northern Halmahera and neighboring islands, northern Maluku, Indonesia), *Loloda* (spoken by 13,000 sp. on the northwestern coast of Halmahera, northern Maluku, Indonesia), *Sahu* (spoken by 9,000 sp. on northern Halmahera Island, northern Maluku, Indonesia), *Ternate* (42,000 sp. on Ternate and neighboring islands and the west coast of Halmahera, northern Maluku, Indonesia), *Tidore* (26,000 sp. on the island of Tidore and the neighboring islands, as well as west coast of Halmahera, northern Maluku, Indonesia), *Tobaru* (spoken by 10,000 to 15,000 sp. in northern Halmahera, northern Maluku, Indonesia), and *Tobelo* (spoken by 20,000 to 25,000 sp. on a chain of islands in northern Maluku and extending as far as Raja Ampat islands of Irian Jaya, Indonesia).

3. EAST BIRD'S HEAD

This family consists of three languages spoken on the Vogelkop (Bird's Head) Peninsula in Western Irian Jaya, Indonesia. The two major languages are *Mantion,* which has about 12,000 speakers, and *Meah,* which has about 10,000.

4. GEELVINK BAY

This family consists of about twelve languages, chief of which are *Barapasi* (spoken by 1,000 sp. on Cenderwasih Bay, in western Irian Jaya, Indonesia), *Bauzi* (spoken by 1,000 sp. around Lake Holmes, Irian Jaya, Indonesia), and *Yawa* (spoken by 6,000 sp. on Central Yapen Island, in western Irian Jaya, Indonesia)

5. SKO

This proposed family consists of eight languages, the chief of which are *Vanimo* (2,200 sp. in West Sepik Province, Papua New Guinea) and *Warapu* (about 3,000 sp. on the coast of West Sepik Province, Papua New Guinea).

6. KWOMTARI-BAIBAI

This family consists of six languages spoken in northwestern Papua New Guinea. The chief representatives are *Fas* (spoken by about 1,600 in West Sepik Province, Papua New Guinea) and *Kwomtari* (spoken by 825 sp. in West Sepik Province, Papua New Guinea).

7. ARAI OR LEFT MAY

This proposed family consists of six languages, none of which is spoken by 500 or more speakers. The chief representative is *Nimo,* spoken by no more than 410 speakers in East Sepik Province, Papua New Guinea.

8. AMTO-MUSAN

This family consists of two languages: *Amto,* spoken by about 230 speakers in West Sepik Province of Papua New Guinea; and *Musan,* which is spoken by 75 speakers in West Sepik Province, Papua New Guinea.

9. TORRICELLI

This proposed family consists of several subbranches, only one of which is listed here:

Kombio-Arapesh

The chief languages in this branch are *Bumbita Arapesh* (spoken by about 2,350 speakers in the Torricelli Mountains, East Sepik Province, Papua New Guinea), *Southern Arapesh* (about 10,500 sp. in the Torricelli Mountains, East Sepik Province, Papua New Guinea), *Bukiyup* (10,300 sp. in the Torricelli Mountains, East Sepik Province, Papua New Guinea), *Kombio* (spoken by about 2,550 sp. in the Torricelli Mountains, East Sepik Province, Papua New Guinea), and *Wom* (spoken by about 1,890 sp. in East Sepik and Maprik Provinces of Papua New Guinea).

10. SEPIK-RAMU

This family consists of a number of subbranches which will not be listed here. The major languages in this family are *Abau* (spoken by about 4,550 sp. in West Sepik Province, Papua New Guinea, also spoken in Irian Jaya, Indonesia), *Ambulas* (spoken by 33,100 sp. in East Sepik Province, Papua New Guinea), *Boikin* (spoken by about 35,200 sp. in East Sepik Province, Papua New Guinea), *Iatmul* (spoken by 12,000 sp. in East Sepik Province, Papua New Guinea), *Kwasengen* (spoken by about 6,000 sp. in East Sepik Province, Papua New Guinea), *Mehek* (spoken by 4,030 sp. in West Sepik Province, Papua New Guinea), *Namia* (spoken by around 3,220 sp. in East Sepik Province, Papua New Guinea), *Sawos* (spoken by 9,000 sp. in East Sepik Province, Papua New Guinea), and *Namsak* (spoken by 3,180 sp. in East Sepik Province, Papua New Guinea).

11. EAST PAPUAN

This language family is subdivided into three major groups.

a. Bougainville

The chief languages belonging to this subgroup are *Buin* (spoken by 17,000 sp. in North Solomons Province, Papua New Guinea), *Siwai* (spoken by 6,600 sp. in North Solomons Province, Papua New Guinea), *Nasioi* (spoken by 17,000 sp. in North Solomons Province, Papua Guinea), and *Rotokas* (spoken by 4,320 sp. in North Solomons Province, Papua New Guinea).

b. Reef Islands-Santa Cruz

This subgroup includes the following: *Ayiwo* (about 3,960 sp. in Santa Cruz Islands, eastern Solomon Islands), *Nangu* (spoken by only 240 sp. on Santa Cruz Islands, Solomon Islands), and *Santa Cruz* (spoken by 3,230 sp. in the Santa Cruz Islands, eastern Solomon Islands).

c. Yele-Solomons-New Britain

The major languages belonging to this subgroup are *Bilua* (spoken by about 4,470 sp. in Western Province, Solomon Islands), *Kol* (spoken by 3,600 sp. in East New Britain Province, Papua New Guinea), *Mali* (spoken by 2,200 sp. in East New Britain Province, Papua New Guinea), *Pele-Ata* (spoken by 1,320 sp. in West New Britain Province, Papua New Guinea), *Qaqet* (spoken by 6,350 sp. in East New Britain Province, Papua New Guinea), *Savo* (spoken by about 1,150 sp. in central Solomon Islands), and *Yele* (spoken by 3,300 sp. in Milne Bay Province, Papua New Guinea).

12. AWERA

Belonging to this group are three small languages found in Irian Jaya, Indonesia, the chief of which are *Awera*, which has only 100 speakers, and *Rasawa*, which has only 200 speakers.

According to Foley (1992), Papuan languages tend to be agglutinating in type and tend to be mainly suffixing. They also tend to have SOV as their basic word order, with modifiers preceding their head nouns and with postpositions instead of prepositions. (The latter two features are the usual concomitant features of SOV languages.)

Although the speakers of all Papuan languages are black, they are quite distinct racially from either Australian aborigines or African blacks. In some places it appears that originally Papuan language speakers were assimilated by Austronesian invaders in both culture and language. It is also typical in the New Guinea and Melanesia to find Austronesian languages on the seacoast, whereas the non-Austronesian languages are spoken inland. There has been some diffusion of linguistic features from Austronesian languages into neighboring Papuan languages and vice-versa.

III. AUSTRALIAN

Australian aborigines differ racially from Austronesian language speakers as well as speakers of the so-called Papuan languages, who are also black like Australian aborigines. (For example, Australian aborigine children are born blond, and only as they grow older does their hair turn dark.) Thus, on the basis of racial similarity, it is not likely that Australian languages will be shown to be related genetically to either Austronesian or Indo-Pacific languages. On the basis of phonological typology there is a very remote possibility that there are genetic ties between Australian and the Dravidian languages of South India: both groups tend to share the somewhat rare three-way contrast between dental, alveolar, and retroflex consonants. However, neither racial characteristics of speakers nor typological considerations are very reliable criteria for establishing genetic relationship among various languages, and therefore the above speculations need not be taken very seriously.

There are about 200 Australian aborigine languages, but about 50 of them are already extinct and most of the rest are spoken by a small number of speakers. The largest languages are *Kala Yagaw Ya (Mabuiag),* spoken by about 3,000 speakers on Torres Strait Islands (off the north coast of Australia), and *Western Desert* (4,000 tot. sp.); this language and its dialects are spread all over Western Australia, but not all parts of Western Australia are Western Desert speaking.

Dixon (1980:225) states that there are two languages spoken in Australia that cannot at present be genetically linked either with the Papuan languages or with the Australian language family. They are *Tiwi,* spoken on Bathurst Island and Melville Island, and *Djingili,* a language spoken on the Barkly Tableland in northern Australia.

The family is divided into 28 separate branches, 27 of which are located in Arnhem Land and the northern part of Western Australia. In the rest of Australia only one branch, the *Pama-Nyungan* branch, is found. Since Proto-Australian has not yet been reconstructed, the aforementioned classification, based as it is on lexicostatistical methods and typological similarities, should be considered as a tentative one: Without knowing what Proto-Australian was like it is not possible to ascertain which linguistic features shared by various languages are *shared retentions* and which are *shared innovations*. Actually, the family tree model of genetic relationship seems to be totally inappropriate for handling the subgrouping of Australian languages because in Australia there did not seem to exist more or less solid divisions among various languages or speech communities, and there was therefore much more diffusion from language to language and more blending of various speech communities than is usually the case. To solve this problem, Heath (1978) has attempted to discover which grammatical features are diffusable and which are not, as well as factors that favor or impede diffusion of grammatical features, at least in the Australian context. However, inasmuch as it is not quite possible to come up with universal criteria as to what may eventually be diffused and what cannot, this problem remains a serious one for the comparative studies on Australian languages. Florey (1988:154), in her overview of the state of comparative Australian studies, concludes that achieving a classification of Australian languages is questionable because of the strong likelihood of diffusion.

Languages of this family exhibit a number of very interesting features. First, one finds very long *dialect chains* that stretch for thousands of miles. (In dialect chains the neighboring dialects are very similar and mutually intelligible, but the dialects at the ends of the chain are very different and not mutually intelligible.)

The sound systems are very uniform in their inventory. There is an almost total absence of fricatives and affricates. Stops do not exhibit voicing contrast. Vowel systems consist of the classical three vowels: *i, u,* and *a*. Some of the languages have contrastive dental, alveolar, and retroflex series of consonants which remind one of the inventories of some Dravidian languages.

The usual word order is SOV, and adjectives follow the nouns they modify, but word order is relatively free. There are also very complicated demonstrative systems, and many languages are *split-ergative languages*. For example, the Western Desert language has accusative case marking in pronouns but has ergative case marking in nouns. (This is also true of Dyirbal. Cf. the "Sketch of Dyirbal" in this chapter.)

In addition, Australian languages are also well known for having very elaborate linguistic taboos. For example, in Guugu Yimidhir, according to Haviland (1979), there is a special way that one must speak to one's brother-in-law. For the most part, the difference between the ordinary language and the "brother-in-law language" consists of difference in the lexical items used for everyday things; in addition, however, there are subjects such as sexual matters that just cannot be talked about with one's brother-in-law.

Sketch of Hawaiian

A. Genetic Affiliation and General Information

Hawaiian belongs to the Polynesian subgroup of the Oceanic branch of Austronesian, along with such languages as Maori, Samoan, Tahitian, and a host of other languages spoken on various islands in the Pacific Ocean, especially in the South Pacific and Central Pacific within the so-called Polynesian triangle bounded by Hawaii in the north, New Zealand in the south, and Easter Island (Chile) in the east.

Like most Polynesian languages Hawaiian has relatively simple phonology (although not as simple as was once thought) and is typologically an analytic isolating language, though it does have some affixation.

Although a fairly large number of Hawaiians and part-Hawaiians (estimated number of speakers is 2,000) still speak Hawaiian, almost all the speakers are bilingual in English (or Hawaiian Creole English) and many do not speak the language on a daily basis any more. Only on the privately owned island of Niʻihau off the coast of Kauʻai is there a small community of Hawaiian speakers (about 200) for whom Hawaiian is truly a native language and among whom there are still monolingual speakers.

In recent years there has been a revival of interest in the Hawaiian language and culture among the people living in Hawaii, and as a result Hawaiian language is studied more widely in schools and spoken Hawaiian is heard more often on the radio. (There has always been much Hawaiian music on the radio in Hawaii, including songs sung in Hawaiian by singers who often did not understand the words they were singing.)

B. PHONETICS, PHONOLOGY, AND ORTHOGRAPHY

Hawaiian is known for having one of the smallest phoneme inventories in the world, mainly because it has so few consonant phonemes. (Rotokas, a Papuan language, is reputed to have the smallest inventory of consonant phonemes—only six.) Table 6.1 lists the consonant phonemes given in current orthography.

The paucity of the consonant phonemes is due to a number of historical mergers of Proto-Polynesian consonants in Hawaiian. For example, both *s and *f have merged into h.

/w/ is pronounced either as [v] or [w]. These two sounds are in free variation in Hawaiian. For more details see Schütz (1980).

/k/ is usually pronounced [t] on the island of Niʻihau except at the beginning of a sentence. On other islands, it is usually pronounced [k]. (But there are words that seem to be pronounced with a [t] everywhere. For example, kūkū 'grandma' or 'grandpa' is usually pronounced as [tūtū] by all speakers of Hawaiian.)

Table 6.1   HAWAIIAN CONSONANT PHONEMES

p		k	ʻ
			h
m	n		
	l		
w			

/'/ represents a glottal stop ([ʔ]).

The vowel inventory is fairly rich (in comparison to the inventory of Hawaiian consonants) and consists of the classical five vowel system which is further enhanced by the presence of the length contrast (see Table 6.2).

Note that the vowel length is not contrastive everywhere. Under certain circumstances vowels are automatically long. This predictable length is sometimes marked and sometimes unmarked in the current orthography. (For the sake of brevity the rules for this predictable length will not be given here.)

In addition to the monophthongs there are also the following short diphthong phonemes:

iu, ei, eu, ai, ae, ao, au, oi, ou

And the following long diphthong phonemes:

āi, āu, āe, āo, ēi, ōu

All other combinations of vowels act as sequences of separate vowel phonemes, not diphthongs (which act as unit phonemes in regard to stress).

As Schütz (1980:25) points out, since there is a large number of vowel nuclei phonemes in Hawaiian, the total number of phonemes adds up to 33 units: 5 short monophthongs + 5 long monophthongs + 9 short diphthongs + 6 long diphthongs + 8 consonants. This is certainly not such a small number of phonemes as phoneme inventories go to deserve special mention as being unusual. However, the number of consonant phonemes is relatively low.

Primary stress is placed on the final syllable if it is long (long monophthong or a long diphthong); if the final syllable is short, the primary stress is placed on the penultimate vowel or diphthong. The placement of secondary accents also follows this rule except that instead of the word boundary being the significant factor, it is units larger than a syllable — what Schütz (1980:20) calls "accent measures" — that determine the placement of other stresses within words.

Prior to World War II few Hawaiian texts marked the presence of a glottal stop, and long vowels were not marked as being different from short vowels even though vowel length is a very important distinction in the language.

Hawaiian has borrowed extensively from various European languages, especially English. It even has several loans from Chinese (Cantonese). (Chinese laborers from South China formed the first wave of indentured workers that came to Hawaii to work on the sugar cane plantations.)

Table 6.2 VOWEL PHONEMES OF HAWAIIAN

i ī		u ū
e ē		o ō
	a ā	

pipi = 'beef'

kālā = 'dollar'

pele = 'bell'

Kalikimaka = 'Christmas'

konohī 'Chinese New Year' < Cantonese *kung hee* 'congrat-
ulations'

Because Hawaiian does not allow any consonant clusters or final consonants, Hawaiian versions of English words and words borrowed from other
languages have vowels inserted between consonants where there are no vowels in the donor language forms or at the end of the word after a consonant.
Another way of dealing with consonant clusters in borrowed words is simply
to drop some of the consonants altogether. Also, since Hawaiian has no apical fricatives or any affricates, usually *k* is substituted for English *s, sh, ch, j*,
and the like, making some of the loanwords from English sometimes almost
unrecognizable.

c. MORPHOLOGY AND SYNTAX

Since Hawaiian is basically an isolating/analytic language and does not have
much affixation or formally marked parts of speech, it is more convenient to
discuss Hawaiian morphology and syntax under a single heading rather than
separating the two.

The basic word order is VSO, and modifiers usually follow the words
they modify. Case relations are signaled primarily by means of prepositions.

Noun Phrase Structure and Nominal Morphology

The elements that form a noun phrase in Hawaiian are as follows:[2] *preposition + determiner + noun + postnominal elements.*
For example,

> *i ka hale nui*
>
> loc. prep./ art. / house/ big
>
> 'to the big house'

Prepositions

i. Nominative: *'o or zero*

This preposition marks the subject of a sentence. It is often overtly marked
by *'o* before the third person singular pronoun. Elsewhere, it may be omitted (zero marking). According to Greg Lee Carter (personal communication), there is also a homophonous preposition *'o* which is used as a topic
marker.

Ua 'ike 'o ia.

perf./ see/ nom. prep./ 3d pers. sing. pron.

'He saw.'

ii. Objective: *i, iā*

This preposition usually marks a direct or indirect object. However, it also has other functions such as agentive, source, instrumental, and causal ('because'), which are also marked by other prepositions. The variant *iā* occurs before all pronouns, names of people and places, and locative nouns, as well as before the interrogative *wai*. Elsewhere, it is realized as *i*.

Hā'awi ke kanaka i ka makana iā Pua

give/ art./ man/ obj. prep./ art./ present, gift/ obj. prep./ Pua
   (fem. proper name)

'The man gives the present to Pua.'

In this sentence the direct object ('present') precedes the indirect object ('Pua'). That is the normal order. Also note that since Pua is a name of a person the allomorph marking the object is *iā*.

iii. Vocative: *ē*

This preposition is used to mark the person (or any entity) being called or addressed.

Ē Pua, hele mai.

voc. prep./ Pua (fem. proper name)/ come, go/ movement toward the speaker

'Pua, come here!'

iv. Agentive: *e*

This preposition marks the agent or actor in passive sentences.

Ua hō'ala 'ia ka lumi e ka pīkake.

perf./ perfume/ pass./ art./ room/ agentive prep./ art./ pikake
   (Hawaiian jasmine)

'The room was perfumed by the pikake (flower).'

v. Comitative/Instrumental: *me*

This preposition marks accompaniment and can be translated by English 'with'. As is the case with English 'with', this preposition not only marks accompaniment but the instrument as well.

Noho 'o Pua me kāna keiki.

stay, live/ nom. prep./ Pua (fem. proper name)/ comit. prep./
   her ('acquired')/ child

'Pua stayed with her child.'

Kākau ʻoe me kēia penikala.

write/ you sing./ comit.-instr. prep./ this/ pencil

'Write with this pencil.'

vi. Possessive: o/a

This preposition is used to mark possession and can be translated by the English preposition 'of'. The alternation of *o* and *a* is not morphophonemic but is semantically conditioned. Basically the distinction signals the nature of the relationship between the possessor and what is possessed. Thus, *a* indicates that possessor caused or had some active control over the ownership, whereas *o* indicates that the possessor had no control over the ownership. Some of the terms used to describe this contrast are "acquired" versus "inherited," "alienable possession" versus "inalienable possession," "active" versus "passive." Note that this contrast is reflected by all possessive words (and is signaled by the vowels *a* and *o* which form parts of the possessives).

However, there are other considerations that override the basic rule as given above. One overriding rule is that personal location uses *o*. Thus, for example, clothing one is wearing, a horse one is riding, involve *o*-marked possession regardless of who ultimately owns the clothing and the horse.

ke kiʻi a Pua

art./ picture/ of ('acquired')/ Pua (fem. proper name)

'the picture (taken or painted) by Pua'

ke kiʻi o Pua

art./ picture/ of ('inherited')/ Pua (fem. proper name)

'the picture of Pua (e.g., a photograph of her)'

ke aliʻi a Kalani

art./ chief/ of ('acquired')/ Kalani (masc. proper name)

'the chief (appointed by) Kalani'

ke aliʻi o ka ʻāina

art./ chief/ of ('inherited')/ art./ land

'the (hereditary) chief'

vii. Subordinate Benefactive/Agentive Focus: na

This preposition marks the entity for the benefit of which an action is performed or to whom an entity belongs. It also marks the agent of a verb that has a passive force but is not marked overtly for passive voice. In other words, *na* not only marks the agent but passivizes the verb at the same time. According to Greg Lee Carter (personal communication), the last usage of this preposition really marks responsibility.

Na wai ka puke?

benefactive prep./ who/ art./ book

'For whom is the book?'

The Hawaiian sentence here is actually ambiguous because it can also mean 'Who wrote the book?' (I.e., 'who is responsible [for] the book?')

viii. Dominate Benefactive/Causative/Locative: no
This preposition has benefactive function similar to *na*. In addition it marks direction of motion (locative) and cause.

No ka lani ka inoa.

benefactive prep./ art./ royal chief/ art./ name-song

'The name song (honors) the royal chief.'

Ua hele a'e nei no Maui.

perf./ go, come/ directional/ this, here (with the preceding morpheme = 'recently')/ *no* in its loc. function

'(He) has just now gone to Maui.'

No laila, maika'i 'ole.

no (in its causal function)/ there/ good/ not

'Therefore, (it is) not good.'

ix. Simulative: pē
This preposition is very rare and is used to mark similitude ('like'). It is most often found in combination with various demonstratives.

x. Locative l: i, iā
Note that this preposition is homophonous with the objective preposition given above and has the same allomorphs as the latter. (Originally the two prepositions were distinct but eventually merged in Hawaiian.) Its chief function is to mark location (in time or space) or direction of an action.

Ua noho ke kanaka i Hilo.

perf./ stay, live/ art./ man/ loc. prep./ Hilo (place name)

'The man stayed in Hilo.'

xi. Locative 2: ma
This preposition signals the location or direction (in time or space) of an action. According to Greg Lee Carter (personal communication), it functions just like the preposition discussed above, although Elbert and Pukui (1979) considered the two prepositions to have somewhat different functions. This preposition also marks instrument, manner, object, and source:

Kāhea akula ʻo Kawelo iā Kamalama ma ka paha.

call/ thither (away from the speaker)/ nom. prep./ Kawelo
(proper name)/ objective prep./ Kamalama (proper
name)/ loc. prep. (instr. function)/ art./ *paha* chant

'Kawelo called to Kamalama in (= by means of) a *paha*
chant.'

ʻAʻole au i hele mai ma ke ʻano ikaika, i hele mai au ma ka
mākaʻikaʻi.

neg./ I/ perf./ go, come/ direction towards the speaker/ loc.
prep. (manner function)/ art./ kind, nature/ forceful/ perf./
go, come/ direction towards the speaker/ I/ loc. prep. (purpose function)/ art./ sightsee

'I did not come in a forceful way, I came to sightsee.'

xii. Allative: ā
This preposition is used to indicate the distance traveled:

Lele ka manu ā luna

fly/ art./ bird/ allat. prep./ top, high

'The bird flies *way* up.'

hele ā Maui

go/ allat. prep./ Maui (name of an island)

'going *as far as* Maui'

xiii. Ablative: mai
This preposition marks the source or origin of movement.

mai Honolulu

ablat. prep./ Honolulu (place name)

'from Honolulu'

Before the names of people or before personal pronouns (except *aʻu* 'I')
this preposition may be followed by a locative preposition or by the possessive preposition *o*.

maiā Pua

ablat. prep. + loc. prep. (contracted form)/ Pua (fem. proper
name)

'from Pua'

It should be noted that the ablative preposition *mai* and the directional *mai* (movement toward the speaker) are completely homophonous. However, because they appear in different syntactic slots there is no confusion between them.

Determiners

Determiners are singular definite article *ke/ka,* plural definite article *nā,* possessives, and various demonstratives. All determiners precede the word they modify.

Articles

The definite article is *ke/ka* in the singular and *nā* in the plural. The *ke* allomorph of the singular definite article is used before words beginning in vowels *a, e,* and *o* and in *k.* It also occurs before some words beginning in a glottal stop or *p.* (In other words, the allomorphy is not predictable everywhere.) Elsewhere, *ka* is used.

> *ke aliʻi* 'the chief' vs. *ka iʻa* 'the fish'
>
> *ke ʻala* 'the fragrance' vs. *ka ʻaka* 'the laugh'

Although the Hawaiian definite article is similar in usage to the definite article in English there are some differences as well. For example, in Hawaiian the definite article is used before abstract and general terms and before names of body parts instead of possessive pronouns.

> *ka hanohano* 'glory' (in general)
>
> *Me ka lima ame ka wāwae lāua i kope hele ai.*
>
> comit.-instr. prep./ def. art./ hand/ and/ sing. def. art./ foot/ they (dual)/ perf.-inceptive aspect/ rake, scratch/ come, go (here = 'continuously')/ particle (part of the perf. aspect marking)
>
> 'They raked on with their hands and feet.' (Lit. 'with the hand and with the foot')

Possessives

We have already encountered the possessive preposition *a/o* above and the *acquired/alienable* versus the *inherited/inalienable* contrast. This contrast extends to the possessive pronouns as well.

There are several kinds of possessives: the zero-possessives, the k-possessives, and the n-possessives. The first series are plain possessives, whereas the k-possessives include the singular definite article and therefore signal that what is possessed is singular and definite. The n-possessives have more of a case marking function and have already been discussed in the sections on prepositions. (See prepositions *na* and *no*.)

Examples of zero-possessives:

'E-lua a'u keiki.

general classifier + two/ my ('acquired' possession)/ child

'I (have) two children.'

'A'ohe a'u keiki.

have not (variant pronunciation of *'a'ole*)/ my ('acquired' possession')/ child

'I don't have any children.'

It would appear that after negatives only zero-possessives are used, but this still requires investigation.

Examples of k-possessives:

ka'u keiki 'my child' ('acquired') vs. *ko'u kupuna* 'my grandparent' ('inherited')

kāna wahine 'his wife' ('acquired') vs. *kona hale* 'his house' ('inherited')

Fronted Possessives

Just as in English, in Hawaiian the possessor noun can precede the noun being possessed. In English this involves a change in the marking of possession as in the following examples:

the pencil *of* the student vs. the student'*s* pencil

Similarly in Hawaiian the possessor NP with its possessive preposition may be inserted after the singular definite article and the possessed NP:

ke keiki a Pua

sing. def. art./ child/ poss. prep./ fem. proper name

'the child of Pua' (focus on the thing possessed)

kā Pua keiki

sing. def. art. + poss. prep. (fused)/fem. proper name/ child

'Pua's child' (focus on the possessor)

Note that in the above example *ke* + *a* fuse into *kā*.

Postnominal elements are modifiers such as adjectives.

Plural Marking

As we have already seen, there is a special plural form of the definite article, *nā*, which makes the NPs plural. In addition there are several plural markers that do not signal definiteness: *mau, po'e,* and *kau*. These precede the noun directly and follow demonstratives or possessives.

kēia mau wāhine

this/ pl. particle/ women (pl. form, see below)

'these women'

The above-mentioned particles are the primary means in Hawaiian of marking plural. However, there are ten nouns, all of them referring to persons (including some kinship terms), which have special plural forms, derived by lengthening the antepenultimate vowel.

> *kahuna* 'priest' vs. *kāhuna* 'priests'
>
> *makua* 'parent' vs. *mākua* 'parents'
>
> *wahine* 'woman' vs. *wāhine* 'women'

Note that in the case of such nouns plurality may be marked redundantly as in the example given earlier for the usage of *mau,* one of the plural markers.

Demonstratives

There are three kinds of demonstrative: (1) *kē*-demonstratives, which may precede nouns as determiners or which substitute for noun phrases; (2) zero-demonstratives, the most common of which, *nei,* usually follows the noun it modifies; and (3) *pē*-demonstratives, which may be called "manner" demonstratives.

kē-demonstratives:

> *kēia* 'this' (near speaker)
>
> *kēnā* 'that' (near addressee)
>
> *kēlā* 'that' (away from both the speaker or addressee)

zero-demonstratives

> *ia* 'this, that, aforementioned' (preposed)
>
> *ua* 'just mentioned' (preposed)
>
> *nā* 'there'

In addition there are some others, but they will not be listed here.

pe-demonstratives

> *pe-nei* 'like this'
>
> *pe-nā* 'like that' (near the addressee)
>
> *pe-ia* 'like that'
>
> *pe-lā* 'like that' (far)

Pronouns

The pronominal system of Hawaiian is relatively complicated since there are dual as well as singular and plural forms as well as the distinction between inclusive (which include persons spoken to) and exclusive pronouns (which exclude persons spoken to (see Table 6.3).

The dual number suffix is derived from *lua* 'two', and the plural marker is derived from *kolu* 'three'.

In addition, as was already mentioned in connection with the so-called possessive preposition, the possessive pronouns exhibit the distinction between 'inherited' (inalienable) and 'acquired' (alienable) possession. Thus what is considered to be one's birthright, God, name, parents, siblings, land, body parts, emotions, and so on, are considered to be inalienable possessions, whereas those items that one acquires through one's own efforts—wife, children, most of one's possessions and actions—are considered alienable. (For brevity's sake the forms of all the possessive pronouns are not listed here.)

There are no gender distinctions in any of the pronominal forms. Thus, *ia* can mean 'he', 'she', or 'it'.

Table 6.3 HAWAIIAN PERSONAL PRONOUNS

PERSON	SINGULAR	DUAL	PLURAL
1st pers. incl.		*kā-ua*	*kā-kou*
1st pers. excl.	*au/wau, a'u*	*mā-ua*	*mā-kou*
2d pers.	*'oe*	*'o-lua*	*'ou-kou*
3d pers.	*ia*	*lā-ua*	*lā-kou*

Verb Phrase Structure and Verb Morphology

The *Verb Phrase* basically has the following structure: *verb marker* + *Verb* (with various derivational affixes) + (directionals and other verbal modifiers).

Negation is generally marked by *'a'ole,* which is a predicate in its own right and can have its own modifiers.

Verb Markers

Verb markers signal aspect or mood. In Hawaiian, there is only marking for aspect, not for tense. In earlier descriptions of the language one can find references to tenses as well, but according to Greg Lee Carter (personal communication), that was the result of misanalysis of certain constructions.

i. Perfective/Inceptive Aspect Marker: ua/zero

This marker signals finished or completed action or a "new situation" (inceptive). (Cf. the perfective particle *le* in the "Sketch of Mandarin Chinese" for comparison.)

In VP's acting as complements (as opposed to predicate VP's) instead of *ua* the allomorph of this marker is *i*, and depending on the type of complement, a particle *ai* must also be added at the end of the VP: *i* + VERB + *ai*

> *Ua hele ke kanaka.*
>
> perf.-inceptive/ go/ sing. def. art./ man
>
> 'The man has gone.' (perf.)

> *Ua maikaʻi au i nehinei, akā, ua maʻi i kēia lā.*
>
> perf.-inceptive/ well/ I/ loc. prep./ yesterday/ but/ perf.-inceptive/ sick/ loc. prep./ this/ day
>
> 'Yesterday I was well (perfective), but today I am sick (inceptive).'

ii. Imperfective Aspect Marker: e

This verb aspect marker usually co-occurs with an aspectual adverb (the most common being *ana*) which follows the verb:

> *iā-ia e ʻau aku ana*
>
> loc. prep. (ref. to time) + 3d pers. sing. pron./ imperef./ swim/ motion away from the speaker/ aspectual adverb
>
> 'while he was swimming away'

iii. Progressive aspect marker: ke

This marker is not to be confused with the singular definite article, which has different allomorphs depending on the first sound of the word it precedes. It is usually translated into English by the present progressive.

This marker is usually followed by a verb plus a directional *nei* which may be considered to be a part of the aspect marking:

> *Ke kali nei au.*
>
> progressive aspect/ wait/ directional/ I
>
> 'I am waiting.'

After the negative marker (actually a verb) and after a noun phrase this marker has the allomorph *e*:

> *ʻAʻole nāu ke keiki āu e pepehi mai nei.*
>
> neg./ for you/ sing. def. art./ child/ your ('acquired')/ progressive aspect/ beat/ movement towards the speaker/ directional
>
> 'The child you are beating now is not yours.'

iv. Affirmative Imperative/Intentive Mood Markers: e/Zero, ō

Ō is politer than *e*. With first and third persons these markers signal intent, purpose, necessity, and probability.

> *E hele ʻoe!*
>
> imper.-intentive/ go/ you sing.
>
> 'Go!' or 'You ought to go!'

> *Ō hoʻi ā ʻōlelo aku . . .*
>
> polite imper.-intentive/ go back/ and/ say/ motion away from the speaker
>
> 'Better go back and say . . .'

> *Malia ō hele au.*
>
> maybe/ polite imper.-inceptive/ go/ motion away from the speaker/ I
>
> 'Maybe I shall go.'

> *Hele akula ʻo Kawelo e³ ʼauʼau*
>
> go/ thither/ nom. prep./ Kawelo (proper name)/ imper.-intentive/ bathe
>
> 'Kawelo went to bathe.'

> *Makemake au e hele.*
>
> want/ I / imper.-intentive/ go
>
> 'I want to go.'

v. Negative Imperative/Intentive Mood Marker: mai

This marker is used only with the second person unlike the above marker that may be used with all three persons.

> *Mai uē ʻoe.*
>
> 'Don't cry.'

Note that Hawaiian personal pronouns are not as likely to be omitted in commands and prohibitions as in equivalent English constructions.

vi. Purposive Mood Marker: i

This marker may mark purpose in subordinate as well as in main clauses.

Hāʻawi ʻo-ia i kālā i kāna keiki e hele i ke kula i loaʻa ka naʻauao.

give, grant/ nom. prep. + 3d pers. sing./ obj. prep./ money/ obj. prep./ his ('acquired')/ child/ inf. complement marker/ go/ loc./ sing. def. art./ school/ purposive/ obtain, get/ sing. def. art./ learning, education

'He gave money to his child to go to school in order to get an education.'

vii. Infinitive Marker: ke
This marker is used only after two common verbs, *hiki* 'be possible' and *pono* 'right, should, must'.

Hiki iaʻu ke ʻai.

able/ obj. prep. (marking indirect obj.) + I (fused)/ inf./ eat

'I can eat.'

The Hawaiian construction above probably means literally 'It is possible for me to eat.'

Pono ke hele.

proper, correct/ inf. / go

'(It's) fine to go.'

viii. Imminence Marker: mai
This marker is somewhat rare. Note that it is homophonous with the negative imperative marker *mai* and that sometimes the two may be confused since they both may occur in the same syntactic slots.

Mai hāʻule ke keiki.

'The child almost fell.'

Directionals
There are four different directionals. The first two are used very much like the German affixes *her* and *hin,* which mark movement toward the speaker and away from the speaker respectively.
i. mai
This directional indicates movement toward the speaker and can therefore be often translated as meaning 'to me' or 'here'.

Hele mai!

go, come/ movement toward the speaker

'Come!'

Note that with verbs of speaking this directional indicates a reply (not necessarily to the speaker).

ii. aku

This directional signals movement away from the speaker.

> *Hele aku!*
>
> go, come/ movement away from the speaker
>
> 'Go away!'

With verbs of speaking this directional indicates that someone else is being addressed. In other words, the speaker is not simply speaking to himself.

iii. iho

This directional signals motion downward as well as reflexive action and near future. (It may be that here, too, we are actually dealing with different morphemes that happen to be homophonous, as is very often the case in Hawaiian.)

> *Hele iho!*
>
> go, come/ movement downward
>
> 'Go down!'

> *Ke nānā nei au i-aʻu iho.*
>
> progressive aspect/ look at, observe/dem. (part of progressive aspect marking)/ I/ obj. prep. + 1st pers. sing. pron. (fused form)/ *iho* (here = 'self')
>
> 'I am looking at myself (now).'

iv. aʻe

This directional signals movement upward or such notions as 'next, adjacent, nearby' in space or time.

> *Hele aʻe!*
>
> go, come/ movement upward
>
> 'Go up!'

Verb Affixes

As we have seen, in Hawaiian there are many particles and prepositions that mark various grammatical functions. Affixation, especially on nouns, is rather limited and is not much more prevalent in the case of verbs. Below are listed some of the more important verbal affixes.

Prefixes

a. Causative-Simulative ho'o-

The addition of this prefix usually causes a verb to become a deliberate transitive class verb.

> *hele* 'go' vs. *ho'ohele* 'to set in motion'
>
> *maka'u* 'to fear' vs. *ho'omaka'u* 'to frighten'

When prefixed to words that can be either nouns or verbs this prefix has a simulative function:

> *haole* 'white person' vs. *ho'ohaole* 'to act like a white person'

b. Approximative Prefix 'ō-

This prefix adds the meaning of 'somewhat':

> *ma'i* 'sick' vs. *'ōma'i* 'sickly'

c. Prefix aka-

This signifies 'carefully, slowly':

> *'ai* 'to eat' vs. *aka'ai* 'to eat slowly'

Nominalizers

The most common nominalizer is the particle *'ana* and suffixes *-Cana/-na* (where $C = h, k$ or l):

> *ka hele 'āwīwī 'ana mai*
>
> sing. def. art./ come/ quick/ nominalizer/ movement toward
> the speaker
>
> 'the quick coming'

The different consonants that appear in the various alternants of the suffixes for this marker, in the case of passive-imperative, and in the various transitivizing suffixes were originally parts of the verb stems which were in the course of time reanalyzed by the speakers as being part of the suffix. This has happened in other Polynesian languages as well.

Passive-Imperative Marker

The *passive-imperative* marker is for the most part a particle or a clitic, not a suffix, because it can be separated from its base by other words. It has a number of alternants, most differing in terms of the initial consonant. (Most of these alternants act as suffixes in that they cannot be split off from the base.) The usual function of *'ia* is to signal passive voice; the imperative function is rare in modern usage and is found mainly in some chants and set phrases in songs.

> *Ua 'āpono wale 'ia ke kānāwai.*
>
> perf.-inceptive/ approve/ unnecessarily/ pass.-imper./ sing.
>   def. art./ law
>
> 'The law was approved unnecessarily.'

Transitivizers

There are a number of suffixes that have the shape -*Ca'i* and -*Ci* that are labeled as being transitivizing suffixes, that is, deriving transitive verbs out of intransitive verbs. However, in many cases the transitivizing function is not the primary one: they sometimes act as derivational suffixes that form new verbs with new meanings that are not predictable:

> *pī-na'i* 'to fill a crack' (compare *pī* 'to sprinkle')

Reduplication

In some cases verb bases are reduplicated either fully or partially. Reduplication signifies frequentative, increased, or plural action. (In some descriptions of American Indian languages such functions are subsumed under the term "augmentative.")

> *nīnau* 'to question' versus *nina-ninau* 'to question repeatedly,
> interrogate; many persons asking questions'

Verb Classes

Elbert and Pukui (1979:46) recognize the following classes of verbs: (a) intransitive verbs (e.g., *hele* 'go'); (b) deliberate transitive verbs (e.g., *'ai* 'eat'); (c) spontaneous transitive verbs (e.g., *aloha* 'love, greet'); (d) adjectival stative verbs (e.g., *maika'i* 'be good'); and (e) *loa'a* stative verbs (e.g., *loa'a* 'obtain, get').

Intransitive verbs are those that do not take an object and include such verbs as 'come' and 'sleep'.

The difference between deliberate and spontaneous transitives is mainly in terms of which class of possessives (alienable or inalienable) may be used with them when they are nominalized. Thus, in the case of deliberate transitives the possessors must be of the *a* or "alienable" class (e.g., *kāna 'ai 'ana* 'his eating'), whereas in the case of spontaneous transitives the *o* or "inalienable" class of possessives must be used (e.g., *kona aloha* 'his love'). It thus looks as if the *a/o* distinction in the possessives also marks the degree of control that a doer has over his or her actions. However, according to Greg Lee Carter (personal communication), this formulation may reflect only a tendency rather than an invariable rule.

Adjectival stative verbs are Hawaiian equivalents of English adjectives. They refer to states rather than actions or processes. They often occur after nouns as modifiers (e.g., *keiki hau'oli* 'a happy child').

The *loa'a* class of stative verbs is a small class of verbs which, however, contains some very common verbs. The 'agents' of such verbs must be marked with the objective preposition:

Loa'a i-a'u ka hale.

have, get/ obj. prep. + I (fused) sing. def. art./ house

'I have got a house.'

Verbless Sentences

Hawaiian sentences expressing location (e.g., 'My book is there') usually do not have any verbs:

Ma 'ane'i ka hale.

loc. prep./ loc. noun ('here')/ sing. def. art./ house

'The house (is) here.'

Subordinate Clauses

There are several ways that English temporal subordinate clauses may be rendered in Hawaiian. One way is by using the preposition *i/iā* 'when, while' (actually locative preposition used in its temporal sense):

ia'u e noho ana me 'oukou

loc. prep. + I (fused)/ imperf./ stay, live/ zero-dem. (goes with the imperf.)/ comit.-instr./ you pl.

'while I was staying with you . . .'

Another way is by means of a nominalized verb phrase and a locative preposition:

i kona hele 'ana mai

loc. prep./ his ('inalienable')/ go, come/ nominalizer/ movement towards the speaker

'at his coming', 'while he was coming'

It may also be rendered by means of words meaning 'time, epoch, era', and so on, which have various modifiers:

I ko'u wā li'ili'i, nui ko mākou le'ale'a.

loc. prep./ my ('inalienable')/ age, period of time/ small, infantile/ big, large/ sing. def. art. + poss. prep. (fused 'fronted' poss.)/ we (exclusive)/ fun, amusement

'When I was small, we had a lot of fun.' ('In my child(hood) age, our fun was great.')

There is also a conjunction *ke* which means 'when' and introduces subordinate clauses that refer to the future (but only in statements, not questions):

> *Ke pōloli, 'ai.*
>
> when/ hunger, hungry/ eat
>
> 'When hungry, eat.'

Hawaiian relative clauses come after their heads (just like attributive adjectives): Head NP + subord. vb. phrase + (subjects, objects, etc. of the subord. clause)

> *Ka manawa i hele mai ai ke ali'i.*
>
> sing. def. art./ time/ perf./ come, go/ movement toward the speaker/ dir. particle (part of perf. marking in complement clauses)/ sing. def. art. / chief
>
> 'The time that the chief came.'

> *I ka manawa i hele mai ai ke kua'āina, pa'a hana au.*
>
> loc. prep./ sing. def. art./ time/ perf.-inceptive/ go, come/ movement toward the speaker/ dir. particle (part of perf. marking in complement clauses)/ sing. def. art./ person from the countryside/ firm, steadfast/ work (with the preceding word = 'busy')/ I
>
> 'At the time the rustic came I was busy.'

Greg Lee Carter (personal communication) provides the following examples of Hawaiian relative clauses:

> *ka moa i 'ai ai 'o Jack.*
>
> sing. art./ chicken/ perf. asp./ eat/ part of perf. asp. marking in rel. clauses/ nom. prep./ Jack
>
> 'The chicken which Jack ate.'

> *ka moa i 'ai iā Jack.*
>
> sing. art./ chicken/ perf. asp./ eat/ obj. prep./ Jack
>
> 'The chicken which ate Jack.'

> *ka lā i 'ai 'ia ai ka moa.*
>
> sing. art./ day/ perf. asp. marker/ eat/ pass./ part of perf. asp. marking in rel. clauses/ sing. art./ chicken
>
> 'The day on which the chicken was eaten.'

It must be pointed out that Elbert and Pukui (1979) consider *ai* to be an "anaphoric particle" which acts as a relative clause marker and not part of imperfective aspect marking as Greg Lee Carter considers it to be.

Interrogative Sentences

Interrogative sentences in Hawaiian either contain a question word or are identical with assertive sentences except for intonation. That is, yes/no questions may be distinguished from statements only by intonation.

> *'Ike 'oe iā Keawe?*
>
> know/ you sing./ obj. prep./ Keawe (proper name)
>
> 'Do you know Keawe?'

Content questions are formed with various interrogative words. The main interrogative words are *aha* 'what', *hea* 'where, which', *wai* 'who', and *-hia* a numeral interrogative.

> *He aha kēlā?*
>
> copula/ what/ that (far)
>
> 'What is that?'

> *'O wai ke kumu?*
>
> copula/ who/ sing. def. art./ teacher
>
> 'Who is the teacher?'

> *'E-hia kālā?*
>
> general numeral classifier + how many/ dollar, money
>
> 'How much money?'

D. SAMPLE TEXT

The superscripted numbers in the literal morpheme-by-morpheme translation refer to the notes which follow that section.

Hawaiian Text

This rather charming little folk tale is taken from Alberta Pualani Hopkins' *Ka lei ha'aheo: Beginning Hawaiian* (University of Hawaii Press, 1992, 190). It may well be that this tale is not only Hawaiian but has wider Polynesian roots. The author recalls that he first heard this story from a

Tongan student at the University of Hawaii who represented it as a Tongan folk tale.

KA HEʻE A ME KA ʻIOLE

(1) I ka wā kahiko ua noho kekahi ʻiole me kona ʻohana ma ka mokupuni ʻo Mokoliʻi. (2) (I kēia manawa, ua kapa ʻia kēia wahi ʻo Chinaman's Hat.) (3) I kekahi lā, makemake ʻo ia e hele aku i Kāneʻohe. (4) Ua loaʻa iā ia he waʻa, a hoe aku la ʻo ia i Kualoa. (5) I kona hiki ʻana mai, ua hoʻopaʻa ʻia ka waʻa ma ke kumu niu, a hele akula ka ʻiole i Kāneʻohe. (6) Akā, ʻaʻole i hoʻopaʻa pono ʻia ka waʻa. (7) No laila, i kona hiki ʻana mai mai Kāneʻohe mai, ua lilo ka waʻa i ke kai. (8) Hū ka pilikia nui! (9) Ua noho ihola ka ʻiole a uē me ka leo nui loa. (10) Ua lohe ʻia kona uē ʻana e kekahi heʻe lokomaikaʻi. (11) Nīnau akula ka heʻe iā ia, "E ia nei, he aha kou pilikia?" (12) A pane maila ka ʻiole, "Ua nalowale koʻu waʻa; ua lilo paha i ke kai, no ka mea ʻaʻole maikaʻi paha koʻu hoʻopaʻa ʻana. (13) ʻAʻole hiki iaʻu ke hoʻi aku i Mokoliʻi no ka mea ʻaʻole hiki iaʻu ke ʻauʻau." (14) Pane maila ka heʻe naʻau palupalu, "ʻAʻole pilikia; hiki paha iaʻu ke kōkua aku iā ʻoe. (15) E piʻi aʻe ʻoe i luna o kuʻu poʻo, a e hoʻihoʻi aku au iā ʻoe i kou home." (16) I ke kau ʻana o ka ʻiole ma luna o kona poʻo, ua hoʻomaka ka heʻe e hoʻi aku i Mokoliʻi. (17) Hū ka nui o ko ka ʻiole makaʻu, akā, kāhea akula ka heʻe, "E noho mālie ʻoe! Mai makaʻu! Kamaʻāina loa au i kēia kai." (18) Ma hope iho, ua hiki akula lāua i Mokoliʻi. (19) Ua iho ihola ka ʻiole mai luna iho o ko ka heʻe poʻo, a haʻi akula ʻo ia iā ia, "Ke mahalo nui loa nei au iā ʻoe no kou lawe ʻana mai iaʻu. (20) Aia kekahi makana nāu ma luna o kou poʻo," a holo ʻāwīwī akula ka ʻiole i uka. (21) Ua hāhā aʻela ka heʻe ma luna o kona poʻo, a loaʻa ke kūkae. (22) Ua kiʻo ka ʻiole ma luna o ke poʻo no ka mea makaʻu loa ʻo ia. (23) Hū ka huhū nui o ka heʻe! (24) Mai kēlā manawa mai, inā ʻike ʻia ka leho e ka heʻe, ua lālau ʻo ia iā ia no ka mea, manaʻo ʻo ia, ʻo ka ʻiole nō ia. (25) Hana ka poʻe Pākīpika i kekahi mea i kapa ʻia "lūheʻe" me ka pōhaku a me ka leho, a loaʻa ka heʻe iā lākou me kēia mea.

Literal Morpheme-by-Morpheme Translation

KA HEʻE AME KA ʻIOLE

art./ **octopus**/ **and**/[1] art./ **rat**/

(1) *I ka wā kahiko ua noho kekahi ʻiole me kona ʻohana ma ka mokupuni ʻo Moko-liʻi.*
loc. prep./ art./ **time**/ **ancient**/ perf.-inceptive/ **live**/ **certain**/ **rat**/ **with**/ his ('inherited')/ **family**/ loc. prep./ art./ cut + surrounded (= **'island'**)/ subj. prep./lizard + little (= place name).

(2) *(I kēia manawa, ua kapa ʻia kēia wahi ʻo Chinaman's Hat.)*
loc. prep./ **this**/ **time**/ perf.-inceptive/ **call**/ pass./ **this**/ **place**/ copula/ **Chinaman's/ Hat**

(3) *I kekahi lā, makemake ʻo ia e hele aku i Kāneʻohe.*
loc. prep./ **some,** certain/ **day**/ **want**/ nom. prep./ 3d pers. sing./ subord. verb marker/ **go**/ away from the speaker/ loc. prep./ **Kāneʻohe** (place name)

(4) *Ua loaʻa iā ia he waʻa, a hoe akula ʻo la i Kualoa.*
perf.-inceptive/ **get**/ loc. prep./[2] 3d pers. sing./ copula/ canoe/ **and**/ **paddle**/ thither/ subj./ 3d pers. sing./ loc. prep./ **Kualoa** (place name)

(5) *I kona hiki ʻana mai, ua hoʻo-paʻa ʻia ka waʻa ma ke kumu niu, a hele akula ka ʻiole i Kāneʻohe.*
loc. prep./ **his** (ʻinalienableʼ)/ **arrive**/ nominalizing particle/ movement towards the speaker/ perf.-inceptive/ caus. + fast, secure (= **ʻfastenʼ**)/ pass./ art./ **canoe**/ loc. prep./ art./ **bottom**/ **coconut** (tree)/ **and**/ **go**/ thither/ art./ **rat**/ loc. prep./ **Kāneʻohe** (place name)

(6) *Akā, ʻaʻole i hoʻo-paʻa pono ʻia ka waʻa.*
however, but/, neg./ perf. asp. marker/ caus. + fast, secure (= **ʻfastenʼ**)/ **well,** properly/ pass./ art./ **canoe.**

(7) *No laila, i kona hiki ʻana mai mai Kāneʻohe mai, ua lilo ka waʻa i ke kai.*
for/ there (with preceding = **therefore**)/ loc. prep./ **his** (ʻinalienableʼ)/ **arrive**/ nominalizing particle/ movement towards the speaker/ **from**/ **Kāneʻohe** (place name)/ movement towards the speaker/ perf.-inceptive/ **be lost**/ art./ **canoe**/ **due to**/ art./ **ocean**

(8) *Hū ka pilikia nui!*
exclamation/ art./ **trouble,** distress/ **big**

(9) *Ua noho ihola ka ʻiole a uē me ka leo nui loa.*
perf.-inceptive/ **sit**/ **downward**/ art./ **rat**/ **and**/ weep, **lament**/ comit.-instr. prep./ art./ **voice,** sound/ big (= **ʻloudʼ**)/ **very**

(10) *Ua lohe ʻia kona uē ʻana e kekahi heʻe loko-maikaʻi.*
perf.-inceptive/ **hear**/ pass./ **his** (ʻinalienableʼ)/ weep, **lament**/ nominalizing particle/ agent of a pass. vb./ **some,** certain/ **octopus**/ character, disposition + good (= **ʻkindʼ**)

(11) *Nīnau akula ka heʻe iā ia, "E ia nei, he aha kou pilikia?"*
ask, question/ thither/ art./ **octopus**/ obj. prep./ 3d pers. sing./, voc. prep./ 3d pers. sing./ here/[3] **be,** exist/ **what**/ **your** (ʻinalienableʼ)/ **trouble,** distress

(12) *A pane maila ka ʻiole, "Ua nalowale koʻu waʻa; ua lilo paha i ke kai, no ka mea ʻaʻole maikaʻi paha koʻu hoʻopaʻa ʻana.*
and/ **answer**/ hither (= **ʻbackʼ**)/ art./ **rat**/, perf.-inceptive/ be lost, **disappear**/ **my** (ʻinalienableʼ)/[4] **canoe**/ perf.-inceptive/ **be lost,** taken away/ maybe, **perhaps**/ loc. prep./ art./ **ocean**/ since/ art./ thing (with previous two morphemes = **ʻbecauseʼ**)/ neg./ **good,** proper/ **perhaps**/ **my**/ caus. + fast, secure (= **ʻfastenʼ**)/ nominalizing particle.

(13) *ʻAʻole hiki iaʻu ke hoʻi aku i Mokoliʻi no ka mea ʻaʻole hiki iaʻu ke ʻauʻau."*
neg./ **be able**/ obj. prep. + **I** (fused form)/ inf. marker/ **leave,** go or come back/ away from the speaker/ loc. prep./ lizard + little (place name)/ since/ art./ thing (with the two preceding morphemes = **ʻbecauseʼ**)/ neg./ **be able**/ obj. prep. + **I** (fused form)/ inf./ **swim,** travel by sea

(14) *Pane maila ka heʻe naʻau palupalu, "ʻAʻole pilikia; hiki paha iaʻu ke kōkua aku iā ʻoe.*
answer, reply/ direction towards the speaker (= **ʻbackʼ**)/ art./ **octopus**/ mind, **heart**/ weak, **soft,** tender/ neg./ **trouble,** distress/; **be able**/ **maybe,** perhaps/

obj. prep. + **I** (fused form)/ inf./ **help**/ movement away from the speaker/ obj. prep./ **you** sing.

(15) *E pi'i a'e 'oe i luna o ku'u po'o, a e ho'iho'i aku au iā 'oe i kou home.* imperat.-exhortative particle/ **climb,** mount/ **upward**/ **you** sing./ loc. prep./ **top**/ **of** (inalienable)/ **my** (neutral possession)/[5] **head**/, **and**/ imperat.-exhortative/ **return,** send back/ thither/ **I**/ obj. prep./ you sing./ loc. prep./ **your** sing. ('inherited')/ **home**

(16) *I ke kau 'ana o ka 'iole ma luna o kona po'o, ua ho'o-maka ka he'e e ho'i aku i Moko + li'i.* loc. prep./ art./ **perch,** board/ nominalizing particle/ **of** ('inalienable')/ art./ **rat**/ loc. prep./ **top**/ **of** ('inalienable')/ **his** ('inalienable')/ **head**/, perf.-inceptive/ caus. + **start,** appear/ art./ **octopus**/ subord. vb. marker/ **return**/ movement away from the speaker/ loc. prep./ lizard + little (= place name).

(17) *Hū ka nui o ko ka 'iole maka'u, akā, kāhea akula ka he'e, "E noho mālie 'oe! Mai maka'u! Kama-'āina loa au i kēia kai."* exclamation/ art./ **big,** great/ poss. prep. (inalienable)/ art. + inalienable poss. prep. (fused)/[6] art./ **rat**/ **fear**/, but, **however**/ call, **cry out**/ thither/ art./ **octopus**/, imperat.-exhortative/ **sit,** keep/ **quiet,** calm/ **you** sing./! neg. command (prohibition)/ fear, **be afraid**/! child + land (= 'native born, old-hand, **experienced**')/ **much,** very/ I/ loc. prep./ **this**/ **ocean.**

(18) *Ma hope iho, ua hiki akula lāua i Moko-li'i.* loc. prep./ after, behind/ down, below (with previous word = **'afterwards'**)/, perf.-inceptive/ reach, **arrive**/ thither/ **they** (dual)/ loc. prep./ lizard + small (place name)

(19) *Ua iho ihola ka 'iole mai luna iho o ko ka he'e po'o, a ha'i akula 'o ia iā ia, "Ke mahalo nui loa nei au iā 'oe no kou lawe 'ana mai ia'u.* perf.-inceptive/ down, **descend**/ **downward**/ art./ **rat**/ **from**/ **top**/ **down**/ **of** ('inalienable')/ art. + inalienable poss. prep. (fused)/[6] art./ **octopus**/ **head**/ **and**/ **say,** tell/ thither/ nom. prep./ 3d pers. sing./ obj. prep./ 3d pers. sing./, progressive aspect/ **thanks**/ **big,** large/ **very**/ here (part of prog. asp. marking)/ I/ obj. prep./ **you** sing./ **for**/ **your** sing./ carry, **bring**/ nominalizing particle/ movement towards the speaker/ obj. prep. + 1st pers. sing. (fused form).

(20) *Aia kekahi makana nāu ma luna o kou po'o," a holo 'āwīwī akula ka 'iole i uka.* exist (= **'there is'**)/ **some,** certain/ **present,** gift/ fusion of benefactive prep. + you sing. (= **'for you'**)/ loc. prep./ **top**/ **of** ('inalienable')/ **your** sing. ('inalienable')/ **head**/, **and**/ **run**/ **quickly,** fast/ thither/ article/ **rat**/ loc. prep./ **inland,** upland, shore.

(21) *Ua hāhā a'ela ka he'e ma luna o kona po'o, a loa'a ke kūkae.* perf.-inceptive/ **grope,** feel/ **upward,** sideways, nearby/ art./ **octopus**/ loc. prep./ **top**/ poss. prep. ('inalienable')/ **his** ('inalienable')/ **head**/ **and**/ get, obtain, **find**/ art./ **excrement.**

(22) *Ua ki'o ka 'iole ma luna o ke po'o no ka mea maka'u loa 'o ia.* perf.-inceptive/ **excrete**/ art./ **rat**/ loc. prep./ **top**/ **of** ('inalienable')/ art./ **head**/ since/ art./ thing (with previous two words = **'because'**)/ **fear**/ **big,** great/ nom. prep./ 3d pers. sing.

(23) *Hū ka huhū nui o ka heʻe.*
exclamation/ art./ **anger**/ **great,** big/ **of** ('inalienable')/ art./ **octopus**

(24) *Mai kēlā manawa mai, inā ʻike ʻia ka leho e ka heʻe, ua lālau ʻo ia iā ia no ka mea, manaʻo ʻo ia, ʻo ka ʻiole nō ia.*
from/ **that**/ **time**/ movement towards the speaker/, **if**/ **see,** recognize/ pass./ art./ **cowry shell**/ agent of the passive verb/ art./ **octopus**/ perf.-inceptive/ seize, **grab**/ nom. prep./ 3d pers. sing./ obj. prep./ 3d pers. sing./ since/ art./ thing (with the two preceding words = **'because'**)/ **think,** suppose/ nom. prep./ 3d pers. sing./ copula/ art./ **rat**/ intensifier/ 3d pers. sing.

(25) *Hana ka poʻe Pākīpika i kekahi mea i kapa ʻia "lūheʻe" me ka pōhaku a me ka leho, a loaʻa ka heʻe iā lākou me kēia mea.*
make, use, work/ art./ **people**/ **Pacific**/ obj. prep./ some, **certain**/ **thing**/ perf. asp. marker/ **call,** name, term/ pass./ **'lūheʻe'** / comit.-instr. prep./ art./ stone, **rock**/ **and**/ comit.-instr. prep./ **cowry shell**/, **and**/ **catch,** get/ art./ **octopus**/ loc. prep.[2]/ 3d pers. pl./ comit.-instr. prep./ **this**/ **thing**

NOTES

1. According to Greg Lee Carter (personal communication), the Hawaiian coordinate conjunction has two allomorphs (*a* and *ame*) whose distribution is determined by the syntactic characteristics of the word that immediately follows this conjunction. Thus, it probably is not quite proper to break up *ame* into its etymological component parts ('and' + comit.-instr. prep.) since it acts syntactically as a single unit.

2. With *loaʻa* and other verbs belonging to this class the subject (more properly, according to Greg Lee Carter, the 'cause of the state'), is marked by the loc. prep. (which in this case looks exactly like the obj. prep.).

3. *E ia nei* (lit. 'oh he/she here') is used as an affectionate way of addressing someone (esp. one's spouse). Here one could perhaps translate it as 'my dear fellow' or some such expression.

4. Canoes, like other conveyances in which one is riding, are regarded as "inalienable" regardless of their actual ownership.

5. There are a few forms like *kuʻu* that are neutral in regard to the 'alienable/inalienable' or 'acquired/inherited' possession contrast.

6. Cf. the "fronted possessive construction" in the sketch.

Idiomatic Translation

The Octopus and the Rat

In ancient times there lived a rat with his family on Mokoliʻi island. (Today this place is called Chinaman's Hat.) One day, he wanted to go to Kāneʻohe. He got a canoe and paddled over to Kualoa. On his arrival he fastened the canoe to the coconut tree and went off to Kāneʻohe. However, the canoe was not fastened very well and therefore by the time the rat returned from Kāneʻohe the canoe was gone, lost in the ocean. Whew, what a big mess!

The rat sat down and wept very loudly. His crying was heard by a kind octopus who asked him: "Hello there! What is your trouble?" The rat replied back saying, "My canoe has disappeared; it may be lost in the ocean because I maybe did not fasten it well. Now it is not possible for me to go back to Mokoliʻi because I can't swim."

The kind-hearted octopus then replied, "That's no problem. Maybe I can help you out. Climb up on top of my head, and let me take you back to your home."

When the rat mounted on top of his head, the octopus set out to return to Mokoliʻi. Oh, how the rat was afraid! However, the octopus called out saying, "Stay calm! Don't be afraid! I am quite at home here in the ocean."

Afterwards they reached Mokoliʻi. The rat jumped down from the top of the octopus' head and then said to the latter, "Thank you very much for bringing me back. There is a present for you on top of your head." Then he ran off inland very quickly.

The octopus groped on top of his head and found excrement. The rat had defecated on top of the octopus' head because he was greatly frightened (during the journey). The octopus then became exceedingly angry. From that time on, if an octopus sees a cowry shell he grabs at it because he thinks that the latter must be the rat. The people of the Pacific make a device called "lūheʻe" with a stone and a cowry shell and they catch octopuses with it.

Sketch of Dyirbal

A. Genetic Relationship and General Background[4]

Dyirbal is spoken in Northeastern Queensland, Australia, by about 40 to 50 speakers in all. Dixon (1972) describes three different dialects: Dyirbal, Giramay, and Mamu. (Dixon now writes the dialect name as Jirrbal.) In this sketch, for the sake of brevity and simplicity, only Dyirbal "proper" will be described.

Dyirbal belongs to the Pama-Nyungan branch of the Australian family of languages. In many respects it is a typical Australian language although it differs from many other Australian languages in some respects, especially syntactic ergativity, which will be discussed in the section on syntax. It is predominantly agglutinative in type and is entirely suffixing. One of its claims to fame is that, according to Dixon (1972), it has "extraordinarily free word order" and is thus of great interest to those linguists who are interested in word order typology since most languages seem to have what may be called "basic" or "unmarked" word order, deviations from which tend to signal at least slight shifts in focus or emphasis.

Another interesting feature of Dyirbal (fairly common among Australian languages) is that it is a *split ergative language* since the case marking on its pronouns is of nominative/accusative type (as in English), whereas the case marking on its nouns is of the absolutive/ergative type. For details, see the discussion of case marking in the section on the morphology of Dyirbal.

Mother-in-Law Language

Australian languages are known for having linguistic taboos which are more complicated than those in other societies. For example, in English one avoids using certain lexical items referring to sex, or sex organs, elimination of bodily wastes, and to a certain extent topics such as death. Instead of using the tabooed words (which are considered to be vulgar, too blunt, or shocking) we use euphemisms, lexical items, or circumlocutions which refer to the same things as the tabooed lexical items but which are not considered to be coarse and vulgar.

In Australian aboriginal languages language taboos are more complicated than that. In Dyirbal, every speaker of the language, until around 1930 when the taboo system broke down, actually had to command two separate languages: a "mother-in-law language," which was used in the presence of certain "taboo" relatives, and an everyday language, which was used in all other situations.

According to Dixon (1972:32), the tabooed relatives were (1) a parent-in-law of the opposite sex or a child-in-law of the opposite sex, and (2) a cross-cousin of the opposite sex (i.e., father's sister's or mother's brother's child).

A person had to use the mother-in-law language when the taboo relative was within earshot and the taboo relative had to do the same. (People were not supposed to approach closely or look directly at a taboo relative, and under no circumstances were they allowed to speak directly to this relative.)

Although the phonology and most of the grammar of the mother-in-law language were the same as that of the everyday language, the two languages had entirely different vocabularies, such that not a single lexical item was common to both the mother-in-law language and the everyday language of the tribe. However, the mother-in-law language had only a quarter or less as many lexical items as the everyday language, but it was possible to express everything in it that everyday language could express. This was possible because a single mother-in-law language word corresponded to many different words in the everyday language. Thus, for example, a single mother-in-law language verb (with the general sense of 'rub') was used instead of four different verbs in the ordinary language: 'wipe or rub', 'massage (by a doctor)', 'paint or draw with a finger', and 'paint with the flat of the hand'.

In this sketch only the everyday Dyirbal variant is described.

B. PHONETICS, PHONOLOGY AND ORTHOGRAPHY

Consonants and Semivowels

Alveopalatal consonants are laminoalveopalatal (articulator = tongue blade), whereas alveolar sounds are apical (articulator = tongue tip). The alveolar nonlateral liquid (/r/) is an alveolar tap between vowels and word-finally, but is an alveolar trill before consonants.

Table 6.4   CONSONANT PHONEMES OF DYIRBAL

	BILABIAL	ALVEOLAR	ALVEO-PALATAL	RETRO-FLEX	VELAR
Stops	b	d	ɖ		g
Nasals	m	n	ɲ		ŋ
Laterals		l			
Nonlateral liquids		r		ɽ	
Semivowels			y		w

Vowels

Because Dyirbal has only three vowel phonemes there is room for wide-ranging allophonic variation. For example, /a/ is realized as [ɛ] after laminoalveolars and as [ɔ] after velars.

Stress is generally placed on the first syllable of a word and all subsequent odd-numbered syllables except the last. There are several complications with stress, but they are not dealt with here.

Table 6.5   VOWEL PHONEMES OF DYIRBAL

i		u
	a	

C. MORPHOLOGY

Nouns

Dyirbal has four noun classes which are not formally marked on the nouns themselves. Instead, noun classes manifest themselves in the so-called *noun markers* (actually a kind of demonstrative) which normally accompany each noun except in general genitive, locative, allative, and ablative forms. The noun markers are affixed with the class marker agreeing with the class of the noun and at the same time indicate the location of the referent of that particular occurrence of the noun. There are three such noun markers:

> *bala-* indicates that the referent of the noun is visible and located at some distance from the speaker;
>
> *yala-* indicates that the referent is visible and located relatively close to the speaker; and
>
> *ŋala-* indicates that the referent is not visible to the speaker.

At first glance, the membership of Dyirbal nouns in the four classes appears arbitrary and haphazard:

> *Class I:* men, kangaroos, possums, mats, most snakes, most fishes, some birds, most insects, moon, storms, rainbow, boomerangs, some spears, and so forth
>
> *Class II:* women, bandicoots (a kind of marsupial), dog, platypus, echidna, some snakes, some fishes, most birds, firefly, scorpion, crickets, hairy mary grub, anything connected with fire or water, sun and stars, shields, some spears, some trees, and so forth
>
> *Class III:* all trees with edible fruit
>
> *Class IV:* parts of the body, meat, bees and honey, wind, yamsticks, some spears, most trees, grass, mud, stones, noises and language, and so forth

However, Dixon (1972:306–11) shows that the membership in the four classes has semantic basis. He lists the following concepts that are associated with each class:

> *Class I:* animateness; (human) masculinity
>
> *Class II:* (human) femininity; water; fire; fighting
>
> *Class III:* edible vegetables and fruit
>
> *Class IV:* residue class dealing with everything else

The major complication is that a noun that would normally be classified as belonging to a particular noun class by virtue of its general semantic features may actually be assigned to another noun class because of a myth or belief that associates that particular noun with a particular characteristic that is the mark of another noun class. In addition, if there is a subset of nouns which has some important characteristic that the rest of the set do not have, then the subset may be assigned to another noun class in order to mark this important characteristic. The important property that most often triggers such class reassignment is "harmfulness."

Case Inflections

Nouns and adjectives have the same case inflections. There are nine cases of which eight are marked overtly by suffixes:

1. Absolutive (Dixon's "Nominative")

This is the case used to indicate an intransitive subject or a transitive object. It has no overt marking; the absolutive form is simply the noun or adjective stem. Since the nominative case in the pronouns (which follow the nominative-accusative pattern instead) is also the unmarked case, it is perhaps reasonable to call both cases by the single name of "nominative" as Dixon does in his description of Dyirbal.

2. Ergative

This case is used to mark a transitive subject. It has the following allomorphs:

-ŋgu after a disyllabic stem ending in a vowel

-gu after a trisyllabic or longer stem ending in a vowel

a homorganic stop plus -u after a stem ending in a nasal or y

-ṭu after stems ending in any of the liquids (-l, -r, or -ṛ), plus deletion of the stem-final liquid

3. Instrumental

The instrumental case is formally completely identical with the ergative case. It signals the instrument by means of which an action is performed.

4. Dative

The dative case is marked by the invariable suffix -gu and is used to indicate direction, as allative, but with an important difference. For example, in the sentence "Man took woman to beans," the goal ('beans') may be marked by either allative case or dative case. Whereas allative case simply indicates motion toward something, dative case marking indicates that the goal ('beans') will be implicated in some imminent action involving 'woman' (as actor). Dixon (1972:65) calls such dative NPs "implicated phrases." Thus, the dative marking implies that in the above example sentence the man took the woman to the beans so that she could eat them or cook them, or for some other purpose.

5. Locative

This case marker has the same allomorphs as the ergative case suffix except that it has -a as the final vowel instead of -u. This case indicates the place where something happens or something is located ('at').

6. Allative

In the case of nouns and adjectives this case is identical in form with the dative case suffix. However, the two cases have contrasting forms in the noun markers and verb markers, and there are also syntactic reasons for distinguishing between this case and the dative case. This case marks the direction of the motion ('to').

7. Ablative

The suffix for this case is -ŋunu. It marks the source or origin ('from').

8. Simple Genitive

This case has two allomorphs:

-u after stems ending in a nasal

-ŋu after all other stems

9. General Genitive

This case is marked by the invariable suffix -mi. The difference between the simple genitive (see above) and the general genitive is that the former signals present possession, whereas the latter signals past or former possession. General genitive is used to describe something that may be abandoned by its owner, something lost by its owner, or something given by its owner, or it is used to describe something that was owned by someone else who is now dead.

Number

Plurality in Dyirbal is marked by full reduplication of the nominal root except in the case of seven nominals which have idiosyncratic plural forms. "Plural" in Dyirbal means 'more than two' since Dyirbal also has a dual number. Both adjectives and nouns may be reduplicated to show plurality. Note that unreduplicated forms (i.e., unmarked forms) may refer to any number of objects and are thus ambiguous as to number, whereas reduplicated forms specifically refer to more than two objects:

> *bala-n ḍugumbil ba-ŋgun ɲalŋga-ɲalŋga-gu bura-n*

> there (noun marker) + Class II, absolutive/ woman (absolutive)/there (noun marker) + Class II, ergative/ girl + reduplication (plural) + ergative/ see + pres.-past

'Girls saw woman/women.'

> *midi* 'small' vs. *midimidi* 'lots of little ones'

Certain stem-forming nominal suffixes also may be reduplicated sometimes with the same force as reduplication of the nominal root, that is, to indicate plurality, and sometimes with the meaning of 'absolutely, excessively'. However, both the suffix and the root may not be reduplicated in the same word. Some examples are:

> *bayi yaṛa-gabun-gabun*

> there (Class I noun marker, absolutive)/ man + another + reduplication 'lots of other men' or 'lots of strangers'

> *bana-ŋaŋgay*

> fresh water + privative suffix

'without water'

> *bana-ŋaŋgay-ŋaŋgay*

> fresh water + private suffix (repeated)

'with absolutely no water at all'

The dual number suffix is -ḍaran. It may be added to nouns or to the demonstrative noun markers that modify them. (But not to both at the same time. However, it may be added both to nouns and their modifying adjectives.) There is also a special dual suffix for some kinship terms.

Note that both of the following sentences mean the same thing even though different things are marked for dual:

bayi-ɖaran baŋguy balay ɲina-ɲu.

there (Class I demonstrative noun marker absolute) + dual/ green frog (Class I, absolutive)/ loc. vb. marker (= 'there')/ sit + pres.-past

'Two frogs are sitting there.'

bayi baŋguy-ɖaran balay ɲina-ɲu.

there (Class I demonstrative noun marker absolute)/ green frog + dual/ loc. vb. marker (= 'there')/ sit + pres.-past

'Two frogs are sitting there.'

Pronouns

Dyirbal does not have pronoun forms for the third person. Pronouns do not occur with the following case forms: general genitive, locative, allative, and ablative.

Table 6.6   **DYIRBAL PERSONAL PRONOUNS**

NOMINATIVE	ACCUSATIVE	DATIVE	SIMPLE GENITIVE	REFERENCE
ŋaɖa	ŋayguna	ŋaygungu	ŋaygu	1st pers. sing.
ŋaliɖi	ŋaliɖina	ŋaliɖingu	ŋaliɖinu	1st pers. dual
ŋanaɖi	ŋanaɖina	ŋanaɖingu	ŋalaɖinu	1st pers. pl.
ŋinda	ŋinuna	ŋinungu	ŋinu	2d pers. sing.
ɲubalaɖi	ɲubalaɖina	ɲubalaɖingu	ɲubalaɖinu	2d pers. dual
ɲuraɖi	ɲuraɖina	ɲuraɖingu	ɲuraɖinu	2d pers. pl.

Unlike nouns, Dyirbal pronouns follow the nominative-accusative pattern of inflection (i.e, subjects of both transitive and intransitive verbs have the same case, nominative, whereas the direct object of a transitive verb takes the accusative case). However, according to Dixon, there is syntactic evidence that both nouns and pronouns of Dyirbal follow an underlying absolutive-ergative pattern. (For more details, see the section on syntax.)

Adjectives

Dyirbal nouns and adjectives show identical case inflections. Adjectives must agree in case with the nouns they modify.

Verbs

There are two verb conjugations in Dyirbal. In one of the conjugations the verb stem ends in *-l*, and in the other the verb stems end in *-y*. (The two endings are sometimes deleted before certain suffixes.) Originally, all transitive roots were probably in the *-l* conjugation, and all intransitive ones in the *-y* conjugation. Thus, at the time this was true, the two endings could have been segmented as transitivity/intransitivity markers. In present-day Dyirbal, however, it is best to consider these endings as part of the verb stem.

Dyirbal verbs must have one of the following final inflectional endings.

1. Tense

Present/past (or nonfuture) which is marked by suffix *-n* after the verb stems ending in *-l* (with the deletion of *-l*), and by *-ɲu* after verb stems ending in *-y* (with the deletion of *-y*).

Future tense which is marked by *-ɲ* in both verb conjugations (with the deletion of the stem final *-l* and *-y*).

2. Imperative

Positive imperative is marked simply by the deletion of the stem-final consonant, whereas negative imperative (prohibition) is marked by *-m* which replaces the stem-final consonant and the addition of particle *galga* which is placed before the verb:

> ŋinda galga wurba-m.
>
> you (nom.)/ prohibitive particle/ speak + neg. imper. suffix
>
> 'Don't you speak!'

3. -ŋura

This suffix indicates that the event marked by the verb to which this suffix is attached follows immediately after the event of the preceding simple sentence. (Verbs must delete the stem final before this ending.)

> bala yugu baŋul yaɽa-ŋu mada-n bayi yaɽa wayɲɟi-ŋura.
>
> there (Class IV, absolutive)/ stick (Class IV, absolutive)/ there (Class I, ergative)/ man (Class I) + ergative/ throw + pres.-past/ there (Class I, absolutive)/ man (Class I, absolutive)/ motion uphill + immediate suffix
>
> 'Man threw the stick and then he (immediately) went uphill.'

4. Purposive

This affix is *-gu* after *-y* stems and *-i* after an *-l* stem. (For the meaning of this verbal suffix see the section on syntax.)

5. Apprehensive

This is usually *-bila* and has a force of warning of an unpleasant result. Thus it may be translated as 'lest'. (Several examples of this suffix appear in the sample text given at the end of this sketch.)

6. Relativizer

This is marked by *-ŋu* and must be followed by a case inflection since presumably it is a kind of a nominalizing suffix. (Examples are given in the description of relative clauses in the syntax section.)

7. Participial Ending

The commonest participial ending is -*muŋa*. Participles are inflected just like nominals and function syntactically just like them.

Thus, from the intransitive root ḍ*anay* 'stand' can be derived ḍ*anaymuŋa* '[someone who] habitually stands (a lot)'. Such a form then can function as an adjective:

> ŋaḍ*a balan* ḍ*ugumbil* ḍ*anay-muŋa buɽa-n*
>
> I (nom.)/ there (Class II, absolutive)/ woman (Class II, absolutive)/ stand + participial suffix/ see + pres.-past
>
> 'I saw the woman who is always standing around.'

Negation

The general negative particle is *gulu,* whereas the negative imperative particle is *galga* (which co-occurs with the negative imperative suffix -*m* on the verb). The negatives occur only with verb forms.

Verb Markers

There are eight verb markers or locative complements of the verb which parallel the noun markers:

> *Allative of place: balu* 'to there (towards a place)'; *yalu* 'to here (toward a place)'
>
> *Allative of direction: bali* 'to there (in a direction)'; *yali* 'to here (in a direction)'
>
> *Ablative: baŋum* 'from there'; *yaŋum* 'from here'
>
> *Locative: balay* '(at) there'; *yalay* '(at) here'

There is also a set of interrogative forms corresponding to the above verb markers:

> *Allative of place: wuɲḍaru* 'to which place?'
>
> *Allative of direction: wuɲḍari* 'in which direction?'
>
> *Ablative: wuɲḍaŋum* 'where from?'
>
> *Locative: wuɲḍay* 'where (at)?'

Verbs may be accompanied by a noun in allative, ablative, or locative case or by a verb marker or both (in which case the verb marker and the locative marker have to agree in case).

D. SYNTAX

Word Order

Although, as was already pointed out, word order is quite free in Dyirbal, there are some rules involving word order as well as favored orders. For example, certain particles (such as the negative) must always precede the verb they negate.

Some of the preferred orders (i.e., nonobligatory but preferred orders) include the following:

a. Noun markers and possessive phrases precede the nouns they qualify.
b. Adjectives and relative clauses, on the other hand, follow the nouns they qualify.
c. Absolutive (Dixons' "Nominative") NPs precede ergative and dative NPs, but ergative NPs precede the verb, whereas dative NPs follow the verb.
d. Time qualifiers precede all other words.
e. Verb markers and locational nominals usually follow the verb.

Case Marking and Syntactic Ergativity

As has already been stated in the section on morphology, case relations in Dyirbal are signaled by case suffixes on nouns, pronouns, and adjectives. It has also been pointed out that Dyirbal may be called a "split-ergative" language since its nouns exhibit the absolutive-ergative pattern of case marking, whereas its pronouns exhibit the nominative-accusative pattern.

However, in spite of the nominative-accusative case marking in Dyirbal pronouns, there is evidence that Dyirbal pronouns, like Dyirbal nouns, follow an underlying absolutive-ergative pattern. In other words, although at the superficial, morphological level Dyirbal can be considered to be a split ergative language, syntactically it behaves like a "pure" absolutive-ergative language.

To understand what is involved one must recall that in English, a nominative-accusative type of language, the subject NP of an intransitive verb and the agent NP of a transitive verb receive the same case marking and behave syntactically in a similar manner. When a sentence contains two verb phrases, one containing a transitive verb and one containing an intransitive verb, the subject NPs of both verbs receive the same case marking:

> 'I (agent) hit the woman and I (subject of an intransitive verb) came here.'

Note that if the two NPs governing the verbs are coreferential, the second one may be omitted:

> 'I hit the woman and came here.'

In Dyirbal the situation is very different from that found in English. In the Dyirbal equivalent of the English sentence 'I hit the woman and I came here,' the second NP cannot be deleted even though it is coreferential with the first NP. If the second NP is deleted, the sentence changes its meaning to 'I hit the woman, and [she] came here.' In other words, the deleted subject NP of the intransitive verb 'come' is understood to be coreferential with the patient (direct object) NP of the transitive verb in the preceding verb phrase, that is, 'woman.'

Now one may think that what is involved in Dyirbal is that Dyirbal does not allow coreferential NP deletion unless the two NPs involved have the same case marking morphologically. Thus, in the Dyirbal equivalent of the English sentence 'The man hit the woman, and the man came here,' the second NP ('the man') would be marked as being in the absolutive case (which marks the subject of an intransitive verb), and the first NP ('the man') would be marked as being in the ergative case (agent of a transitive verb), and therefore the second NP, having different case marking from its coreferent, could not be deleted. However, this turns out to be incorrect, since in sentences involving pronoun NPs (which morphologically exhibit the nominative-accusative pattern) the coreferential NP deletion rule ignores morphological case marking and follows the same absolutive-ergative pattern as with NPs which consist of nouns:

(a) ŋaḍa ŋinuna balgan.

   I (nom.) you (acc.) hit

   'I hit you.'

(b) ŋaḍa baniɲu

   I (nom.) came-here

   'I came here.'

(c) ŋinda baniɲu

   you (nom.) came-here

   'You came here.'

(d) ŋaḍa ŋinuna balgan, ŋinda baniɲu

   I (nom.) you (acc.) hit, you came-here

   'I hit you, and [you] came here.'

(e) ŋaḍa ŋinuna balgan, baniɲu

   I (nom.) you (acc.) hit, came-here

   'I hit you, and [you] came here.'

Note that in Dyirbal sentence (e) does not mean 'I hit you and [I] came here' as the equivalent English sentence would if the second NP is deleted. In spite of the morphological case difference between the two NPs (ŋinuna vs. ŋinda), Dyirbal identifies the deleted subject NP as being coreferential with the patient NP of the preceding verb phrase. That is, Dyirbal identifies a patient NP with the subject NP of an intransitive verb regardless of the differences in the morphological case marking.

For a very clear and more detailed discussion of the facts and issues concerning syntactic ergativity in Dyirbal, one should consult Comrie (1989:110–16).

Implicated Verb Complexes

Any NP which is in nominative case (absolutive case) can be identified as a "topic" NP. (In a simple sentence any Subject or Object NP may be so identified.) Furthermore, a common topic may be then recognized for more then consecutive sentences (sometimes up to twenty), forming a "topic chain."

The second or succeeding verb complexes in any topic chain may be then marked as being "implicated." Each verbal form is inflected with the purposive suffix instead of a tense suffix. This type of marking implies that the action referred to as being implicated is possible only as a necessary or natural consequence of an event referred to in the previous sentence of the discourse.

The purposive inflection has two allomorphs:

> *-i* after *-l* stems
>
> *-gu* after *-y* stems
>
> ŋaɖa ɖiŋali-ɲu bili-gu
>
> I (nom.)/ run + pres.-past/ climb + purposive
>
> 'I am running [to a tree] to climb [it].'

Relative Clauses

Relative clauses in Dyirbal are formed by inflecting the verbs and adverbals of the embedded clauses with a special relativizing suffix -ŋu which is then followed by a case ending (or zero in the absolutive) which must agree with the case of the qualified NP.

> ŋaɖa balan ɖugumbil ɲina-ŋu buṛa-n.
>
> I (nom.)/ there (Class II, absolutive)/ woman (Class II, absolutive)/ sit + relativizer (absolutive)/ watch + pres.-past
>
> 'I am watching a woman who is sitting down.'
>
> bayi yaṛa ba-ŋgu-n ɖugumbi-ṛu wayɲɖi-ŋu-ru buṛa-n.
>
> there (Class I, absolutive)/ man (Class I, absolutive)/ there + ergative + Class II marker/ woman + ergative/ move uphill + rel. + ergative/ see + pres.-past
>
> 'Woman who was going uphill saw a man.'

Other Types of Clauses

According to Dixon (1972:361), Australian languages lack precise equivalents for English logical connectors such as 'if', 'because', 'or'. However, that does not mean that Dyirbal and other Australian languages are incapable of expressing such notions by other means. For example, "entailment" ('since', 'because') is sometimes signaled in Dyirbal by means of implicated verb complexes that have been already discussed, or by the particle -ŋuri ('in turn'):

> ŋayguna baŋgul ḏilwa-n ɲuri ŋaḏa bayi biḏin

> me (acc.)/ there (Class I, ergative)/ kick + pres.-past/ 'in turn'/ there (Class I, absolutive)/ hit with rounded object + pres.-past

> 'I punched him because he had kicked me.'

In the preceding sentence the noun marker for Class I nouns acts as a third person masculine pronoun. (There are no third person pronouns in Dyirbal.)

In the same way, the notion of 'if' can be rendered in Dyirbal by various means one of which involves future tense inflection in the main clause and a relative clause which represents the equivalent of the English 'if' clause:

> bayi yaṛa ṛudu balga-ŋu guyibi-ŋ

> there (Class I, absolutive)/ man (Class I, absolutive)/ hollow in the back of the neck (Class IV, absolutive)/ hit with a long rigid instrument + relativizer (absolutive)/ die + future

> 'If a man is hit in the hollow in the back of his neck, he will die.' (Lit., 'Man who is hit in the back of the neck will die.')

Interrogative Sentences

Content questions in Dyirbal contain various question words: pronominal interrogatives, verbal interrogatives, interrogative verb markers, and so forth.

> waɲḏu ŋinuna balga-n?

> who (pronominal interrog.)/ you (acc.)/ hit + pres.-past

> 'Who hit you?'

> bayi yaṛa wiyama-ɲu?

> there (Class I)/ man/ do what (verbal interrog.) + pres.-past

> 'What was man doing?'

wuɲɖin yaṯa miyanda-ɲu?

where (Class I interrog. noun marker)/ man/ laugh + pres.-
  past

'Where is the man who is laughing?'

Yes-or-no questions may be signaled by rising intonation as in English or by a sentence clitic *-ma*[5] which is added to the end of the first word of the sentence. Note that this clitic may be redundantly added to the content questions as well.

ŋinda-ma bala-n ɖugumbil balga-n?

you + interrog. clitic/ there (Class II)/ woman/ hit + pres.-
  past

'Did you hit the woman?'

Antipassive Construction with -ŋay

In Dyirbal, just as in English, there are different ways of encoding the same case relations (or semantic roles) of NPs. For example, in English we may change a sentence which has a transitive verb into its passive voice equivalent where the patient appears as a subject, and the agent appears as an oblique object marked with the preposition 'by':

'The man hit the woman.' (Act. voice)
'The woman was hit by the man.' (Pass. voice)

In Dyirbal there is a special construction that is called "antipassive" whereby the agent NP of the basic voice acts syntactically as if it were a subject of an intransitive verb.

Any simple transitive sentence may be transformed into a -ŋay form. This involves (a) adding the suffix -ŋay (-y stems delete the stem-final -y and add -nay) to verbal forms, and (b) changing the case marking such that the ergative marking is substituted for the absolutive inflection of the object NP and the absolutive inflection is substituted for the ergative inflection of the agent NP. For example:

Simple transitive sentence:

balan ɖugumbil baŋgul yaṯa-ngu balga-n

there (Class II, absolutive)/ woman (Class II, absolutive)/
  there (Class I, ergative)/ man (Class I) + ergative/ hit with
  a long rigid instrument + pres.-past

'Man is hitting woman.'

Corresponding -ŋay form:

> *bayi yaṛa baŋgun ḍugumbil-ṛu balgal-ŋa-ɲu*
>
> there (Class I, absolutive)/ man (Class I, absolutive)/ there (Class II, ergative)/ woman (Class II) + ergative/ hit with a long, rigid instrument + ŋay + pres.-past
>
> 'Man is hitting woman.'

Alternatively, dative case marking may be substituted for the nominative inflection of the NP which functions as the object:

> *bayi yaṛa bagun ḍugumbil-gu balgal-ŋa-ɲu*
>
> there (Class I, absolutive)/ man (Class I, absolutive)/ there (Class II, dat.)/ woman (Class II) + dat./ hit with a long, rigid instrument + -ŋay + pres.-past
>
> 'Man is hitting woman.'

The difference between the two sentences cannot be expressed by giving different English glosses. According to Dixon (1972:66), the plain sentence simply reports an event involving an actor, a goal, and an action, whereas the -ŋay construction counterpart implies something more—that the actor is positively implicating the goal in the event, the difference being essentially one of topic.

The antipassive voice in Dyirbal allows what is otherwise an agent (subject of a transitive verb) to be identified as a subject of an intransitive verb. Thus, in the antipassive version of the sentence 'The man came here and [he] hit the woman,' the subject of the verb 'hit' (agent) may be deleted even though its coreferential NP is a subject of an intransitive verb 'come':

> *bayi yaṛa baniɲu, bagun ḍugumbilgu balgalŋnaɲu*
>
> there (Class I, absolutive)/ man (Class I, absolutive) came-here, there (Class II, dat.) woman (Class II, dat.) hit
>
> 'The man (intransitive sub.) came here and [he (agent)] hit the woman.'

Instrumental and Comitative Constructions

There are two ways in Dyirbal of describing an event which involves an object, an actor, and an instrument. The first way involves simply including in a normal sentence an NP which is marked for ergative-instrumental case. The second way is to mark the verbal stems with the instrumentive suffix -*mal* (-*mbal* in some environments), replace by absolutive case marking the instrumental-ergative case marking on the NP which refers to the instrument, and replace the absolutive inflection of the object NP with dative case inflection:[6]

bala yugu baŋgul yaṛa-ŋgu balgal-ma-n bagun ḍugumbil-gu

there (Class IV, absolutive)/ stick (Class IV, absolutive)/ there (Class I, ergative)/ hit with a long, rigid instrument + instrumentive + pres.-past/ there (Class II, dative)/ woman (Class II) + dat.

'Man is hitting woman with a stick.'

Comitative constructions are identical in form to the instrumentive but differ in their function (they indicate accompaniment rather than instrument whereby an action is performed) and in that in such constructions the suffix *-mal* is attached to intransitive verbal stems which then function as transitive verbal stems:

bala yugu baŋgul yaṛa-ŋgu ḍanay-ma-n

there (Class IV, absolutive)/ stick, wood, tree (Class IV, absolutive)/ there (Class I, ergative-instr.) man (Class I) + ergative-instr./ stand + comit. (instrumentive) + pres.-past

'Man is standing with some wood (i.e., either standing on a block of wood, or leaning against a tree, or standing under a tree, or standing holding a stick).'

This of course does not exhaust all the complexities of Dyirbal syntax. What has been presented is a mere sampling of the major constructions that occur in the cited examples and in the sample Dyirbal text which follows.

E. SAMPLE TEXT[7]

Unlike most of the other sample texts in this book, this particular text is an example of unedited oral literature, presented just as the linguistic field worker (R. M. W. Dixon) recorded it from a native informant with just a few changes (e.g., addition of punctuation). For that reason, it may seem rather rough and unpolished. One should keep in mind that oral presentations are very much different from written communication. For example, in cases of oral presentations like story telling, the audience may ask the storyteller for clarifications, whereas in written communication the writer must anticipate what possible points of confusion and misunderstanding may arise and therefore must be more specific and precise than he or she might be in an oral communication situation.

This is an autobiographical story in which the storyteller recounts one of her experiences as a little girl. While sitting in the camp with the tribe one night she heard a strange noise and was told by the old people that the noise was made by the Dambun spirit. In spite of the warnings not to do so, she went looking for the source of the noise and discovered that it was none other than a curlew. The following night she heard another strange noise and was told by the old people that that was Dambun spirit also. She looked again and this time she found that the noise had been made by the mopoke owl.

The superscripted numbers in the literal morpheme-by-morpheme translation refer to the notes which follow that section.

Dyirbal Text

(1) dambunda ŋananga muguru ɲina! (2) wuɳɖananga? (3) ŋan bangaluŋunu yalgayɖaru wandin. (4) ɲiralbila! (5) muymba buni buṛalbila dambundu! (6) ŋanaɖina ɖindi ɲiraɲ. (7) wuɳɖan? (8) gilaɲunda ŋalan ŋalan ŋandaɲ mulgu. (9) ŋaɖa walmawalmagaliɲu baŋum maŋgalmbarigu duɖugu gindalmali. (10) ɖaɲɖa ŋaɖa yanu. (11) baŋgumaŋgandu gindimban: (12) 'ɛ! galga ban dambun gindam banimbila!' (13) ŋaɖa bala gulu ŋamban baŋgumaŋganu guwal; miɖuganiɲu. (14) baliɖilu ŋaɖa yanu bagun gindalŋaɲu dambungu. (15) ŋaɖa ban buṛali dambun banɖana dambun gilagiɲan yaṛaŋarumban balan muray ɖuda biguŋgalugalu margimargi wirmban dayidayigala. (16) balubawal ŋaɖa yanu. (17) yimba bangalu buṛan ŋaɖa guyibara yambiɲu. (18) 'giyu, giyu, giyu,' ŋangalu ban yambin. (19) baɲum balan yuŋgugan; ɖagungabunda ŋaɖa ŋamban; bangalu mulgubiŋgu; balan ŋamban guɲu dambun. (20) yanu ŋaɖa. (21) maŋgalmban ŋaɖa duɖu gindalmali. (22) dambunda yaŋgun 'gindagindamalbila dambun! (23) ŋanaɖi ɖaɲɖa manmaygu yalugungari.' (24) baliɖilu ŋaɖa yanu gindalŋaɲu. (25) buṛan giɲanbaydi gugu ɲinaɲu mulgumbaɲu: (26) 'mm, mm, mm.' (27) yalamaɲu bangali. (28) yidiṛa ɲinaɲu buybayriɲu gaygabu bulgan ŋaɖa ŋaṛban. (29) banagayaraɲu ŋaɖa buṛalaygu ŋuymalaygu gaygagu bagun. (30) balan buṛan gugu ɲinaɲu. (31) ɖaɲɖa ŋaɖa miyandaɲu balaydilu. (32) baŋngumaŋgandu ŋayguna ŋundaɲu dambundu gidimbaɲu. (33) ban—ŋaɖa ban miyandaɲu bagun dambu-ŋambiyagu gugugu.

Literal Morpheme-by-Morpheme Translation

(1) *dambun-da ŋa-na-ŋga muguru ɲina!*
Dambun (Class II) + loc.[1]/ unseen + nominal affix -ɲa (+ Class II marker, fused) + loc./ **quiet** (adj. in absolutive case)/ **sit** (imperat. form)

(2) *wuɳɖa-naŋ-ga?*
where + nominal affix -ɲa (+ Class II marker, fused) + loc.

(3) *ŋan ba-n-galu-ŋunu yalgay-ɖa-ru wandi-n.*
unseen + Class II (absolutive)/ there + Class II + **out in front** + ablat./ **road,** path + loc. + motion/ **move upriver** + pres.-past tense

(4) *ɲiral-bila!*
pin[2] + apprehensive

(5) *muymba buni buṛal-bila dambun-du!*
extinguish (imper.)/ **fire** (Class II, absolutive)/ **see** + apprehensive/ **Dambun** (Class II) + ergative

(6) *ŋanaɖi-na ɖindi ɲira-ɲ.*
us (1st pers. pl. pron.) + acc./ **chest** (Class IV, absolutive)/ **pin** + fut. tense

(7) *wuɳɖa-n?*
where + Class II (absolutive)

(8) *gila-ŋunda ŋala-n ŋala-n ŋanda-ɲ mulgu*

somewhere (loc. vb. marker) + somewhere (suffix)/ unseen + Class II (absolutive)/ unseen + Class II (absolutive)/ **call out** + fut. tense/ **noise** (Class I/Class II, absolutive)

(9) *ŋaḍa walma-walma-gali-ɲu ba-ŋum maŋgal-mbari-gu duḍu-gu gindal-mal-i*

I (nom.)/ **get up** + reduplication[3] + **quick** + pres.-past/ there (Class II) + ablat./ **pick up** + reflexive[4] + purposive/ **torch**[5] + dat.[6]/ **look with a light** + instr. + purposive

(10) *ḍaɲḍa ŋaḍa yanu.*

now/ **I** (nom.)/ **go** (irreg. pres.-past form)

(11) *baŋgumaŋgan-du gindimba-n:*

many people + ergative/ **warn** + pres.-past

(12) '[ɛ]*! galga ba-n dambun ginda-m bani-mbila!'*

exclamation/ neg. imperat. sentence particle/ there + Class II (absolutive)/ **Dambun** (Class II, absolutive)/ **look with a light** + neg. imperat. suffix/ **come** + apprehensive

(13) *ŋaḍa bala gulu ŋamba-n baŋgumaŋgan-u guwal; miḍu-gani-ɲu.*

I (nom.)/ there (Class IV, absolutive)/ neg. particle/ **listen** + pres.-past/ **many people** + simple gen./ language, **speech** (Class IV, absolutive)/; take no notice, **ignore** + repeated or continued action + pres.-past

(14) *ba-li-ḍilu ŋaḍa yanu ba-gu-n gindal-ŋa-ɲu dambun-gu.*

there + allat. of direction + intensifier/ **I** (nom.)/ **go** (irreg. pres.-past form)/ there + dat. + Class II/ **look with a light** + -ŋay[7] + pres.-past/ **Dambun** (Class II) + dat.

(15) *ŋaḍa ba-n buṛal-i dambun, miɲa-ŋaru-mba-n dambun, ba-n-ḍana dambun gila-giɲa-n yaṛa-ŋaru-mb-an bala-n muray ḍuda biguɲ-galu-galu margi-margi wirmban dayi-dayi-gala.*

I (nom.)/ there + Class II (absolutive)/ **see** + purposive/ **Dambun** (Class II, absolutive)/, **what** + **look like** + transitive verbalizer + pres.-past/ **Dambun** (Class II, absolutive)/ there + Class II (absolutive) + emphatic/ **Dambun** (Class II, absolutive)/ **somewhere** + this one here (dem.) + Class II (absolutive)/ **man** + **look like** + transitive verbalizer + pres.-past/ there + Class II (absolutive)/ **head hair** (Class IV, absolutive)/ **bushy** (absolutive)/ **nail** + **out in front** + reduplication[8] (absolutive)/ **thin** + reduplication[9] (absolutive)/ **skin and bones** (absolutive)/ up + reduplication[9] + vertically up (absolutive)

(16) *ba-lu-bawal ŋaḍa yanu.*

there + allat. of place + **long way** (in any direction)/ **I** (absolutive)/ **go** (irreg. pres.-past form)

(17) *yimba ba-n-galu buṛa-n ŋaḍa guyibara yambi-ŋu.*

no, **nothing** (interjection)/ there + Class II (absolutive) + **out in front**/ **see, look at** + pres.-past/ **I** (nom.)/ **curlew** (Class II, absolutive)/ **fly** + relativizer (absolutive)

(18) *'giyu, giyu, giyu,' ŋa-n-galu ba-n yambi-n.*

'noise made by the curlew × 3'/ unseen + Class II (absolutive) + **out in front**/ there + Class II (absolutive)/ **fly** + pres.-past

(19) *ba-ŋum bala-n yuŋgugan; ḏagun-gabun-da ŋaḏa ŋamba-n; ba-n-galu mulgu-bi-ŋgu; bala-n ŋamba-n guɲu dambun.*
there + ablat./ there + Class II (absolutive)/ **another one** (absolutive)/ **night, sleep** + **another** + loc./ **I** (nom.)/ **hear,** listen to + pres.-past/ there Class II (absolutive) + **out in front**/ **indistinct noise** + intransitive verbalizer + relativizer (absolutive)/ there + Class II (absolutive)/ **hear** + pres.-past/ **new** (absolutive)/ **Dambun** (Class II, absolutive)

(20) *yanu ŋaḏa.*
go (irreg. pres.-past)/ **I** (nom.)

(21) *maŋgal-mba-n ŋaḏa duḏu gindal-mal-i.*
pick up + instrumentive[10] + pres.-past/ **I** (nom.)/**torch**[5] (absolutive)/ **look with a light** + instrumentive[10] + purposive

(22) *'dambun-da ya-ŋgu-n ginda-ginda-mal-bila dambun!*
Dambun (Class II) + loc./ here + ergative + Class II/ **look with a light** + reduplication[3] + instrumentive[10] + apprehensive/ **Dambun** (absolutive)

(23) *ŋanaḏi ḏaɲḏa manmay-gu ya-lu-guŋgari.'*
we (nom.)/ **now**/ **shift camp** + purposive/ here + allat. of place + **north**

(24) *bal-i-ḏilu ŋaḏa yanu gindal-ŋa-ɲu*
there + allat. of direction + emphatic/ **I** (nom.)/ **go** (irreg. pres.-past)/ **look with a light** + -ŋay[7] + pres.-past[11]

(25) *buṛa-n giɲa-n-bayḏ-i gugu ɲina-ŋu mulgu-mba-ŋu:*
see + pres.-past/ **this here** (dem.) + Class II (absolutive) + **downhill** + **short way**/ **mopoke owl** (Class II, absolutive)/ **sit** + relativizer (absolutive)/ indistinct noise + intransitive verbalizer + relativizer (absolutive)

(26) *'mm, mm, mm.'*
noise made by owl

(27) *yalama-ŋu ba-n-gali.*
do like this + relativizer (absolutive)/ **there** + Class II (absolutive) + **downhill**

(28) *yidiṛ-a ɲina-ŋu buyba-yiri-ŋu gayga-bu bulgan ŋaḏa ŋaṛba-n.*
grass (Class IV) + loc./ **sit** + relativizer (absolutive)/ **hide** + reflexive + relativizer (absolutive)/ **eye**[12] (Class IV, absolutive) + **only**/ **big** (absolutive)/ **I** (nom.)/ **be frightened** + pres.-past

(29) *banagay-ara-ɲu ŋaḏa buṛal-ay-gu ŋuymal-ay-gu gayga-gu ba-gu-n.*
return + **again** + pres.-past/ **I** (nom.)/ **see** + -ŋay[7] + purposive/ **do properly** + -ŋay[7] + purposive/ **eye**[12] (Class IV) + dat./ there + dat. + Class II

(30) *bala-n buṛa-n gugu ɲina-ŋu.*
there + Class II (absolutive)/ **see** + pres.-past/ **mopoke owl** (Class II, absolutive)/ **sit** + relativizer (absolutive)/

(31) *ḏaɲḏa ŋaḏa miyanda-ɲu bala-y-ḏilu.*
now/ **I** (nom.)/ **laugh** + pres.-past/ **there** + loc. + emphatic

(32) *baŋgumagan-du ŋayguna ŋunḏa-ɲu dambun-du gidimba-ŋu.*
many people + ergative/ **me** (acc.)/ **blame** + pres.-past/ **Dambun** (Class II) + ergative/ **tickle** + relativizer (absolutive)

(33) *ba-n ŋaḍa ba-n miyanda-ɲu ba-gu-n dambu-ŋambiya-gu gugu-gu.*
there + Class II (absolutive)/ **I** (nom.)/ there Class II (absolutive)/ **laugh** +
pres.-past/ there + dat. + Class II/ **Dambu** + **what's** **it** **called** + dat./
mopoke owl (Class II) + dat.

NOTES

1. Locative case may mark cause, especially if the cause involves something fright-ening. Thus, here we can translate Dambun in the locative case as 'for fear of Dambun'.

2. Dixon (383) has ŋiral for 'pin', but in the glossary (405) he cites ɲiral for 'pin'. According to Dixon (personal communication), ɲiral is the correct form.

3. Reduplication here marks an 'action performed to excess'.

4. Reflexive affix has no semantic content in some situations.

5. The cited Dyirbal word for 'torch' is an ad hoc loan from English.

6. Dative here marks an "implicated" NP. (See the discussion of the dative case in Dyirbal.)

7. For the function of this affix consult the syntax section in the sketch.

8. Here reduplication signals plural number ('nails') even though it is the affix, not the stem that is reduplicated.

9. Here reduplication marks intensity.

10. Instrumentive affix on the verb indicates that an NP in the sentence (which is in the absolutive case, not in the ergative-instrumental case) is the instrument of the ac-tion expressed by the verb.

11. Since Dixon (386) glosses this affix as being the present-past tense suffix, I have corrected the Dyirbal ending to the expected -ɲu instead of what is actually given (-ŋu).

12. Dyirbal nouns unmarked for number are not necessarily singular. That is, they are actually indeterminate in number.

Idiomatic Translation

Sit quiet for the fear of Dambun, who can be heard (now)! Where is she that we fear? She can be heard going along the road up alongside the river there. She might pin [our chests, with her claw-like hands]! Put out the fire lest Dambun see it! She would pin our chests. Where is she? She can be heard somewhere out there; she will call out her noise.

I quickly got up from there [from where I was sitting in the camp] to pick up a torch, so that I could look by its light. Then I went out.

They all [all the old people of the camp] warned [me]: "Hey! Don't look for Dambun with the light, lest she come here!"

I did not listen to what they were saying; I took no notice at all. I went in that direction, looking for Dambun by [torch]light. I wanted to see Dambun; to see what Dambun looked like. That Dambun somewhere out there [is sup-posed to] look something like a man, with bushy hair, long finger and toe nails, very skinny and emaciated, all bones and no flesh, very very tall.

I went over there. Oh no! I saw the curlew flying. "Giyu, giyu, giyu," she could be heard flying.

Then the next night I heard another [noise]; something was making an indistinct noise out there; it was another Dambun [I] heard. I went out. I picked up the torch, to look [for Dambun] with it.

[All the old people said:] "This girl might shine a light on Dambun! And we might all have to move camp to the north [to escape Dambun]."

I went out there looking with a light. I saw a mopoke owl sitting down there [in the grass] making a noise: "Mm, mm, mm." That's the way it [was making a noise], down on the ground.

[Seeing] just [two] big eyes sitting hiding in the grass frightened me. [But] I went back again to have a proper look at the eyes. [And] saw a mopoke owl sitting there. I laughed, right there. All the people [in the camp] put the blame [for the laughing] on me being tickled by Dambun. I was laughing at that Dambu—what's it called—that owl.

EXERCISES

1. Possession Marking in Hawaiian

Read the description of the distinction between 'alienable/acquired' and 'inalienable/inherited' possession in the "Sketch of Hawaiian." Contrary to our expectations, however, the following Hawaiian nouns are always treated as being 'inalienable/inherited' possessions: *hale* 'house', *wa'a* 'canoe', *'āina* 'land', words referring to items of clothing such as *kāma'a* 'shoe', and sometimes terms for adzes. Suggest a plausible explanation for this situation.

2. Focus in Tagalog[8]

In *Tagalog (Austronesian)* there is a way of shifting attention to the various constituents of the sentence. Some linguists call this "focus." Examine the Tagalog sentences below and then describe the morphosyntactic mechanisms whereby this "focus" effect is signaled in Tagalog. More specifically, how does Tagalog mark what type of focus is involved and which constituent of the sentence is being focused on?

a. *Agent focus*

    Bumili ang bata ng tinapay.

    but (stem = *bili*)/ grammatical marker/ child/ some/ bread

    '*The child* bought some bread.'

b. *Patient focus*

    Bilhin mo ang tinapay.

    buy (stem = *bil*)/ you/ grammatical marker/ bread

    'You buy *(some) bread.*

c. *Benefactive focus*

Ibili mo ang nanay ng sapatos.

buy (stem = *bili*)/ you/ grammatical marker/ mother/ some/ shoes

'(You) buy shoes *for mother.*'

d. *Instrumental focus*

Ipanghiwa mo ang kutsilyo.

cut (stem = *hiwa*)/ you/ grammatical marker/ knife

'(You) *use the knife* to cut.'

e. *Locative focus*

Puntahan mo ang bahay niya.

go (stem = *punta*)/ you/ grammatical marker/ house/ their

'You go *to their house.*'

3. Noun Classes in Fijian[9]

In Fijian (Austronesian) there are three noun classes which manifest themselves only in that each class determines the allomorph of the possessive pronoun which modifies a given noun:

Class I:

na ke-na uvi 'his/her yam'
na ke-na raisi 'his/her rice'
na ke-na dalo 'his/her taro'
na ke-na ika 'his/her fish'
na ke-na vonu 'his/her turtle'
na ke-na bulamakau 'his/her beef'
na ke-na vuaka 'his/her pig'
na ke-na toa 'his/her fowl'

Class II:

na me-na tī 'his/her tea'
na me-na yaqona 'his/her kava (ceremonial drink)'
na me-na moli 'his/her citrus'
na me-na bia 'his/her beer'
na me-na suvu 'his/her soup'

na me-na wai 'his/her water'

na me-na kove 'his/her coffee'

na me-na bū 'his/her drinking coconut'

Class III:

na no-na waqa 'his/her canoe'

na no-na motokā 'his/her car'

na no-na vale 'his/her house'

na no-na tūraga 'his/her chief'

na no-na ivola 'his/her book'

na no-na peni 'his/her pen'

na no-na bilo 'his/her 'cup'

na no-na kato 'his/her basket'

na no-na ibe 'his/her mat'

Membership in the noun classes is not arbitrary but is based on the semantic features of the nouns. What are the semantic features that determine to which noun class a given Fijian noun belong?

4. Buang Morphophonemics[10]

Buang is an Austronesian language spoken in the Morobe Province of Papua New Guinea. Examine the *Buang* data given below and then set up an invariable underlying shape for each morpheme as well as the necessary phonological rules by which the surface forms in question can be derived. (Hint: You will need some critically ordered rules.) [G] is a voiced uvular stop, and [R] is a voiced uvular fricative. Remember also that in very many languages third person is not marked.

Table 6.7

	MY . . .	YOUR . . .	HIS . . .
1. 'father'	amaG	amam	ama
2. 'child'	naluG	nalum	nalu
3. 'face'	malaG	malam	mala
4. 'knee'	luk	lup	lus
5. 'tail'	Ruk	Rup	Rus
6. 'head'	yuG	yum	yu
7. 'neck'	kwaG	kwam	kwa
8. 'brother'	ariG	arim	ari
9. 'name'	areG	arem	are
10. 'breath'	saRɛG	saRɛm	saRɛn
11. 'cousin'	gadɛG	gadɛm	gadɛ

5. Kiwai Morphology

Kiwai is a Papuan language belonging to the Trans-New Guinea group of languages and is spoken in the Western Province of Papua New Guinea.

This language has a highly complicated verb morphology. Try to make a morphological analysis (as far as it is possible on the basis of the data given) of the following Kiwai verb forms. The data for this exercise was taken from Capell (1969:73–5).

You should know that this language does not make a difference between second and third persons as far as person marking on verbs. Also, the system of affixation is not entirely symmetrical, and there are some morphophonemic changes involving vowels.

noruso	'I eat/ate one.'
norusodurudo	'We two eat one.'
norusurudo	'We two ate one.'
roruso	'You or he eat one.'
rorusodurudo	'You two or they two eat one.'
goruso	'You or he ate one.'
nidorusori	'I shall eat one.'
nidudorusori	'We two shall eat one.'
niriso	'I eat/ate many.'
ririsodurumo	'They (more than three) eat many.'
ririso	'You or he eats many.'
norusobidurumo	'We three eat one.'
norusodurumo	'We (more than three) eat one.'

NOTES

1. The presentation here is based on Clark's (1992) overview of the family and Blust's (1983–84) subgrouping hypothesis.

2. This account of the structure of Hawaiian is based chiefly on that found in Elbert and Pukui (1979). Where it deviates from the latter work, it follows the as yet unpublished analysis of Greg Lee Carter, a graduate student in linguistics at the University of Hawaii currently working on a new description of the Hawaiian language. I am very much indebted to Carter for letting me include his analyses and some of his examples in my sketch.

3. Greg Lee Carter (personal communication) considers this to be simply an infinitive marker that happens to be homophonous with the imperative marker.

4. This sketch is based entirely on R. M. W. Dixon's (1972) description of Dyirbal.

5. A clitic is a type of morpheme similar to an affix, except that whereas particular affixes are attached to particular parts of speech, clitics attach to any word regardless of its class.

6. The difference involved here looks very much like a difference in *focus* such as that found in the various languages of the Philippines for example.

7. This Dyirbal text and its English translation are cited from R. M. W. Dixon, *The Dyirbal language of North Queensland,* pp. 382–87. © Cambridge University Press 1972. Reprinted with the permission of Cambridge University Press.

8. The examples for this exercise are taken from Ramos (1971:88–91).

9. I am very grateful to Prof. Albert J. Schütz of the Linguistics Department at the University of Hawaii for the examples used in this exercise.

10. This exercise is Problem 70 in Merrifield et al. (1987). Used with permission, *Laboratory Manual for Morphology and Syntax, Revised Edition,* Merrifield et al. eds.; Summer Institute of Linguistics.

SELECTED BIBLIOGRAPHY

General

Capell, A. 1969. *A survey of New Guinea languages.* Sydney: Sydney University Press. (This survey covers both the Austronesian and non-Austronesian languages spoken in New Guinea and, although somewhat dated, contains still very interesting and useful information about the typological features of various languages spoken there.)

Wurm, Stephen A., and Shirō Hattori. 1981–84. *Language atlas of the Pacific area.* Canberra: Australian Academy of the Humanities.

Austronesian

Arakin, V. D. 1965. *Indonezijskie jazyki.* Moscow: Izdatel'stvo "Nauka".

———. 1973. *Samoanskij jazyk.* Moscow: "Nauka."

Bellwood, Peter. 1991. The Austronesian dispersal and the origin of languages. *Scientific American* July: 88–93.

Besnier, Niko. 1992. Polynesian languages. In William Bright et al., eds., *International encyclopedia of linguistics.* Vol. 3:245–51. New York: Oxford University Press.

Blust, Robert. 1983–84. More on the position of the languages of eastern Indonesia. *Oceanic Linguistics* 22/23:1–28.

———. 1984–85. The Austronesian homeland: A linguistic perspective. *Asian Perspectives* 26.1:45–67.

———. 1990. Summary report: Linguistic change and reconstruction methodology in the Austronesian language family. In Philip Baldi, ed., *Linguistic change and reconstruction methodology,* 133–53. New York: Mouton de Gruyter.

Clark, Ross. 1987. Austronesian languages. In Bernard Comrie, ed., *The world's major languages,* 899–912. New York: Oxford University Press.

———. 1992. Austronesian languages. In William Bright et al., eds., *International encyclopedia of linguistics.* Vol. 1:142–5. New York: Oxford University Press.

Keenan, Edward Louis, and Elinor Ochs. 1979. Becoming a competent speaker of Malagasy. In Timothy Shopen, ed., *Languages and their speakers,* 113–158. Cambridge, Mass.: Winthrop Publishers.

Krupa, Viktor. 1973. *Polynesian languages: A survey of research.* Paris: Mouton.

Prentice, D. J. 1987. Malay (Indonesian and Malaysian). In Bernard Comrie, ed., *The world's major languages,* 913–35. New York: Oxford University Press.

———. 1992. Malay and Indonesian. In William Bright et al., eds., *International encyclopedia of linguistics.* Vol. 2:374–80. New York: Oxford University Press.

Ramos, Teresita V. 1971. *Tagalog structures.* Honolulu: University of Hawaii Press.

Schacter, Paul. 1987. Tagalog. In Bernard Comrie, ed., *The world's major languages,* 936–58. New York: Oxford University Press.

————. 1992. Tagalog. In William Bright et al., eds., *International encyclopedia of linguistics*. Vol. 4:123–6. New York: Oxford University Press.

Sugita, Hiroshi. 1981. Ōsutroneshia shogo. In Hajime Kitamura, ed., *Sekai no gengo*, 199–230. Kōza gengo, vol. 6. Tokyo: Taishūkan shoten.

Papuan Languages

Foley, William A. 1986. *The Papuan languages of New Guinea*. New York: Cambridge University Press.

————. 1992. New Guinea languages. In William Bright et al., eds., *International encyclopedia of linguistics*. Vol. 3:86–91.

Greenberg, Joseph H. 1971. The Indo-Pacific hypothesis. In Thomas A. Sebeok, ed., *Current trends in linguistics*. Vol. 8, 1963–76. The Hague: Mouton.

Haiman, John. 1979. Hua: A Papuan language of New Guinea. In Timothy Shopen, ed., *Languages and their status*, 35–89. Cambridge, Mass.: Winthrop Publishers.

Leont'ev, A. A. 1974. *Papuasskie jazyki*. Moscow: Izdatel'stvo "Nauka."

Wurm, Stephen. 1982. *Papuan languages of Oceania*. Ars linguistica, Vol. 7. Tübingen: Narr.

Australian

Blake, Barry J. 1981. *Australian aboriginal languages*. London: Angus & Robertson. (This is a more popularized, easy-to-read presentation than the following works.)

Blake, Barry J., and R. M. W. Dixon, eds. 1979–91. *Handbook of Australian languages*. 4 vols. Amsterdam: John Benjamins.

Dixon, R. M. W. 1980. *The languages of Australia*. Cambridge: Cambridge University Press.

————. 1992. Australian languages. In William Bright et al., eds., *International encyclopedia of linguistics*. Vol. 1:1.134–7. New York: Oxford University Press.

Florey, Margaret J. 1988. A review of the classification of Australian languages. *Working papers in linguistics* (Dept. of Linguistics, University of Hawaii at Manoa) 20(2):137–62. (This is a very clearly written review of the work done in the area of establishing the Australian family of languages and the difficulties encountered in this task.)

Haviland, John B. 1979. How to talk to your brother-in-law in Guugu Yimidhirr. In Timothy Shopen, ed., *Languages and their speakers*, 161–239. Cambridge, Mass.: Winthrop Publishers. Among other things, this work discusses the special language one must use when speaking within earshot of the "tabooed" relatives and how that language differs from the ordinary language.)

Heath, Jeffrey. 1978. *Linguistic diffusion in Arnhem Land*. Canberra: AIAS.

————. 1981. A case of intensive lexical diffusion: Arnhem Land, Australia. *Language* 57(2):335–67.

Wurm, Stephen A. 1972. *Languages of Australia and Tasmania*. Paris: Mouton.

Hawaiian

Elbert, Samuel H. 1970. *Spoken Hawaiian*. Honolulu: University of Hawaii Press.

Elbert, Samuel, and Mary Kawena Pukui. 1979. *Hawaiian grammar*. Honolulu: University of Hawaii Press. (A good reference grammar of the language, but needs updating in several areas.)

Hopkins, Alberta Pualani. 1992. *Ka lei ha'aheo: Beginning Hawaiian*. 2 vols. Honolulu: University of Hawaii Press.

Kahananui, Dorothy M., and Alberta P. Anthony. 1974. *E. kama'ilio Hawai'i kakou: Let's speak Hawaiian*. 2d rev. ed. Honolulu: The University Press of Hawaii. (This is a pedagogical grammar of the language.)

Krupa, Victor. 1979. *Gavajskij jazyk.* Moscow: Izdatel'stvo "Nauka."

Pukui, Mary K., and Samuel H. Elbert. 1971. *Hawaiian dictionary.* Honolulu: University of Hawaii Press.

Schütz, Albert J. 1980. A reanalysis of the Hawaiian vowel system. *Oceanic Linguistics* 20(1):1–43.

Dyirbal

Dixon, R. M. W. 1972. *The Dyirbal language of North Queensland.* Cambridge Studies in Linguistics, vol. 9. Cambridge: Cambridge University Press. (This is the grammar on which the "Sketch of Dyirbal" is based.)

Chapter 7   Native Languages of the Americas

In North, Central, and South America there are three groups of languages: (1) the native or aboriginal languages of the Americas, (2) the varieties of languages imported into the Americas from the Old World (primarily Europe) and which now predominate in the region, and (3) some important contact languages which arose on the soil of the American continent. Contact languages in general, as well as those that arose in the Americas, are discussed in Chapter 8. The languages imported to the Americas from Europe have over the years developed traits that mark them as being somewhat different from their European antecedents; however, these differences will not be discussed here. In this chapter only the native American languages will be discussed.

Most authorities seem to agree that the original population of the Americas came over from Asia, most likely across the Bering Strait or even across the land bridge which, geologists say, connected Asia and America in the remote past. One basis for this claim is that the native Americans share some racial traits in common with peoples of Asia, for example, the Mongolian spot which appears on the back and buttocks of newborn babies and disappears as they grow into adulthood.

It is not known just how long ago the migrations from Asia began, but some recent evidence suggests that the first wave may have come over about 40,000 B.C. Kaufman (1990:26) is more conservative and cites 20,000 B.C. as the more established earliest date for the settlement of the New World. It is also reasonable to assume that there were many waves of migrations from Asia. Some scholars believe, for example, that the Eskimo-Aleut migration from Asia took place about 3000 B.C. However, the fact that there are still Eskimo settlements in Asia (on the Chukchi peninsula) does not necessarily prove that Eskimos migrated to Alaska from Asia: the Eskimo settlements in Asia appear to be the result of a migration going the other way.

Not long ago Joseph Greenberg (1987) proposed on the basis of his mass comparison studies that *all* aboriginal languages of North, Central, and South America, except the Eskimo-Aleut language family and the Na-Dene language family (see below), form a large super language family which he calls "Amerind." Because most linguists reject the validity of Greenberg's mass comparison methodology (some even say that Greenberg actually has no methodology) this claim has received little acceptance. See, for example, the very negative review of Greenberg's Amerind hypothesis by Lyle Campbell (1988) and Kaufman's (1990:15–7) comments on Greenberg's methodology.

A. LANGUAGES OF NORTH AMERICA

Native language groups of North America will be listed roughly in terms of their geographical location from north to south and in terms of their possible interconnections. The language classification follows in the main the list given by Campbell and Mithun (1979:39–46), which is rather conservative in its genetic classification of languages, and, with one exception (Haida language isolate), the following list keeps the numbers assigned by Campbell and Mithun to each language group.[1]

I. ESKIMO-ALEUT FAMILY

As far as is known, this is the only native language family that has speakers in both Asia and America. According to Kaplan (1992, 1:415–9), this family is divided into the following branches and subbranches.

1. ALEUT

This branch of the family is spoken by very small groups of inhabitants on various islands in the Aleutian chain and on the Commander Islands. There are now fewer than about 500 speakers of various Aleut dialects, the chief of which is the dialect of Atka. All of the Aleut dialects have been heavily influenced by Russian. (Most of the technical and religious vocabulary was borrowed from Russian.)

2. ESKIMO

This branch of the family consists of two subbranches.

a. Inuit

(This subbranch called *Inupiaq* in Alaska, *Inuktitut* in eastern Canada, and *Kalaallisut* in Greenland) stretches in a dialect chain from Greenland to Alaska and contains the following groups.

Greenlandic Inuit (43,000 sp. in Greenland and about 7,000 in Denmark), *Eastern Canadian Inuit* (about 14,000 sp. in northeastern Canada), *Western Canadian Inuit* (around 4,000 sp. in central and northwestern Canada), *North Alaskan Inuit* (about 3,500 sp. in northern Alaska to the Mackenzie River Delta in Canada), and *Seward Peninsula Inuit* (about 700 sp. on the Seward Peninsula in Alaska).

b. Yupik

This subbranch, according to Reuse (1994:1), consists of five mutually unintelligible language groups found in Alaska and Siberia.

i. Sirenikski

This language was originally spoken in the villages of Sireniki and Imtuk to the west of the *Chaplinski* dialect of *Central Siberian Yupik* on the tip of the Chukchi Peninsula, Siberia. It is highly divergent from any other Yupik language. It is now probably extinct since there were only two elderly speakers in 1980. The descendants of the *Sirenikski* speakers now speak *Chaplinski, Chukchi,* or Russian.

ii. Naukanski

Until 1958 this language was spoken in the village of Naukan near east Cape, Siberia, when the entire village was evacuated, and *Naukanski* speakers were relocated to other villages down the coast. The total number of speakers is estimated to be around 75.

iii. Central Siberian Yupik

This group has around 1,400 speakers, of which 1,000 are on St. Lawrence Island, Alaska, and about 400 on the eastern tip of the Chukchi Peninsula, Siberia, who speak the *Chaplinski* dialect of *Central Siberian Yupik.*

iv. Central Alaskan Yupik

This group has about 15,000 speakers on the northern Alaskan coast from Bristol Bay to Norton Sound and inland along Nushagak, Kuskokwim, and Yukon Rivers.

v. Pacific Yupik or Alutiiq

This group has about 600 speakers on the Alaskan Peninsula, Kodiak Island, and the Alaskan coast from Cook Inlet to Prince William Sound, Alaska.

Both *Aleut* and *Eskimo* languages are polysynthetic. There are hypotheses that *Eskimo-Aleut* family is related to Indo-European, Uralic, as well as to some Paleo-Siberian languages, especially Chukchi, but so far convincing evidence for any of these relationships is lacking.

IIA. Na-Dene Family

It has been proposed that this language family is also a relative newcomer to the American continent just like the *Eskimo-Aleut* family. However, there are no widely recognized relatives of *Na-Dene* languages in Asia as is the case with *Eskimo-Aleut.* Edward Sapir and later Robert Shafer both attempted to establish a genetic link between Na-Dene and *Sino-Tibetan,* but regardless of the ultimate truth of this hypothesis, their attempts to prove it remain unconvincing. (In the case of Sapir the attempt was premature since little was known at the time either about Proto-Sino-Tibetan or about Proto-Na-Dene, and some knowledge of both is needed for a truly scientific attempt to establish a genetic link between the two families. In the case of Robert Shafer, who took on the task of gathering evidence for the relationship after Sapir, the haphazard nature of the various comparisons he adduced in support of this hypothesis made the task itself fall into disrepute.

This family is subdivided into two branches.

1. TLINGIT

This branch is represented by only one language: *Tlingit* (spoken by about 2,000 sp. in the Alaskan panhandle and inland into Canada).

2. ATHABASKAN-EYAK

This branch is split into two main subbranches.

a. Eyak

This branch, represented by only one language, *Eyak,* which is said to have recently become extinct. It was spoken at the mouth of Copper River, Alaska.

b. Athabaskan

This branch includes a number of very important languages which, according to Cook (1992,1:122–8), are found in three separate areas.

i. Western Subarctic (interior Alaska and northwestern Canada)
This group includes the following major languages: *Babine* or *Northern Carrier* (around 1,600 sp. in west central British Columbia, Canada), *Central Carrier* (around 1,500 sp. in central British Columbia, Canada), *Chilcotin* (around 1,200 sp. in south central British Columbia, Canada), *Chipewyan* (around 8,000 sp. in Northwest Territories, Saskatchewan, Alberta, and Manitoba, Canada), *Dogrib* (2,300 to 2,400 sp. between Great Slave Lake and Great Bera Lake, Northwest Territories, Canada), *Gwich'in* or *Kuchin* (around 1,500 sp. in northeastern Alaska on the Yukon River, and in the Old Crow and MacKenzie River areas in Canada), and *Slavey* (around 4,000 sp. in northwestern Canada).

ii. Northwest Coast (California and Oregon)
Most of the languages in this group have become extinct. The following are some of the surviving ones: *Hupa* (50 or fewer elderly sp. in northwestern California), *Kato* (10 or fewer elderly sp. in northwestern California), and *Tutuni* (10 or fewer elderly sp. in southwestern Oregon).

iii. Southwest (Arizona and New Mexico)
This region contains perhaps the most influential Native American language in the United States: *Navaho,* or *Navajo,* which has over 130,000 speakers in the Arizona, Utah, and New Mexico region. This may be the only aboriginal language of United States and Canada whose native speakers are actually *increasing* rather than rapidly diminishing in numbers. A number of newspapers and periodicals are published in this language.

Other languages belonging to this group are *Jicarilla Apache* (around 1,500 sp. in northern New Mexico), *Kiowa Apache* (10 sp. or fewer in western Oklahoma), *Mescalero-Chiricahua Apache* (around 1,800 sp. in New Mexico, some in Oklahoma), and *Western Apache* (around 11,000 sp. in east central Arizona).

Languages belonging to the Na-Dene family possess complicated grammars that exhibit fusional, synthetic, and polysynthetic traits. Many of the languages are tonal. In addition, most of these languages have complicated consonant systems which include glottalized ejectives, and various complex lateral sounds (such as are found in many other native languages of North America).

IIB. HAIDA ISOLATE

Haida (spoken by about 295 sp. on Queen Charlotte Island and the opposite coast of Alaska) is thought by some to be distantly related to the Na-Dene languages, but Campbell and Mithun (1979) prefer to list it as a language isolate. (However, they do not give it its own index number in their list of language families and language isolates.)

III. ALGONQUIAN-RITWAN FAMILY

This family is subdivided into two groups, *Ritwan* and *Algonquian (Algonkian)*, but there is strong doubt that the *Ritwan* branch, which consists of *Wiyot* and *Yurok*, is indeed a viable genetic grouping since these two languages do not seem to be more closely related to each other than to the languages belonging to the *Algonquian* branch. Here, we shall treat *Wiyot* and *Yurok* as being separate branches of this family; the rest of the subgrouping follows Goddard (1992, 1:44–8).

1. WIYOT

Wiyot is now extinct, the last speaker having died in 1962. It used to be spoken in northwestern California.

2. YUROK

Yurok is spoken by 10 or fewer speakers in northwestern California.

3. ALGONKIAN

This is subdivided into three major branches.

a. Eastern

The major languages in this group are *Micmac* (around 8,100 sp., of which 6,000 are in Nova Scotia, Prince Edward Island, New Brunswick, and Quebec provinces of Canada, 2,000 in Boston, Massachusetts, and 10 to 100 in New York City) and *Maliseet-Passamaquoddy* (around 1,500 sp. in New Brunswick, Canada, and Maine, United States).

b. Central

This group includes *Central Cree* (4,500 sp. from James Bay, Ontario, north-westward in Manitoba, Canada), *Coastal Eastern Cree* (around 5,000 sp. in Quebec, Canada), *Inland Eastern Cree* (around 2,200 sp. in Quebec, Canada), *Western Cree* (around 35,000 sp. in north central Manitoba, westward into Saskatchewan and Alberta, Canada, and in Montana, United States), *Montag-nais* (around 7,000 sp. on the north shore of the Gulf of St. Lawrence, along the St. Lawrence River, and in Labrador, Quebec, Canada), *Eastern Ojibwa* (around 8,000 sp. around Lake Huron and southeastern Ontario, Canada), *Northern Ojibwa* (around 8,000 sp. in Manitoba and northern Ontario, Canada), *Western Ojibwa* (around 35,000 sp. from Lake Superior westward and northwestward into Saskatchewan, Canada, and from Lake Superior to North Dakota and Montana in the United States; in Canada, there are outly-ing groups as far west as British Columbia), *Algonkin* (around 3,000 sp. in southwestern Quebec and adjacent areas of Ontario, Canada), *Menominee* (50 sp. in northeastern Wisconsin), *Potowatomi* (500 sp. in Michigan, Wiscon-sin, Kansas, and Oklahoma, United States, and in Ontario, Canada), *Fox* (800 sp. in Iowa, on the Kansas-Nebraska border, and in central Oklahoma), *Kick-apoo* (around 1,200 sp., of which 500 are in Coahuilla, Mexico, and the rest in northeastern Kansas and central Oklahoma), and *Shawnee* (200 sp. in central and northeastern Oklahoma).

c. Plains

This group consists of *Blackfoot* (around 9,000 sp. in southern Alberta, Canada, and in Montana, United States), *Arapaho* (around 1,500 sp. in Wyoming), *Atsina* or *Gros Ventre* (10 or fewer sp. in north central Montana), and *Cheyenne* (around 2,000 sp. in southeastern Montana and in western Oklahoma).

IV. MUSKOGEAN FAMILY

According to Haas (1979:303), this family is divided into two branches.

1. WESTERN MUSKOGEAN

This consists of *Choctaw-Chickasaw* (12,000 sp. in southeastern Oklahoma and central Mississippi.

2. EASTERN MUSKOGEAN

This branch includes *Alabama-Koasati* (700 sp. in southeastern Texas and southwestern Louisiana, *Mikasuki* or *Hitchiti* (around 1,000 sp. in southern Florida), and *Muskogee* (around 10,000 sp. mainly in east central Oklahoma). *Muskogee* is spoken by the Creek and Seminole tribes; some Seminoles are also found in Florida, and some Creek are found in southern Alabama.)

V. Natchez Isolate

This language is now extinct. The last speakers were located in Oklahoma.

VI. Atakapa Isolate

This language also is now extinct. It used to be spoken in southwestern Louisiana.

VII. Chitimacha Isolate

The *Chitimacha* language is now extinct. There are about 300 Chitimacha Indians living in southern Louisiana.

VIII. Tunica Isolate

Tunica is now extinct. It was originally spoken in central Louisiana.

Muskogean, Natchez, Atakapa, Chitimacha, and *Tunica* have been considered by some linguists to belong to a language family called "Gulf," but at present there is no clear evidence for such a grouping.

IX. Tonkawa Isolate

This language also is now almost extinct as there are no more fluent speakers left of the language. It was spoken in north central Oklahoma.

X. Siouan Family

This family, according to Rood (1992b, 3:449–52) is divided into following groups.

1. Southeastern

This group consists of *Ofo, Biloxi,* and *Tutelo,* which are all extinct but were once spoken from western Carolinas to Louisiana.

2. Mississippi Valley

This group is in turn subdivided into four subbranches.

a. Dhegiha

This subbranch includes: *Quapaw* (now extinct), *Osage* (25 elderly fluent sp. and few semifluent ones in north central Oklahoma), *Kansa* (few, if any sp. left in north central Oklahoma), and *Omaha-Ponca* (around 1,500 sp. of *Omaha* in eastern Nebraska, and 25 fluent elderly sp. of *Ponca* in north central Oklahoma).

b. Chiwere

This subbranch includes *Iowa* (20 elderly sp. in north central Oklahoma and northeastern Kansas) and *Oto* (50 sp. in north central Oklahoma).

c. Winnebago

This consists of one language: *Winnebago* has around 1,500 speakers in central Wisconsin and eastern Nebraska.

d. Dakotan

This group includes *Dakota* (around 19,000 sp. in Nebraska, Minnesota, North and South Dakota, and Montana, and in southern Manitoba and Saskatchewan, Canada), *Lakota* (around 6,000 sp. in Nebraska, Minnesota, and North and South Dakota), *Assiniboin* (150 to 200 fluent sp. in central Alberta and west central Saskatchewan, Canada, and in Montana), and *Stoney* (1,000 to 1,500 sp. in Alberta, Canada).

3. MANDAN

Mandan has only six elderly speakers in North Dakota.

4. MISSOURI RIVER

This includes *Hidatsa* (125 sp. in North Dakota) and *Crow* (around 5,500 sp. in southern Montana).

Siouan languages tend to have SOV as their basic word order. *Dhegiha* languages have developed typologically rare contrasts in stops: *lenis* (or voiced in some languages), *fortis unaspirated* (geminate intervocalically), *aspirated,* and *glottalized.* In *Chiwere* and *Dhegiha* branches there is a system of definite articles that mark the position of the NP to which they are attached according to the NP in question is standing, sitting, lying down, or moving.

XI. IROQUOIAN FAMILY

According to Marianne Mithun (1992, 2:233–6), this family is divided into two branches.

1. SOUTHERN

This branch is represented by a single language: *Cherokee* (also called *Tsalagi*), spoken by about 11,000 speakers, of which 10,000 are in northeastern Oklahoma and 1,100 in western North Carolina).

2. NORTHERN

This branch includes, among others, the following: *Cayuga* (380 sp. in Six Nations, Ontario, Canada, and in New York and Oklahoma), *Mohawk* (about 3,000 sp. in southwestern Quebec and southern Ontario, Canada, and in northern New York), *Oneida* (250 sp. in central New York and eastern Wisconsin), *Onondaga* (100 sp. in southern Ontario, Canada, and south of Syracuse, New York), *Seneca* (200 sp. in western New York, and mixed with Cayuga in northeastern Oklahoma; also spoken on the Six Nations Reserve in Ontario, Canada), *Tuscarora* (30 elderly sp. on the Six Nations Reserve in Ontario, Canada, and near Niagara Falls, New York), and *Huron* (once a very important language, now extinct; originally spoken in the Great Lakes area of Canada and in northeastern Oklahoma).

Iroquoian languages are somewhat unusual in that they lack bilabial consonant phonemes. The Oklahoma dialect of *Cherokee* is reported to have developed contrasting tones. The languages are polysynthetic; verbs, especially, have elaborate morphological structure.

XII. CADDOAN FAMILY

Caddoan was originally represented by languages covering central United States from Dakota to northern Louisiana and Texas but is now represented by only four surviving languages: *Arikara* (200 sp. in northern Dakota), *Caddo* (300 speakers in western Oklahoma), *Pawnee* (200 sp. in Oklahoma), and *Wichita* (50 sp. in west central Oklahoma).

Chafe (1973:1189–98) presented some evidence that *Siouan, Iroquian,* and *Caddoan* may be distantly related. Campbell and Mithun (1979:41), however, feel that the evidence presented so far is not compelling and that more work needs to be done.

XIII. YUCHI ISOLATE

Yuchi is spoken by 50 speakers who live among Creek-speaking people in central Oklahoma.

XIV. YUMAN FAMILY

This family is divided into two major branches.

1. DELTA-CALIFORNIAN

Major languages belonging to this branch are *Cocopa* (450 sp. in Baja California, Mexico, as well as some in Arizona), *Diegeño* (350 to 400 sp. in Baja California, Mexico, and possibly 50 to 100 in California), and *Paipai* (240 sp. in northern Baja California, Mexico).

2. RIVER YUMAN

Major languages belonging to this group are *Mojave* (700 sp. on the California-Arizona border), *Quechan* or *Yuma* (500 sp. in southeastern California), and *Upland Yuman* (about 1,200 sp. in central and northwestern Arizona).

This family may be related to *Pomoan* family. (cf. XVI.)

XV. SERI ISOLATE

Seri is spoken by 500 speakers on Sonora coast, Mexico.

XVI. POMOAN FAMILY

Pomo is spoken in a variety of dialects, many of which may be separate languages, by 100 or fewer speakers in northern California. This family may be related to *Yuman*.

XVII. PALAIHNIHAN FAMILY

This family is almost extinct since both languages constituting this family are spoken by very few people: *Achumawi* (10 sp. in California) and *Atsugewi* (4 sp., all over 50, in northeastern California).

XVIII. SHASTAN FAMILY

Only one language of this family survives: *Shasta* (10 or fewer sp. in northern California). Possible genetic relationship of this family to *Palaihnihan* family is a controversial issue according to Campbell and Mithun (1979:41).

XIX. YANAN FAMILY

This family is extinct. It included *Yahi* (formerly spoken in the upper Sacramento Valley).

XX. CHIMARIKO ISOLATE

This language is extinct. It was formerly spoken in northwestern California.

XXI. WASHO ISOLATE

Washo is spoken by 100 speakers on the California-Nevada border southeast of Lake Tahoe.

XXII. SALINAN FAMILY

This language family is now extinct. Two Salinan languages were originally spoken on the central coast of California.

XXIII. KAROK ISOLATE

Karok or *Karuk* is spoken by 100 speakers in northwestern California along the Klamath River.

Yuman, Seri, Pomoan, Palaihnihan, Shastan, Yanan, Washo, Chimariko, Salinan, and *Karok* are considered by some to be "Core *Hokan*" languages. Campbell and Mithun (1979:42) feel that it is an open question whether any of these languages are genetically related.

XXIV. CHUMASHAN FAMILY

This family is now extinct. Languages belonging to it were once spoken on the coast of southern California.

XXV. COTONAME ISOLATE

This is an extinct language spoken originally in southern Texas and northwestern Mexico.

XXVI. COMECRUDO ISOLATE

This is an extinct language originally spoken in Tamaulipas, Mexico.

XXVII. COAHUILTECO ISOLATE

This language, now extinct, was spoken in southern Texas in the eighteenth century.

XXVIII. ARANAMA-TAMIQUE ISOLATE

This language, originally spoken in Texas, is now extinct.

XXIX. SOLANO ISOLATE

This language is also extinct. It was spoken in Texas.

XXX. ESSELEN ISOLATE

This language, now extinct, used to be spoken near Carmel, on the coast of central California. Data on this language is insufficient to establish genetic ties of this language to any others.

XXXI. Jicaque Family

Tol or *Jicaque* is spoken in Honduras by 250 to 300 speakers. This family is probably related to the *Tequistlatecan* family. (Cf. XXXIII.)

XXXII. Subtiaba-Tlapanec Family

This family consists of *Subtiaba,* spoken originally in Nicaragua, which is now extinct; and *Tlapanec,* which is spoken by 40,000 speakers in Guerrero, Mexico.

Campbell and Mithun (1979:42) consider that genetic relationship of this family with the so-called Hokan languages cannot be established, in spite of Sapir's claims to the contrary. Instead, they suggest that this group may perhaps be related to the *Otomanguean* languages of Meso-America.

XXXIII. Tequistlatecan Family

This includes *Highland Tequistlatec* (around 5,000 sp. in southeastern Oaxaca State, Mexico) and *Lowland Tequistlatec* (4,000 to 5,000 sp. in southeastern Oaxaca State, Mexico). This family and *Jicaque* family are probably related.

Language groups from XIV to XXXIII have all been classified earlier as being branches of the Hokan language family, but Campbell and Mithun (1979:43) consider the evidence for this family to be extremely tenuous.

XXXIV. Yokuts Family

This family consists of several closely related languages lumped together under the name of *Yokuts. Chukchansi Yokuts* seems to be the only surviving language. It is spoken by 10 or fewer speakers in southern San Joaquin Valley and Sierra foothills, California.

XXXV. Maiduan Family

Only one language survives in this group: *Maidu* (20 elderly sp. in western foothills of northern Sierras, California).

XXXVI. Wintuan Family

The languages belonging to this family, *Nomlaki, Patwin,* and *Wintu,* are all spoken by very few speakers in Sacramento Valley, California.

XXXVII. Miwok Family

The only surviving language, *Miwok,* is spoken by 10 or fewer speakers from Marin County to the Central Valley and southern Sierra foothills, California.

XXXVIII. Costanoan Family

This family is now extinct. Languages belonging to this family were once spoken in coastal central California from San Francisco Bay southward.

XXXIX. Klamath-Modoc Isolate

Klamath-Modoc is spoken by 150 speakers in south central Oregon.

XL. Sahaptian Family

This family includes *Nez Perce* (500 sp. in northern Idaho), *Tenino* (200 sp. in Oregon), *Umatilla* (about 50 sp. in Oregon), *Walla Walla* (100 sp. in Oregon), and *Yakima* (around 3,000 sp. in south central Washington state).

XLI. Cayuse Isolate

This language was formerly spoken in Washington and Oregon near the headwaters of Wallawalla, Umatilla, and Grande Ronde rivers.

XLII. Molala Isolate

Molala or *Molale* was originally spoken in Washington and Oregon in the valley of Deschutes River.

XLIII. Coos Family

This family is now probably extinct since only 1 or 2 elderly speakers were reported in 1962 on the southern Oregon coast.

XLIV. Alsea Isolate

This is an extinct language once spoken on the Oregon coast.

XLV. Siuslaw-Lower Umpqua Isolate

Siuslaw-Lower Umpqua is spoken by 1 or 2 speakers on southern Oregon coast.

XLVI. Takelma Isolate

This extinct language was once spoken in southwestern Oregon.

XLVII. KALAPUYA FAMILY

Kalapuya is now probably extinct as only 1 or 2 speakers, over 50 years old, were found in 1962 in northwestern Oregon.

XLVIII. CHINOOKAN FAMILY

This consists of two languages: *Chinook* (now extinct, formerly spoken on the lower Columbia River, Oregon and Washington) and *Wasco-Wishram* (10 sp. in north central Oregon and south central Washington). *Chinook* was the basis of *Chinook jargon,* a pidgin, which served as an important trade language among different native peoples living in northwestern United States and British Columbia, Canada.

XLIX. TSIMSHIAN ISOLATE

Tsimshian is spoken by 1,435 mother tongue speakers on the northern coast of British Columbia, Canada, and Alaskan coast. *Tsimshian* is closely related to *Nass-Gitskan* (2,500 sp. in west central British Columbia, Canada).

L. ZUNI LANGUAGE ISOLATE

Zuni or *Zuñi* isolate is spoken by 5,000 speakers in New Mexico, south of Gallup.

The language groups from XXXIV to L are considered by some to form the Macro-Penutian language family. According to Campbell and Mithun (1979:44–5), although some of the California groups may turn out to be genetically related, it is very doubtful that genetic connections with the rest of Penutian languages (which in addition to the language groups listed here are supposed to include *Mayan, Mixe-Zoquean,* and *Totonacan* as well as some languages spoken in South America as far as Chile) can be firmly established.

LI. KIOWA-TANOAN FAMILY

Kiowa-Tanoan includes *Kiowa* (Oklahoma, 2,000 sp.), *Tiwa* and *Towa* (each spoken by 2,000 sp. in central New Mexico), and *Tolowa* (spoken by 1,000 sp. in New Mexico).

LII. UTO-AZTECAN FAMILY

According to Miller (1992, 4:212), there is some controversy about the genetic subclassification of this family. Some linguists prefer to recognize only three major branches (*Shoshonean, Sonoran,* and *Aztecan*), whereas others prefer to recognize up to nine primary branches, splitting the subbranches within Sonoran and Shoshonean branches into separate branches of Uto-Aztecan. Here we shall follow the former classification without necessarily claiming that it is more correct than the alternative one.

1. SHOSHONEAN

This branch has the following subbranches.

a. Numic

This subbranch consists of the following languages in addition to some others: *Mono* (20 sp. in east central California reported in 1977, all elderly), *Shoshone* (around 3,000 sp. in Nevada, Idaho, and Wyoming), *Comanche,* (500 sp. in western Oklahoma), *Kawaiisu* (10 or fewer sp. reported in 1962, all of them over 50 years of age, south central California), and *Ute-Southern Paiute* (around 2,500 sp.; *Ute* in Colorado and Utah, *Southern Paiute* in Utah, Arizona, and Nevada, *Chemehuevi* on the lower Colorado River, California).

b. Tubatulabal

This subbranch consists of a single language: *Tubatulabal* (spoken by 6 or fewer sp. in southern California, reported in 1972, all over 50 years of age).

c. Takic

This subbranch includes *Serrano* (now very likely extinct, but spoken until recently in southern California), *Cahuilla* (50 sp. in southern California), and *Luiseño* (100 sp. in southern California).

d. Hopi

This subbranch contains only one language: *Hopi* (spoken by around 5,000 sp. in northeastern Arizona).

2. SONORAN

This branch has the following subbranches.

a. Cáhita

This subbranch consists of *Mayo* (spoken by around 50,000 sp. in coastal Sonora and Sinaloa, Mexico) and *Yaqui* (spoken by 17,000 to 25,000 sp., of which 12,000 or more are in Mexico and 5,000 or more in Arizona).

b. Corachol

This subbranch consists of *Cora* (spoken by around 15,000 sp. in Nayarit, Mexico) and *Huichol* (spoken by 12,500 or more sp. in Nayarit and Jalisco, Mexico).

c. Opatan

The languages of this subbranch are all extinct. They were once spoken in northwestern Mexico.

d. Tepiman

This subbranch includes *Papago-Pima* (around 15,000 sp. in south central Arizona and adjacent Mexico), *Chihuahua Pima Bajo* (spoken by 1,000 or more sp. on the central Sonora-Chihuahua border area, Mexico), *Sonora Pima Bajo* (spoken by about 1,000 sp. in scattered groups on the central Sonora-Chihuahua border area, Mexico), *Northern Tepehuán* (5,000 to 8,000 sp. in southern Chihuahua, Mexico), *Southeastern Tepehuán* (5,000 or more sp. in southern Durango, Mexico), and *Southwestern Tepehuán* (4,000 to 6,000 sp. in southwestern Durango, Mexico). *Tepehuan* languages are tonal, but most Uto-Aztecan languages are not.

e. Tarahumaran

This subbranch consists of the following languages. *Guarijío* (2,000 to 3,000 sp. in the western Sierra Madre of Chihuahua and Sonora, Mexico), *Central Tarahumara* (30,000 to 40,000 sp. in southwestern Chihuahua, Mexico), *Northern Tarahumara* (500 or more sp. in Chihuahua, Mexico), *Southwest Tarahumara* (100 or fewer sp. in Chihuahua, Mexico), and *Western Tarahumara* (5,000 to 10,000 sp. in Chihuahua, Mexico).

3. AZTECAN

a. Nahuatl

This subbranch contains a large number of languages including *Classical Aztec,* which was the chief language of the Aztec empire at the time of Spanish conquest. The modern languages belonging to this subgroup are all varieties of *Nahuatl.* Here only the major *Nahuatl* languages will be listed.

Guerrero Nahuatl (80,000 to 90,000 sp. in Guerrero, Mexico), *Eastern Huasteca Nahuatl* (around 410,000 sp. in Hidalgo, Puebla, and Vera Cruz, Mexico), *Western Huasteca Nahuatl* (around 300,000 sp. in San Luis Potosí and Hidalgo, Mexico), *Isthmus Nahuatl* (16,000 to 20,000 sp. in southern Veracruz, Mexico), *Morelos Nahuatl* (80,000 to 90,000 sp. in Morelos, Mexico), *North Puebla Nahuatl* (55,000 to 60,000 sp. in northern Puebla, Mexico), *Orizaba Nahuatl* (90,000 to 100,000 sp. in Veracruz, Mexico), *Sierra de Puebla Nahuatl* (around 125,000 sp. in northeastern Puebla, Mexico), and *Southeast Puebla Nahuatl* (30,000 to 50,000 sp. in southeastern Puebla, Mexico).

b. Pipil

This consists of a single language: *Pipil* (around 20 elderly sp. out of 190,000 ethnic group in El Salvador).

c. Pochutec

Pochuteco is an extinct language formerly spoken in Pochutlán, Oaxaca, Mexico.

There are also some who recognize an extra branch consisting of one language, *Giamina,* but since Giamina is extinct and there is little data on it, there is not much basis for this claim.

In general, grammatical structure of languages belonging to this family is less elaborate than, for example, that of the Na-Dene languages. Most of the languages are agglutinative in type and have elaborate suffixation. The Shoshonean languages are strongly verb-final, and it is believed that this feature ought to be reconstructed for Proto-Uto-Aztecan.

Evidence for the genetic relationship of this language family to the *Kiowa-Tanoan* language family is "disappointingly inconclusive" according to Campbell and Mithun (1979:45).

LIII. KERESAN FAMILY

This family consists of two languages: *Eastern Keresan* (around 4,000 sp. in north central New Mexico) and *Western Keresan* (around 4,500 in north central New Mexico). There is a possibility that this family may be related to the *Uto-Aztecan* language family.

LIV. YUKIAN FAMILY

This family consists of two languages: *Wappo* (1 sp. north of San Francisco Bay, California) and *Yuki* (now probably extinct; originally spoken in northern California).

LV. BEOTHUK ISOLATE

Since this language (originally spoken in Newfoundland, Canada) became extinct very early there is too little data on this language to permit reliable classification. Some scholars speculate that it was an Algonquian language.

LVI. KUTENAI ISOLATE

Kutenai is spoken by a total of 200 speakers in southeastern British Columbia. This language isolate may be distantly related to the Salish family. (Cf. LIX.)

LVII. KARANKAWA ISOLATE

This language isolate is now extinct. It was originally spoken in Texas.

LVIII. CHIMAKUAN FAMILY

This family includes two languages: *Chimakum* (now extinct, but formerly spoken on the Olympic Peninsula in the state of Washington) and *Quileute* (possibly 10 sp. on the Olympic Peninsula, Washington).

LIX. SALISH FAMILY

According to Kinkade (1992, 3:359–63), this family is divided into five branches.

1. BELLA COOLA

This branch consists of a single language: *Bella Coola* (fewer than 50 sp. on the central British Columbia coast, Canada).

2. CENTRAL SALISH

Excluding the extinct languages, this branch includes *Comox-Sliammon* (400 sp. in British Columbia, Canada, most of them middle-aged or older), *Clallam* (fewer than 20 sp., all elderly, on northeastern portion of the Olympic Peninsula, Washington), *Halkomelem* (500 sp. in southwestern British Columbia, Canada), *Lushootseed* or *Puget Sound Salish* (60 sp. or fewer in the Puget Sound area, Washington), *Sechelt* (fewer than 40 sp. on the British Columbia coast north of Vancouver, Canada), *Squamish* (fewer than 20 sp., all middle-aged or older, in southwestern British Columbia, Canada), and *Straits Salish* (fewer than 30 sp., all elderly, on southeastern Vancouver Island, Canada, and the adjoining portions of Washington state).

3. INTERIOR SALISH

Coeur d'Alene (20 or fewer sp. in northern Idaho), *Columbian* (75 or fewer sp. in north central Washington state), *Kalispel-Flathead* (800 sp. in northeastern Washington and northwestern Montana), *Spokane* (fewer than 50 sp. in northeastern Washington; closely related to the preceding language), *Lillooet* (300 to 400 sp. in southern British Columbia, Canada), *Okanagan-Colville* (500 sp. in south central British Columbia, Canada, and on the Colville Reservation in Washington state), *Shuswap* (500 sp. in south central British Columbia, Canada), and *Thompson* (fewer than 50 sp. in south central British Columbia, Canada).

4. TILLAMOOK

This branch consists of a single language: *Tillamook* (extinct since 1970; originally spoken in northwestern Oregon).

5. TSAMOSAN

Lower Chehalis (fewer than 5 sp. on southwestern coast of Washington state), *Upper Chehalis* (maximum 2 sp. in Washington state, south of Puget Sound), *Cowlitz* (possibly 2 sp. remaining in southwestern Washington state), and *Quinalt* (fewer than 6 sp. on the Pacific side of the Olympic Peninsula, Washington).

Most Salish languages are spoken only by small numbers of speakers, most of whom are middle-aged or older.

Salish languages, especially the *Interior Salish* languages, have very rich consonantal systems (glottalized ejectives, uvular consonants, pharyngeal resonants, voiceless laterals). Several Interior Salish languages have in addition glottalized resonant consonants and pharyngeal resonant consonants. The grammar of these languages is very complicated and shows clear polysynthetic tendencies.

Salish languages belonging to branches other than Interior Salish tend to be simpler phonologically and seem to have been strongly influenced by their non-Salish neighbors.

Sapir considered this family as well as the following one *(Wakeshan)* to be distantly related to Algonquian, but there is no convincing evidence that he was correct in this hypothesis. Campbell and Mithun (1979) do not even bother mentioning this hypothesis in their list.

LX. WAKASHAN

Wakashan languages are spoken by a total of about 4,000 speakers on Vancouver Island and the adjacent coast of British Columbia. Chief representatives of this family are *Nootka* (1,800 speakers) and *Kwakiutl* (1,000 speakers). These languages exhibit a number of similarities with their Salish neighbors in structure and phonology. (As already mentioned, Sapir considered *Wakashan* to be related to both *Salish* and *Macro-Algonquian*.)

LXI. TIMUCUA ISOLATE

This language is now extinct. It was spoken formerly in Florida.

LXII. ADAI ISOLATE

This language is also extinct. It is mentioned by Spanish explorers of the sixteenth century and later by others as being spoken from the Red River in Louisiana southward beyond the Sabine River in Texas.

Although this language is usually listed as belonging to the *Caddoan* family, it is so poorly known that available data do not support any kind of genetic classification of this language.

B. LANGUAGES OF MESO-AMERICA[2]

Besides the Meso-American languages and language families listed in this section, there are following language families represented in the region: *Uto-Aztecan* (listed with the language families of North America), *Chibchan* (listed with the language families of South America), and *Misumalpan* (also listed with the languages of South America).

I. Oto-Manguean Family

The languages belonging to this family are spoken exclusively in Central America, for the most part in Central Mexico. According to Campbell (1979:915–6), this family is subdivided into the following branches.

1. Amuzgoan

This branch consists of two languages: *Guerrero Amuzgo* (around 25,000 sp. in southeastern Guerrero, Mexico) and *Oaxaca Amuzgo* (5,000 to 7,500 sp. in southwestern Oaxaca, Mexico).

2. Chiapanec-Mangue

The languages belonging to this branch are now both extinct. They were spoken in Chiapas, Mexico, and in Costa Rica.

3. Chinantecan

This branch includes 14 languages of which the following are the major ones: *Lalana Chinanteco* (around 10,000 sp. on the Oaxaca-Vercruz border, Mexico), *Ojitlán Chinanteco* (around 10,000 sp. in northern Oaxaca, Mexico), *Palantla Chinanteco* (around 10,600 sp. in Oaxaca, Mexico), *Quiotepec Chinanteco* (around 5,000 sp. in northwestern Oaxaca, Mexico), and *Usila Chinanteco* (around 10,000 sp. in Oaxaca, Mexico).

4. Mixtecan

This branch contains a very large number of languages of which the following ones have the largest number of speakers: *Teuitila Cuicateco* (16,000 to 20,000 sp. in northwestern Oaxaca, Mexico), *Eastern Mixteco* (12,000 to 14,000 sp. in west central Oaxaca, Mexico), *Eastern Jamiltepec-Chayuco Mixteco* (around 30,000 sp. in southwestern Oaxaca, Mexico), *Eastern Juxtlahuaca Mixteco* (14,500 to 15,000 sp. in Oaxaca, Mexico), *Highland Guerrero Mixteco* (around 10,000 sp. in eastern Guerrero, Mexico), *Metlatonoc Mixteco* (10,000 to 15,000 sp. in eastern Guerrero, Mexico), *Northern Tlaxiaco Mixteco* (around 10,000 sp. in Oaxaca, Mexico), *San Juan Colorado Mixteco* (around 12,000 sp. in Oaxaca, Mexico), *Santiago Yosondua Mixteco* (around 15,000 sp. in Oaxaca, Mexico), *Silacayoapan Mixteco* (around 15,000 sp. in Oaxaca, Mexico), and *Western Jamiltepec Mixteco* (10,000 to 15,000 sp. in Oaxaca, Mexico).

5. Otopamean

This branch is further subdivided into three subbranches.

a. Chichimec

The language representing this branch is *Chichimeca-Jonaz* (around 1,200 sp. in Guanajuato, Mexico).

b. Otomian

This branch is represented primarily by *Mazahua* (250,000 to 400,000 sp. in the states of México and Michoacán, and in the Federal District, Mexico), *Eastern Otomí* (17,500 to 20,000 sp. in Huehuetla, Hidalgo, Mexico), *Mezquital Otomí* (80,000 to 100,000 sp. in Mezquital valley, Hidalgo, Mexico), *Northwestern Otomí* (30,000 to 40,000 sp. in Querétaro, Guanajuato, Hidalgo, and the state of México, Mexico), *Temoaya Otomí* (30,000 or more sp. in the state of México, Mexico), and *Tenango Otomí* (8,000 to 10,000 sp. in Hidalgo and Puebla states, Mexico).

c. Pame

This consists of *Central Chichimeca Pame* (around 3,000 sp. in San Luis Potosí, Mexico) and *Northern Chichimeca Pame* (1,000 to 2,000 sp. in San Luis Potosí, Mexico).

6. POPOLOCAN

The major languages belonging to this group are *Huautla de Jiménez* (50,000 to 60,000 sp. in northern Oaxaca, Mexico), *San Felipe Jalapa de Díaz Mazatec* (10,000 to 15,000 sp. in northern Oaxaca and Veracruz, Mexico), *San Jerónimo Tecoatl Mazatec* (around 40,000 sp. in Oaxaca, Mexico), and *Western Popoloca* (around 10,000 sp. in Puebla, Mexico).

7. ZAPOTECAN

A very large number of languages belong to this branch. The major ones are *Nopala Chatino* (around 10,000 sp. in southeastern Oaxaca, Mexico), *Zenzontepec Chatino* (around 10,000 sp. in southeastern Oaxaca, Mexico), *Central Miahuatlán Zapotec* (around 80,000 sp. in south central Oaxaca, Mexico), *Central Tlacolula Zapotec* (around 15,000 sp. in Mitla Valley, Oaxaca, Mexico), *Choapan Zapotec* (around 17,000 sp. in north central Oaxaca, Mexico), *Isthmus Zapotec* (around 75,000 sp. in the Isthmus of Tehuantepec, Oaxaca, Mexico), *Northern Villa Alta Zapotec* (around 15,000 sp. in north Oaxaca, Mexico), *Western Ocotlán Zapotec* (around 20,000 sp. in central Oaxaca), and *Western Tlacolula Zapotec* (around 30,000 sp. in central Oaxaca, Mexico).

Most of Oto-Manguean languages are tonal and have nasal vowels. In addition they tend to have a verb-initial sentence structure.

II. TOTONACAN FAMILY

According to Campbell (1979:924–6), this family has two major branches.

1. TOTONAC

The major languages belonging to this branch are *Coyutla Totonac* (30,000 to 40,000 sp. in Puebla, Mexico), *Filomeno Mata-Coahuitlan Totonac* (10,000 to 12,000 sp. in Veracruz, Mexico), *Northern Totonac* (10,000 sp. or more in northeastern Puebla and in Veracruz, Mexico), *Papantla Totonac* (around

80,000 sp. in Veracruz, Mexico), and *Sierra Totonac* (around 120,000 sp. in Puebla and Veracruz, Mexico).

2. TEPEHUA

This branch consists of three languages: *Huehuetla Tepehua* (around 3,000 sp. in northeastern Hidalgo, Mexico), *Pisa Flores Tepehua* (2,000 to 2,500 sp. in Puebla, Mexico), and *Veracruz Tepehua* (3,000 to 4,000 sp. in Veracruz, Mexico).

III. MIXE-ZOQUEAN FAMILY

According to Campbell (1979:902–1000), this family is divided into two major branches.

1. MIXE

This is subdivided into the following subbranches.

a. Eastern

This branch is represented by several languages of which the major ones are *Coatlán Mixe* (around 5,000 sp. in east central Oaxaca, Mexico), *Guichicovi Mixe* (15,000 to 18,000 sp. in northeastern Oaxaca, Mexico), and *Juquila Mixe* (around 8,500 sp. in east central Oaxaca, Mexico).

b. Tapachultec

The *Tapachultec* language is now extinct. It used to be spoken in southern Chiapas, Mexico.

c. Veracruz Mixe

This branch consists of two languages: *Oluta* (100 to 200 sp. in southeastern Veracruz, Mexico) and *Sayula* (around 6,000 sp. in Veracruz, Mexico).

d. Western

This consists of *Tlahuitoltepec Mixe* (around 8,000 sp. in northeastern Oaxaca, Mexico) and *Totontepe Mixe* (around 6,000 sp. in northeastern Oaxaca, Mexico).

2. ZOQUE

This is further subdivided into three subbranches.

a. Chiapas Zoque

This consists of three languages: *Copainalá Zoque* (around 5,650 sp. in Chiapas, Mexico), *Francisco León Zoque* (around 5,000 sp. in Chiapas, Mexico), and *Rayón Zoque* (around 1,200 sp. in Chiapas, Mexico).

b. Oaxaca Zoque

This is represented by one language: *Santa Maria Chimalpa* (5,000 to 6,000 sp. in Oaxaca, Mexico).

c. Veracruz Zoque

This consists of three languages of which the most important one is *Sierra Popoluca* (around 25,000 sp. in Veracruz, Mexico).

IV. MAYAN FAMILY

This family has the following branches.

1. CHOLAN-TZELTLALAN

This branch is subdivided into two subbranches.

a. Cholan

This subgroup consists of *Chol* (about 90,000 sp. in Chiapas, Mexico; spoken in two varieties) and *Chontal of Tabasco* (30,000 to 40,000 sp. in Tabasco, Mexico).

b. Tzeltlalan

This subbranch includes *Bachajón Tzeltal* (around 20,000 sp. in Chiapas, Mexico), *Highland Tzeltal* (about 25,000 sp. in Chiapas, Mexico), *Southeastern Tzeltal* (about 500 sp. in Chiapas, Mexico), *Chamula Tzotzil* (50,000 sp. in Chiapas, Mexico), *Chenalhó Tzotzil* (around 10,000 sp. in Chiapas, Mexico), *Huixtán Tzotzil* (5,000 to 7,000 sp. in Chiapas, Mexico), *San Andrés Larrainzar Tzotzil* (30,000 sp. in Chiapas, Mexico), and *Zinacanteco Tzotzil* (10,000 sp. in Chiapas, Mexico).

2. HUASTECAN

This subbranch consists of *San Luis Potosí Huastec* (around 38,300 sp. in San Luis Potosí, Mexico) and *Veracruz Huastec* (around 35,000 sp. in Veracruz, Mexico).

3. KANJOBALAN-CHUJEAN

This branch is subdivided into two subbranches.

a. Chujean

This consists of *Chuj* (about 25,000 tot. sp. of two varieties, mostly in Guatemala, about 2,000 in Chiapas, Mexico) and *Tojolabal* (about 40,000 sp. in Chiapas, Mexico).

b. Kanjobalan

Acatec (about 18,000 sp. in Guatemala), *Eastern Jacaltec* (around 6,000 sp. in Guatemala on the border with Mexico), *Western Jacaltec* (9,800 to 10,000 in Guatemala, a few in Chiapas, Mexico), *Kanjobal* (around 60,000 sp. in Huehutenango department in Guatemala), and *Mochó* (500 sp. in Chiapas on the border between Guatemala and Mexico).

4. QUICHEAN-MAMEAN

This branch is further subdivided into two subbranches.

a. Mamean

This includes *Aguacatec* (about 20,000 sp. in Guatemala), *Ixil* (55,000 tot. sp. of different dialects, in Guatemala), and *Mam* group: *Northern Mam* (126,000 sp. mostly in Guatemala and about 1,000 in Mexico), *San Martín Sacatepéquez Mam* (about 8,000 sp. in northwestern Guatemala), *Southern Mam* (around 100,000 sp. in Guatemala and about 20,000 sp. in Chiapas, Mexico), *Todos Santos Cuchumatán* (around 16,000 sp. in Guatemala), and *Western Mam* (around 10,000 sp. in Guatemala).

b. Quichean

This includes *Cakchiquel,* which has a number of varieties. Only the major ones will be listed here: *Central Cakchiquel* (around 126,000 sp. in southern Guatemala), *Eastern Cakchiquel* (around 100,000 sp. near Guatemala City), *South Central Cakchiquel* (around 56,000 sp. west of Guatemala City), *Southern Cakchiquel* (around 42,000 sp. south of Antigua, Guatemala), and *Western Cakchiquel* (around 69,200 sp. on the northern and eastern shores of Lake Atitlán, Guatemala.

In addition, it includes *Kekchí* (272,000 to 282,000 tot. sp. mostly in Guatemala, about 20,000 or fewer in Belize), *Eastern Pokomchí* (around 20,000 sp. in Baja Verapaz department, Guatemala), *Western Pokomchí* (around 28,000 sp. around San Cristobal, Guatemala), *Central Quiché* (210,000 sp. in Guatemala), *Coastal Quiché* (around 152,000 sp. in Guatemala), *Cunén Quiché* (around 5,000 sp. in Quiché department, Guatemala), *Eastern Quiché* (around 13,000 sp. in Quiché department, Guatemala), *Joyabaj Quiché* (around 40,000 sp. in Quiché department, Guatemala), *West Central Quiché* (around 355,000 sp. in Guatemala), *Western Quiché* (around 99,000 sp. in Quezaltenango and Totonicapan departments, Guatemala), *Eastern Tzutujil* (around 25,000 sp. on the southern shore of Lake Atitlán, Guatemala), and *Western Tzutujil* (around 25,000 sp. on the southwestern shore of the same lake in Guatemala).

5. YUCATECAN

This includes *Yucatec* (500,000 sp. mostly in Mexico on the Yucatan peninsula, some in Belize), *Mopán Maya* (8,000 sp. of whom 6,000 are in Belize and the rest in Guatemala), and *Lacandón* (about 550 sp. in northeastern Chiapas, Mexico).

Ancient Mayas were the only native American people who developed a writing system before the coming of the Europeans. This script, which has been deciphered relatively recently, began as a logographic system that eventually evolved into a syllabic system whose signs typically had a CV value. Closed syllables (CVC) were written with two CV signs in which case the vowel of the second sign was silent but was chosen to match the vowel of the root. For example, the Yucatec word *ku:ts* 'turkey' was spelled *ku-tsu*.

It was first used by Cholan speakers who were the principal bearers of the Classic Lowland Maya culture (A.D. 300–900) and later by Yucatecans mainly to record dynastic histories.

V. TARASCAN ISOLATE

There are 57,000 to 60,000 speakers in Michoacán, Mexico.

VI. CUITLATEC ISOLATE

Cuitlatec is now extinct. It was spoken in Oaxaca, Mexico.

VII. TEQUISTLATEC ISOLATE

Tequistlatec or *Chontal of Oaxaca* is spoken by about 5,000 speakers in southeastern Oaxaca, Mexico. Some consider this language to belong to the Hokan language family, which is not recognized by Campbell and Mithun (1979) as a valid entity.

VIII. HUAVE ISOLATE

About 13,000 speakers of *Huave* are found in Oaxaca, Mexico.

IX. XINCAN ISOLATE

About 20 speakers of *Xinca* have been reported in southeastern Guatemala.

C. LANGUAGES OF SOUTH AMERICA

An estimated 11.2 million people in South America speak an American native language. Unfortunately, only recently has the study of South American native languages begun to make significant progress. As a result, the genetic classification of these languages is still in quite a primitive state: On the one hand, we have Joseph Greenberg's (1960) classification that lumps all South American Indian languages into three macrogroups with very little evidence to support it; on the other, we have Čestimir Loukotka's (1968) classification (which originally appeared in 1935) that lists 113 stocks and language isolates. Even in the case of a supposedly safely established genetic relationship between Quechuan languages and Aymaran, a number of Andeanists now express their doubts concerning this genetic link.

The following presentation of genetic relationships is based on the rather careful and conservative work by Kaufman (1990:39–50) which lists 118 genetic units (families, stocks, language areas, and language isolates), many of which are now extinct. The different terminology used by Kaufman reflects the degree of certainty or closeness of the genetic relationship among the languages belonging to each grouping with the term "families" referring to the more closely related languages, and "stocks" referring to the more distantly related ones.

Seventy of Kaufman's genetic units are language isolates and 48 are groups consisting of at least two related languages. I have retained Kaufman's numbering of the languages as well as their grouping into various regions of South America, except that his Arabic numerals are changed into Roman numerals for the sake of uniformity with this book's other lists.

A. NORTHWESTERN REGION

I. YURIMANGI LANGUAGE

Now extinct. Originally spoken in Colombia.

II. TIMÓTEAN FAMILY

This consists of 2 languages, both dead, originally spoken in Venezuela.

III. HIRAHÁRAN FAMILY

This consists of 3 languages, now all extinct. Originally spoken in Venezuela.

IV. CHOKÓ LANGUAGE AREA

This consists of 5 languages (of which two are extinct) spoken in Panama and Colombia. The major representative are *Catío* (spoken by 10,000 to 20,000 sp. in Colombia and about 40 sp. in Panama), *Northern Embera* (9,000 to 10,000 sp., of which 7,000 to 8,000 are in southeastern Panama, and 2,000 in Colombia), and *Southern Embera* (around 2,500 sp. on the southern Pacific coast, Colombia).

V. BETOI LANGUAGE

Now extinct. Originally spoken in Colombia.

VI. PÁESAN SUBSTOCK

This consists of 7 languages of which 5 are extinct. The chief representative of this group is *Paez* (spoken in Colombia by 40,000 sp. in the Central Andes Range near Popayán).

VII. Barbakóan Family

This family consists of 6 languages, of which 3 are extinct. These languages are spoken in Colombia and Ecuador. Their chief representatives are *Cuaiquer* (spoken by 20,000 sp. in Colombia and undetermined number of sp. in Ecuador in the Pacific slopes of the Andes) and *Chachi* or *Cayapa* (spoken by 5,000 sp. in Esmeraldas province of Ecuador).

According to Kaufman (1990:39), there is a universal agreement that *Páesan* and *Barbakóan* should be grouped into a *Páes-Barbakoa* stock since there are clear lexical similarities in these languages.

VIII. Chíbchan (Sub)Stock

This consists of 24 languages of which 6 are extinct. The languages belonging to this group stretch from Honduras, Nicaragua, Costa Rica, Panama, Colombia, and Venezuela. The major languages belonging to this genetic grouping are *Guaymí* or *Ngäbere* (spoken by around 45,000 sp. in northeastern Panama and few in Costa Rica), *San Blas Cuna* (around 35,000 sp. on San Blas Islands and adjoining mainland, Panama), *Cogui* (from 3,000 to 5,000 sp. in Sierra Nevada de Santa Marta, Colombia), and *Bribri* (spoken by about 4,000 sp. in Costa Rica).

IX. Misumalpa Family

This consists of 4 languages (of which 2 are extinct) found in El Salvador, Honduras, and Nicaragua. The chief representatives of this family are *Mískito* (spoken by 77,000 to 160,000 sp. of which about 10,000 are in Honduras and the rest in Nicaragua), and *Sumo* (7,200 sp. of which 500 are in Honduras, the rest being in Nicaragua).

According to Kaufman (1990:39), there is a good chance that *Chíbchan* substock and *Misumalpa* family are genetically related, and there is already some evidence for this.

X. Kamsá Language

This language is spoken by 2,000 sp. in Colombia. According to some, this language belongs to Macro-Chibchan.

B. WESTERN AMAZONIA I

XI. Tiníwan Family

This family consists of 2 languages both of which are extinct. Both were originally spoken in Colombia.

XII. OTOMÁKOAN FAMILY

This family consists of 2 extinct languages, both of which were originally spoken in Venezuela.

XIII. WAMO LANGUAGE

This language is extinct. It used to be spoken in Venezuela.

XIV. CHAPAKÚRAN FAMILY

This family consists of 8 languages, 5 of which are now extinct, found in Brazil and Bolivia. The chief representative is *Pakaás-novos* or *Jaru* (spoken by 990 to 1,150 sp. in Rondônia, Brazil).

According to Kaufman (1990:40), the *Wamo* language and *Chapakúran* family are very likely genetically related and may form *Wamo-Chapakúran* stock.

XV. WAHÍVOAN FAMILY

This family consists of 4 languages, 1 of which is extinct, spoken in Colombia and Venezuela. The main representative is *Guahibo* or *Wahibo* (spoken by 20,000 sp., of which 15,000 are in Colombia and the rest in Venezuela).

XVI. MAIPÚREAN (SUB)STOCK

This genetic grouping consists of 65 languages of which 31 are extinct. This is the biggest stock in the whole New World. It is spoken in every country of South and Central America except El Salvador, Costa Rica, Panama, Uruguay, and Chile. Normally the term "Arawakan" is applied to this stock, but Kaufman (1990:40) cites reasons why this practice should be abandoned.

According to Derbyshire (1992, 1:102–8), this family has the following branches.

1. CENTRAL

The chief representative of this branch is *Parecís* (800 sp. in Matto Grosso State, Brazil).

2. EASTERN

This branch is represented by *Palikúr* (spoken by about 1,200 sp. of which 800 are in northern coastal Amapá, Brazil, and 400 in French Guiana).

3. NORTHERN

This is subdivided into two major subbranches and one minor one.

a. Caribbean

This subbranch is represented by the following languages: *Black Carib* (spoken by as many as 100,000 tot. sp., of which 14,700 are in Guatemala, 13,000 to 15,000 in Belize, perhaps 70,000 in Honduras, and 1,500 in Nicaragua), *Guajiro* (127,000 sp. of which around 82,000 are in Colombia, the rest in Venezuela) and *Arawak* or *Lokono* (2,400 sp. of which 1,500 are in Guyana, 700 in Surinam, 150 to 200 in French Guiana, and a few in Venezuela). *Taino,* a language which is now extinct, but used to be very widely spoken in West Indies, belongs to this group.

b. Inland

This is represented chiefly by *Curripaco* (2,550 to 4,210 sp., of which 340 to 1,500 are in Brazil, 210 in Venezuela, and the rest in Colombia) and *Piapoco* (3,100 sp., of which 100 are in Venezuela and the rest in Colombia).

c. Wapishana

This subbranch consists of one language: *Wapishana* (5,500 sp., of which 4,000 are in Guyana and the rest in Brazil).

4. SOUTHERN

This branch is further subdivided into three major subbranches.

a. Bolivia-Paraná

The chief representatives of this branch are *Ignaciano* (around 4,000 sp. in south central El Beni department, Bolivia), *Terêna* (20,000 sp. in southern Matto Grosso, Brazil), and *Trinitario* (5,000 sp. in south central El Beni department, Bolivia).

b. Campa

The major representatives of this group are *Asháninca Campa* (15,000 to 18,000 sp. in Peru), *Ashéninca Campa* (12,000 to 15,000 sp., most of whom are in Peru and about 212 to 235 are in Brazil), *Machiguenga* (6,000 to 8,000 sp. on Urubamba River in Peru), *Nomatsiguenga* (2,500 to 4,000 sp. in Junín department, Peru), and *Pajonal Campa* (2,000 to 4,000 sp. in Gran Pajonal area of Peru).

c. Purus

This consists of 2 languages: *Apurinã* (around 1,500 sp. scattered along the Purus River from Rio Branco to Manaus, Brazil) and *Piro* (1,700 to 2,500 sp. most of which are in the Urubamba River area, Peru, and 265 to 530 in Brazil).

5. WESTERN

This branch is represented mainly by *Amuesha* (4,000 to 8,000 sp. in eastern Peru).

XVII. Arawán Family

This family is found in Peru and Brazil and consists of 5 languages, one of which is extinct. The chief representative is *Culina* (780 to 1,265 tot. sp., of which 631 to 865 are in Brazil and 150 to 400 in Peru).

XVIII. Harákmbut Language Area

Two Harákmbut languages are spoken in Peru. The chief of the two is *Amarakaeri* (500 sp. in Peru around Madre de Dios and Colorado rivers).

C. WESTERN AMAZONIA II

XIX. Puinávean Stock

This stock consists of 6 languages of which 2 are extinct. The languages of this stock are found in Brazil, Colombia, and Venezuela. The chief among them is *Puinave* (2,240 sp. of which 2,000 are in Colombia and 240 in Venezuela).

XX. Katukínan Family

This family consists of 5 languages of which 3 are extinct. Languages belonging to this group are found in Brazil. The chief among them is *Kanamari* (580 to 645 sp. in Amazonas, Brazil).

XXI. Tekiraka Language

This language is now extinct. It was spoken in Peru.

XXII. Kanichana Language

This language is spoken by only about 25 speakers in Bolivia.

XXIII. Tukánoan Stock

This consists of 14 languages of which two are extinct. The languages belonging to this stock are found in Colombia, Ecuador, Peru, and Brazil. The ones with the largest number of speakers are *Tukano* (4,100 to 4,600 sp., of which 2,630 are in Amazonas, Brazil, and the rest in Colombia), *Cubeo* (around 2,150 sp., of which 2,000 are in Colombia, and the rest in Amazonas, Brazil), *Desano* (around 2,400 sp., of which 1,590 are in northwestern Amazonas, Brazil, and the rest in Colombia), and *Guanano* (1,070 sp., of which 620 are in northwestern Amazonas State, Brazil, and the rest in Colombia).

XXIV. Tikuna Language

This language is spoken by a total of 25,000 speakers, of which 6,000 are in Peru, 14,000 in Brazil, and 5,000 in Colombia. The region where this language is spoken stretches from Chimbote in Peru to San Antonio do Iça in Brazil.

XXV. Jurí Language

This language is extinct. It was spoken in Colombia and Brazil. According to Kaufman (1990:41), *Tikuna* and *Jurí* are very likely to be genetically related as there is lexical evidence in support of this.

XXVI. Munichi Language

This language is spoken by only about 10 speakers in the town of Muniches on the Paranapura River in Peru.

D. NORTHERN FOOTHILLS REGION

XXVII. Ezmeralda Language

This language is extinct. It used to be spoken in Ecuador.

XXVIII. Jaruro Language

This language is spoken by 2,000 to 3,000 speakers in Venezuela, near the Orinoco, Sinaruco, Meta, and Apure rivers.

According to Kaufman (1990:42), the extinct *Ezmeralda* language and the *Jaruro* language are very likely to be genetically related since there are lexical similarities between them.

XXIX. Kofán Language

This language is spoken by 400 speakers in Ecuador and 300 in Colombia, on the border between these two countries.

XXX. Kandoshi Language

This language is spoken by 3,000 speakers in Peru on the Morona, Pastaza, Huitoyacu, and Chapuli rivers.

XXXI. Hívaro Language Area

This includes 2 languages spoken in Ecuador: *Shuar* and *Candoshi* (around 3,000 sp. in Peru).

Shuar has the following varieties: *Achuar-Shiwiar* (5,000 to 5,500 sp., of which 3,000 to 3,500 are in Peru, and 2,000 in Ecuador), *Aguaruna* (25,000 sp.

in Peru), *Huambisa* (around 6,000 sp. in Peru), and *Shuar* (proper) (30,000 to 32,000 sp. in the southeastern jungle of Ecuador).

XXXII. KAWAPÁNAN FAMILY

This family consists of 2 languages spoken in Peru: *Chayahuita* or *Cahuapa* language (6,000 sp. in Peru) and *Jebero* (2,300 to 3,000 sp. in the District of Jeberos, Peru). According to Kaufman (1990:42), *Hívaro* and *Kawapánan* may perhaps form a *Hívaro-Kawapana* stock.

XXXIII. SÁPAROAN FAMILY

This family consists of 6 languages, 1 of which is extinct. These languages are found in Ecuador and Peru.

Most of the languages of this family have very few speakers. The following 3 are the major ones: *Arabela* (150 sp. on a tributary of Napo River in Peru), *Iquito* (150 sp. in northern Nanay River area, Peru), and *Záparo* (150 sp. in Pastaza Province, Ecuador).

XXXIV. YÁWAN FAMILY

This family consists of 3 languages of which 2 are extinct. The surviving language is *Yagua* (3,000 to 4,000 sp. in the northeastern Amazon River region, from Iquitos to the Brazilian border). According to Kaufman (1990:42), *Saparoan* family and *Yáwan* family may perhaps be genetically related.

XXXV. OMURANO LANGUAGE

This language is extinct. It used to be spoken in Peru.

XXXVI. SABELA LANGUAGE

According to Kaufman (1990:43), this language is spoken in Peru, but if this language is indeed the same language as *Waorani* or *Auca,* as is claimed by Voegelin and Voegelin (1977:22), it is also spoken in Ecuador between Napo and Curaray rivers by 750 to 800 speakers.

XXXVII. URARINA LANGUAGE

This language is spoken by 2,000 to 3,500 speakers in Urarina district, Peru.

XXXVIII. BÓRAN FAMILY

This family consists of 2 languages. One of them is *Bora,* which is spoken by 1,000 to 1,500 in Peru, 500 in Colombia, and 457 in Brazil.

XXXIX. Witótoan Family

This family consists of 7 languages, of which 4 are extinct. These languages are found in Colombia, Peru, and Brazil. The major languages in this group are *Meneca Huitoto* (2,500 sp. in Colombia and only 5 in Peru) and *Murui Huitoto* (2,000 to 2,800 tot. sp., of which 1,200 to 1,500 are in Peru, 500 to 1,000 in Colombia, and 261 in Brazil).

XL. Andoke Language

This language is spoken by 75 to 100 speakers in Colombia. There used to be some speakers in Peru, but Peruvian *Andoque* is now extinct. According to Kaufman (1990:43), there is a chance that *Bóran* and *Witótoan* families and the *Andoke* language form *Bora-Witoto* stock.

E. ANDES REGION

XLI. Chimúan Family

This family consists of 3 languages all of which are now extinct. They were spoken in Ecuador and Peru.

XLII. Cholónan Family

This family consists of 2 languages both of which are now extinct. They used to be spoken in Peru.

XLIII. Kulyi Language

This language is extinct. It used to be spoken in Peru.

XLIV. Sechura Language

This language is also extinct. It used to be spoken in Peru.

XLV. Katakáoan Family

This language consists of 2 languages both of which are extinct. According to Kaufman (1990:43), it is very likely that *Sechura* language and the *Katakáoan* family form *Sechura-Katakao* stock since there is supporting lexical evidence.

XLVI. Leko Language

This language is extinct. It used to be spoken in Bolivia.

XLVII. KECHUA LANGUAGE COMPLEX

Also spelled Quechua, this complex consists of 7 languages spoken in Colombia, Ecuador, Peru, Bolivia, and Argentina. (For details on the languages of this group, see "Ayacucho Quechua Sketch" at the end of this chapter.)

XLVIII. HAKI (JAQUÍ) LANGUAGE COMPLEX

This complex consists of 2 languages found in Peru Bolivia, Chile, and Argentina: *Aymara* (about 2 million sp., of which 1,790,000 or more are in Bolivia, 300,000 to 500,000 sp. in Peru, and others in Chile and Argentina) and *Jaqaru* (about 2,000 sp. in Yauyos province, Peru).

Although there seems to be general agreement that *Kechua* and *Haki* are genetically related and form *Kechumara* stock, there is also some argumentation to the contrary.

XLIX. CHIPAYA LANGUAGE AREA

This consists of 2 languages spoken in Bolivia: *Uru* (spoken by only a few older people in department of Oruro, province of Atahuallpa, Bolivia) and *Chipaya* (1,000 sp. in the same region as Uru).

L. PUKINA LANGUAGE

This language is extinct. It used to be spoken in Bolivia.

LI. KOLYAWAYA JARGON

Kolyawaya is spoken in Bolivia. This is a jargon used by *Kechua* speakers who used to speak *Pukina* or a language related to Pukina. Since it is not known where all of its components come from, Kaufman (1990:44) lists it as a separate genetic unit with its own number.

Kaufman (1990:44) also thinks that if it were shown that *Kolyawaya* is descended from a sister of Pukina rather than Pukina itself, there is a possibility of establishing Pukina-Kolyawaya family.

F. SOUTHERN FOOTHILLS REGION

LII. YURAKARE LANGUAGE

This language is spoken by 2,500 sp. in Beni and Cochabamba departments of Bolivia.

LIII. PÁNOAN FAMILY

This family consists of 28 languages of which 13 are extinct. These languages are spoken in Bolivia, Peru, and Brazil. According to Ruhlen (1987:376), this family has the following branches.

1. Eastern Panoan

This is represented by Kaxararí (130 sp. in Acre, Rondônia, and Amazonas, Brazil).

2. North-Central Panoan

This branch is represented by *Capanahua* (350 to 500 sp. on the Tapiche and Buncuya rivers, Peru), *Marúbo* (500 to 595 sp. in Amazonas, Brazil, near the Peruvian border), and *Shipibo-Conibo* (11,300 to 15,000 sp. in the Ucayali River area, Peru).

3. Northern Panoan

This is represented by 3 languages of which the major one is *Matsés* (940 to 1,285 sp., of which 800 are in Yaquerana, Peru, and 140 to 485 in Brazil).

4. South-Central Panoan

This includes *Amahuaca* (720 to 1,720 sp., of which 500 to 1,500 are in Peru and 200 in Brazil), *Nukuini* (240 to 250 sp. in northwestern Acre, Brazil), *Poyanáwa* (225 sp. in Acre, Brazil), *Sharanahua* (850 to 950 sp. of which 500 to 600 are in Peru and 350 in Acre, Brazil), *Yaminahua* (1,200 to 1,600 sp., of which 700 to 1,100 are in Peru, 360 in Brazil, and 150 in Bolivia), *Yora* (200 or more sp. in or near Manu Park, Peru), and *Yawanáwa* (195 sp. in Acre, Brazil).

5. Southeastern Panoan

This includes *Cashinahua* (1,600 to 2,000 sp., of which 850 to 1,200 are in Peru and the rest in Brazil), *Panoan Katukína* (around 1,000 sp. in Amazonas, Brazil), and *Moranahua* (150 sp. at the headwaters of the Embira River, Peru; possibly some speakers are also in Brazil).

6. Southern Panoan

This includes, among other languages, *Chácobo* (250 sp. in northwestern El Beni, Bolivia) and *Karipúna do Guaporé* (20 sp. in Rondônia, Brazil).

7. Western Panoan

This is represented by *Cashibo* (around 1,000 to 1,500 sp. on the Aguaytia and San Alejandro rivers, Peru).

8. Unclassified Panoan

Panobo, an extinct language which was once spoken along Ucayali River in Peru, was placed by Kaufman in this category because there is not enough data on it to group it with some other Panoan languages.

LIV. TAKÁNAN FAMILY

This family consists of 5 languages spoken in Bolivia and Peru. The major representatives of this family are *Tacana* (3,000 sp. in the Beni and Madre de Dios River areas of Bolivia), *Cavineña* (around 1,000 sp. along the Beni River in Bolivia), and *Ese Ejja* (850 to 1,050 sp., of which 600 to 650 are in the foothills above the Beni River, and 250 to 400 are around Puerto Maldonado in Peru).

According to Kaufman (1990:45), there is a very good chance that *Pánoan* family and *Takánan* family are genetically related and form *Pano-Takana* stock.

LV. MOSETÉN LANGUAGE AREA

This consists of 2 languages spoken in Bolivia. This language group is represented by *Tsimané* and *Moseten* (5,500 sp., of which 500 speak the latter language; in southwestern Beni department and along Maniqui River as well as in nearby towns, Bolivia).

LVI. CHON FAMILY

This family consists of 3 languages, 2 of which are extinct. These languages are found in Argentina and Chile. The surviving language is *Tehuelche,* which has only 24 speakers in Patagonia, Argentina. Originally this language was spoken in Chile.

According to Kaufman (1990:45) there is a fairly good chance that *Mosetén* languages and *Chon* family are genetically related and form *Mosetén-Chon* stock, although various authorities seem to disagree on the genetic affiliation of these languages groups.

G. THE CONE

LVII. YÁMANA LANGUAGE

This language is extinct. It used to be spoken in Chile.

LVIII. KAWÉSKAR LANGUAGE (AREA)

This contains 2 emergent languages, of which one is extinct. Located in Chile. The surviving language is Kawesqar (47 sp. in western Patagonia, Isle of Wellington, Chile).

LIX. MAPUDUNGU LANGUAGE (AREA)

This is in Chile and Argentina. The representative of this group is *Mapudungun* or *Araucano* (440,000 tot. sp. of various dialects, of which 400,000 are in Chile, and 40,000 or more in Argentina).

LX. Puelche Language

This language is extinct. It used to be spoken in Argentina.

LXI. Warpe Language Area

This consists of 2 languages both of which are extinct. They used to be spoken in Argentina.

H. CHACO REGION

LXII. Matákoan Family

This family consists of 4 languages spoken in Argentina, Paraguay, and Bolivia. The major languages of this family are *Iyo'wujwa Chorote* (around 7,870 sp. in Argentina; also spoken by a few sp. in Bolivia and Paraguay), *Chalupí* (around 12,500 sp. of which 12,300 are in the Chaco of Paraguay, and 200 in Argentina), and *Wichí Lhamtes Vejoz* (around 25,000 sp. along the upper Bermejo and Pilcomayo rivers in Argentina).

LXIII. Waikurúan Family

This family consists of 8 languages of which 4 are extinct. It is found in Paraguay, Brazil, Argentina, and Bolivia. The major languages of this family are *Mocoví* (around 3,000 to 4,000 sp. in the southern Chaco, northeastern Santa Fe Province, Argentina), *Pilagá* (2,000 sp. or more in Formosa Province and in Chaco and Salta provinces, Argentina), and *Toba* (15,500 to 20,500 sp. in eastern Formosa and Chaco provinces, Argentina; also spoken in Paraguay and possibly Bolivia).

LXIV. Charrúan Family

This family consists of 2 languages both of which are extinct. They were spoken in Uruguay.

LXV. Lule Language

This language is extinct. It was spoken in Argentina.

LXVI. Vilela Language

This language is spoken by five families in east central Chaco province of Argentina near Paraguay border. According to Kaufman (1990:46), there is a very good chance that *Lule* and *Vilela* languages are genetically related and form *Lule-Vilela* stock since there is lexical evidence to support the connection.

LXVII. Maskóian Family

This family consists of 4 languages, 1 of which is extinct. The major languages belonging to this family are *Angaite* (2,370 sp. in Paraguay), *Lengua* (8,500 to 10,000 tot. sp. in the Chaco of Paraguay), and *Maskoy* (around 1,400 sp. in Puerto Victoria, Paraguay).

LXVIII. Samúkoan Family

This family consists of 2 languages spoken in Paraguay and Bolivia: *Ayoreo* (2,200 to 2,700 sp., of which 1,000 to 1,500 are in southeastern Bolivia, and 1,225 in Chaco and northern Alto Paraguay Departments, Paraguay) and *Chamacoco* (1,000 sp. in the northeastern Chaco along the Paraguay River, in Paraguay).

LXIX. Gorgotoki Language

This language is extinct. It was spoken in Bolivia.

I. EASTERN BRAZIL

LXX. Chikitano Language

This language is spoken by 20,000 speakers in the eastern region of Bolivia, east of Santa Cruz.

LXXI. Boróroan Family

This family consists of 3 languages, one of which is extinct. The chief language in this family is Borôro (800 sp. in central Mato Grosso, Brazil).

LXXII. Aimoré Language Complex

This complex consists of 3 languages 1 of which is extinct. All are located in Brazil. *Xokleng* or *Botocudos* (250 sp. along the tributary of Itajaí River, Brazil) is the representative language of this group.

LXXIII. Rikbaktsa Language

This language is spoken by 500 to 800 speakers in the Mato Grosso region of Brazil.

LXXIV. Je or Ge Stock

This stock consists of 13 languages of which 6 are extinct. All are found in Brazil. The major representatives of this group are *Xávante* (around 7,000 sp. in Mato Grosso, Brazil) and *Xerénte* (755 to 850 in Goiás, Brazil).

LXXV. Jeikó Language

This language is extinct. It was spoken in Brazil.

LXXVI. Kamakánan Family

This family consists of 4 languages all of which are extinct. They used to be spoken in Brazil.

LXXVII. Mashakalían Family

This family consists of 3 languages of which two are extinct. The representative language is *Maxakalí* (600 sp. in Minas Gerais, Brazil).

LXXVIII. Purían Family

This family consists of 2 languages, both of which are extinct. They were spoken in Brazil.

LXXIX. Fulnió Language

This language is spoken by 1,526 to 3,500 speakers in Pernambuco, Brazil. According to Grimes (1988:94), the speakers are all bilingual in Portuguese and use *Fulnió* mainly in a three-month annual religious retreat.

LXXX. Karajá Language Area

This consists of 2 languages located in Brazil. *Karajá* (around 2,700 sp. in the vicinity of the Bananal Island, Araguaia River, Brazil) is the representative of this group.

LXXXI. Ofayé Language

This language is spoken by 23 people in Mato Grosso do Sul, Brazil.

LXXXII. Guató Language

This language is spoken by 220 to 300 speakers in Mato Grosso do Sul, Brazil, near the Bolivian border, banks of the Paraguai and going up the São Lourenço rivers.

According to Kaufman (1990:47), the genetic groups from *Chikitano* (LXX) to *Guató* (LXXXII) are probably genetically related and form *Macro-Je*. There is already some evidence which links various of these groups together, but more detailed comparative work is needed.

LXXXIII. Otí Language

This language is extinct. It used to be spoken in Brazil.

LXXXIV. Baenã Language

This language is extinct. It used to be spoken in Brazil.

LXXXV. Kukurá Language

This language is extinct. It used to be spoken in Brazil.

J. NORTHEASTERN BRAZIL

LXXXVI. Katembrí Language

This language is extinct. It used to be spoken in Brazil.

LXXXVII. Karirí Language (Area)

This language is extinct. It used to be spoken in Brazil.

LXXXVIII. Tushá Language

This language is extinct. It was spoken in Brazil.

LXXXIX. Pankararú Language

This is extinct. It was spoken in Brazil.

XC. Natú Language

This language is extinct. It was spoken in Brazil.

XCI. Shukurú Language

This language is extinct. It was spoken in Brazil.

XCII. Gamela Language

This language is extinct. It was spoken in Brazil.

XCIII. Wamoé Language

This language is extinct. It was spoken in Brazil.

XCIV. Tarairiú Language

This language is extinct. It was spoken in Brazil.

XCV. Shokó Language

This language is extinct. It was spoken in Brazil.

K. CENTRAL AMAZONIA

XCVI. Múran Family

This family consists of 2 languages, of which 1 is extinct. The surviving language is *Múra-Pirahã* (150 sp. in Amazonas, along the Maici River, Brazil).

XCVII. Matanawí Language

This language is extinct. It was spoken in Brazil. According to Kaufman (1990:48), it is probable that *Múran* family and *Matanawí* form *Mura-Matanawí* family.

XCVIII. Itonama Language

This language is spoken by 110 speakers in Beni department and Itonamas River in Bolivia.

XCIX. Kunsa Language

This language is extinct. It used to be spoken in Chile and Bolivia.

C. Kapishaná Language

This language is said to be spoken by 100 speakers in Mato Grosso, Brazil, but it may be now extinct. According to Kaufman (1990:49), *Kunsa* language and *Kapishaná* language may be genetically related and form *Kunsa-Kapishaná* stock since lexical evidence looks promising.

CI. Jabutían Family

This family consists of 3 languages spoken in Brazil. The following languages belong to this group: *Arikapú* (15 sp. in Rondônia, near the headwaters of Rio Branco, Brazil) and *Jabutí* (60 sp. in Rondônia, Brazil).

CII. Koayá Language

This language is extinct. It was spoken in Brazil.

CIII. Aikaná Language

Aikaná or *Tubarão* is spoken by 90 speakers in Rondônia, Brazil.

CIV. Nambikuara Family

This family consists of the following 4 languages spoken in Brazil: *Manairisu* (450 sp. in Mato Grosso, Brazil), *Nambikuára* (1,100 sp. mostly in Mato Grosso, Brazil), *Sabanês* (40 to 50 sp. in Mato Grosso, Brazil), and *Sararé* (150 sp. in Mato Grosso, Brazil).

CV. Iranshe Language

This language is spoken in Mato Grosso, Brazil, by 150 to 194 speakers.

CVI. Trumai Language

This language is spoken by 60 to 71 speakers along the Xingú River, Mato Grosso, Brazil.

CVII. Movima Language

This language is spoken by about 500 speakers in central Beni, Bolivia.

CVIII. Kayuvava Language

This language is spoken by 25 speakers in Beni, Bolivia.

CIX. Tupían Stock

This stock consists of 37 languages of which 12 are extinct. The majority of the languages belong to a single branch, the Tupí-Guaraní family. The languages of this genetic unit stretch from Venezuela, Colombia, Brazil, Bolivia, Argentina, and Paraguay. According to Jensen (1992, 4:182–7), this stock is divided into two major groups.

1. Tupí-Guaraní Family

This is further subdivided into eight branches.

a. Guaranian

This branch includes a number of languages with a relatively large number of speakers: *Chiriguano* (70,000 tot. sp., of which 50,000 are in the Gran Chaco, Bolivia, 15,000 in Jujuy and Salta, Argentina, and 5,000 in the Chaco of Paraguay), *Mbyá Guaraní* (8,000 to 8,500 sp., of which 2,500 to 3,000 are in a number of Brazilian states and 5,500 in Paraguay; some in Argentina),

Paraguayan Guaraní (over 3 million sp. in Paraguay, plus some in adjacent areas of Argentina and Brazil), *Kaiwá* (around 18,000 sp. in Mato Grosso do Sul, Brazil, plus 11,000 sp. in eastern Paraguay and in Argentina), and *Ñandeva* (around 9,200 sp., of which 2,500 are in Mato Grosso do Sul and São Paulo states, Brazil, and 6,799 in eastern Paraguay).

Old Guaraní or *Classical Guaraní* is now extinct but used to be spoken during the colonial period (1604–1767) by about 300,000 speakers in Jesuit missions. There are grammars and dictionaries of this language compiled by colonial missionaries during that period.

In Paraguay, *Guaraní* has the status of a second national language, although Spanish is considered the "official language."

b. Guarayu, etc.

The chief language belonging to this branch is *Guarayu* (around 5,000 sp. in the northeastern Guarayos River, Bolivia).

c. Tupinambá, etc.

The chief languages representing this branch are *Cocama-Cocamilla* (around 15,000 to 18,200 sp. in Peru, plus 20 sp. in Colombia and 176 in Amazonas, Brazil) and N*heengatú* (around 3,000 sp. in Amazonas, Brazil).

d. Tapirapé, etc.

The chief language in this branch is *Guajajára* (about 10,000 sp. in Maranhão, Brazil).

e. Kayabí, etc.

The chief language in this branch is *Kayabí* (500 sp. in the Xingú Park, Mato Grosso, and in southern Pará, Brazil).

f. Parintintín, etc.

The major language here is *Parintintín* (215 sp. in Amazonas, Brazil).

g. Kamayurá

This branch contains only *Kamayurá* (200 to 210 sp. in the Xingú Park, Mato Grosso, Brazil).

h. Tukunyape, etc.

The main languages here are *Urubú-Kaapor* (500 sp. in Maranhão, Brazil), *Amapari Wayampi* (320 sp. in west central Amapá, Brazil), and *Oiapoque Wayampi* (400 sp. in French Guiana).

2. NON-TUPÍ-GUARANÍ

This is in turn subdivided into the following eight languages.

a. Arikem

The representative language of this division is *Karitiâna* (123 sp. in Rondônia, Brazil).

b. Aweti

Awetí has 35 speakers in Xingú Park, Mato Grosso, Brazil.

c. Jurúna

Jurúna has 125 speakers in Xingú Park, Mato Grosso, Brazil.

d. Monde

Mondé has 30 to 200 speakers in Rondônia, Brazil.

e. Mundurukú

Mundurukú has 2,000 to 3,760 speakers in Pará and Amazonas, Brazil.

f. Ramarama

This is represented by *Rondônia Arára* (92 sp. in Rondônia and Acre, Brazil).

g. Sateré

Sateré-Mawé has 5,000 speakers in Pará, Brazil. There may be more speakers in Amazonas.

h. Tuparí

Tuparí is spoken by 56 or more speakers in Rondônia, Brazil.

L. NORTHERN AMAZONIA

CX. KÁRIBAN FAMILY

This family consists of 43 languages of which 19 are extinct. This genetic unit is found in Venezuela, Colombia, Surinam, Guyana, French Guiana, and Brazil. There are many subgroups in this family that do not appear to group together into major divisions. According to Rodrigues (1985), this family may be related to *Tupian* languages.

The major languages belonging to this family are *Akawaio* (3,500 to 4,500 sp., of which 3,000 to 4,000 are in Guyana, 500 in Brazil, and a few in Venezuela), *Carib* (around 20,000 sp., of which 10,000 are in Venezuela near the mouth of Orinoco River, 2,500 in Surinam, 1,200 in French Guiana, 900 in Brazil, and 475 or more in Guyana), *Makushi* (around 5,700 sp., of which 3,000 are in northeastern Roraima and Rio Branco, Brazil, 1,300 in west central Guyana, and 600 in southern Venezuela), *Panare* (1,200 sp. in Bolivar, Venezuela), *Patamona* (3,000 to 4,000 sp. in west central Guyana), *Pemón* (5,930 sp., of which 4,850 are in Bolivar, Venezuela, 400 to 500 in Guyana, and 680 in Brazil), *Waiwai* (885 to 1,060 sp. in Amazonas and Pará, Brazil, and in Guyana), *Wayana* (950 sp., of which 600 are in southeastern Surinam, 200 in French Guiana, and 150 in Brazil), *Ye'cuana* (5,240 sp., of which 4,970 are in

Venezuela and 270 in Brazil) and *Yukpa* (3,000 sp., of which 2,500 are in Colombia on the Colombia-Venezuela border, and 500 in Venezuela).

Hixkaryâna, a Kariban language spoken by 350 speakers in the Amazonas state of Brazil near Manaus, is rather famous among linguists because it has a very rare basic word order: Object + Verb + Subject (OVS). Derbyshire (1977) has written an article on the significance of the existence of OVS word order for linguistic typology.

The Carib or Island Carib language which used to be spoken on a number of Caribbean islands was a language belonging to the Arawakan language family, not Kariban. It got its name because the Carib invaders from the mainland of South America imposed their nationality and name on their Arawakan subjects, even though they were unable to totally displace the native Arawakan language of their subjects.

CXI. Yanomáman Family

This family consists of 4 languages found in Venezuela and Brazil. The chief representative of this family is *Yanomamö* or *Yanomame* (10,500 to 11,000 sp., of which 9,000 are in Venezuela and 1,500 to 2,000 are in Brazil).

CXII. Warao Language

This language is spoken by 15,000 speakers, most of whom are in Venezuela, with a few in Guyana and Surinam.

CXIII. Taruma Language

This language is extinct. It used to be spoken in Brazil and Guyana.

CXIV. Sálivan Family

The 2 languages are *Piaroa* (12,000 sp. south bank of Orinoco River, Amazonas, Venezuela; perhaps some in Colombia) and *Sáliba* (2,022 sp., of which 2,000 are in Colombia and others in Venezuela).

CXV. Awaké Language

This language is spoken by a total of 23 speakers of whom 17 are in Brazil and the rest in Venezuela.

CXVI. Kaliana Language

Also called *Sapé,* this language is spoken in Venezuela by 60 to 100 speakers, with a few more in Brazil. According to Kaufman (1990:50), chances are very good that *Awaké* language and *Kaliana* language are genetically related and form *Awaké-Kaliana* family since there is some lexical evidence to support this.

CXVII. Maku Language

This language is extinct. It used to be spoken in Brazil and Venezuela. According to Kaufman (1990:50), there is some chance that *Maku, Kaliana*, and *Awaké* are all genetically related and form Kaliánan stock.

CXVIII. Hotí Language

Also called *Yuwana* and *Waruwaru*, this language is spoken in Central Venezuela by 300 to 500 speakers.

Sketch of Yup'ik Eskimo

A. Genetic Affiliation and General Information

Central Yup'ik Eskimo is a language belonging to the Eskimo-Aleut family of languages. This family stretches across the Aleutian island chain to Alaska, across northern Canada and all the way to Greenland. This is also the only known language family that straddles both North America and Asia since there are Eskimos speakers on the Chukchi (Chukotka) peninsula in Siberia.

The main branches of the family are Aleut and Eskimo. The Eskimo subbranch is further subdivided into the Inupiaq and Western Eskimo subbranches. Inupiaq dialects are found from northern Alaska to Greenland in a long dialect chain. Western Eskimo is subdivided into Siberian Yup'ik (Chukchi Peninsula and St. Lawrence Island), Sugpiaq (Southern Alaska Peninsula), and Central Yup'ik (Central Alaska Peninsula).

It is estimated that about 15,000 speakers speak Central Yup'ik out of the population of about 17,000 which is spread from Nunivak Island, and on Alaska coast from Bristol Bay to Norton Sound and inland along Nushagak, Kuskokwim, and Yukon rivers.

The center of this family is definitely in Alaska, and there are scholars who believe that the Eskimos migrated from Alaska to Siberia in relatively recent times although they may have originally all come from Siberia to Alaska at an even earlier time. It is clear that Inupiaq has spread across northern Canada into Greenland relatively recently because its dialects are mutually intelligible to a very high degree, which means that they did not have time to develop significant local differences in language.

The Eskimo-Aleut family has been linked by some to Uralic and by others to the Paleo-Siberian languages, but both links are rather tenuous and speculative at this time.

Eskimo languages spoken in Alaska have been influenced by Russian and have borrowed extensively from that language:

staalista, estaalista < Russian *starosta* 'church elder'

tupuuluq < Russian *topor* 'axe'

kuulicaq < Russian *kurica* 'chicken'

In Canada, and in recent years in Alaska, there has been more borrowing from English:

pelumessaq 'women's underpants' < English 'bloomers'

minaq < English 'miner'

tiiviiq < English 'T.V.'

Greenlandic Eskimo has borrowed words mainly from Danish.

B. PHONETICS, PHONOLOGY, AND ORTHOGRAPHY[3]

Central Yup'ik is now written in the Roman alphabet using an orthography designed by American linguists. Some Inupiaq dialects, however, are written in a special syllabary which was designed by missionaries to write the Cree Indian language in Canada. Table 7.1 gives the Central Yup'ik segments in their orthographic transcription; the phonetic values are given in square brackets.

Yup'ik voiceless stops are unaspirated except in the final position. The lateral phonemes are actually fricatives rather than sonorants. /c/ is an alveopalatal or alveolar affricate.

Table 7.1 CENTRAL YUP'IK CONSONANTS

	LABIAL	ALVEOLAR	ALVEOPALATAL
Stops	p	t	
Affricatives			c [tʃ/ts]
Voiced fricatives	v [v/w]	s [z]/y [j]	
Voiced laterals		l [ɭ]	
Voiceless fricatives	vv [f]	ss [s]	
Voiceless laterals		ll [ɬ]	
Voiced nasals	m	n	
Voiceless nasals	ṁ [m̥]	ń [n̥]	

	VELAR	ROUNDED VELAR	UVULAR	ROUNDED UVULAR
Stops	k		q	
Affricatives				
Voiced fricatives	g [ɣ]	ûg [ɣʷ]	r [ʀ]	ûr [ʀʷ]
Voiced laterals				
Voiceless fricatives	gg [x]	w [xʷ]	rr [χ]	ûrr [χʷ]
Voiceless laterals				
Voiced nasals	ng [ŋ]			
Voiceless nasals	ńg [ŋ̥]			

Table 7.2   Central Yup'ik Vowels

i ii		u uu
	e [ə]	
	a aa	

There are geminate consonants which are marked by an apostrophe. Table 7.2 shows, for example, a geminate *p* (as in *Yup'ik*) is written *p'*.

e represents a *schwa* (unrounded lax mid central vowel). *i* and *u* have allophones *e* and *o* in the neighborhood of uvular consonants.

Stress in Central Yup'ik is predictable by a somewhat complicated rule. A word gets multiple stresses in a roughly alternating pattern of stressed and unstressed syllables.

Besides phonemically long vowels and long (geminate) consonants, Yup'ik also has predictable vowel lengthening and consonant lengthening. The rule for consonant lengthening is somewhat complex and will not be cited here. The rule for rhythmic vowel lengthening is that any vowel (except a schwa) is lengthened if it is found in the second of a series of two open syllables unless it comes at the end of the word.

c. Morphology

Central Yup'ik has the very rich morphology of a typical polysynthetic language. A typical noun or verb has the following morphological structure—parentheses mark the nonobligatory elements of the structure:

base or stem + (post bases) + ending + (enclitic)

Primarily it is the ending that determines whether the word is a noun or a verb because many stems and postbases can be either. Below is an example of a verb form that has in its structure all the required and optional elements:

angya-li-ciq-sugnar-quq-llu

angya = boat (BASE)/ *li* = make (POSTBASE)/ *ciq* = future action (POSTBASE)/ *sugnar* = probability (POSTBASE)/ *quq* = 3d pers. sing. subj., intrans. (ENDING)/ *llu* = also, and (ENCLITIC)

'also, he will probably make a boat'

Theoretically at least there is no limit on how many postbases may follow the stem or base. The type of stem or postbase immediately preceding the ending usually determines the part of speech. Thus, *kuig-* 'river' is a nominal stem, and *cali-* 'work' is a verbal stem. In the same way, postbase *-vig-* 'place where' must be followed by a nominal ending, and postbase *-li-* 'to make preceding nominal' by a verbal ending. However, there are some stems that are either verbal or nominal: *nutg-* 'shoot'/'gun'.

It should be pointed out here that Central Yup'ik has very complicated morphophonemics which cause almost every morpheme in the language to have many allomorphs some of which are, strictly speaking, not phonologically conditioned.

Nouns

Nouns in Eskimo are inflected for case, number, and possession. The case endings will be cited below. There are three numbers: singular, dual, and plural. Sometimes the case, number, and possessor markers are so fused together that it is difficult, if not impossible, to say where one ends and the other begins. In any case, all three constitute part of the ending.

Case Endings

1. Absolutive
singular: unmarked, plural: -*t*, dual: -*k*.

Actually, since the latter two endings are actually plural and dual endings respectively, it would be more accurate to simply say that this case is unmarked everywhere.

This case is used for the direct object of a transitive verb and the subject of an intransitive verb:

> *Angyaa tak'uq.*
>
> his boat (absolutive case)/long
>
> 'His boat (subj. of an intransitive vb.) is long.'

> *Angyaa tangrraat.*
>
> his boat (absolutive case)/they see
>
> 'They see his boat (direct obj. of a transitive vb.).'

2. Relative
singular: -*m*, plural: -*t*, dual: -*k*.

(This time it may be pointed out that this case has overt marking only in the singular; the plural and dual forms of this case are identical to the absolutive case forms.)

This case marks the subject of transitive verbs as well as the possessor (like a possessive case):

> *Angute-m ner-aa neqa.*
>
> man + relative case/ eat + transitive 3d pers. sing./ fish (absolutive)
>
> 'The man (subj. of a transitive verb) is eating the fish.'

Angute-m qimugt-ii ner'-uq.

man + relat. case/ dog-his/ eat + intransitive 3d pers. sing.

'The man's dog is eating.'

In the second example we should note that the possessed NP is suffixed with the third person possessive suffix in addition to having the possessor NP ('man's') expressed. Moreover, since the direct object is not expressed, the verb 'eat' is suffixed with an intransitive personal ending.

3. Ablative/Modalis

singular: *-mek,* plural: *-nek,* dual *-gnek.*

This case suffix marks the point of origin ('from') and an indefinite direct object. In addition, some verbs of giving (but not all) use the direct object in the absolutive to tell to whom something is given and specify the object given by a noun in the ablative/modalis case. It may also mark the subject matter of speaking and thinking. (In other words, it functions like the English preposition 'about'.)

Tegullrua nuussi-ni estuulu-mek.

he took/ knife-his/ table + ablat. case

'He took his knife from the table.'

Tanger-tuq imarmiutar-mek.

see + intransitive 3d pers. sing./ mink + ablat. case

'He sees a mink.'

Contrast the foregoing sentence with the following one:

Tangrr-aa imarmiutaq.

see + transitive 3d pers. sing./ mink (absolutive case)

'He sees the mink.'

(For brevity's sake not all the usages of this case will be illustrated here.)

4. Localis

singular: *-mi,* plural: *-ni,* dual: *-gni.*

This case suffix marks location ('at, in') and the object of comparison:

Ner'-uq ne-m'i.

eat + intransitive 3d pers. sing./ house + localis case

'He is eating in the house.'

Una ena assi-nru-uq ne-vni.

this/ house (absolutive)/ to be good, nice, fine + comparative + intransitive 3d pers. sing./ house + 2d pers. sing. localis case (fused)

'This house is better than yours.'

5. *Vialis*

singular: *-kun,* plural: *-tgun,* dual *-gnegun.*

This case marks the route by which a movement is performed, 'via, by way of', the instrument by which an action is performed, and also has the function of marking the partitive. (That is, it marks the object when only a part of a whole is affected.) Finally, this case also marks the instrument whereby an action is performed.

Ayag-tuq Kui-pag-kun.

go + intransitive 3d pers. sing./ river + big + vialis case

'He is going by way of the Yukon River.'

Navg-aa angya-ni kingua-kun.

break + transitive 3d pers. sing./ boat + his (absolutive)/ stern + vialis case

'He broke his boat on its stern.'

Angya-mi-kun tekitellr-uuq.

boat + 3d pers. sing. possessor + vialis case/ arrive + intransitive 3d pers. sing.

'He arrived using his boat.'

6. *Aequalis*

singular: *-tun,* plural: *-cetun,* dual: *-gtun.*

This case indicates similarity and is usually translated by English prepositions 'like' and 'as'. It is also used to mark language specification or price specification. (That is, in what language one is speaking; at what price one is selling something.)

Kass'aq Yup'ig-tun yurar-tuq.

white man (absolutive case)/ Eskimo + aequalis case/ dance + intransitive 3d pers. sing.

'The white man is dancing like an Eskimo.'

Camek ate-ngqer-ta tauna Yup'ig-tun?

what/ name + have + be/ that/ Eskimo + aequalis case

'What is the name of that in Eskimo?'

7. *Terminalis*

singular: *-mun.*

This case ending marks motion to or into something.

> *Arna-m ekellru-a nuusiq yaassiig-mun.*
>
> woman + relat./ place, put + transitive 3d pers. sing./ knife (absolutive case)/ box + terminalis case
>
> 'The woman put the knife into the box.'

Possessive Suffixes

Besides being inflected for case, nouns can also be inflected for possession. For the sake of keeping things simple and brief only a few examples of possessive endings will be shown here.

> *nuna* 'land' (absolutive case)
>
> *nunaa* 'his land' < *nuna-nga* (absolutive case)
>
> *nuniin* 'his land' (relative case)
>
> *uinga* 'her husband' (absolutive case)
>
> *uingan* 'her husband' (relative case)
>
> *uingit* 'their husbands' (absolutive case)

Pronouns

Personal Pronouns

Since the subject of the verb and the pronominal object are both marked on the verbs, personal pronouns are not used as much in Yup'ik as they are in English. It must be pointed also that Yup'ik pronouns and person markers do not distinguish gender but do distinguish three numbers: singular, dual, and plural. Like nouns, pronouns are also inflected for various cases. (The various forms will not be listed here.)

Unlike English, Yup'ik distinguishes two kinds of third person, the third person that is coreferential with the subject of a preceding clause and the one that is not coreferential with the said subject. In English, a sentence like 'When John entered he saw the book' is ambiguous because the pronoun 'he' could be referring to John or to someone else mentioned before. In Yup'ik there is no such ambiguity since Yup'ik has different markings for coreferential and non-coreferential third person pronouns and person marking.

In addition, Yup'ik has demonstrative pronouns which indicate several "exotic" parameters. For example, there are three different forms for the demonstrative which means 'the one down the river, on the coast, or by the exit':

unegna ('extended', that is, indicating large expanses of land or water, or objects that are lengthy or moving)

ugna ('restricted', that is, indicating objects that are stationary or moving within a confined area, or are fairly small in extent, relatively near and visible)

cakemna ('obscured', that is, indicating objects that are farther away and not clearly in sight)

Verbs

Yup'ik verbs take endings which mark (a) transitivity and intransitivity, (b) person/number of subject (and object, if transitive), (c) mood.

These markers also show a strong tendency toward fusion, and it is often very difficult to make clear morpheme cuts between the various markers. However, in some cases, at least, it is possible to observe the sequencing of the various markers in verbal endings:

kiput-a-k-0

buy + transitive marker + dual obj. + 3d pers. sing. subj.

'He buys them (two).'

tangrr-a-i-t

see + transitive marker + 3d pl. obj. + 3d pl. subj.

'They see them.'

But sometimes it is not possible to isolate various elements:

nallu-uq

not know + 3d pers. sing. intransitive

'He doesn't know.'

nallu-a

not know + 3d pers. sing. transitive subj., 3d pers. sing. obj.

'He doesn't know it.'

It should be noted that incorporated nominal objects do not necessarily make verbs grammatically transitive. Transitivity depends on whether there is a direct object NP (at least understood one) outside the verb form itself. Thus, for example, with the postbase *-li-* 'to make an N' ('N' here refers to the incorporated nominal stem preceding this postbase) one can have either an intransitive or a transitive verb:

angya-li-uq

boat + make + 3d pers. sing. intransitive

'He is making a boat.'

angya-li-a

boat + make + 3d pers. sing. transitive subj., 3d pers. sing.
    obj. (marked by zero)

'He is making a boat for him.'

Moods

There are many mood forms in Yup'ik: (a) indicative (unmarked), (b) interrogative, (c) optative (used to mark wishes and commands), (d) subordinate.

Although yes/no questions in Yup'ik use the indicative mood verb forms (along with the interrogative enclitic *-llu*), content questions must use main verbs marked for interrogative mood.

The subordinate mood involves a variety of participial-like constructions or dependent clause VPs which can be translated into English by subordinate clauses such as 'while I was doing X', 'when I was doing X', or 'before I did X'.

calinginaurnani

'while he works'

calivailgan

'before he works'

D. Syntax

Eskimo syntax is rather simple because much of the grammatical work is done by morphology. The basic word order is SVO (although examples of OV order are commonly found in the various grammars if there is no subject NP in the sentence), and case relationships are marked primarily by case endings.

As can be seen from the discussion of case endings above, Eskimo is an ergative language in which the subject of the intransitive verb and the direct object of a transitive verb are marked by the same case ending whereas the subject of a transitive verb is marked by a different ending.

Negation

Negation is expressed primarily by various postbases. In addition some verbs have very different lexical items for their negative counterparts. That is, there are different stems for 'to know' *(nallunrite-)* and 'not to know' *(nallu-)*.

Interrogative Sentences

Yes/no sentences add the interrogative enclitic *-qaa* to the first word in the sentence:

angut-em-qaa ner-aa neqa?

man + relat. case + interrog. enclitic/ eat + 3d pers. sing. transitive subj. (3d pers. sing. obj. expressed by zero)/ fish (absolutive case)

'Is the man eating the fish?'

However, content questions require a question word ('what?', 'how?', etc.) and the main verb of such sentences must also be inflected for interrogative mood instead of the indicative mood:

ciin ner'-a?

why/ eat + 3d pers. sing. intransitive subj., interrog. mood

'Why is he eating?'

ciin ner-au?

why/ eat + 3d pers. sing. transitive subj., interrog. mood (3d pers. sing. obj. marked by zero)

'Why is he eating it?'

Relative Clauses

Yup'ik relative clauses are formed by means of various postbases which basically nominalize the VPs to which they are attached. For example, the postbase -*llr*- with unpossessed ending marks the subject of the underlying verb taken intransitively, that is, 'the one who V-ed'. For example:

pai-lleq < *pai* + *llr*

babysit + *llr* (absolutive case)

'the one who babysat'

But if a possessor ending is added, the expressed word denotes the *object* of the underlying verb taken transitively: 'the one that the grammatical possessor V-ed'.

pai-llr-a

babysit + *llr* + 3d pers. sing. poss.

'the one she babysat'

E. SAMPLE TEXT

There are very few original texts in Central Yup'ik. Most of those available are actually translations from English done by linguists and their native informants. The text given here is a very simple self introduction that a native teacher of Central Yup'ik gave to me in St. Mary's, Alaska, in 1978 when I was training some Central Yup'ik native speakers to become elementary school teachers of that language.

Eskimo Text

Waqaa! Wiinga atengqertua Lena L-amek. Yup'iugna. Yugtun qaneryuumaunga. Elicariciqua mikelnguarnek yugtun. Yuurtellruunga nunacuarmi atengqerrluni Anipaunguarvigmek. Elicartua qayugga elicallerkamnek mikelnguarat yugtun.

Literal Morpheme-by-Morpheme Translation

(1) *Waqaa! Wiinga ate-ngqer-tu-a Lena L-amek.*
hello!/ **I**/ **name** + **have** + intransitive indic. + 1st pers. sing. intransitive/ **Lena** (proper name)/ **L** (abbreviated last name) + ablat. modalis case

(2) *Yup'i-ug-na. Yug-tun qaner-yuuma-u-nga.*
Yup'ik (lit. 'real person')/. **Eskimo** (language) + aequalis case/ **speak** + **be able** + intransitive indic. + 1st pers. sing. intransitive

(3) *Elicar-i-ciq-u-a mikel-nguar-nek yug-tun.*
teach + half-transitive (used with indefinite objects) + future + intransitive indic. + 1st pers. sing. intransitive/ small + one who is (= **'child'**) + modalis ablat. pl.

(4) *Yuurte-llru-u-nga nuna-cuar-mi ate-ngqerr-lu-ni Anipa-unguar-vig-mek.*
be born + perf. asp. + intransitive indic. + 1st pers. sing. intransitive/ land, **village** + **small** + localis sing./ **name** + **have, possess** + appositional (intransitive ending) + 3d pers. sing./ **owl** + **be false** + **place** + modalis ablat. sing.

(5) *Elicar-tu-a qayugga elica-ller-kam-nek mikel-nguara-t yug-tun.*
learn + intransitive indic. + 1st pers. sing. intransitive/ **how**/ **teach** + act of V-ing + future act + ablat. modalis plural (with the sense of 'about')/ small + one who is + (= **'child'**) + plural (absolutive)/ **Eskimo** (language) + aequalis

Idiomatic Translation

Hello! My name is Lena L. I am Yup'ik. I can speak Yup'ik. I shall be teaching Yup'ik to children. I was born in a small place called Owl Village. I am learning how to teach the children.

SKETCH OF AYACUCHO QUECHUA

A. GENETIC RELATIONSHIP AND GENERAL INFORMATION

Quechua has been classified by some scholars as being a member of the so-called Quechumaran language family, which, besides various Quechua languages and dialects, also includes Aymara, its dialects, and Aymara's close relatives such as Jaqaru. In other words, Quechumaran consists of what Kaufman (1990) calls *Kechua* and *Hakí (Jaqui)* language complexes, but Kaufman himself appears to be neutral on whether such classification is correct. This classification is currently somewhat controversial because there are some linguists who doubt that Aymara and Quechua groups are genetically related: Nobody argues that there has been some diffusion between the Aymara and Quechua languages, and it is now a question of whether the putative cognates that were used to link the two groups genetically are also due to diffusion.

It is claimed by those who question the Quechumaran hypothesis that the latter was based primarily on the comparison of Aymara and the Cuzco Quechua (usually considered to be the "standard" Quechua of the ancient Inca empire) and the geographically close Bolivian Quechua, both of which clearly have been influenced by Aymara. In addition, those scholars who have attempted to establish the genetic link between Aymara and Quechua seem have assumed that the Cuzco dialect of Quechua and Bolivian Quechua were very conservative in that they alone preserved the original three-way contrast between plain voiceless stops, voiceless aspirated stops, and voiceless glottalized ejectives—a contrast that was presumed lost in other Quechua dialects. (Ayacucho Quechua, for example, has only the plain voiceless stop/affricate series). This three-way contrast is the hallmark of all the Aymara languages and dialects, and there is no doubt that it should be reconstructed for Proto-Aymara. If the three-way contrast goes back to Proto-Quechumaran, it is somewhat suspicious (although not necessarily impossible) that the only Quechua languages that seem to have preserved it are those in close proximity of Aymaran languages. On the other hand, if the three-way contrast in some of the Quechua languages is due to diffusion, then there is no mystery as to why only the particular Quechua languages in proximity of Aymara have it.

Adelaar (1992:303), in summarizing the difficulties of grouping Quechua languages with Aymara, states that Quechua shares about 25% of its vocabulary with Aymara, including some basic lexical items, and that the two languages share a number of similarities in their sound systems and basic morphological structure. On the other hand, the greater part of their lexicons shows no similarlity, and the shapes of grammatical morphemes show no systematic correspondences.

The Quechuan languages stretch from the southern part of Colombia (Putumayo) in the north to Chile and Argentina (Santiago del Estero) in the south. According to Grimes (1992), the total number of speakers of some kind of Quechua may be as high as 8.5 million or more. The same source estimates that 41.3% of the population of Ecuador or 4,320,000 people speaks a Quechuan language. The largest Quechua speaking groups of population are as follows:

> *Central or South Bolivian Quechua* is spoken by a total 3,632,000 speakers, of whom 2,782,000 are in Bolivia and 850,000 are in Argentina.
>
> *Cuzco Quechua* has 1,250,000 speakers and has official status in Peru. (Since Cuzco was the capital of the Inca empire, this dialect acquired prestige and was considered to be the "purest" Quechua dialect.)
>
> *Ayacucho Quechua (Chanka)* with 1,000,000 speakers is also spoken in Peru generally to the west of Cuzco Quechua.

Chimborazo Highland Quichua is spoken by 1,000,000 speakers in Ecuador.

Ancash Quechua is spoken in Peru by about 500,000 speakers.

Other Quechua groups are smaller, though some of them number in the hundreds of thousands. In Ecuador the term *Quichua* is preferred over *Quechua*.

According to Parker (1963), Quechua dialects are divided into two major groups: Quechua A, which includes several dialect groups of Central Peru such as Ancash, Huánuco, Junín, Lima, and Pasco, and Quechua B, which includes all the rest. It is reported that there is no mutual intelligibility between the Quechua A dialects and Quechua B dialects. According to Torero (1964), Quechua A (which he calls Quechua II) is further subdivided into three groups.

Quechua IIA includes a number of Quechua varieties in Cajamarca and Lambayeque in northern Peru and some dialects spoken in mountain villages of the department of Lima. Adelaar (1992:305), however, questions this particular grouping.

Quechua IIB, according to Adelaar (1992), is a much more firmly established subgroup and includes the varieties of Quechua spoken in Ecuador and Colombia as well as the dialects spoken in Chachapyas in Amazonas, Peru, and a coastal variety, also found in Peru.

Quechua IIC includes a large number of Quechua varieties spoken to the southeast of Quechua B (Torero's Quechua I). This includes Ayacucho Quechua as well as the dialects of Cuzco and southern Peru, and all the Quechua varieties spoken in Bolivia, Chile, and Argentina.

Ayacucho Quechua is closest to Cuzco Quechua, its neighbor to the east, and is to a high degree mutually intelligible with that dialect. The major difference between the two dialects has already been mentioned: Cuzco Quechua has a three-way distinction in the consonants that is not found in Ayacucho Quechua.

In some areas there are still very large numbers of monolingual Quechua speakers, and some non-Quechua Indians are learning Quechua as a second language. (Some groups of Quechua speakers are reported to be trilingual in Quechua, Spanish, and Aymara.) In general, however, most Quechua speakers are to a certain extent bilingual in Spanish, and the latter language has greatly influenced Quechua. In both Cuzco and Ayacucho Quechua there are not only many borrowed simple vocabulary items from Spanish but also some borrowed grammatical words such as prepositions (which originally did not exist in Quechua as a grammatical category),[4] and Quechua mediopassive construction is sometimes used like the Spanish passive, most likely because of Spanish influence. (For the use of the mediopassive in Ayacucho Quechua, see *Verbs* in the section on morphology.)

B. PHONETICS, PHONOLOGY AND ORTHOGRAPHY

Consonants

The consonant symbols which are preceded by an asterisk in Table 7.3 are found almost exclusively in loanwords (from Spanish). The symbols in paren-

Table 7.3   QUECHUA CONSONANTS

	LABIAL	ALVEOLAR	PALATAL	VELAR	UVULAR
Voiceless stops	p	t	tʃ (č)	k	
Voiced stops	*b	*d		*g	
Voiceless fricatives	*f	s		x (h)	χ (q)
Nasals	m	n	ɲ (ñ)		
Laterals		l	ʎ (ĺ)		
Tap		ɾ (r)			
Retroflex fricatives		*ʐ (ř)			
Glides	w		j (y)		

theses are those used in Parker (1969) for the sounds in question. In the usual orthography used in Peru and other countries where Quechua is spoken, [tʃ] is usually written as *ch*, [ʎ] as *ll*, and [ɲ] as *ñ*.

The retroflex phoneme /ř/ which is found only in Spanish loanwords is often written as *rr* in the usually accepted orthography.

The voiceless aspirated series of consonants and the voiceless glottalized ejective series of consonants which are found in Cuzco and Central Bolivian dialects of Quechua are usually marked in the orthography by a double apostrophe following the consonant symbol (e.g., *p"*) and a single apostrophe following a consonant symbol (e.g., *p'*) respectively.

The voiceless uvular fricative phoneme /χ/ corresponds to a voiceless uvular stop [q] in other Quechuan dialects and languages, and therefore Parker (1969) prefers to transcribe it as *q*. Actually, even in Ayacucho Quechua after *n* this phoneme may also be realized as a stop. The phoneme /h/ varies in value from [h] to [x] (voiceless velar fricative). Phoneme /n/ is realized as a velar nasal [ŋ] syllable-finally except before apical consonants /t, tʃ, d, s, ʐ/ where it is realized as an apicoalveolar nasal [n]. Finally, in the following environments the phoneme /s/ is realized as /ʃ/: between vowel *i* and followed by either tʃ or *k*.

Vowels

The vowel phonemes /e/ and /o/ are contrastive only in loanwords (mostly from Spanish); otherwise, [e] and [o] may be considered to be allophones of /i/ and /u/ respectively in the environment next to the uvular (or postvelar) fricative /χ/. In Parker's (1969) phonemic transcription (which will be used throughout the rest of this sketch) *e* and *o* are differentiated only in the situations where they contrast with *i* and *u*; otherwise, they are transcribed as *i* and *u* respectively.

Some Quechua speakers who are not sufficiently exposed to Spanish sometimes substitute *i* and *u* for *e* and *o* respectively in their pronunciation of the Spanish loanwords.

Stress is generally placed on the penultimate syllable, except in a few cases (morphologically determined) in which the stress falls on the final syllable.

Table 7.4   QUECHUA VOWELS

i		u
*e		*o
	a	

C. MORPHOLOGY

Generally speaking Quechua morphology may be characterized as being of the agglutinative type in the sense that relatively long strings of affixes are quite common; however, there is at the same time a number of allomorphic irregularities that are not so typical of agglutinative languages. The degree of morphological irregularity, however, is not so high as to qualify Quechua as a polysynthetic language according to the definition of the term "polysynthetic" given in Chapter 1.[5]

Nouns

Basically the morphological structure of a Quechua noun is as follows: Noun stem + (person suffix) + (plural marker) + (case suffixes).

Many stems are ambiguous in that without any additional morphological markers they can be used either as noun or verb stems. Person suffixes added to nouns function as possessive pronouns. Number marking is not obligatory and is usually used only when it is necessary to emphasize plurality. More than one case suffix may be attached to the nominal complex. Since the nominative case is unmarked, a bare stem may appear as an independent word.

i. Person Marking Suffixes on Nominals

Person suffixes on nouns have the force of possessive pronouns. On nominalized verb forms they indicate the subject of the nominalized verb phrase.

First person singular is marked by -niy after consonants and -y after vowels:

> ñan-niy 'my road'; wasi-y 'my house'

Second person singular is marked by -niki (from ni-yki after consonants and -yki after vowels, but y is lost after the vowel i:

> ñan-niki 'your (sing.) road'; wasi-ki 'your (sing.) house'; ima-yki 'your possession'

Third person singular is marked by -nin after consonants and -n after vowels:

> ñan-nin 'his, her road'; wasi-n 'his, her house'

Note that what all the preceding forms have in common is a connective element -ni after consonants which is not present after stems ending in vowels.[6]

The plural marking for persons is somewhat more complicated. There are two pluralizing morphemes. The first, -ninčik/-nčik, refers to a group that includes the addressee and also the speaker unless it is preceded by second person marker (in which case it only includes the addressee):

ñan-ninčik 'our (incl.) road'   *wasi-nčik* 'our (incl.) house'

ñan-niki-čik 'your (pl.) road'   *wasi-ki-čik* 'your (pl.) house'

The other pluralizing morpheme *-ku* excludes the addressee(s):

ñan-ni-ku 'our (excl.) road'   *wasi-y-ku* 'our (excl.) house'

ñan-nin-ku 'their road'   *wasi-n-ku* 'their house'

The suffix *-ku* may refer only to human beings.

ii. Number Marking

Number, except in person marking suffixes and independent pronouns, is not an obligatory category in Quechua. Nouns are optionally pluralized by the addition of the suffix *-kuna* which precedes case suffixes, if any.

iii. Case Endings

Case relations in Ayacucho Quechua are signaled primarily by case suffixes on the nouns and nouns acting like postpositions, as well as a few prepositions borrowed from Spanish. The case suffixes are as follows:

> a. *Nominative: zero marker*
>
> b. *Accusative: -ta*

This case suffix marks the direct object NP; with verbs of motion an object marked with this suffix is the goal of the motion. (In addition, this suffix is also used to derive adverbs from adjectives.)

> *Wasi-ta qawa-n.*
>
> house + acc./ watch + simple pres. tense
>
> 'He watches the house.'

> *Wasi-ta ri-n.*
>
> house + acc./ go + simple pres. tense
>
> 'He goes to the house.'

> *Alĩn-ta ruwa-n.*
>
> good + acc./ do, make + simple pres. tense
>
> 'He does well.'

> c. *Possessive or Genitive: -pa*

This case marks simple possession.

> *ñuqa-pa tayta-y-pa wasi-n*
>
> 1st pers. sing. pronoun + gen. case/ father + 1st pers. sing. (poss.) + gen. case/ house + 3d pers. sing. (poss.)
>
> 'my father's house'

Note that the possessed noun has to have person agreement with the possessor. Thus, the above phrase is literally 'my father's his house'.

  d. *Locative: -pi*

This suffix signals general location: 'in, at, on, within'. More precise locations (e.g., above, under) are signaled by means of various nouns used as postpositions which have the locative suffix attached to them. With names of days and months it may be translated as 'during'.

> *wasi-pi*
>
> house + locative
>
> 'in, at, on the house'

> *setembri-pi*
>
> September + locative
>
> 'in, during September'

  e. *Illative/Directional: -man*

This suffix indicates direction and can be translated as 'to, toward, into, onto' or 'according to' with *hina* 'like'. With verbs of motion it marks the goal just like *-ta* accusative. (Note that the latter cannot be used if the subject is non-human.)

> *Ñuqa-man qumu-wa-y.*
>
> 1st pers. sing. pronoun + illat./directional/ give + 1st pers. sing. obj. + imperat.
>
> 'Give it to me!'

> *pay-man hina*
>
> 3d pers. sing. + illat./directional/ like
>
> 'according to him'

  f. *Ablative: -manta*

This case suffix marks the origin of an action and in addition has many idiomatic uses. It may be translated as 'from, about, concerning, instead of, made of, by' as well as 'than' in comparative constructions (cf. *Adjectives*).

> *Wasi-manta ĩuqsi-n.*
>
> house + ablat./ leave + simple pres. tense
>
> 'He leaves the house.'

Wasi-manta rima-n.

house + ablat./ speak + simple pres. tense

'He speaks about the house.'

Pay-mi ri-nqa ñuqa-manta.

3d pers. sing. pronoun + personal experience comment en-
clitic/ go + future tense/ 1st pers. sing. pronoun + ablat.

'He will go in my stead.'

Feřu-manta-m.

iron + ablat. + personal experience comment enclitic

'It is made of iron.'

    g. Limitational/Terminative: -kama
This suffix means 'up to, as far as, until':

wasi-kama

house + limitational

'as far as the house'

    h. Interactive: -pura
This suffix marks location of a thing *among others of its kind:*

Amigu-pura ka-čka-n.

friend + interlocative/ be + durative + simple pres. tense

'They are among friends.'

   When the things involved are not of the same kind the stem *čawpi* 'center,
midst' plus locative case suffix marks similar relationship:

Wasi čawpi-pi ka-čka-n.

house + midst + loc./ be + durative + simple pres. tense

'He is among the houses.'

    i. Causal: -rayku
This suffix means 'because, because of'.

ñuqa-rayku

1st pers. sing. pronoun + causal

'because of me'

j. Purposive/Benefactive: -paq

This suffix indicates purpose or beneficiary:

Qam-ĩa-paq-mi.

2nd pers. sing. pronoun + limiting suffix 'only, merely' + purposive/benefactive + personal experience comment enclitic

'It is just for you.'

miku-na-m-paq.

eat + nominalizer + 3d pers. sing. + purposive/benefactive

'in order for him to eat'

k. Comitative/Instrumental/Associative: -wan

This case suffix signals accompaniment (comitative function), or means or instrument (instrumental function).

Ñuqa-wan-mi ri-n.

1st pers. sing. pronoun + comit. + personal experience comment enclitic

'He goes with me.'

Lampa-wan ĩamka-čka-n.

hoe + instr./ work + durative + simple pres. tense

'He is working with the hoe.'

The same suffix *-wan* also appears after other case suffixes as an additive construction marker or conjunction, that is with a meaning of 'and'. (Cf. below.)

It should be noted that some of the case suffixes may occur in combination with other case suffixes. For example, the genitive case suffix may be followed by other case suffixes, especially the locative/directional ones when an NP which is possessed is merely understood, but is not overtly present:

kura-pa-pi

priest/gen./loc.

'at the priest's (house)'

Similarly, the comitative case suffix may follow all other suffixes where it merely connects two NP's as a conjunction 'and':

wasi-ta-wan tuři-ta

house + obj. marker + comit./ tower + obj. marker

'to (with the verb of motion understood) the house and to the tower'

Pronouns

Person is marked on most verb forms, and therefore independent pronouns are used less than in English. They are used for emphasis and in situations where the subject/object verbal suffix system has structural gaps. The independent forms are shown in Table 7.5.

Note that there is no gender distinction in the third person pronouns or in person marking elsewhere in Quechua. Thus *pay* may mean either 'he' or 'she.' The first person plural has two different forms: *exclusive,* which excludes the addressee, and *inclusive,* which includes the addressee.

Table 7.5 QUECHUA PERSONAL PRONOUNS

1st pers. sing.	*ñuqa*	1st pers. pl. incl.	*ñuqa-nčik*
		1st pers. pl. excl.	*ñuqa-y-ku*
2d pers. sing.	*qam*	2d pers. pl.	*qam-kuna*
3d pers. sing.	*pay*	3d pers. pl.	*pay-kuna*

Adjectives

For the most part Quechua adjectives behave very much like other substantives; in fact some stems may act either as nouns or as adjectives. Comparison of adjectives does not involve any special affixes on the adjectives themselves.

Equality Comparison:

Qaqa hina kapka-m kay tanta-qa.

rock, boulder/ like/ hard + comment enclitic/ this/ bread + topic enclitic

'This bread is as hard as a rock.'

Comparative of Superiority/Inferiority:

Qaqa-manta aswan kapka-m kay tanta-qa.

rock + ablat. 'from'/ more/ hard + comment enclitic/ this/ bread + topic enclitic

'This bread is harder than a rock.'

L̃ama-kuna-manta pisi hatun-mi al̃qu-kuna-qa.

llama + plural + ablat. 'from'/ little, few (= 'less') + comment enclitic/ dog + plural + topic enclitic

'Dogs are smaller than the llamas.'

Superlatives:

> *Kay sača-qa l̃iw-manta (aswan) hatun-in-mi.*
>
> this/ tree + topic enclitic/ every + ablat. 'from'/ (more)/ big + 3d pers. sing. + comment enclitic
>
> 'This tree is the biggest of all.'

> *Kay sača-qa l̃iw sača-kuna-manta pisi hatun-mi.*
>
> this/ tree + topic enclitic/ every/ tree + pl. + ablat. 'from'/ little, few/ big + comment enclitic
>
> 'This tree is the smallest of all trees.'

Quechua comparison of adjectives is fairly similar to that found in many other languages that do not have special comparative and superlative affixes on adjectives (e.g., Japanese).

Verbs

Tense/Aspect Markers

According to Parker (1969), Ayacucho Quechua has the following aspect markers.

> *-n* aspect does not seem to have much meaning by itself.
>
> *-r* is perfective or completive aspect marker.
>
> *-p* appears only before the subordinate verb marker *-tin* to indicate that the subject of this form is different from the subject of the verb in the main clause.
>
> *-s* aspect marker appears only in combination with tense and subordination markers and is hard to assign meaning to. (However, in quotative past, discussed later, it appears to have "hearsay" force similar to the comment enclitic *-si*, which also has that force.)

Tense and aspect suffixes combine in the following ways to form the following tenses:

1. stem + *n* aspect marker alone = simple present tense
2. stem + *n* aspect marker + *qa* (nonpresent) = future tense
3. stem + *r* aspect marker + *qa* (nonpresent) = simple past
4. stem + *s* aspect marker + *qa* (nonpresent) = quotative past tense
5. stem + *q* (agentive nominalization) + *ka* (verb 'to be') + (optional simple past marking *-rqa-*) + subject marking = iterative or habitual past tense

Note that the present or past form of 'to be' is used only with the first and second persons; in the case of the third person singular, the auxiliary verb is entirely dropped, and in the third person plural the third person plural marker is added directly after *-q*, not to a form of the verb 'to be':

> *riku-q* 'he used to see'; *rikuq-ku* 'they used to see'.

Examples:

> *riku-n* 'he sees'
>
> *riku-n-qa* 'he will see'
>
> *riku-r-qa* 'he saw'
>
> *riku-s-qa* 'he saw (I am told)'
>
> *riku-q ka-ni* or *riku-q ka-rqa-ni* 'I used to see'.

Person Marking on Verbs

Person marking on verbs is very similar to person marking in nouns except that somewhat different allomorphs are used; also, besides subject marking (possessor marking in nouns) the verbs are also inflected for object.

Table 7.6 shows that the plural marking is somewhat complex: *-čik* is not simply a plural marker but refers to a group that includes the addressee and which, unless preceded by a second person marker, may also include the speaker; *-ku* is also not simply a plural marker but refers to a group that excludes the addressee and may include the speaker if it is preceded by first person marking. *-ku* may be used only in reference to human beings.

The first person singular has two allomorphs: *-y* after vowels in compound forms and *-ni* after consonants and in noncompound affixes.

In the future tense only the first person subject is marked irregularly by a suffix *-sa*:

> *Riku-sa-q.*
>
> see + 1st pers. + future
>
> 'I shall see.'

Table 7.6 SUBJECT MARKERS

1st pers. sing.	*-y/-ni*	1st pers. pl. incl.	*-čik*
		1st pers. pl. excl.	*-i-ku*
2d pers. sing.	*-ki*	2d pers. pl.	*-ki-čik*
3d pers. sing.	unmarked	3d pers. pl.	*-ku*

Object Markers

There are two special object suffixes: *-wa*, which indicates that the first person is the object, and *-su*, which, if followed by a second person suffix, indicates that the addressee is the object of a third person action. These two suffixes usually precede all other suffixes.

In addition, there are some other allomorphic complications involving irregular allomorphs and sequencing of the suffixes, but for the sake of brevity they will not be mentioned here.

Table 7.7   OBJECT MARKERS

1st pers. sing. subj.–2d pers. sing. obj.	*riku-y-ki*	'I see you (sing.).'
1st pers. sing. subj.–2d pers. pl. obj.	*riku-y-ki-čik*	'I see you (pl.)'
1st pers. pl. excl. subj.–2d pers. sing. obj.	*riku-y-ki-ku*	'We (excl.) see you (sing.).'
2d pers. sing. subj.–1st pers. sing. obj.	*riku-wa-n-ki*	'You (sing.) see me.'
2d pers. pl. subj.–1st pers. sing. obj.	*riku-wa-ni-ki-čik*	'You (pl.) see me.'
2d pers. sing. subj.–1st pers. pl. excl. obj.	*riku-wa-n-ki-ku*	'You see us (excl.).'
3d pers. sing. subj.–1st pers. sing. obj.	*riku-wa-n*	'He/she sees me.'
3d pers. sing. subj.–1st pers. pl. incl. obj.	*riku-wa-n-čik*	'He sees us (incl.).'
3d pers. sing. subj.–1st pers. pl. excl. obj.	*riku-wa-n-ku*	'He sees us (excl.).'
3d pers. sing. subj.–2d pers. sing. obj.	*riku-su-n-ki*	'He sees you (sing.).'
3d pers. sing. subj.–2d pers. pl. obj.	*riku-su-n-ki-čik*	'He sees you (pl.).'

Subject/object suffix combinations other than those listed above are not allowed by the rules. When the actor is third person plural, or if the object is third person, or if both the subject and the object are plural, the relationship must be expressed by independent pronoun forms.

Reflexive or Mediopassive
Reflexive construction is formed by adding the mediopassive modal *-ku* suffix to the verb stem:

Riku-ku-ni.

see + mediopassive + 1st pers. sing.

'I see myself.' (or 'I see for myself.')

Mediopassive has either a reflexive function (as in our example) or signals an action that the subject performs for himself or on behalf of himself.

Note that mediopassive is sometimes also used as an equivalent to English passive because of influence from Spanish. However, there is a native quasi-passive construction that is apparently not imported from Spanish and which does not use the mediopassive suffix:

Pay-qa qawa-sqa ka-sqa huwansitu-wan-mi.

3d pers. sing. (pron.) + topic marker enclitic/ watch, see + *sqa* vb. nominalizer/ be + *sqa* verb nominalizer/ Johnny + comit./instr. case + personal experience comment enclitic

'He was seen by Johnny.'

Moods
     i. Imperative
Imperative mood is signaled by the suffix *-y* which usually follows right after the stem or the object person suffix *-wa* ('me'):

riku-y

see + imperative

'see!'

ii. Conditional

Conditional mood is signaled by the suffix *-man* added to the present tense of the verb, following all suffixes except the plural nonsecond person suffix *-ku*. Besides the usual conditional meaning ('would'), it may also mean 'should', 'may', and 'might'.

Wakin-ku taki-n-man-ku.

other + 3d pers. pl./ sing. + simple pres. + conditional + 3d pers. pl.

'Others would sing.'

Past conditional adds the past tense form of the verb 'to be' to the present conditional form:

Čay mesa-ta ãlin-ta ruwa-n-man ka-rqa.

that/ table + acc./ good + acc. (= 'well')/ make, do + simple pres. tense + conditional/ be + simple past tense

'He should have made that table well.'

iii. Injunctive

Injunctive indicates a wish for some action to take place and is signaled by the suffix *-ču* which follows the stem or object *-wa* but precedes the *-n-* aspect marker:

Riku-ču-n.

see + injunctive + simple pres. tense

'May he see.'

Subordinate Verb Forms

There are three different subordinate verb forms which function somewhat like English participles.

a. p-ti Subordinate Verb Marker

The *p-* part of this marker indicates that the subject of this verb form is different from the subject of the verb in main clause. This subordinate form therefore must always be inflected for person (as opposed to the other two subordinate verb forms). It indicates an action that begins before the action expressed by the verb in the main clause and is usually translatable into English by a clause introduced by 'if', 'when', or 'because'.

Ñuqa ni-pti-y-mi ri-rqa.

1st pers. sing. (pron.)/ say + *pti* subord. vb. marker + 1st
   pers. sing. + personal experience comment enclitic/ go +
   simple past

'He went because I said it.'

b. *spa Subordinate Verb Marker*

The subordinate verb form derived with this marker is different from the *pti*
subordinate form only in that its subject and the subject of the verb of the
main clause are the same. It is usually translatable into English by an *-ing*
participial form the tense of which depends on the tense of the main verb.
Person marking on this form is optional.

Miku-spa-n ĩuqsi-rqa.

eat + *spa* subord. vb. marker + 3d pers. sing./ leave, depart + simple past tense

'Having eaten, he left.' or 'When he had eaten, he left.'

c. *s-tin Subordinate Verb Marker*

This marker also signals that the subordinate verb form it derives has the
same subject as the verb of the main clause. It marks action that takes place
at the same time as the action of the main verb and is usually translatable by
a phrase introduced by 'while' or simply by a participle in *-ing*. This form is
never inflected for person.

Tuma-stin puriku-čka-n-ki.

drink + *stin* subord. vb. form marker/ walk around + durative + simple pres. + 2d pers. sing.

'You are walking around drinking.'

Simultaneous action of two different actors must be expressed by a construction in which a *stin* subordinate form is in attributive relationship to a *pti*
subordinate form of the durative stem of *ka-* 'to be':

Ŵaqa-stin ka-čka-pti-n ĩuqsi-rqa-ni.

cry + *stin* subord. vb. marker/ be + durative + *pti* subord.
   vb. marker + 3d pers. sing./ leave, depart + simple past
   tense + 1st pers. sing.

'I left while she was crying.'

Verb Derivation and Modal Suffixes

Verb derivation is very richly developed in Quechua. Verbs can be fairly easily derived from noun stems or adjective stems by means of various derivational suffixes:

wasi-ča

house + deriv. verb marker

'to make a house'

sumaq-ya

pretty, beautiful + deriv. verb marker

'to become pretty'

According to Parker (1969:31) Ayacucho Quechua has sixteen modal suffixes which occur in various combinations to yield thousands of derived forms from a single verb stem. Only a few of such derivations will be cited below as an illustration:

riku-pa-n: 'he sees again' (repetitive)

riku-raya-n: 'he sees continually' (continuative)

riku-ru-n: 'he has just seen, he sees urgently' (sudden or urgent action)

riku-ku-n: 'he sees himself, he sees it for himself' (mediopassive)

riku-či-n: 'he has someone see' (caus.)

riku-ysi-n: 'he helps someone see' (auxiliary)

riku-pu-n: 'he sees it for someone' (benefactive)

riku-na-ku-n: 'he and someone else see each other' (reciprocal + mediopassive)

riku-mu-n: 'he sees there, he goes to see' (loc./motion)

riku-čka-n: 'he is seeing' (durative or progressive)

To Have

Quechua does not have a verb corresponding to the English verb 'to have'. Predication of possession is made by means of the verb 'to be, to exist' and personal suffixes on nouns (which have possessive pronoun value), and sometimes genitive case marking.

Bisinti-pa-qa ka-čka-n-ña-s musuq wasi-n.

Vicente (prop. noun) + gen. suffix + topic marker enclitic/ be, exist + durative + simple pres. tense + already + hearsay enclitic/ new/ house + 3d pers. sing. (poss.)

'They say Vicente already has a new house.'

More literally this sentence means something like 'Vicente's new house already exists (it is said)'.

Lapis-niy ka-n.

pencil + 1st pers. sing. (poss.)/ be, exist + simple pres. tense

'I have a pencil.' (Lit. 'My pencil exists')

A more emphatic predication of possession is made by means of the bene-factive verb suffix *pu-:*

Lapis-niy ka-pu-wa-n.

pencil + 1st pers. sing. (poss.)/ be, exists + benefactive suf-
    fix + 1st pers. sing. obj. + simple pres. tense

'I have a pencil.' (Lit. 'My pencil exists for me.')

Enclitics

Clitics are morphemes which have many features in common with affix mor-phemes. For example, they are bound morphemes that usually have rela-tional/modal function rather than referential meaning. They differ from af-fixes in that they can be attached to words belonging to different parts of speech and may follow any morphemes, whereas specific affixes are usually limited to particular parts of speech and must appear in particular sequences in relation to other affixes. For example, the English comparative suffix *-er* can be attached only to adjective stems, and not even all adjective stems at that.

There are thirteen *enclitics* (clitics that are attached at the end of words, as opposed to *proclitics,* which are attached to the beginning of a word) in Quechua; a partial list follows. Note that there may be more than one clitic attached to the same word.

a. -puni Definite Statement Enclitic

Wasi-puni-m.

house + def. enclitic + comment enclitic

'It is definitely a house.'

b. -ña 'already, yet'

Karu-ña-m.

far + already enclitic + comment enclitic

'It is already far.'

This enclitic very often combines with the following one.

c. -taq Sequential/Contradictory Enclitic

This enclitic can be translated as 'so, then, and so'. It is also used to mark con-tradictory statements:

Yana-taq.

black + contradictory enclitic

'(You are wrong); it is black!'

d. *-ču Interrogative/Negative Enclitic*

For more details concerning this particular enclitic see "Negation" and "Interrogative Sentences" in the syntax section.

e. *-mi Personal Experience Comment Enclitic*

This enclitic has an allomorph *-m* which appears after vowels. It usually cannot be directly translated into English. It can occur only once in a given clause and indicates that the speaker is commenting from personal experience, not from hearsay, and has a certain degree of conviction that what he says is true. Thus, it contrasts with the following enclitic and does not occur together with it. In questions it occurs only with the phrase which is introduced by an interrogative stem or which adds the interrogative enclitic *-ču.*

Ima-ta-m muna-n-ki?

what + acc. + comment enclitic/ want + simple pres. tense + 2d pers. sing.

'What do you want?'

f. *-si Hearsay Enclitic*

This enclitic has the shape *-s* after a vowel. It indicates that what is being said is either hearsay (somebody else's report) or the speaker is not sure about what he is reporting because he may have dreamed it or have been drunk at the time he observed it, and so on.

Wasi-m-pi-ču-s ka-čka-n?

house + 3d pers. sing. (poss.) + loc. + interrog. enclitic + hearsay enclitic/ be + durative + simple pres. tense

'Do they say that he is at home?'

g. *-ča Conjectural Enclitic*

Mana-m ãlin-ča.

general negative + comment enclitic/ good + conjecture enclitic

'It's no good, I guess.'

h. *-qa Topic Marker Enclitic*

This enclitic marks the phrase whose referent is to be commented upon. Note that there may be more than one topic in a sentence.

Wasi-qa sumaq-mi.

house + topic enclitic/ beautiful + personal experience
comment enclitic

'The house (topic) is beautiful (comment)'

Note that in equational sentences in which the subject or topic is a third person, the verb 'to be' is not used, but the topic and comment markers are obligatory. A topic is what one is talking about, and comment is the new information about the topic that one wants to impart to the listener. Note that topic is not necessarily identical with the subject:

Mana-m karu-ču-qa.

general negative + personal experience comment enclitic/
far + negative enclitic + topic marker enclitic

'It is not far.'

More literally translated, the preceding Quechua sentence is 'As for being far (topic), it (subject) is not (the whole phrase after the comma is the comment).'

i. -ya Regret or Resignation Enclitic

Wasi-y-ya.

house + 1st pers. sing. (poss.) + regret enclitic

'Oh my poor house!'

j. -á General Emphatic Enclitic

This enclitic is realized as *-á* after comment enclitics; elsewhere it is realized simply as a shift of stress onto the last syllable of the word. It occurs only in polite and intimate address.

Wasi-n-s-á

house + 3d pers. sing. (poss.) + hearsay comment enclitic +
emphatic enclitic

'He says it is his house!'

D. SYNTAX

Word Order

The basic word order in Quechua is SOV, and modifiers usually precede the words they modify, but adverbial phrases may often follow the verb they modify, and SVO order is not entirely uncommon (due to Spanish influence?):

Wallpa-kuna sara-ta miku-čka-n-ku.

chicken + pl./ maize, corn + acc./ eat + durative + simple pres. tense + (3d pers.) pl. sub.

'The chickens are eating corn.' (SOV)

anča aĩin wasi

very/ good/ house

'a very good house' (adv. + adj. + noun)

Hawka yača-n.

peaceful(ly)/ live + simple present tense

'He lives peacefully.' (adv. + vb.)

Ri-n wayna + m + pa + ta.

go + simple pres. tense/ lover, young man + 3d pers. sing. poss. + gen. + acc. (here marking the direction of movement)

'She goes to her lover's (house).' (vb. + noun used adverbially)

Case Relations

Case relationships are signaled primarily by (a) noun suffixes, (b) nouns in conjunction with case suffixes used as postpositions, (c) subject/object suffixes on verbs, and, much more rarely, (d) few prepositions borrowed from Spanish:

(a) *wasi-pi*

house + loc.

'in the house'

(b) *wasi uku-pi*

house/ interior + loc.

'inside the house'

(c) *Riku-y-ki*

see + I + you

'I see you.'

(d) *(asta) uktubri-kama*

(until)/ October + limitational/terminative case

'until October'

Note that in the last example *asta* (< Spanish *hasta*) is an optional element.

Agreement

Gender agreement is foreign to Quechua, but a small number of nouns borrowed from Spanish preserve Spanish gender distinctions, and an even smaller number of borrowed adjectives actually show gender agreement:

> *amigu* 'friend' (masc.) vs. *amiga* 'friend' (fem.)
>
> *loko* 'crazy' (masc. agreement) vs. *loka* 'crazy' (fem. agreement)

Agreement in person is mandatory, however, between the subject of a verb and the subject suffix attached to the verb:

> *Qamqa ačka-ta-m miku-n-ki.*
>
> you (sing.)/ much + acc. + comment enclitic/ eat + simple pres. tense + 2d pers. sing. sub.
>
> 'You eat a lot.'

However, the subject and the verb *do not* have to agree in number in all situations. Thus both of the following sentences are acceptable:

> *Runa-kuna pukĩa-čka-n-ku.*
>
> man, person + pl./ play + durative + simple pres. tense + (3d pers.) pl.
>
> 'The men are playing.'
>
> *Runa-kuna pukĩa-čka-n.*
>
> man, person + pl./ play + durative + simple pres. tense
>
> 'The men are playing.'

Note that **Runa pukĩa-čka-n-ku* is not grammatical because it is not possible to have plural subject agreement suffix on the verb when its subject is not overtly marked for plurality.

Subordinate Clauses

Instead of being introduced by various subordinate conjunctions as in English, Quechua subordinate clauses for the most part consist of participle-like subordinate verb forms:

> *Miku-spa-n ĩuqsi-rqa.*
>
> eat + *spa*-subord. vb. marker + 3d pers. sing./ + leave, depart + simple past tense
>
> 'When he had eaten he left' or 'After eating he left.'

For other, similar subordinate verb constructions, see under "Verbs" in the morphology section.

Other types of subordinate clauses involve various nominalized verb forms:

> *Yac ă-n-i wasi ruwa-na-n-ta.*
>
> know + simple pres. tense + 1st pers. sing./ house/ do, make + nominalizer expressing potential state of an action + 3d pers. sing. + acc.
>
> 'I know that he will build a house.'

Relative Clauses

Relative clauses are not introduced by relative pronouns as in English and Spanish. Quechua equivalents of relative clauses consist of a verb phrase whose verb has been nominalized by one of the Quechua nominalizing suffixes, some of which have rather specialized functions. For example, -*q* a suffix which derives agent or instrument nouns from verbs can be used in the following construction to render one type of a relative clause:

> *l̃amka-q runa*
>
> work + agent nominalizer/ man, person
>
> 'man who works'

In addition to such nominalizations Quechua nouns may be suffixed with several suffixes which may be translated into English as relative clauses:

> *wasi-yuq*
>
> house + possessor suffix
>
> 'person who owns a house or houses, a landlord'

> *wasi-sapa*
>
> house + multiple possession of a referent
>
> 'a man who has many houses'

> *wasi-ntin*
>
> house + adjacence of position suffix
>
> 'that which has a house next to it'

Interrogative Sentences

Yes-or-no questions are formed by adding the interrogative enclitic -*ču* to the word being questioned (as in the case of Russian interrogative particle *li*) and moving the questioned word to the front of the sentence:

Ayakuču-ta-ču paqarin ri-nqa-ku?

Ayacucho + acc. + interrog. enclitic/ tomorrow/ go + future + (ed pers.) pl.

'Will they be going to Ayacucho (and not some other place) tomorrow?'

Paqarin-ču Ayakuču-ta ri-nqa-ku?

'Is it tomorrow that they will be going to Ayacucho?'

Negative interrogative sentences have the *-ču* enclitic being added to the general negative morpheme:

Mana-ču hamu-n-ki?

general negative + interrog. enclitic/ come + simple pres. + 2nd pers. sing.

'Aren't you coming?'

Content questions use interrogative words and usually do not add the interrogative enclitic:

Ima-ta-taq tayta-yki ruwa-čka-n?

what + acc. + an anclitic that appears to be a focus marker in questions/ father + 2nd pers. sing. possessor + do, make + durative + simple pres. tense

'What is your father doing?'

Negation

Negation is signaled by the general negative morpheme *mana* and the prohibitive marker (negative imperative marker) *ama,* and *-ču* negative enclitic is added to the main verb (but not to a subordinate verb form) or to the simple substantive that acts as a predicate (but not to substantives that have certain suffixes):

Mana-m ri-nqa-ču

general negative + comment enclitic (added for a certain degree of emphasis)/ go + future + negative enclitic

'He won't go.'

mana ri-spa-n

general negative/ go + *spa* subord. vb. marker + 3d pers. sing.

'not going, without going'

Mana-m wasi-ču.

general negative + comment enclitic (added for some emphasis)/ house + negative enclitic

'It is not a house.'

mana wasi-yuq

general negative/ house + possessor

'one who has no house, houseless'

Negative words such as 'nobody' and 'nothing' are formed with interrogative words acting as indefinite pronouns which are negated and then suffixed with the suffix meaning 'even'. (This construction is very similar to its Japanese equivalent.)

Mana pi-pas rima-n-ču

general negative/ who, someone + even/ speak + simple pres. tense + negative enclitic (Lit. 'Not someone even speaks.')

'Nobody speaks.'

E. SAMPLE TEXT

This sample text is from Parker (1969), who does not indicate where he got it from. (The Quechua text as well as its idiomatic translation, both of which are quoted here, are to be found at the end of Parker's grammar on unnumbered pages. Had the pages been numbered they would have been 224 and 225, respectively. It is published here with the permission of Mouton de Gruyter, a Division of Walter de Gruyter & Co.) The morpheme-by-morpheme translation and the accompanying notes are my own.)

The superscripted numbers in the literal morpheme-by-morpheme translation refer to the notes that follow that section.

Quechua Text

ADRIAN WARMAČA

(1) Huk siñuras huk warmata uywasqa wasimpi yanapanampaq, Adriyan sutiyuqta. (2) Siñuraqa kamačiq ĺapa imata čay warmačata, (3) warmačañataq mana imatapas ruwaqču aĺintaqa. (4) Sapa triguta akĺaspan, kutaspan, waki-wakiĺanta akĺaykuq, kutaykuq; (5) wakintañataq maraypa ladun qučaman wisčuykuq. (6) Mikuykunatapas wisčuykariq wakiĺanta mikuspan. (7) Warmaqa pukĺayĺa pukĺakuq sapa punčaw mana kasukuspan. (8) Quĺqitawan pukĺanakunata suwakamun bisinun wasikunamanta, (9) hinaspan maray qipapi pakan sapa patrunan ĺuqsiptin pukĺanampaq.

(10) Kayna kačkaspan, warmačaqa unqurun yana muruwan; (11) hinaspan wañukun čay unquywan manaña imawampas alinyayta atispan. (12) Čay wañusqanmanta pača, mančačikuyta qalaykun huk yana bultu quča čawpipi sapa tuta. (13) Kayta rikuruspa warmiqa mančarikun, hinaspan rin tayta kuraman wilaq. (14) Tayta kurañataq yačačin krusta hapiykuspa pim kasqanta tapunampaq. (15) Warmiqa kutiykun wasinta čay ruwaq, (16) tutačaykuptin suyan čay yana bultu rikurimunanta. (17) Rikuriramuptin, mančarikuspan pampaman kumpakun; (18) hinaspa čayna pampapi wisčusqa ačikyarun. (19) Paqarinnintinta kaqla rin tayta kurapata, hinaspa kikinta pusaramun. (20) Kuraqa krusta apaykuspa suyan, (21) rikuriramuptinñataq tapun "Pim kanki, imatam munanki?" nispan.

(22)   Čay bultu kontestan: "Adriyanmi kani, taytačam kutičimuwan; (23) kay qučapim lapa ima talisqay kačkan, (24) wak maray qipapiñataqmi lapa suwakusqa pakasqay. (25) Ama hina kaspaykičik urquruyčik, mana čayqa supay wasipaqmi taytača unančawanman."

(26) Čay řatula urquyta qalaykunku, ña tukuruptinkuñataq tayta kura nin: (27) "Kananqa hawka kutiriy taytačaman, ñam urqurumikuña." (28) Čaynapi čay yana bultuqa činkarikurun "grasyas" nispan.

Literal Morpheme-by-Morpheme Translation

ADRIYAN WARMA-ČA

Adrian (prop. noun)/ boy (5–10 years of age) + diminutive/

(1) *Huk siñura-s huk warma-ta uywa-s-qa wasi-m-pi yanapa-na-m-paq, Adriyan suti-yuq-ta.*

once, one/ **lady** + hearsay comment enclitic/ **one/ boy** + acc./ **raise,** care for + hearsay? + nonpresent (with the preceding morpheme = quotative past)/ **house** + **her**[1] + at, **in** (loc. case)/ aid, **help** + nominalizer + 3d pers. poss. (= **'her'**) + purpose, **for the purpose of**/ **Adrian** (prop. noun)/ **name** + possessor + acc./[2]

(2) *Siñura-qa kamači-q lapa ima-ta čay warma-ča-ta,*

lady + topic marker/ **command,** order + iterative past tense/ all/ what + acc. (with preceding word = **'everything'**)/ **that** (dem. pron.)/ **boy** + diminutive + acc./,

(3) *warma-ča-ñataq mana ima-ta-pas ruwa-q-ču alin-ta-qa.*

boy + diminutive + and so, **then** (enclitic)/ negative/ what, which + acc. + even, too also (with preceding negative = **'nothing'**/ **do,** make + iterative past + negative/ **well,** good + acc.[3] + topic marker/.

(4) *Sapa trigu-ta akla-spa-n, kuta-spa-n, waki-waki-lan-ta akla-yku-q, kuta-yku-q;*

each, **every (time)**/ **wheat** + acc./ **choose,** select + subord. vb. marker[4] + 3d pers. sing./, **grind,** mill + subord. vb. marker[4] + 3d pers. sing./, part, fraction + reduplication of the preceding + only, merely + acc.[3] (= **'just a little'**)/ **choose,** select + action differ, from the usual[6] + iterative past tense/, **grind,** mill + action differ, from the usual[6] + iterative past tense/;

(5) *waki-n-ta-ñataq maray-pa ladun quča-man wisču-yku-q.*
part, **fraction,** small amount + 3d pers. poss. (= **'its'**) + acc. + **and so,** then/ millstone + gen. marker/ side/ **well** + to, towards, **into**/ discard, **throw away** + action differ. from the usual[6] + iterative past tense/.

(6) *Mikuy-kuna-ta-pas wisču-yka-ri-q waki-l̃an-ta miku-spa-n.*
food, meal + pl. + acc. + even, **also,** too/ discard, **throw away** + action differ. from the usual[7] + inceptive + iterative past tense/ part, **fraction,** small amount + merely, **only** + acc./ **eat** + subord. vb. marker[4] + 3d pers. sing./

(7) *Warma-qa pukl̃ay-l̃a pukl̃a-ku-q sapa punčaw mana kasu-ku-spa-n.*
boy + topic marker/ **play** + merely, just, **only**/ play + mediopassive + iterative past tense/ **every,** each/ **day**/ negative/ **obey,** pay attention to + mediopassive + subord. vb. marker[4] + 3d pers. sing./

(8) *Qul̃qi-ta-wan pukl̃a-na-kuna-ta suwa-ka-mu-n bisinu-n wasi-kuna-manta.*
money, silver + acc. + and/ play + instr. nominalizing suffix (= **'toy'**) + pl. + acc./ **steal,** rob + mediopassive[8] + action involving movement in reference to the subject + simple pres. tense[5]/ **neighbor** + 3d pers. sing. possessor/ house + pl. + **from** (ablat. case marker)/,

(9) *hina-spa-n maray qipa-pi paka-n sapa patruna-n l̃uqsi-p-ti-n pukl̃a-na-m-paq.*
be thus, do thus + subord. vb. marker[4] + 3d pers. sing. (= **'so, then'**)/ **millstone**/ **behind,** rear + in, at (loc. marker)/ **hide** + simple pres. tense[5]/ **every (time)**/**patroness,** lady boss + 3d pers. poss. (= **'his'**)/ leave, **depart** + actor differs from sub. of the main clause + subord. vb. marker[9] + 3d pers. sing./ **play** + nominalizer (= 'playing') + 3d pers. possessor + for, **for the purpose of**/.

(10) *Kay-na ka-čka-spa-n, warma-ča-qa unqu-ru-n yana muru-wan;*
this + thing, **situation**/ **be** + durative + subord. vb. marker[4] + 3d pers. sing./, **boy** + diminutive + topic marker/ **get sick** + sudden, urgent or surprising action + simple pres. tense[5]/ black/ seed, speckled + comit. 'with' (with the previous word = **'with smallpox'**)/;

(11) *hina-spa-n wañu-ku-n čay unqu-y-wan mana-ña ima-wam-pas al̃in-ya-y-ta ati-spa-n.*
be thus, do thus + subord. vb. marker[4] + 3d pers. sing. (= **'so, then'**)/ **die** + mediopassive + simple pres. tense[5]/ that (dem. pron.)/ get sick + nominalizer (= **'sickness'**) + comit. 'with' (= **'from'**)/ negative + more (= **'no more'**)/ what + comit. 'with'[1] + even (= **'in respect to anything'**)/ good, well + become (= **'improve,** get well') + nominalizer + acc./ be able + subord. vb. marker[4] + 3d pers. sing./

(12) *Čay wañu-sqa-n-manta pača, mančači-ku-y-ta qal̃a-yku-n huk yana bultu quča čawpi-pi sapa tuta.*
that (dem. pron.)/ die + past tense nominalizer + 3d pers. sing. poss. + ablat.: 'from'/ time (with previous word = **'since his death . . .'**)/, **frighten** + mediopassive + nominalizer + acc./ **begin,** start + action differ. from the usual[6] + simple pres. tense[5]/ one, **a**/ **black**/ **spirit**/ **well**/ **middle,** center + **in,** at (loc.)/ **each,** every/ **night**/.

(13) *Kay-ta riku-ru-spa warmi-qa mančari-ku-n, hina-spa-n ri-n tayta kura-man wiĩa-q.*
this + acc./ **see** + urgent, sudden, surprising action + subord. vb. marker[4]/
woman (approx. 30–40 years of age) + topic marker/ fear, **be afraid** +
mediopassive + simple pres. tense[5]/, be thus, do thus + subord. vb.
marker[4] + 3d pers. sing. (= **'so, then'**)/ go + simple pres. tense[5]/ father, mister, sir/ **priest** + directional: **'to'**/ tell, inform + nominalizer of purpose
(= **'for the purpose of informing'**)/.

(14) *Tayta kura-ñataq yačači-n krus-ta hapi-yku-spa pi-m kasqan-ta tapu-na-m-paq.*
father, mister, sir/ **priest** + and so, **then**/ **teach** + simple pres. tense[5]/ **cross** +
acc./ **hold** + action differ. from the usual[6] + subord. vb. marker[4]/ **who** + personal exper. comment clitic/ **again** + acc./[3] **ask** + nominalizer + 3d pers.
poss.[1] + purpose/.

(15) *Warmi-qa kuti-yku-n wasi-n-ta čay ruwa-q,*
woman + topic marker/ **return** + action differ. from the usual[6] + simple
pres. tense[5]/ **house** + 3d pers. poss. + acc./[12] this/ do, make + nominalizer of
purpose (= **'in order to do this'**)/,

(16) *tuta-ča-yku-p-ti-n suya-n čay yana bultu riku-ri-mu-na-n-ta.*
night, dark + verbalizer + action differ. from the usual[6] (= **'become dark'**) +
different subject from the main clause + subord. vb. marker[9] + 3d pers. sing./
await, **wait for** + simple pres. tense[5]/ **this**/ **black**/ **spirit**/ see + inceptive (= **appear,** come into view) + action involving movement in reference to the
speaker + nominalizer + 3d pers. sing. poss. + acc./.

(17) *Riku-ri-ra-mu-p-ti-n, manča-ri-ku-spa-n pampa-man kumpa-ku-n;*
see + inceptive (= **appear,** come into view) + sudden, surprising action[13] +
action involving movement in reference to the speaker + actor differ. from
the main clause + subord. vb. marker[9] + 3d pers. sing./ **frighten** + inceptive + mediopassive + subord. vb. marker[4] + 3d pers. sing./ ground, **earth** +
to/ thrown down + mediopassive (= **'throw down herself'**) + simple pres.
tense/;

(18) *hina-spa čayna pampa-pi wisču-sqa ačikya-ru-n.*
to be thus, do thus + subord. vb. marker[4]/ do thus (with previous word =
'and so she remained thus')/ **earth,** ground + **on** (loc. marker)/ abandon,
throw away + past tense nominalizer (passive sense?)/ become light, dawn,
awaken + urgent, surprising action + simple pres. tense[5]/.

(19) *Paqari-nnintin-ta kaqĩa ri-n tayta kura-pa-ta, hina-spa kiki-n-ta pusa-ra-mu-n.*
dawn, be born + adjacence of position or accompaniment + acc.[3] (= **'on the
following day'**)/ **again** / go + simple pres. tense[5]/ father, mister, sir/ **priest** +
gen. + acc./[14] be thus, **do thus** + subord. vb. marker[4]/ self + 3d pers. sing.
(= **'himself'**) + acc./ **lead,** take (a person) + urgency, surprise + action involving motion in relation to the sub. + simple pres. tense/.[5]

(20) *Kura-qa krus-ta apa-yku-spa suya-n,*
priest + topic marker/ **cross** + acc./ **take,** bring, carry + action differ. from
the usual[6] + subord. vb. marker[4]/ wait, **await** + simple pres. tense[5]/,

(21) *riku-ri-ra-mu-p-ti-n-ñataq tapu-n "Pi-m ka-n-ki, ima-ta-m muna-n-ki?" ni-spa-n.*
see + inceptive (= **appear,** come into view) + urgent, surprising action[13] + action involving movement in respect to the sub. + actor differ. from the sub. of the main clause + subord. vb. marker[9] + 3d pers. sing. + and so, **then** (enclitic)/ **ask** + simple pres. tense[5]/ **who** + personal exper. comment clitic/ **be,** exist + simple pres. tense[5] + 2d pers. sing./, **what** + acc. + personal exper. comment clitic/ **want,** need like + simple pres. tense[5] + 2d pers. sing./ **say,** tell + subord. vb. marker[4] + 3d pers. sing./

(22)*Čay bultu kontesta-n: "Adriyan-mi ka-n-i, tayta-ča-m kutiči-mu-wa-n;*
that (dem. pron.)/ **spirit**/ **answer** + simple pres. tense[5]/ **Adrian** (proper noun) + personal exper. comment clitic/ **be**, exist + simple pres. tense[5] + 1st pers. sing./ **father,** mister, sir + diminutive + personal exper. comment clitic (here = 'the Lord, **God**')/ **return** (transitive verb) + action involving movement in respect to the sub. + 1st pers. sing. obj. + simple pres. tense/,[5];

(23) *kay quča-pi-m ĩapa ima talĩ-sqa-y ka-čka-n,*
this/ **well** + **in,** at (loc.) + personal exper. comment clitic/ all/ what, how (with previous word = **'everything'**)/ **throw out** + past tense nominalizer + 1st pers. sing./ be + durative + simple pres. tense[5]/,

(24) *wak maray qipa-pi-ñataq-mi ĩapa suwa-ku-sqa paka-sqa-y.*
that (distant or out of sight)/ **millstone**/ **behind,** rear + at (loc.) + and so, **then** + personal exper. comment clitic/ **all**/ **steal,** rob + mediopassive + past tense nominalizer/ **hide** + past tense + 1st pers. sing./.

(25) *Ama hina ka-spa-y-kičik urqu-ru-y-čik, mana čay-qa supay wasi-paq-mi tayta-ča unanča-wan-man."*
negative (prohibition)/ like, such, always/be + subord. vb. marker[4] + I + you pl. (obj.) (whole phrase = **'please'**)/ **remove, take out** + urgent action + imperat. marker + pl. (2d pers. pl., referent)/, negative/ that (dem. pron.) + topic marker (with preced. negative = 'without that, **otherwise**)/ evil spirit, devil/ house + purpose + (with previous word = **'for hell'**) + personal exper. comment clitic/ father, mister, sir + diminutive (here = the Lord, **God**)/ announce, **designate** + 1st pers. sing. obj. + simple pres. tense[5] + conditional suffix/.

(26) *Čay řatulã urqu-y-ta qalã-yku-n-ku, ña tuku-ru-p-ti-n-ku-ñataq tayta kura ni-n:*
that (dem. pron.)/ **immediately**/ remove, **take out** + nominalizer (infinitive) + acc./ begin, start + action differ. from the usual[6] + simple pres. tense[5] + (3d pers.) pl./, **already**/ **finish** + urgent action + actor differ. from the main clause + subord. vb. marker[9] + 3d pers. sing. + and so, **then**/ father, mister, sir/ **priest**/ **say,** tell + simple pres. tense[5]/:

(27) *"Kanan-qa hawka kuti-ri-y tayta-ča-man, ña-m urqu-ru-niku-ña."*
now, this day + topic marker/ **peaceful(ly),** tranquil(ly)/ **return to a place** + inceptive + imperat./ father, mister, sir + diminutive + directional 'to' (here = **'to God'**)/, already + personal exper. comment clitic/ remove, **take out** + urgent action + first person pl. exclusive + **already**/."

(28) *Čay-na-pi čay yana bultu-qa činka-ri-ku-ru-n "grasyas" ni-spa-n.*
that + matter, thing + at, in (loc.) (= **'in that situation, then'**)/ **that** (dem. pron.)/ **black**/ **spirit** + topic marker/ **disappear** + inceptive + mediopassive + sudden, urgent or surprising action + simple pres. tense[5]/ **thanks**/ **say, tell** + subord. vb. marker[4] + 3d pers. sing./

NOTES

1. Before bilabial consonants the nasal *-n* of various affixes regularly becomes *-m* by assimilation.

2. The entire noun phrase is in apposition to *warma-ta* 'boy': '. . . boy . . . Adrian name possessor' = '. . . boy . . . Adrian by name.'

3. Accusative or object suffix *-ta* is often used to derive adverbs from nominal stems, but especially from adjectival stems.

4. This subordinate verb marker indicates that its subject is the same as that of the main clause. It can often be translated into English by a participle in *-ing* or by *having* + past participle.

5. Simple present tense replaces other tenses in story telling when the context is unambiguous.

6. It is usually not possible to translate this suffix into English. In many cases the meaning is very idiomatic: *rima-* 'to speak', but *rima-yku-* 'to greet'. According to Parker (1969:67), it may indicate cordiality, severity, fear, surprise, and so on, depending on context.

7. The form *-yka-* is the allomorph of *-yku-* before *-mu* and few other suffixes. There are several affixes in which *-a* and *-u* alternate in identical morphological environments. The phonological motivation for this alternation is unclear.

8. The form *-ka-* is the allomorph of *-ku-* (mediopassive) before *-mu* and a few other suffixes. Cf. note 7.

9. This subordinate verb marker always indicates that the subject of the verb is a different one from that of the main verb. It usually may be translated into English by a phrase beginning with "if." "when," or "because."

10. With demonstrative pronouns, the stem *na-* has the force of a transitive verb which means 'to do thus, be thus, treat thus'.

11. Lit. 'time from his having died' = 'since his death'.

12. With verbs of motion the accusative or object marker *-ta* indicates the goal or destination.

13. The form *-ra-* is the allomorph of *-rqu-/-ru-* before *-mu* and certain other suffixes. Cf. note 7.

14. Lit., 'to the priest's (house)'. In Quechua several case endings may follow the same nominal.

Idiomatic Translation

The Boy Adrián

Once a woman kept a boy named Adrian in her house to help her. The woman ordered the boy to do everything, but the boy never did anything well. Every time he selected and ground wheat, he selected and ground it little by little and he threw a part of it away into the well beside the millstone. He also threw away food after eating only part. The boy just played and played every day without ever being obedient. He went to steal money and toys from his neighbors' houses, and then hid them behind the millstone, to play with each time his mistress left.

In this state of affairs the boy got sick with smallpox; and then he died of this disease before he could improve in anything. Soon after he died, a black spirit began to frighten (people) around the well each night. Seeing this, the woman became frightened, and she went to the priest to tell him. The priest taught her to hold a cross and ask who it was. The woman returned home to do that, and when it became dark she waited for the black spirit to appear. When it appeared she became frightened and threw herself to the ground, and she stayed like that lying on the ground till dawn. On the following day she went again to the priest's, and brought him himself. The priest waited carrying a cross, and when it appeared he asked: "Who are you, and what do you want?" The spirit answered: "I am Adrián; God has made me return here; in this well is everything I threw away, and behind that millstone everything I stole is hidden. Please take it out, otherwise God would destine me for hell."

Immediately they began to take it out, and when they had finished the priest said: "Now you can return in peace to God; we have taken it out." Then the black spirit disappeared, saying "Thank you."

EXERCISES

1. Hixkaryana and Language Typology[7]

Hixkaryana is a Carib language spoken by a small group of people in the Amazonas province of Brazil not far from Manaus. Its basic word order, Object + Verb + Subject, is rather rare among the languages of the world, and at one time many linguists believed that it did not occur at all. For that reason this language is of great interest to language typologists.

Carefully examine the *Hixkaryana* data given below and then try to answer the following questions.

a. How are case relations signaled in *Hixkaryana*? (In your answer be sure to indicate how you reached your conclusions.)

b. What is the order of the various types of modifiers in this language? In what ways is this language's order of constituents similar to that of a typical SOV language and in what ways is it different? (If you do not remember what the typical order of constituents in an SOV language is supposed to be, you may want to refer to Greenberg's 1966 article on the word order universals.)

    i. namryehtxowɨ totokomo

       they-went-hunting people

       'The people have gone hunting.'

ii. totokomo yonyetxkonɨ roro hatɨ kamar-yana komo

people they-used-to-eat-them permanent hearsay jaguar-person collective

'The jaguar people used to eat people all the time.'

iii. asak kanawa wenyo

two canoe I-saw-it

'I saw two canoes.'

iv. anaro owto hona kahatakeko

another village to I-came-out

'I arrived at another village.'

v. bɨryekomo yoknɨ

boy pet-of

'the boy's pet'

vi. bɨryekomo y-otaha-no ɨnyo

boy 3d pers. sub. 3d pers. obj.-hit her-husband

'Her husband hit the boy.'

vii. toto yahosɨye kamara

man it-grabbed-him jaguar

'The jaguar grabbed the man.'

viii. toto yahosɨye

man it-grabbed-him

'It (jaguar) grabbed the man.'

ix. kamara nahosɨye (or: nahosɨye kamara)

jaguar it-grabbed-him

'The jaguar grabbed him.'

x. toto nahosɨye (or: nahosɨye toto)

man he-grabbed-it

'The man grabbed it (the jaguar).'

xi. nahosɨye

it/he-grabbed-it/him

'It (jaguar) grabbed him (man).' or 'He (man) grabbed it (jaguar).'

xii. ehonomnɨ me rmahaxa naha yaskomo, totokomo wya

important-one denominalizer very-much he-is shaman, people to

'The people think the shaman is a very important person.'

xiii. ɨwahathɨyamo, aknyohnyenhɨyamo tho, oske nketxkonɨ

his-killers, ones-who-had-burned-him devalued,[8] thus they-said-it

'His killers, the ones who had burned him, said thus.'

xiv. txetxa waha ntetxhe onokna komo

forest through they-go creature collective

'Creatures go through the forest.'

2. Michoacan Aztec Morphology[9]

1.	nikočik	I slept.
2.	kočik išolul	His child slept.
3.	tiyuli	You live.
4.	yuli mosiwal	Your wife lives.
5.	nečlamačiltia	He informs me.
6.	kilamačiltik nosiwal	He informed my wife.
7.	tiwehkawa	You endure.
8.	wehkawa nočkawalisli	My strength holds out.
9.	nilamik	I finished.
10.	lami molamačiltilisli	Your news ends.
11.	lamik ičikawalisli	His strength gave out.
12.	mihčikawak	He strengthened you.
13.	kičikawa	He strengthens him.
14.	kičikawa nošolul	He strengthens my child.
15.	kipolua	He loses it.
16.	kipolua kočilisli	He loses sleep.
17.	kipoluk ičikawalisli	He lost his strength.
18.	nečwililtia	He empowers me.
19.	mičwililtik	He empowered you.
20.	kiwililtia mošolul	He empowers your child.

21. nečneki	He loves me.
22. kineki yulilisli	He wants life.
23. kineki isiwal	He loves his wife.
24. kinekik nowililtilisli	He wanted my power.

3. Huave Morphology and Syntax[10]

Examine the *Huave* (a language that is spoken in Mexico) data given below and then answer the following questions.

1. What is the basic word order of this language?
2. How does it signal case relations?
3. What is the morphological structure of the Huave verb?
4. To what general language type does it belong? (Be sure to cite specific examples in support of your claim.)

1. tandok tišem	He netted shrimp.
2. tahond kìet nop našey	A man dried fish.
3. tehanc	He washed (something).
4. apmahanc kìet	He will wash fish.
5. aaga nenč apmehanc	That boy will wash something.
6. apmandok tišem aaga nenč	That boy will net shrimp.
7. nop nenč tendok	A boy netted (something).
8. aaga našey tehond	That man dried (something).
9. nop nenč apmahond kìet	A boy will dry fish.
10. nop našey apmehond	A man will dry (something).
11. aaga našey tahanc tišem	That man washed shrimp.
12. apmendok	He will net (something).
13. nop našey apmandok kìet	A man will net fish.
14. tahond tišem	He dried shrimp.
15. nop našey tahond kìet	A man dried fish.
16. aaga nenč apmehond	That boy will dry (something).
17. nop nenč apmehanc	A boy will wash (something).
18. aaga nenč apmandok tišem	That boy will net shrimp.

NOTES

1. The information on the numbers of speakers and their location is taken from various entries in the *International encyclopedia of linguistics* (Oxford University Press, 1992), where such data was available. Otherwise, as in the case of most language isolates cited here and elsewhere in this textbook, such data was taken from Grimes (1992).

2. The following is based on Campbell (1992: 3.415–7).

3. The following sketch of Yup'ik Eskimo is based mainly on Reed et al. (1977).

4. One such borrowed preposition is *asta* 'until' (< Spanish *hasta*) which is optionally used with nouns to which the Quechua suffix *-kama* 'until' is attached. In other words, the idea "until" may be expressed redundantly.

5. It should be emphasized that my definition of the term *polysynthetic* differs markedly from the original definition developed by Duponceau and later employed by Humboldt and others. Originally this term was applied to languages whose words

tend to be made up of long strings of morphemes, *any* types of morphemes. Cf. the section on morphological typology in Chapter 2.

6. Basically, *-ni-* is an empty morph which is inserted after stems ending in consonants. This empty morph is found not only with pronominal endings but elsewhere as well.

7. This exercise is based on the data and description given in Derbyshire (1979) and Derbyshire (1985).

8. According to Derbyshire (1985:245), the "devalued" particle marks the items it modifies as having undergone some change of state or relationship usually involving loss of value.

9. This exercise is Problem 179 in Merrifield et al. (1987). Used with permission, *Laboratory Manual for Morphology and Syntax, Revised Edition,* Merrifield et al. eds.; Summer Institute of Linguistics.

10. This exercise is Problem 250 in Merrifield et al. (1987). Used with permission, *Laboratory Manual for Morphology and Syntax, Revised Edition,* Merrifield et al., eds.; Summer Institute of Linguistics.

SELECTED BIBLIOGRAPHY

General

Aoki, Haruo. 1981. Amerika-indian shogo. In Hajime Kitamura, ed., *Sekai no gengo* 311–62. Tokyo: Taishūkan shoten.
Campbell, Lyle. 1988. Review of *Language in the Americas,* by Joseph A. Greenberg. *Language* 63(3):591–615.
Campbell, Lyle, and Ives Goddard. 1990. Summary report: American Indian languages and principles of language change. In Philip Baldi, ed., *Linguistic change and reconstruction methodology,* 15–30. New York: Mouton de Gruyter.
Cook, Eung Do, and Donna B. Gerdts, eds., 1984. *Amerindian syntax.* Orlando, Fla.: Academic Press.
Greenberg, Joseph A. 1987. *Language in the Americas.* Stanford, Calif.: Stanford University Press. (Presents more evidence for his hypothesis that all Native American Indian languages are genetically related except Na-Dene and Eskimo-Aleut.)
Matisoff, James A. 1990. On megalocomparison. *Language* 46(1):106–20.
Mithun, Marianne. 1990. The role of typology in American Indian historical linguistics. In Philip Baldi, ed., *Linguistic change and reconstruction methodology,* 31–53. New York: Mouton de Gruyter.
Sebeok, Thomas A., ed. 1977. *Native languages of the Americas.* 2 vols. New York: Plenum Press.

North America

Campbell, Lyle, and Marianne Mithun, eds. 1979. *The languages of Native America: Historical and comparative assessment.* Austin: University of Texas Press. (Excellent overview of North American native language families.)
Cook, Eung-do. 1992. Athabascan languages. In William Bright et al., eds., *International encyclopedia of linguistics.* Vol. 1:122–28. New York: Oxford University Press.
Goddard, Ives. 1992. Algonkian languages. In William Bright et al., eds., *International encyclopedia of linguistics.* Vol. 1:44–48. New York: Oxford University Press.

Kaplan, Lawrence D. 1992. Eskimo-Aleut languages. In William Bright et al., eds. *International encyclopedia of linguistics*. Vol. 1:415–19. New York: Oxford University Press.

Kinkade, M. Dale. 1992. Salishan languages. In William Bright et al., eds., *International encyclopedia of linguistics*. Vol. 3:359–62. New York: Oxford University Press.

Matthews, G. Hubert. 1958. *Handbook of Siouan languages*. Philadelphia: University of Pennsylvania Press.

Miller, Wick R. 1992. Uto-Aztecan languages. In William Bright et al., eds., *International encyclopedia of linguistics*. Vol. 4:212–16. New York: Oxford University Press.

Mithun, Marianne. 1992. Iroquoian languages. In William Bright et al., eds., *International encyclopedia of linguistics*. Vol. 2:233–6. New York: Oxford University Press.

Mithun, Marianne, and Wallace L. Chafe. 1979. Recapturing the Mohawk language. In Timothy Shopen, ed., *Languages and their status,* 3–33. Cambridge, Mass.: Winthrop Publishers.

Rood, David S. 1979. *Siouan. The languages of Native America*. Austin: University of Texas Press.

———. 1992a. North American languages. In William Bright et al., eds., *International encyclopedia of linguistics*. Vol. 3:110–15. New York: Oxford University Press.

———. 1992b. Siouan languages. In William Bright et al., eds., *International encyclopedia of linguistics*. Vol. 3:449–52. New York: Oxford University Press.

Sherzer, Joel. 1976. *An areal-typological study of Amerindian languages north of Mexico*. Amsterdam: North Holland Publishing.

Thompson, Laurence C., and M. Terry Thompson. 1992. *The Thompson language*. University of Montana Occasional Papers in Linguistics, No. 8. Missoula, Montana: The University of Montana. (An excellent description of a typologically interesting Salish language.)

Central America

Campbell, Lyle. 1979. Middle American languages. In Lyle Campbell and Marianne Mithun, eds., *The languages of Native America: Historical and comparative assessment,* 902–1000. Austin: University of Texas Press.

———. 1992a. *Mayan languages*. In William Bright et al., eds., *International encyclopedia of linguistics*. Vol. 2:401–6. New York: Oxford University Press.

———. 1992b. Meso-American languages. In William Bright et al., eds., *International encyclopedia of linguistics*. Vol. 2:415–7. New York: Oxford University Press.

Craig, Colette Grinevald. 1977. *The structure of Jacaltec*. Austin: University of Texas Press. (A very readable descriptive grammar of an interesting Mayan language.)

———. 1979. Jacaltec: Fieldwork in Guatemala. In Timothy Shopen, ed., *Languages and their speakers,* 3–57. Cambridge, Mass.: Winthrop Publishers.

McQuown, Norman A., ed. 1967. *Handbook of Middle American Indians*. Austin: University of Texas Press.

South America

Derbyshire, Desmond C. 1979. *Hixkaryana*. Amsterdam: North Holland Publishing. Lingua Descriptive Studies, vol. 1. (This work attracted much attention when it first appeared because the language in question is typologically very interesting.)

———. 1985. *Hixkaryana and linguistic typology*. Dallas, Texas, and Arlington, Texas: Summer Institute of Linguistics and University of Texas at Arlington Press. Summer Institute of Linguistics Publications in Linguistics vol. 76.

Derbyshire, Desmond C., and Geoffrey K. Pullum, ed. 1986. *Handbook of Amazonian languages.* New York: Mouton de Gruyter.

Greenberg, Joseph A. 1960. The general classification of Central and South American languages. In Anthony F. C. Wallace, ed., *Men and cultures. Selected papers of the 5th International Congress of Anthropological and Ethnological Sciences, September 1956,* 791–4. Philadelphia: University of Pennsylvania Press.

Hoff, Bernard. 1992. Cariban languages. In William Bright et al., eds., *International encyclopedia of linguistics.* Vol. 1:213–6. New York: Oxford University Press.

Jensen, Cheryl J. 1992. Tupian languages. In William Bright et al., eds., *International encyclopedia of linguistics.* Vol. 4:182–6. New York: Oxford University Press.

Kaufman, Terry. 1990. Language history in South America: What we know and how to know more. In Doris L. Payne, ed., *Amazonian linguistics: Studies in lowland South American languages.* Austin: University of Texas Press.

Key, Marie Ritchie. 1979. *The grouping of South American Indian languages.* Ars linguistica Vol. 2, Commentationes analyticae et criticae. Tübingen: Gunter Narr Verlag.

Loukotka, Čestimir. 1968. *Classification of South American languages.* 4th ed. Reference series, vol. 7. Los Angeles: Latin American Center, UCLA. (Original Spanish edition published in 1935 in Prague.)

Manelis Klein, Harriet E. South American languages. In William Bright et al., eds., *International encyclopedia of linguistics.* Vol. 4:31–8. New York: Oxford University Press.

Manelis Klein, Harriet E., and Louisa R. Stark, eds., 1985. *South American Indian languages: Retrospect and prospect.* Texas Linguistic Series. Austin: University of Texas Press.

Payne, David L. 1990. Some widespread grammatical forms in South American languages. In Doris L. Payne, ed., *Amazonian Linguistics: Studies in lowland South American Languages,* 75–87. Austin: University of Texas Press.

Urban, Greg, and Joel Sherzer. 1988. The linguistic anthropology of Native South America. *Annual Review of Anthropology* 17:283–307.

Central Yup'ik Eskimo

Basse, Bjarne, and Kirsten Jensen, eds., 1979. *Eskimo languages: Their present day conditions.* Aarhus: Arkona Publ.

Jacobson, Steven A., comp. 1984. *Yup'ik Eskimo dictionary.* Fairbanks: University of Alaska, Alaska Native Language Center.

Krauss, Michael. 1979. Na-Dene and Eskimo-Aleut. In Lyle Campbell and Marianne Mithun, eds., *The languages of Native America: Historical and comparative assessment,* 803–901. Austin: University of Texas Press.

Krauss, Michael. 1980. *Alaska native languages: Past, present, and future.* Fairbanks: University of Alaska, Alaska Native Language Center.

Miyaoka, Osahito. 1978. *Eskimō no gengo to bunka.* Tokyo: Kōbundō.

Reed, Irene, et al. 1977. *Yup'ik Eskimo grammar.* Fairbanks: University of Alaska, Alaska Native Language Center.

Quechua

Adelaar, Willem F. H. 1992. Quechuan languages. In William Bright et al., eds., *International encyclopedia of linguistics.* Vol. 4:303–10. New York: Oxford University Press.

Cerrón-Palomino, Rodolfo M. 1976. *Grammática Quechua: Junin-Huanca.* Lima: Instituto de Estudios Peruanos.

———. 1976a. *Diccionario Quechua: Cuzco-Callao.* Lima: Instituto de Estudios Peruanos.

Cusihuaman Gutiérrez, Antonio. 1976b. *Grammática Quechua: Cuzco-Collao.* Lima: Instituto de Estudios Peruanos.

Finch, Roger. 1983. The velar and uvular series in Quechua. *Sophia Linguistica (Working Papers in Linguistics)* 13:1–17.

Hardman, M. J. 1985. Aymara and Quechua. In Harriet E. Manelis Klein and Louisa R. Stark, eds., *South American Indian languages: Retrospect and prospect,* 617–43. Austin: University of Texas Press. (The author expresses his doubts concerning the Quechumaran hypothesis.)

Mannheim, Bruce. 1985. Contact and Quechua external genetic relationships. In Harriet E. Manelis Klein and Louisa R. Stark, eds., *South American Indian languages: Retrospect and prospect.* 644–88. Austin: University of Texas Press.

Middendorf, E. W. 1890. *Das Runa Simi oder die Keshua-Sprache. (Wie sie gegenwärtig in der Provinz von Cusco gesprochen wird).* Leipzig: Brockhaus.

Orr, Carolyn, and Robert E. Longacre. 1968. Proto-Quechumaran. *Language* 44(3):528–55. (In this article the authors present their evidence in support of the hypothesis that Quechua varieties and Aymara form a language family.)

Parker, Gary J. 1963. Clasificación de los dialectos quechuas. *Revista del Museo Nacional* (Lima) 32:241–52.

———. 1969. *Ayacucho Quechua grammar and dictionary.* The Hague: Mouton.

Perroud, Pedro Clemente. 1961. *Gramatica Quechwa: Dialecto de Ayacucho.* Santa Clara, Peru: Seminario San Alfonso de los Padres Redentoristas.

Soto Ruiz, C. 1974. *Quechua manual de enseñanza.* Lima: Instituto de Estudios Peruanos.

———. 1976a. *Diccionario Ayacucho-Chanca.* Lima: Instituto de Estudios Peruanos.

———. 1976b. *Gramática Ayacucho-Chanca.* Lima: Instituto de Estudios Peruanos.

Torero Fernández de Cordova, Alfredo. 1964. Los dialectos quechuas. *Anales Cientificos de la Universidad Agraria* (Lima) 2:446–78.

———. 1970. Lingüística e historia de la sociedad andina. *Anales Cientificos de la Universidad Agraria* (Lima) 3/4:231–64.

Chapter **8**   # Pidgin and Creole Languages

▩

WHAT ARE PIDGINS AND CREOLES?

Pidgin and creole languages used to be referred to as "mixed languages," but in recent years this term has been abandoned in favor of "contact languages." The reason for this is perhaps that the term "mixed" suggests hodgepodge, chaos, and lack of norms, whereas not all pidgins and none of the creoles are in fact chaotic mixtures, nor are they in most major respects any different from the established languages that most of us are familiar with. Also, if by "mixed" we mean "influenced by other languages," the term is really empty of meaning since *all* languages have at some time been influenced by some language or other.

The term "mixed languages" is now back in use and refers to a very special type of contact language in which grammar is originally from one language and the lexicon from another. Examples of such languages are *Michif,* spoken in North Dakota and nearby parts of Canada, in which the lexicon is largely French in origin and the grammar is largely Plains Cree in origin, and *Media Lengua,* spoken in Ecuador, in which most of the lexicon is of Spanish origin and the grammar is almost identical to that of local Quechua.

Both pidgins and creoles arise out of a particularly close contact between groups of people who do not speak each other's language at all or do not speak it well enough, yet who for some reason or other simply must work out a means of communicating with each other.

Often, when groups of people speaking different languages come into contact and have to communicate with each other, there may be a language which all of the people involved may know. That language is then used for communication among them. Such "intermediary" languages are called *lingue franche* (singular *lingua franca*, lit., "language of the Franks," originally the name of a medieval pidgin spoken between European traders, and later the crusaders, and the people of the eastern Mediterranean region such as Arabs and Turks). For example, in refugee camps in the Free Territory of Trieste (now part of Italy), where I spent the year 1950, there were many different nationalities—Russians, Hungarians, Bulgarians, Greeks, and so on. To communicate with each other they used Serbo-Croatian, which all knew to some extent because all these refugees came from Yugoslavia or from somewhere else by way of Yugoslavia. Thus, even though Serbs and Croats in the camp were a very small ethnic minority their language served as a *lingua franca* for all because that happened to be the language that all the ethnic groups in the camp knew at least to some extent.

It also happens occasionally that when people speaking different languages come into contact they may not share a language in common and have somehow to create an ad hoc lingua franca in a hurry. Such a lingua franca, without native speakers, is termed a *pidgin*. Eventually, a pidgin may fade away because, for various reasons, it is no longer needed, as when the linguistically diverse groups break off contact with each other or when the groups in contact learn each other's language. For example, as immigrants acquire the language or languages of their host countries, they no longer need to depend on some makeshift language in order to communicate with their neighbors.

Some of the various situations that lead to creation of pidgins are discussed in the following list.

1. Trade

Trade usually involves brief but periodic contacts between trading partners. If there are just too many different languages spoken by their customers, itinerant traders just cannot learn all of them, and some kind of general makeshift pidgin for trading purposes is likely to develop. An example of such a trade pidgin is *Chinook Jargon*, which used to be spoken in the Pacific Northwest region of the United States, the adjacent regions of Canada, and as far away as Alaska. This pidgin was based on the Native American language called *Chinook* spoken in the states of Oregon and Washington. When white traders reached the area, they found this pidgin quite useful for their purposes and enriched Chinook jargon with many words from the European languages, especially from French since many of these early white traders were the so-called *voyageurs* from French Canada. (This pidgin is now no longer used, but some older people, mostly Indians, still remember it, and loanwords from this pidgin are found in many native languages of the region.)

2. Tourism

Even relatively brief encounters between temporary visitors from foreign countries and the host populations may lead to development of pidgins. For example, there is *Cicerone Jargon* spoken in some parts of Italy by unofficial tourist guides who do not have training in foreign languages but who want to earn money by taking foreign tourists on tours. This pidgin consists of very simplified Italian, which such guides hope that the foreign tourists will be able to understand.

3. Conquest and Wars

During wars and during military occupations large numbers of soldiers come into contact with other soldiers and civilians who do not speak their language. Since numbers of trained interpreters are usually very limited, ordinary soldiers often have to create makeshift means of communication, which leads to development of pidgins, some very short-lived. For example, during the occupation of Japan by American troops after World War II there developed a pidgin called *Bamboo English,* used mostly by GIs to communicate with Japanese bar girls, bartenders, and other Japanese who had frequent contacts with GIs.

4. Plantations

When large numbers of workers speaking different languages are brought together on a plantation a pidgin of some kind develops not only for communication between the bosses and the laborers but for communication among the laborers themselves. Such situations have produced a large number of contact languages during the era of European colonial expansion, especially in the Caribbean region where there were many plantations employing slave labor from Africa, and the salves came from a variety of African ethnic groups, speaking a wide variety of mutually unintelligible languages.

Under the right conditions, and such conditions seem to exist especially in the plantation situation just described, the pidgin speakers intermarry and have children who are mainly exposed to pidgin, rather than a noncontact language. Partially on the basis of the pidgin to which these children are exposed a second generation contact language develops. Such a contact language which has native speakers is termed a *creole*. (Further differences between *pidgins* and *creoles* are discussed later.)

PIDGINS

Pidgins evolve through various stages. In the initial stage when the various linguistic groups enter into contact, a pidgin is usually very highly variable and idiosyncratic: Anything at all goes, as long as it somehow helps communication. Depending on the background and knowledge of an individual speaker of such incipient pidgin, the vocabulary and grammar may show great variation. At this state a pidgin is usually called a *jargon.*

If the contact between the different linguistic groups is prolonged but the conditions are not such that one noncontact language in the region becomes a lingua franca for the community, a pidgin may evolve into a *stable pidgin,* a pidgin which does have some steady grammatical rules and a steady core of vocabulary. To be sure, even such a stable pidgin is a rather rudimentary means of communication in many respects. For example, it usually still has a very limited vocabulary (reflecting the fact that the pidgin may be used in a very highly restricted social context), and it may not have a rich enough grammatical structure to express anything very complicated, at least not with the ease with which the non-pidgin languages express it.

Some scholars also recognize another evolutionary stage called "expanded pidgin" which in complexity is much closer to a noncontact language. The development of this stage is triggered by the expansion of the use of a stable pidgin when the usage of the latter becomes less restricted, that is, when it begins to be used in all the situations in which the noncontact languages are used. (This happens, for example, when a pidgin ceases to be used solely in the marketplace, but begins to be used in the community everywhere that the native languages are used.) Thus, when a pidgin is called upon to fulfill the role of a full-fledged language, it somehow manages to "fill the gaps" in its structure.

All pidgins have a good deal of polysemy—their words must serve many functions. For example, *long* in *Tok Pisin* (Papua New Guinea) serves as a preposition which may mean 'of', 'at', 'to', 'from', and so on. In addition, the gaps in the vocabulary are filled by rather ingenious phrases and circumlocutions. For example, also in *Tok Pisin,* "beard" is *gras bilong chin* and "ashes" is *shit bilong fire.*

Besides having very reduced vocabularies and grammars, stable pidgins exhibit some other features in common. Their grammatical structure, what little there is of it, is not only very simple but shows certain influences of the *substratum* language or languages, that is, the influence of the language or languages of the group or groups that have a lower socioeconomic status than some other socioeconomic group or groups within the same community. On the other hand, the vocabulary or lexicon of such pidgins is usually to a large extent adapted from the *superstratum* language, the language of social prestige in the community. Thus, for example, the European languages of the plantation overseers and owners were the superstratum languages and provided most of the vocabulary for the various plantation pidgins, whereas the languages of the slaves or indentured laborers on the plantations were the *substratum* languages which provided some grammatical structures, and, of course, vocabulary pertaining to the local culture and environment (since the superstratum languages tend to be languages of newcomers to the area).

Since there are not only structural but lexical similarities among pidgins spoken in widely scattered parts of the globe, some scholars have come up with a hypothesis that many, if not all pidgins now in use, are "relexified" versions of an earlier Portuguese-based nautical jargon, that is, a pidgin developed originally by Portuguese sailors and then spread around the world by Portuguese pilots and sailors. It was then relexified by new users—English, Dutch, Spanish, and so forth—who kept the overall structure of the Portuguese pidgin and some Portuguese words such as *pequeninho* for 'small' (used in various pidgins to mean 'child' or 'baby') and *saber* for 'to know', which appear in many European-language-based pidgins in Africa, Oceania, and the Americas. These same speakers, however, replaced most of the words of Portuguese origin with those of their own language. (Words like 'pick-aninny' and 'savvy', which are found in American English, have very likely been borrowed from some contact languages that flourished in the various parts of the United States in the past.)

Although many linguists discount the relexification theory, it does seem plausible that there was indeed such a Portuguese protopidgin, since the Portuguese were at the forefront of European nations searching for new trade routes to India. Thus, by the time explorers from other European nations decided to follow the Portuguese explorers such as Vasco da Gama around the continent of Africa to reach India, they very likely already found a number of places on the coast of Africa where Portuguese had landed for water and provisions and perhaps even encountered natives who had learned a few Portuguese words learned from the Portuguese explorers who had come that way. It also stands to reason that rather than spending time either to learn the local native language or teach the natives Dutch, English, and so on, the new-comers would simply take advantage of whatever knowledge they and the natives had of Portuguese language (neither party speaking that language well at all—a situation highly conducive to the creation of a pidgin).

A process of relexification similar, though ultimately unrelated to Portuguese protopidgin may explain some very strange features of various Russian-based pidgins. For example, according to Jabłońska (1957), the Russian-based Russo-Chinese pidgin which was spoken as a lingua franca between Chinese and Russian speakers along the borders of China and Russia in the nineteenth century and until 1950 in northeastern China (Manchuria) has several features that make no sense from the point of view of either Chinese grammar or Russian grammar:

1. The word order of the Russo-Chinese pidgin is Subject + Object + Verb, whereas *both* Russian and Mandarin Chinese (the Sinitic language in contact with Russian) are Subject + Verb + Object languages.

2. In the pidgin either the Chinese Mandarin morphemes or the Russian morphemes may be used for the pronouns, but regardless of their language of origin, pronouns that function as ordinary subjects and objects are etymologically equivalent to *possessive pronouns*. In other words, if one wants to say in this pidgin, 'I see you', one has to say something like 'My your see', which makes no sense from the point of view of either Russian or Chinese grammar.

Similar features are also found in Russenorsk, a Russian-based pidgin developed out of contact between Norwegian and Russian fishermen in the White Sea in the nineteenth century. There too, the basic word order and the possessive forms of the pronouns make very little sense from the point of view of either Russian or Norwegian grammar.

The answer to this puzzle seems to be that before the development of either Sino-Chinese pidgin or Russenorsk, there were apparently already many Russian-based pidgins which had developed out of contact between Russian speakers and speakers of various Tartar and other Turkic peoples as well as various Uralic peoples. Since the languages of all these ethnic groups are overwhelmingly SOV in structure, these pidgins also had SOV word order. (A few samples of such pidgins are found in the Russian novels written in the early nineteenth century.) As Russians continued meeting new peoples and needed to communicate with them, they remembered that "foreigners seem to prefer SOV word order," and that is what they used as they tried to teach the newly encountered people how to communicate in "contact Russian."

The use of Russian possessive pronouns to represent the plain personal pronouns can also be explained on the basis of the structure of Turkic and Uralic languages, where both pronominal possession suffixes and subject marking suffixes on the verbs are identical or almost identical in form. For example, consider the following data from Turkish:

> *ev* + *im*
>
> hand + 1st pers. sing. poss. suffix
>
> 'my hand'
>
> *ver* + *im*
>
> give + 1st pers. sing. sub. suffix
>
> 'I give.'

Thus, a Turkic-language speaker who has been exposed to Russian phrases such as *moja ruka* ('my hand') may very easily jump to the wrong conclusion that *moja* can also be used to represent the first person singular pronoun subject of a verb as well. The resultant mistakes in Russian in turn convince the Russian speakers that "that is how foreigners prefer to talk," and eventually they also adopt this type of construction when talking to the non-Russians regardless of what language group the latter belong.

CREOLES

Under the proper sociolinguistic and demographic conditions in language contact situations, there may come into being a second generation contact language called a *creole*. A creole usually arises in a community where a pidgin is spoken in the home (because the parents come from different ethnic groups and share only pidgin as their lingua franca) and therefore children are exposed mainly, if not entirely, to pidgin.

Through the process of *creolization* (or, as some prefer to call it, *depidginization*) the children exposed to the highly variable and idiosyncratic pidgin of their parents and other adults in their environment introduce not only more uniformity but more complexity into their language. In other words, they introduce grammatical rules where there may have been very few or even none before. Where do these rules, the uniformity, and the complexity come from? According to the "bioprogram hypothesis" of Derek Bickerton (see the bibliography at the end of this chapter under Bickerton for several references), the children fall back on the genetically preprogrammed default set of grammatical rules: Since all human children are genetically predisposed to learn a full-fledged human language, in situations where they are exposed to a very rudimentary and limited pidgin of their environment, they must fall back on the natural tendencies (the "bioprogram") as the latter emerge during the maturation processes of these children.

How much of the bioprogram is eventually contained in the creole depends to some extent on how 'stable' was the pidgin on which the creole is based. That is, if the pidgin already had at least some set rules, the nascent creole might incorporate the latter even if these rules are not really a part of the "bioprogram set." If the pidgin had not yet become stable, all or almost all the grammar would then come from the bioprogram.

The evidence for the bioprogram hypothesis comes from the comparative studies of various creoles which are based on very diverse languages and are spoken in widely scattered areas of the world. Such studies show that creoles everywhere share a number of grammatical features in common which cannot be explained on the basis of such things as "simplification" or features of the languages that have come into contact to produce the creoles in question or diffusion from one contact language into another. In addition, many of the features shared by the creoles also appear as tendencies which manifest themselves in the speech of all children as they learn their first language, no matter what that language may be.

Among such shared features among various creoles cited by Bickerton (1983) is the marking of various special modal, aspectual, and temporal distinctions by the use of auxiliaries preceding the main verb.

For example, note the structural similarities among Hawaiian Creole English (an older variant, now almost obsolete), Haitian Creole (French-based), and Sranan (English-based creole of Surinam) in respect to the marking of the categories of *anterior, irreal,* and *nonpunctual* and their combinations in Table 8.1. The unmarked or "base form" represents past tense for nonstative

Table 8.1

VERB FORM	HAW. CREOLE	HAIT. CREOLE	SRANAN
Base form	He walk	Li maché	A waka
Anterior	He bin walk	Li té maché	A ben waka
Irreal	He go walk	L'av(a) maché	A sa waka
Nonpunctual	He stay walk	L'ap maché	A e waka
Anterior + irreal	He bin go walk	Li t'av(a) maché	A ben sa waka
Anterior + nonpunctual	He bin stay walk	Li t'ap maché	A ben e waka
Irreal + nonpunctual	He go stay walk	L'av ap maché	A sa e waka
Anterior + irreal + Nonpunctual	He bin go stay walk	Li t'av ap maché	A ben sa e waka

verbs but present tense for stative ones such as 'love' and 'want'. Anterior tense in the examples in Table 8.1 represents something that is roughly equivalent to English past perfect tense for nonstative verbs and past tense for stative ones. The irreal mode includes the English future tense and conditional and subjunctive modes. ('He will/would walk.') Nonpunctual aspect signals something similar to the English progressive tense: 'He is/was walking'. The anterior + irreal + nonpunctual combination translates roughly into English 'He would have been walking'.

One should note especially the fact that in all of the foregoing creole languages, the anterior particle precedes the irreal particle, and the irreal particle precedes the nonpunctual particle. Thus, it is not only the existence of the particular categories of verb marking in all creole languages that is so striking but the *order* in which these markers appear in each creole (anterior + irreal + nonpunctual) that forms yet another piece of evidence that Bickerton's hypothesis is correct.

Actually, as Bickerton notes in his discussion of the above example, in Hawaiian Creole 'He bin go walk' now means 'He walked' instead of 'He would have walked', and the forms 'He bin stay walk', 'He go stay walk' and 'He bin go stay walk', which were prevalent before World War II, are now almost extinct due to the growing influence of English (Standard American English, henceforth SAE) in Hawaii. In fact, due to this strong influence of English, Hawaiian Creole is now in a state of decreolization (with English structures slowly replacing the original creole structures). In other words, one may observe in Hawaii an example of what linguists call a *post-creole continuum:* SAE, which is taught in schools, is the *acrolect,* that is, the socially prestigious *lect,* or language variant, at the top of social hierarchy. At the bottom socially is the *basilect*—"heavy pidgin" or more accurately "heavy creole," a *lect* least influenced by SAE, usually spoken by people of low economic and social status who had very little education and very little chance to learn the acrolect in school. Between the two there is a continuum of *mesolects* ("inbetween" variants) which range from being very close to the acrolect to those which are very close to the basilect. Many people in Hawaii control various parts of this continuum. For example, most educated, professional people born in Hawaii, able to speak SAE at work in the office, switch to Hawaiian Creole when relaxing at home with friends and neighbors. There are also many speakers who cannot speak the acrolect perfectly but can approach it to a certain degree: Some speakers, for example, speak SAE using the correct SAE grammar and vocabulary but at the same time using Hawaiian Creole intonation patterns (which are very different from those of SAE).

It should be emphasized here that Bickerton's bioprogram hypothesis is not accepted by all linguists, and that some of the evidence which he adduces in its support has been challenged. In addition, readers should be cautioned that the above account of a post-creole continuum has been somewhat simplified. For example, SAE itself is not as uniform as one imagines it to be, and decreolization proceeds in different ways in different communities depending on different factors.

As time goes by and as more and more people gain access to educational opportunities, which in turn give them a better chance to learn the acrolect, it is clear that the basilect and the mesolects will continue to be influenced by SAE and the differences between the basilect and the acrolect will keep shrinking, until very few original creole features will be left. The differences may not disappear entirely, however, since Hawaiian Creole plays a positive role of creating and maintaining group identity among Hawaii-born people in spite of its being a variant with lower social prestige. For example, there are reports that young immigrants in Hawaii are learning SAE in school "to please their teachers" and at the same time are learning Hawaiian Creole English from their classmates in order to be accepted by their Hawaii-born fellow students.

To sum up our discussion of the development of contact languages, it may be helpful to study Mühlhäusler's (1986:11) chart in which he summarizes the various developments of contact language (see Figure 8.1).

In Figure 8.1 the development of contact languages is viewed as consisting of two parameters: the parameter of development or expansion from a very rudimentary jargon to a creole, that is, a contact language which is a full-fledged human language with native speakers, and the parameter of restructuring in the direction of the *lexifier language* or the acrolect. The first parameter involves increased complexity of the language; the second one does

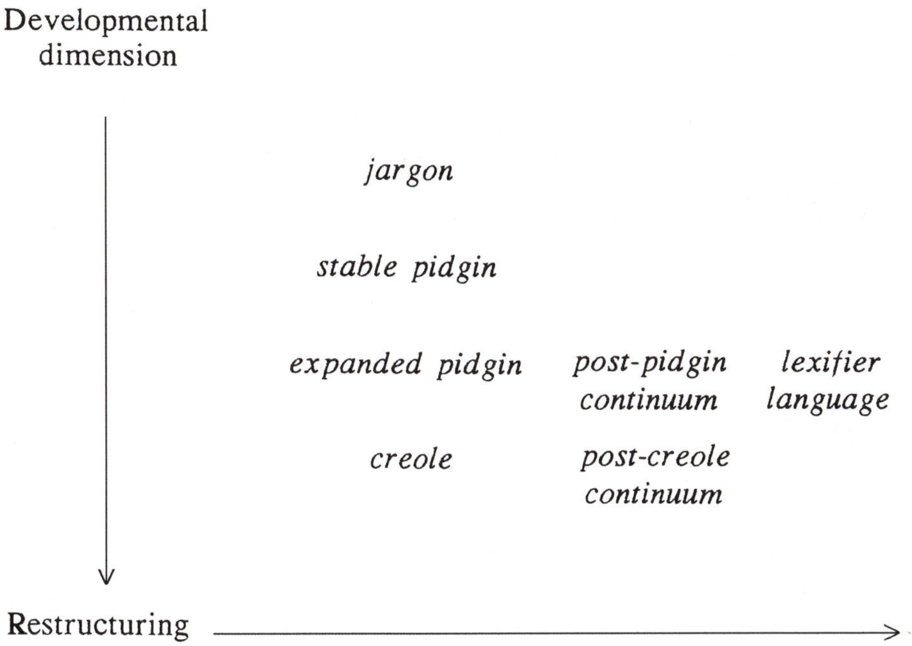

Developmental
  dimension

jargon

stable pidgin

expanded pidgin   *post-pidgin*   *lexifier*
                      continuum   *language*

creole   *post-creole*
             continuum

Restructuring ⟶

Figure 8.1

not. The second parameter merely involves evolution of structure and lexicon toward those of the socially more prestigious language.

CONTACT LANGUAGES OF THE WORLD

The information in the following list is taken, with a few exceptions, from Rickford (1992). It is by no means an exhaustive list of contact languages but is meant to be geographically representative as well as to show variety of languages coming into contact all over the world. Thus it is not limited only to those contact languages that have the most speakers or to those that are currently spoken.

EUROPE

Since Europe was not colonized by anyone in recent times, there are relatively speaking few contact languages currently spoken in Europe. (In some countries, for example, Germany, the presence of large immigrant worker population from various countries of Europe and even Asia creates favorable conditions for the development of contact languages of various kinds, especially since immigrants to Germany typically do not know much German before their arrival.)

Note also that some of the Romani (Gypsy) languages spoken in Europe are reported to be pidginized versions of the more mainstream Romani languages. For a brief overview of such Romani-based contact languages, see Jacques Arends et al. (1994:47–9).

Gastarbeiterdeutsch or Guest Worker German

This is a very simplified or "pidginized" German used (more so during the West German industrial boom of the 1950s and 1960s) in what was West Germany by foreign workers and even by Germans who deal with the latter; it is used especially by the new arrivals who haven't yet had a chance to learn the standard German language. The number of speakers of this pidgin fluctuates greatly.

Russenorsk

This is a pidgin developed for communication between Norwegian and Russian fishermen in the North Sea in the latter half of the nineteenth century. It is no longer in use.

ASIA

Chinese Pidgin English

This was a pidgin developed in the last century from the contact between Chinese and English speakers especially in the coastal cities of central and southern China. It is now no longer spoken in China but is found only in Nauru.

Indo-Portuguese

This is a Portuguese-based creole which has 2,250 speakers in Sri Lanka, but was formerly found also in India. It is spoken only in the home since its speakers are all fluent in Tamil and some are trilingual in English or Sinhalese.

Macanese

This is also a Portuguese-based creole which was originally spoken in the Portuguese colony of Macao. It is no longer spoken in Macao, but about 4,000 speakers are reported to be in Hong Kong.

Naga Pidgin

This is a creole based on Assamese (an Indo-Aryan language of northeastern India). It is spoken by the Kachari ethnic group in Kohima District, Dimapur Subdivision, and is also used by others in Nagaland as a lingua franca. (There are no estimates of the numbers of speakers.)

Russo-Chinese Pidgin

This was a pidgin once spoken in various places in the border region between Russia and China, wherever Russians came into contact with Chinese and later especially in Manchuria between 1920 and the end of World War II, that is, the period when large numbers of White Russians who had fled to Manchuria from Russia after the Russian revolution lived in northeastern China.

Sri Lankan Creole Malay

This is a Malay-based creole spoken by about 50,000 speakers in the cities of Sri Lanka. All the speakers are reported to be bilingual in Tamil.

AFRICA

Cameroons Pidgin

This English-based pidgin spoken by 2,000,000 speakers in Cameroon is reported to be very similar to other English-based pidgins found in other West African countries.

Crioulo or Portuguese Creole

This Portuguese-based creole is spoken by a total of 400,000 speakers, of which 100,000 are in the Bijagos Islands, Guinea Bissau, and other former Portuguese possessions in West Africa, 50,000 in Senegal, 250,000 speakers in the Cape Verde Islands, and some speakers in Gambia.

Fanagalo

This is a Xhosa-based (Bantu) pidgin spoken in South Africa and Zambia especially in the mines and surrounding areas where laborers from different ethnic groups work. Its vocabulary is reported to be a mixture of Xhosa (70%), English (24%), and Afrikaans (6%).

Kituba

This is a Kongo-based (Bantu) creole spoken by 4,200,000 speakers in Zaire.

Krio

This is an English-based creole spoken by 350,000 or more first-language speakers in Sierra Leone; some speakers are also found in Senegal, Guinea, Equatorial Guinea, and Gambia. It has been estimated that there may be as many as 3,230,000 second-language speakers.

Liberian English

This is an English-based pidgin spoken by 1,500,000 second-language speakers in Liberia.

Morisyen or Mauritius Creole French

This a French-based creole spoken on the island of Mauritius by 600,000 or more speakers.

Manukutuba

This is another Kongo-based (Bantu) contact language with about 1,160,000 speakers in south Congo. It is reported to be close to Kituba, which is spoken in Zaire.

Nigerian Pidgin English

This is spoken by a large number of speakers in Nigeria, some of whom speak it as their native language. Grimes (1992) and other sources, however, fail to give an estimate of the total number of speakers.

Réunion Creole French

This French-based creole is spoken by around 555,000 speakers on Réunion Island. There are two dialects: The urban one is said to resemble French more closely than the rural one, which exhibits more influences from Bantu and various West African languages.

Sango

This a creole which has about 200,000 first-language speakers mostly in the Central African Republic and some in Zaire, Chad, and Cameroon. It is also spoken and written informally by 4,900,000 second-language speakers. It is based on *Ngbandi,* a language belonging to the *Niger-Congo* language family spoken by 210,000 speakers in Zaire.

Seselwa

This is a French-based creole spoken by a total of about 76,600 speakers, of which 74,600 are on Tromelin and Aglega in the Seychelles, and the rest mostly on Mauritius. It is reported that in the Seychelles the first four years of education are in *Seselwa,* and it is used for some subjects for five additional years.

Sudanese Creole Arabic or Juba Arabic

This Arabic-based creole is spoken in Southern Sudan by 20,000 or more first-language speakers and an additional 44,000 second-language speakers. It is reported not to be mutually intelligible with Sudanese, the Arabic spoken in the north of the country, or Modern Standard Arabic.

OCEANIA

Bislama

This is an English-based creole which has few first-language speakers but is used by the majority of the 128,000 inhabitants of Vanuatu, and by 1,200 immigrants from Vanuatu in Noumea, New Caledonia.

Chavacano or Zamboangeño

This is a Spanish-based (some argue that it was originally Portuguese-based) creole spoken by 280,000 or more people in the Philippines around Zamboanga on Mindanao, as well as elsewhere.

Hawaii Creole English

This an English-based creole spoken by about 500,000 speakers in Hawaii. It is estimated that anywhere from 100,000 to 200,000 speakers do not control standard or near-standard English.

Hiri Motu or Police Motu

This is a Motu-based contact language of Papua New Guinea with a very few first-language speakers, but is used by as many as 250,000 second-language speakers in and around Port Moresby and throughout Oro, Central, Gulf, part of Milne Bay, and Western provinces. *Motu* is an Austronesian language spoken by 15,000 people in and around Port Moresby.

Kriol

This is an English-based creole which has 2,000 or more first-language speakers but is used by up to 30,000 speakers if second-language speakers are included. It is spoken in the Roper River and Katherine areas, Ngukurr, Northern Territory, and around Hall's Creek, Western Australia. All speakers are bilingual in English and various Australian aborigine languages of the region.

Pijin or Solomons Pijin

This is an English-based creole, not a pidgin (in spite of its name), spoken in the Solomon Islands by 1,300 first-language speakers. About 100,000 use it as a second language.

Tok Pisin or Neo-Melanesian

This is an English-based expanded pidgin of Papua New Guinea which now has 50,000 first-language speakers (and is thus in the process of being creolized) and about 2,000,000 second-language speakers. The number of first-language speakers is increasing in the urban areas. (Cf. "Sketch of Tok Pisin" in this chapter.)

Torres Strait Pidgin

This is an English-based pidgin spoken by up to 15,000 speakers, including second-language speakers, on Torres Straight Islands, Queensland, Australia. It is based on *Tok Pisin* and *Kala Yagaw Ya* an Australian aboriginal language.

AMERICAS

Aukaans or Ndjuka

This is an English-based creole spoken by 20,000 speakers along the Marowijne and Tapanahonij Rivers in Surinam.

Bahamas Creole English

This English-based creole is spoken by 225,000 speakers in the Bahamas.

Belize Creole English

This English-based creole is spoken by about 114,000 speakers in Belize, Central America. The first-language speakers are found mainly in the urban areas, whereas second-language speakers are found mainly in the rural areas. It is reported to be very close to the Jamaican, Nicaraguan, and Tobago creoles.

Chinook Jargon

It is estimated that somewhere from 10 to 100 older speakers of this Chinook-based trade pidgin remain in British Columbia, Canada, and in northwestern United States. *Chinook* is a Native American Indian language spoken in Oregon. This pidgin originated in times before the contact of the native population and the white traders; however, after white traders appeared in the area, this pidgin incorporated a large number of loanwords from French and some from English. It is estimated by some that at its peak almost 100,000 speakers used this trade jargon.

French Guianese

This is a French-based creole language of French Guiana with about 59,000 speakers. Most speakers are bilingual in French.

Guyanese Creole English

This English-based creole is spoken by a total of 700,000 speakers, of whom 650,000 are in Georgetown and coastal Guyana, and 50,000 in Surinam. There may also be some speakers in French Guiana.

Haitian Creole French

This French-based creole is spoken by 6,070,000 speakers, of whom 5,740,000 are in Haiti, 112,000 in the Dominican Republic, and the rest in other countries, including the United States. It is estimated that this is the only language for 95% of the population in Haiti.

Lesser Antillean Creole English

This English-based creole has around 192,000 speakers, of which 43,000 are in Grenada, 36,000 in Tobago, 17,500 in the British West Indies, and some speakers in six additional countries.

Lesser Antillean Creole French

This French-based creole is spoken by a total of 1,010,000 speakers, of which 335,000 are in Guadeloupe, 325,000 in Martinique, 121,000 in St. Lucia, 83,700 in Dominica, 150,000 in France, and possibly some in Grenada.

Louisiana Creole French

This French-based creole is spoken by 40,000 speakers in Louisiana, in parts of East Texas, and a small community in Sacramento, California. It is reported to be different from both standard French and Cajun French of Louisiana, but it may be mutually intelligible with Haitian Creole French and other French-based creoles of the Antilles. A small percentage are monolingual in the creole, others are bilingual in English.

Mitchif or French Cree

This creole is spoken by an indeterminate number of elderly speakers at Turtle Mountain Reservation, North Dakota, and scattered communities in the adjacent areas of Canada. It is a contact language based on French and Plains Cree.

Mobilian Jargon

This pidgin, which became extinct about 100 years ago, was based on various Muskogean languages of the Gulf region of the United States, such as Choctaw and Chikasaw, with an admixture of English, French, and Spanish. It was used as a lingua franca among the various native groups in the area.

Palenquero

This is a Spanish-based creole of Colombia spoken by about 3,000 speakers southeast of Cartagena. It is said to be entirely unintelligible to Spanish speakers.

Papiamentu

This Portuguese-based creole, with many Spanish and Dutch elements, is spoken by a total of 262,000 speakers, of which 227,000 are in the Netherlands Antilles (84% of the population), 35,000 in the Netherlands, and the rest in Puerto Rico and the U.S. Virgin Islands.

Saramaccan

This English-based creole is spoken in central Surinam by about 15,000 to 20,000 speakers.

Sea Islands Creole English or Gullah

This English-based creole is spoken by about 125,000 speakers who are found from North Carolina to Florida but are mostly concentrated on the Sea Islands off the coast of Georgia. There are reported to be from 7,000 to 10,000 monolinguals.

Sranan or Surinam Creole English

This is an English-based creole spoken by a total of anywhere from 310,000 to 350,000 speakers, of whom 130,000 to 170,000 are found on the Surinam coast (300,000, if second-language speakers are included), and 180,000 in the Netherlands and Netherlands Antilles. It is the lingua franca for 80% of the population of Surinam.

Western Caribbean Creole English

This English-based creole is spoken by 2,220,000 or more speakers, of which 1,670,000 are in Jamaica, 498,000 in five Central American countries, and 12,000 to 18,000 on San Andrés and Providencia Islands, Colombia. It is the language of the home for 70% of the population of Jamaica.

SKETCH OF TOK PISIN

A. GENERAL BACKGROUND

Tok Pisin is an expanded stable pidgin language that is in the process of acquiring native speakers. (It is estimated that there are already 50,000 first-language speakers of Tok Pisin, and that as much as 2 million people use it as their second language.)

It has developed to the point that is now used as one of the official languages, along with English and Hiri Motu (a pidgin based on an Austronesian language spoken around Port Moresby) of Papua New Guinea, a country which contains a multitude of tribal languages spoken by a few scattered villages each. A number of newspapers, magazines and an increasing number of books are published in it. Without Tok Pisin, in spite of its humble origins as a contact language, it probably would be very difficult to govern the country. It would probably cause much strife and unrest if one of the native languages of the country were to be chosen as the official language, and to make all or a dozen languages official would encourage chaos and regional separatism.

Although the bulk of Tok Pisin vocabulary comes from English, there are also significant numbers of words which are German in origin and words that are borrowed from the various languages of Papua New Guinea, especially Tolai. The words of German origin were incorporated during the time of German influence and colonization in Papua New Guinea; even after World War I, when German influence waned, there remained in the country a significant number of German missionaries thanks to whom some German influence continued. However, most German loanwords have now been replaced by loanwords from English:

> *tinte* < German Tinte 'ink' (now *ing* < English ink)
>
> *karaide* < German Kreide 'chalk' (now *sak* < English chalk)
>
> *kartopel* < German Kartoffel 'potato' (now *poteto* < English potato)

From Tolai and related languages come such words as:

> *balus* 'pidgeon'
>
> *liklik* 'small'
>
> *tamboran* 'ghost'

There is also a difference in vocabulary (and very likely some difference in grammar as well) between Rural Tok Pisin spoken in the countryside and less influenced by English and the Urban Tok Pisin spoken in Port Moresby and a few other large centers of population where English influence is rather strong. Thus, for example, in Urban Tok Pisin the words for 'jet plane' (*setplen*), 'orange' (*orins*), and 'lemon' (*lemen*) are clearly direct loans from English, whereas in Rural Tok Pisin their equivalents are not: *smokbalus* (< smoke + balus = 'smoke + plane, pigeon'), *switmuli* (< sweet + muli = 'sweet lime'), and *solmuli* (< sour + muli = 'sour lime').

Tok Pisin, like most contact languages, is an analytical/isolating language. Its basic word order is SVO as in English. The non-English elements involve the presence of inclusive/exclusive contrast in the pronouns, and the transitive verb marking (both of which features are also found in the indigenous languages of the area where Tok Pisin was formed).

B. Phonetics, Phonology and Orthography

The phonological system of Tok Pisin is influenced greatly by both English and the Melanesian languages of Papua New Guinea.

Consonants

Table 8.2 shows the consonant phonemes of Tok Pisin which are represented in the standard orthography of Tok Pisin (which is based on the variety of Tok Pisin spoken in Madang district).

The voiceless stops of Tok Pisin are unaspirated in all positions. In some dialects of Tok Pisin the voiced stops are strongly prenasalized due to the influence of the local Melanesian languages.

Because Tok Pisin has the final obstruent devoicing rule only voiceless obstruents are found in the word-final position. (This is reflected in the orthography even though this devoicing is completely automatic.) According to Mihalic (1971:8), the only exception to this rule is the word *God.*

The alveopalatal affricate *j* ([dʒ]) is found only at the beginning of words: elsewhere *s* is substituted for an English *j*: *bris* 'bridge', *jas* 'judge'. Most rural speakers do not use *j* but substitute *s* for it everywhere.

The voiceless labiodental fricative is also found only at the beginning of words, and actually there are very few words that have this sound at all. English words beginning with *f* are usually pronounced with a voiceless bilabial fricative initial ([Φ]) which is represented by the letter *p* in the orthography. Its voiced counterpart, *v*, is sometimes replaced by *b* in the middle of words.

Table 8.2   **Tok Pisin Consonants**

LABIAL	DENTAL	ALVE-OLAR	ALVEO-PALATAL	RETRO-FLEX	PALA-TAL	VELAR	GLOT-TAL
p	t					k	
b	d					g	
			j [dʒ]				
f	s						h
v							
m	n					ng	
		l					
				r			
w					y [j]		

The semivowel *w* is often replaced by *v* in the middle of words.

The velar nasal is written *n* when it stands before *k* and *g*: *anka* [aŋka] 'anchor'. (Actually, the spelling *ng* is ambiguous, just as in English: [ŋ] or [ŋg].)

Vowels

The vowel system of Tok Pisin is relatively simple and consists of five monophthong phonemes and three diphthong phonemes (see Table 8.3). The diphthongs are ai (as in *taim* 'time'), au (as in *maus* 'mouth'), and *oi* (as in *boi* 'boy').

Table 8.3 TOK PISIN VOWELS

i		u
e		o
	a	

The vowel phonemes have tense allophones in open syllables and lax allophones in closed syllables. However, the tense allophones are not pronounced with an offglide as in English. Thus the tense allophone of /o/ is [o], not [oṵ].

C. MORPHOLOGY

Pronouns

The personal pronouns are shown in Table 8.4. Note that there are no gender differences in the third person pronoun: *em* can stand for 'he', 'she' or 'it'.

Third person pronouns are usually followed by the third person agreement particle *i* which comes between the pronoun and the verb. (No such agreement particle exists for other persons. However, the particle *i* also appears in some constructions after other persons. See the section on the verb morphology below. Also, some dialects of Tok Pisin use this particle after other personal pronouns.)

> *Em i luk-im mi.*
>
> He/ 3d pers. agreement/ look + transitive/ 1st pers. sing.
> personal pronoun
>
> 'He looks at me.'

> *Mi luk-im em.*
>
> 1st pers. sing. personal pronoun/ look + transitive/ he
>
> 'I look at him.'

Reflexive pronouns are the same as the personal pronouns cited above with the addition of the reflexives particle *yet:*

Table 8.4 TOK PISIN PERSONAL PRONOUNS

1st pers. sing.	mi	1st pers. inclus.	yumi
		1st pers. pl. exclus.	mipela
2d pers. sing.	yu	2d pers. pl.	yupela
3d pers. sing.	em	3d pers. pl.	(em) ol

Mi pait-im mi yet. (Or: *Mi yet mi paitim mi.*)

1st pers. sing. pers. pron./ fight + transitive/ 1st pers. sing. pers. pron./ reflexive particle

'I hit myself.'

Emphatic forms of the personal pronouns are derived from the personal pronouns by means of various particles:

Mi yet 'I myself'

Mi tasol 'Only I, only me'

Mi wanpela 'I alone, me alone'

Numbers are usually attached to the personal pronouns as suffixes:

Mitupela (mitla in fast speech) 'Two of us'

Mitripela 'Three of us'

Adjectives and Adverbs

Tok Pisin adjectives usually end in suffix *-pela* and most precede the nouns they modify:

bikpela maunten 'big mountain'

yangpela meri 'young woman'

When used predicatively most adjectives retain the suffix *-pela,* but some do not:

maunten i bikpela 'the mountain is big'

dispela haus i gutpela 'this house is good'

dispela haus i klin 'this house is clean'

A few adjectives mean different things when they have the suffix and when they appear without it:

dispela mari is stret 'this woman is *honest*'

dispela mari is stretpela 'this woman is well-postured, has a straight posture'

A few adjectives (mostly of non-English origin) never take the suffix *-pela:*

liklik 'small'

lapun 'old'

Some adjectives *follow* the nouns they modify:

man nating 'just an ordinary person'

ples tambu 'forbidden place'

samting nogut 'something bad'

Comparison of adjectives and adverbs is signaled not by affixation but by the word *moa* (< more) and various circumlocutions:

> *Dispela moran i longpela moa long dispela.*
>
> this/ python/ 3d pers. sub. agreement/ long/ more/ general
>   prep. (= 'than')/ this
>
> 'This python is longer than this one.'

> *Tasol, dispela moran i longpela long olgeta.*
>
> but/ this/ python/ 3d pers. sub. agreement/ long/ than/ all
>
> 'But this python is longest of all.'

> *Em i digim boret hariap long mi.*
>
> he/ 3d pers. sub. agreement/ dug/ trench/ fast/ general prep.
>   (= 'than')/ I
>
> 'He dug the trench faster than me.'

> *Em i digim boret hariap olsem mi.*
>
> he/ 3d pers. sub. agreement/ dug/ trench/ fast/ as, like/ I
>
> 'He dug the trench as fast as me.'

> *Em i digim boret hariap winim olgeta.*
>
> he/ 3d pers. sub. agreement/ dug/ trench/ fast/ superlative
>   marker/ all
>
> 'He dug the trench the fastest.'

Verbs

Verbs in Tok Pisin that are not marked for tense can refer to present, past, or future depending on the context. Thus, for example, *'Mi go long taun'* may mean 'I am going to town', 'I went to town', or 'I shall go to town'.

Past tense may be marked by the preposed particle *bin:*

> *Ol kakaruk i bin ranawe i go long bus.*
>
> pl./ chicken/ 3d pers. agreement/ past/ run away/ 3d pers.
>   agreement/ into (general prep.)/ bush
>
> 'The chickens ran away into the bush.'

The future tense may be marked by a preposed particle *bai* which is usually shortened to *ba* or even *b* in fast speech:

Bai mi go long taun. (*'Mi bai go long taun'* is also possible.)

future / 1st sing. pers. pron. / go / into (general prep.) / town

'I shall go to town.'

The future particle usually precedes short subject NPs, but it usually follows long ones. In the latter case, the particle *i* (which normally shows third person agreement with the subject) may follow it:

Mi bai i go long taun.

1st sing. pers. pron. / future / *i* / to (general prep.) / town

'I shall go to town.'

Transitive verbs usually, but not always, have the suffix *-im* attached to them. This suffix may be used to derive transitive verbs from intransitive ones or transitive verbs out of other parts of speech in general:

bos 'boss' (noun) vs. bosim 'to boss, oversee'

wok 'work' vs. wokim 'to make, build'

orait 'okay' vs. oraitim 'to fix up'

bihain 'later' vs. bihainim 'to follow'

op 'to be open' (stative verb) vs. opim 'to open'

kros 'to be angry' vs. krosim 'to scold somebody'

singaut long 'to call out to (somebody)' vs. singautim 'to call (somebody)'

There is, however, a fairly large number of transitive verbs that do not have the transitive suffix *-im* attached:

kaikai 'to eat' (but some people use *'kaikaim'* instead)

gat 'to have'

save 'to know'

pekpek 'to defecate'

Mi pekpek wara.

1st sing. pers. pron. / defecate / water, liquid

'I have diarrhea.'

Various particles are used to mark aspectual and modal differences.

Perfective aspect is marked by the particle *pinis,* which is added after the verb or even after the direct object:

Olpela pat bilong ka i bagarap pinis.

old/ part/ of (poss. prep.)/ car 3d pers. agreement particle/
break, wear out/ perf. aspect

'The second hand parts of the car have worn out.'

Mi rit-im Wantok niuspepa pinis.

1st sing. pers. pron./ read + transitive/ Wantok (proper
name)/ newspaper/ perf.

'I have finished reading Wantok.'

Continuative aspect is marked by postposing *i stap* after the verb. Note
that *stap* is a general locative verb in Tok Pisin meaning something like 'stay,
be located'.

Mi raun i stap bilong pain-im wok.

1st sing. pers. pron./ go around/ *i*/ continuative aspect/ purpose marking prep./ find + transitive/ work

'I am walking around looking for work.'

Habitual action is expressed by *save* ('know' used as an auxiliary) + verb:

Em i save kaikai ol man.

it/ 3d pers. agreement/ habitual action/ eat/ pl./ person

'It used to eat people.'

'About to' is rendered by either *laik* + verb or *klostu* + verb.
Finally, physical ability is expressed by *inap* + verb:

Mi bai inap wok.

I /future/ able/ work

'I shall be able to work.'

D. SYNTAX

Word Order

The basic word order is Subject + Verb + Object as in English. As already
noted, most adjectives precede the nouns they modify, but there are some
that follow what they modify. The case relations in Tok Pisin are marked entirely by word order and the prepositions, since Tok Pisin pronouns do not
have different forms when they are used as subjects and objects of verbs.
(Compare English 'he' versus 'him', 'I' versus 'me', etc.)

Case Relations

Case relationships are signaled, as in English, by word order and prepositions.

Relative Clauses

There are three different types of relative clause constructions in Tok Pisin:

1. Relative clauses that do not have any overt relativizers except for intonational markers. The relative clauses in this type of constructions may be said to be embedded sentences in apposition to the head NPs in the matrix sentence.

> *Dispela man i kam asde em i papa bilong mi.*
>
> this/ man/ 3d pers. sub. agreement/ came/ yesterday/ he/ 3d pers. sub. agreement/ father/ gen. prep./ I
>
> 'This man who came yesterday is my father.'

2. Relative clauses that are bracketed by the marker *ya*:

> *Dispela man ya em i stap long bus ya em i redi na em i kisim bonara.*
>
> this/ man/ relative clause bracket/ he/ live, stay/ general prep. (= 'in')/ bush/ relative clause bracket/ he/ 3d pers. sub. agreement/ ready/ and/ he/ 3d pers. sub. agreement/ get/ bow and arrows
>
> 'This man who lived in the bush was ready to get his bow and arrows.'

3. The third type of relative construction is found in the varieties of Tok Pisin which are in close contact with English and have been much influenced by the latter. This type of construction employs relative pronouns just as in English:

> *Pablik seven em i man husat i gat strong long wok bilong en.*
>
> public/ servant/ he/ 3d pers. sub. agreement/ who/ 3d pers. sub. agreement/ have/ strength (?)/ general prep. (= 'in')/ work/ gen. prep./ 3d pers. pron.
>
> 'A public servant is someone who knows his job.'

> *Ol i go long wanpela ples we i gat bikpela tais long en.*
>
> they/ 3d pers. sub. agreement/ general prep. (= 'to')/ place/ where/ 3d pers. sub. agreement/ have/ big/ swamp/ general prep. (= 'in, at')/ 3d pers. pron.
>
> 'They went to a place where there is a big swamp.'

The relative clauses of this type are more common in constructions whose English equivalents have 'whosoever', 'whatsoever' rather than 'who' or 'which' as the relative pronouns:

> *Husat ol man i laik kam i ken i kam.*

> who/ pl./ pers./ 3d pers. sub. agreement/ want/ come/ 3d pers. sub. agreement/ can, may/ 3d pers. sub. agreement/ come

> 'Whosoever wants to come can come.'

Direct and Indirect Speech

Direct speech:

> *Em i tok: mi bagarap pinis.*

> he/ 3d pers. sub. agreement/ said:/ I/ exhausted/ perf. aspect

> 'He said, "I am really tired." '

Indirect speech uses the marker *olsem* to introduce the indirect quotation:

> *Em i tok olsem em i bagarap pinis.*

> he/ 3d pers. sub./ said/ that/ he/ 3d pers. sub./ exhausted/ perf. aspect

> 'He said that he was tired.'

Interrogative Sentences

Yes-and-no questions differ from their noninterrogative equivalents only by intonation. Content questions have interrogative words such as *husat* 'who' and *wanem* 'what, which' to indicate that they are questions.

E. SAMPLE TEXT

I am very much indebted to Gillian Sankoff for providing the following story. She recorded it in July 1971 in Papua New Guinea, annotated it, and explained it to me in August 1992. It is a folktale told by an informant who is identified only as Lina Z., a native speaker of Tok Pisin, which explains why it contains some complicated syntactic structures which are usually absent from the speech of non-native Tok Pisin speakers.

As in the case of the story cited in the sketch of Dyirbal, this is not a highly polished, literary piece, but an oral presentation which was transcribed by a field linguist and must be taken as such. Sankoff did take out some hesitations and normalized some of the spelling, and I made a few changes on the advice of Craig Volker, a graduate student in linguistics at the University of Hawaii who has done field work in Papua New Guinea; otherwise, the story is cited as it was recorded by her. (Therefore, the spelling and some of the word usage do not always conform with Standard Tok Pisin.) The idiomatic English translation at the end was also kindly provided by Sankoff.

As usual, the superscripted numbers in the literal morpheme-by-morpheme translation refer to notes that follow that section.

Tok Pisin Text

(1) Long taim bifo, wanpela ailan, draipela pik i save stap ya, na em i save kaikai ol man. Em i save kaikai ol man nau; wanpela taim, wanpela taim nau ol man go tokim bikpela man bilong ol, bos bilong ol, ol i go tokim em nau, em i tok: "Orait yumi mas painim nupela ailan."

(2) Nau, ol i stretim ol samting bilong ol na i go painim nupela ailan. Na wanpela meri, pik, pik ya bin kaikai man bilong en bifo na, em i gat bel. I-gat pikinini insait long bel bilong en. Nau, em go askim ol man long kisim em long kanu na ol man tok: "Nogat, fulap ya, yu go painim narapela!"

(3) Ol i toktok 'sem nau, em i go long narapela, ol tok 'sem. Em i go nau, las kanu nau, em i tok: "Nogat, mi fulap, mi gat pikinini bilong mi, na meri bilong mi yet. Yu go . . ."

(4) Ol man i tok, "Yu stap, yu gat bel, na nogat inap spes long yumi go."

(5) Na ol i go painim nupela ailan na em i stap long olpela peles.

(6) Nau, wampela taim nau em bonim, em karim tupela pikinini boi, long insait long bel bilong en—olsem tupela pikinini, tupela boi, man. Tupela man nau, em i save wokhat long painim kaikai na abus bilong tupela. Em i wokim olsem i go nau, tupela kamap bikpela yangpela man. Bikpela man nau, em tokim tupela stori long, pik ya, husat ya, em ol man, long ol man ronewe i go ya. Em stori long tupela pinis nau, em wokim supia na soim tupela long ol na sutim na ol sutim na yusim holim gut.

(7) Nau bihain nau, em i go soim ples long we pik i save slip long en ya. Ol i go antap long bikpela diwai na em i soim tupela, long pik, draipela pik ya i save stap long en ya. Nau ol i kam bek nau, wokim planti supia tru. Wokim planti supia nau, bihain ol i go bildim flatfom antap long diwai. Fom antap long diwai nau, narapela moning nau, ol i go antap long diwai ya. Kisim supia na ol i go antap long flatfom long diwai. Ol i lukim, pik i go na i kam bek, dring wara na, waswas long wara.

(8) Na ol tripela man ya, pikinini na mama bilong tupela ya, i go antap long wanpela bikpela diwai. Nau ol tripela i stap nau, pik ya laik kam, dring wara na waswas. Ol tripela, i tromoe supia na ol samting long . . .

(9) Em pik i win olsem ya, em kalap antap, na flatfom daunbelo ya bruk. Nau tripela kalap i go long antap wanpela flatfom antap long diwai, strongpela. Nau ol tromwe spia i go na pik i sotwin na em i laik i dai nau. Na tupela boi ya, i kam daun long seken flatfom na siutim em long supia. Na em i dai nau. Ol tripela kam daun na siutim em na brukim het bilong en long ston.

(10) Nau, ol i stap nau, mama bilong tupela tok: "Bai yu wokim wanem long pik ya?" Na, tupela tok: "Yu mas katim skin bilong en na tromwe long solwara. Em bai karim i go long narapela ailan na ol man bilong yumi bai i kam bek."

(11) Nau ol katim skin bilong pik ya na ol karim i go long haus. Karim i go long haus nau, ol tromwe long solwara na karim i go.

(12) Na draipela win na, wara i save—, i go, olsem, si bruk. Long moning-taim, si wokim olsem nau, solwara karim dispela skin bilong pik ya i go daun long, ailan, narapela ailan ya.

(13) Nau, wanpela lapun man, em i laik go, em i laik go we? Em i laik go long toilet o, we, nau em lukim disfela samting, bikpela samting, skin bilong pik ya long solwara. Na em singautim olgeta man long ples bihain kam luk, sanap na lukluk.

(14) Nau, ol sampela man tok olsem: "Ol meri mas karim pikinini na stap insait long haus, no ken kam arasait, ol man tasol kam arasait!"

(15) Nau, ol man kam sanap lukluk nau, ol i lukim olosem skin bilong pik bifo save kaikai ol man ya. Nau, ol i go kisim disfela skin bilong pik ya na tromwe i go antap long, wesan . . .

(16) Ol tingting bek long meri ya i gat bel bifo ya. Nau, tupela i tok: "Na-ting tumoro samting yumi mas i go bek long ples, bilong mitupela ya na lukim husat kilim disfela pik na tromwe."

(17) Nau long moningtaim nau, ol i kisim olgeta samting bilong ol i go long ples. Ol i go nau, lukim, na tripela man ya, tupela man ya na mama bilong en tupela, ol kam sanap long nambis na lukluk long ol.

(18) Ol i lukim kanu na olgeta samting. Ol man ya long kanu ol i lukluk i go na lukim tripela sanap. Ol i wokim kaikai na redi i stap long ol man kam bek na kaikai.

(19) Em, ol i kam nau, ol i wokim, kaikai. Ol tripela wokim kaikai na ologeta i stap. Ol man i kam kaikai nau, ol tripela bai i go daun, ol i go, ol i go daun na i go, i go daunbilo tru. Bai ol tripela i go insait long solwara na, pik ya ol kilim bipo ya bai kamap olsem draipela ston, blakpela ston.

(20) Em tasol.

Literal Morpheme-by-Morpheme Translation

(1) *Long taim bifo, wan-pela ailan, drai pela pik i save stap ya, na em i save kaikai ol man.*
prep. (= **'In'**)/ **time**/ before (= **'past'**)/, **one** + adj./ **island**/, **huge** + adj./ **pig**/ 3d pers. sub./ **used to**/ **live**/ det./, **and**/ **he**/ 3d pers. sub./ **used to**/ **eat**/ pl./ man (= **'people'**).

Em i save kaikai ol man nau;[1] *wan-pela taim, wan-pela taim nau ol man go tok-im*[2] *bik-pela man bilong ol, bos bilong ol, ol i go tok-im*[2] *em nau, em i tok: "Orait yumi mas pain-im nu-pela ailan."*
He/ 3d pers. sub./ **used to**/ **eat**/ pl./ man (= **'people'**)/ **then**/; one + adj./ **time**/, one + adj./ **time**/ **then**/ pl./ man (= **'men'**)/ **talk** + transitive/ **big** + adj./ **man**/ of/ 3d pers. pl. (with preceding = **'their'**)/, **boss**/ of/ 3d pers. pl. (= **'theirs'**)/, **they**/ 3d pers. sub./ **go**/ **talk** + transitive/ **him**/ **then**/, **he**/ 3d pers. sub./ talk, **say**/: "**All right**/ **we** (inclus.)/ **must**/ **find** + transitive/ **new** + adj./ **island**/."

(2) *Nau, ol i stret-im ol samting bilong ol na i go pain-im nu-pela ailan.*
Then/, **they**/ 3d pers. sub./ **gather together** + transitive/ **some thing(s)**/ of/ they (= **'their'**)/ **and**/ 3d pers. sub./ **go**/ **find** + transitive/ **new** + adj./ **island**/.

Na wan-pela meri, pik, pik ya[3] bin kaikai man bilong en[4] bifo na, em i gat bel.
And/ **one** + adj./ **woman**/, **pig**/, **pig**/ det./ imperf. aux./ **eat**/ man, **husband**/ of/ she (= **'her'**)/ before, **previously**/ **and**/, **she**/ 3d pers. sub./ get/ belly (= **'get pregnant'**)/.

I-gat pikinini insait long bel bilong en.[4] Nau, em go ask-im ol man long kis-im em long[5] kanu na ol man tok: "Nogat, fulap ya, yu go pain-im nara-pela!"
3d pers. sub./ **Get**/ child, **baby**/ **inside**/ prep. (= **'in'**)/ **belly**/ of/ she (= **'her'**)/. **Then**/ **she**/ **go**/ **ask** + transitive/ pl./ man (= **'men'**)/ prep. (= **'to, for'**)/ **take** + transitive/ prep. (= **'into'**)/ **canoe**/ and, **but**/ pl./ man (= **'men'**)/ **say**/: "**No**/ **full**/ det./, **you**/ **go**/ **find** + transitive/ **another** + adj./!"

(3) *Ol i toktok 'sem[6] nau, em i go long nara-pela, ol tok 'sem.[6] Em i go nau, las kanu nau, em i tok: "Nogat, mi fulap, mi gat pikinini bilong mi, na meri bilong mi yet.[7] Yu go . . ."*
They/ 3d pers. sub./ **say**/ **same**/ **then**/, **She**/ 3d pers. sub./ **go**/ prep. (= **'to'**)/ **other** + adj./, **they**/ **say**/ **same**/. **she**/ 3d pers. sub./ **go**/ **then**/, **last**/ **canoe**/ **then**/, **he**/ 3d pers. sub./ **say**/: "**No**/, **I**/ **full**/, **I**/ **have**/ **child**/ of/ I (= **'my'**)/, **and**/ woman (= **'wife'**)/ of/ I / self (with the preceding two morphemes = **'my own'**)/. **You**/ **go**/ . . ."

(4) *Ol man i tok, "Yu stap, yu gat bel, na nogat inap spes long yumi go."*
pl./ man (= **'Men'**)/ 3d pers. sub. + **say**/, "**You**/ **stay**/, **you**/ have/ belly (= **'are pregnant'**)/, **and**/ **there is not**/ **enough**/ **space**/ prep. (= **'for'**)/ **us** (inclusive)/ **go**/."

(5) *Na ol i go pain-im nu-pela ailan na em i stap long ol-pela peles.*
And/ **they**/ 3d pers. sub./ **go**/ **find** + transitive/ **new** +/ **island**/ and, **but**/ **she**/ 3d pers. sub. **stay**/ prep. (= **'in'**)/ **old** +/ **place**/.

(6) *Nau, wam-pela taim nau em bon-im, em kar-im tu-pela pikinini boi, long insait long bel bilong en[4]—olsem tu-pela pikinini, tu-pela boi, man.*
Then/, **one** + adj./ **time**/ **then**/ **she**/ **give birth** + transitive/, **she**/ **bear** + transitive/ **two** + adj./ **baby**/ **boy**/, prep. (= **'in'**)/ **inside,** interior/ prep. (= **'in'**)/ **belly**/ of/ she (= **'her'**)/—**like**/ **two** + adj./ **boy**/, man, **male**/.

Tu-pela man nau, em i save wokhat long pain-im kaikai na abus[8] bilong tu-pela.
Two + adj./ **man**/ **then**/, **she**/ 3d pers. sub. + **used to**/ **work hard**/ prep. (= **'to'**)/ **seek,** find/ **food**/ **and**/ **game**/ of (= **'for'**)/ **two** + adj./.

Em i wok-im olsem i go[9] nau, tu-pela kamap bik-pela yang-pela man.
She/ 3d pers. sub./ **do** + transitive/ like, **thus**/ 3d pers. sub./ **go**/ **then**/, **two** + adj./ **grow**/ **big** + adj./ **young** + adj./ **man**/.

Bik-pela man nau, em tok-im tu-pela stori long, pik ya,[3] husat ya, em ol man, long[5] ol man ronewe i go ya.[3]
Big + adj./ **man**/ **then**/, **she**/ **tell,** speak + transitive/ **two** + adj./ **story**/ prep. (= **'about'**)/, **pig**/ det./, **who**/ det./, 3d person/ plural/ man (= **'men'**)/, prep. (= **'from'**)/ pl./ man (= 'men')/ **run away**/ 3d pers. sub. + **go**/ det./.

*Em stori long tu-pela pinis nau, em wok-im supia na so-im tu-pela long ol[10]
na sut-im na ol sut-im na yus-im hol-im gut.*
She/ **story**/ prep. (= **'to'**)/ **two** + adj./ **finish,** perf. aspect/ **then**/, **she**/ **make** +
transitive/ **spear**/ **and** / **show** + transitive/ **two** + adj./ prep. (= **'to'**)/ **them**/
and/ **shoot** + transitive/ **and**/ **they**/ **shoot** + transitive/ **and**/ **use** + transitive/
handle/ good, **well**/.

(7) *Nau bihain nau, em i go so-im ples long we pik i save slip long en[4] ya.[3]*
Then/ afterwards, **later**/ **then**/, **she**/ 3d pers. sub./ **go**/ **show** + transitive/
place/ prep. (loc. function)/ **where**/ **pig**/ 3d pers. sub./ **used to**/ **sleep**/ prep.
(loc. function)/ **it**/ det./.

*Ol i go antap long bik-pela diwai na em is so-im tu-pela, long pik, drai pela
pik ya[3] i save stap lon en[4] ya.[3]*
They/ 3d pers. sub./ **go**/ **up**/ prep. (= **'on'**)/ **big** + adj./ **tree**/ **and**/ **she** 3d pers.
sub./ **show** + transitive/ **two** + adj./, prep./ **pig**/, **huge** + adj./ **pig**/ det./ 3d
pers. sub./ **used to**/ **stay**/ prep. (= **'at'**)/ 3d pers. pron./ det./.

*Nau ol i kam bek nau, wok-im planti supia tru.[11] Wok-im planti supia nau,
bihain ol i go bild-im flatfom antap long diwai.*
Then/ **they**/ 3d pers. sub. + **come**/ **back**/ **then**/, **make** + transitive/ **many**/
spear/ **very** (intensifier)/. **make** + transitive/ **many**/ **spear**/ **then**/, later, **after-**
ward/ **they**/ 3d pers. sub./ **go**/ **build** + transitive/ **platform**/ **up**/ prep. (=
'on')/ **tree**/.

*Fom antap long diwai nau, nara-pela moning nau, ol i go antap long diwai
ya.*
Platform/ **up**/ prep (= **'on'**)/ **tree**/ **then**/, **another,** different + adj./ **morning**/
then/, **they**/ 3d pers. sub./ **go**/ **up**/ prep. (= **'on'**)/ **tree**/, det./.

*Kis-im supia na ol i go antap long flatfom long diwai. Ol i luk-im, pik i go
na i kam bek, dring wara na, waswas long wara.*
Take + transitive/ **spear**/ **and**/ **they**/ 3d pers. sub./ **go**/ **up**/ prep. (= **'on'**)/
platform/ prep. (= **'on'**)/ **tree**/. **they**/ 3d pers. sub./ **look** + transitive/, **pig**/ 3d
pers. sub./ **go**/ **and**/ 3d pers. sub./ **come**/ **back**/, **drink**/ **water**/ and/, **wash**/
prep. (= **'in'**)/ **water**/.

(8) *Na ol tri-pela man ya, pikinini na mama bilong tu-pela ya, i go antap
long wan-pela bik-pela diwai.*
And/ **they**/ **three** + adj./ **man** (= **'people'**)/ det./, baby, **child**/ **mother**/ **of**/
two + adj./ det./, 3d pers. sub./ **go**/ **up**/ preposition (= **'on'**)/ **one** + adj./ **big**
+ adj./ **tree**/.

*Nau ol tri-pela i stap nau, pik ya laik kam, dring wara na waswas. Ol tri-
pela, i tromoe supia na ol samting long . . .*
Then/ **they**/ **three** + adj./ 3d pers. sub./ **stay**/ **then**/, **pig**/ det./ **about to**/
come/, **drink**/ **water**/ **and**/ **wash**/. **They**/ **three** + adj./, 3d pers. sub./ **throw**/
spear/ **and**/ plur./ something, thing (= **'things'**)/ prep. (= **'at (him)'**) . . .

(9) *Em[12] pik i win olsem ya, em kalap antap, na flatfom daunbelo ya bruk.*
he (= **'The'**)/ **pig**/ 3d pers. sub./ **win**/ **thus,** like/ det./, **he**/ **climb**/ **up**/, **and**/
platform/ below, **bottom**/ det./ **break**/.

*Nau tri-pela kalap i go long antap wan-pela flatfom antap long diwai,
strong-pela. Nau ol tromwe spia i go na pik i sotwin na em i laik i dai nau.*

Then/ **three** + adj./ **climb**/ 3d pers. sub./ **go**/ prep. (= **'on'**)/ det./ **top, up**/ **one** + adj./ **platform**/ up, **upper**/ prep. (= **'on'**)/ **tree**/, **strong** + adj./. **Then**/ **they**/ **throw**/ **spear**/ 3d pers. sub./ **go**/ **and**/ **pig**/ 3d pers. sub./ **be winded**/ **and**/ **he**/ 3d pers. sub./ **about to**/ 3d pers. sub./ **die**/ **then**/.

Na tu-pela boi ya, i kam daun long seken flatfom na siut-im em long[13] *supia. Na em i dai nau.*

And/ **two** + adj./ **boy**/ det./, 3d pers. sub./ **come**/ **down**/ prep. (= **'to'**)/ **second**/ **platform**/ **and**/ **shoot** + transitive/ **him**/ prep. (= **'with'**)/ **spear**/. **And**/ **he**/ 3d pers. sub./ **die**/ **then**/.

Ol tri-pela kam daun na siut-im em na bruk-im het bilong en[4] *long*[13] *ston.*

They/ **three** + adj./ **come**/ **down**/ **and**/ **shoot** + transitive/ **him**/ **and**/ **break**/ **head**/ of/ he (with previous = **'his'**)/ prep. (= **'with'**)/ **stone**/.

(10) *Nau, ol i stap nau, mama bilong tu-pela tok: "Bai yu wok-im wanem long pik ya?"*

Then/, **they**/ 3d pers. sub./ stay, **be**/ **then**/, **mother**/ **of**/ **two** + adj./ **say**/: "future/ **You**/ make, **do** + transitive/ **what**/ prep. (= **'with'**)/ **pig**/ det./?"

Na, tu-pela tok: "Yu mas kat-im skin bilong en[4] *na tromwe long solwara.*

And/, **two** + adj./ **say**/: "**you**/ **must**/ **cut** + transitive/ **skin**/ of/ he (= **'his'**)/ **and**/ **throw**/ prep. (= **'into'**)/ **ocean**/.

Em bai kar-im i go long nara-pela ailan na ol man bilong yumi bai i kam bek."

It/ future/ **carry** + transitive/ 3d pers. sub./ **go**/ prep. (= **'to'**)/ another, **other** + adj./ **island**/ **and**/ pl./ man (= **'people'**)/ of/ us (= **'our'**)/ inclus.)/ future/ 3d pers. sub./ **come**/ **back**/."

(11) *Nau ol kat-im skin bilong pik ya na ol ol kar-im i go*[9] *long haus. Kar-im i go long haus nau, ol tromwe long solwara na kar-im i go.*

Then/ **they**/ **cut** + transitive/ **skin**/ of/ **pig**/ det./ **and**/ **they**/ **they**/ **carry** + transitive/ 3d pers. sub./ **go**/ prep. (= **'to'**)/ **house**/. **Carry** + transitive/ 3d pers. subj./ **go**/ prep. (= **'to'**)/ **house**/ **then**/, **they**/ **throw**/ prep. (= **'into'**)/ **ocean**/ **and**/ **carry** + transitive/ 3d pers. sub./ **go**/.

(12) *Na drai pela win na, wara i save—, i go, olsem, si bruk. Long moning-taim, si wok-im olsem nau, solwara kar-im dis-pela skin bilong pik ya i go daun long, ailan, nara-pela ailan ya.*

And/ **huge, great** + adj./ **wind**/ **and**/, **water**/ 3d pers. sub./ know how to, **do frequently**/—3d pers. sub./ **go**/ like, **as if**/ **sea**/ break, **burst**/. prep. (= **'In'**)/ **morning**/ **time**/, **sea**/ work, **do** + transitive/ **thus,** like/ **then**/, **ocean**/ **carry** + transitive/ **this** + adj./ **skin**/ of / **pig**/ det./ 3d pers. sub./ **go**/ **down**/ prep. (= **'to'**)/, **island**/, another, **other** + adj./ **island**/ det./.

(13) *Nau, wan-pela lapun man, em i laik go, em i laik go we? Em i laik go long toilet o, we, nau em luk-im dis-fela samting, bik-pela samting, skin bilong pik ya long solwara.*

Then/, **one** + adj./ **old,** elderly/ **man**/, **he**/ 3d pers. sub./ **want**/ **go**/, **he**/ 3d pers. sub./ **want**/ **go**/ **where**/? **He**/ 3d pers. sub./ **want**/ **go**/ prep. (= **'to'**)/ **toilet**/ **or**/, **somewhere,** where/, **then**/ **he**/ **see** + transitive/ **this** + adj./ **(some)thing**/, **skin**/ **of**/ **pig**/ det./ prep. (= **'in'**)/ **ocean**/.

Na em singaut-im olgeta man long ples bihain kam luk, sanap na luk-luk.

And/ **he**/ **call** + transitive/, **all**/ **man**/ prep. (= **'in'**)/ **village**/ later, **afterward**/ **come**/ **look**/, **stand up**/ **and**/ **look**/.

(14) *Nau, ol sam-pela man tok olsem: "Ol meri mas kar-im pikinini na stap insait long haus, no ken kam arasait, ol man tasol kam arasait!"*

Then/, pl./ **some** + adj./ **man**/ **say**/ **thus**/: "pl./ woman (= **'Women'**)/ **must**/ **carry** + transitive/ **child,** baby/ **and**/ **stay**/ **inside**/ prep. (= **'of'**)/ **house**/, negat./ **can**/ **come**/ **outside**/, pl./ man (= **'men'**)/ **only**/ **come**/ **outside**/!"

(15) *Nau, ol man kam sanap luk-luk nau, ol i lukim olosem skin bilong pik bifo save kaikai ol man ya.*

Then/, pl./ **man** (= **'men'**)/ **come**/ **stand up**/ look + look (= **'stare'**)/ **then**/ thus, **just like**/ **skin**/ **of** / **pig**/ before, **previously**/ **used to**/ **eat**/ plur./ man (= **'men'**)/ det./.

Nau, ol i go kis-im dis-fela skin bilong pik ya na tromwe i go antap long, wesan . . .

Then/, **they** 3d pers. sub./ **go**/ **take** + transitive/ **this** + adj./ **skin**/ **of**/ **pig**/ det./ **and**/ **throw**/ 3d pers. sub./ **go**/ **top,** on/ prep. (= 'of')/, **sand**/ . . .

(16) *Ol tingting bek long meri ya[3] i gat bel bifo ya.[3] Nau tu-pela i tok: "Nat-ing tumoro samting yumi mas i go bek long ples, bilong mi tu-pela ya na luk-im husat kil-im dis-fela pik na tromwe."*

They/ **think**/ **back**/ prep. (= **'about'**)/ **woman**/ det./ 3d pers. sub./ have/ belly (= **'pregnant'**)/ before, **previously**/ det./. **Then**/, **two** + adj./ 3d pers. sub./ **say**/: "**Perhaps,** maybe/ **tomorrow**/ or so,/ **we** (inclus.)/ **must**/ 3d pers. sub./ **go** / back/ prep. (= **'to'**)/ **(own) place**/, of/ **us** + **two** + adj./ det./ **and**/ **see** + transitive/ **who**/ **kill** + transitive/ **this** + adj./ **pig**/ **and**/ **throw**/."

(17) *Nau long moning-taim nau, ol i kis-im olgeta samting bilong ol i go long ples.*

Then/ preposition (= **'in'**)/ **morning** + **time**/ **then**/, **they**/ 3d pers. sub./ **take** + transitive/ **all**/ **thing(s)**/ of/ they (= **'their'**)/ 3d pers. sub./ **go**/ prep. (= **'to'**)/ (own) place, **home**/.

Ol i go nau, luk-im, na tri-pela man ya, tu-pela man ya na mama bilong-en tu-pela, ol kam sanap long nambis na luk-luk long ol.

They/ 3d pers. sub./ **go**/ **then**/, **look** + transitive/, **and**/ **three** + adj./ **man, person**/ det./, **two** + adj./ **man**/ det./ **and**/ **mother**/ **of** + **them**/ **two** + adj./, **they**/ **come**/ **stand**/ prep. (= **'on'**)/ det./ **beach,** shore/ **and**/ look + look (= **'stare'**)/ prep. (= **'at'**)/ **them**/.

(18) *Ol i luk-im kanu na olgeta samting. Ol man ya long kanu ol i luk-luk i go[9] na luk-im tri-pela sanap.*

They/ 3d pers. sub./ **look** + transitive/ **canoe**/ **and**/ all/ thing, something (with the preceding = **'everything'**)/. plur./ **man** (= **'Men'**)/ det./ prep. (= **'in'**)/ **canoe**/ **they**/ 3d pers. sub./ look + look (= **'stare'**)/ 3d pers. sub./ **go**/ **and**/ **look** + transitive/ **three** + adj./ stand up, **standing**/.

Ol i wok-im kaikai na redi i stap long ol man kam bek na kaikai.

They/ 3d pers. sub./ **make,** do + transitive/ **food**/ **and**/ **ready**/ 3d pers. sub./ **wait,** stay, be, sit/ prep. (= **'for'**)/ det./ plur./ **man** (= **'men'**)/ **come**/ **back**/ **and**/ **eat**/.

(19) *Em, ol i kam nau, ol i wok-im, kaikai. Ol tri-pela wok-im kaikai na ologeta i stap.*
3d pers. pron./, **They**/ 3d pers. sub./ **come**/ **then**/, **they**/ 3d pers. sub./ **make** + transitive/ **food**/. **they**/ **three** + adj./ **make** + transitive/ **food**/ **and**/ **all**/ 3d pers. sub./ **stay**, be (there)/.

Ol man i kam kaikai nau, ol tri-pela bai[14] *i go daun, ol i go, ol i go daun na i go, i go taunbilo tru.*
plur./ **man** (= **'People'**)/ 3d pers. sub./ **come**/ **eat**/ **then**/, **they**/ **three** + adj./ somewhat later, **after a while**/ 3d pers. sub./ **go**/ **down**/ **and**/ 3d pers. sub./ **go**/, 3d pers. sub./ **go**/ below, deep/ intensifier (with the previous word = **'very deep'**)/.

Bai ol tri-pela i go insait long solwara na, pik ya[3] *ol kil-im bipo ya*[3] *bai*[14] *kamap olsem drai pela ston, blak-pela ston.*
After a while/ **they**/ **three** + adj./ 3d pers. sub./ **go**/ **inside**/ prep. (= **'into'**)/ **ocean**/ **and**/, **pig**/ det./ **they**/ **kill** + transitive/ **earlier**, before/ det./, **after a while**, somewhat later/ **become**, grow, appear/ **like**/ **huge** + adj./ **stone**/, **black** + adj./ **stone**/.

(20) *Em tasol.*
It/ **only**/.

NOTES

1. *Nau* may be translated as 'then' in narratives about past events. According to Sankoff, *nau* here is a marker of "punctual" aspect.

2. *Tokin* takes a direct object in Tok Pisin, unlike its English counterpart 'talk' which requires the preposition 'to'.

3. *Ya* is a determiner that marks those items that have been mentioned before. Thus, it can be translated as 'the aforementioned' or 'the one we are talking about'. However, according to Sankoff, *ia* is also used as a kind of bracket for relative clauses. See the discussion of the Tok Pisin relative clauses in the sketch.

4. *Long* here is not a preposition but a complementizer.

5. *En* is a variant of *em*, the third person pronoun, after *bilong* or *long*. In Standard Tok Pisin this variant is used only for nonmasculine and nonfeminine noun referents such as 'gras', 'haus', 'God'.

6. *'Sem* is a phonological reduction of *olsem* 'like'.

7. *Yet* here is reflexive.

8. *Abus* is a word meaning 'bit of meat or game' borrowed into Tok Pisin from Tolai, an Austronesian language spoken by 80,000 speakers in the New Britain Province of Papua New Guinea.

9. *I wokim . . . i go* construction: i *go, i kam,* and *i stap* suffixed to the main verb add continuous aspect or directional 'vector' on main verb.

10. *Na soim tupela long ol* = 'And she showed them [spears] to the two [sons].' The Tok Pisin construction is actually very different from the English equivalent since *tupela* in the Tok Pisin sentence is the *direct object* of *soim,* and *ol* ('them') is an *indirect object* which has to be marked by the preposition *long.* In English, however, 'them' (spears) is the direct object, and 'the two' (sons) is the indirect object that has to be marked by the preposition 'to'.

11. *Tru* is an intensifier modifying *planti.* Note that it does not come directly before or after the word it modifies as an ordinary adverb would.

12. *Em pik* = 'the pig'. According to some authorities on Tok Pisin, the third person pronoun before a coreferential noun acts as a definite article.

13. *Long,* a preposition which has many uses in Tok Pisin, is used here in instrumental sense.

14. *Bai,* according to Sankoff, usually acts as a future tense marker, but here it is being used in innovative way as a past punctual marker.

Idiomatic Translation

Once upon a time, on a certain island, a huge pig used to live and it used to eat people. It used to eat the people, and one time, the people went and said to their big man, their leader, they went and talked to him. He said: "All right, we must find a new island."

Then, they got their belongings together and went to seek a new island. And one woman whose husband had been eaten by the pig was pregnant. She had a child in her belly. Then, she went and asked everybody to take her in their canoe, and the people said, "No, we're full, go look for another one!" That's what they said, and she went to another, [but] they said the same.

So she went to the last canoe, and he [the canoe's owner] said, "No, mine's full. I have my own children and my wife. You go . . ." The people said, "You stay here, you're pregnant, and there is not enough space for you to come with us." So they went to look for a new island, and she stayed in the old place.

Now, one time she gave birth, she gave birth to two boy babies, inside her belly—like, two babies, two boys, males. [She gave birth to] two male children, and she worked hard to seek food and game for the two of them.

Thus she kept doing, until the two of them grew into fine young men. Once they were grown, she told the two of them the story of the pig who, that the people had run away from. Having told them the story she made spears and showed them to them and shot them and they shot them and used them, handled them well. Then later, she showed the place at which the pig used to sleep.

They went up a big tree, and she showed the two of them [the place that] the pig, the huge pig used to sleep at. So they came back then and made a very large number of spears. Having made a lot of spears, they then went and built a platform up in the tree. Once the platform was in the tree, another morning then, they went up the tree. Taking the spears they went up on the platform in the tree.

They saw the pig leaving and then coming back, drinking water and washing in the water. And these three people, the children and their mother, went up a big tree. And the three of them stayed there, and the pig came to drink water and wash. The three threw their spears and things at [the pig].

The pig was winning. He climbed up, and the bottom platform broke. And the three climbed up on a platform high up in the tree, a strong one. And they threw their spears at him and the pig was winded, and he was about to die right then. And these two boys came down to the second platform and shot him with their spears. And he died then.

The three of them then came down and shot him and broke his head with a stone. So there they were, and their mother said to them, "What will you do with the pig?" And the two said, "You must cut off its skin and throw it in the ocean. It [the ocean] will carry it off to the other island, and our people will return."

So they cut the pig's skin and carried it to the house, then they threw it into the ocean, and the latter carried it off. And there was a tremendous wind, and the water was—going, as if the sea were raging.

In the morning, the sea had been like that; the sea had carried the pig's skin off to the island, the other island.

Now, one old man wanted to go . . . Where was he going? He was going to the toilet or something, and he saw this thing, this big thing, this pig skin, in the ocean. And he called everybody from the village to come then and look, stand up and look. And some of the men said, "The women must carry the children and stay indoors, they mustn't come outside, only the men can come outside!"

So the men came and stood and stared, they looked at the skin of the pig that had been eating the people before. Now, they went and took this pig skin and threw it on top of the sand. They thought back to the woman who had been pregnant before. And the two [?] said, "Maybe tomorrow or so we should go back to our own place and see who killed this pig and threw it away."

And in the morning they took all their belongings and went home. They went, looked, and the three people, the two men and their mother, they had come to stand on the beach and look at them. They looked at the canoes and everything.

The people in the canoes looked towards the three people standing there. The latter had prepared some food, and it was sitting there ready for all the people to come back and eat. So, they came [to the beach] and made food 'for the returnees]. The three of them made food, and they were all there. Then the people came and ate and the three of them went down into the sea. They went down, down, down, down to the very depths. The three of them went down into the sea, and the pig that they had killed turned into an enormous stone, a black stone.

The end.

EXERCISES

1. Tok Pisin Passage

After reading the "Sketch of Tok Pisin" in this chapter, try to translate the following Tok Pisin passage into English. For those words whose meaning you cannot guess you may consult F. Mihalic (1971). (The passage below is a fragment from a news story which appeared in the Tok Pisin newspaper magazine *Wantok* on 3 September, 1975.)

MOA BIA TAKIS

Mista Julius Chan, Minista bilong Fainens, i bin putim strongpela takis long bia na wiski na olkain siga na sigaret. Nau wanpela katon bia bai kostim wan kina moa; na olgeta peket sigaret bai kostim 8t moa.

Olsem tasol gavman i ting long winim 6 milien kina moa long yia.

Dispela yia Australia bai no givim mani inap long yi i go pinis. Na olsem gabman hia i mas painim sampela we o rot bilong wanim mani. Na bikpela rot oltaim em kain kain takis.

Mista Chan i tok bia na sigaret i no samting bilong ol tumbuna o samting tru bilong pasin bilong PNG. Nogat.

Na Mista Somare i tok tu: Sapos man i no gat bia o sigaret, bai em i no hangre.

Na plenti meri tu bai i hepi long harim gavman i mekim hat liklik long ol man i lusim mani long bia. Planti i laik rausim bia, long wanem em i as bilong planti trabel long ples na long famili.

2. Sociolinguistic Aspects of Contact Languages

Although a number of contact languages (e.g., Tok Pisin) are widely used for serious purposes and even have some official status, there are many that have a very low social status in the communities in which they are used and are restricted in their use in the public media.

For example, in Hawaii, Hawaiian Creole English (HCE) is seldom used in public except by various local comedians. Thus, one gets the impression that HCE is fine to amuse people in public but is not appropriate for, say, political speeches or church sermons, even when the audiences consist entirely of HCE speakers.

Finally, although most people would not even think of making fun of anyone who speaks a foreign language like Spanish or Russian, many people react with great amusement to contact languages which are based on their own native languages. What, for example, was your own reaction, as a speaker or reader of Standard English, when you first encountered Tok Pisin?

Suggest some reasons that might explain (a) the low social status of many contact languages, (b) the restricted use of such languages for certain purposes such as entertainment, and (c) why many people react to contact languages with amusement.

3. Hawaiian Creole English (HCE)

Examine the following short fragment (taken from Ronald Nishihara's story *Lady's Man,* which appeared in the May 1979 edition of the *Ad Hoc* magazine published by Iolani School, Honolulu, Hawaii) which is an attempt to write down Hawaiian Creole English. Actually, this is an example of HCE containing some elements of Standard American English.

Is there anything in this fragment to indicate that what we are dealing with here is a creole and not simply another dialect of American English? If so, point out the typical creole features and discuss them briefly. If not, point out some of the major features which differentiate HCE from Standard American English.

Afta we come out of 'Sleeping Beauty', we went someplace for grind. Ho man! Da snack bar at Kaimuki Bowling alley got good kine food.

Den we went go around in da small parking lot doing about thirty. Ho man, she got turn white one time when I almost went hit one other car.

Afta, she started saying something about one headache, so I go toss her one aspirin I found on da floor of da car and said "Take dis den you gon' feel mo betta." Den she went go say "No, I really don't feel very well, I think I should just go home and rest a little while."

So I went go take her home at about one twenty on da straightways. Den she go turn white one time when I went go make one U-turn in her neighbor's front lawn and pulled up right in front of her house.

. . . As I was driving home, I told myself what I told myself when I was twelve years old, I said "Eh, I ste [stay] one lady's man."

SELECTED BIBLIOGRAPHY

General

Arends, Jacques et al., eds. 1994. *Pidgins and creoles. An introduction.* Amsterdam and Philadelphia: John Benjamins Publishing Co. A companion series to the *Journal of Pidgin and Creole Languages,* vol. 15.

Bickerton, Derek. 1983. Creole languages. *Scientific American* 249, no. 1 (July) 116–22. Reprinted in Virginia P. Clark et al., eds., *Language: Introductory readings.* 4th ed. New York: St. Martin's Press, 1985, 134–51. (In this article Bickerton outlines in very simple terms the reasoning which led him to set up his "bioprogram" hypothesis concerning the genesis of creole languages.)

———. 1984a. The language bioprogram hypothesis. *The Behavioral and Brain Sciences* 7:173–221.

———. 1984b. The language bioprogram hypothesis and second language acquisition. In W. E. Rutherford, ed., *Language universals and second language acquisition.* Amsterdam: John Benjamins, 141–61.

Gilbert, Glenn G. 1987. *Pidgin and creole languages: Essays in memory of John E. Reinecke.* Honolulu: University of Hawaii Press.

Hall, R. A., Jr. 1969. *Pidgin and creole languages.* Ithaca: Cornell University Press.) (Hall is one of the pioneers in contact language studies.)

Holm, John A. 1988. *Theory and structure.* Vol. 1 of *Pidgins and creoles.* Cambridge Language Surveys. Cambridge: Cambridge University Press.

———. 1989. *Reference survey.* Vol. 2 of *Pidgins and creoles.* Cambridge Language Surveys. Cambridge: Cambridge University Press. (Holm's two volumes are a comprehensive survey of contact language studies.)

Mühlhäusler, P. 1986. *Pidgin and creole linguistics.* Oxford: Blackwells.

Reinecke, J. E., David De Camp, Ian Hancock, and Richard E. Wood, eds. 1975. *A bibliography of pidgin and creole languages.* Honolulu: University of Hawaii Press. (This is a very good, comprehensive bibliography for studies published before 1975. However, since the field has expanded so rapidly in recent years, it is now very much out of date.)

Rickford, John R. 1992. Pidgins and creoles. In William Bright et al., eds., *International encyclopedia of linguistics.* Vol. 3:224–32. New York: Oxford University Press.

Romaine, Suzanne. 1988. *Pidgin and creole languages.* New York: Longman. Longman Linguistics Library. (This is an excellent, up-to-date, and very readable overview of the field with a very rich bibliography.)

Sankoff, Gillian. 1980. *The social life of language.* Philadelphia: University of Pennsylvania Press. (This work contains a number of very important esays on Tok Pisin and language contact in general.)

Todd, Loretto. 1984. *Modern Englishes, pidgins and creoles.* Oxford: Basil Blackwell.

———. 1990. *Pidgins and creoles.* 2d ed. New York: Routledge. (A very good, readable introduction into the field.)

Valdman, Albert, ed. 1977. *Pidgin and creole linguistics.* Bloomington: Indiana University Press.

Pidgins

Jabłońska, Antonina. 1957. Język mieszany chińsko-rosyjski w Mandżurii *Przeglad Orientalistyczny* 2:157–68. Translated by Anatole Lyovin as "The Sino-Russian mixed language in Manchuria by Alina Jablońska" in *Working Papers in Linguistics* (University of Hawaii) 1969, 3:135–64.

Kozinskij, I. Š. 1974. K voprosu o proisxoždenii kjaxtinskogo (russko-kitajskogo) jazyka. In Akademija Nauk SSSR, Institut Vostokovedenija, *Genetičeskie i areal'nye svjazi jazykov Azii i Afriki: Tezisy dokladov:* (Diskussija na rasširennom zasedanii Filologičeskoj sekcii Učenogo Soveta Instituta Vostokovedenija. Dekabr' 1973 goda.) Moscow: Izdatel'stvo "Nauka" 1973, 36–8. (This is a brief summary of Kozinskij's thesis that Russian-based pidgins are in essence variants of the Russo-Tartar pidgin.)

Mühlhäusler, P. 1984. Syntax of Tok Pisin. In S. A. Wurm and P. Mühlhäusler, eds., *Handbook of Tok Pisin (New Guinea pidgin),* (Pacific Linguistics, C-70), 341–421. Canberra, Australia: Department of Linguistics, Research School of Pacific Studies, the Australian National University.

Nagara, Susumu. 1972. *Japanese pidgin English in Hawaii: A bilingual description. Oceanic Linguistics* Special Publication, No. 9. Honolulu. The University of Hawaii Press.

Simons, Linda, and Hugh Young. 1978. *Pijin blong yumi: A guide to Solomon Islands pijin.* Honiara, Solomon Islands: Solomon Islands Christian Association Publications Group. (Describes a pidgin that is very similar to Tok Pisin.)

Šprincin, A. G. 1968. O russko-kitajskom dialekte na Dal'nem Vostoke. *Strany i Narody Vostoka,* vyp. VI, pp. 86–100. (In this article the author discusses Jabłońska's article on the Russo-Chinese pidgin and adds more materials.)

Thomas, Edward Harper. 1970. *Chinook: A history and a dictionary.* 2d ed. Portland, Oregon: Binfords & Mort. (Chinook jargon was a very important trade pidgin of the Pacific Northwest coast and the adjacent areas of Canada.)

Creoles

Bickerton, Derek. 1975. *Dynamics of a creole system.* Cambridge: Cambridge University Press.

Crowley, Terry, and Bruce Rigsby. 1979. Cape York creole. In Timothy Shopen, ed., *Languages and their status.* Cambridge, Mass.: Winthrop, 153–207.

D'jačkov, M. V. 1981. *Jazyk krio.* Moscow: Izdatel'stvo "Nauka".

———. 1987. *Kreol'skie jazyki.* Moscow: Izdatel'stvo "Nauka".

Tok Pisin

D'jačkov, M. V., A. A. Leont'ev, and E. I. Torsueva. 1981. *Jazyk tok-pisin.* Moscow: Iz-date'stvo "Nauka".

Dutton, Tom, in collab. with Dicks Thomas. 1985. *A new course in Tok Pisin (New Guinea Pidgin).* Australian National University, Pacific Linguistics Series D, Special publications, 0078–7866 No. 67. Canberra, Australia: Department of Linguistics, Research School of Pacific Studies, the Australian National University.

Hall, Robert Anderson, Jr., 1980. *Melanesian pidgin English.* New York: AMS Press. (Originally published in 1943 as an LSA Special Series volume by Waverly Press, Baltimore.) (Includes many sample texts, a short grammar, and a vocabulary.)

Mihalic, F. 1971. *The Jacaranda dictionary and grammar of Melanesian Pidgin.* Brisbane: Jacaranda Press.

Sankoff, Gillian, and Penelope Brown. 1980. The origin of syntax in discourse: A case study of Tok Pisin relatives. In Gillian Sankoff, *The social life of language,* Philadelphia: University of Pennsylvania Press, 211–55.

Sankoff, Gillian, and Suzanne Laberge. 1980. On the acquisition of native speakers by a language. In Gillian Sankoff, *The social life of language.* Philadelphia: University of Pennsylvania Press, 195–209.

Appendix   LANGUAGE MAPS

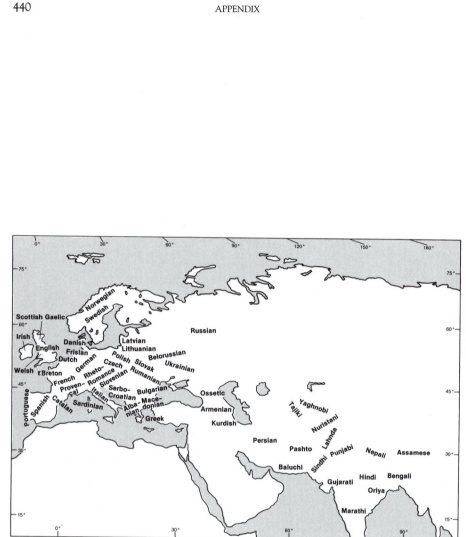

Map I. *Indo-European Languages*

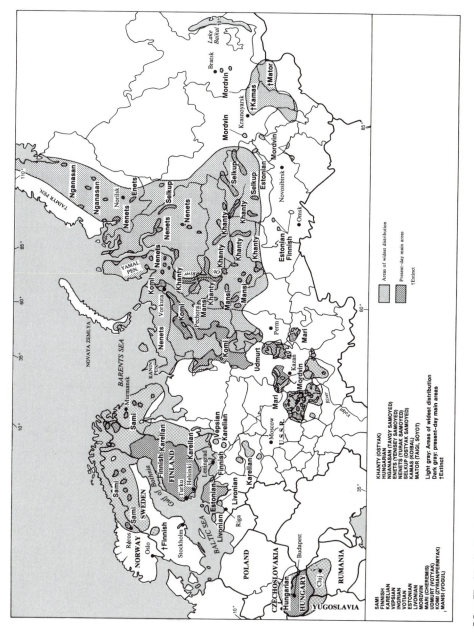

Map II. *Uralic Languages*

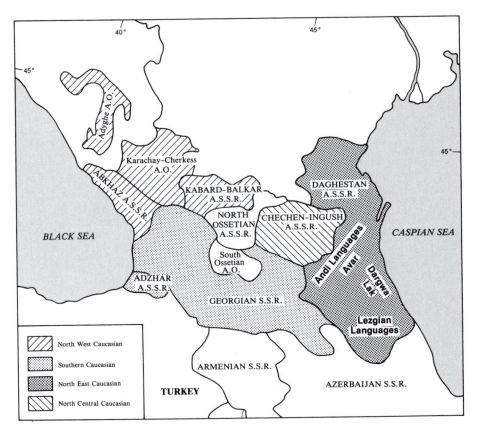

Map III. *Politico-Linguistic Divisions in the Caucasus*

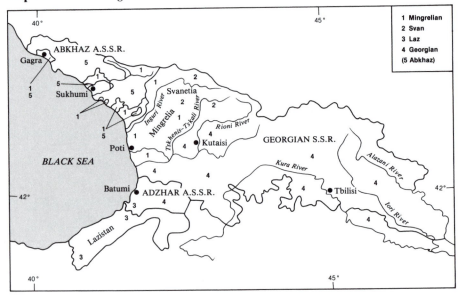

Map IV. *Distribution of South Caucasian Languages*

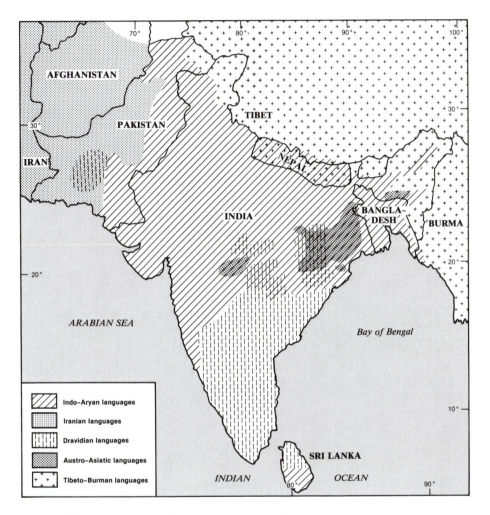

Map V. *Distribution of South Asian Languages*

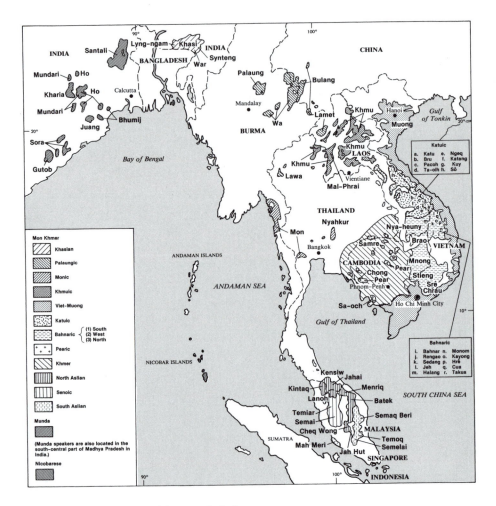

Map VI. *Distribution of Austroasiatic Languages*

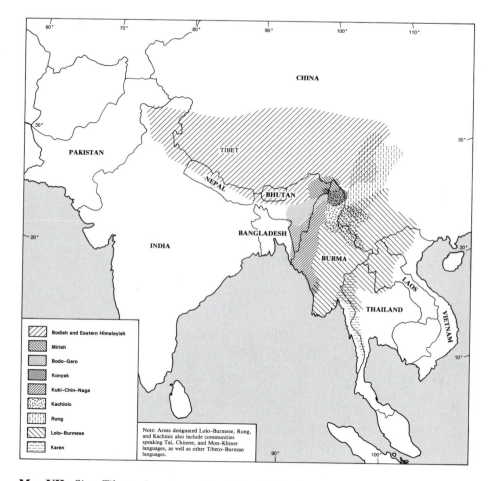

Map VII. *Sino-Tibetan Languages (excluding Sinitic Branch)*

Map VIII. *Sinitic Languages and Dialects*

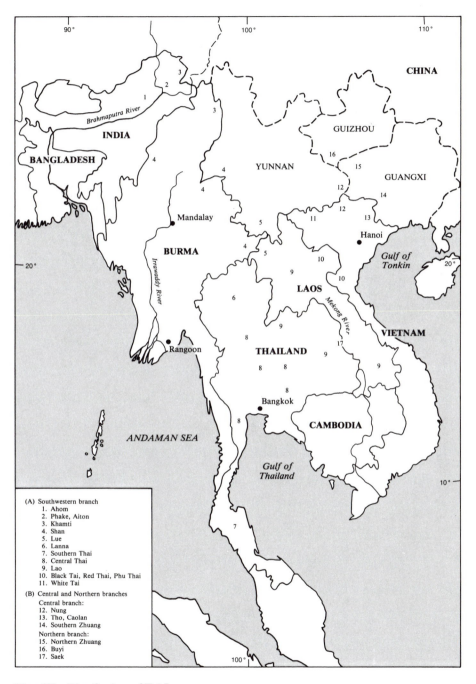

90°　　　　　　　　　100°　　　　　　　　110°

CHINA

3
2
1
Brahmaputra River

INDIA

BANGLADESH

GUIZHOU

16
15

YUNNAN

GUANGXI

4
4
4
12
14
12

Mandalay

5
11
12
13

BURMA

Hanoi

4
5

Irrawaddy River

10

Gulf of Tonkin

20°　　　　　　　　　　　　　　　　　　　　　　20°

5
9
10

LAOS

6

Mekong River

9
17

8

VIETNAM

Rangoon

THAILAND

9
9

8
8

Bangkok

8

CAMBODIA

8

ANDAMAN SEA

Gulf of Thailand

10°

(A) Southwestern branch
  1. Ahom
  2. Phake, Aiton
  3. Khamti
  4. Shan
  5. Lue
  6. Lanna
  7. Southern Thai
  8. Central Thai
  9. Lao
  10. Black Tai, Red Thai, Phu Thai
  11. White Tai

(B) Central and Northern branches
  Central branch:
  12. Nung
  13. Tho, Caolan
  14. Southern Zhuang
  Northern branch:
  15. Northern Zhuang
  16. Buyi
  17. Saek

7

100°

Map IX. *Distribution of Tai Languages*

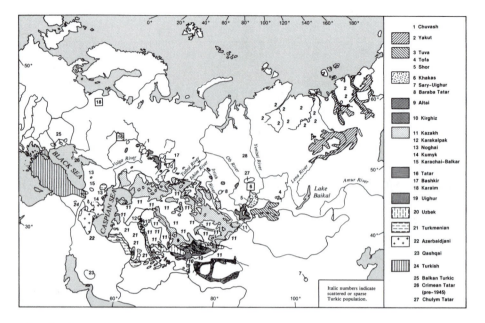

Map X. *Turkic Languages*

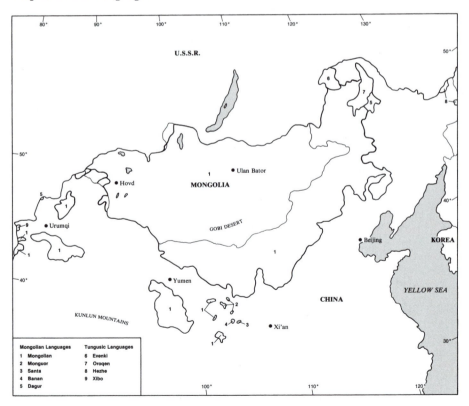

Map XI. *Distribution of Mongolian and Tungusic Languages of China and Mongolia*

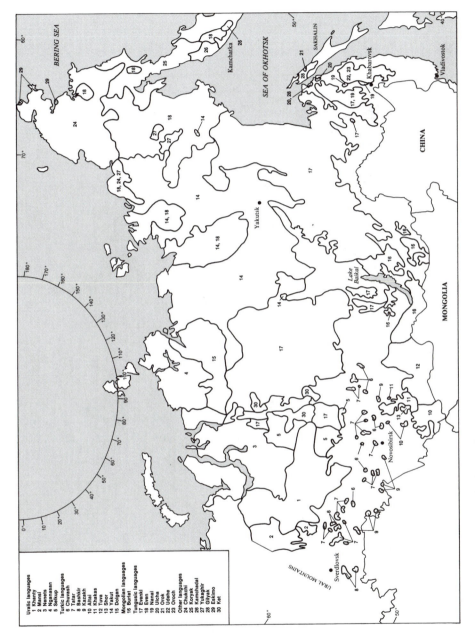

Map XII. *Distribution of Siberian Languages*

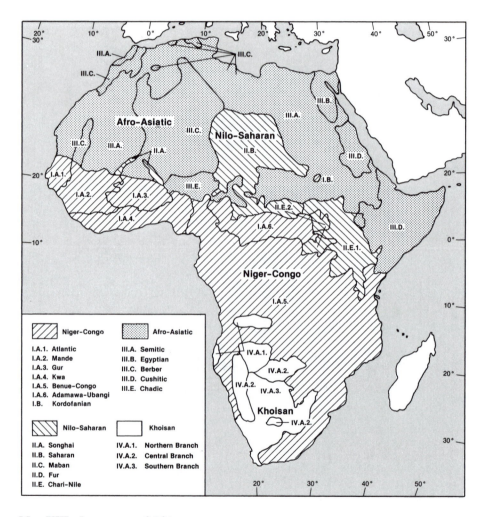

Map XIII. *Languages of Africa*

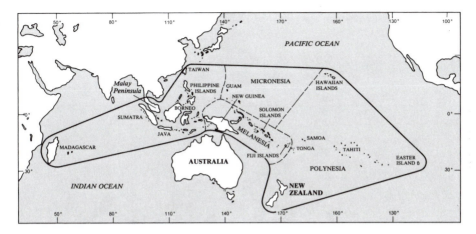

Map XIV. *Austronesian Languages*

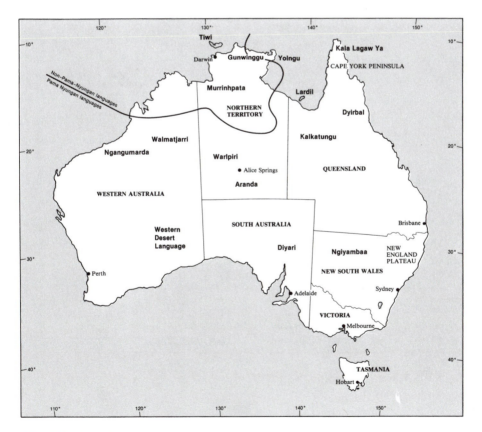

Map XV. *Australian Languages*

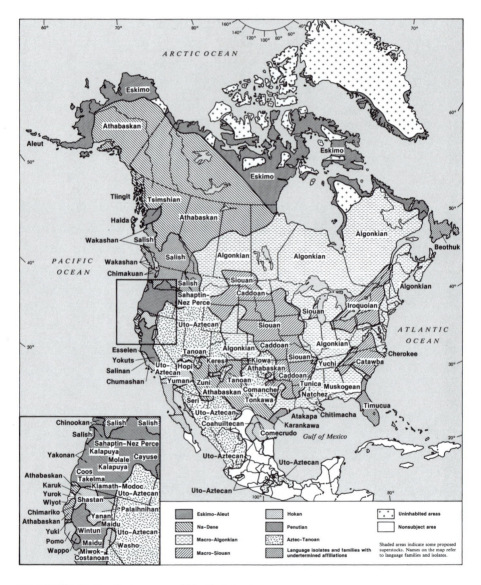

Map XVI. *Native Languages of North America*

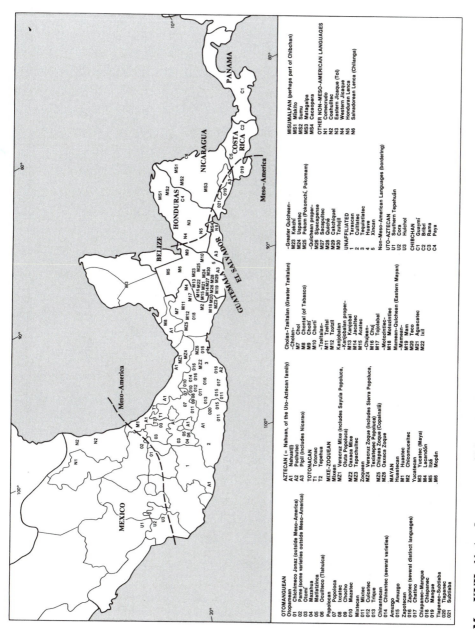

OTOMANGUEAN
Otopamean
01 Chichimeco Jonaz (outside Meso-America)
02 Pame (some varieties outside Meso-America)
03 Otomí
04 Mazahua
05 Matlatzinca
06 Ocuilteco (Tlahuica)
Popolocan
07 Popoloca
08 Ixcatec
09 Chocho
010 Mazatec
Mixtecan
011 Mixtec
012 Cuicatec
013 Trique
Chinantecan
014 Chinantec (several varieties)
Amuzgo
015 Amuzgo
Zapotecan
016 Zapotec (several distinct languages)
017 Chatino
Chiapanec-Mangue
018 Chiapanec
019 Mangue
Tlapanec-Subtiaba
020 Tlapanec
021 Subtiaba

AZTECAN (= Nahuan, of the Uto-Aztecan family)
A1 Nahuatl()
A2 Pochutec
A3 Pipil (includes Nicarao)
TOTONACAN
T1 Totonac
T2 Tepehua
MIXE-ZOQUEAN
Mixean
MZ1 Veracruz Mixe (includes Sayula Popoluca)
MZ2 Oaxaca Mixe
MZ3 Oluta Mixe
MZ24 Tapachultec
Zoquean
MZ4 Veracruz Zoque (includes Sierra Popoluca,
MZ5 Texistepec Popoluca)
MZ5 Chiapas Zoque (Copainalá)
MZ6 Oaxaca Zoque
MAYAN
Huastecan
M1 Huastec
M2 Chicomuceltec
Yucatecan
M3 Yucatec (Maya)
M4 Lacandón
M5 Itzá
M6 Mopán

Cholan-Tzeltalan (Greater Tzeltalan)
-Cholan-
M7 Chol
M8 Chontal (of Tabasco)
M9 Chortí
M10 Chortí
-Tzeltalan-
M11 Tzeltal
M12 Tzotzil
Kanjobalan
-Kanjobalan proper-
M13 Kanjobal
M14 Jacaltec
M15 Acatec
-Chujean-
M16 Chuj
M17 Tojolabal
-Motozintlec-
M18 Motozintlec
Mamean-Quichean (Eastern Mayan)
-Mamean-
M19 Mam
M20 Teco
M21 Aguacatec
M22 Ixil

-Greater Quichean-
M23 Kekchí
M24 Uspantec
M25 Pokom (Pokomchí, Pokomam)
-Quichean proper-
M26 Sipacapense
M27 Sacapultec
M28 Quiché
M29 Cakchiquel
M30 Tzutujil

UNAFFILIATED
1 Tarascan
2 Cuitlatec
3 Tequistlatec
4 Huave
5 Xincan

Non-Meso-American Languages (bordering)
UTO-AZTECAN
U1 Southern Tepehuán
U2 Cora
U3 Huichol

CHIBCHAN
C1 Guaymí
C2 Bribri
C3 Rama
C4 Paya

MISUMALPAN (perhaps part of Chibchan)
MS1 Miskito
MS2 Sumu
MS3 Matagalpa
MS4 Cacaopera

OTHER NON-MESO-AMERICAN LANGUAGES
N1 Comecrudo
N2 Coahuiltec
N3 Eastern Jicaque (Tol)
N4 Western Jicaque
N5 Honduran Lenca
N6 Salvadorean Lenca (Chilanga)

Map XVII. *Native Languages of Meso-America*

Map XVIII. *Some Major Groups of South American Native Languages*

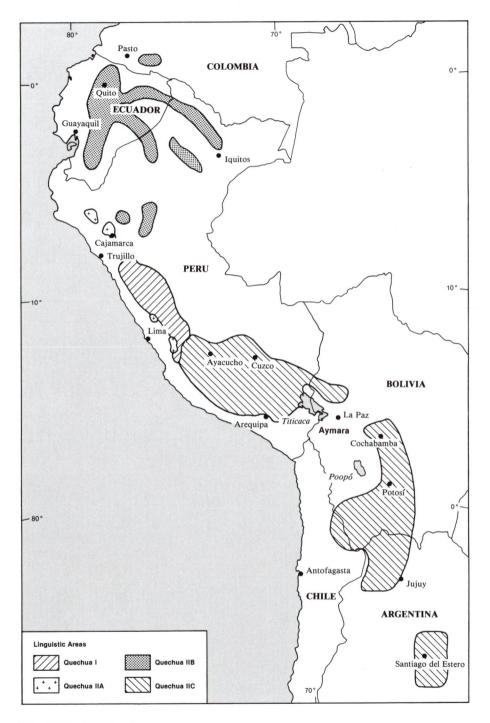

Map XIX. *Quechua Languages*

BIBLIOGRAPHY

Abondolo, Daniel. 1987. Hungarian. In Bernard Comrie, ed., *The world's major languages,* 577–92. New York: Oxford University Press.

Adelaar, Willem F. H. 1992. Quechuan languages. In William Bright et al., eds., *International encyclopedia of linguistics.* Vol. 4:303–10. New York: Oxford University Press.

Anderson, E. 1978. Lexical universals of body-part terminology. In J. H. Greenberg, ed., *Universals of human language.* Vol. 3:335–68. Stanford: Stanford University Press.

Andronov, M. S. 1970. *Dravidian languages.* Moscow: Izdatel'stvo "Nauka."

Aoki, Haruo. 1981. Amerika-Indian shogo. In Hajime Kitamura, ed., *Sekai no gengo,* 311–62. Kōza Gengo, Vol. 6. Tokyo: Taishūkan shoten.

Arakin, V. D. 1965. *Indonezijskie jazyki.* Moscow: Izdatel'stvo "Nauka."

———. 1973. *Samoanskij jazyk.* Moscow: Izdutel'stvo "Nauka."

Arends, Jacques, et al., eds., 1994. *Pidgins and creoles. An introduction.* Amsterdam and Philadelphia: John Benjamins Publishing Co. A companion series to the *Journal of Pidgin and Creole Languages,* Vol. 15.

Arlotto, Anthony. 1972. *Introduction to historical linguistics.* Boston: Houghton Mifflin.

Austerlitz, Robert. 1966. *Finnish reader and glossary.* Indiana University Publ., Uralic and Altaic Series, Vol. 15. Bloomington: Indiana University Press.

———. 1987. Uralic languages. In Bernard Comrie, ed., *The world's major languages,* 567–76. New York: Oxford University Press.

Avanesov, R. I. 1984. *Russkoe literaturnoe proiznošenie.* Moscow: Prosveščenie.

Awde, Nicholas, and Putros Samano. 1987. *The Arabic alphabet, how to read and write it.* London: Al Saqui Books.

Baldi, Philip. 1983. *An introduction to the Indo-European languages.* Carbondale: Southern Illinois University Press.

———. 1987. Indo-European languages. In Bernard Comrie, ed., *The world's major languages*, 33–67. New York: Oxford University Press.

Basse, Bjarne, and Kirsten Jensen, eds., 1979. *Eskimo languages: Their present day conditions.* Aarhus: Arkona.

Bateson, Mary Catherine. 1967. *Arabic language handbook.* Washington, D.C.: Center for Applied Linguistics.

Bellwood, Peter. 1984–85. A hypothesis for Austronesian origins. *Asian Perspectives* 26.1:107–17.

———. 1991. The Austronesian dispersal and the origin of languages. *Scientific American* (July) 88–93.

Bender, Marvin Lionel, ed. 1989. *Nilo-Saharan language studies.* Vol. 2. Hamburg: Buske.

Bendor-Samuel, John. 1992. Niger-Congo languages. In William Bright et al., eds., *International encyclopedia of linguistics*, 93–100. New York: Oxford University Press.

Bendor-Samuel, John, and Rhonda L. Hartell, eds. 1989. *The Niger-Congo languages.* Lanham, Md: University Press of America.

Benedict, Paul. 1942. Thai, Kadai and Indonesian: A new alignment in Southeastern Asia. *American Anthropologist* 44:576–601.

———. 1972. *Sino-Tibetan: A conspectus.* Contrib. ed. James A. Matisoff. Cambridge: Cambridge University Press.

———. 1975. *Austro-Thai languge and culture, with a glossary of roots.* New Haven: Human Relations Area Files Press.

———. 1986. *Japanese/Austro-Tai.* Ann Arbor: Karoma Press. (Here Benedict proposes that Japanese is also a part of Austro-Tai.)

Berger, Hermann. 1974. *Das Yasin-Burushaski (Werchikwar): Grammatik, Texte, Wörterbuch.* Wiesbaden: Otto Harrassowitz.

Bergsland, Knut. 1959. The Eskimo-Uralic hypothesis. *Journal de la Société Finno-ougrienne* 61:1–29.

Bergsträßer, G. 1983. *Introduction to the Semitic languages.* Winona Lake, Ind.: Eisenbrauns. (Translation of the German original by P. T. Daniels. *Einführung in die semitischen Sprachen.* 2nd ed. 1963 [1928]. Munich: Max Hueber.)

Berlin, Brent, and Paul Kay. 1969. *Basic color terms: Their universality and evolution.* Berkeley and Los Angeles: University of California Press.

Berman, Ruth A. 1992. Hebrew: Modern Hebrew. In William Bright et al., eds., *International encyclopedia of linguistics*, 118–23. New York: Oxford University Press.

Besnier, Niko. 1992. Polynesian languages. In William Bright et al., eds., *International encyclopedia of linguistics.* Vol. 3:245–51. New York: Oxford University Press.

Bickerton, Derek. 1975. *Dynamics of a creole system.* Cambridge: Cambridge University Press.

———. 1983. Creole languages. *Scientific American* 249, no. 1 (July):116–22. Reprinted in Virginia P. Clark et al., eds. 1985. *Language: Introductory readings.* 4th ed. New York: St. Martin's Press, 134–51.

———. 1984a. The language bioprogram hypothesis. *The Behavioral and Brain Sciences* (7):173–221.

———. 1984b. The language bioprogram hypothesis and second language acquisition. In W. E. Rutherford, ed., *Language universals and second language acquisition.* Amsterdam: John Benjamins, 141–61.

Binnick, Robert I. 1992. Mongolian languages. In William Bright et al., eds., *International encyclopedia of linguistics.* Vol. 2:434–7. New York: Oxford University Press.

Bird, Charles, and Timothy Shopen. 1979. Maninka. In Timothy Shopen, ed., *Languages and their speakers,* 59–111. Cambridge, Mass.: Winthrop Publishers.

Blake, Barry J. 1981. *Australian Aboriginal languages.* London & Sydney: Angus & Robertson.

Blake, Barry J., and R. M. W. Dixon, eds., 1979–91. *Handbook of Australian languages.* 4 vols. Amsterdam: John Benjamins.

Blust, Robert. 1983–84. More on the position of the languages of eastern Indonesia. *Oceanic Linguistics* 22/23:1–28.

———. 1984–85. The Austronesian homeland: A linguistic perspective. *Asian Perspectives* 26.1:45–67.

———. 1990. Summary report: Linguistic change and reconstruction methodology in the Austronesian language family. In Philip Baldi, ed., *Linguistic change and reconstruction methodology,* 133–53. New York: Mouton de Gruyter.

Branch, Michael. 1987. Finnish. In Bernard Comrie, ed., *The world's major languages,* 593–617. New York: Oxford University Press.

Bright, William, et al., eds. 1992. *International encyclopedia of linguistics.* 4 vols. New York: Oxford University Press.

Campbell, George L. 1991. *Compendium of the world's languages.* 2 vols. New York: Routledge.

Campbell, Lyle, 1979. Middle American languages. In Lyle Campbell and Marianne Mithun, eds., *The languages of Native America: Historical and comparative assessment,* 902–1000. Austin: University of Texas Press.

———. 1988. Review of *Language in the Americas,* by Joseph Greenberg. *Language* 63(3):591–615.

———. 1992. Meso-American languages. In William Bright et al., eds., *International encyclopedia of linguistics.* Vol. 3:415–7. New York: Oxford University Press.

Campbell, Lyle, and Ives Goddard. 1987. Summary report: American Indian languages and principles of language change. In Philip Baldi, ed., *Patterns of change, change of patterns: Linguistic change and reconstruction methodology,* 15–30. New York: Mouton de Gruyter.

Campbell, Lyle, and Marianne Mithun. 1979. Introduction: North American Indian historical linguistics in current perspective. In Lyle Campbell and Marianne Mithun, eds., *The languages of Native America: Historical and comparative assessment,* 3–69. Austin: University of Texas Press.

Campbell, Lyle, Terrence F Kaufman, and Thomas Smith-Stark. 1986. Meso-America as a linguistic area. *Language* 62:530–70.

Cǎo, Cuì-yún. 1987. Miáoyáoyǔ tèdiǎn gàiyào. In Zhōngyāng Mínzúyuàn Shǎoshǔ Mínzú Yǔyán Yánjiùsuǒ, ed., *Zhōngguó shaoshǔ mínzú yǔyán,* 403–5. Chengdu: Sìchuān Mínzú Chubǎnshè.

Capell, A. 1969. *A survey of New Guinea languages.* Sydney: Sydney University Press.

Cardona, George. 1987a. Indo-Aryan languages. In Bernard Comrie, ed., *The world's major languages,* 440–7. New York: Oxford University Press.

———. 1987b. Sanskrit. In Bernard Comrie, ed., *The world's major languages,* 448–69. New York: Oxford University Press.

Cardona, George. 1992. Indo-European languages. In William Bright et al., eds., *International encyclopedia of linguistics.* Vol. 2:206–13. New York: Oxford University Press.

Carter, Greg Lee. 1994. Hawaiian prepositions and the word *he. Working Papers in Linguistics* (University of Hawaii) 23.1–44.

Cerrón-Palomino, Rodolfo M. 1976. *Grammática Quechua: Junin-Huanca.* Lima: Instituto de Estudios Peruanos.

Chafe, Wallace L. 1973. Siouan, Iroquoian and Caddoan. In Thomas A. Sebeok, ed., *Current trends in linguistics.* Vol. 10 *(Linguistics in North America)*:1164–1209. The Hague: Mouton.

————. 1987. Review of *Language in the Americas,* by Joseph Greenberg. *Current Anthropology* 28:652–3.

Chang, Kun. 1992. Tibetan. In William Bright et al., eds., *International encyclopedia of linguistics.* Vol. 4:156–60. New York: Oxford University Press.

Chang, Kun, and Betty Shefts. 1964. *Manual of spoken Tibetan (Lhasa dialect).* Seattle: University of Washington Press.

Chao, Yuen Ren. 1930. A system of tone letters. *Le Maître Phonétique,* troisième série, 30.24–7.

————. 1957. *Mandarin primer: An intensive course in spoken Chinese.* Cambridge: Harvard University Press.

————. 1968. *A grammar of spoken Chinese.* Berkeley and Los Angeles: University of California Press.

Clark, Ross. 1987. Austronesian languages. In Bernard Comrie, ed., *The world's major languages,* 899–912. New York: Oxford University Press.

————. 1992. Austronesian languages. In William Bright et al., eds., *International encyclopedia of linguistics.* Vol. 1:142–5. New York: Oxford University Press.

Clauson, Sir Gerard. 1956. The case against the Altaic theory. *Central Asiatic Journal* 2(3):181–7.

Coleman, R. G. G. 1987. Latin and the Italic languages. In Bernard Comrie, ed., *The world's major languages,* 180–202. New York: Oxford University Press.

Collinder, Björn. 1965. *An introduction to the Uralic languages.* Berkeley and Los Angeles: University of California Press.

Collinder, Björn, et al. comps. 1969 [1957]. *Survey of Uralic languages. Grammatical sketches and commented texts with English translations.* Stockholm: Almquist & Wiksells.

Comrie, Bernard. 1979. Russian. In Timothy Shopen, ed., *Languages and their status,* 91–151. Cambridge, Mass.: Winthrop.

————. 1981. Altaic languages. In Bernard Comrie et al., eds., *The languages of the Soviet Union,* 39–91. Cambridge: Cambridge University Press.

————. 1981. Paleosiberian and other languages. In Bernard Comrie et al., eds., *The languages of the Soviet Union,* 238–78. Cambridge: Cambridge University Press.

————. 1987a. Russian. In Bernard Comrie, ed., *The world's major languages,* 329–47. New York: Oxford University Press.

————. 1987b. Slavonic languages. In Bernard Comrie, ed., *The world's major languages,* 322–8. New York: Oxford University Press.

————. 1989. *Language universals and linguistic typology: Syntax and morphology.* 2d ed. Chicago: University of Chicago Press.

————. 1992. Altaic languages. In William Bright et al., eds. *International encyclopedia of linguistics.* Vol. 1:48–51. New York: Oxford University Press.

————. 1992. Siberian languages. In William Bright et al., eds., *International encyclopedia of linguistics.* Vol. 3:429–32. New York: Oxford University Press.

————. 1992. Turkic languages. In William Bright et al., eds., *International encyclopedia of linguistics.* Vol. 4:187–90. New York: Oxford University Press.

Comrie, Bernard, ed. 1987. *The world's major languages.* New York: Oxford University Press.

Comrie, Bernard et al., eds., 1981. *The languages of the Soviet Union.* Cambridge: Cambridge University Press.

Cook, Eung Do, and Donna B. Gerdts, eds. 1984. *Amerindian syntax.* Orlando Fla.: Academic Press.

Coulmas, Florian. 1989. *The writing systems of the world.* Oxford: Blackwell Publishers.

Craig, Colette Grinevald. 1977. *The structure of Jacaltec.* Austin: University of Texas Press.

———. 1979. Jacaltec: Fieldwork in Guatemala. In Timothy Shopen, ed., *Languages and their speakers,* 3–57. Cambridge, Mass.: Winthrop.

Croft, William. 1990. *Typology and universals.* Cambridge: Cambridge University Press.

Crowley, Terry, and Bruce Rigsby. 1979. Cape York creole. In Timothy Shopen, ed., *Languages and their status,* 153–207. Cambridge, Mass.: Winthrop.

Cusihuaman Gutiérrez, Antonio. 1976a. *Diccionario Quechua: Cuzco-Callao.* Lima: Instituto de Estudios Peruanos.

———. 1976b. *Grammática Quechua: Cuzco-Callao.* Lima: Instituto de Estudios Peruanos.

Daniels, Peter T. 1990. Fundamentals of grammatology. *Journal of the American Oriental Society* 110(4):727–31.

Daniels, Peter T., and William Bright, eds. 1995. *The world's writing systems.* New York: Oxford University Press.

Das, Sarat Chandra (Rai Bahadur). 1960. *Tibetan-English dictionary.* Alipore, West Bengal: West Bengal Government Press. (Originally published in 1902.)

De Francis, John. 1984. *The Chinese languages: Fact and fantasy.* Honolulu: University of Hawaii Press.

———. 1989. Writing: *Its diversity and essential oneness.* Honolulu: University of Hawaii Press.

DeLancey, Scott. 1987. Sino-Tibetan languages. In Bernard Comrie, ed., *The world's major languages,* 797–810. New York: Oxford University Press.

———. 1992. Sino-Tibetan languages. In William Bright et al., eds., *International encyclopedia of linguistics.* Vol. 3:445–9. New York: Oxford University Press.

Derbyshire, Desmond C. 1979. *Hixkaryana.* Amsterdam: North Holland Publishing Co.

———. 1985. *Hixkaryana and linguistic typology.* Summer Institute of Linguistics and the University of Texas at Arlington publication.

Derbyshire, Desmond C., and Geoffrey K. Pullum, eds. 1986. *Handbook of Amazonian languages.* New York: Mouton de Gruyter.

de Rijk, Rudolf P. G. 1992. Basque. In William Bright et al., eds., *International encyclopedia of linguistics.* Vol. 1:162–9. New York: Oxford University Press.

Diakonoff, Igor M. 1965. *Semito-Hamitic languages: An essay in classification.* Moscow: Nauka Publ.

Diffloth, Gérard, and Norman Zide. 1992. Austro-Asiatic languages. In William Bright et al., eds., *International encyclopedia of linguistics.* Vol. 1:137–42. New York: Oxford University Press.

Diller, Anthony. 1992. Thai. In William Bright et al., eds., *International encyclopedia of linguistics.* Vol. 4:149–56. New York: Oxford University Press.

———. 1992. Tai languages. In William Bright et al., eds., *International encyclopedia of linguistics.* Vol. 4:128–31. New York: Oxford University Press.

Dimmendaal, Gerrit J. 1992. Nilo-Saharan languages. In William Bright et al., eds., *International encyclopedia of linguistics,* 100–4. New York: Oxford University Press.

Dixon, R. M. W. 1972. *The Dyirbal language of North Queensland.* Cambridge Studies in Linguistics, no. 9. Cambridge: Cambridge University Press.

———. 1980. *The languages of Australia.* Cambridge Language Surveys. Cambridge: Cambridge University Press.

———. 1992. Australian languages. In William Bright et al., eds., *International encyclopedia of linguistics.* Vol. 1:134–7. New York: Oxford University Press.

D'jačkov, M. V. 1981. *Jazyk krio.* Moscow: Izdatel'stvo "Nauka."

———. 1987. *Kreol'skie jazyki.* Moscow: Izdatel'stvo "Nauka."

D'jačkov, M. V., A. A. Leont'ev, and E. I. Torsueva. 1981. *Jazyk tok-pisin.* Moscow: Izdate'stvo "Nauka."

Donegan, Patricia Jane, and David Stampe. 1983. Rhythm and the holistic organization of language structure. In John F. Richardson et al., eds., *Papers from the parasession on the interplay of phonology, morphology and syntax,* 337–53. Chicago: Chicago Linguistic Society.

Dörfer, Gerhard. 1985. *Mongolo-Tungusica.* Wiesbaden: Otto Harrassowitz.

Duranti, Alessandro. 1988. Ethnography of speaking: Towards a linguistics of the praxis. In Frederick J. Newmeyer, ed., *Language: The socio-cultural context.* Vol. 4 of *Linguistics: the Cambridge survey,* 210–28. Cambridge: Cambridge University Press.

Dutton, Tom, in collab. with Dicks Thomas. 1985. *A new course in Tok Pisin (New Guinea Pidgin).* Pacific Linguistics Series D, Special publications, 0078–7866, No. 67. Canberra, Australia: Department of Linguistics, Research School of Pacific Studies, the Australian National University.

Dzidziguri, Shota. 1969. *The Georgian language.* Tbilisi: Tbilisi University Press.

Egerod, Søren. 1991. Far Eastern languages. In Sydney M. Lamb and E. Douglas Mitchell, eds., *Sprung from some common source,* 205–31. Stanford: Stanford University Press.

Elbert, Samuel H. 1970. *Spoken Hawaiian.* Honolulu: University of Hawaii Press.

Elbert, Samuel, and Mary Kawena Pukui. 1979. *Hawaiian grammar.* Honolulu: University of Hawaii Press.

Finch, Roger. 1983. The velar and uvular series in Quechua. *Sophia Linguistica (Working Papers in Linguistics)* 13.1–17.

Fischer, Wolfdietrich. 1992. Arabic. In William Bright et al., eds., *International encyclopedia of linguistics,* 91–8. New York: Oxford University Press.

Fleisch, H. 1956. *L'Arabe classique: esquisse d'une structure linguistique.* Beirut: Imprimerie catholique.

Florey, Margaret J. 1988. A review of the classification of Australian languages. *Working Papers in Linguistics* (Dept. of Linguistics, University of Hawaii at Manoa) 20(2):137–62.

Foley, William A. 1986. *The Papuan languages of New Guinea.* New York: Cambridge University Press.

———. 1992. New Guinea languages. In William Bright et al., eds., *International encyclopedia of linguistics.* Vol. 3:86–91.

Forrest, R. A. D. 1965. *The Chinese language.* 2d, rev. ed. London: Faber & Faber.

Fraenkel, Gerd. 1967. *Languages of the world.* Boston: Ginn.

Gelb, I. J. 1963. *A study of writing.* 2d, rev. ed. Chicago: University of Chicago Press.

Gilbert, Glenn G. 1987. *Pidgin and creole languages: Essays in memory of John E. Reinecke.* Honolulu: University of Hawaii Press.

Gilyarevskiy, R. S., and V. S. Grivnin. 1970. *Language identification guide.* Moscow: Nauka Publishing House.

Goddard, Ives. 1992. Algonkian languages. In William Bright et al., eds., *International encyclopedia of linguistics.* Vol. 1:44–8. New York: Oxford University Press.

Green, John N. 1987. Romance languages. In Bernard Comrie, ed., *The world's major languages,* 203–9. New York: Oxford University Press.

Greenberg, Joseph H. 1960. A quantitative approach to the morphological typology of language. *International Journal of American Linguistics* 26:178–94.

———. 1960. The general classification of Central and South American languages. In Anthony F. C. Wallace, ed., *Men and cultures: Selected papers of the 5th International Congress of Anthropological and Ethnological Sciences, September 1956.* Philadelphia: University of Pennsylvania Press, 791–4.

———. 1963. *The languages of Africa.* Bloomington: Indiana University Press.

———. 1966. Some universals of grammar with particular reference to the order of meaningful elements. In Joseph Greenberg, ed., *Universals of language,* 73–113. 2d ed. Cambridge: M.I.T. Press.

———. 1971. The Indo-Pacific hypothesis. In Thomas A. Sebeok, ed., *Current trends in linguistics.* Vol. 8:1963–76. The Hague: Mouton.

———. 1975. Research on language universals. *Annual Review of Anthroplogy* 4:75–94.

———. 1978. Generalizations about numeral systems. In J. H. Greenberg, ed., *Universals of human language.* Vol. 3:249–95. Stanford: Stanford University Press.

———. 1987. *Language in the Americas.* Stanford, Calif.: Stanford University Press.

Gregersen, E. A. 1977. *Language in Africa: An introductory survey.* New York: Gordon and Breach.

Grimes, Barbara. 1992. *Ethnologue: Languages of the world.* 12th ed. Dallas, Texas: Summer Institute of Linguistics, Inc. (Also a separate index volume.)

Grimes, Joseph Evan, and Barbara Grimes. 1993. *Ethnologue: Language family identity.* Dallas, Texas: Summer Institute of Linguistics.

Gumperz, John J., and Dell Hymes, eds. 1972. *Directions in sociolinguistics: The ethnography of communication.* New York: Holt, Rinehart & Winston.

Haas, Mary R. 1969. *The prehistory of languages.* Janua Linguarum, series minor, no. 57. The Hague: Mouton.

Haddon, Ernest B. 1955. *Swahili lessons.* Cambridge: W. Heffer and Sons.

Haiman, John. 1979. Hua: A Papuan language of New Guinea. In Timothy Shopen, ed., *Languages and their status,* 35–89. Cambridge, Mass.: Winthrop.

Hakulinen, L. 1961. *The structure and development of the Finnish language.* Indiana University Publ., Uralic and Altaic Series, Vol. 3. Bloomington: Indiana University Press.

Hale, A. 1982. *Research on Tibeto-Burman languages.* The Hague: Mouton.

Hall, Robert Anderson, Jr. 1969. *Pidgin and creole languages.* Ithaca: Cornell University Press.

———. 1980. *Melanesian pidgin English.* New York: AMS Press. (Originally published in 1943 as an LSA Special Series volume by Waverly Press, Baltimore.)

Hardman, M. J. 1985. Aymara and Quechua. In Harriet E. Manelis Klein and Louisa R. Stark, eds., *South American Indian languages: Retrospect and prospect,* 617–43. Austin: University of Texas Press.

Hashimoto, Mantarō. 1981. Shina-chibetto shogo. In Hajime Kitamura, ed., *Sekai no gengo,* 149–70. Kōza Gengo, Tokyo: Taishūkan shoten. Vol. 6.

Haviland, John B. 1979. How to talk to your brother-in-law in Guugu Yimidhirr. In Timothy Shopen, ed., *Languages and their speakers,* 161–239. Cambridge, Mass.: Winthrop.

Hawkins, John A. 1987. Germanic languages. In Bernard Comrie, ed., *The world's major languages,* 68–76. New York: Oxford University Press.

Heath, Jeffrey. 1978. Linguistic diffusion in Arnhem Land. Canberra: AIAS.

———. 1981. A case of intensive lexical diffusion: Arnhem Land, Australia. *Language* 57(2):335–67.

Heine, Bernd. 1976. *A typology of African languages: Based on the order of meaningful elements.* Kölner Beiträge zur Afrikanistik, Band 4. Berlin: Dietrich Reimer Verlag.

———. 1992. African languages. In William Bright et al., eds., *International encyclopedia of linguistics.* Vol. 41:31–6. New York: Oxford University Press.

Heine, Bernd, Thilo C. Schadeberg, and Ekkehard Wolff, eds., 1981. *Die Sprachen Afrikas, mit zahlreichen Karten und Tabellen.* Hamburg: Helmut Buske Verlag.

Hetzron, Robert. 1987a. Afroasiatic languages. In Bernard Comrie, ed., *The world's major languages,* 645–53. New York: Oxford University Press.

———. 1987b. Hebrew. In Bernard Comrie, ed., *The world's major languages,* 687–704. New York: Oxford University Press.

———. 1987c. Semitic languages. In Bernard Comrie, ed., *The world's major languages,* 654–63. New York: Oxford University Press.

———. 1992. Semitic languages. In William Bright et al., eds., *International encyclopedia of linguistics,* 412–7. New York: Oxford University Press.

Hewitt, B. G. 1981. Caucasian languages. In Bernard Comrie et al., eds., *Languages of the Soviet Union,* 196–237. New York: Cambridge University Press.

———. 1987. Georgian: Ergative or active? *Lingua* 71:319–340.

———. 1992. Caucasian languages. In William Bright et al., eds., *International encyclopedia of linguistics.* Vol. 1:220–7. New York: Oxford University Press.

Hinnebusch, Thomas J. 1979. Swahili. In Shopen, Timothy, ed., *Languages and their status,* 204–93. Cambridge, Mass.: Winthrop.

———. 1992. Swahili. In William Bright et al., eds., *International encyclopedia of linguistics.* Vol. 4:99–106. New York: Oxford University Press.

Hoberman, Robert D. 1992. Aramaic. In William Bright et al., eds., *International encyclopedia of linguistics.* Vol. 1:98–102. New York: Oxford University Press.

Hock, Hans Heinrich. 1991. *Principles of historical linguistics.* 2d ed. Berlin: Mouton de Gruyter.

Hockett, Charles. 1955. *Manual of phonology.* Indiana University Publications in Anthropology and Linguistics, Memoir 2. Bloomington: Indiana University Press. (Reprinted in 1979 by the University of Chicago Press.)

Hodge, Stephen. 1990. *An introduction to Classical Tibetan.* Warminster, Wiltshire, U.K.: Aris & Phillips.

Hoff, Berend J. 1992. Cariban languages. In William Bright et al., eds., *International encyclopedia of linguistics.* Vol. 1:213–17. New York: Oxford University Press.

Holm, John A. 1988. Theory and structure. Vol. 1 of *Pidgins and creoles.* Cambridge Language Surveys. Cambridge: Cambridge University Press.

———. 1989. *Reference survey.* Vol. 2 of *Pidgins and creoles.* Cambridge Language Surveys. Cambridge: Cambridge University Press.

Hopkins, Alberta Pualani. 1992. *Ka lei ha'aheo:* Beginning Hawaiian. 2 vols. Honolulu: University of Hawaii Press.

Horne, Kibbey M. 1966. *Language typology: 19th and 20th century views.* Washington: Georgetown University Press.

Hu, Tan. 1988. A comparative study of tonal and toneless Tibetan dialects. [In Chinese.] In Paul K. Eguchi, ed., *Languages and history in East Asia: Festschrift for Tatsuo Nishida on the occasion of his 60th birthday,* 75–92. Kyoto: Shokado.

Hudak, Thomas John. 1987. Thai. In Bernard Comrie, ed., *The world's major languages,* 757–75. New York: Oxford University Press.

Hymes, Dell. 1974. *Foundations in sociolinguistics: An ethnographic approach.* Philadelphia: University of Pennsylvania Press.

Jabłońska, Antonina. 1957. Język mieszany chińsko-rosyjski w Mandżurii. *Przegląd Orientalistyczny* 2:157–68. Translated by Anatole Lyovin as "The Sino-Russian mixed language in Manchuria by Alina Jabłońska" in *Working Papers in Linguistics* (University of Hawaii) 1969.3:135–64.

Jacobson, Steven A., comp. 1984. *Yup'ik Eskimo dictionary.* Fairbanks: University of Alaska, Alaska Native Language Center.

Jaeschke, H. A. 1958. *A Tibetan-English dictionary (with an English-Tibetan vocabulary).* London: Kegan Paul. (Reprint of the 1881 original edition.)

Janhunen, Juha. 1992. Uralic languages. In William Bright et al., eds., *International encyclopedia of linguistics.* Vol. 4:205–10. New York: Oxford University Press.

Jensen, Cheryl J. 1992. Tupian languages. In William Bright et al., eds., *International encyclopedia of linguistics.* Vol. 4:182–7. New York: Oxford University Press.

Joseph, Brian D. 1987. Greek. In Bernard Comrie, ed., *The world's major languages,* 410–39. New York: Oxford University Press.

Kahananui, Dorothy M., and Alberta P. Anthony. 1974. *E kamaʻilio Hawaiʻi kakou: Lets speak Hawaiian.* 2d, rev. ed. Honolulu: The University Press of Hawaii.

Kaiser, M., and V. Shevroshkin. 1988. Nostratic. *Annual Review of Anthropology* 17:309–29. (An overview of the Nostratic hypothesis written by its proponents.)

Kamei, Takashi, and Rokurō Kōno, eds. 1988–92. *Gengogaku daijiten. Sekai gengo hen.* 4 vols. Tokyo: Sanseidō Press.

Kaplan, Lawrence D. 1992. Eskimo-Aleut languages. In William Bright et al., eds., *International encyclopedia of linguistics.* Vol. 1:415–9. New York: Oxford University Press.

Karlsson, Fred. 1992. Finnish. In William Bright et al., eds., *International encyclopedia of linguistics.* Vol. 2:14–17. New York: Oxford University Press.

Katzner, Kenneth. 1986. *The languages of the world.* Rev. ed. London: Routledge & Kegan Paul.

Kaufman, Terry. 1990. Language history in South America: What we know and how to know more. In Doris L. Payne, ed., *Amazonian linguistics: Studies in lowland South American languages,* 13–73. Austin: University of Texas Press.

Kaye, Alan S. 1987. Arabic. In Bernard Comrie, ed., *The world's major languages,* 664–85. New York: Oxford University Press.

Keenan, Edward Louis, and Elinor Ochs. 1979. Becoming a competent speaker of Malagasy. In Timothy Shopen, ed., *Languages and their speakers,* 113–58. Cambridge, Mass.: Winthrop.

Key, Marie Ritchie. 1979. *The grouping of South American Indian languages.* Ars linguistica 2, Commentationes analyticae et criticae. Tübingen: Gunter Narr Verlag.

Kim, Nam-Kil. 1987. Korean. In Bernard Comrie, ed., *The world's major languages,* 881–98. New York: Oxford University Press.

Kincade, Dale. 1992. Salishan languages. In William Bright et al., eds., *International encyclopedia of linguistics.* Vol. 3:359–63. New York: Oxford University Press.

Klein, Harriet E. Manelis. 1992. South American languages. In William Bright et al., eds., *International encyclopedia of linguistics.* Vol. 4:31–8. New York and Oxford: Oxford University Press.

Klein, Harriet E. Manelis, and Louisa R. Stark, eds., 1985. *South American Indian languages: Retrospect and prospect.* Austin: University of Texas Press. (Texas Linguistic Series.)

Klimov, Georgij Andreevič. 1965. *Kavkazskie jazyki.* Moscow: Nauka Publishing House.

Klimov, Georgij Andreevič, and M. E. Alekseev. 1980. *Tipologija kavkazskix jazykov.* Moscow: Nauka Publishing House.

Klimov, G[eorgij] A[ndreevič], and D. I. Èdel'man. 1970. *Jazyk burušaski.* Moscow: Izdatel'stvo "Nauka."

Kloss, Heinz. 1968. Notes concerning a language-nation typology. In Fishman, J. A., C. A. Ferguson, and J. Das Gupta, eds., *Language problems of developing nations.* New York. John Wiley & Sons.

Kloss, Heinz, and Grant McConnell, gen. eds., 1974–84. *Linguistic composition of the nations of the world.* Québec: Les Presses de l'Université Laval.

Koizumi, Tamotsu. 1981. Uraru shogo. In Hajime Kitamura, ed., *Sekai no gengo,* 81–111. Kōza Gengo, Vol. 6. Tokyo: Taishūkan shoten.

Koo, John H., and Robert N. St. Clair. no date. *Languages of the world.* Seoul: Hanshin Publishing Co.

Kornfilt, Jaklin. 1987. Turkish and the Turkic languages. In Bernard Comrie, ed., *The world's major languages,* 619–44. New York: Oxford University Press.

———. 1992. Turkish. In William Bright et al., eds., *International encyclopedia of linguistics.* Vol. 4:190–6. New York: Oxford University Press.

Koval', A. I. and G. B. Zubko. 1986. *Jazyk fula.* Moscow: Nauka Publ.

Kozinskij, I. Š. 1974. K voprosu o proisxoždenii kjaxtinskogo (russko-kitajskogo) jazyka. In Akademija Nauk SSSR, Institut Vostokovedenija, *Genetičeskie i areal'nye svjazi jazykov Azii i Afriki: Tezisy dokladov.* (Diskussija na rasširennom zasedanii Filologičeskoj sekcii Učenogo Soveta Instituta Vostokovedenija. Dekabr' 1973 goda.) Moscow: "Nauka" Publishing, 36–8.

Kratochvil, Paul. 1968. *The Chinese language today: Features of an emerging standard.* London: Hutchinson University Library.

Krauss, Michael. 1979. Na-Dene and Eskimo-Aleut. In Lyle Campbell and Marianne Mithun, eds., *The languages of native America: Historical and comparative assessment,* 803–901. Austin: University of Texas Press.

Krauss, Michael. 1980. *Alaska native languages: Past, present, and future.* Fairbanks: University of Alaska, Alaska Native Language Center.

Krishnamurti, Bh. 1992a. Dravidian languages. In William Bright et al., eds., *International encyclopedia of linguistics.* Vol. 1:373–8. New York: Oxford University Press.

———. 1992b. Telugu. In William Bright et al., eds., *International encyclopedia of linguistics.* Vol. 4:137–41. New York: Oxford University Press.

Kropp Dakubu, M. E., ed. 1988. *The languages of Ghana.* International African Institute, African languages/Languages Africaines, occas. publ. no. 2. London: Kegan Paul International.

Krupa, Viktor. 1973. *Polynesian languages: A survey of research.* The Hague, Paris: Mouton.

———. 1979. *Gavajskij jazyk.* Moscow: Izdatel'stvo "Nauka."

Kuipers, Aert H. 1976. *Typologically salient features of some North-West Caucasian languages.* Lisse: Peter de Ridder Press.

Ladefoged, Peter. 1982. *A course in phonetics.* New York: Harcourt Brace Jovanovich.

Lalou, Marcelle. 1950. *Manuel élémentaire de tibétain classique.* Paris: Librarie d'Amérique et d'Orient, Adrien Maisonneuve.

Lehmann, Winfred P., ed. 1978. Syntactic typology: *Studies in the phenomenology of language.* Austin: University of Texas Press.

———. 1992. *Historical linguistics.* 3d ed. New York: Routledge.

Lehtinen, Meri. 1962. *Basic course in Finnish.* Indiana University Publ., Uralic and Altaic Series, Vol. 27. Bloomington: Indiana University Press.

Leont'ev, A. A. 1974. *Papuasskie jazyki.* Moscow: Izdatel'stvo "Nauka."

Lhalungpa, Lobsang Phuntsok, transl. 1984. *The life of Milarepa.* Boulder, Colo.: Shambhala.

Li, Charles N. 1992. Chinese. In William Bright et al., eds., *International encyclopedia of linguistics.* Vol. 1:257–63. New York: Oxford University Press.

Li, Charles N., and Sandra A. Thompson. 1979. Chinese: Dialect variations and language reforms. In Timothy Shopen, ed., *Languages and their status,* 295–335. Cambridge, Mass.: Winthrop.

———. 1981. *Mandarin Chinese: A functional reference grammar.* Berkeley and Los Angeles: University of California Press. (A more modern approach than that used in Chao's reference grammar; more emphasis on syntax.)

———. 1987. Chinese. In Bernard Comrie, ed., *The world's major languages,* 811–33. New York: Oxford University Press.

Liu, Y. C. 1960. *Fifty Chinese stories, selected from classical texts, romanized and translated into Modern Chinese.* London: Lund Humphries.

Lockwood, W. B. 1972. *A panorama of Indo-European languages.* London: Hutchinson University Library.

Loogman, Alfons. 1967. *Swahili readings with notes, exercises and key.* African Series no. 2. Pittsburgh, Penn.: Duquesne University Press.

Loukotka, Čestimir. 1968. *Classification of South American languages.* Reference series, Vol. 7. 4th ed. Los Angeles: Latin American Center, UCLA. (Original Spanish edition published in 1935 in Prague.)

Lyovin, Anatole. 1981. Bibliography of linguistic topology. *Working Papers in Linguistics* (Dept. of Linguistics, University of Hawaii at Manoa) 13(2):75–94.

Mallory, J. P. 1989. *In search of Indo-Europeans: Language, archeology and myth.* London: Thames and Hudson.

Mannheim, Bruce. 1985. Contact and Quechua external genetic relationships. In Harriet E. Manelis Klein and Louisa R. Stark, eds. *South American Indian languages: Retrospect and prospect,* 644–88. Austin: University of Texas Press.

Martin, Samuel E. 1991a. Morphological clues to the relationships of Japanese and Korean. In Philip Baldi, ed., *Patterns of change, change of patterns: Linguistic change and reconstruction methodology,* 483–510. New York: Mouton de Gruyter.

———. 1991b. Recent research on the relationships of Japanese and Korean. In Sydney M. Lamb and E. Douglas Mitchell, eds., *Sprung from some common source,* 269–92. Stanford: Stanford University Press.

Mason, J. A. 1950. The languages of South American Indians. *Handbook of South American Indians* 6:157–317.

Matisoff, James A. 1991. Sino-Tibetan linguistics: Present state and future prospects. *Annual review of Anthropology* 20:469–504.

Matthews, G. Hubert. 1958. *Handbook of Siouan languages.* Philadelphia: University of Pennsylvania Press.

McQuown, Norman A., ed. 1967. *Handbook of Middle American Indians.* Austin: University of Texas Press.

Meillet, Antoine, and Marcel Cohen, eds. 1924. *Les langues du monde, par un groupe de linguistes sous la diréction de A. Meillet et Marcel Cohen.* Paris: E. Champion

Menges, Karl H. 1968. *The Turkic languages and peoples: An introduction to Turkic studies.* Wiesbaden: Otto Harrassowitz.

Merrifield, William B., et al., eds. 1987. *Laboratory manual for morphology and syntax.* 4th rev. ed. Santa Ana, Calif.: Summer Institute of Linguistics.

Middéndorf, E. W. 1890. *Das Runa Simi oder die Keshua-Sprache. (Wie sie gegenwärtig in der Provinz von Cusco gesprochen wird).* Leipzig: Brockhaus.

Mihalic, F. 1971. *The Jacaranda dictionary and grammar of Melanesian Pidgin*. Brisbane: Jacaranda Press.

Milewski, Tadeusz. 1948. *Atlas lingwistyczny języków świata*. Prace Etnologiczne, Vol. 1. Krakow: Wydawnictwo Polskiego Towarzystwa Ludoznawczego.

Miller, Roy Andrew. 1956. *The Tibetan system of writing*. American Council of Learned Societies, Program in Oriental Languages, Publ. ser. B, Aids No. 6. Washington, D.C.: American Council of Learned Societies.

———. 1970. A grammatical sketch of Classical Tibetan. *Journal of the American Oriental Society* 90:74–96.

———. 1971. *Japanese and other Altaic languages*. Chicago: University of Chicago Press. (In this book the author presents evidence for including Japanese in Altaic.)

———. 1991. Genetic connections among the Altaic languages. In Sydney M. Lamb and E. Douglas Mitchell, eds., *Sprung from some common source*, 293–327. Stanford: Stanford University Press.

Miller, Wick R. 1992. Uto-Aztecan languages. In William Bright et al., eds., *International encyclopedia of linguistics*. Vol. 4:212–16. New York: Oxford University Press.

Mithun, Marianne. 1992. Iroquoian languages. In William Bright et al., eds., *International encyclopedia of linguistics*. Vol. 2:233–6. New York: Oxford University Press.

Mithun, Marianne, and Wallace L. Chafe. 1979. Recapturing the Mohawk language. In Timothy Shopen, ed., *Languages and their status*, 3–33. Cambridge, Mass.: Winthrop.

Miyaoka, Osahito. 1978. *Eskimō no gengo to bunka*. Tokyo: Kōbundō.

———. 1981. Kyū ajia shogo. In Hajime Kitamura ed., *Sekai no gengo*, 393–411. Kōza Gengo, Vol. 6. Tokyo: Taishūkan shoten.

Moscati, Sabatino, et al., eds. 1964. *An introduction to the comparative grammar of the Semitic languages: Phonology and morphology*. Porta linguarum orientalium, n.s. 6. Wiesbaden: Otto Harrassowitz.

Moseley, C., and R. E. Asher, gen. eds. 1994. *Atlas of the world's languages*. London: Routledge.

Mühlhäusler, P. 1984. Syntax of Tok Pisin. In S. A. Wurm and P. Mühlhäusler, eds., *Handbook of Tok Pisin (New Guinea pidgin)*, Pacific Linguistics, C-70. Canberra, Australia Department of Linguistics, Research School of Pacific Studies, the Australian National University, 341–421.

———. 1986. *Pidgin and creole linguistics*. Oxford: Blackwell.

Myachina, E. N. 1981. *The Swahili language: A descriptive grammar*. Boston: Routledge and Kegan Paul. Languages of Asia and Africa series, Vol. 1. Translated from original Russian by G. L. Cambell.

Nagara, Susumu. 1972. *Japanese pidgin English in Hawaii: A bilingual description*. *Oceanic Linguistics* Special Publication No. 9. Honolulu: University of Hawaii Press.

Nakanishi, Akira. 1982. *Writing systems of the world: Alphabets, syllabaries, pictograms*. Rutland, Vt.: Charles E. Tuttle.

Newman, Paul. 1992a. Chadic languages. In William Bright et al., eds., *International encyclopedia of linguistics*. Vol. 1:253–4. New York: Oxford University Press.

———. 1992b. Hausa. In William Bright et al., eds., *International encyclopedia of linguistics*. Vol. 2:103–9. New York: Oxford University Press.

Nguyễn, Đình-Hoà. 1987. Vietnamese. In Bernard Comrie, ed., *The world's major languages*, 777–96. New York: Oxford University Press.

Nikiforova, L. A. 1981. *Jazyk volof*. Moscow: Nauka Publ.

Nishie, Masayuki. 1981. Afurika no shogengo. In Hajime Kitamura, ed., *Sekai no gengo*, 261–308. Kōza Gengo, Vol. 6. Tokyo: Taishūkan shoten.

Norman, Jerry. 1988. *Chinese.* Cambridge: Cambridge University Press. Cambridge Language Surveys.

Ono, Susumu. 1970. *The origin of the Japanese language.* Tokyo: Kokusai Bunka Shinkokai.

Osgood, Cornelius, ed. 1946. *Linguistic structures of Native America.* New York: Viking Fund in Publications in Anthropology, No. 6.

Oxotina, N. V. 1961. *Jazyk zulu.* Moscow: Nauka Publ.

Parker, Gary J. 1963. Clasificación de los dialectos quechuas. *Revista del Museo Nacional* (Lima) 32:241–52.

———. 1969. *Ayacucho Quechua grammar and dictionary.* The Hague: Mouton.

Parpola, Asko. 1994. *Deciphering the Indus script.* New York: Cambridge University Press.

Patrie, James. 1982. *The genetic relationship of the Ainu language.* Oceanic Linguistics Special Publication, Vol. 17. Honolulu: University of Hawaii Press.

Payne, David L. 1990. Some widespread grammatical forms in South American languages. In Doris Lander Payne, ed., *Amazonian linguistics: Studies in Lowland South American languages,* 75–87. Austin: University of Texas Press.

Payne, Doris Lander, ed. 1990. *Amazonian linguistics: Studies in Lowland South American languages.* Austin: University of Texas Press.

Payne, J. R. 1987. Iranian languages. In Bernard Comrie, ed., *The world's major languages,* 514–22. New York: Oxford University Press.

Perrott, D. V. 1951. *Teach yourself Swahili.* London: English Universities Press.

———. 1965. *Concise Swahili and English dictionary.* New York: David McKay. *(Teach Yourself Books)*

Perroud, Pedro Clemente. 1961. *Gramatica Quechwa: dialecto de Ayacucho.* Santa Clara, Peru: Seminario San Alfonso de los Padres Redentoristas.

Philipsen, G., and D. Carbaugh. 1986. A bibliography of fieldwork in the ethnography of speaking. *Language in Society* 15:387–97.

Pike, Kenneth L. 1948. *Tone language: A technique of determining the number and type of pitch contrasts in a language, with studies in tonemic substitution and fusion.* Ann Arbor: University of Michigan Press.

Polomé, E. C. 1967. *Swahili language handbook.* Washington, D.C.: Center for Applied Linguistics.

Poppe, Nicholas. 1960. *Vergleichende Grammatik der altaischen Sprachen. Teil 1, Vergleichende Lautlehre.* Wiesbaden: Otto Harrassowitz.

Prentice, D. J. 1987. Malay (Indonesian and Malaysian). In Bernard Comrie, ed., *The world's major languages,* 913–35. New York: Oxford University Press.

———. 1992. Malay and Indonesian. In William Bright et al., eds., *International encyclopedia of linguistics.* Vol. 2:374–80. New York: Oxford University Press.

Pukui, Mary K., and Samuel H. Elbert. 1971. *Hawaiian dictionary.* Honolulu: University of Hawaii Press.

Pulleyblank, Douglas. 1987a. Niger-Kordofanian languages. In Bernard Comrie, ed., *The world's major languages,* 959–70. New York: Oxford University Press.

———. 1987b. Yoruba. In Bernard Comrie, ed., *The world's major languages,* 971–90. New York: Oxford University Press.

Pullum, Geoffrey K. 1991. *The great Eskimo vocabulary hoax, and other irreverent essays in the study of language.* Chicago: University of Chicago Press.

Ramos, Teresita V. 1971. *Tagalog structures.* PALI language texts: Philippines. Honolulu: University of Hawaii Press.

Reed, Irene, et al. 1977. *Yup'ik Eskimo grammar.* Fairbanks: University of Alaska, Alaska Native Language Center.

Reid, Lawrence A. 1984–85. Benedict's Austro-Tai hypothesis—an evaluation. *Asian Perspectives* 26.1:19–34.

Reinecke, J. E., David De Camp, Ian Hancock, and Richard E. Wood, eds. 1975. *A bibliography of pidgin and creole languages.* Honolulu: University of Hawaii Press.

Rerix, Ju. N. 1961. *Tibetskij jazyk.* Moscow: Izdatel'stvo "Nauka."

Reuse, Willem Joseph de. 1994. *Siberian Yupik Eskimo: The language and its contacts with Chukchi.* Studies in the Indigenous Languages of the Americas. Salt Lake City: University of Utah Press.

Rickford, John R. 1992. Pidgins and creoles. In William Bright et al., eds., *International encyclopedia of linguistics.* Vol. 3:224–32. New York: Oxford University Press.

Romaine, Suzanne. 1988. *Pidgin and creole languages.* New York: Longman. (Longman Linguistics Library.)

———. 1994. *An introduction to sociolinguistics.* New York: Oxford University Press.

Rodrigues, Aryon Dall'Igna. 1985. Evidence for Tupi-Karib relationships. In Harriet E. M. Klein and Louisa R. Stark, eds., *South American Indian languages: Retrospect and prospect,* 371–404. Austin: University of Texas Press.

Rood, David S. 1979. *Siouan. The languages of Native America.* Austin: University of Texas Press.

———. 1992. North American languages. William Bright et al., eds., *International encyclopedia of linguistics.* Vol. 3:110–15. New York: Oxford University Press.

Ruhlen, Merritt. 1987. *A guide to world's languages. Vol. 1, Classification.* Stanford: Stanford University Press.

Saltarelli, Mario. 1988. *Basque.* Croom Helm Descriptive Grammar Series, London: Croom Helm.

Sampson, Geoffrey. 1985. *Writing systems: A linguistic introduction.* London: Hutchinson.

Sankoff, Gillian, ed. 1980. *The social life of language.* Philadelphia: University of Pennsylvania Press.

Sankoff, Gillian, and Penelope Brown. 1980. The origin of syntax in discourse: A case study of Tok Pisin relatives. In Gillian Sankoff, ed., *The social life of language,* 211–55. Philadelphia: University of Pennsylvania Press.

Sankoff, Gillian, and Suzanne Laberge. 1980. On the acquisition of native speakers by a language. In Gillian Sankoff, ed., *The social life of language,* 195–209. Philadelphia: University of Pennsylvania Press.

Sapir, Edward. 1921. *Language.* New York: Harcourt, Brace and World.

Sasse, Hans-Jürgen. 1992. Cushitic languages. In William Bright et al., eds., *International encyclopedia of linguistics.* Vol. 1:326–30. New York: Oxford University Press.

Saville-Troike, Muriel. 1989. *The ethnography of communication: An introduction.* 2d ed. Oxford and New York: Basil Blackwell.

Schacter, Paul. 1987. Tagalog. In Bernard Comrie, ed., *The world's major languages,* 936–58. New York: Oxford University Press.

———. 1992. Tagalog. In William Bright et al., eds., *International encyclopedia of linguistics.* Vol. 4:123–6. New York: Oxford University Press.

Schmalsteig, W. R. 1980. *Indo-European linguistics: A new synthesis.* University Park: Pennsylvania State University Press.

Schütz, Albert J. 1980. A reanalysis of the Hawaiian vowel system. *Oceanic Linguistics* 20:1.1–43.

Scollon, Ronald, and Suzanne B. K. Scollon. 1979. *Linguistic convergence: An ethnography of speaking at Fort Chipewyan, Alberta.* New York: Academic Press.

Sebeok, Thomas A., ed. 1977. *Native languages of the Americas.* 2 vols. New York: Plenum.

Shafer, Robert. 1966–73. *Introduction to Sino-Tibetan.* Wiesbaden: Otto Harrassowitz.

Sherzer, Joel. 1976. *An areal-typological study of Amerindian languages north of Mexico.* Amsterdam: North Holland Publishing.

Simons, Linda, and Hugh Young. 1978. *Pijin blong yumi: A guide to Solomon Islands pijin.* Honiara, Solomon Islands: Solomon Islands Christian Association Publications Group.

Smirnova, M. A. 1960. *Jazyk hausa.* Moscow: Nauka Publ.

Snyman, J. W. 1970. *An introduction to the !Xũ language.* Cape Town: A. A. Balkeme. (Published for the Department of African Languages, School of African Studies, University of Capetown.)

Solženicyn, A. I. 1968. *V pervom krugu.* London: Flegon Press.

Soto Ruiz, C. 1974. *Quechua manual de enseñanza.* Lima: Instituto de Estudios Peruanos.

———. 1976a. *Diccionario Ayacucho-Chanca.* Lima: Instituto de Estudios Peruanos.

———. 1976b. *Gramática Ayacucho-Chanca.* Lima: Instituto de Estudios Peruanos.

Šprincin, A. G. 1968. O russko-kitajskom dialekte na Dal'nem Vostoke. *Strany i Narody Vostoka,* vyp. VI:86–100. Moscow: Izdatel'stvo "Nauka."

Steiner, Richard C. 1992. Hebrew: Ancient Hebrew. In William Bright et al., eds., *International encyclopedia of linguistics.* Vol. 2:110–8. New York: Oxford University Press.

Stevick, E. W., J. G. Mlela, and F. N. Njenga. 1963. *Swahili basic course.* Washington, D.C.: Department of State, Foreign Language Institute.

Stewart, William A. 1962. An outline of linguistic typology for describing multilingualism. In *Study of the role of second languages in Asia, Africa, and Latin America.* 15–25. Washington, D.C.: Center for Applied Linguistics of the Modern Language Association of America.

Suárez, Jorge A. 1983. *The Mesoamerican Indian languages.* New York: Cambridge University Press.

Sugita, Hiroshi. 1981. Ōsutroneshia shogo. In Hajime Kitamura, ed., *Sekai no gengo,* 199–230. Kōza Gengo, vol. 6. Tokyo: Taishūkan shoten.

Sussex, Roland. 1992. Russian. In William Bright et al., eds., *International encyclopedia of linguistics.* Vol. 3:350–8. New York: Oxford University Press.

Szemerényi, O. 1980. *Einführung in die vergleichende Sprachwissenschaft.* 2d ed. Darmstadt: Wissenschaftliche Buchgesellschaft.

Tennant, Edward A. 1977. *Central Yupik: A course in spoken Eskimo.* Albuquerque, N. Mex.: Educational Research Associates.

Thomas, Edward Harper. 1970. *Chinook: A history and a dictionary.* 2d ed. Portland, Ore.: Binfords & Mort.

Thurgood, Graham. 1993. Tai-Kadai and Austronesian: The nature of the historical relationship. Paper presented at the *Conference of Asia-Mainland/Austronesian Connections,* Honolulu, May 10–13, 1993.

Todd, Loretto. 1984. *Modern Englishes, pidgins and creoles.* Oxford: Basil Blackwell. 2d ed. Routledge.

Tokarskaja, V. P. 1964. *Jazyk malinke (mandingo).* Moscow: Nauka Publ.

Torero Fernandez de Cordova, Alfredo. 1964. Las dialectas quechuas. *Anales Cientificos de la Universidad Agraria* (Lima) 2:446–78.

———. 1970. Lingüística e historia de la sociedad andina. *Anales Científicos de la Universidad Agraria* (Lima) 3/4:231–64.

Tovar, Antonio. 1957. *The Basque language.* Transl. from Spanish by H. P. Houghton. Philadelphia: University of Pennsylvania Press.

Trager, George L. 1972. *Language and languages.* San Francisco: Chandler.

Tritton, Arthur Stanley. 1943. *Teach yourself Arabic.* Philadelphia: D. McKay for the English University Press.

Trubetzkoy, N. S. 1969. *Principles of phonology.* Transl. by Christiane A. M. Baltaxe of

Grundzüge der Phonologie, which originally appeared in 1939. Berkeley and Los Angeles: University of California Press.

Tucker, A. N. 1940. *The Eastern Sudanic languages.* Publ. for the International Institute of African Languages and Cultures. London: Oxford University Press.

Urban, Greg, and Joel Sherzer. 1988. The linguistic anthropology of native South America. *Annual Review of Anthropology* 17:283–307.

Uspenskij, L. 1957. *Slovo o slovax.* Moscow: Molodaja Gvardija.

Valdman, Albert, ed. 1977. *Pidgin and creole linguistics.* Bloomington: Indiana University Press.

Vinokur, G. O. 1971. *The Russian language: A brief history.* London: Cambridge University Press. (Translation from the 1957 Russian edition.)

Voegelin, Carl F., and Florence M. Voegelin. 1977. *Classification and index of the world's languages.* New York: Elsevier.

Wald, Benji. 1987. Swahili and the Bantu languages. In Bernard Comrie, ed., *The world's major languages.* 991–1014. New York: Oxford University Press.

Wáng, Fùshì, ed. 1985. *Miàoyŭ jiǎzhì.* Beijing: Mínzú Chūbǎnshè.

Watkins, Calvert. 1992. Indo-European languages. In William Bright et al., eds. *International encyclopedia of linguistics.* Vol. 2:206–12. New York: Oxford University Press.

Welmers, William E. 1973. *African language structures.* Berkeley and Los Angeles: University of California Press.

Whitley, W. H. 1969. *Swahili: The rise of a national language.* London: Methuen.

Whitney, Arthur H. 1956. *Finnish.* Sevenoaks, Kent: Hodder and Stoughton. *(Teach Yourself Books)*

Williamson, Kay. 1989. Niger-Congo overview. In John Bendor-Samuel and Rhonda L. Hartell, eds., *The Niger-Congo languages,* 3–45. Lanham, Md.: University Press of America.

Windfuhr, Gernot L. 1987. Persian. In Bernard Comrie, ed., *The world's major languages,* 524–46. New York: Oxford University Press.

Wirth, J. R. 1982. Toward universal principles of word formation: A look at antonyms. Paper delivered at the International Congress of Linguistics in Tokyo, Japan.

Wright, W. 1896. *A grammar of the Arabic language.* 3d ed. Cambridge: Cambridge University Press.

Wurm, Stephen A. 1972. *Languages of Australia and Tasmania.* The Hague: Mouton.

———. 1982. *Papuan languages of Oceania.* Ars linguistica, no. 7. Tübingen: Narr.

Wurm, Stephen A., and Shirō Hattori. 1981–84. *Language atlas of the Pacific area.* Canberra: Australian Academy of the Humanities.

Wylie, Turrell. 1959. A standard system of Tibetan transcription. *Harvard Journal of Asiatic Studies* 22:261–7.

Yushmanov, N. V. 1961. *The structure of the Arabic language.* Transl. from Russian by Moshe Perlmann. Washington, D.C.: Center for Applied Linguistics.

Zaborski, Andrzej. 1992. Afro-Asiatic languages. In William Bright et al., eds., *International encyclopedia of linguistics.* Vol. 1:36–7. New York: Oxford University Press.

Zavadovskij, Ju. N. and E. B. Smagina. 1986. *Nubijskij jazyk.* Moscow: Nauka Publ.

Zhōngyāng Mínzúyuàn Shǎoshŭ Mínzú Yánjiùsuǒ, ed. *Zhōngguó shǎoshŭ mínzú yŭyán.* Chengdu: Sìchuan Mínzú Chūbǎnshè.

Language Index

Subject Index